TEACH

POWERPOINT 4

Oxford Computer Training

OXFORD COMPUTER TRAINING

Hodder & Stoughton

A MEMBER OF THE HODDER HEADLINE GROUP

Acknowledgements

A number of products have been referred to in this book, many of which are registered trademarks. These are acknowledged as being the property of their owners.

The trademarks mentioned in this book include:

Microsoft: Windows, MS-DOS, PowerPoint 4, Word for Windows 6, Excel 5, Access.

IBM: PC

Intel: i486, Pentium

British Library Cataloguing in Publication Data

ISBN 0 340 63945 8

First published 1995

Impression number	10	9	8	7	6	5	4	3	2	1
Year	1999		1998		1997		1996		1995	

Typeset by Oxford Computer Training.
Printed in Great Britain for Hodder & Stoughton Educational, a division of Hodder Headline Plc, 338 Euston Road, London NW1 3BH by Cox & Wyman, Reading, Berks.

CONTENTS

List of Contributors

Ross Bentley, Jon Collins, Andrew O'Connell, Gary Powell, Brian Reid, Shona McLeod, Narinderpal Singh Thethi, Pamela Stanworth, Donald Taylor, Hugh Simpson-Wells, Peter Ferry, Peter Othen, Duncan Young.

1

— INTRODUCTION —

This chapter covers:

- Conventions used in this book.
- The aims of this book.

Welcome

This book is intended for first time users of Microsoft PowerPoint version 4; it assumes that you understand a few fundamental computer concepts, such as a 'file' and an 'application' and that you know how to use Windows controls such as menus, dialogs and, of course, a mouse. You should also know how to start PowerPoint (you may do this by following the instructions in the PowerPoint manual or as instructed by whoever installed it).

This book is not a definitive source of information – it is intended as an introduction to PowerPoint and a supplement to the User Guide. It will help you in great detail at first, but less and less so as you progress, encouraging you to use the manual or on-line Help for further information.

Note that this book uses PowerPoint version 4. This requires Windows version 3.1 or later.

Conventions

Throughout this book, instructions which you should carry out are written in italics, like this:

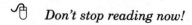

Don't stop reading now!

Anything which you are to type on the keyboard is written `like this`.

Key words are shown like this: **text placeholder, slide view, master**

File names and directories appear like this:

    C:\POWERPNT\PRESENT1.PPT

Special keys are shown like this:

[Home], [PgDn], [Ctrl][F1] or [Alt][Shift][↑], etc.

On screen 'buttons' are shown like this: [OK]

[Enter] means the return key (also known as: carriage return, enter, CR, etc.)

A guide to show you an easier way to achieve something is shown by the thumbs-up hint.

> *Text appearing in square brackets and this small font within a box is usually a little technical or simply a 'closer look' at a feature, or a trivial aside.*

From time to time you will see a box summarising the text above, like this:

Summary : PowerPoint introduction

- Instructions and questions appear in *italics*.
- You should type text that appears like this: **`Oxford Computer Training`**
- Keys to press are shown as: [Esc] or [Ctrl][Home]
- Buttons appear as [OK] or 
- File names appear in a special font: `PRESENT1.PPT`
- This is a summary box, intended to reinforce the points made in the main body of the text.

2

BASIC PRINCIPLES

This chapter covers:

- Typical uses of PowerPoint.
- Starting PowerPoint.
- The constituent parts of the screen.

What is PowerPoint?

Increasingly, conference speakers, lecturers and business people are improving the quality of their presentations by making use of professional-looking graphics and pictures. Presentations are usually structured by displaying only relevant points during the talk, the speaker outlining these points in greater detail. The completed presentation can be shown in many ways: it can be printed out on paper for handouts, transparent acetate sheets or 35mm slides, or displayed directly from PowerPoint, perhaps through a projector of some kind. Printed output can be either black and white (including shades of grey) or full colour. Colour printing can be done by yourself if you have the equipment, or by using a high street printing bureau, while the photographic quality 35mm slides and computer screen shows will tend to be in colour.

Using a computer based presentation package will help you produce slides and notes that are striking and have a good layout - 'a picture paints a thousand words'!

A PowerPoint presentation is made up of **slides**, each slide typically (but not always) carrying a **title**, with supporting text (often in the form of **bullets**) and/or pictures. The pictures might be created within PowerPoint, imported from a drawing/painting application or be picked from a large library of prepared pictures that are supplied with PowerPoint - **ClipArt**.

Microsoft supplies **applets** (little applications) with PowerPoint (in common with other Microsoft applications), these include MSGraph and OrgChart. The MSGraph utility allows you to produce detailed chart information and OrgChart to produce organisation layouts and family tree type structures.

Presentations can be made more attractive by the use of: **transitions** - using special effects to switch from one slide to another; and **builds** - using effects to reveal bullet points one at a time, rather than displaying them all at the beginning.

Screen shows also have the advantage that they do not require PowerPoint to be installed on the computer that will run the show. PowerPoint comes with a **PowerPoint Viewer**, this is licence free, and can be distributed freely. Therefore you can send out presentations on computer floppy disks including the Viewer, without the need to know if your recipients have a copy of PowerPoint 4 .

A sample presentation and screen show

The next few pages show a presentation from its outline through to displaying it on the monitor during a sales conference.

The presentation will cover an introduction to a series of teach yourself books from Hodder Headline and Oxford Computer Group, and then discuss PowerPoint 4, the book of which you are now holding.

The presentation will consist of just three slides (an unusually short presentation, but good enough to set the scene and explain the terminology):

1. The four books and a summary
2. Contributors and what they have done
3. Focus on PowerPoint 4

Additional summary information will be included on each slide relevant to the above points.

The following screenshots show a copy of the presentation before starting, and also the first slide just after the text is entered. The presentation was based on a predesigned presentation known as a **template** that was supplied with PowerPoint.

This is how the presentation looks before any data has been added (the graphics are part of the template upon which this slideshow is based):

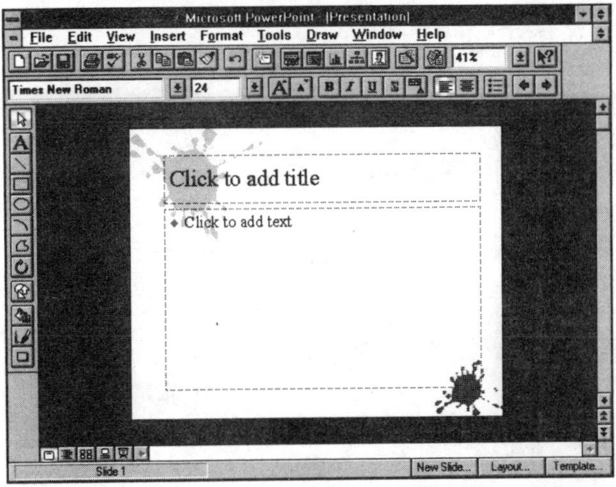

This is the first slide after text has been added.

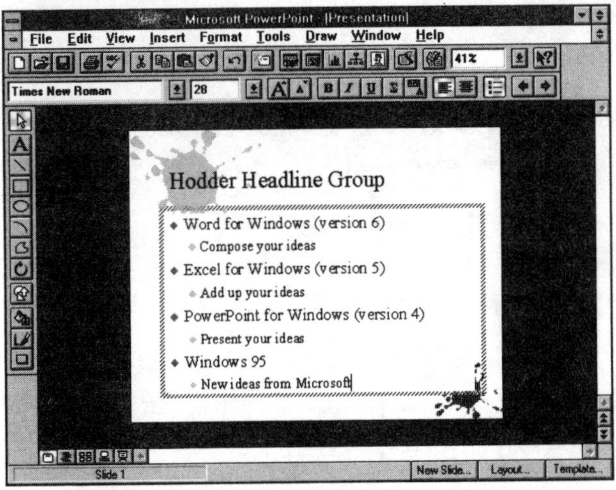

The first slide is then altered to take on certain appearances, such as the **emboldened**, *italicised* and underlined title, and changes in size of different parts of the bullet text.

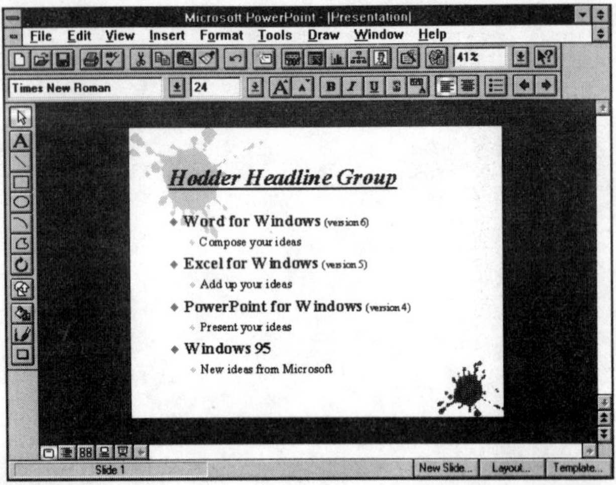

The second slide in the presentation may be added with New Slide... at the bottom right of the PowerPoint window. The following dialog is displayed, requesting the type of slide to add:

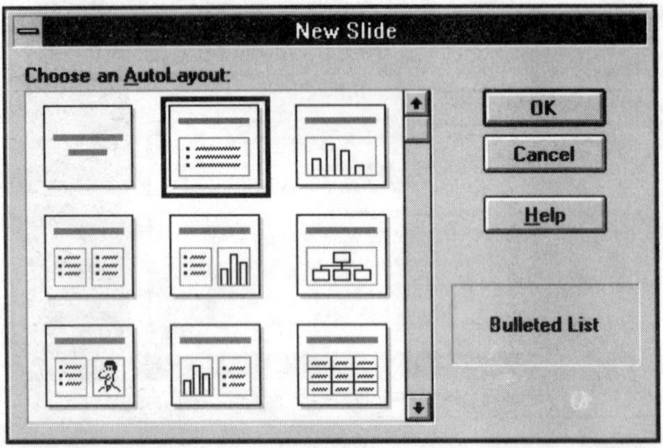

The Bulleted List option is selected and the second slide is created. Text is added and the format changed to match the styles of the previous slide.

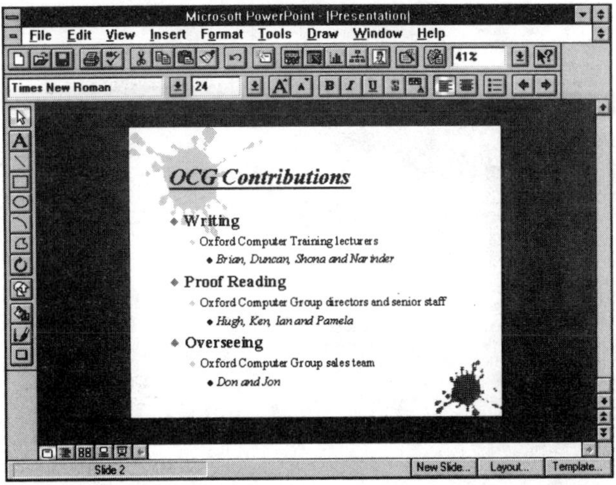

The third slide is added, edited and the format changed as with the second slide.

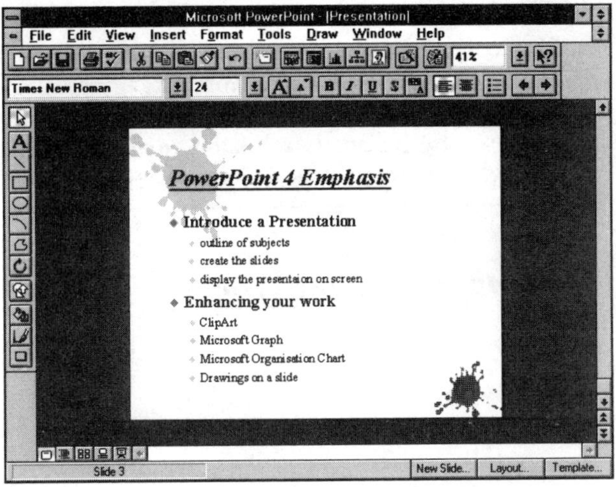

As you can see in the above screenshots, the appearance of the layout and text is consistent across the three slides.

Any editing can be done in Slide View as above, or in Outline View as below. Outline View shows only the text, and many slides together, and may be accessed using [icon] at the bottom of the PowerPoint window.

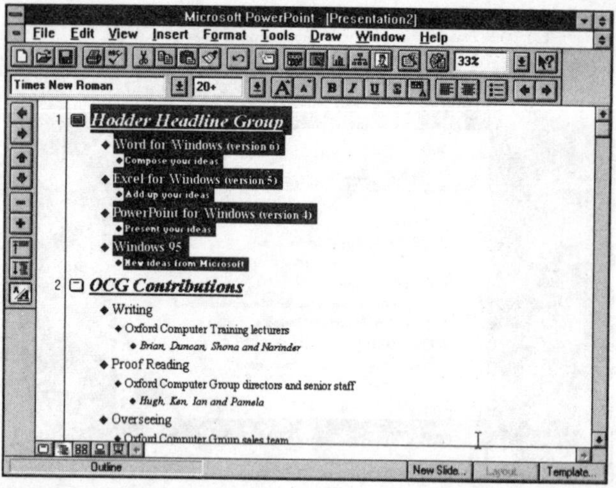

In the above screenshot, the contents of the first slide have been selected by clicking the slide icon displayed next to the slide number.

Now that all is complete, you can run the slide show on screen using the slide show button. The slideshow will start from the presently active slide; so, in this example, it will begin from slide one. The presenter can use the left mouse button to move to the next slide (and the right one to go back a slide).

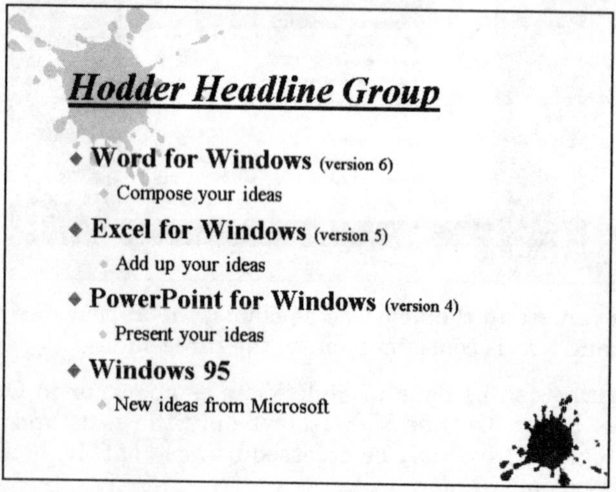

An annotate feature exists within slideshows to highlight selected parts of the presentation as the presenter sees fit. The following screenshot has highlighted those members of Oxford Computer Group that have overseen these book projects.

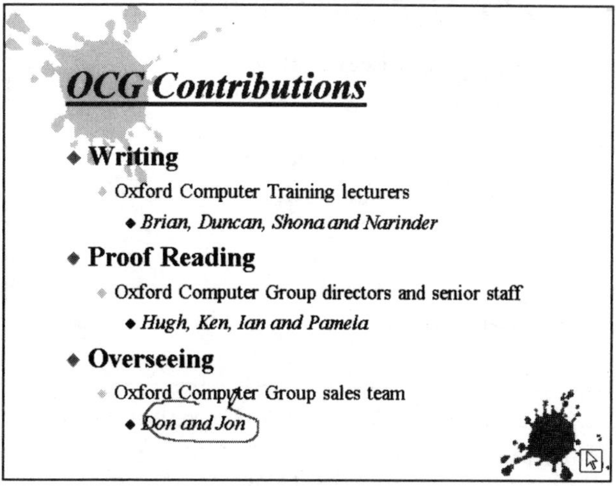

And then, the last screen of this slideshow:

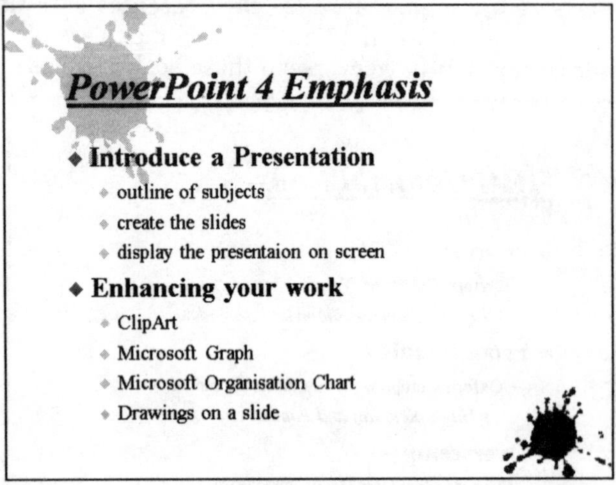

The slideshow might be designed to repeat, or to finish at this point. Many presenters use the trick of having an extra slide at the end, blank apart from the template graphics – a slightly less harsh finish than dropping out of the viewer mode altogether:

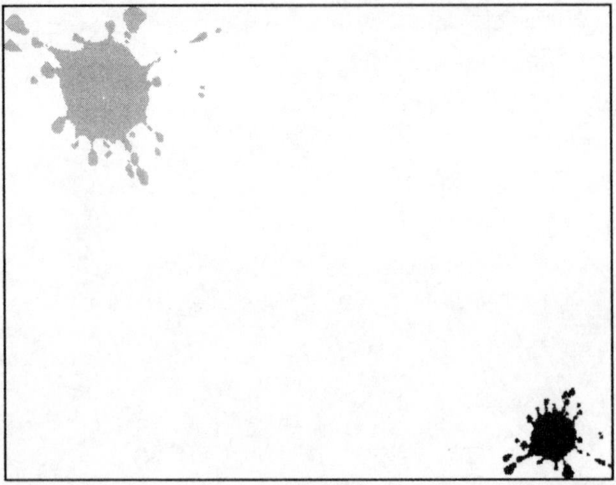

Aims when creating presentations

With PowerPoint, you may create your presentation in the form of an on-screen display, or print the slides out onto acetate for overhead projection (OHP), which may be in colour or black & white, depending on the printer available to you, or have them made up as 35mm slides, or simply print them out on paper for posters or signs.

On-screen displays have the advantage that they can be set up to require no user intervention. They can be run repeatedly until [Esc] is pressed, and if the keyboard and mouse are disconnected or hidden after starting, a rolling demonstration can be produced – ideal for a shop windows or an exhibition.

When you are making a presentation to a number of people, a powerful technique is to emphasise the verbal points you are making with visual information. PowerPoint provides a means to create these pictorial aids, and to synchronise them with the verbal part of the presentation. It has been designed so that you can create a workable, professional-looking presentation very quickly, and then if you do have more time available you may want to continue adding special features and effects.

PowerPoint has a wealth of included work (samples, ClipArt, pre-designed templates) and wizards to speed up creating a presentation.

Tools are provided so that you can easily change the appearance (the format) of your text or graphics - the colours, lettering style, patterns and so on can be important aids to creating the right mood, and thus increasing the impact of your presentation.

Starting to use PowerPoint

Starting PowerPoint

It is assumed that you have loaded PowerPoint in whichever way is appropriate to your system. If your system has been installed by someone other than you then you should follow their instructions for loading PowerPoint.

Tip of the Day

The first thing that appears will be the Tip of the Day (unless it has been turned off). This is one aspect of Microsoft's 'IntelliSense' feature, which is intended to offer you help on screen as you need it. Usually, a different Tip will appear each time you start PowerPoint. This one is a variation on the tip we gave earlier:

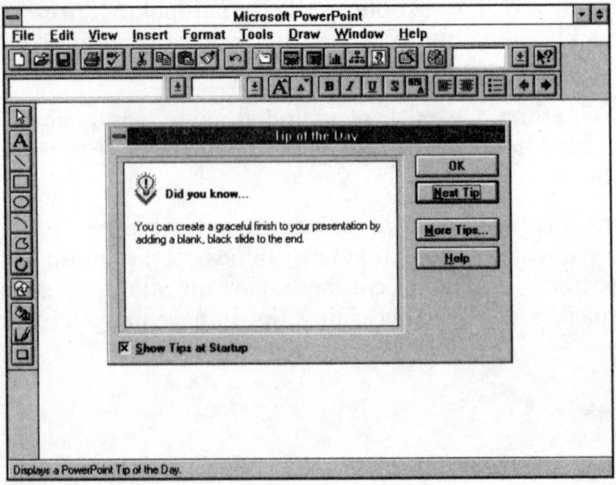

If you are interested in seeing more, click [More Tips...]. If you don't want to see these tips in future, click ☒ Show Tips at Startup to clear the checkbox and suppress display of future tips.

Click [OK]

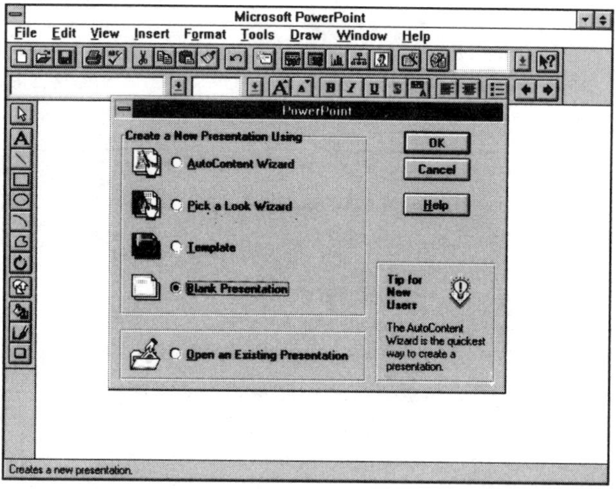

The resulting dialog offers several options for creating a new presentation or continuing work on an existing one. Ordinarily you would probably use one of these options, but first a short tour of the screen is in order.

Click [Cancel]

A tour of the screen

Title bar

As is usual with Windows applications, there is a title bar at the top of the application window. It carries the usual buttons for controlling the application window: on the right are  or  for maximising or restoring (depending on whether currently maximised) and  for minimising the application window, while on the left is , a menu that contains various commands to do with the window.

> *A fast way of closing PowerPoint is to double-click its control menu (); a convenient way of maximising/restoring a window is to double-click its title bar.*

Menu bar

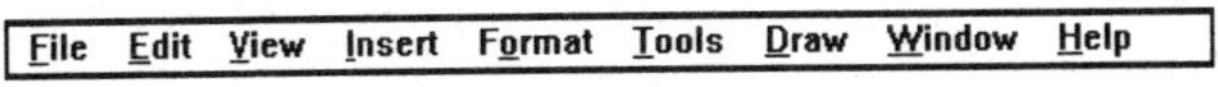

The commands and options are grouped under a series of menus. The menus give access to much of the functionality of PowerPoint, although you will be surprised at how much you can do without using the menus.

As is usual with Windows applications, there are alternative methods for using menus. For instance, point to a menu name with the mouse pointer, and click to make the menu drop down. Then point to an option and click. When you release the mouse, the option is selected.

In each menu name, one letter is underlined. This provides a method of using menus with the keyboard, rather than with the mouse. This is done by holding down [Alt] while typing the underlined letter. This makes the chosen menu drop down. It is then possible to choose a menu option by typing the appropriate underlined letter from the menu.

Note that with this method you do not have to press [Alt] a second time when typing a letter for the individual command on a menu.

Toolbars

There are three toolbars on display at present. At the top of the screen shown above are the Standard toolbar and, below it, the Formatting toolbar. On the left edge of the screen is the Drawing toolbar.

The toolbars provide easy access to a variety of useful commands. These same commands are also available via the menus, but the toolbars provide often-used commands more directly. Various tools will be introduced as they are required.

PowerPoint has seven predesigned toolbars available, and these will be displayed as needed. You can design your own collection of tools on a customised toolbar if you wish.

Toolbars may be displayed at different positions around the screen – at the edges (**docked**) or over the working area (**floating**). This is covered in more detail in the chapter 'Graphics and Drawings'.

Status bar

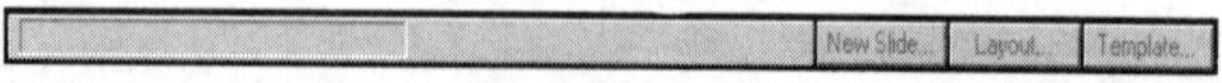

The status bar at the bottom of the screen offers (perhaps unsurprisingly) status information. When a presentation is open, it reminds you which slide you are looking at, and which view is in use. It also provides help messages – for example, when you leave your mouse pointer over a tool on a toolbar.

At the right-hand end of the status bar are three buttons, allowing you to create a new slide, alter the layout of a slide, or apply a new template to a presentation. These are dimmed at present as these commands are only available when you are working on a presentation.

Summary : Basic Principles

- PowerPoint may be used to produce screen shows, sets of overhead slides or paper posters.
- The PowerPoint window has many familiar Windows features: title bar, menu bar, toolbars.
- A completed slide show can be opened and run on screen.
- PowerPoint comes with a copy of PowerPoint Viewer which can be freely distributed with your presentations. The Viewer can be used to ensure you can show your presentation on computers and at locations without a licensed copy of PowerPoint 4.
- The status bar offers help information and shows the current status of the machine as appropriate.

3

GETTING STARTED

> **This chapter covers:**
>
> - Creating a new presentation.
> - Making corrections to text.
> - Seeing the your embryonic slideshow in use.

Before beginning basic editing, you will, of course, need something to edit. The first step then, will be to create a presentation for *Aviation Monthly*, a new monthly magazine. This presentation will start with quite a plain-looking slide, which will provide an opportunity to consider some important techniques for working with text.

Creating a new presentation

Click [icon] *to display the New Presentation dialog.*

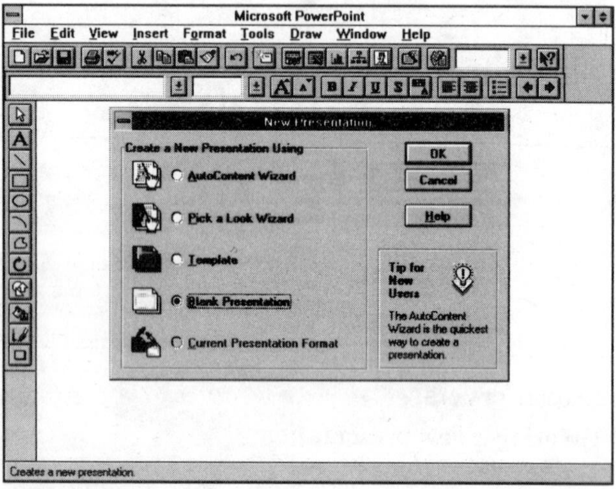

Later on we will use some Wizards and Templates, but for our first, very simple example we'll start with a blank presentation.

Select ◉ Blank Presentation and click [OK]

Creating the first slide

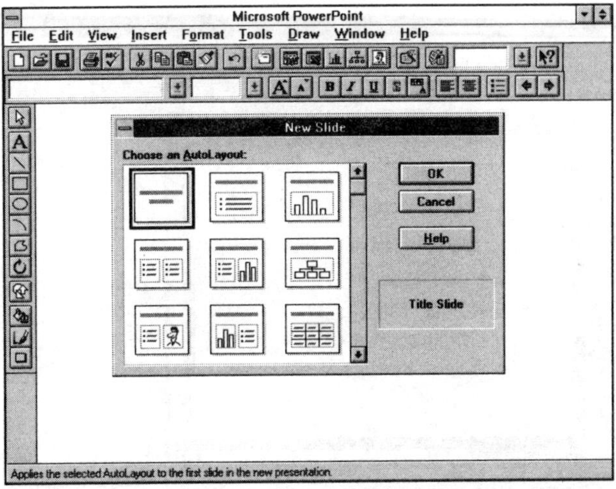

The New Slide dialog provides twenty-one different types of slide to choose from. You select a slide layout by scrolling (as necessary) then clicking once on the type you want. The selected slide type is described on the right of the dialog. In the screenshot above, a **Title Slide** is selected.

> *As we have started a new presentation, the default choice of the new slide is the Title Slide. Later, when we see this dialog again, the default choice may be different.*

The presentation describing *Aviation Monthly* will begin with a title page followed by a list of the new magazine's attributes. The title page can use the suggested default as shown above, with the second slide containing a list of sales points, for which a bullet list would be suitable.

Select the first slide on the top row – the Title Slide – and click OK

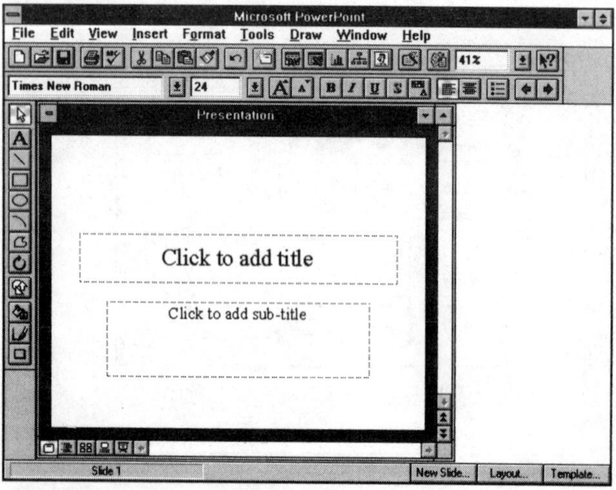

Your first slide has been created! At present it contains no 'real' text, but rather areas where you can place your own text. The area in the middle of the slide, where it says 'Click to add title' is the **title placeholder**, while the area underneath containing the words 'Click to add sub-title' is the **sub-title placeholder**.

You will notice that the three buttons previously dimmed on the status bar have become available, and that five smaller buttons have appeared on the lower left-hand edge of the document window:

These buttons are used to alter the view of the slide. At present you are in **Slide View**, which allows editing of individual slides. You can return to Slide View at any time by clicking . Other views available using these buttons include the Outline , Slide Sorter and Notes Views . The right-most button runs a Slide Show . Slide Shows and the different types of view are examined in detail later in this book.

If it's not already maximised, you may now like to increase the working area of the document window by maximising it:

Click [▲] on the document title bar.

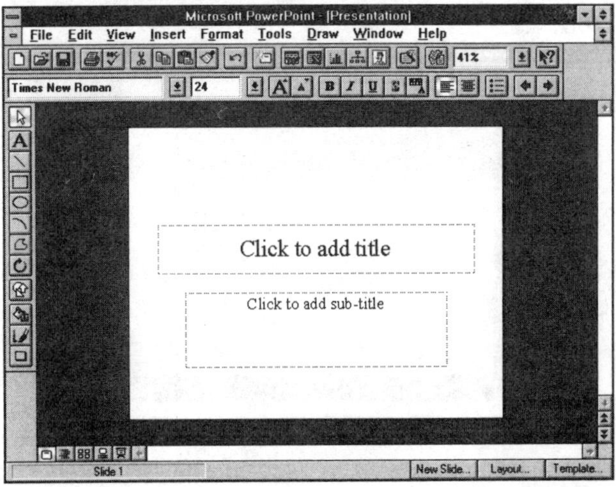

Adding a title

This is as simple as it looks.

Move the mouse pointer over the words 'Click to add title', so that it becomes the I-beam I, *and click.*

You must actually click – it isn't enough just to move the mouse pointer (the I-beam) over the area.

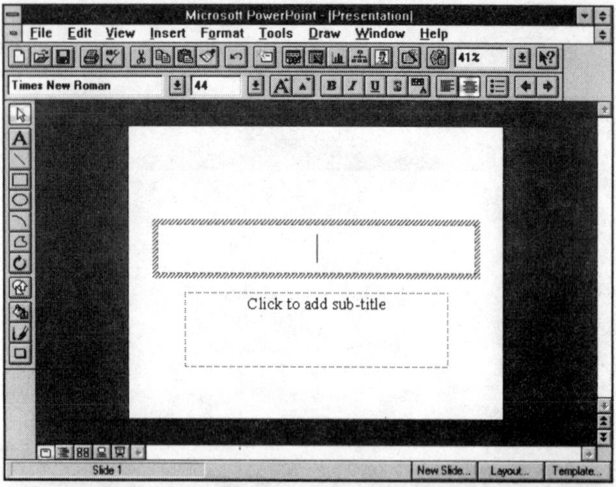

The grey border indicates the edge of the **title placeholder**. The flashing vertical line in the middle is the **insertion point.** Any text that you type now will be inserted at the insertion point.

Type `Aviation Monthly`*, but do not finish the line with* Enter*, as this would add an extra blank line.*

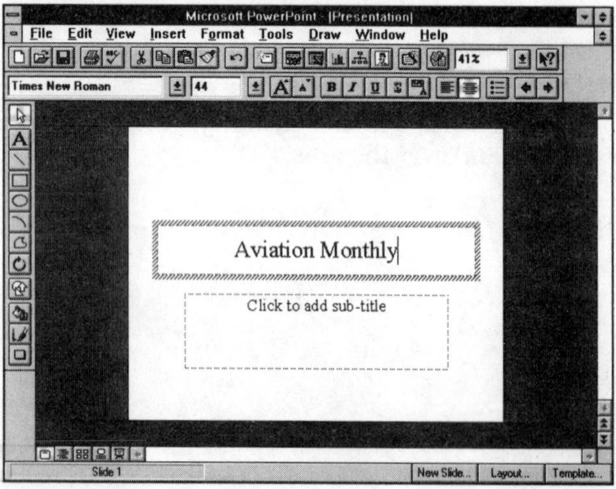

Note that the text has, by default, been centred within the title placeholder (this can be changed). The insertion point continues to flash after the newly-entered text.

Creating a sub-title

Adding a sub-title to a title slide follows the same method as adding the title: move the mouse pointer over the text 'Click to add sub-title' and click the left mouse button. Then, type some text.

Click the sub-title placeholder

Type **Available Now, Priced £2.50**

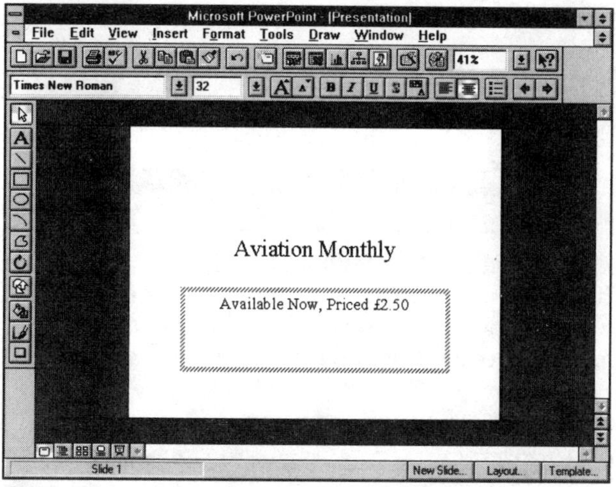

Adding a new slide

It is very easy to insert a new slide into a presentation: simply click [icon] on the standard toolbar – you could also do this by taking the Insert Slide... from the Insert menu, or by pressing Ctrl M.

Click [icon] on the Standard Toolbar.

The New Slide dialog appears presenting you with a choice of standardised Layouts (as before):

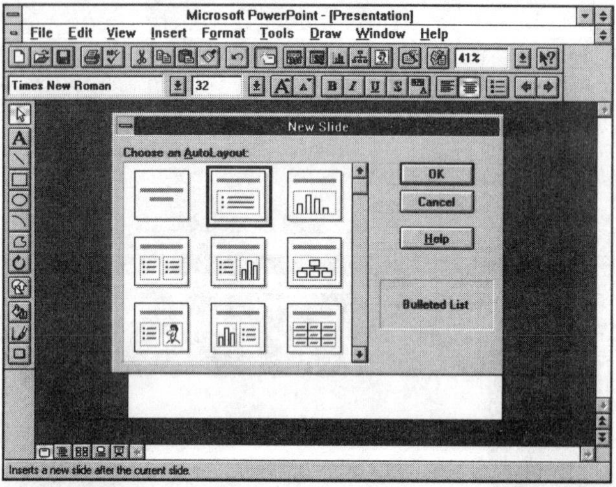

A slide layout called **Bulleted List** has already been selected for you. This is a different choice to that offered earlier, as this is not the first slide in a presentation. You could choose a different layout by clicking the illustration of the one you want.

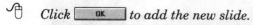

Click OK *to add the new slide.*

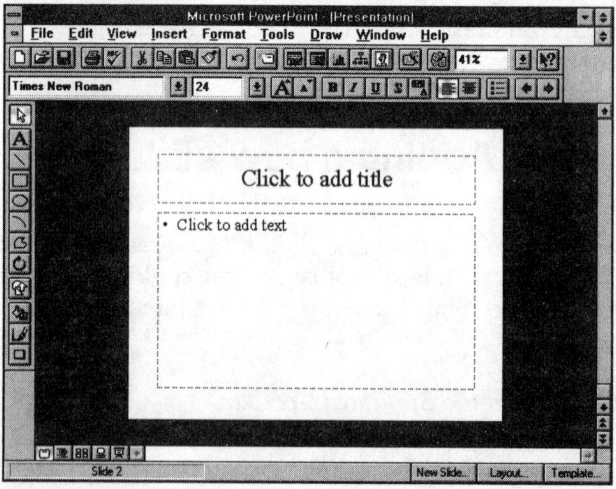

As you have now moved to slide two of the presentation, you will need to add another title. For this slide, you can use the name of the magazine again.

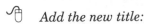

Add the new title:

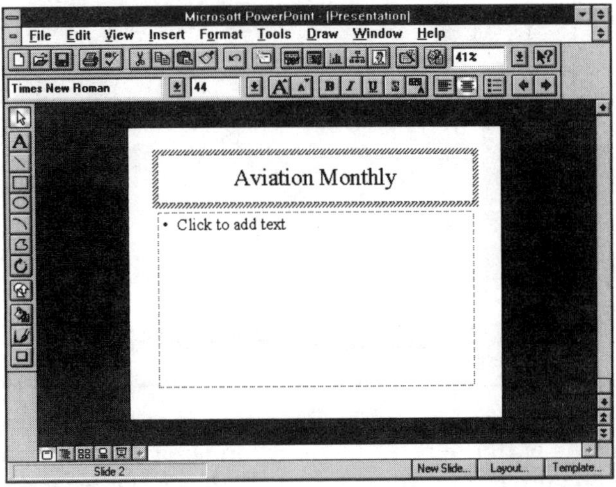

Adding a bullet point

A list of statements or phrases on a slide is known as a set of **bullet points**. A later section will consider how you can arrange to remove the bullet symbols if necessary, and how to set-up sub-points. For now, you will enter a simple set of bullet points with standard appearance.

Adding text to the body of the slide is done in a similar manner to titles. Note that, as for titles or any text editing, you can use the normal Windows editing features of [Home], [Esc], [Ctrl][↑], [Ctrl][↓], or double-clicking within a word to select it.

Click over the text 'Click to add text', and type the following text:

```
First issue this month[Enter]
Comprehensive[Enter]
```

```
Full Colour[Enter]
Free 'Plane Included
```

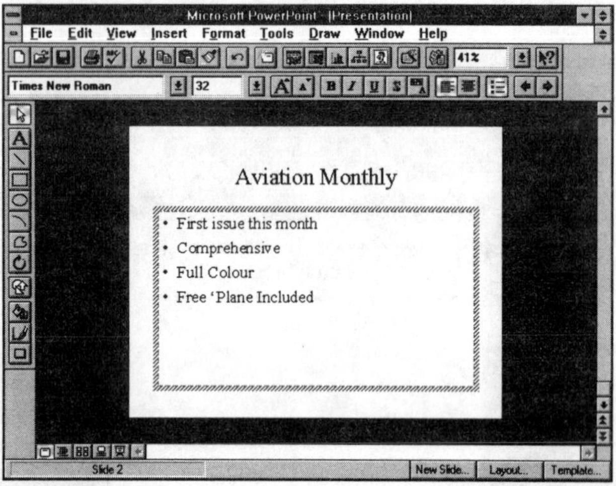

Each time [Enter] is pressed while typing, a new bullet point is created. As with the title, the insertion point continues flashing at the end of your typed text, and there is a border around the **text placeholder**.

If you have pressed [Enter] once too often and created an extra bullet point, press [←Back] to delete the extra point.

Even at this early stage you can run the slideshow to see your slides taking shape (though we have to do a lot more work if our presentation is to look at all impressive).

Click [button] and you will see current slide as it will appear in a slide show:

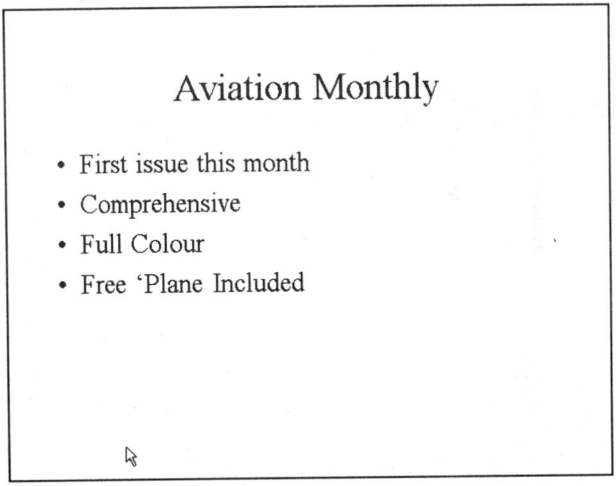
Aviation Monthly
• First issue this month
• Comprehensive
• Full Colour
• Free 'Plane Included

You may use the right mouse button to change to the first slide, and the left mouse button to change back to the second.

Esc takes you out of the slideshow and back to the slide view.

Summary: Getting started

- A standard slide consists of a title, plus a body object. The body object will have a number of bullet points.
- Until you enter some text in a text object, its position is marked by a text placeholder. To add text to the placeholder, click anywhere in it and type.
- A new slide can be added by clicking .
- Press Enter at the end of a bullet point to create another point.
- Press to see your slideshow, and Esc to finish it.

4

SELECTING AND FORMATTING

This chapter covers:

- Text formatting using tools or menus – font styles and typefaces.
- Changing the colours of text.
- Selecting a whole object or part of the text it contains.

The Formatting Toolbar

The text is very plain, so you can jazz it up a bit. The first step is to ensure that you can see the Formatting toolbar. It may be that your formatting toolbar has been switched off:

If the formatting toolbar is not already present, activate the View menu and select Toolbars...

A dialog will display the names of the available toolbars: those that are visible will be checked ☒.

Ensure that ☒ Formatting is checked.

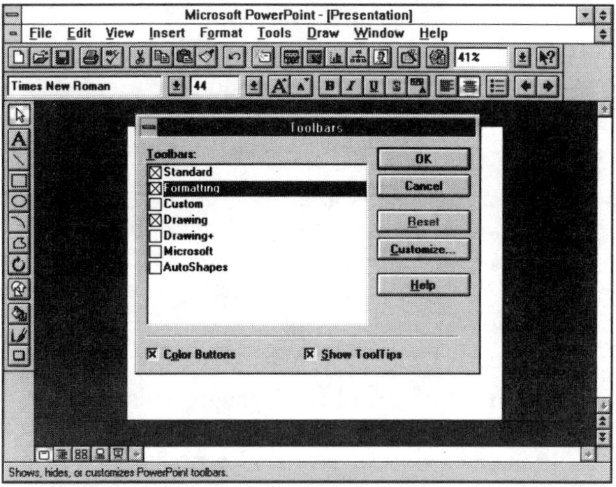

Alternatively you could right-click any toolbar:

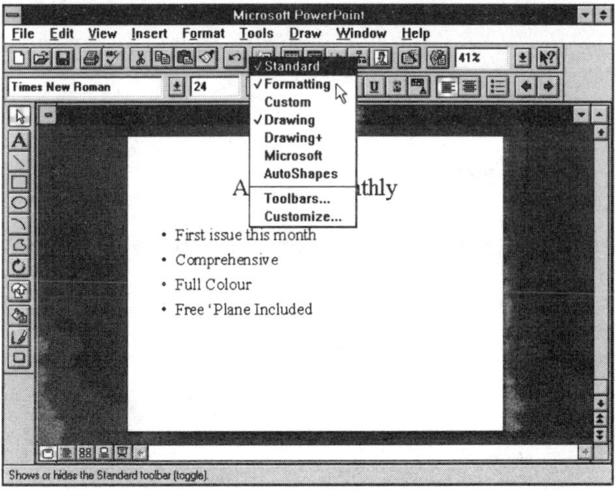

There are often several ways to do things – you will just have to work out the method with which you are most comfortable.

Selecting an object

If you plan to make changes to an object on a slide, use the normal Windows method 'select then do'. First, select the object or collection to be changed (usually by clicking it or dragging over it using the mouse). Then, choose a command.

New users often find selecting the right part of the screen tricky, so it is worth spending some time experimenting. Taking the title as an example, there are two sorts of selection with which you must become familiar: selecting the text, and selecting the placeholder.

You may find it easier to start off by ensuring that nothing is already selected. You can always ensure this by pressing Esc twice – this will deselect any selected objects and placeholders (although it may be only necessary to press it once, or not at all).

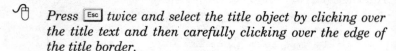

Press Esc *twice and select the title object by clicking over the title text and then carefully clicking over the edge of the title border.*

Selecting Text

If you click the text of the title (once) you will see something like this:

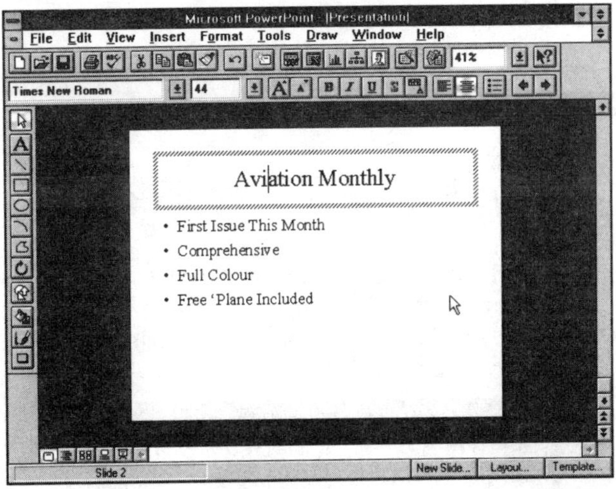

An insertion point appears beside the title text so you can edit the text or format parts of the text in the usual way – selecting parts of the text if necessary, as here:

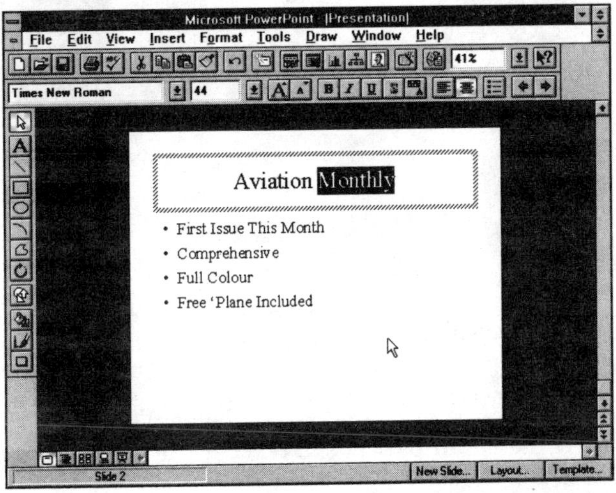

Such selection can be performed using either the mouse or the keyboard. The mouse method involves using the left mouse button to click one side of the item to select it, then dragging the mouse over to the other end of the selection. The keyboard method is to use the arrow keys (↑↓←→) to move to the object or text; then, move to the end of the text while holding down [Shift]. Various other keys can be used in conjunction with [Shift] and the arrow keys to alter the amount that you select in one go. For example, try [Shift][Ctrl] and either [←] or [→] to select words at a time.

Selecting Placeholders

A grey selection border also appears around the text – known as the **title placeholder**. Pressing [Esc] once, or carefully selecting the grey selection border around the title text selects the title placeholder:

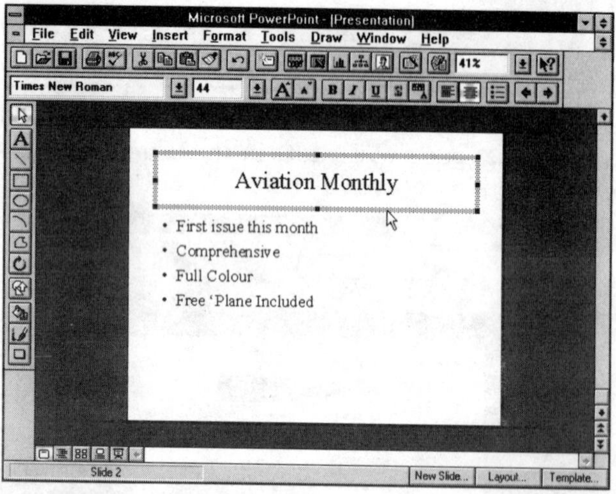

When the whole title placeholder is selected, black blocks called **selection handles** appear at the corners and halfway along the side of the selection border.

Now, any changes that you make will be applied to the whole of the title (rather than part of the text) or the whole item can be moved, sized or deleted.

Practise selecting the text itself, the title placeholder, and deselecting altogether.

The shape of your pointer will depend upon where it is on screen. When the pointer is over the background of the slide it shows as ↖, but when over the text it becomes the I-beam pointer (I). If an object is selected, a few other shapes may appear. The four-headed arrow (✥) is associated with bullet symbols, and if the placeholder is selected, a two headed arrow indicates that the pointer is over a selection handle.

Formatting a text object

With the whole title selected, try out **B** *(bold),* U *(underline),* *I* *(italic), and* S *(text shadow) on the Formatting toolbar.*

The Formatting toolbar also includes buttons (A and A) to increase or decrease the font size and a drop-down ⬇ to change font.

Try changing the font and point size of the title.

≡ and ≡ are easy to interpret – they align the text in the selected object at the left or centrally. To see what the other tools do, hold the mouse pointer over a them for a few seconds: a yellow flag appears naming the tool. These are called ToolTips. For example, the ToolTip displayed for 📂 is Open

Change the title alignment between centred and left-aligned and back again, as you wish (in this illustration, the title text is left-aligned and the words are shadowed).

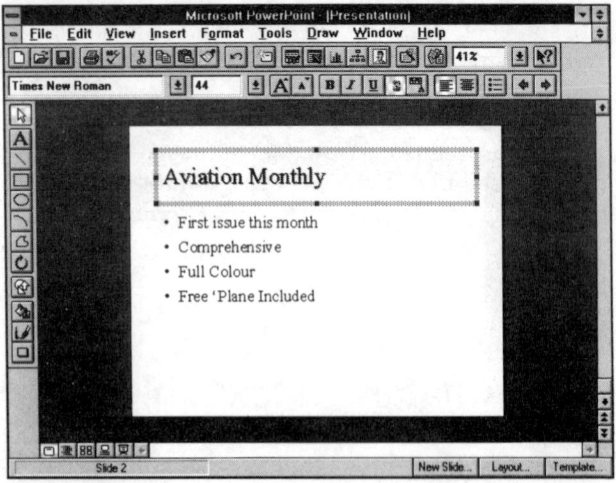

Selecting text within a text placeholder

As already mentioned, you select (and format) part of the text within a placeholder.

Click inside the text of the body placeholder (looking for the insertion point which shows that you are able to edit), then use the mouse and click anywhere within one word which you wish to format – we'll choose the word 'Colour'.

In Windows there is a standard quick way of selecting a whole word – double-clicking it – but even this is unnecessary if you wish to format a particular word. Formats are understood to apply to whole words unless you explicitly select just a character or characters.

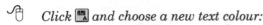

Click and choose a new text colour:

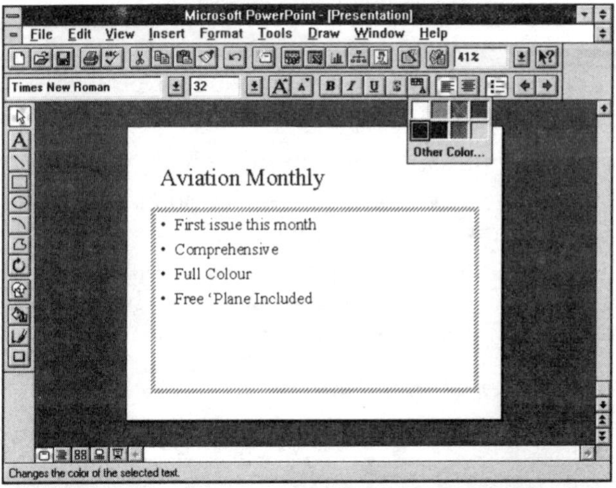

After selecting your colour:

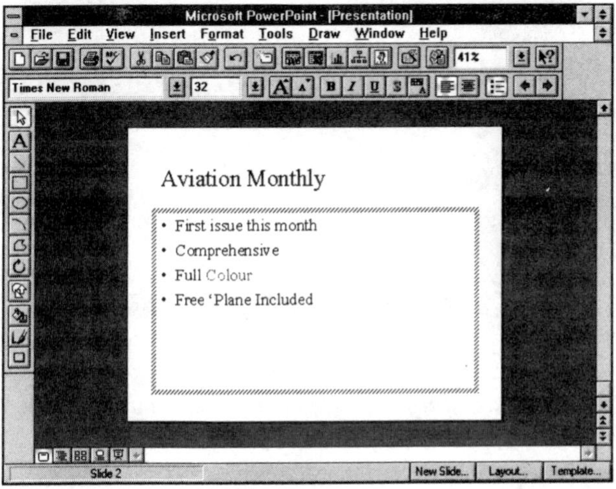

Any colour text can be used anywhere, but beware that some colours work better than others in the various media (paper, colour screen, monochrome screen, etc.).

If you plan to change the appearance of more than one word, select them using the mouse or keyboard.

You may want to change the appearance of a whole bullet, in which case you must select it. There are several ways of doing this:

- Hold Γ and click anywhere in the bullet point text.
- Triple-click anywhere in the bullet point text - this would also select any sub-points (see later).
- Click the bullet point itself (again including sub-points) - although this only works if you are already editing the body text, so an initial click may be necessary.

Triple-click the first bullet:

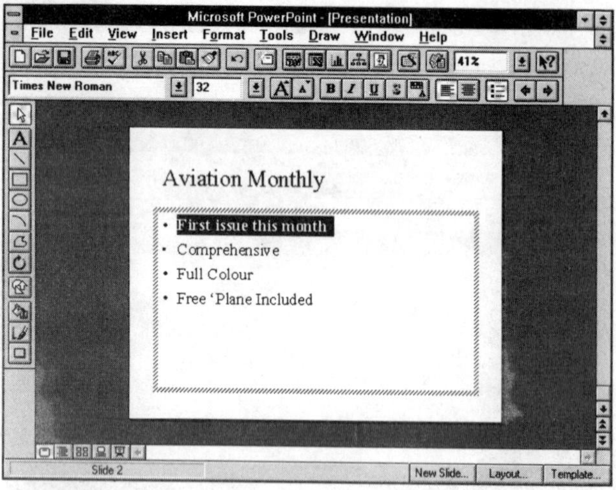

Make some simple change, like italicising it, then put it back as it was (remember you can use Γζ to undo changes)

Formatting changes can be made to all the text within a text object by clicking the border of the text object (i.e. all the bullets together, in this case).

Select the text object by clicking its border (look for the selection border with sizing handles). Then, experiment with text formatting using the tools.

You should find will remove or replace the bullet symbols themselves.

Click twice to see them removed and replaced again.

If you click inside the box, so that you do not have the whole set of bullet points selected (and you do not see the selection border with sizing handles) then only the bullet symbol for the point where you clicked is changed.

Change the text colour of all the bullet points by selecting the body object and choosing a colour from the Text Colour tool

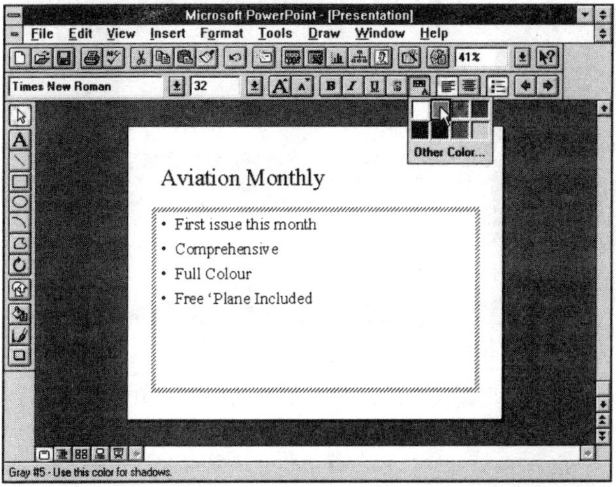

This has overridden our previous choice of colour for one word.

Text formatting using the menu

The Format menu offers more options for changing the appearance of text.

Select a few words and try out the various options under Format Change Case...

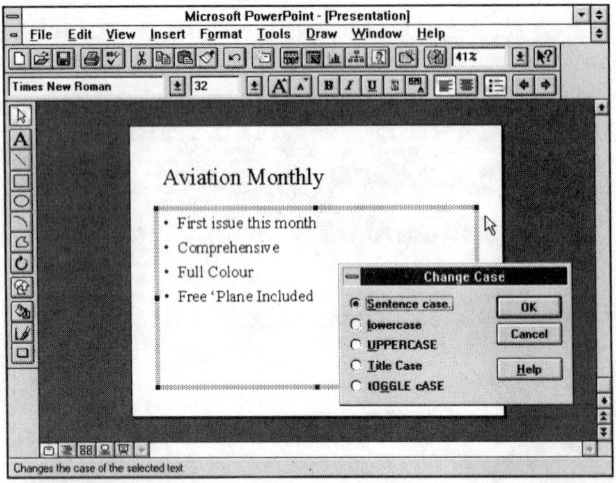

The keyboard shortcut for changing the case of your text is H, *which you can press repeatedly to cycle through the options (though you should note that neither Sentence case nor Toggle case are available using this method).*

You should also experiment with the Periods command on the Format menu - this adds or removes full stops at the ends of bullet points, and can be useful if you need to harmonise a set of bullet points that haven't been entered in a consistent fashion.

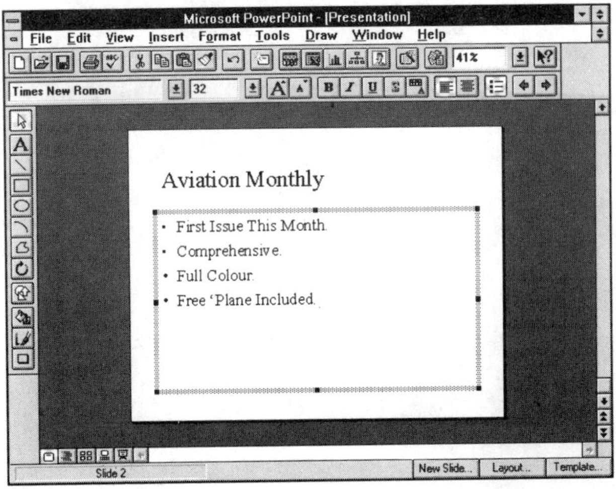

The above screenshot shows all points ending in full stops and the first bullet point has been changed to title case to make it consistent with the remaining items.

Adding further slides

Click on the Standard toolbar.

As before, a dialog appears which presents you with a choice of standardised layouts. Again, Bulleted List is selected for you.

Click OK *to add the new slide.*

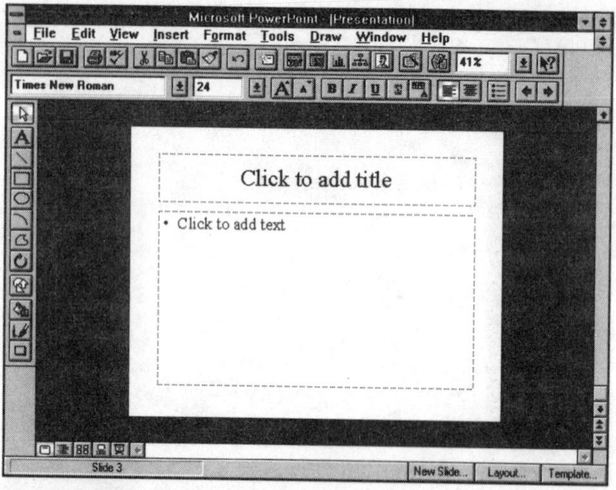

As before, a slide appears with dashed lines marking the positions of the title and text objects – just follow the instructions on the screen:

Click the title area and type `Assembly Instructions`

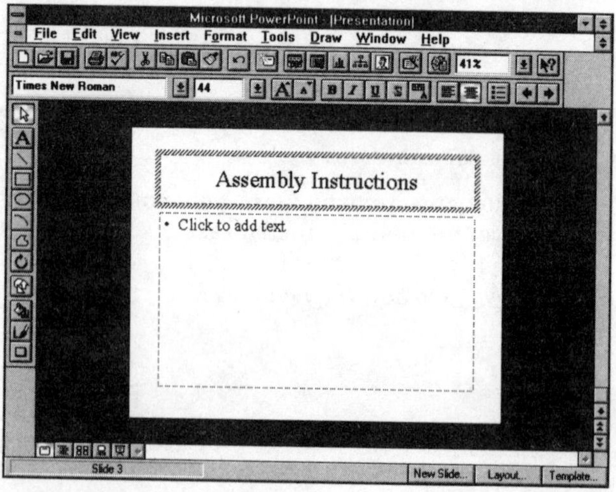

Click the text area to add bullet points.

Type `Join wings to fuselage` [Enter]
`Place tail at back` [Enter]

```
Learn to fly[Enter]
Acquire fare paying passengers
```

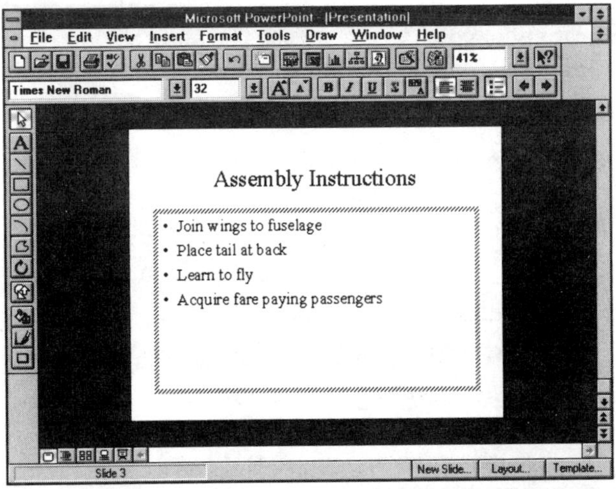

Add a further slide in the same way:

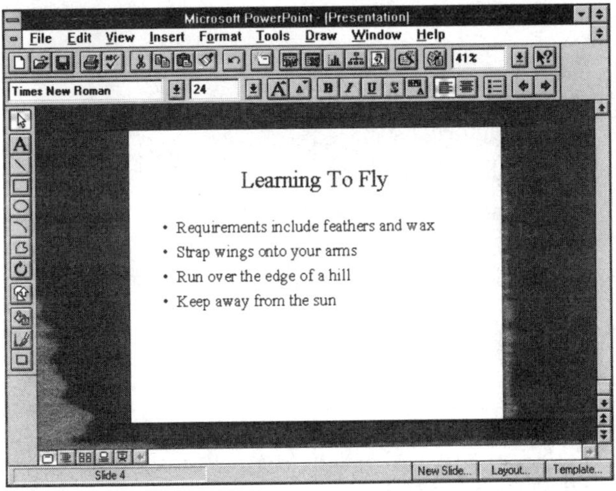

We will cover many of the other new slide options later in the book, so don't worry about them for now.

You could at this stage add additional slides of your own.

Now is the ideal time to try out your slide show, but remember that a slide show will always start on the current slide, which is likely to be the last one, as we have just entered it! To move to the first slide, you can either use the slide bar on the right or press PgUp on the keyboard the required number of times until the status bar at the bottom of the screen shows 'Slide 1'.

Find the first slide, and run the slide show by clicking

Use the mouse buttons to change slides:

- Next slide: left mouse button, Δ or Space
- Previous slide: right button, E or ←Back

Add any 'on the fly' emphasis, as shown on the earlier example by wiggling the mouse a bit (which makes appear) clicking and using the mouse to mark features to which you wish to draw attention:

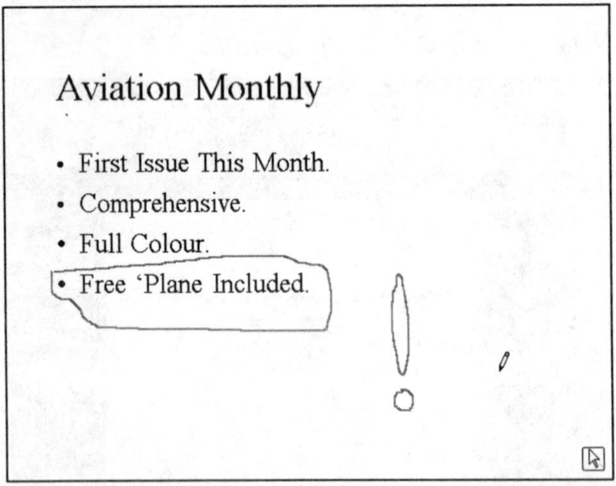
Aviation Monthly
• First Issue This Month.
• Comprehensive.
• Full Colour.
• Free 'Plane Included.

When you have finished highlighting clicking at the bottom right of the screen, to return to normal.

Pressing Esc will return you to PowerPoint.

Pressing during the show to display the help screen relating to the keys you can use during a presentation (as shown below).

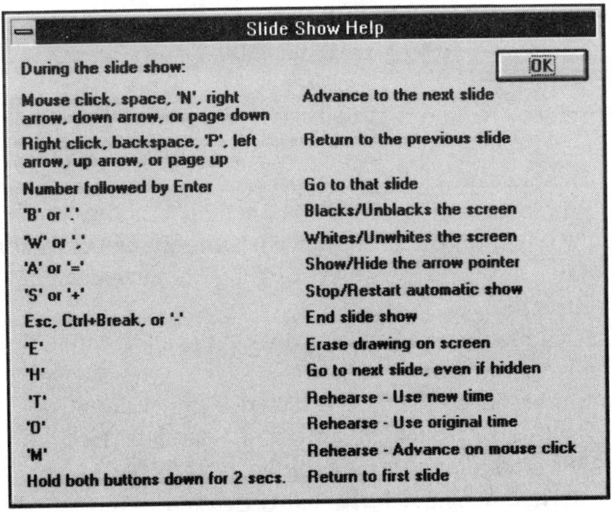
Slide Show Help
OK
During the slide show:
Mouse click, space, 'N', right arrow, down arrow, or page down
Advance to the next slide
Right click, backspace, 'P', left arrow, up arrow, or page up
Return to the previous slide
Number followed by Enter
Go to that slide
'B' or '.'
Blacks/Unblacks the screen
'W' or ','
Whites/Unwhites the screen
'A' or '='
Show/Hide the arrow pointer
'S' or '+'
Stop/Restart automatic show
Esc, Ctrl+Break, or '-'
End slide show
'E'
Erase drawing on screen
'H'
Go to next slide, even if hidden
'T'
Rehearse - Use new time
'O'
Rehearse - Use original time
'M'
Rehearse - Advance on mouse click
Hold both buttons down for 2 secs.
Return to first slide

Note the last entry especially – hold both buttons for 2 seconds to return to the first slide.

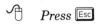

Press [Esc]

Summary: Selecting and formatting

- When formatting text, use the 'Select then Do' approach.
- Select a whole text object by clicking its border (look for the special selection border with handles at the corners and along the sides).
- When editing text, use the normal Windows methods for selecting it: dragging with the mouse or holding down Shift and moving over the chosen text using the cursor keys.
- If you have no text selected, changes are made to the current word.
- Bullet points can be selected by clicking the bullet itself, triple-clicking any bullet point text or holding Ctrl and clicking any bullet point text (this final method does not include any sub-points).
- If the format toolbar is not present, use View Toolbars to display a menu of the available toolbars.
- Most formatting can be done using buttons and drop-down lists on the Formatting toolbar.

5

COLOUR SCHEMES AND SLIDE MASTER

This chapter covers

- Using a different colour scheme.
- Working on the Slide Master.
- Adding page numbers to the Slide Master.
- Closing and saving the presentation.

Colour schemes

Behind the title and body objects is the slide itself. We refer to this part of the slide as the **background**. It is the background upon which all objects on the slide are placed. One of the most striking things you can do to a slide is colour this background.

In this next section, you will review the colour scheme that has been set, and alter it.

Pull down the Format menu and choose Slide Color Scheme.

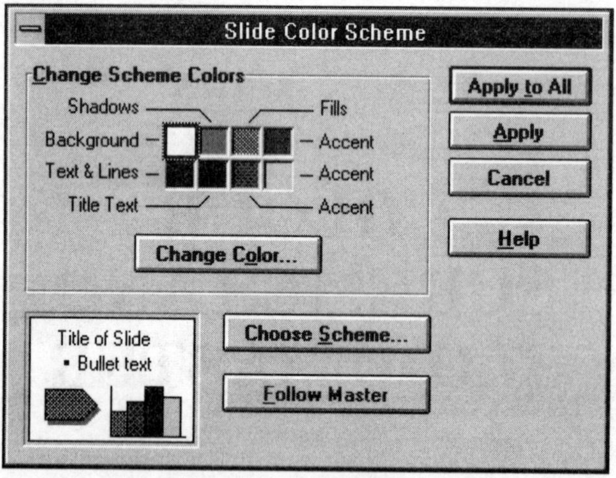

Look at the grid of eight colours. Each of the colours has a specified role, and the set of eight colours is known as a **colour scheme**. You can apply this chosen colour scheme to some, or all, of your slides.

Some of the colours are self explanatory, the remainder cover the default colour of filled in objects (Fills), and secondary colours such as those used in charts (Accent). These will be discussed later, but a sample of how a chart would look with the present colour scheme is shown in the bottom left-hand corner of the dialog.

PowerPoint has predefined sets of colour schemes available. Each scheme contains a set of colours which complement each other. You can choose different schemes and even make up your own but you ought to be aware that there are over fifty predefined schemes which have been professionally designed, and you may find it difficult to improve on these!

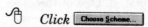

Click 

Initially, the list of possible background colours is shown. Pick one you like as the background colour, using ↓ or ↑ or the mouse to select different colours.

Choose a background colour from the Background list.

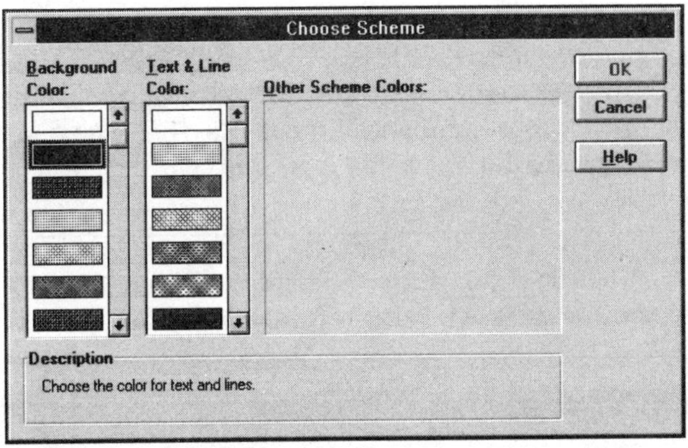

See how the list of possible text & line colours appear as soon as PowerPoint knows which background colour you are currently considering.

Choose a text colour from the Text & Line list.

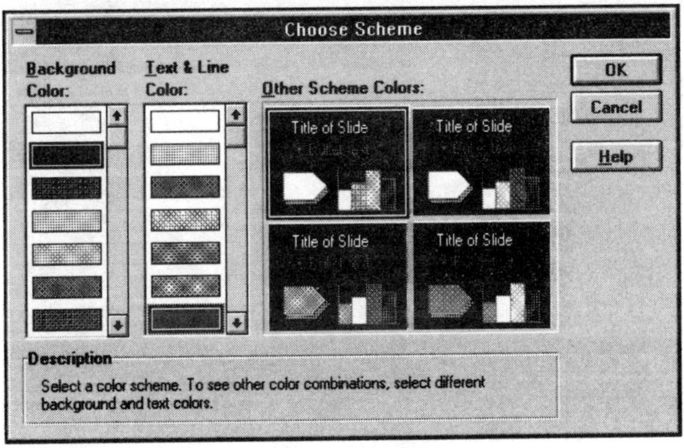

When you select a text & line colour, PowerPoint then offers a further set of colours which would probably complement the text, line and background choices. Each of these sets of colours, together with the background and text & line colours you have just chosen, is a **colour scheme**.

Click one of the sets of Other Scheme Colors, then click OK. *Alternatively double-click your scheme of choice.*

You are now presented with two options: Apply or Apply to All. Apply will only change your current slide; Apply to All will apply to all slides, except that specific colours that you may have applied to particular text (as you did earlier) will be unchanged.

> *If you wish to keep a consistent appearance across all your slides, then use* Apply to All.

Click Apply to All *to apply your new colour scheme to all your slides and return to the slide.*

The slide will now take on the new colour scheme:

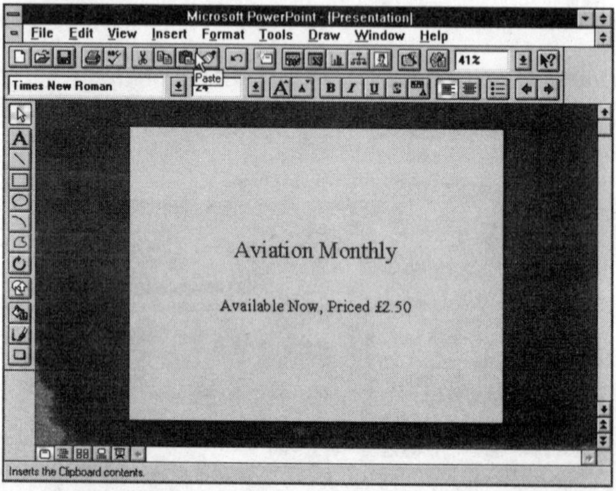

Most of the colours on your slides should now have changed, although any local re-colouring of text which you may have done earlier should have survived. Choosing a different colour scheme will only change the **default** colours, the colours used if no others are specified. If you were to add new slides now, they would follow the revised colours. When you come to add shadows, charts and shapes onto a slide, the new Scheme Colours will be used by default.

The Slide Master

Every PowerPoint slide show includes a Slide Master. Any design choices made on the Master will be the defaults for all slides in this show – effectively, when we used [Apply to All] (above) we were changing the master, and hence affecting all slides (except those that had explicitly been set to some other colour). You may have noticed a [Follow Master] button, allowing a particular slide to be re-harmonised with the Slide Master.

The Slide Master covers other formatting options in addition to colour, such as: text formatting, positioning of the title and body objects, and any decorative graphics such as borders, shapes or drawings.

The new presentation consists of four slides, and it may seem as though it is quite easy to make any changes to each of the slides, but since it is likely that more slides may be added, it makes sense to put changes on the Master (assuming they need to be consistent amongst all slides).

You can view the Slide Master by holding [Shift] while clicking the Slide View button or by choosing Slide Master from the Master section of the View menu.

Hold Shift *and click to switch to the Slide Master.*

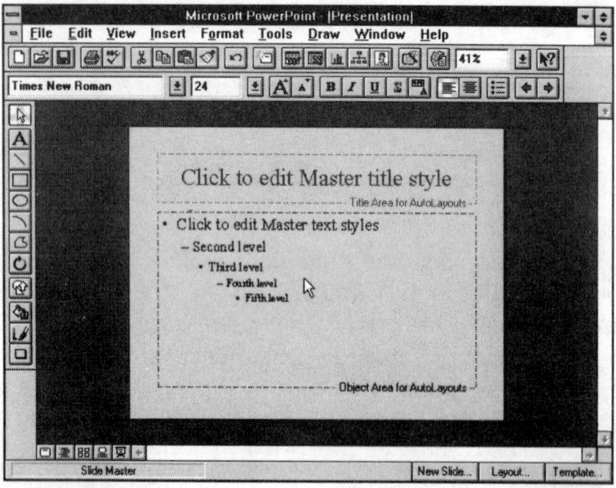

The Slide Master produces an effect similar to pre-printed letterhead paper. You add your own text on individual letters but the printed address and logo stay the same. As an example, you will add a text object and page number code to the Master. This will then appear on each slide in the current presentation (and on any other slides you may add to it later).

Creating a text object

To create a text object, use A on the Drawing toolbar (not to be confused with the text sizing tools A and A on the Formatting toolbar). You simply click where you want the text, and start typing. Thereafter you can treat it like the standard title and bullet points that you have already used, except that it is much more likely that you will want to reposition it. We are going to add a sort of header to the slide master – this will then appear on every slide.

Click A *and move to the top left corner of the Slide Master, then click again. At the insertion point, type* **`Fly-A-Way Publishing`** *as a company name.*

Press Esc *when you have finished typing.*

When you see the selection border, you can move (or reformat) the piece of text just as you did in the presentation slide earlier.

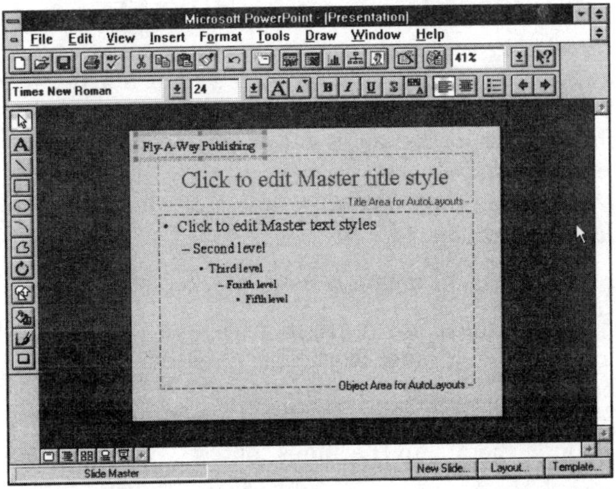

Don't forget – if you want to move it, click the border itself, **not** the black handles. You use the black handles when you wish to re-size it, for instance like this:

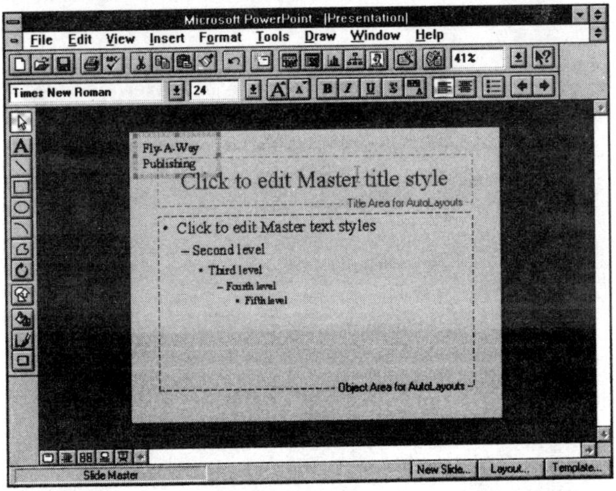

Adding page numbers

Page number codes can only be placed on a Master. The code appears as "" in Slide View, but will display proper page numbers when you print the slides out or run a screen show.

Click the desktop (the dark area behind the slide) to deselect the text object (or press Esc*).*

From the Insert menu, choose Page Number.

You can place the page number anywhere on the Master by dragging the placeholder border, but be careful that neither this nor the text object overlaps the placeholders for the title or the body object, otherwise their contents may overlap your titles and bullet points on the slides themselves.

If you want to centre the Page Number on the Master, drag the border of the page number code to your desired location and use the sizing handles to make it as wide as possible. Now use [icon] *to centre the code. This is much easier than trying to centre the page numbers by eye (the selection border will not be visible on the slides themselves).*

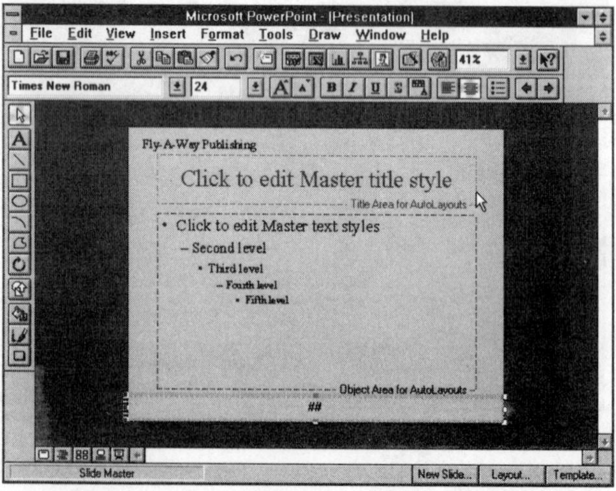

You could also edit the page number like another text object, for instance, like this:

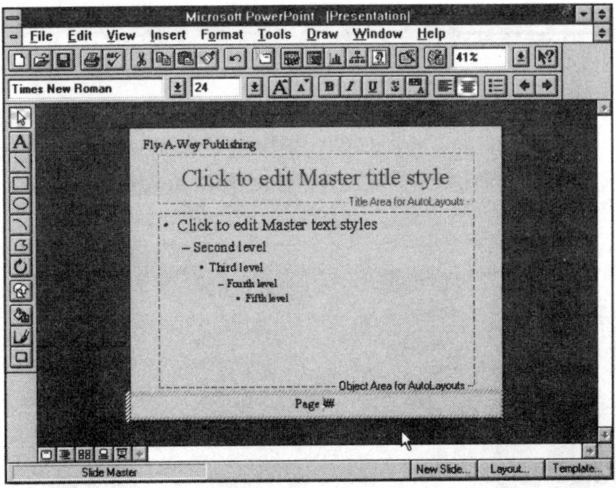

You may decide to change the colour or size of it too, of course.

Effect of slide master changes

Switch back to the presentation by clicking

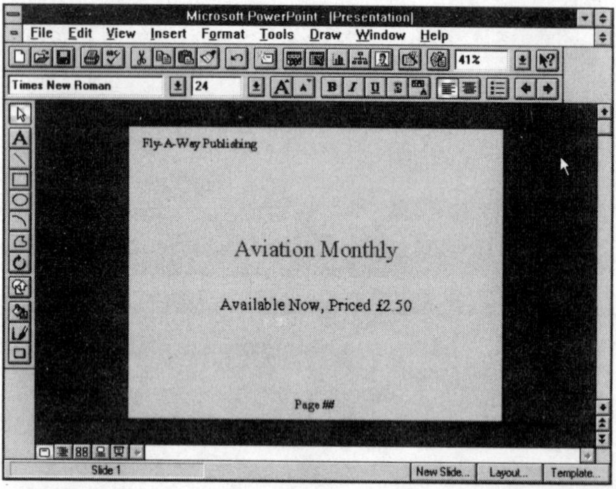

The text object and the page number code should now appear on the slide. Objects like the page numbers are always displayed as ## when in Slide View, and only take on the correct numbers during printing or in a slide show

Click to see how your slide show will look:

Formatting choices and objects added to the Slide Master will affect every slide in this presentation, and if more slides are added later these will also be affected. Working on the Slide Master is a good way to ensure that the same design is carried right through the presentation. It also makes it easy to revise your design.

You can specify that an individual slide has a different layout or background shading, or indeed omit background objects altogether (like our 'header' and page number).

Take the Slide Background option from the Format menu:

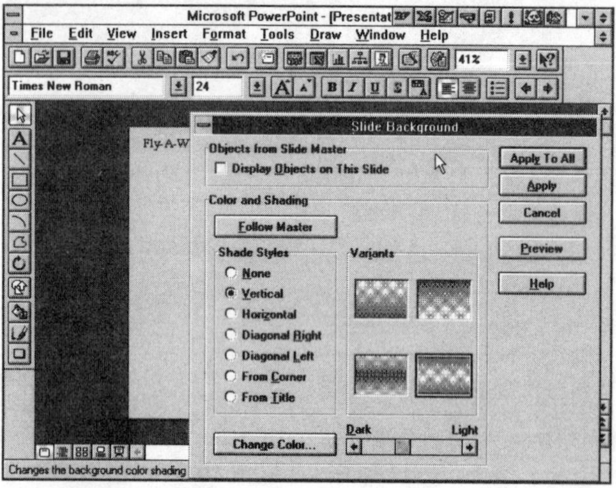

From this dialog you can (for instance) deselect ⊠ Display Objects on This Slide (this refers to the objects you placed on the Slide Master), and choose a shading variant of your background colour (as above). Click Apply, to apply the changes just to this slide:

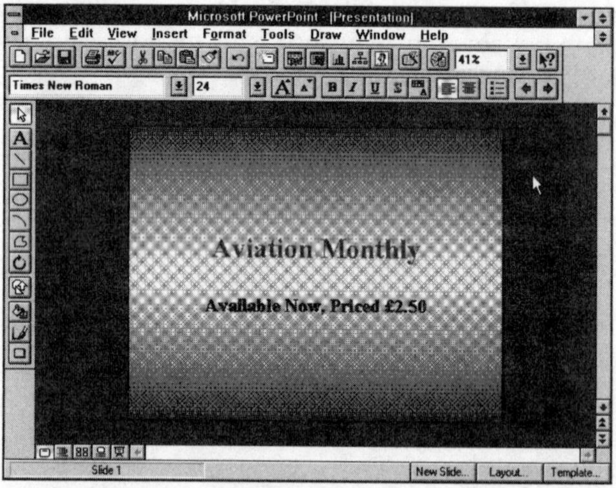

Summary: Colour schemes and the Slide Master

- The default colours used for the slide background, text, graphics objects and so on are set in the Colour Scheme.
- The Slide Colour Scheme dialog offers a sequence of choices so you can easily choose a colour scheme that is effective (but no guarantee of good taste!).
- This colour scheme can be applied to all slides in the current show or to just one slide.
- Shift – click the Slide View button (▣) to see the Slide Master.
- Anything on the Slide Master appears on all slides, unless expressly inhibited (using Format Slide Background...).
- Put background objects such as text or a page number at the edge of the Slide Master so they don't interfere with the contents of the slides proper.

Saving the slide show

If you were to switch off the machine before saving this slide show, or for some reason PowerPoint were to crash before you save it, you would lose your work and have to re-do it. The slide show on the screen is only in the computer's 'RAM' (i.e. its non-permanent memory) – this will be forgotten by the computer if it is switched off before the information has been saved onto a disk (which does store information after the power is switched off).

Click ▣

Save and Save As

Once a presentation has been named and saved, clicking [save icon] will save it again. This presentation has not been named, so the Save As dialog is presented. This dialog can be invoked in future by using File Save As..., allowing you to save the slide show under a different name and/or in a different location:

You are prompted to give the presentation a name and directory location:

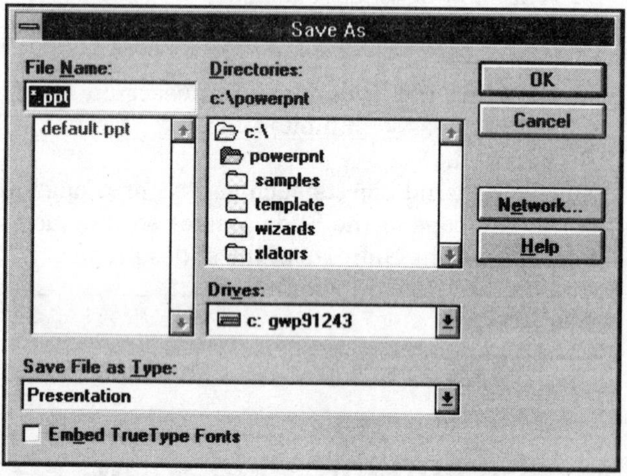

You can use the list boxes to navigate around the drives and directories to choose the most appropriate place for the presentation to be stored. After the document has been saved, you should be returned to your presentation, ready for more editing.

Save your presentation, in a suitable directory, as AVIATOR.PPT.

Filenames – a reminder

You may know that in Windows, which runs on top of MS-DOS (on which most users run Windows), you are allowed only up to eight letters for the name and an optional three letters for the extension which comes after a full stop. The name should be unique in the chosen directory. No spaces are allowed.

Certain special characters (including [Space], [*], [/] and [\]) are not allowed in filenames.

We suggest that you restrict your filenames to normal letters and numbers. If you would like to have a space you can use the underscore [_] character (for example `SALES_94.PPT`), which looks quite like a space. Incidentally, you can type filenames in upper or lower case – PowerPoint, like all programs running under Windows, does not distinguish between the two cases and it will accept either.

Summary Info

At this point you will normally be presented with the Summary Info dialog (this actually depends on how PowerPoint is configured – whether or not you have ☒ Prompt for Summary Info enabled in Tools Options). Here you should fill in as much as you find useful; the fields are discretionary, offering you an opportunity to record data about the presentation which might help with locating and identifying this presentation file at a later date.

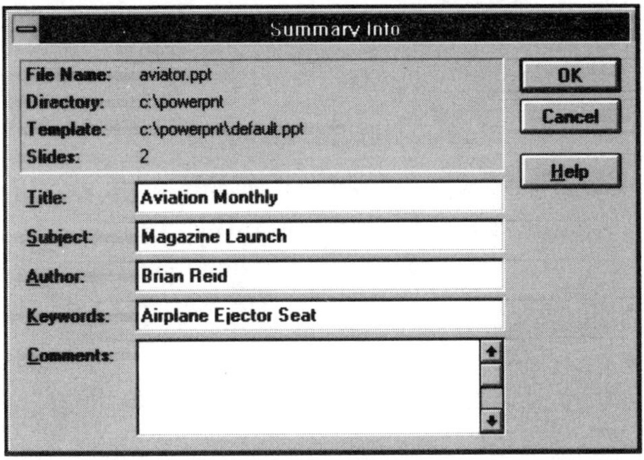

Fill in suitable data in the Summary Info dialog, as you have done in the screenshot above, using [Tab] *or the mouse to move between edit boxes.*

> *The Cancel button on this dialog doesn't cancel the Save, it just cancels any changes you make to the Summary Info.*

As already mentioned, if the presentation already has a name, when [save] is clicked, the latest version of the work is saved with that name and at that location, overwriting the earlier version. It is good practice to save frequently in this way, just in case of a power break or unexpected computer crash.

Closing the slide show

Now that the presentation has been saved on disk, you can safely close the document.

Double-click the document control menu, [−], or choose File Close.

In this chapter you created a very simple slide show from scratch. In the following chapters, you will explore PowerPoint further, to show you more of PowerPoint's many features that make your slide shows impressive and enjoyable to look at.

Summary: Saving and Closing a Slide Show

- When you first use [save], you invoke the Save As dialog, allowing a name and location to be chosen.
- Once a presentation has been saved, clicking [save] saves the current version of the work using the existing filename and path.
- Save your work frequently to avoid accidental data loss.
- The current document can be closed in the usual way, such as by using Exit from the File menu or double-clicking the document control icon [−].

6

THE AUTO CONTENT WIZARD AND CUE CARDS

This chapter covers:

- creating a presentation with a theme using Auto Content Wizard
- getting help from Cue Cards
- running an on-screen slide show

Using the AutoContent Wizard

Until now we have relied on our own material entirely – simply starting with a blank Presentation (slide show) and adding new (more or less blank) slides to which we add our own text. PowerPoint has some features that can make producing a presentation even easier.

Click ▢ *to create a new slide show.*

From the alternatives offered, choose the AutoContent Wizard.

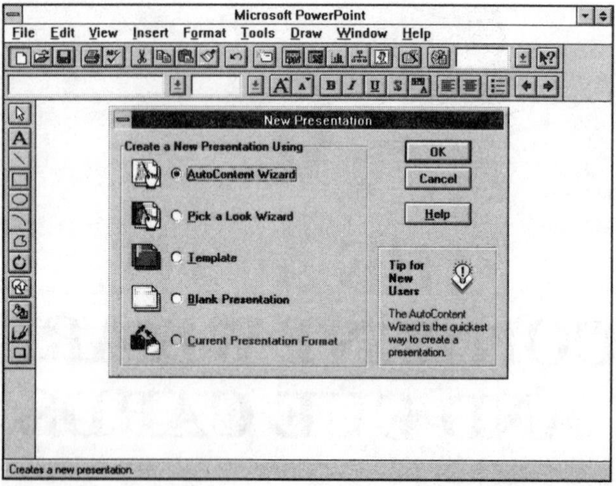

The AutoContent Wizard offers plenty of guidance if you are putting together a new presentation, with suggestions for what to say in a series of slides and some basic layout and design choices.

We will use this to make a new presentation for Rondo Tyres Ltd (an imaginary company, we hope), introducing the company and presenting some ideas on uses of The Wheel. Then we will see how to customise a presentation and add formatting and graphics to suit your own needs.

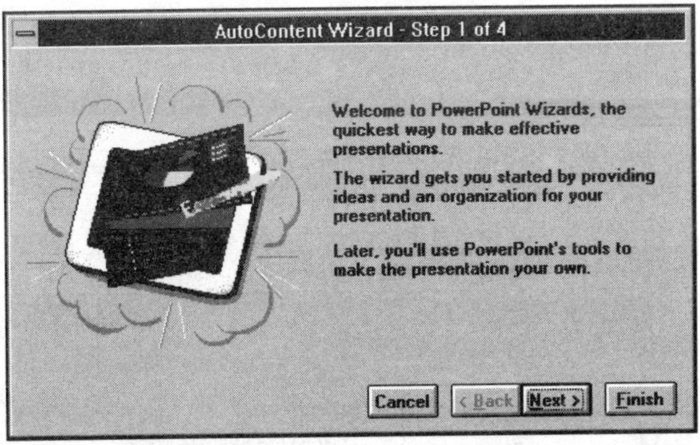

The first screen of the AutoContent Wizard is just an introduction, so after you have read this, click Next> to move to step 2 of 4.

In Step 2, create a topic for your presentation by using the title `The Wheel`*, your name and perhaps a company name or slogan.*

To move between the boxes (**fields**) of the Step 2 dialog, either click in the box with the mouse, or, if you prefer, use Tab to move forwards (Shift Tab moves backwards).

This data will be used in your presentation (you can always change it later, if necessary):

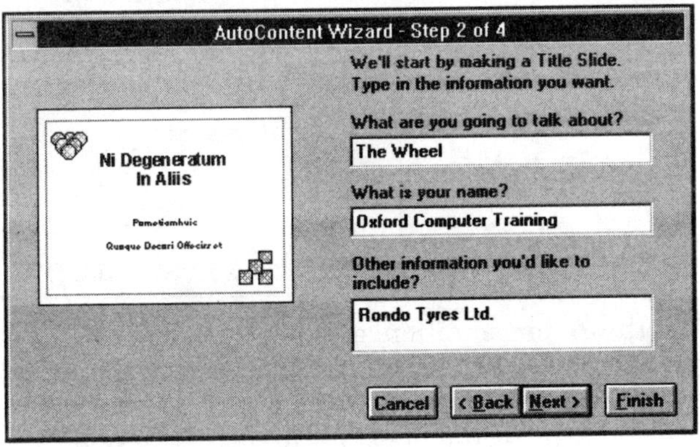

When ready, click Next>

Step 3 offers several presentation types. These are intended to provide guidelines and suggested text for each type of presentation.

Click the option button for each type in turn, to examine the outlines available.

For example, 'Recommending a Strategy'...

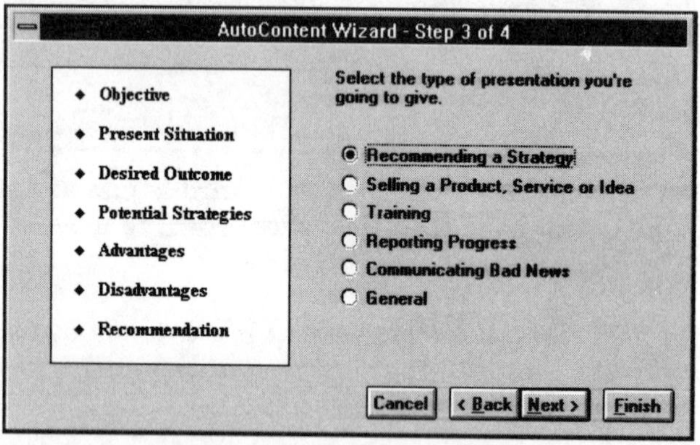

...or 'Communicating Bad News':

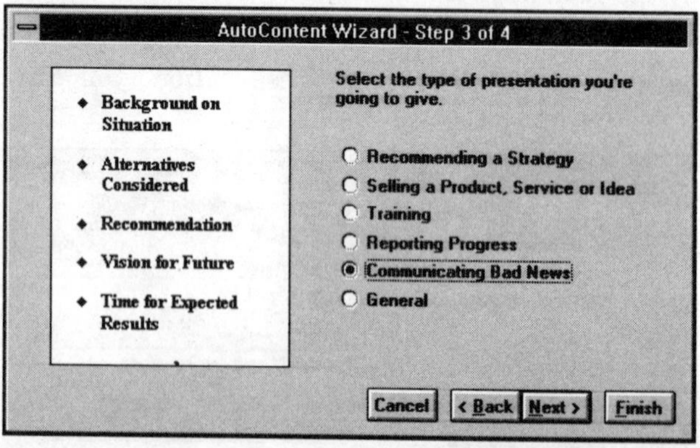

Each of the 6 presentation outlines is task-specific and the chances are none of them will match your needs exactly. But that doesn't matter, as the whole point of the Wizard is that it will give you a good starting point to further develop your presentation. It's not intended to do all the work for you!

In this case, we are trying to present some information about the wheel. This doesn't really fall into any of the special categories above, so we'll use the General category. You can, of course, come back later, and try any of the other Wizards that take your fancy.

Choose ◉ General.

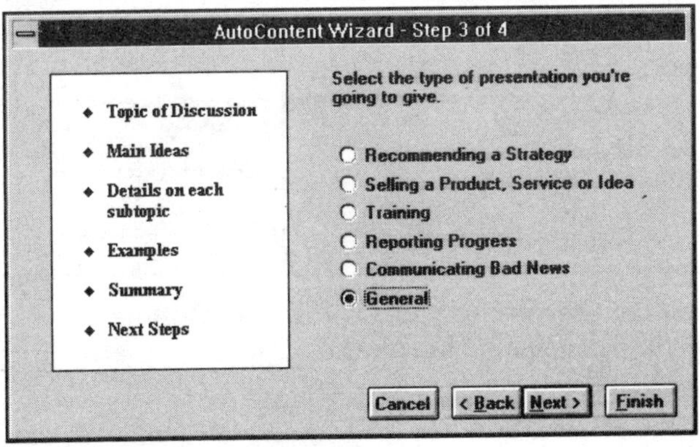

After you select the presentation type, click Next> *to show you a final, information dialog:*

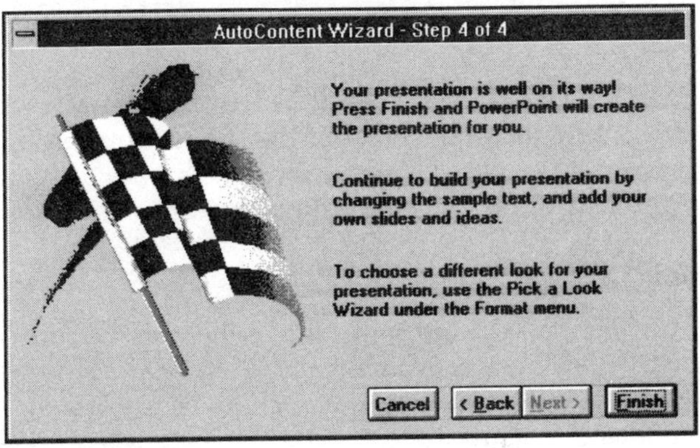

Click Finish *to finish the Wizard.*

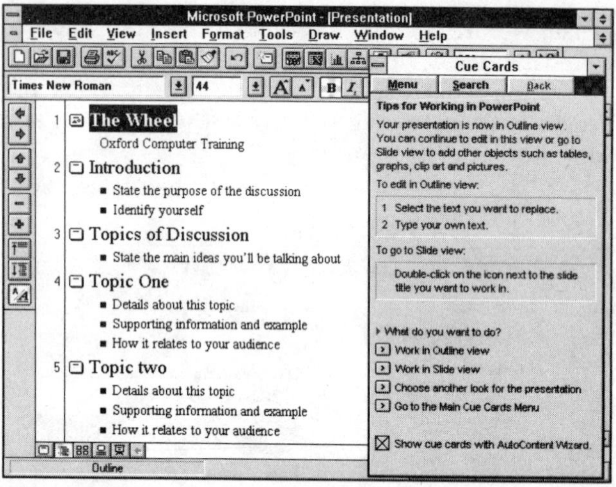

At the end of the Wizard you are taken to **Outline View** and the **Cue Cards** window appears on the screen.

Cue Cards

PowerPoint's Cue Cards are designed to help new users and offer useful guidance on carrying out important tasks. They stay visible while you follow a list of simple instructions, helping you learn how to do everyday tasks.

Read the Cue Card.

As the Card says, 'the presentation is now in Outline View'. Outline View is a view in which you can see only the raw text of each slide. As you can see, each slide is presented in the following form:

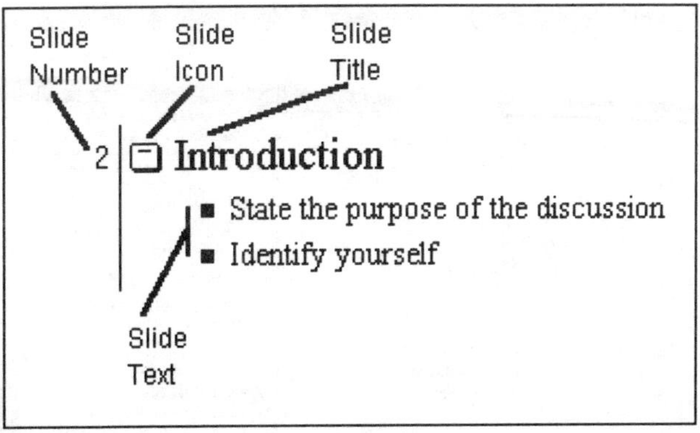

We can only briefly introduce Outline View here: each slide is represented by a numbered icon with the **slide title** next to it. The text for that slide is shown indented to the right. This hierarchical view helps you see which text belongs to which slide. We will look at Outline View in a lot more detail in a later chapter.

Returning to the cue card again, there is a checkbox which determines whether this Card is displayed every time you use the AutoContent Wizard.

Clear the checkbox if you don't want to see the Cue Cards next time you use the AutoContent Wizard.

Note also that the Cue Card says: 'to edit the text, select the text you want to replace and type your own text.' That sounds quite easy, so let's try it. You'll find that if you click in any slide text, the Cue Card window stays on top so that you can still read the Cards.

Click at the end of the Slide 1 title 'The Wheel'. Type **`(An Introduction)`**

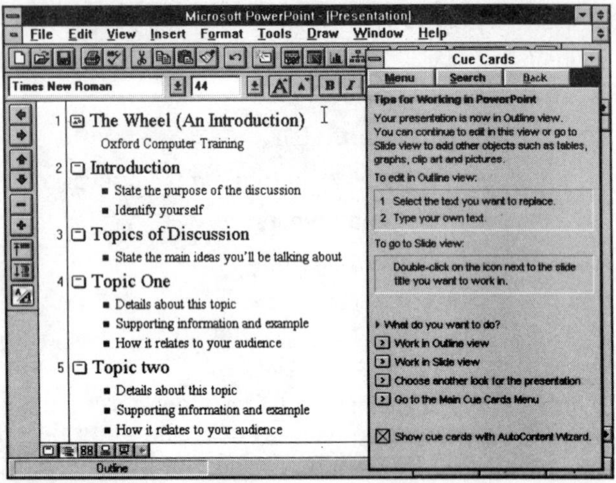

As you can see, the Cue Card stayed visible as you worked on your slide.

You could, of course, do further editing at this point, but let's look at another topic in Cue Cards, to help us get a better idea of what this feature will do for us. Cue Cards have a menu page, giving you an overview of what is available.

Click **Menu** *to get to the Cue Cards menu.*

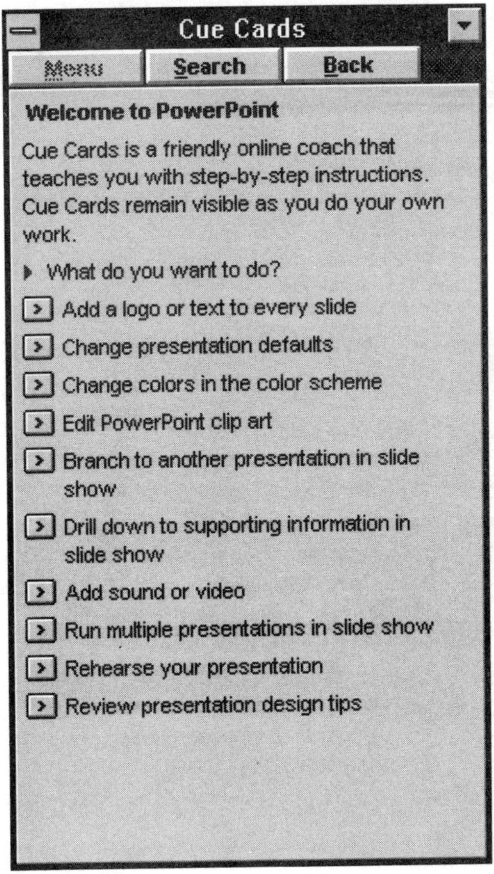

Let's take a look at one of the topics in Cue Cards: 'Review presentation design tips'.

Click [>] *Review presentation design tips.*

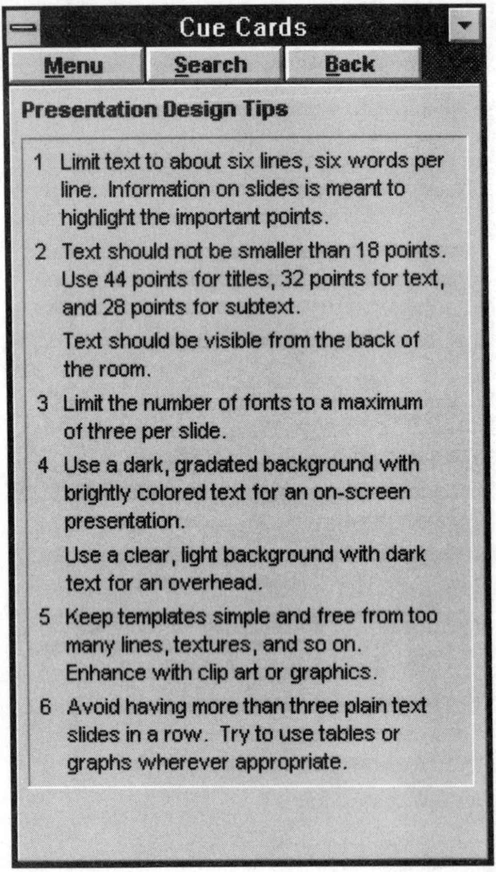

This Card gives you a list of design tips for your presentations. If you're new to presentations, you might like to read these tips.

The Search button takes you into the general help system. Using this is just like using the help for any other Windows application – in this particular case, the facility would be invoked, allowing you to find help on a particular topic (as if you had used the Search for Help on... option from the Help menu).

The Back button allows you to return to previous Cards.

Click Back *until you return to the original Cue Card.*

When you have finished reading a cue card, you could minimise the Window using (rather than closing the Window altogether), in which case you can quickly recall the same card by double-clicking the icon. Even if you close the Window, Cue Cards can be recalled quickly by taking the Cue Cards option from the Help menu, in which case you will be presented with the Menu Cue Card.

For now, we suggest you close Cue Cards (if you prefer to leave them there as you work, you may do so).

To close Cue Cards, double-click the window control button of the Cue Cards window:

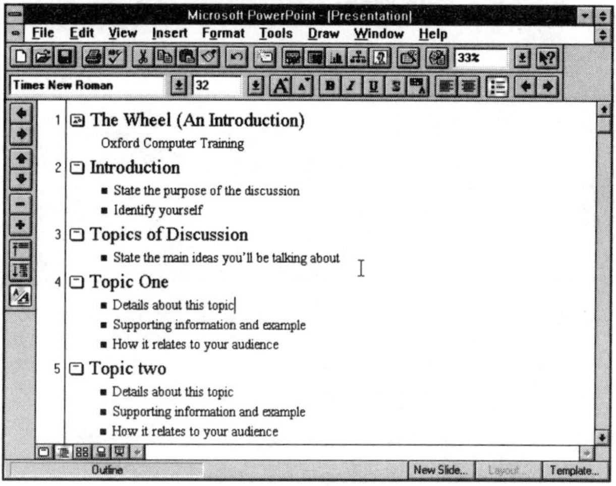

Running a slide show on screen

Before going on to enter and format our own text, let's see what the AutoContent Wizard did for us – by running a Slide how you can preview the work (even if you are going to print it out as hard copy eventually).

First click anywhere among the text of Slide 1, to make sure the show starts at the beginning.

Click *to start the slide show, then (as before) click the left mouse button (anywhere on the screen) to move between the slides (you can right-click to move backwards).*

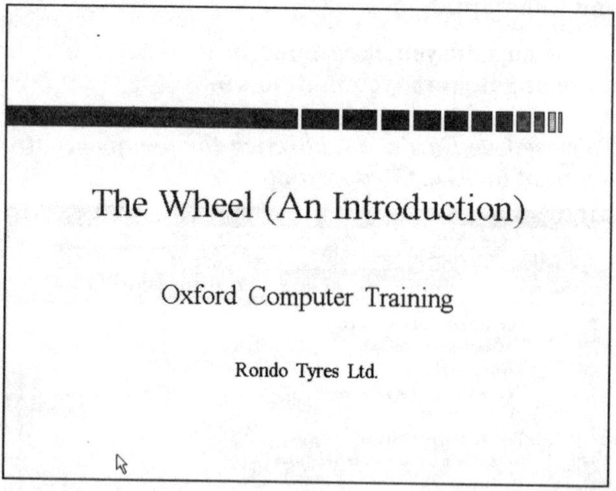

(Your slide may look a little different – we have colours that reproduce well in this book.)

After this title slide, you will see:

- A slide to introduce the presentation and presenter
- A slide to introduce the topics of discussion
- A topic slide (with suggestions of what you might include on it)
- Another topic slide (further ones can be added as necessary)
- A suggested 'Real Life' slide
- A concluding 'What This Means' slide
- A 'Next Steps' (next actions) slide

You may depart from this as much as you like, editing, adding or deleting slides as necessary. Other choices of AutoContent presentation would have given different ideas for slides.

Summary: The AutoContent Wizard and Cue Cards

- The AutoContent Wizard offers the swiftest way to create a presentation from scratch.
- A Wizard takes you through the process of creating a slide show, one easy step at a time.
- A number of standardised outlines are offered, suitable for different occasions.
- Dummy text is set up on a series of slides, to guide you in deciding what sort of thing to say.
- Cue Cards can offer guidance on screen as you try out other PowerPoint tasks.
- The slide show can be shown on screen immediately, (e.g. using ).

7

ALTERING AND REARRANGING TEXT

This chapter covers:

- altering slide text in Outline View
- altering slide text in Slide View
- changing between slides in Slide View
- rearranging items on a slide

Entering text in Outline View

If necessary, use ▤ *to switch back to Outline View.*

Slides created using the AutoContent Wizard have dummy text to guide you in deciding what to say in your presentation. We will replace it with 'real' text. The AutoContent Wizard may give you a few ideas, but it rarely provides a perfect structure for your presentation.

Navigating using arrows or mouse

The insertion point is probably positioned in Slide 1. You can move over the slide titles and bullet points using the arrows ↑, → and so on, or else use the mouse and point to the text you want to change and click once. After this, you could work your way through the entire presentation, replacing the dummy text with your own ideas, and deleting bullet points that are completely unwanted.

We will replace the bullet-point text of the 'Introduction' and 'Topics of Discussion' slides:

Under 'Introduction', change the points to `Introducing the Wheel` *and* `Its uses and variants`.

Next, we will change the 'Topics of Discussion' slide so that it has three bullet points:

`Some applications old and new`

`Some modern facts and figures`

`Rondo Tyres' contribution to world progress`

To do this: type the first line of text and then press Enter *in order to start each new line.*

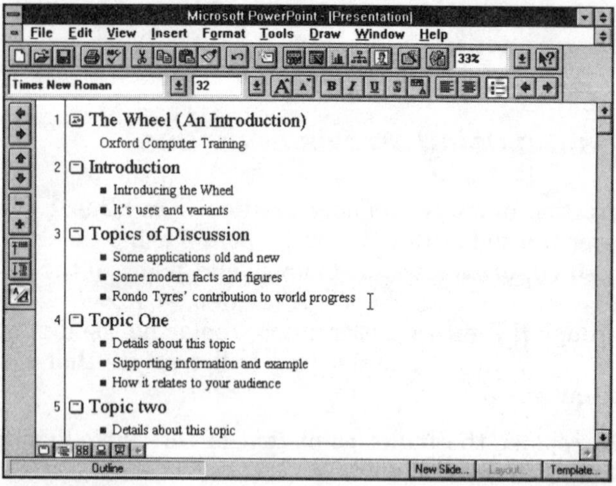

If you press ←Back when the insertion point is at the very start of a line, the text on the current line is appended to the previous line. If this happens press Enter to break the line again, or choose Edit Undo to undo your last action.

Entering text in slide view

Sometimes you may prefer to enter text in Slide View instead of Outline View. Outline view is great when you have large quantities of text to work with, as you can clearly see several slides at the same time, helping you to get a feel for the flow of the presentation. As you will see later, it is also great for rearranging text between slides. The Slide View gives you a better feel for an individual slide, showing the complete slide, and not just the slide title and text.

Click on Slide 4 ('Topic One') in Outline View (as though you are ready to change the text), then switch to Slide View.

> *You may have noticed earlier on one of the cue cards, that you can change to the slide view by double-clicking the appropriate ▭, in addition to the method you already know - clicking ▭.*

The Topic One slide should now be displayed in detail (remember yours may not look the same, but we can change that later).

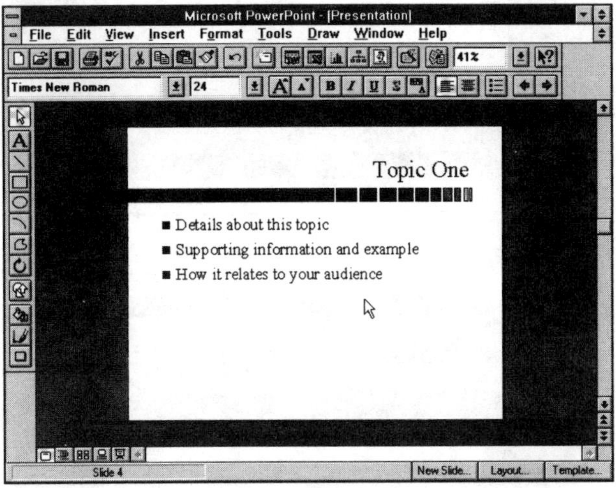

As before, we can edit text in this view.

Select the title 'Topic One'

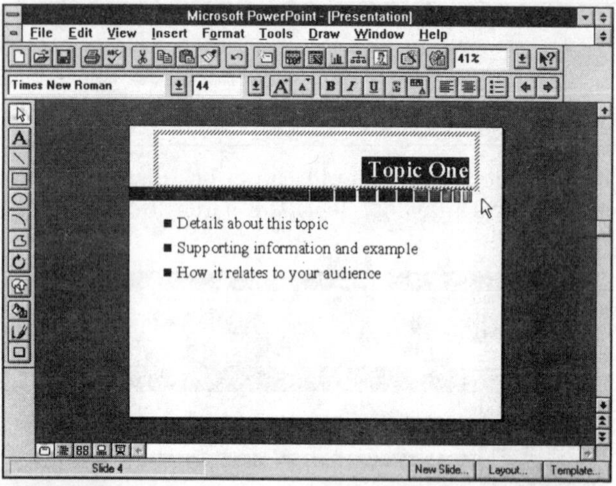

Type the title **Gears**

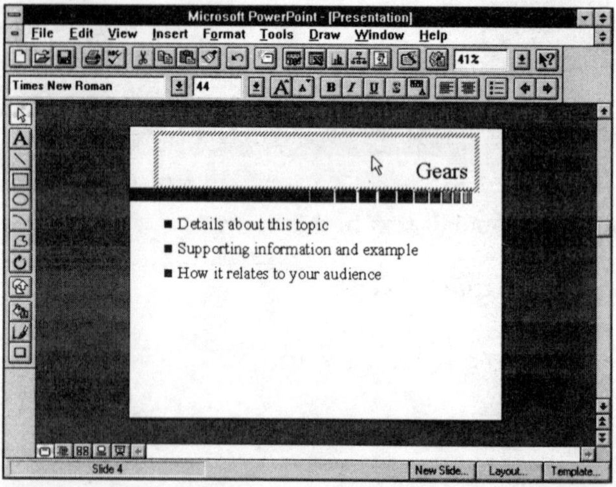

Now we will replace the previous bullet points by clicking the bullet symbol and replacing the text by typing over the selection.

Click the first bullet point to select that text (you may need to click twice, depending on what you had selected previously).

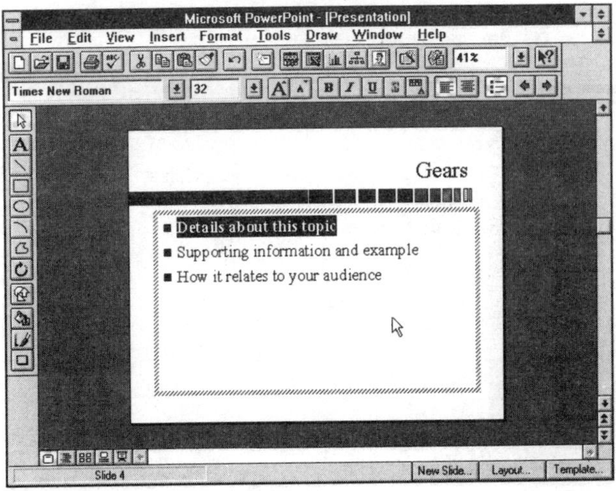

Type the text of the first point:

If you put teeth on wheels you can make them drive each other

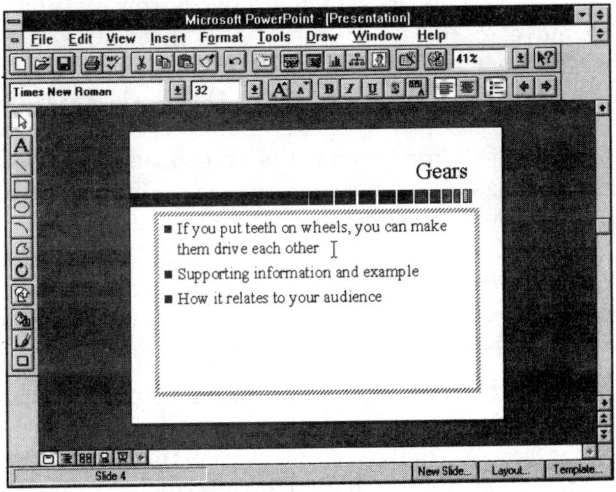

Repeat this process for the other two points:

One person can move very heavy loads...

...but very slowly

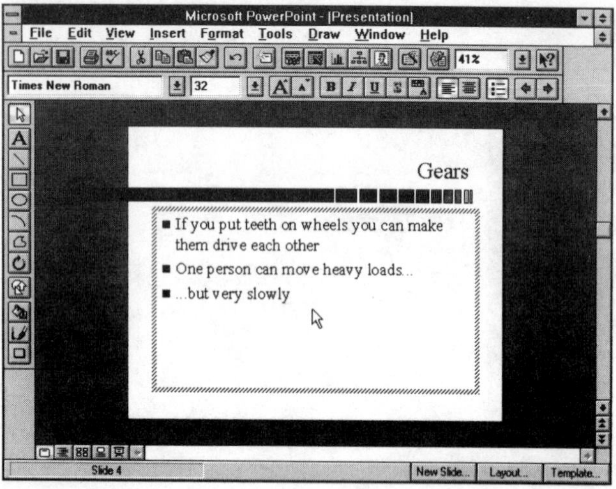

Navigating between slides in slide view

At the bottom right of the screen are two buttons and , use these to move to the next or previous slides. Currently, the vertical scroll bar can be used to do this too, but only because the zoom control is set just right (so that a slide occupies the available space exactly). In general, the scroll bar is used to move the current slide around the screen, useful if you have increased the size of the slide in order to see it more clearly, in which case some of the slide may not be visible.

Try this: use the zoom control to change the size of the slide, perhaps to 66%. Then experiment with the vertical scroll bar.

You should find that clicking and buttons on the scroll bar moves the slide around on the screen. If you move the slide too far, the screen changes to show you the next or previous slide. As usual with scroll bars, clicking the background of the scroll bar achieves the same sort of effect, but moves the slide more quickly. You should also discover an unusual behaviour of the vertical scroll bar: drag the elevator (the plain scroll box on the scroll bar) slowly up or down and a flag appears naming the current slide; as you drag, it indicates which slide you are on.

Practise moving between slides using ⏶ and ⏷, and also using the vertical scroll bar.

— Rearranging objects on the slide —

Move back to the Gears slide if necessary (it should be number 4, but you may have moved it). Also, change the zoom size back to 50% (for instance) so that you can see the whole slide.

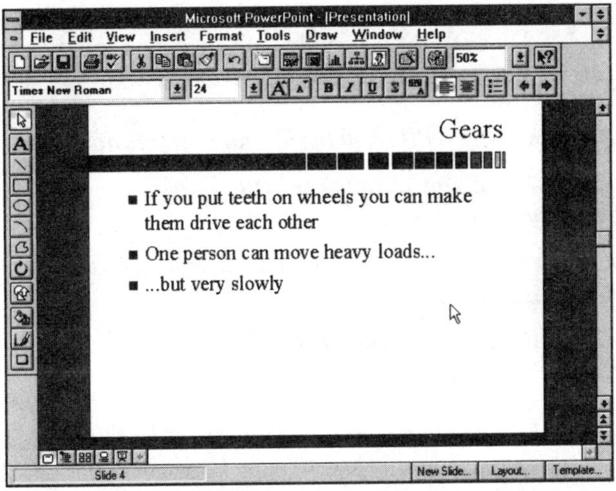

You do not necessarily have to settle for the layout you were given by the AutoContent Wizard. Suppose we want to change the layout of the slide to make room for an illustration (we will add the illustration in the next chapter).

Select the whole title (look for the selection border and handles to confirm that you have the whole object selected):

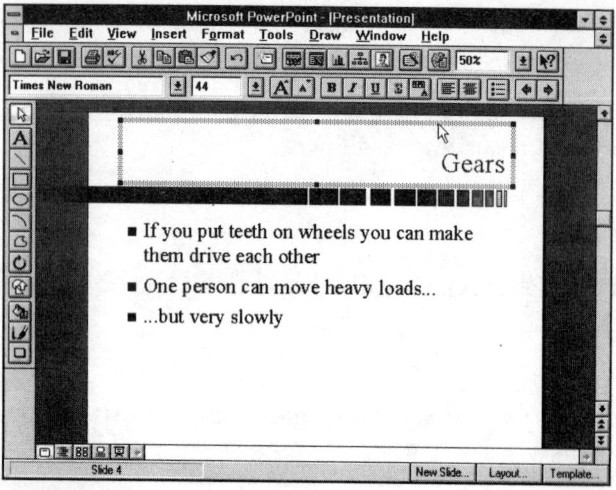

The title can be moved around by dragging, provided you drag from the border and not a handle – the pointer must remain as a pointer( ) not a double-headed arrow (e.g. ↔).

Drag the title by its border to move it around on the slide.

If you drag one of the handles on the border, the title object is re-sized (shrunk or stretched).

If you re-size, or move, an object accidentally, don't forget to undo it with Ctrl Z.

We will reduce the width of this object before moving it to the right hand side of the slide

Drag the middle handle on the left of the title border (you should see the ↔pointer if you have correctly positioned the mouse) to re-size the title object.

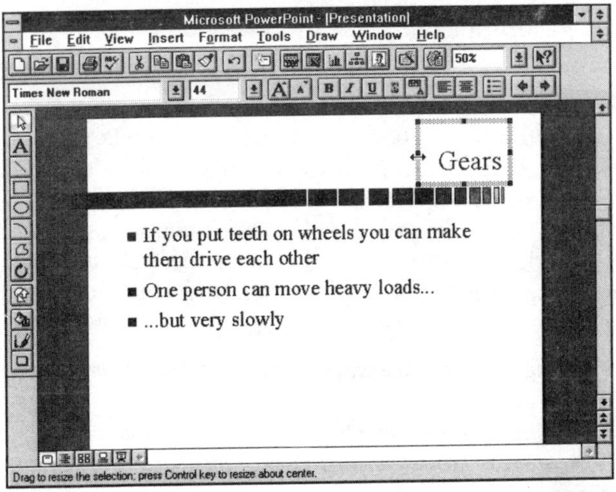

You should now find that you can use the same techniques with the body object containing the bullet points.

Experiment with rearranging the set of bullet points – re-size it and move it elsewhere on the slide.

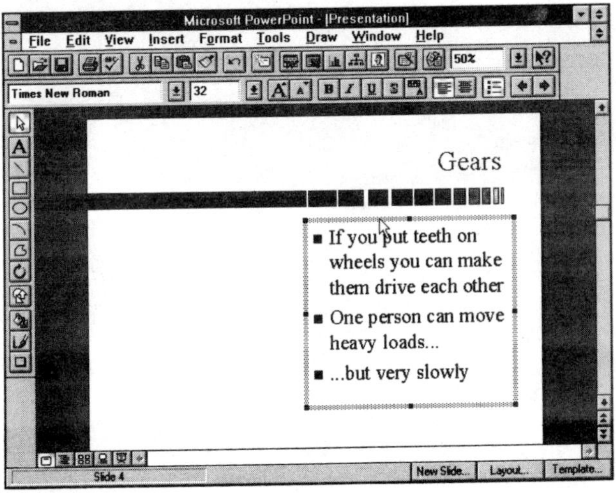

As you can see, if you re-size the body object so that it is much narrower, the text is word-wrapped, much in the manner of a wordprocessor.

This is a general technique with PowerPoint objects on a slide: select an object, then drag it to move it, or drag a handle to resize it.

As mentioned before, there are various methods of deselecting the current object (good practice when you have finished, as it may save you making accidental changes). Either click the slide background once, or press Esc (sometimes you may have to press Esc twice, as the first Esc selects the title border). When you deselect, notice that the handles and selection border disappear.

Pressing Esc twice is always guarantees that nothing is selected.

Experiment with selecting and deselecting various objects on the slide, until you are satisfied that you know what's going on.

Finally, press Esc twice to deselect everything.

Summary: Altering and rearranging slide text

- The dummy text from the AutoContent Wizard is intended to give some guidance – like any other slide text, it can be deleted or replaced by your own material.
- Switch between views of the work using the view changer buttons at bottom left of the screen, depending whether you want detail of one slide (Slide View) or an overview of the presentation (Outline View).
- Outline View displays the titles and bullet point text of the presentation. In Outline View, use the mouse or arrow keys to navigate over the text.
- Slide View displays one slide in detail, and text can be entered or altered here too.
- In Slide View, the title or text placeholder can be moved around the slide by dragging and dropping the selection border.
- The vertical scroll bar can be used to scroll the view of the current slide, or to switch slides –  and  can always be used to move to the previous or next slide respectively.
- Dragging one of the sizing handles (at the corners and along the sides of the selection border) re-sizes an object.
- It is good practice to deselect an object when you have finished work on it. This can always be done by pressing Esc twice (although sometimes only one press is strictly necessary).

8

THE PICK A LOOK WIZARD

This chapter covers:

- Transforming the Slide Master using the Pick a Look Wizard

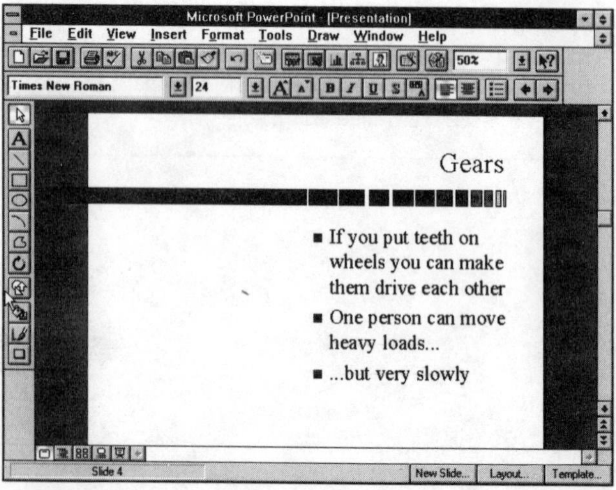

As we have seen, the overall appearance of the slide show is controlled by the Slide Master. The Pick a Look Wizard allows you to make changes very quickly from a list of pre-defined 'looks'.

This Wizard is intended to help you choose a completely different look for your slides, plus adding one or two features such as page numbers onto the slides, and also onto Notes, Outlines and Handouts if needed.

Click , and read the introduction shown on the screen.

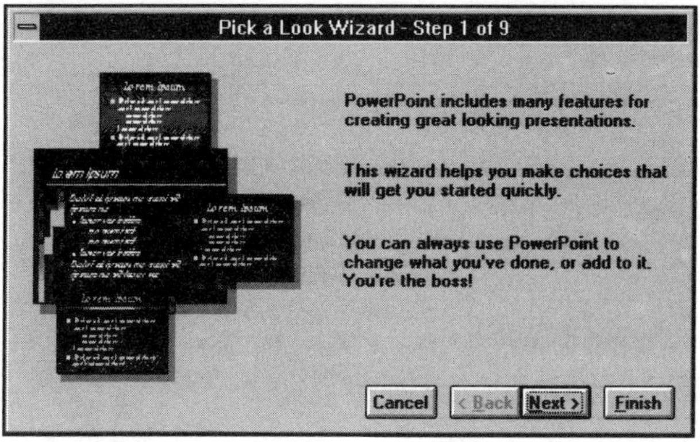

Click Next> *to move to the next page of the Wizard, where you can change the output of your presentation.*

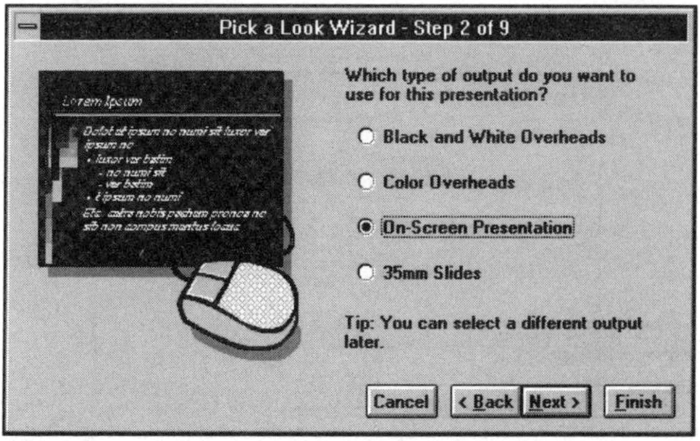

The different choices here are appropriate for different types of presentation. For example, ◉ Black and White Overheads is most appropriate when you intend to print to a monochrome printer. ◉ 35mm Slides provides colour schemes well-suited to the 35mm slide medium. More on this in a moment.

For the sake of argument you will choose the option for Color Overheads (perhaps you can print these in colour, later) and click [Next>] *to go to the next Wizard step.*

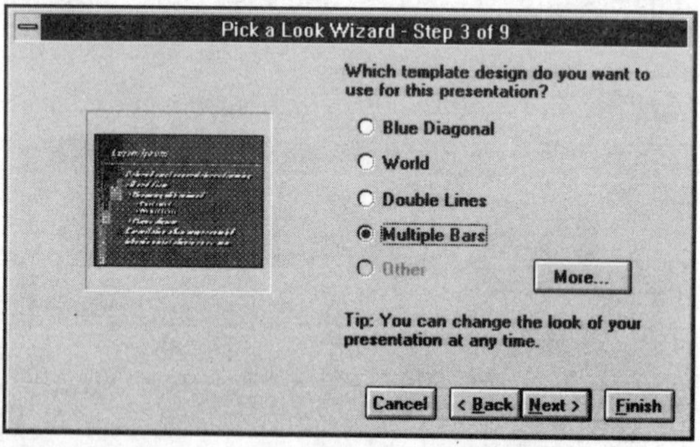

You are offered just a few templates, and one of these might suit you.

Try the different options to see what happens to the preview.

Otherwise, clicking [More...] will lead to a dialog offering further choices:

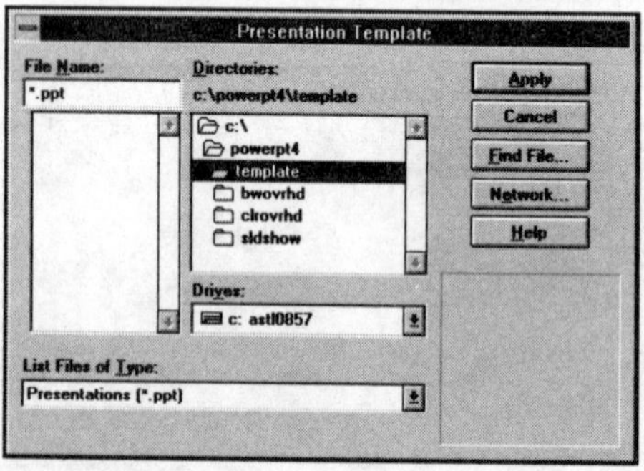

From here you may choose to navigate to another directory and locate **any** .PPT file of your choice.

Click once on a filename in the Presentation Template dialog, to see a preview of that template. Use ↓ to browse through the filenames to see the alternatives.

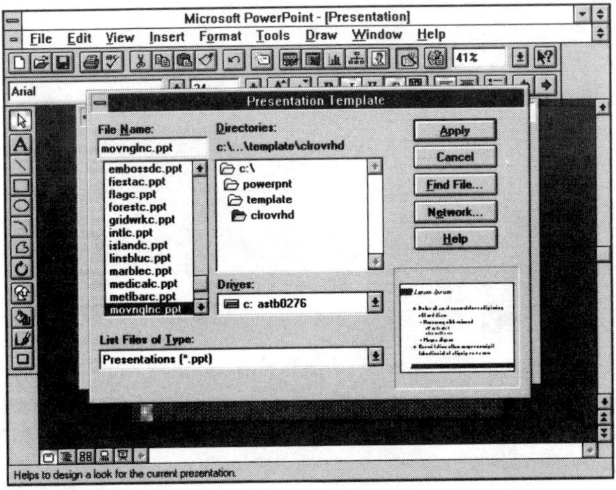

Over 160 sample templates are available in the three subdirectories of the TEMPLATE directory. These are divided up into

- Black and White for overheads (BWOVRHD)
- Colour for overheads (CLROVRHD)
- Those especially suited for On-Screen shows (SLDSHOW).

> *It is important to know that with PowerPoint a template is not a special sort of document (as in Word or Excel, for instance). Any other PowerPoint file that you admire can be used as a template. This means that you could navigate now to any other PowerPoint file on your network, and lift its appearance to transform your own work.*

When you find a file with an appearance you like, select it and click Apply *(or double-click the file of your choice).*

We chose *SLDSHOW\NEONLITC.PPT*:

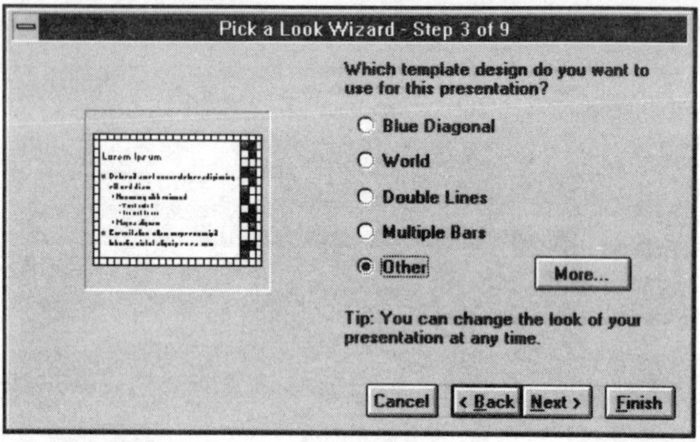

Click [Next>]

In the next part of the Wizard you decide whether you are likely to want to produce your presentation in any of a number of printed formats. Depending on your choices, the Wizard will ask for more information in later dialogs.

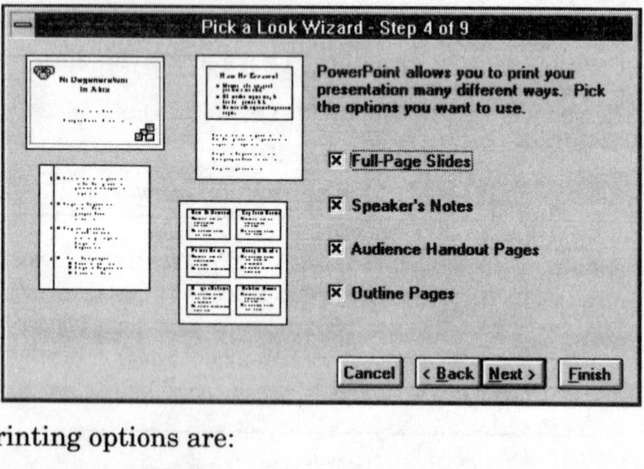

The printing options are:

- Full-page slides (if you are creating an on-screen presentation, then even if you don't intend printing it, this option is important, as it affects the screen version).
- Speaker's notes – for the presenter, detailing slide order and providing guidelines for comments.
- Audience handout pages, so that you can give the audience copies of your slides, with additional notes (see later).

- Outline pages: an outline of the title and text on each slide.

Of course, you may not need any hard copy at all, but when you do, this Wizard is a tremendous help. We'll look at all the options, so that you will know what's available.

Request all four types of layout and click Next>

Following on from this selection are dialogs asking for information for each of the layout choices you have just made.

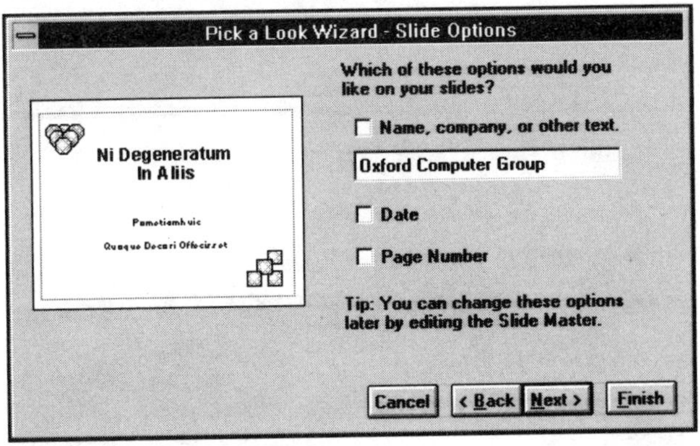

These next stages of the Wizard are all basically the same. Each page asks whether you want to print company or name details, date and/or page numbering. The defaults reflect the most likely choices, for instance, page numbering on notes but not on slides.

Select and give information for those items you wish to see included on each respective type of layout.

The importance of these options may not become obvious until we reach the section on printing.

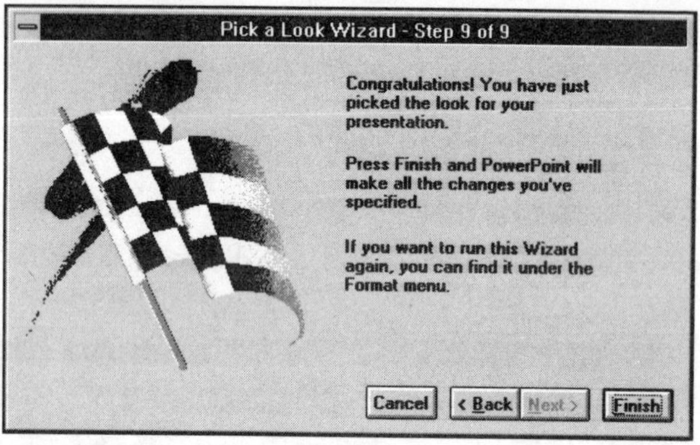

When you reach this dialog you have almost finished the Wizard.

Click Finish *to finish the Wizard.*

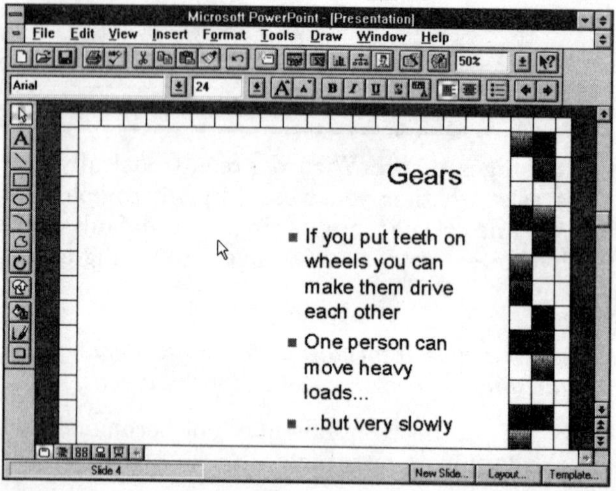

Working in the Slide Master

In Slide View, at this stage you should be able to see the effect that the Pick a Look Wizard has had on your slide. These changes were quite easy to make, via the Wizard, but you could have made those changes directly in the masters yourself, if you preferred.

Look at the transformed Slide Master (Shift-click the Slide View button).

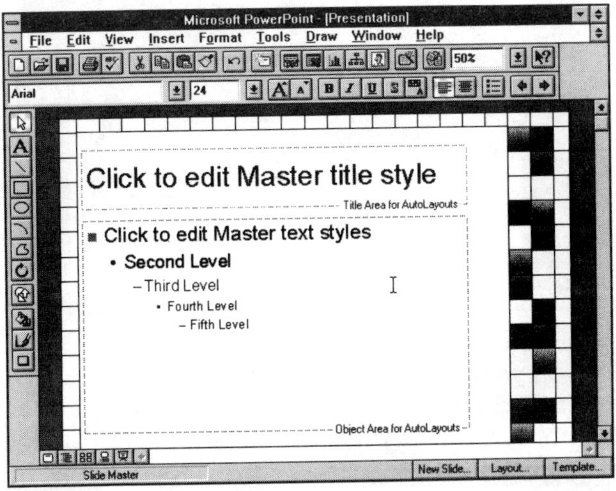

The template applied has completely changed the Slide Master. If at this stage some of the details of this design do not suit you, you can change them here. The screenshot below shows the company name in a new location. You are now changing the Slide Master of your own presentation, the original 'template' will not be affected.

Change the alignment of the title using and until you are happy with the effect.

Remember: changes in the Slide Master will affect all slides (unless a specific slide overrides or ignores features of the master). If you like, change back to a slide to confirm this.

Change some text formatting of the title, perhaps making it shadowed or italicised.

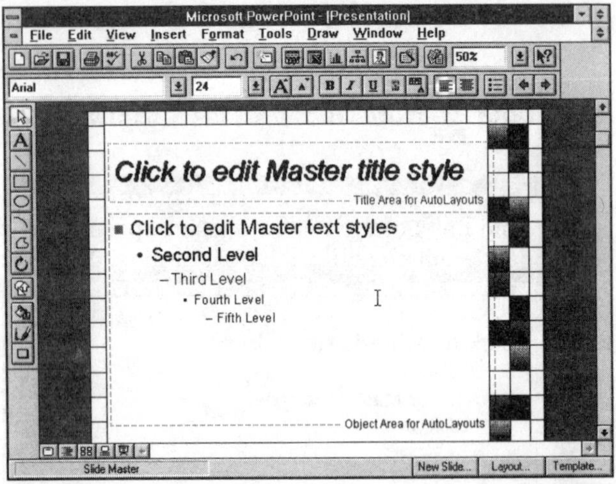

After making changes to the Slide Master, you should look at the effect on your slides in Slide View. Much of the formatting and design will have changed, although of course local variations set up on one slide will have survived – for instance:

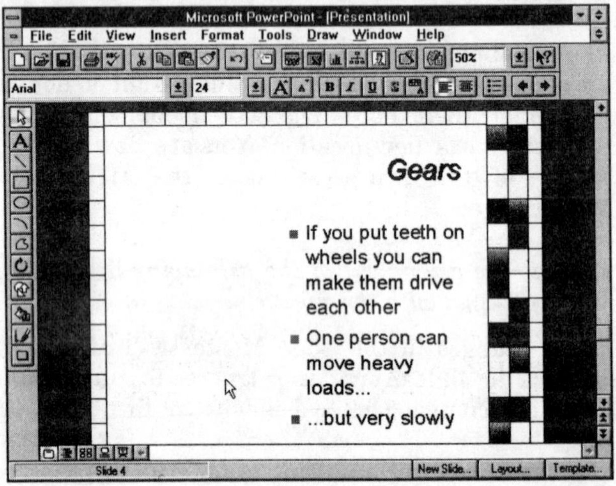

Saving the wheel presentation

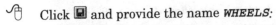

As always, you should save your work before going too far. Since no filename has been given, you must specify a filename and location now from the File Save As dialog. However, because this is a new, unsaved presentation, clicking , pressing Ctrl S or using Save from the File menu will take you to that dialog:

Click and provide the name ***WHEELS***:

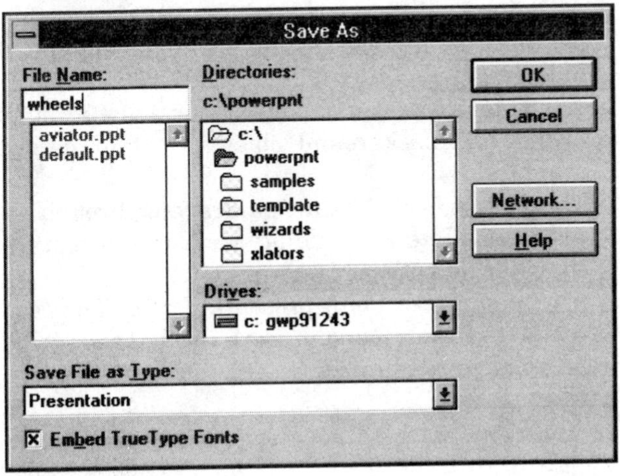

You can use the list boxes to navigate around the drives and directories, to choose the most appropriate place for the document to be stored. After the document has been saved, you should be returned to your presentation, ready for more editing.

There is a useful checkbox to Embed TrueType Fonts on this dialog: with this you can embed the fonts you used in your slides in the saved file. Then you can take the presentation away to another computer, for a sales demonstration for instance, without worrying whether the system at the other site has the right fonts available. However, if you have used lots of different fonts, this will increase the size of your presentation.

Summary: The Pick a Look Wizard

- Applying a different template transforms the appearance of a presentation by replacing the Slide Master.
- A new template can change colours, text formatting, layout and background objects (text or decorative graphics).
- The Pick a Look Wizard guides you through applying a template and adding some useful features to the Slide and other Masters.
- Any other PowerPoint presentation can be used as a template so your current work can be made to match previous presentations.

9

GRAPHICS AND DRAWINGS

This chapter covers:

- Adding a fill colour, border and shadow to a text object
- Reshaping a graphic object
- A quick way to create 'regular' shapes such as circles, squares and so on
- The Drawing toolbars; managing toolbars
- Some more formatting tools on the Drawing+ toolbar
- Inserting ClipArt
- Copying and pasting a picture from one presentation to another

Graphical formatting for text objects

Now we will improve the title slide by adding a text object, some formatting and a simple graphic.

Ensure that you are in Slide View, on the first slide of `WHEELS.PPT`

You are going to work on the title object 'The Wheel' in order to learn how to apply graphical formatting to a text object (in this case the title object).

You may like to move the other text object downwards a little to make some space. In order to move it you will remember that you have to **select** it – click the text, then click the edge border to see the handles.

Select the object for 'Oxford Computer Training' (or your name) and move it down slightly.

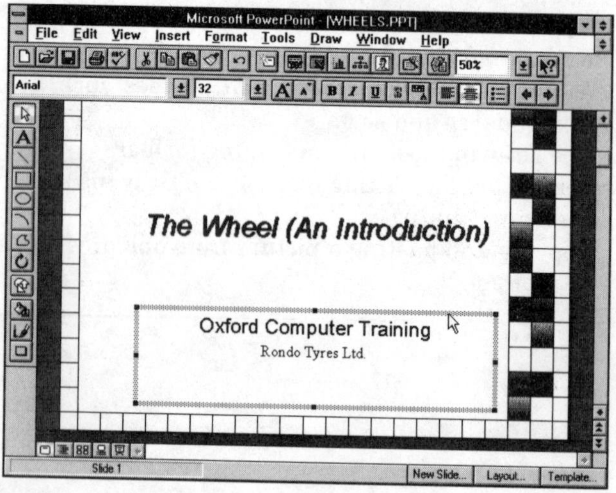

Now select the title object, ready to format it.

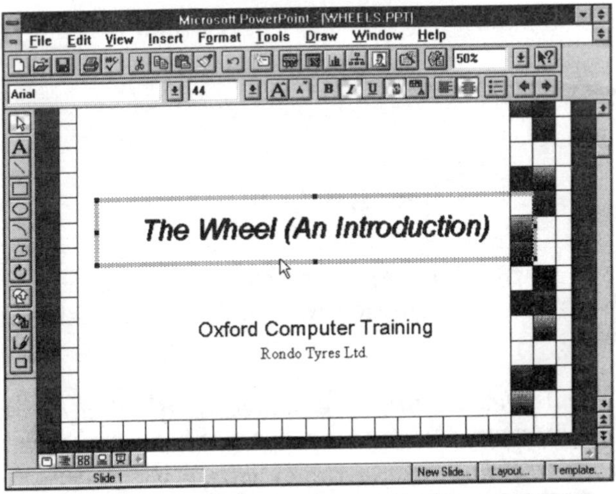

In order to see some of the ways we can format a text object we are going to try switching coloured fill, border and shadow on and off using the tools on the Drawing toolbar.

Try out [icon] [icon] *and* [icon] *– they toggle on and off Fill, Line and Shadow respectively. Finish with the fill and line and shadow all on.*

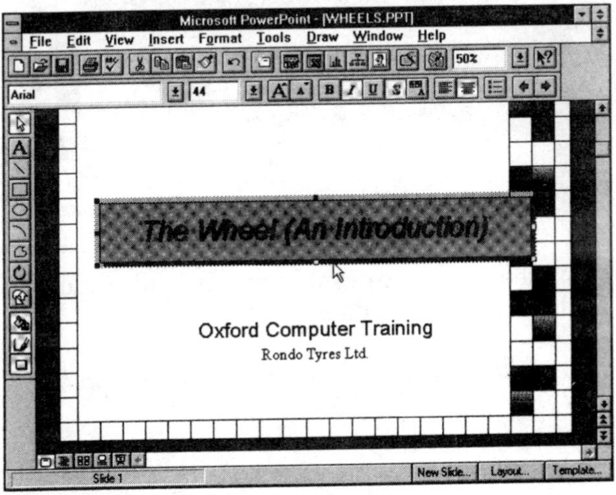

These tools only turn the features on and off – the actual colours and other format options used have been decided by your choice of template – later we will see how to change these 'defaults'.

Changing shapes

Let's change the shape of the title object to be a circle. We do this by choosing an ellipse (oval) and then adjusting it to be circular.

Ensure that the title placeholder is still selected. From the Draw menu choose Change AutoShape and pick the ellipse shape.

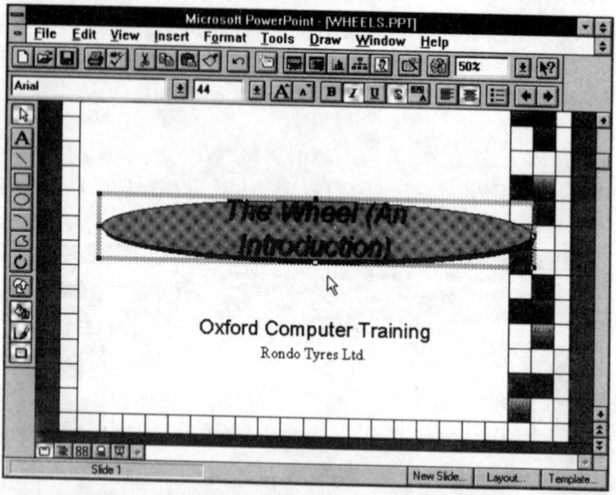

Having got the ellipse we could stretch it to a more rounded shape by dragging the handles.

Increase the height of the ellipse using the top handle.

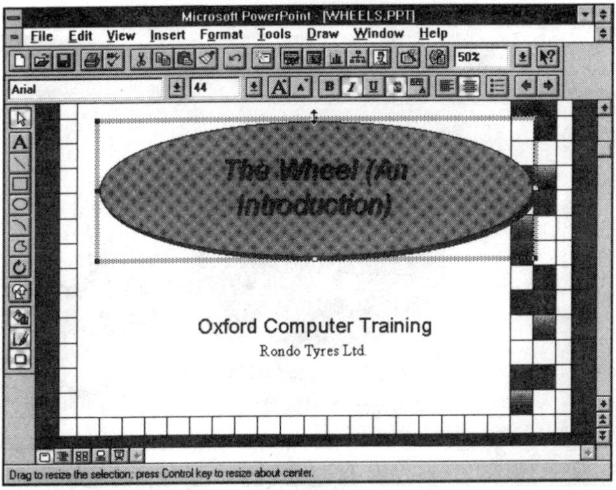

You can get an exact circle by double-clicking a handle (the final position of the circle depends on which handle you use). This technique works for rectangles too, turning them into squares.

Remember, if you make a mistake, Undo it immediately (i.e. before doing anything else) using or Ctrl Z or the Edit Undo menu command.

Double-click one of the handles to make the wheel circular, then drag the whole shape to the centre of the slide. Adjust the size if necessary.

Notice that when you re-size the shape, the point size of the text is maintained – it is only the shape itself that is stretched or shrunk.

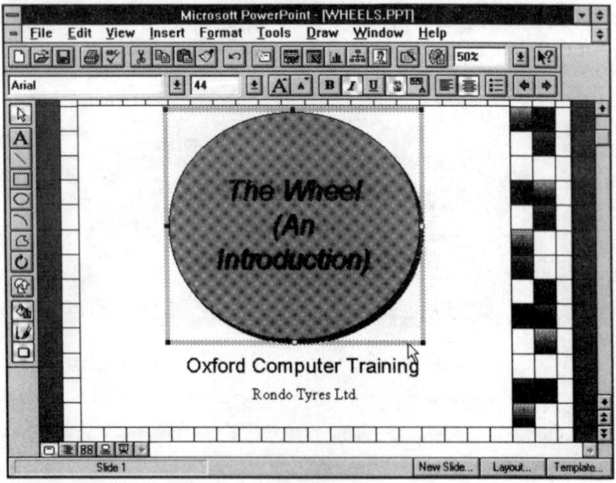

More graphical formatting options

The Drawing toolbar gives us those drawing features most commonly used. The Drawing+ toolbar offers a greater range of formatting options, so we will display this extra toolbar.

Displaying Other Toolbars

PowerPoint comes with a number of toolbars, each offering a collection of (approximately) related commands.

Using a Dialog

One method of displaying a list of toolbars is to choose Toolbars from the View menu. This method is described in an earlier chapter.

Using a Shortcut Menu

Another way of listing alternative toolbars is to use a **shortcut menu:** display this by right-clicking any visible toolbar.

Right-click one of the toolbars you can see.

A shortcut menu appears close to the place where you right-clicked. Ticks are shown beside the names of any toolbars which are already displayed.

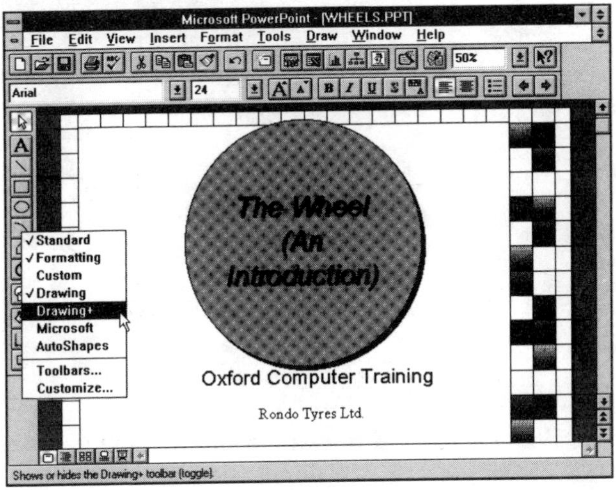

Now you can choose to display one of the other toolbars by clicking its name using the left mouse button.

Choose the Drawing+ toolbar.

There are a number of shortcut menus available in PowerPoint. Each one is displayed by right-clicking some object or screen feature: the menu that then appears contains commands that are relevant to the object or feature you clicked.

You may like to take a few moments to find some shortcut menus by right-clicking various areas on your PowerPoint screen. Be careful not to choose a menu command inadvertently – use Esc *to close an unwanted menu.*

Examining the Drawing+ Toolbar

You can discover the function of the tools on the Drawing+ toolbar using the ToolTips:

Position the mouse pointer over a tool and pause until the yellow ToolTip appears, describing the tool function.

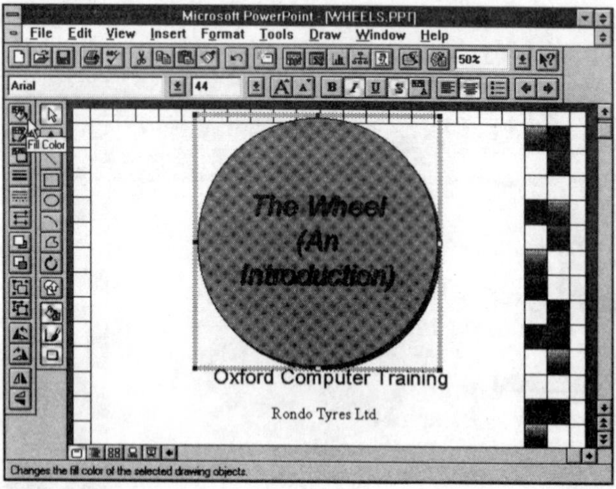

Use the Fill Color tool to change the fill colour of the title object:

Select the title object, click the Fill Color tool and choose a colour.

As always, if you change the wrong object, or do the wrong thing to the right object, use the undo feature immediately (e.g. Ctrl Z).

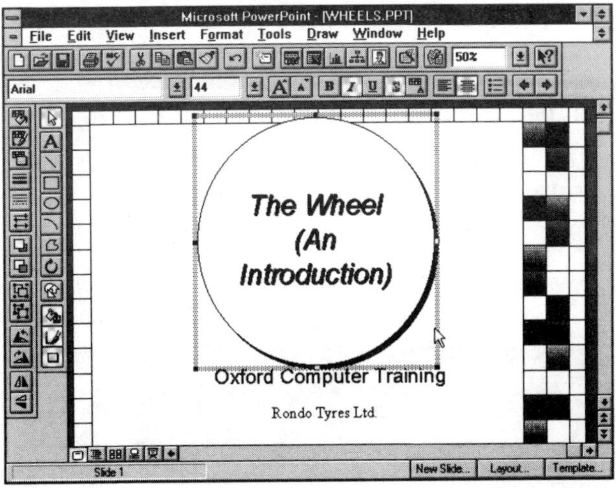

Notice that the choice of colours you are given seems very limited. These colours are the 'theme' colours of your presentation and depend on the Colour Scheme you have chosen. The idea is that if you stick to a few co-ordinating colours, your presentation will look less 'gaudy'.

You may recall that you can change the colour scheme for a whole slide show using the Slide Color Scheme dialog.

If you only want a different fill colour for the selected object (in this case, the wheel), then choose Other Color... from the Fill Color tool. A palette of colours is offered, from which you can select something more to your taste.

> *When you are editing a piece of text, the fill colour will temporarily revert to a solid colour which may look different from the normal fill colour. Don't worry! This is done to make your text more legible while you are editing it, and the correct colours will reappear as soon as you stop editing.*

Moving and Re-sizing Toolbars

Now might be an opportune moment to remind you about positioning the toolbars. Currently your toolbars are probably

docked at the sides or top of the screen. Toolbars can also be floating (undocked). There are two main reasons for docking/undocking toolbars: first, your preference, and secondly, to make best use of space.

To move a toolbar, drag the grey background. Be careful not to click any of the buttons, or you may carry out a command by mistake!

Drag the background of the Drawing+ toolbar away from the edge of the window and release the mouse button.

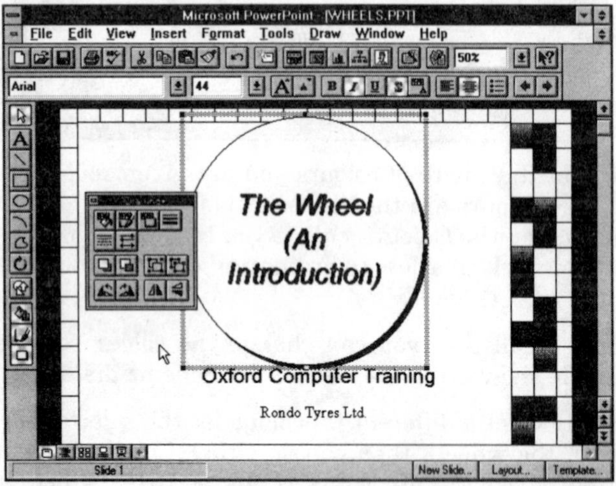

In this **floating** state a toolbar can be re-sized in the same way that you would re-size a window: by dragging the border of the window.

Try re-sizing the toolbar by dragging its border.

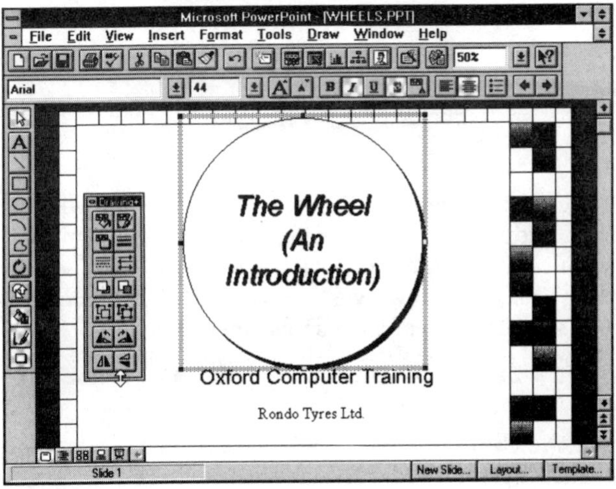

To re-dock a toolbar, drag the background of the toolbar towards the edge of the window until the thick grey outline changes to a thinner outline. When the mouse is released, the toolbar will be 'docked' on that edge of the window. (Some toolbars include drop-down list boxes, and these can be docked at the top or bottom of the window, but they will not dock at the sides.)

Try docking the Drawing+ toolbar on the right hand edge of the screen.

Toolbars can be undocked and docked more quickly by double-clicking the toolbar background. If the toolbar is in a dock, double-clicking will restore it to its previous floating position; if the toolbar is floating, double-clicking will dock it in its most recent dock.

Using the double-click method, dock and undock the toolbar.

To hide a toolbar, either right-click and choose the toolbar that you wish to hide from the shortcut menu, or (if the toolbar is floating) click ▭ at the top-left of the toolbar.

Pictures

Before you have used PowerPoint for long, you will probably want to include a graphic or picture of some description. There are several ways to do this, as we will see in more detail in later chapters. For now, we'll outline the methods that are available, and use two of the easiest methods:

- By drawing the picture using the PowerPoint drawing tools.
- From the ClipArt Gallery, which is a large collection of pictures that come ready-drawn with PowerPoint. This will be discussed shortly.
- From another document: if you have previously included a picture in another document, the quickest way to make use of the same picture may be to copy and paste it onto the PowerPoint slide.
- By drawing the picture in another application, such as PaintBrush, and copying it to PowerPoint.

The means you choose will depend on your requirements. First we will briefly introduce the ClipArt Gallery; then later we will copy a picture from another presentation.

The ClipArt Gallery Introduced

You may remember that earlier we made space on the 'Gears' slide for a picture. Let's go back to that slide and put the picture in. There may be something suitable in the ClipArt Gallery.

Find the 'Gears' slide (slide 4) again and re-size the text object to make space as necessary.

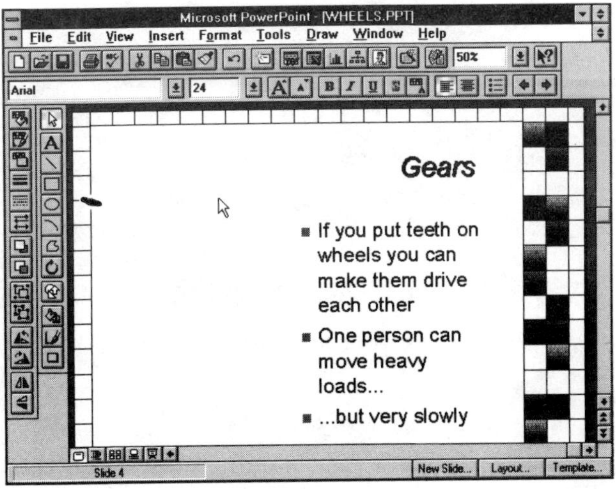

Starting the ClipArt Gallery

To insert a ClipArt picture, choose Insert ClipArt.

Choose Insert ClipArt.

Don't worry if you get a dialog like this:

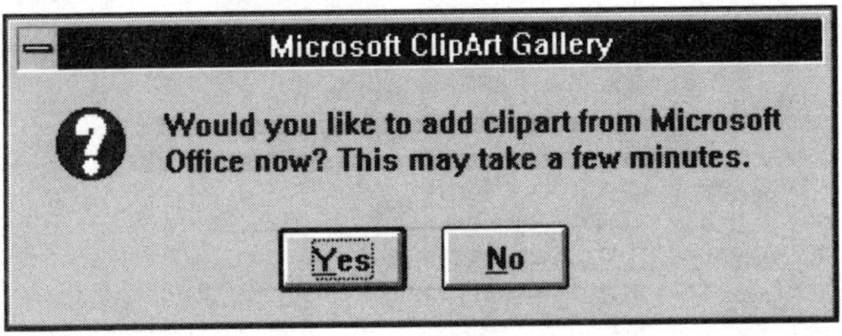

If this is the first time that ClipArt has been used since the software was installed, you may see this dialog (depending on how your installation was performed).

Click Yes

The next stage may take a few minutes. You will see several of the following dialogs as the ClipArt Manager scans your hard disk, looking for, installing and categorising your clipart.

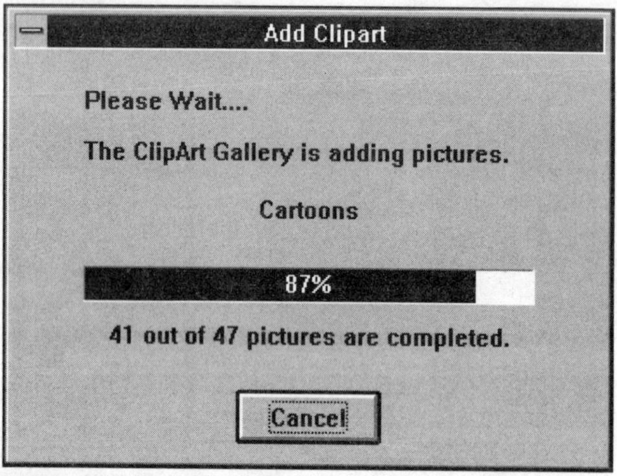

Choosing ClipArt

Eventually, you should see the following:

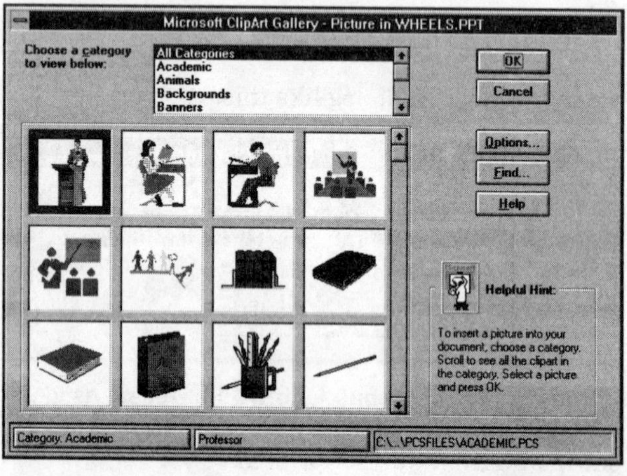

The ClipArt Gallery provides a categorised collection of pictures. The categories available to you are listed near the top of the dialog.

Explore some of the different categories, by choosing category names from the list. Try and find a picture appropriate to 'Gears'.

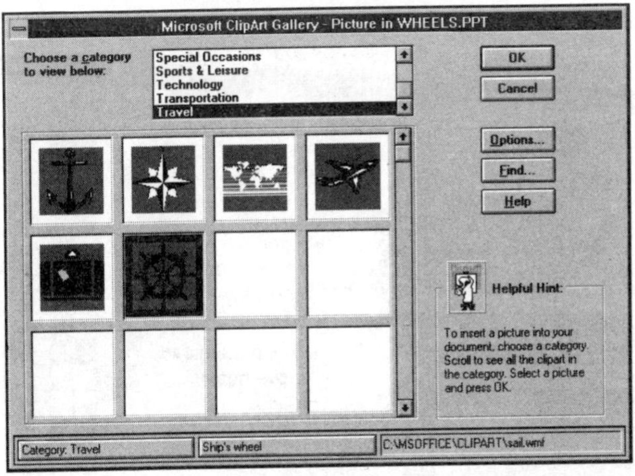

As it happens in this case, there is no clipart picture that is perfect. We will see later that we could take a car (for example) and break up the picture so that we would be left with the wheels!

Inserting ClipArt on a Slide

For now, let's take the 'Ship's wheel', shown above, in the Travel category.

Insert the wheel by clicking OK *You may need to move and re-size the picture slightly on the slide.*

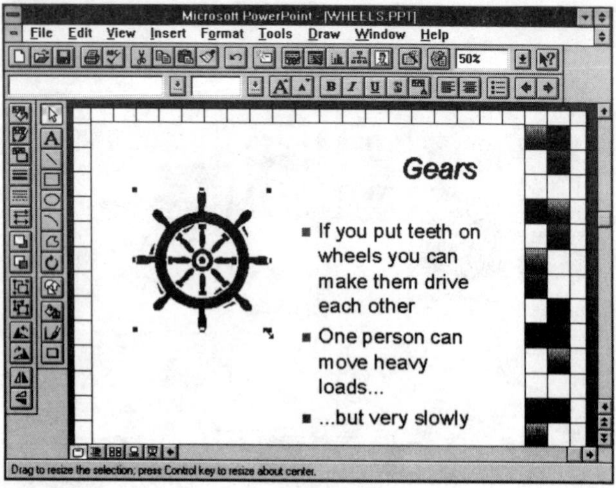

Choosing a Different Piece of ClipArt

If you wanted to change the picture for a different one, you could simply double-click the ClipArt you had on the slide. The ClipArt Gallery would be displayed and you could choose something else. But we'll come back to the ClipArt Gallery later.

Copy and Paste

As the picture is not quite ideal as an illustration of gears, let's look in some other presentations to see what we can find. Often it is convenient to copy a picture from an existing presentation to the presentation that we are developing – in this example we will copy a picture (of some circles, to substitute for gears) from the slideshow `FLOWCHRT.PPT` into the current one.

The flowchart presentation can be found included amongst the sample presentations supplied with PowerPoint. The file is usually stored in the `\SAMPLES` subdirectory of the `\POWERPNT` directory.

Leave WHEELS.PPT *open.*

Open FLOWCHRT.PPT *and change to Slide View.*

The circles graphic is on Slide 7 (as the file is supplied), so you will need to use the slide changer buttons (▲ and ▼) or vertical scroll bar to find it.

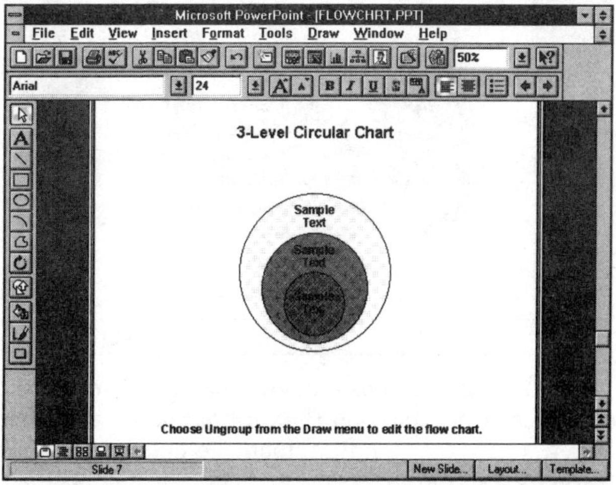

This picture is not quite an ideal gears illustration either, but it does serve to illustrate the principle of Copy and Paste. Copy and Paste works just as it does in any Windows application. There are four steps:

- select the object to copy
- click the copy button (or press Ctrl C, or choose Edit Copy)
- locate the slide on which you want to place the copied objectclick the paste button (or press Ctrl V, or choose Edit Paste)

Let's do this:

Locate and select the circles picture, and click - *be careful to get the whole of it, not just one of the pieces of text.*

Switch back to the Wheel presentation by choosing WHEEL.PPT *from the Window menu.*

When you have moved onto the correct slide, click [paste button] *to paste the picture.*

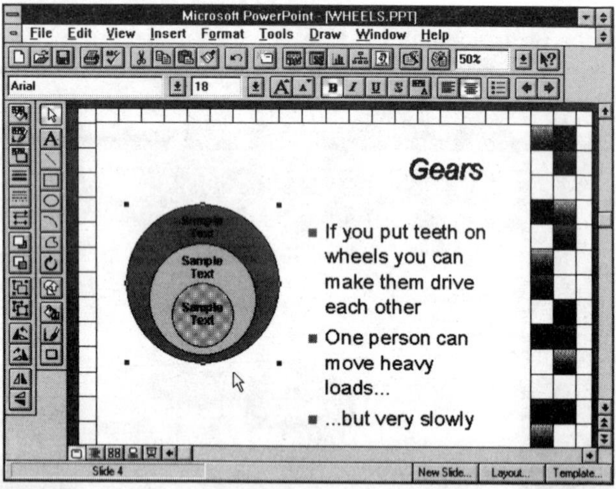

Notice that the picture is pasted onto the new slide in the same position which it occupied on the original slide, though colours are liable to change depending upon the default colour scheme of the target presentation.

You can now reposition and re-size the picture to a more convenient location on the screen. To maintain the aspect ratio of the graphic, use the Shift key while dragging a corner handle.

You no longer need the flowchart presentation:

Switch back to this presentation by choosing `FLOWCHART.PPT` *from the Window menu; close it by using Close from the File menu.*

If you are feeling brave, try the following (or perhaps you may like to return to this slide later, when you have learned about grouping and ungrouping graphical objects):

The graphical objects are 'grouped' (linked) together, for ease of positioning and sizing – we need to get at the component parts.

Take the Ungroup option from the Draw menu.

This ungroups the three circles, but leaves each circle grouped with its text.

Select each circle in turn and Take the Ungroup option from the Draw menu again.

Select the unwanted objects (the little text objects) and press Delete *to remove them – when you select, make sure it is the placeholder you select, not the text itself.*

Rearrange the wheels in a somewhat more 'gearlike' manner, as shown below:

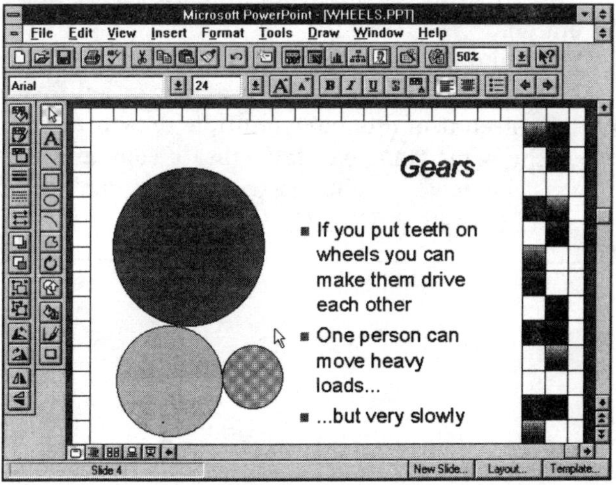

Summary: Graphical formatting and Copy & Paste

- When changing the appearance of a shape – its colour, border, shadow and so on – use the procedure 'Select then Do'.
- Double-click a corner handle to convert a shape to a 'regular' form (e.g. an ellipse becomes a circle).
- The Drawing toolbar offers tools for applying a default fill colour, border and shadow to a selected object.
- The Drawing+ toolbar offers more colour and style options.
- Several different toolbars can be displayed: they may be docked at the edge of the window or left floating.
- It is often useful to have multiple presentations open at the same time, e.g. to facilitate copy and paste of existing work – but close any you don't need, to avoid clutter.

10

— DRAWING SHAPES —

This chapter covers:

- Drawing geometrical shapes
- Attaching text to shapes
- Aligning text within a shape
- Selecting several objects on a slide
- Aligning several items

You will not always be able to copy graphics and ClipArt ready-drawn: sometimes you will need to draw your own. For this, you must master PowerPoint's shape-drawing tools and also know how to attach text to a shape.

Find the 'Topic Two' slide: it should be found just after the gears slide.

Replace the title text with **`Rondo Tyres`**

Type in a slogan as the one and only bullet point. Resize the text object so it just contains the words without extra space.

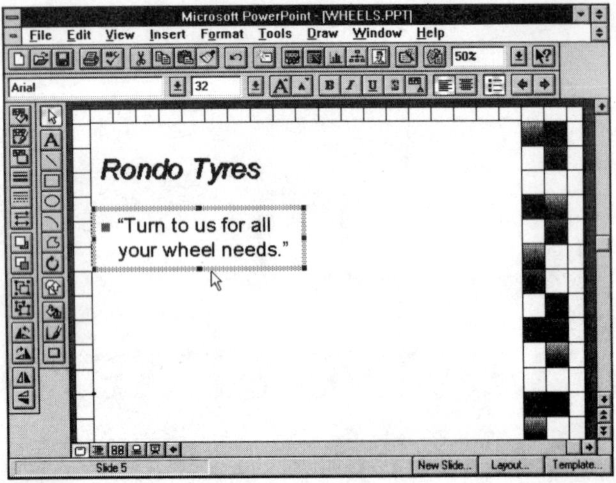

Why do you bother resizing the text object? If you only have one or two bullet points, it is good practice to resize the text object to fit snugly around the text, even if no border or shading is visible. Then you can be sure that the text object will not be in your way when you are manipulating graphic shapes in the 'empty' part of the slide.

AutoShapes

The next step will be to design a logo for Rondo Tyres Ltd., using the AutoShapes tool.

Before starting to draw any new objects, make sure that nothing on the slide is selected already – press Esc *as necessary.*

Click [AutoShapes button]*, select a suitable shape from the resulting AutoShapes toolbar, and drag out an area on the slide to create the object.*

Move the shape about and resize it until you have a satisfactory effect.

Recall that you can convert a shape to its 'regular' version by double-clicking a corner handle. For instance, a squashed star becomes a star based on a perfect circle.

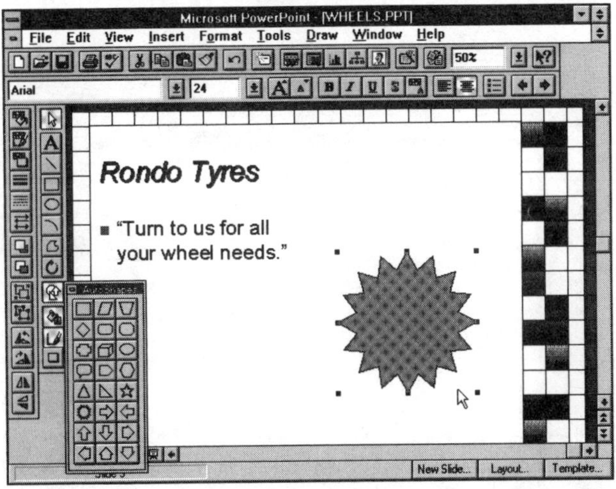

At this point, you will probably want to make some changes to the fill colour and line type and even use a pattern or shaded fill – these last are available from the Fill Color tool 

Work on the formatting of your shape using the appropriate tools on the Drawing+ toolbar:

 *Fill colour*

 *Line colour*

 *Shadow colour*

 *Line style*

 *Dashed lines*

Attached text to a shape

You may often need to 'write on' a graphic object. This process is known as 'attaching text', as the text is attached to a particular object. Then if the object is moved around or even rotated the text moves with the shape. It is very easy to attach text: simply select the shape and start typing.

Select the graphic object and type RONDO

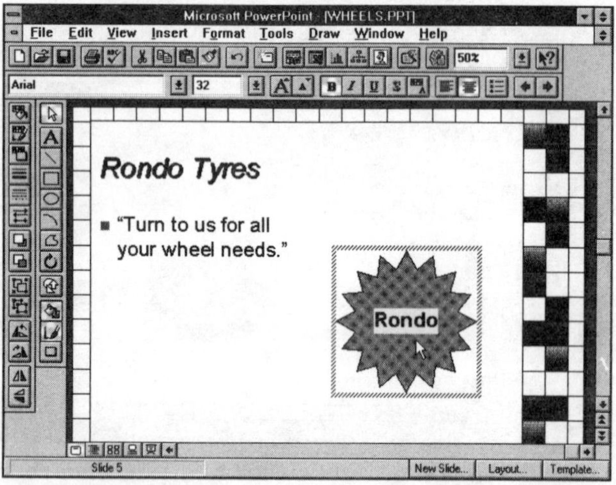

If you want to change the text colour use as before, not forgetting to select the text object first.

Experiment with some different text colours using

Anchoring text within a shape

One problem you might notice is that the text may not at first be properly aligned within the graphic object. To align the text, you select the shape or any of the text and use the Format Text Anchor command.

Select some of the text or the shape and choose Format Text Anchor. Pick the Middle or Middle Centered option in the Anchor Point list and click OK

A little PowerPoint vocabulary is needed here: when you are considering the way text is aligned within a shape, 'Middle' means with respect to Top and Bottom, whereas 'Centred' means with respect to Left and Right.

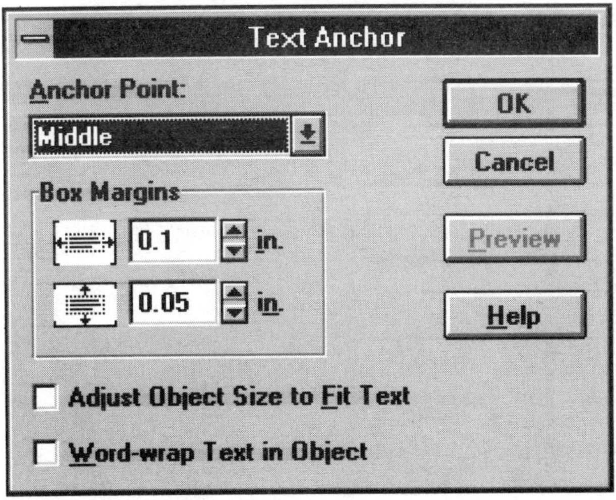

Other options here allow you to determine the margins, i.e. how close to the edge of the shape can the text be, and a word-wrap option, useful for long phrases attached to shapes.

Rotating and flipping the picture

The Drawing+ toolbar offers tools which can be used to flip and rotate a picture: and for rotating, and for flipping.

Try some of these tools, not forgetting to select the object first.

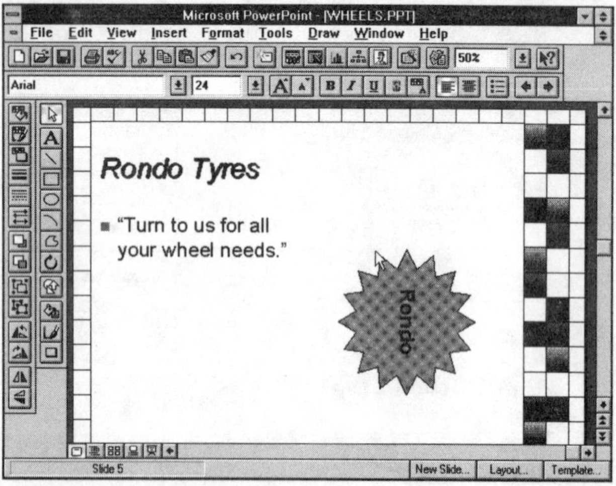

If you are feeling adventurous, you could try the Free Rotate tool –

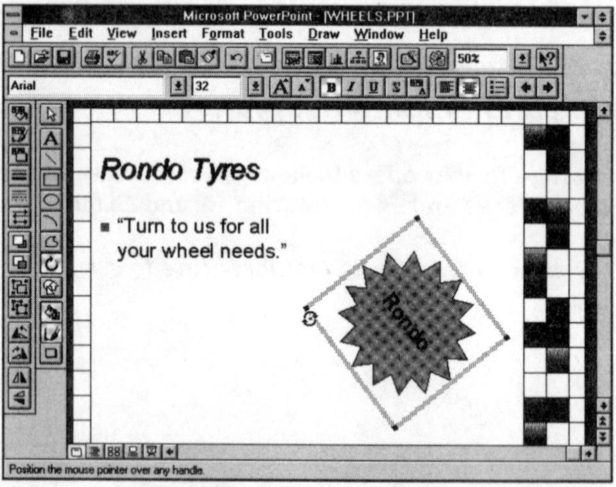

Aligning objects

Ideally you want the title, slogan and logo to be aligned so that their centres are vertically in a line. Before trying to align several objects, you need to have all of them selected at once. One method of multiple selection is to click the first, then hold Shift and click each of the others in turn. When you succeed at this, you will see selection handles around each selected object.

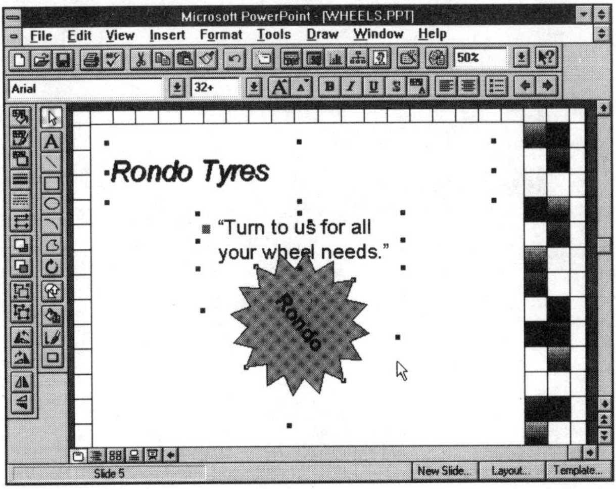

Select the title, slogan and logo by Shift-clicking, then use Draw Align Centres (be cautious – use ↶ *or* Ctrl Z *if you get the wrong Align option!).*

Another way to select several objects is to drag an imaginary 'rubber band' around them on the slide. Click well away from the object you want to select and start dragging the mouse (i.e. holding the left button down). A fine box appears on the screen so you can see where you are dragging. When you stop dragging and let go of the mouse button, anything that was completely enclosed in the box is selected. This is a useful technique when you need to select a number of small or overlapping objects.

For practice, deselect the 3 objects (title, text and shape) by clicking on the slide background, then try to select them by the 'rubber banding' method.

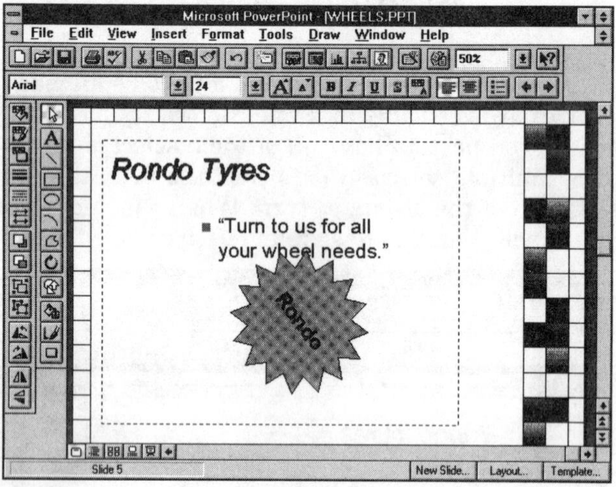

Use whichever seems appropriate!

Summary: Drawing and manipulating objects

- The AutoShapes tool offers a choice of ready-made shapes to draw on your slides.
- Attach text to a shape by selecting the shape and typing directly.
- Attached text is moved and rotated with its shape and can be word-wrapped inside the shape.
- Select several objects on a slide by holding down Shift and clicking each object in turn.
- Select a number of objects together by dragging a 'rubber band' around them on the slide – any objects entirely enclosed will be selected.
- Line up a number of objects by selecting them all and choosing the appropriate alignment point from the Align choice on the Draw menu.
- If you align your objects the wrong way, or make any mistake, use Undo (, Edit Undo or Ctrl Z) – but do this before you do anything else!

11

INTRODUCING AUTOLAYOUTS

This chapter covers:

- inserting a new slide
- using AutoLayouts
- choosing and inserting ClipArt
- modifying a piece of ClipArt

Inserting a new slide

We're going to add a slide about shopping trolley wheels, just after the one about gears.

It is very easy to insert a new slide into a presentation: click New Slide... on the status bar (or you could click on the Standard Toolbar, take the New Slide... option from the Insert menu or press Ctrl M).

Make sure the gears slide is the current one, and insert a new slide (it will be added after the current one):

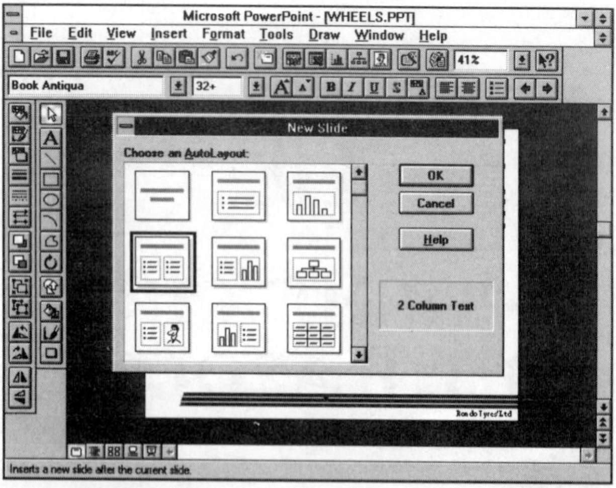

This dialog presents you with a choice of standardised AutoLayouts. There would be no reason why you couldn't start every slide with any old slide layout – you can always modify them, and add objects as necessary, but AutoLayouts give you a starting point appropriate to the intended layout of that slide. If you intend to put a chart on to the slide, why not make use the appropriate AutoTemplate, rather than having to work out how to insert a chart later?

There are 21 AutoLayouts: title slide, bulleted list, graph, 2 column text, text & graph, OrgChart, text & ClipArt, graph & text, table, ClipArt & text, text & object, object, text & 2 objects, object & text, object over text, 2 objects & text, 2 objects over text, text over object, 4 objects, title only, blank.

So, when you are about to insert a new slide, think for a moment and choose the best starting point. You will undoubtedly save yourself quite a lot of time in the long run!

Two column text

Let's choose one with two columns of bullets, as indicated above.

Double-click the two-column option shown.

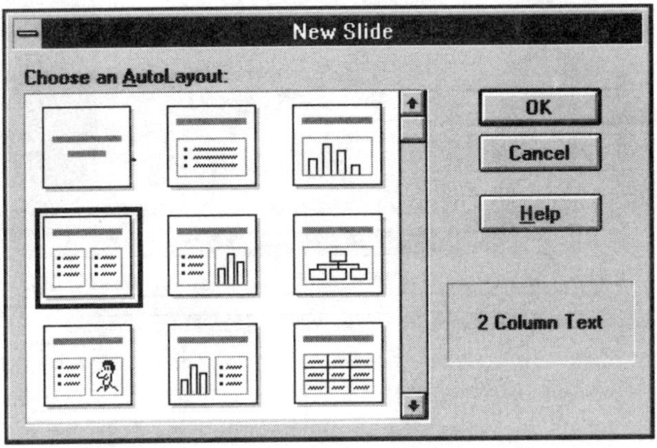

Enter a title and list some of the advantages and disadvantages of supermarket trolley wheels, as in the following slide.

Remember: you should press Tab to demote the text to the next level of bullet point (or Shift Tab to promote it).

> *In the outline view this can be done by dragging, but only the first set of bullets appears in Outline View.*

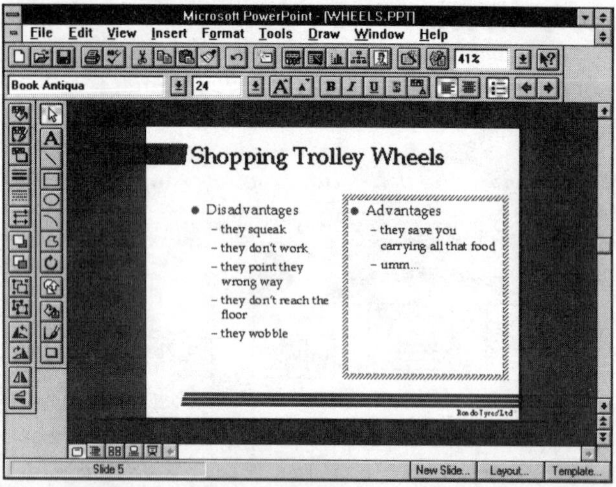

> *These two columns of bullet points look the same but only the left one is a real text placeholder. The right hand one is a text object, not part of the fundamental structure of the slide, i.e. the text won't appear on Outline View with the bullet points and titles, but will appear on the slide.*

ClipArt

You were introduced to the ClipArt gallery in a previous chapter. Let's take a closer look.

PowerPoint comes with a library of illustrations, cartoons and miscellaneous art which is easily available to liven up your presentations. The drawings are organised into a gallery which is managed by the ClipArt Applet. You will take advantage of a ClipArt drawing to illustrate a slide about bicycles.

Add another new slide, in the same way, but this time choosing the Text & Clip Art layout.

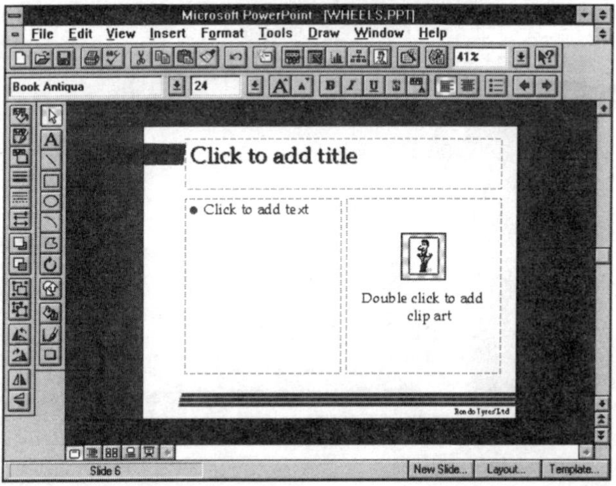

You could also use the Insert Slide tool New Slide... (or), which also inserts a new slide immediately after the current slide.

The slide appears with title and body placeholders, as you have seen before, plus a ClipArt placeholder which shows where the drawing will be (at first at least).

Give the slide a title '`The Bicycle`' *and fill in some bullet points as shown below.*

```
The bicycle

Still the cheapest way of getting around

... on two wheels
```

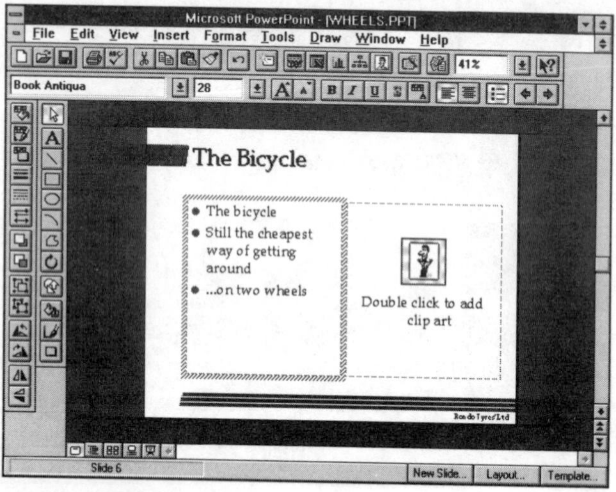

The ClipArt gallery

Double-click the ClipArt place-holder in order to launch the ClipArt applet.

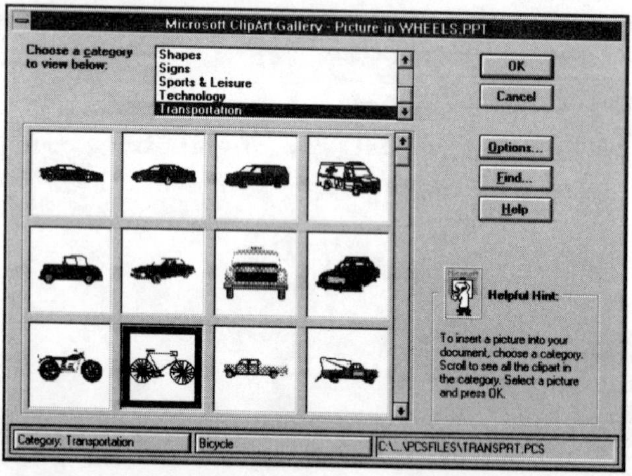

An `Applet` is a subsidiary application that comes with a main application. The ClipArt applet is in effect a ClipArt manager and is used to retrieve a particular image. The drawings are organised into categories which may help you track down something useful. It is possible to add your own works of art to the ClipArt library, building up a resource for others to use, too.

Choose the Transportation category and the picture of the bike. Click OK

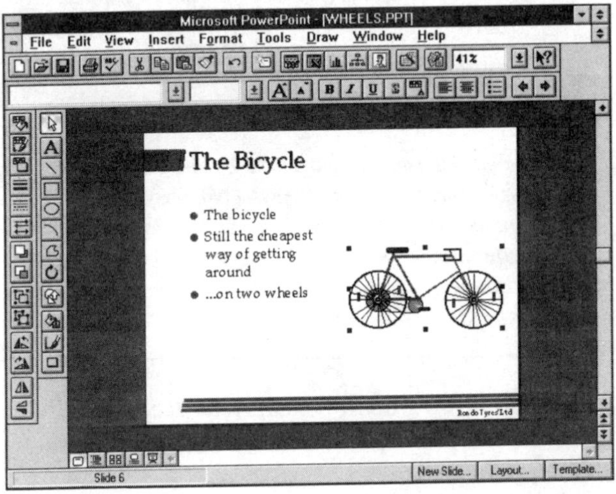

Resize and reposition the picture on the slide (by dragging).

If you have time you may like to experiment with the Tools Recolor... menu option which allows you to modify certain colours and patterns on the picture. Specifically, you may want to change the colours so that the illustration blends in well with your slide show Colour Scheme.

Personalising ClipArt

Typically, ClipArt pictures are made up of lots of smaller pictures – so other pictures can be made up from these parts. In a finished piece of ClipArt, the constituent parts will be grouped together, so as to facilitate formatting of the entire item. If you want to 'dismantle' the bike, click on the Drawing+ toolbar to **ungroup** them, and confirm by clicking OK when the following dialog appears:

> *Be warned that ungrouping the picture makes a permanent change – the picture becomes a set of PowerPoint objects and no longer has any 'knowledge' of its ClipArt origins. This means that having ungrouped a picture, you will not readily be able to change it for another. However, you can always insert another ClipArt picture using Insert ClipArt.*

Just for fun, try this for the bicycle. It is actually made up of dozens of pictures. You could even try to make a tandem!

You will probably find this difficult, as the bicycle is quite complex. For a simpler example (which has no connection with wheels!), we'll start another new slide:

Create a new slide using the same 'Text & ClipArt' AutoLayout, but this time choose the 'piggy bank' ClipArt (under 'Animals').

Again, the 'piggy bank' is made up of a lot of pieces of ClipArt, which when ungrouped can be handled individually.

Ungroup it and you can remove the slot and coin (by selecting and deleting parts) or copy the coin (using Copy and Paste).

Thus you could make a pig (removing the coin and slot, and grouping the remainder), or a coin (either by copying and pasting the coin, or by removing the pig!). In the picture, the pig on the right has been ungrouped, and the coin and slot moved; the coin has then been copied a number of times:

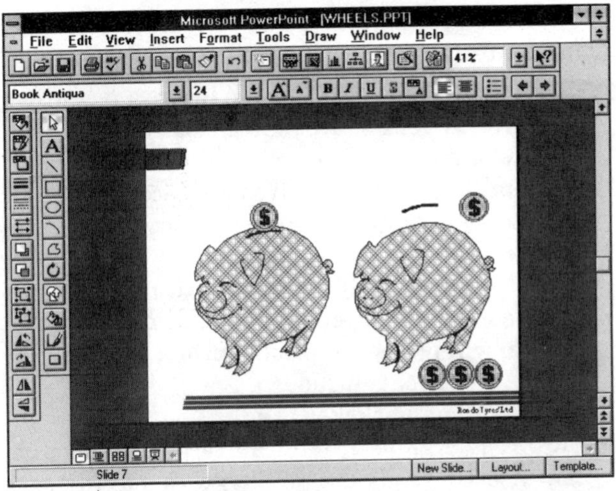

You will need some practice, and you should certainly feel free to experiment. You can add a new slide, insert ClipArt and experiment. Small mistakes can be undone (immediately) with Ctrl Z. Larger mistakes can be dealt with by removing the slide! To remove a slide, use Edit Delete Slide.

Summary: Introducing AutoLayouts

- Click New Slide... (for instance) to insert a new slide just after the current slide, then choose one of the Auto-Layouts offered.
- The AutoLayout dialog gives a choice of 21 standard layouts. Choose the nearest to your intended layout – you can always change it later.
- The two-column layout automatically sets up two columns for bullet points, but text in the right-hand column will not be shown in Outline View.
- If an AutoLayout includes a graphic object (e.g. Clip Art), just double-click it to edit it.
- ClipArt is organised into categories from which you can choose a ready-drawn illustration or cartoon.
- ClipArt (like any other object) can be dragged to a new location on the slide.
- For detailed redrawing, the constituent parts of a ClipArt object can be ungrouped, and deleted, copied and pasted in any way.

12

GRAPHS

This chapter covers:

- creating and altering a graph with the MSGraph applet
- the use of graph formats

New slide with a graph

One of the other AutoLayouts is a Graph. In general a graph (or chart) could be copied and pasted from Excel or another source (and could even maintain a link to the original data, responding to it if it changes), but assume that you don't have such a source. The graph in an AutoLayout is embedded in the slide show, with data you must provide.

Click 

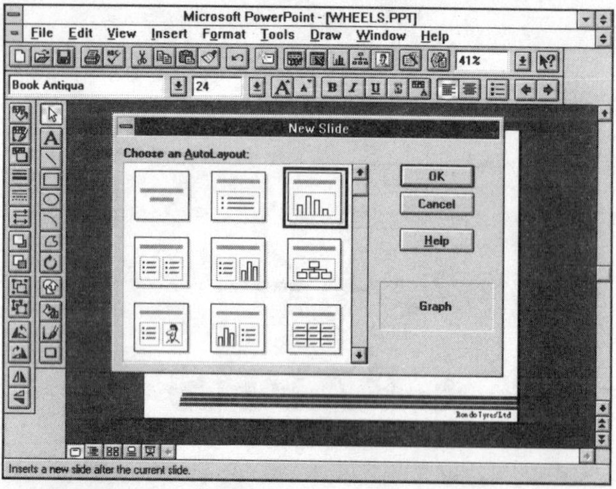

Choose the Graph type (row 1, column 3):

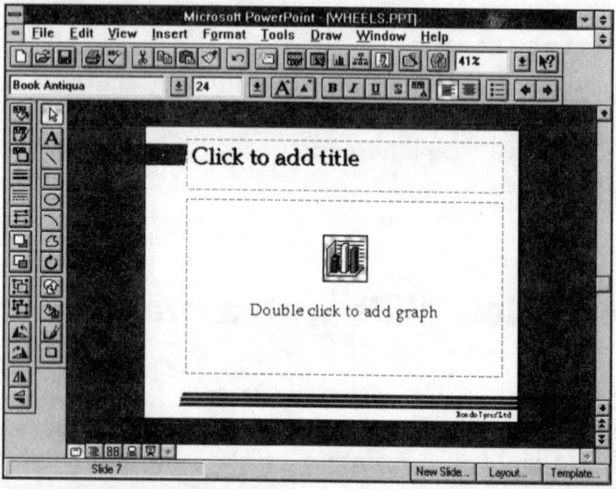

Double-click the graph icon, as invited, to launch the Microsoft Graph applet.

MSGraph is an applet that comes bundled with many of the Microsoft applications, including PowerPoint. Notice that the toolbar has changed and that a datasheet with some dummy data has appeared. Without going into every detail of

MSGraph's commands, here are a few of the more useful features.

Setting up the graph data

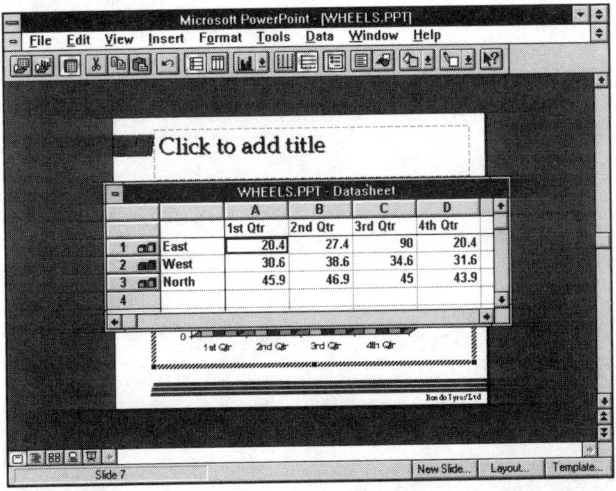

When MSGraph appears, the PowerPoint toolbars and menu bar are replaced by those for MSGraph. You are using **In-Place Editing**, and it is intended that you use all of Graph's functions while the graph can still be seen in its proper context on the PowerPoint slide. As soon as you click anywhere outside the grey graph border, you are clicking back into PowerPoint and the Graph features (toolbars, etc.) will be replaced. So be careful not to click the mouse outside the graph until you are ready to return to PowerPoint. Eventually, the finished graph will be embedded in the PowerPoint slide, but it will retain its association with MSGraph. Simply double-click to edit it again (indeed, you will always need to use MSGraph to edit the graph).

Initially, a dummy graph is displayed, with a datasheet containing the dummy data. So let's replace the dummy data with proper values for a simple graph.

Click 'East' (the row heading) in the datasheet, type 'Car' and press Enter*. Overtype the other headings in the same way, replacing them with 'Bicycle' and 'Commercial'.*

You may find the following keys useful: instead of using the mouse, you could use the arrow keys or Tab and Shift Tab to move around the datasheet.

Add numerical data as follows:

	China	India	USA	Europe
Car	15	17	271	180
Bicycle	300	183	17	30
Commercial	88	124	45	130

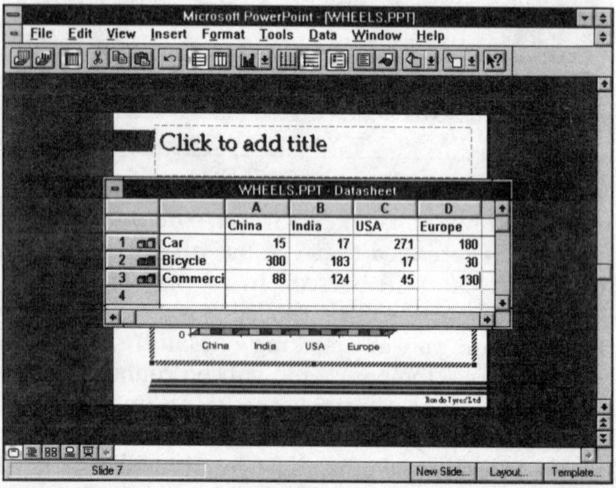

The graph is redrawn immediately, indicating any new values or titles. The (view datasheet) button is useful if you manage to hide the datasheet and want to display it again!

If you want to hide certain **series** (rows of data, producing bars of one colour) or **categories** (e.g. USA) in the graph, by preventing them from being displayed, double-click the appropriate grey row or column header in the datasheet (double-clicking again to show it).

For example, double-click the grey header above 'USA' in the datasheet and drag the datasheet slightly out of the way using its title bar.

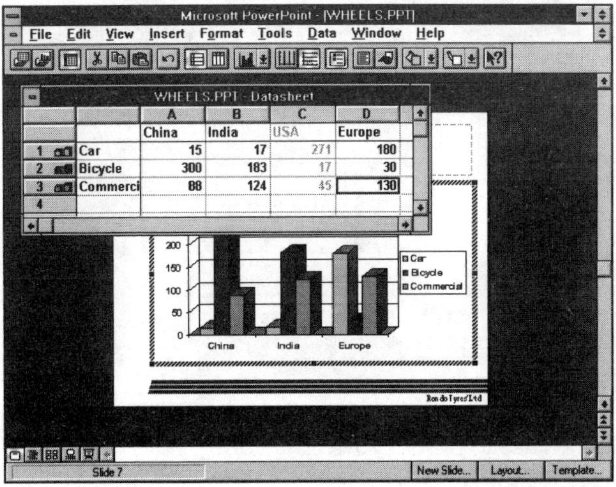

Double-click again to see the category return.

Chart layout options and some different types

The By Row/By Column tools and enable you to make a choice as to which way the data is to be plotted.

Try clicking these buttons to see what effect they have on the graph.

Here it is with the 'by column' option:

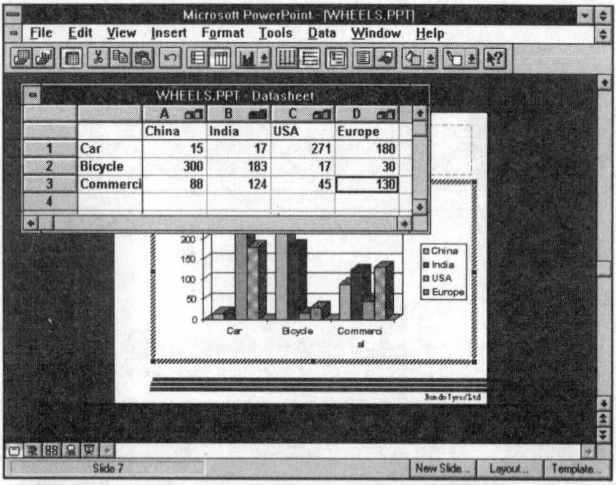

 gives access to other types of graph.

Note that Pie charts only use the first row or column of data ('Car' in the present case). Some chart types, e.g. the Radar chart, would not be meaningful here.

Click this button and try some!

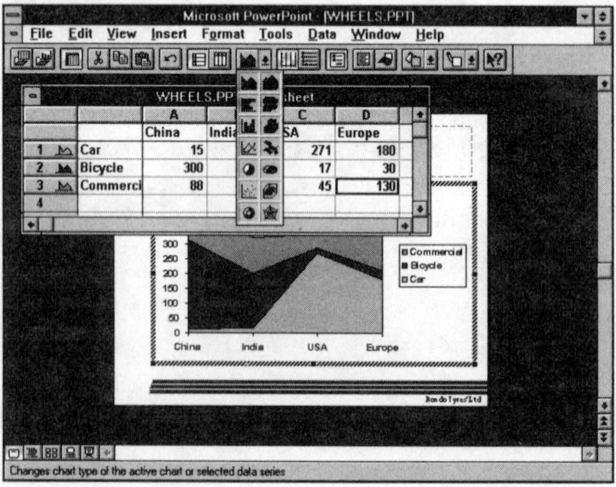

Click ▤ and ▥ to apply horizontal and vertical gridlines respectively. Click ▤ to turn the legend on and off. The legend can be resized by selecting it and dragging the handles. At this stage, now that the graph data has been entered, you may also choose to hide the datasheet window by clicking inside the graph window so that it does not obscure the graph itself, as illustrated below.

Another way of showing and hiding the datasheet is by clicking the ▦ button.

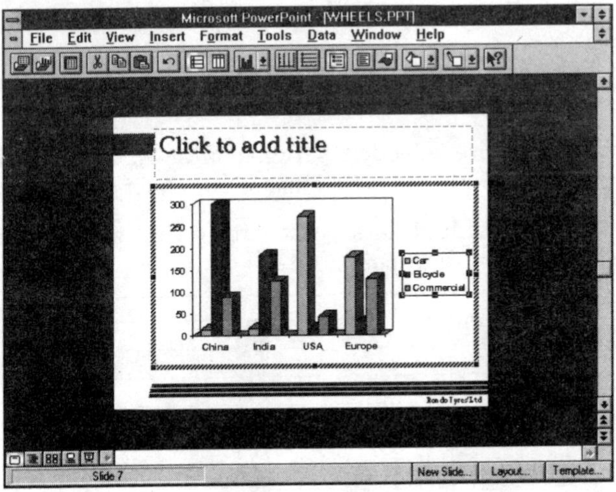

Colours and formatting for a graph

In order to format the various components of the graph, you must first select the component of interest. When it comes to selecting data bars, there are one or two things to note. Firstly, the first time you click a data bar, you actually end up selecting the entire series. The reason for this is that more often than not, you actually want to format entire series, rather than individual data points.

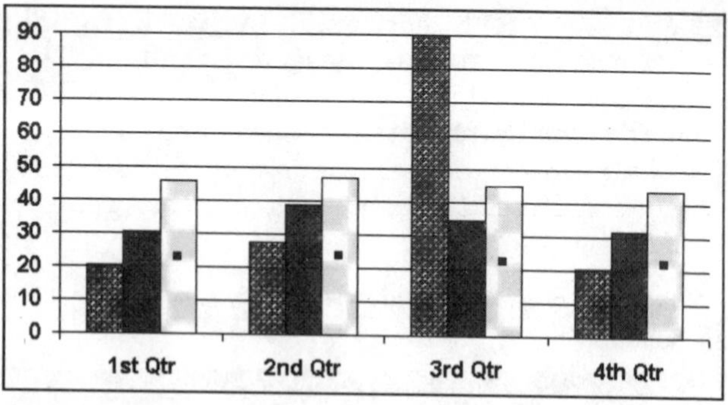

*Click one of the data bars **once** to select the entire series, as shown above.*

Note that there are selection handles on **each** data bar (here a 2-dimensional graph has been chosen, for clarity).

To select an individual data point within that series, you must click again on that data point:

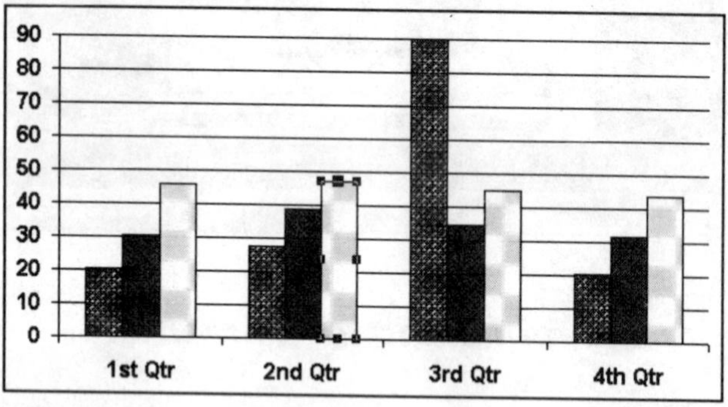

Click again on one data point, within the same series.

Notice, this time, that only the one data bar is selected. Having selected one bar, you can format it independently of the other bars in that series, or even resize it. To resize a bar, get hold of the handle in the middle of the top of the bar and drag (the datasheet figures will be changed accordingly):

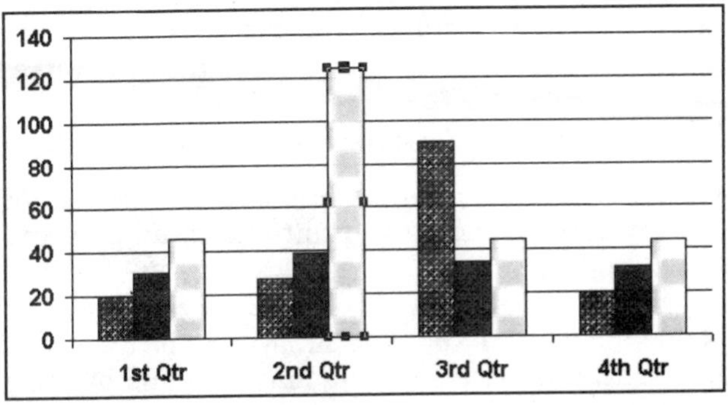

To get from this state, where only one data point is selected, to that in which the entire series is selected, do the following: deselect the point, by selecting the graph background, and then reselect the series by clicking once.

Spend some time, ensuring that you are happy with the process of selecting data series and data points.

Let's put that selection technique into practice now:

Click one of the 'Bicycle' data bars and click (Color Fill).

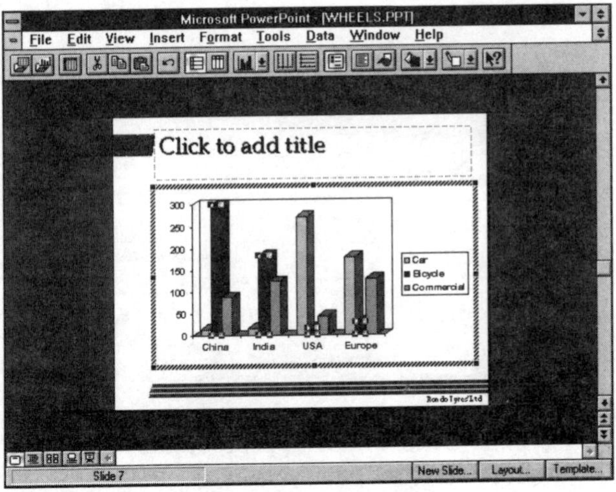

This palette is used to choose a fill colour for the currently selected data element of the graph, whether that be a data series or a graph object. For instance, you can set interesting fill colours for the title box or for the plot area of the graph itself.

Choose a colour and see the effect on the graph.

Clearly some of the black and white options may be more appropriate if you're intending to print out on a black and white printer, although many of the colours will be rendered fairly well as greys on a printer. The patterns pulldown works in much the same way. If your graph is to be printed in black & white, the most impressive results may be found by assigning a variety of black and white patterns (e.g. diagonal stripes, cross-hatching, dots) to the different data series.

Labels for the axes

The graph means very little without some labels to explain what the two axes represent. Axis titles may be added by using the Insert Titles menu.

Choose Insert Titles and check the boxes for the appropriate axis titles (not for Chart Title since you can have a title on the slide within the title placeholder).

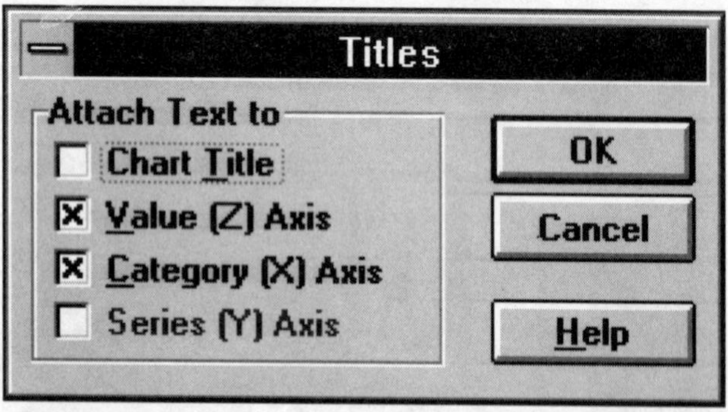

Rudimentary labels appear beside whichever axis/axes you chose. The Chart Title would appear at the top of the chart. Axis titles appear next to the appropriate axes:

- the Value Axis is the axis containing the values of the data, and may be vertical (Y or Z) or horizontal (X), depending on the type of chart chosen.
- the Category Axis is the axis containing the categories, e.g. 'January' or 'Cars', or in the present case, 'China', etc.
- the Series Axis, for some graph types, contains the names of the series.

The picture below might help:

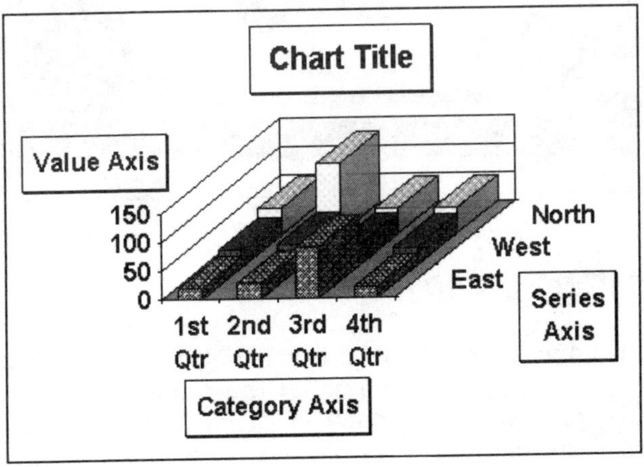

Select the titles and, in turn, overtype them with the titles '`Sales`' *and* '`Country`'.

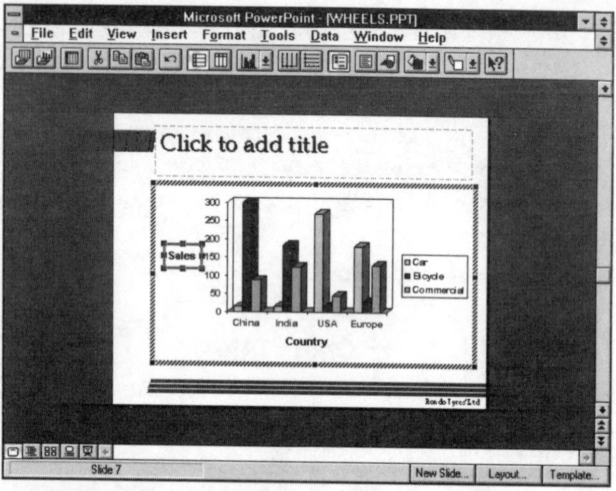

Formatting graph elements

This introduces an important rule-of-thumb for formatting elements of a graph. Of course all these commands are available through the menus, but you should be able to go a long way with the dictum 'If an element of a graph looks wrong, double-click it to get the relevant dialog to change it'.

A good example of this would be the label on the vertical axis. The text would look neater if it was oriented vertically. If you want to format the y-axis labels so that the writing is vertical:

Select 'Sales' and double-click the selection border to get the Format dialog. Choose the Alignment tab and the desired text alignment.

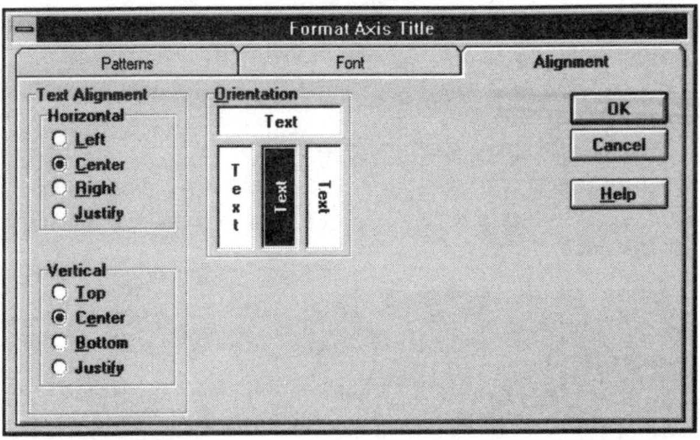

If you want to change patterns or the font used for the labels, click the appropriate tabs and make the changes, then click OK.

An important formatting issue for any values axis is the range of values plotted. You can control the scaling of the vertical axis from the Format Axis dialog.

Double-click the 'Sales' axis (or right-click and choose Format Axis). On the Scale tab set the maximum to 500*, minimum to* 0 *and major unit to* 100.

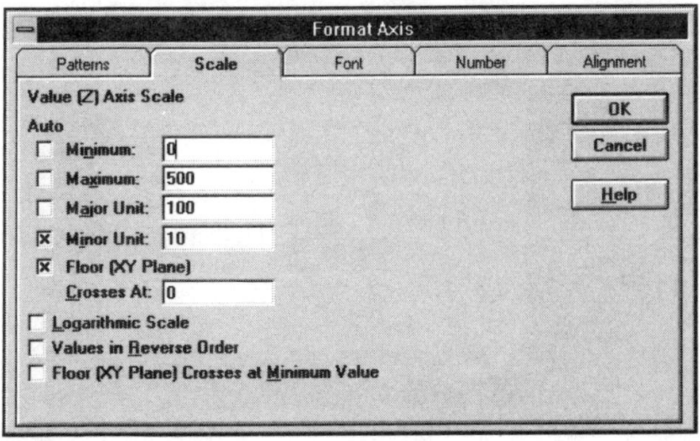

This technique is necessary, for instance, to get a sequence of charts to have matching plot ranges, when they might otherwise be different as each graph will be scaled automatically.

When you type in a value to any of the boxes, the Auto checkbox switches off; to return the value to the automatically calculated one, click the mouse pointer over this box.

There is a lot more formatting to try. Use the general rule that to get formatting dialogs you double-click (or right-click) the element of the graph e.g. axis, data series, graph area, etc. then use the dialog tabs.

Try formatting some other elements of the graph using this rule.

Switching between MSGraph and PowerPoint

The controls for MSGraph remain on the screen until you click outside the graph area.

When you have finished formatting the graph, click the slide away from the graph and you will see the PowerPoint toolbars and controls reappear.

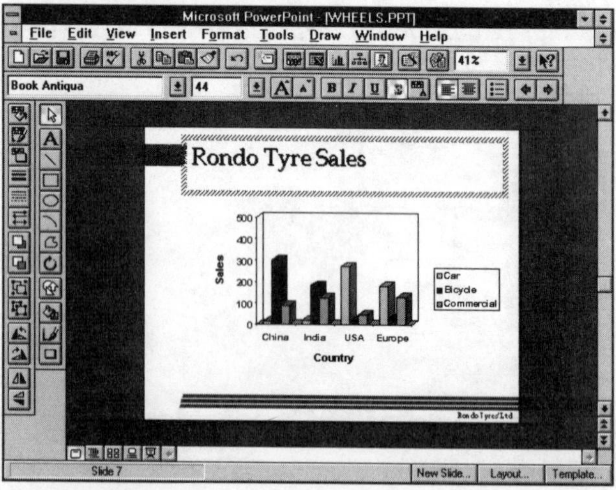

Now would be a suitable time to give the slide a title, as you may not have included a title in the actual graph.

Click in the title placeholder and type '**`Rondo Tyre Sales`**'.

If you decide that you need to do further editing of the graph, double-click the graph and the MSGraph controls will appear. You may need to use the View Datasheet tool to display the datasheet.

Summary: Graphs

- The Graph AutoLayout includes the MSGraph icon which can be double-clicked to launch the Graph applet.
- You can insert a graph at any time using Insert Microsoft Graph..., or you can paste a graph from another source.
- MSGraph offers in-place editing: while you are working on the graph, MSGraph's menu and toolbar replace those of PowerPoint. When you have finished the graph just click the slide away from the graph to close MSGraph and display the PowerPoint controls again.
- In MSGraph you replace dummy data with real data and a graph is created automatically.
- Tools make it easy to change graph type, add or remove gridlines and a legend, and change fill colours and patterns.
- When formatting any part of a graph, double-click the graph element to display a relevant formatting dialog, then use the tabs to switch between parts of compound dialogs.

13

ORGANISATION CHARTS

This chapter covers:

- Using Microsoft Organisation Chart to design charts displaying the structure of organisations
- Changing the slide background

Organisation charts have traditionally been a real headache to produce on slides, involving lots of little text boxes and separate lines, not to mention the problems of trying to add another senior manager or fit in an extra staff member. Now PowerPoint includes an applet, OrgChart, which makes the task much easier.

Add a new slide and choose OrgChart layout. Click OK *and enter a title.*

Remember: you can always add an OrgChart to any slide by choosing Insert Object and Microsoft Organisation Chart 1.0.

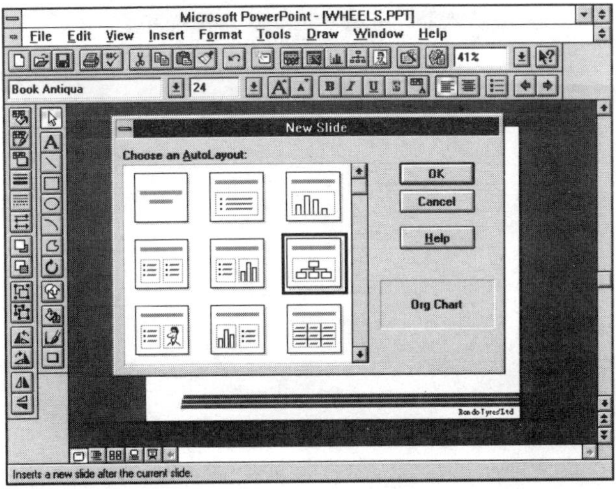

The AutoLayout includes a placeholder for an organisation chart, with an invitation to double-click it to work on the organisation chart itself. Here you are seeing once again a general feature of the way object linking and embedding (OLE) works in Windows – when an object (a piece of work or data made up in another application) is embedded in a Windows document, you should expect to be able to double-click the embedded object or icon to launch the appropriate application (or **Applet**, a mini-application that can only be launched from within another) and start making changes to the data.

Creating and modifying an organisation chart

For this example, you will design a slide showing the management structure for Rondo Tyres.

- *Give the slide a title, such as* '`Rondo Management Structure`'.

- *Double-click the OrgChart icon to edit the organisation chart.*

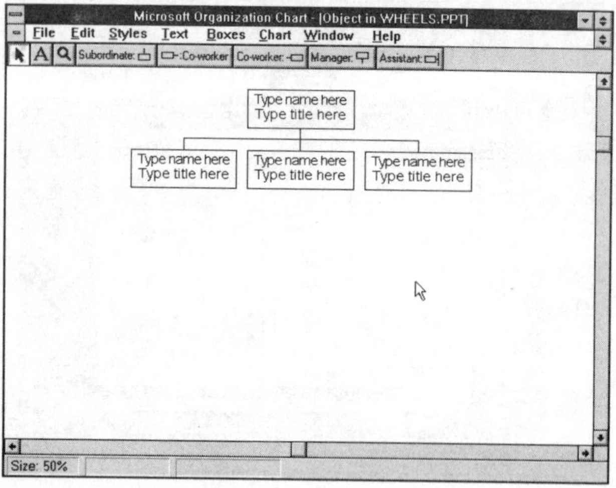

The basic idea is to click in any box and type in name, title and comments for a member of staff as desired.

Try adding some names with job-titles to the chart.

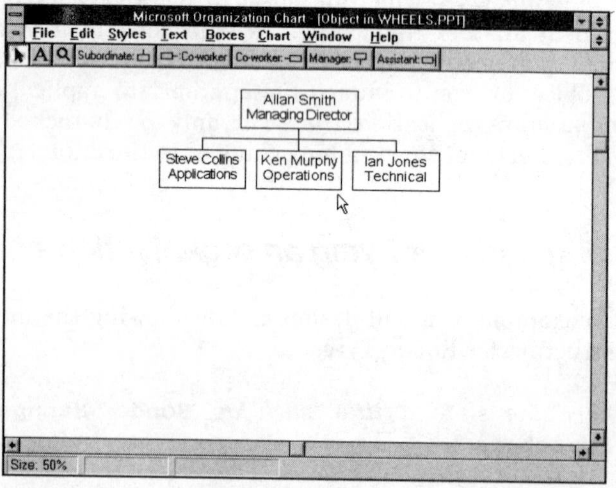

No doubt you will want to add extra people to the chart, so click a box type from the toolbar, e.g. Subordinate (Subordinate:), click it and type in the name of the new person.

Add some extra people to the chart.

Notice that you can equally well give a senior person another subordinate or give one of their staff a co-worker, and that you can choose whether the co-worker is to be shown on the left or the right of the existing person (Co-worker & Co-worker).

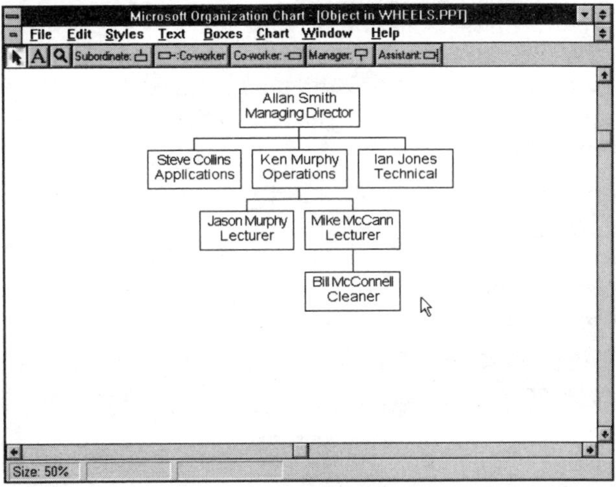

If a senior person has an assistant, say a PA, who reports entirely to them but is not part of the general hierarchy, use the Assistant button (Assistant).

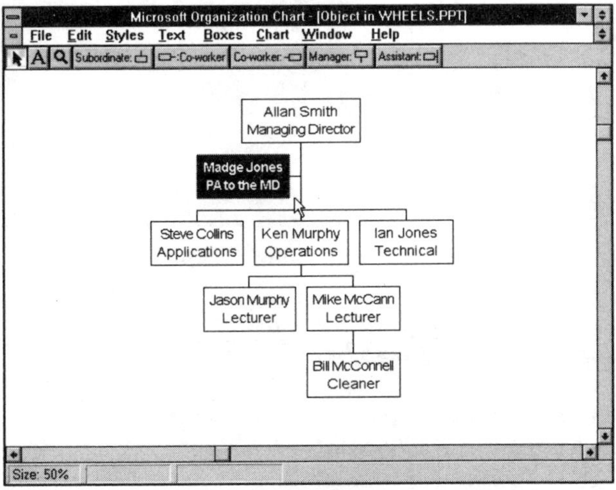

Changing the appearance of the organisation chart

As usual, formatting is achieved by selecting an item, then applying the formats. Selecting can be done by the usual means (e.g. Shift – click, dragging out a 'rubber-band', etc.) but also note the Select submenu of the Edit menu, through which you can select groups of boxes and the connecting lines of the boxes, and format them.

The boxes are formatted by selecting a box and using options on the Text and Boxes menus.

Select some boxes and lines and experiment with some of the options.

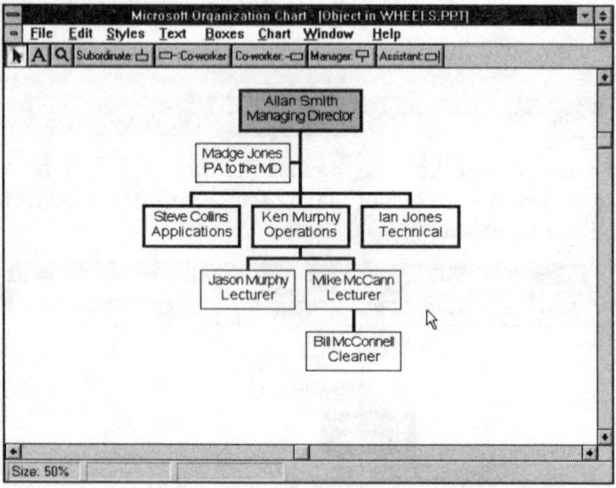

To achieve the diagram above the main steps were:

Select the connecting lines using Edit Select Connecting Lines and then Boxes Line Thickness 3pt.

Select the MD and his 3 subordinates by choosing Edit Select Levels 1-2. This also selects the PA. Deselect her by Shift *– clicking her box.*

> *Note the general method of selecting several items and then deselecting some, rather than explicitly selecting the item you want.*

Then choose Boxes Box Border and pick an appropriate border style.

Finally, the MD's box was coloured, by selecting it and using Boxes Box Colour.

In order to see the effect of layout styles you need to select a group of boxes.

Select all the senior managers and try out the styles using the Styles menu.

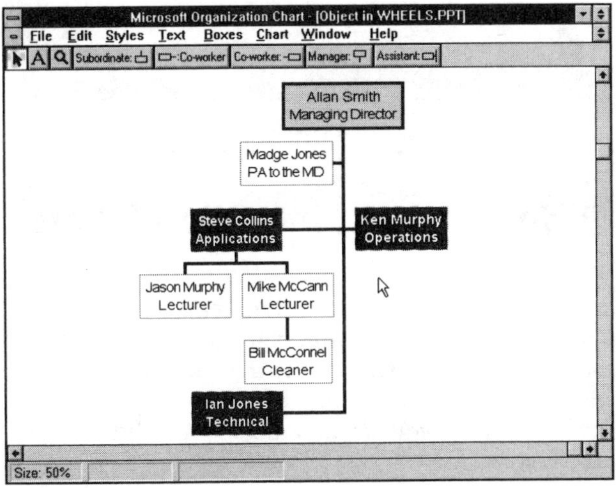

If necessary, the background colour for the chart can be changed via the Chart menu.

When you're ready, choose File Exit and Return (alternatively double-click ▭ - the control menu for the OrgChart applet), say Yes to the Update message and you will return to PowerPoint.

You will see the organisation chart on the slide and it can be resized and moved as required. For any further modifications, simply double-click the Organisation Chart to re-launch the Applet and close as before, either accepting or cancelling the changes.

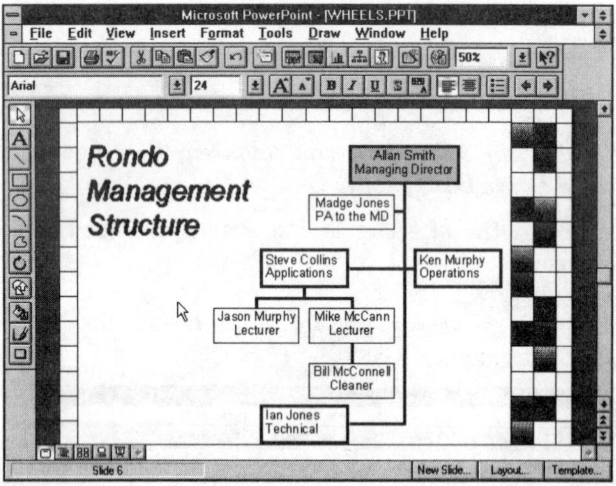

Differing from the Slide Master

It's quite likely that with this slide you may not want all the default background shading and objects from the Slide Master, as the background pattern looks rather odd in this context – in other words, you may not want this slide to follow the Master. In general, you may well want some of your slides not to follow the Slide Master.

Choose Format Slide Background (e.g. by right-clicking the desktop).

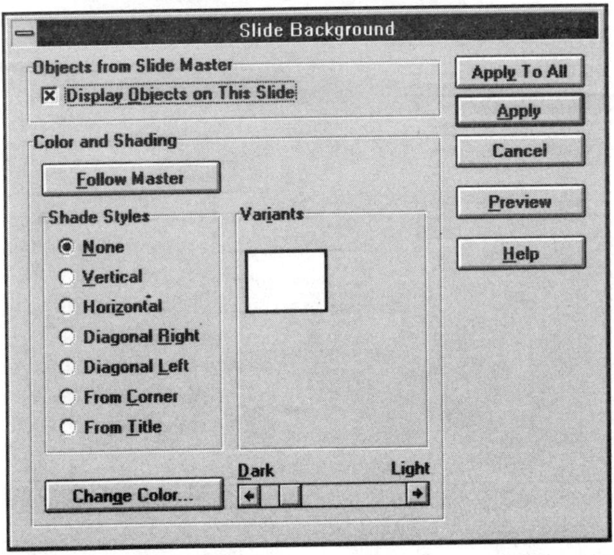

The background of a slide is, as it were, the paper on which the slide is to be drawn. In this dialog, different shade styles can be chosen (or None). There is the opportunity to change the background colour entirely, via the [Change Color...] button, or just to alter the light/dark level.

A useful option comes from the Display Objects on This Slide checkbox – for just one slide, you may prefer to leave out the background objects such as company logo or jolly slogan text, in which case this checkbox should be cleared.

Choose the Shade Style to be Vertical, choose a Variant, and clear the ☒ Display Objects on This Slide checkbox.

If you make changes in this dialog and then regret them, pressing [Follow Master] returns the slide to matching the Slide Master.

Click [Apply]

Don't be tempted to click the [Apply to All] button without careful thought, as this will apply these settings to ALL your slides in this presentation! i.e. it alters the background on the Slide Master.

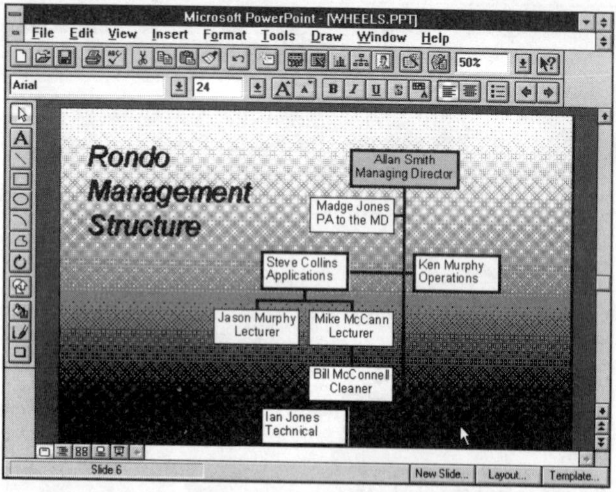

Summary: Organisation chart

- There are 2 ways to include an OrgChart on your slide: choose a new slide with an OrgChart AutoLayout or choose Insert Object Microsoft Organisation Chart to include an OrgChart on an existing slide.
- The text, boxes and connecting lines of the OrgChart can all be formatted by using the Style, Text and Boxes menus.
- To return to PowerPoint having made the necessary changes, choose File Exit and Return from the OrgChart menu.

14

— SOME DRAWING TOOLS —

This chapter covers:

- Using some drawing tools to create your own drawings
- Some useful drawing shortcuts

Although the Clip Art offers quite a variety of illustrations, it is by no means exhaustive, and for some presentations you do need to create your own drawings or diagrams. PowerPoint has some useful tools for this and you will look at some of the important techniques.

Drawing Your Own Pictures

Even though PowerPoint contains lots of Clip Art items, there are times when you will need to create your own pictures. It may be worth asking 'Isn't there *something* that I or one of my colleagues has already done, that I can copy and adapt'? And if this is the case then you have already seen how to retrieve pictures from one presentation to another, if it is not the case – as in the example that follows – you will need to use the drawing facilities of PowerPoint to assist. You can use the buttons on the Drawing and Drawing+ toolbar.

The goal is the following picture:

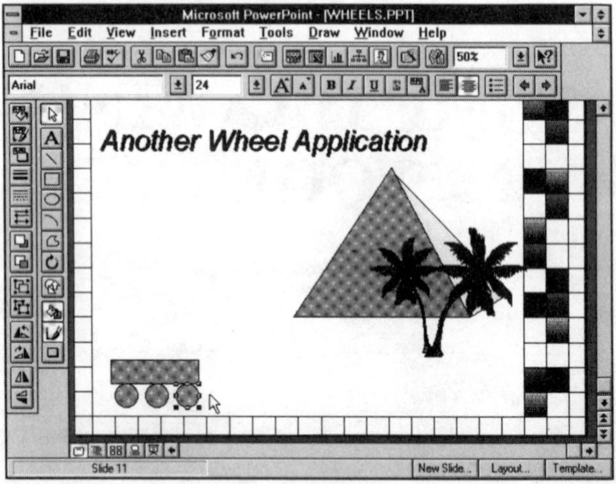

Building a pyramid

Create a new slide with a title only (look at the bottom of the AutoLayout list) and enter a title 'Another Wheel Application'.

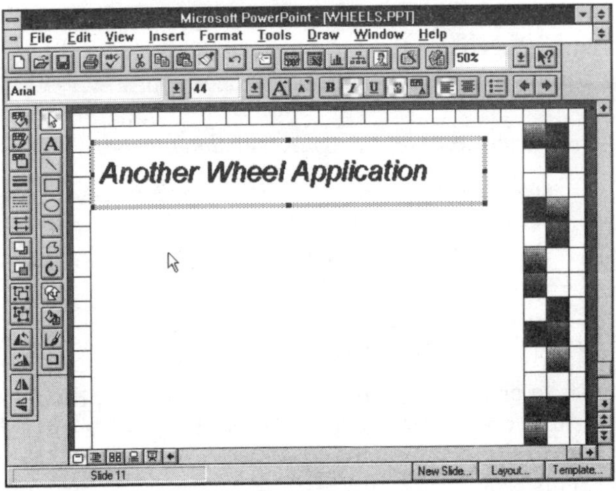

As you are going to draw a pyramid, you can start by selecting the Isosceles Triangle Tool (△) from the AutoShapes toolbar.

First click the (AutoShapes) button on the Drawing toolbar and click the triangle button (△). Then draw a triangle on the slide.

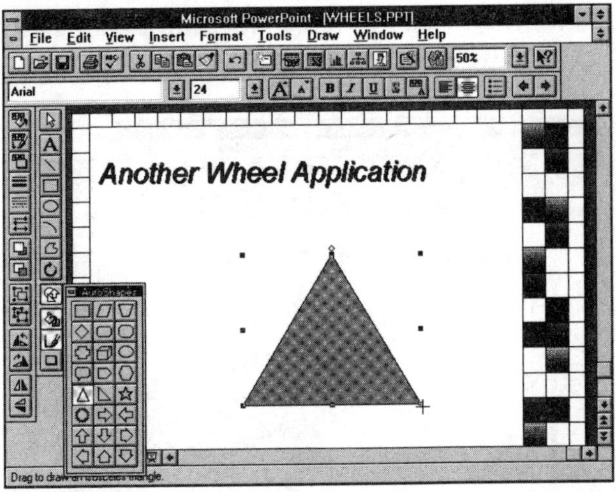

The triangle will fill automatically with the default colour associated with 'Fills' and will probably need changing to a brown or sandy yellow colour. This is done using and selecting a suitable colour from the defaults at the top of the list or selecting one from the Other Colour... option. This presents you with a dialog from which to choose the colour you prefer!

If necessary, change the colour of the 'pyramid'.

You will now notice that the lines around the pyramid (triangle) are the default line colour and they can also be changed to the selected fill colour by using the Line Color tool ( ).

Change the line colour to black.

If you wish to change any aspect of your drawing, then some of the tools included with PowerPoint will assist with this. So here is a good opportunity to experiment again with the rotate and flip tools (and), and also with the ability to move the individual parts of the picture around. To use any of the rotate and flip tools, you need to select the specific object first.

For example, in the picture below a palm tree was first inserted from Clip Art and then flipped using the appropriate button.

Choose Insert Clip Art, locate the palm trees (Plants category), insert them into the slide and reposition as appropriate.

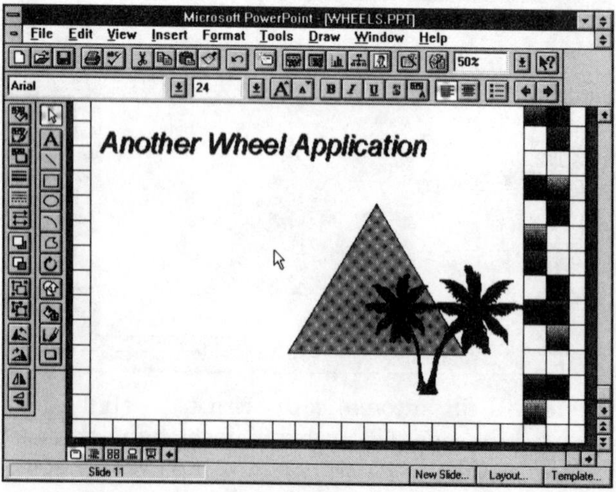

Remember: moving an object is done by dragging it to its new location on the presentation and releasing the mouse button, taking care **not** to try moving the object by dragging either the black handles or the diamond shaped object anchor. The handles will re-size the object and the anchor will tilt the object.

Remember that you can always undo the last revision you make by clicking on [undo button], selecting Undo from the Edit menu or pressing Ctrl Z on the keyboard.

Try inserting another triangle and tilting , rotating and formatting it to achieve the following:

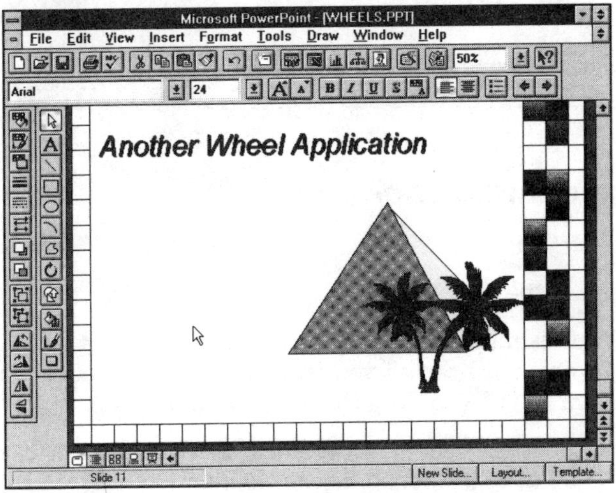

Let's start drawing the stone block and it's rollers. For the stone block we'll start with a rectangle.

Click [rectangle button] on the Drawing toolbar, then click and drag on the slide to drag out the shape.

If it is not in the right place, move it about and re-size.

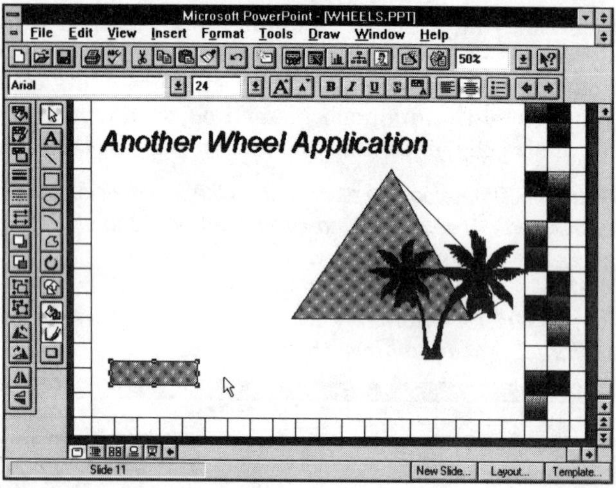

Some drawing shortcuts

Reshaping the object

Trying to reshape an object symmetrically about it's middle can be awkward. However, if you want to do this, a quick way is to hold down Ctrl as you drag the sizing handles.

Ctrl has another use. A very quick way to make a copy of a shape is **by drag and drop**. If you hold down the Ctrl key as you drag the shape PowerPoint makes a copy rather than moving the object.

If you drag a corner handle with Shift held down, you will find the aspect ratio maintained (angles stay the same). If you drag a sizing handle while holding Ctrl, you will find that the object remains centred in the same position (i.e. all the corners move in opposition).

Try out these uses of Ctrl *and* Shift

Holding down the Shift key will usually constrain your pointer movement. If you try to move an object whilst holding Shift you will find that you can only drag it vertically or horizontally.

Use this when drawing decision trees or flow charts to ensure that lines are truly vertical or horizontal, and use [Shift] while creating a rectangle to force 45 degree movement and ensure that the shape will be a true square.

Finally, double-clicking the corner handle of an object will adjust that object to its regular shape, i.e. a rectangle will become a square and an ellipse (oval) will become a circle.

Try double-clicking the corner handle on the rectangle.

Snap-to-Grid

You may notice that any shapes you draw seem to be constrained to fit to an invisible grid. This **snap-to-grid** behaviour is very useful if you are trying to line up different objects, e.g. the parts of a flow chart.

The snap-to-grid command on the Draw menu will switch the feature off altogether if you prefer not to use it. However, holding down [Alt] as you drag will temporarily override the snap-to-grid, which can sometimes be more useful. Both of these forms of behaviour have their uses.

Practise moving the rectangle around (slowly) to see it snapping to grid, then move it while holding [Alt] to see the smooth non-snapping movement.

Selecting

Selecting smaller objects can be a bit fiddly. Try these tips sometime:

- to select a very small object, try 'rubber-banding' it instead – it's a lot easier.
- to select several items at once, select the first item normally, then hold down [Shift] as you select further items.
- alternatively, 'rubber-band' to select all the items, then [Shift] – click to deselect the unwanted items.

Use some of these methods to make the first 'wheel' under the stone block (i.e. draw an ellipse, double-click the cor-

ner handle to make it into a circle and move it to the correct location under the building block).

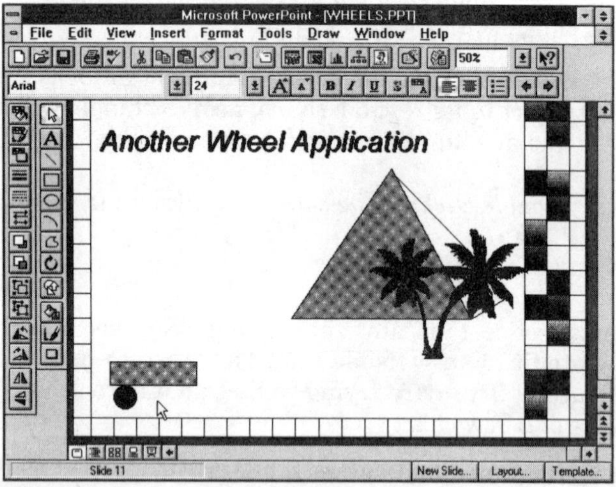

The last stage is to copy the circle. Holding down Ctrl whilst dragging will make a copy and holding down Shift constrains the circles to be horizontally aligned, so holding both Ctrl and Shift will do both.

Ctrl Shift *drag the circle to the right to make a copy of it.*

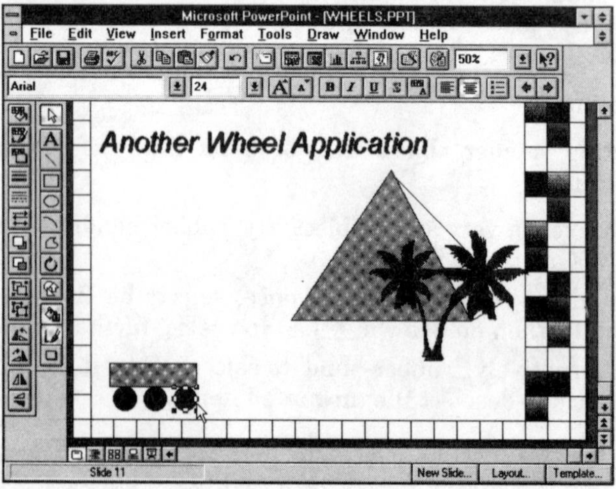

An evenly spaced set of circles

The Edit menu offers a Duplicate command, which you could have used for making that second circle. When only one copy is needed, there is no advantage to this, but if you need a series of identical drawn objects the Edit Duplicate method offers something extra: the duplicates can be spaced evenly in a row. This would look good for the rollers under the building block.

First delete the extra circles.

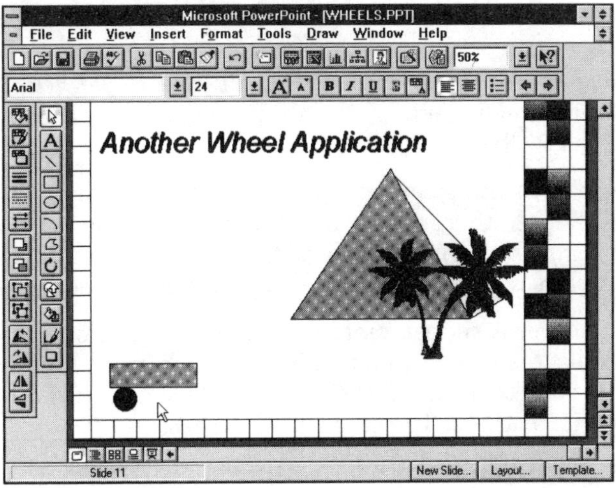

Using the Edit Duplicate procedure it is important to move smoothly through the commands without getting diverted. If you interrupt the sequence and click somewhere else on the slide, you are liable to lose contact with the set of duplicates and the procedure falls apart.

- select the first circle
- choose Edit Duplicate (or Ctrl D)
- a second circle appears, slightly offset from the first, so drag it carefully into place beside the first, and leave it selected
- choose Edit Duplicate Again (or Ctrl D) – if the command Duplicate Again doesn't appear you have lost the thread and you may have to go back and start again

- the third circle appears neatly lined up beside the second
- now use Edit Duplicate Again as many times as necessary

Use this procedure to draw a set of rollers aligned below the building block.

Formatting shapes with the Format Painter

You have seen how to change the fill colour, pattern, border style, border colour, etc. of the shapes using the different buttons on the toolbars.

If you are formatting several shapes, the easiest way is to select all the shapes, then either use the different buttons on the Drawing and Drawing+ toolbars or right-click the shapes and choose Colors & Lines from the shortcut menu to see the dialog.

To make several shapes match, i.e. have the same formatting, you can also use the Format Painter. The Format Painter button is used to 'pick up' the style and formatting of an object and copy it to others. The steps involved are:

- Select the object whose formatting you wish to copy.
- Click the button.
- Select the other object to which you wish to apply formatting – as you do so the format will be applied.

If you want to make several copies of the formats then the procedure is slightly different:

- Select the object whose formatting you wish to copy.
- **Double**-click the button.
- Select the other objects to which you wish to apply the format – again, as you do so the format will be applied.
- When you have finished click again to switch the Format Painter off (or press Esc).

The same principle is also implemented in a slightly different way from the shortcut menu:

- Right-click the object whose formatting you wish to copy and choose Pick Up Object Style.
- Right-click the other objects that you want to apply the format to and choose Apply Object Style.

Change the fill colour and other attributes of the building block, then use the Format Painter to get all the rollers to match it.

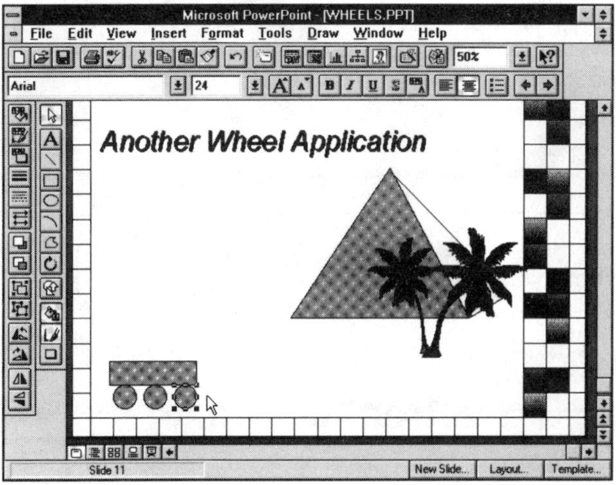

Grouping and ungrouping

Having selected several objects you may decide to group them so that they will subsequently behave as one compound object (you have already ungrouped in a previous exercise). This will make it a lot easier when it comes to moving and/or formatting the different objects. Click [group button] to do this. [ungroup button] is the ungroup button and is used to remove grouping from objects.

Try this: using one of the above methods select the entire block and rollers, then click [group button] to group all the objects. Try moving the objects now – you will find that it behaves as one.

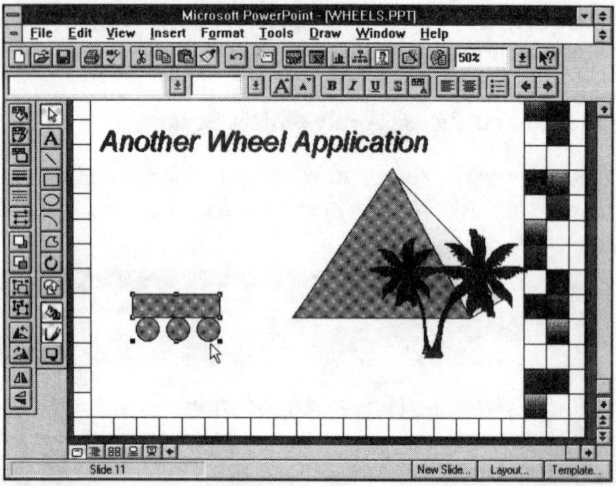

You can also re-size a group, thus keeping the components in proportion, with no risk of the elements 'falling apart'.

In front or behind?

The next item to add to this pyramid slide is a setting sun, disappearing behind the trees. This will raise another issue of the way shapes are positioned.

Draw a circle for the sun, and colour it orange by changing both the fill and line colour.

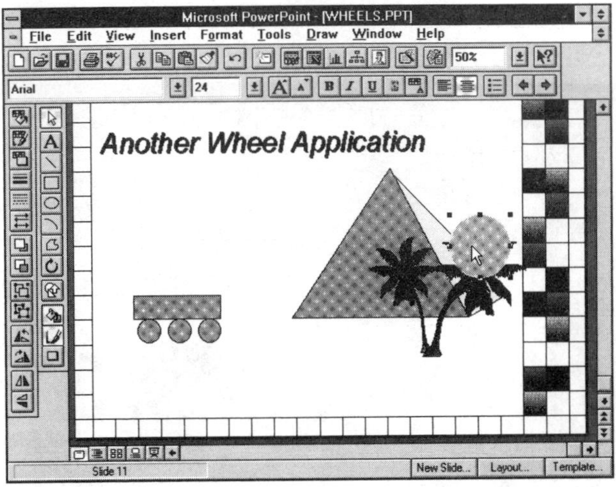

You will probably find that the sun is in front of the other objects, which looks most peculiar! What you need here is the Send to Back tool. When dealing with multiple overlapping objects you need to consider which one is at the front and which are behind. With several objects you may need to think in terms of several layers. The Send to Back () and Bring to Front () tools are very useful in this respect.

Click until the setting sun looks right.

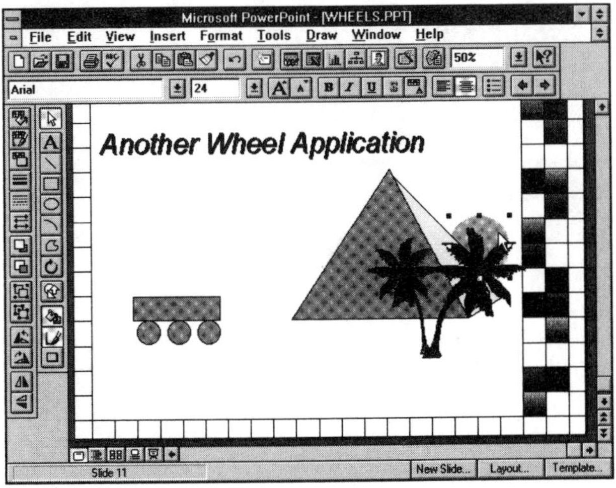

In practice, you will usually need to experiment with [icon] and [icon] a few times to get the 'stacking sequence' that you want. A little trial and error should get you there!

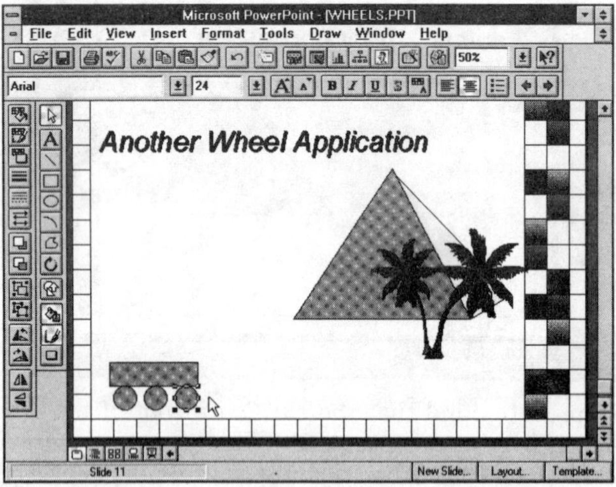

The slide sorter view

Switch to the Slide Sorter View [icon] to look over the slides.

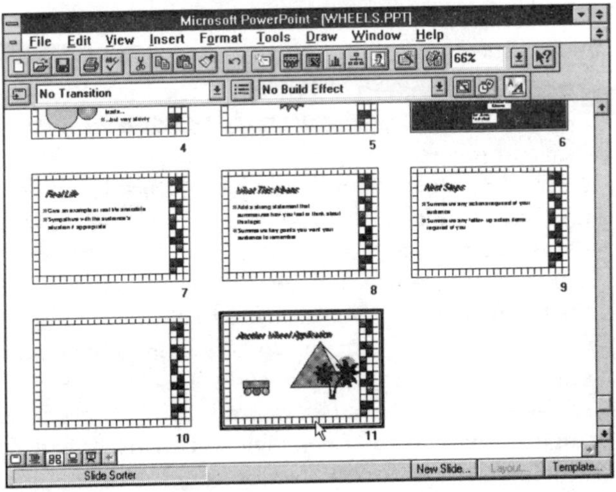

Don't worry if yours looks a little different (you have been experimenting) – in fact, now is your chance to sort things out!

This view (of which you will see more later) offers an overview of the sequence of the slides – it is not too late to make changes! You can remove any unwanted slides by selecting them and pressing [Del]. Use Drag & Drop to rearrange the order of the slides.

Remember you can always save your presentation under a different name, using File Save As, if you are worried about any of your changes being too severe!

Save the presentation as `WHEEL.PPT` *and close it.*

You'll be adding some finishing touches later.

Summary: Drawing Tools

- You can add shapes of your own, then move, size and format them to get surprisingly convincing results.
- You can incorporate ClipArt.
- Normally, moving and sizing conforms to an invisible grid; this can be overcome by holding Alt while using the mouse.
- The Format Painter button ( ) can be used to transfer the formatting of one object to others.
- Objects can be grouped, so that they subsequently stay together (including re-sizing).
- Objects can be moved in behind or in front of others – using the Send to Back ( ) and Bring to Front ( ) tools
- The Slide Sorter View ( ) gives an overview of your presentation allowing quick rearrangement of your slides, or even the removal of unwanted ones.

15

SLIDE NOTES

This chapter covers:

- exploring the Notes View
- adding note text
- setting up the Note Master, including formatting note text

Notes view

Reading the notes

When creating presentations in PowerPoint there is quite often the need for lecturer's or audience notes to accompany each slide, either to remind you what to say, or to remind the audience what you've said!

In the Notes View you can set up such notes pages, i.e. extra text to go with the slides. The PowerPoint Notes facility lets you attach such notes to each slide in a presentation. Each page of notes usually includes a small version of the slide plus space for more text to be typed in.

Open your WHEELS.PPT *presentation.*

Don't worry if your presentation looks slightly different (you may have made your own choices in the previous chapters).

You may like to review the slides first, in Slide Sorter View:

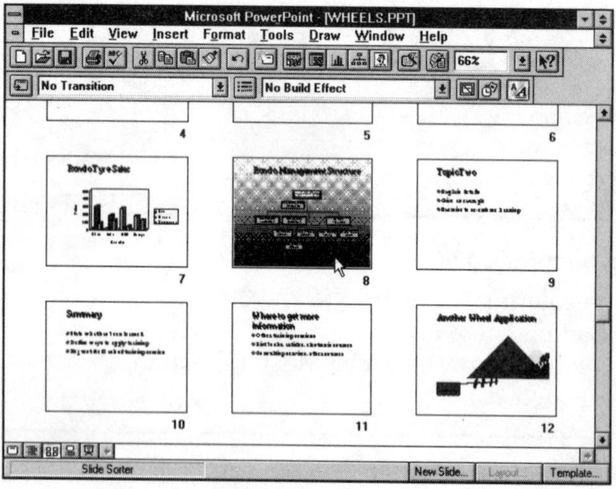

The 'pyramid' slide, above, has a few extras – you can try this as an extra exercise but it is not important. A line was added, then two shapes, to give the impression of a figure (a parallelogram and trapezoid, with suitable flips and rotates), grouped these two, duplicated them, and sized them (holding Alt to suppress the snap to grid, and Shift to keep the aspect ratio). Using the tools you have already used you will probably soon find that you can improve on the rather crude attempt at a line of workers dragging the block of stone!

View Notes or [icon] will switch to Notes View.

Switch to Notes View, and look through the slides again.

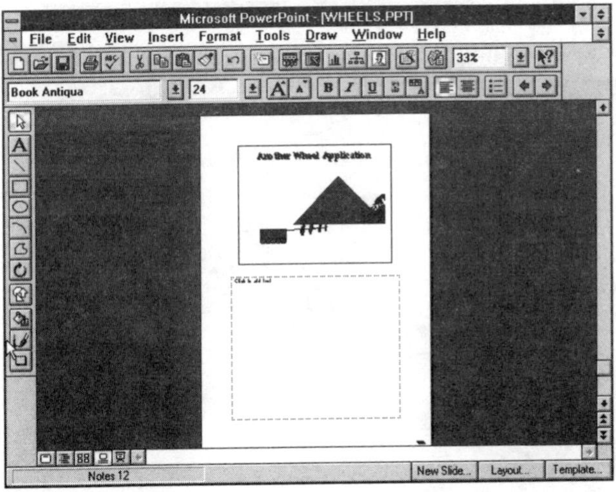

Notice that the slides can still be presented (and are worked with) in the usual way, regardless of whether or not there are notes.

Zoom

You may find it helpful to be able to increase or decrease the display scale using Zoom. The Standard toolbar includes an edit box where you can enter a percentage of zoom scaling so as to enlarge or reduce the screen display. This can be used in all the four editing views. In Notes and Slide Views, the zoom percentage has no effect on the size of the work as printed out (beware that this is not the case in Outline View!). At 75% zoom:

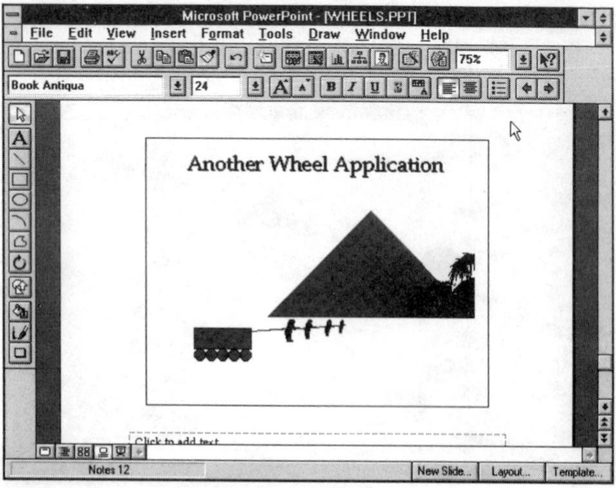

In what follows use varying levels of zoom as appropriate.

Adding note text

You can now see a piece of paper on screen containing objects representing the current slide (at the top) and some explanatory notes (near the bottom).

Try adding some text to one set of notes – click in the Notes area of one page, press Enter *for a new line and invent something interesting to add!*

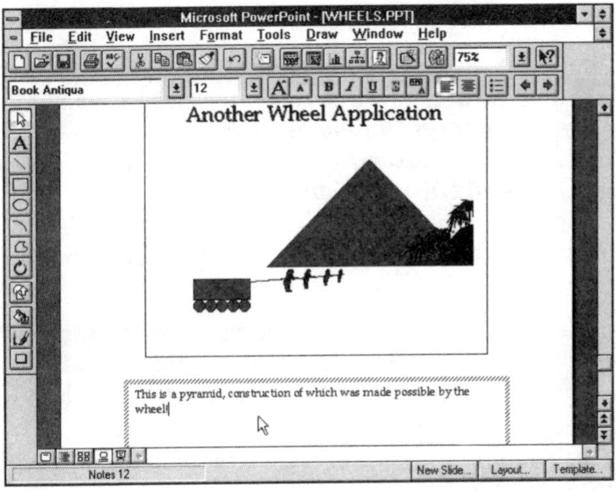

Notes master

In the same way that slides have a Slide Master (in which you can make changes to common elements of all slides), the common elements on all the pages of explanatory notes for a presentation can be set up on the Notes Master.

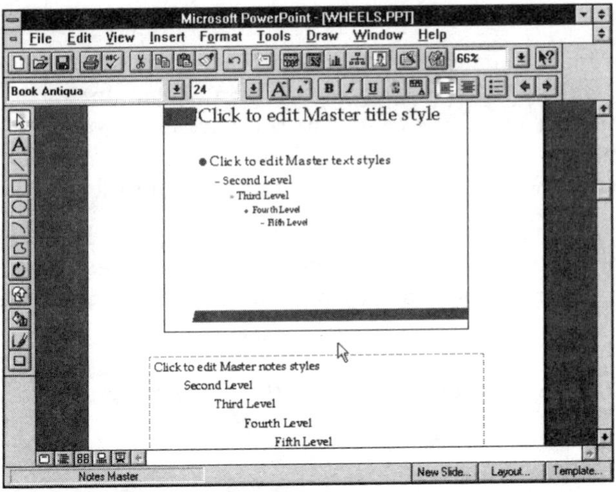

You can switch to the Notes Master by Shift-clicking .

View the Notes Master.

You might want to position the slide object on each page nearer the upper left corner, place a company slogan near one edge, then move and re-size the Notes object to fill whatever space remains at the bottom (being careful not to cover the slogan). You could also add a page number object, so that the Notes pages are correctly numbered. In this case you are going to reduce the size of the slide and increase the area allowed for the notes.

You can accomplish the moving and re-sizing in the same way you moved/sized any of the other PowerPoint objects, i.e. selecting the object, then dragging the object or one of its handles.

Rearrange the slide and notes objects to your taste (for example, add a bullet to the First Level note style).

You can add a page number code in the same way that you did on a Slide Master earlier – use Insert Page Number.

Insert a page number code and move the ## object to a suitable place near the edge of the page.

If you prefer the page number object to read 'Page 3' and so on, click carefully with the mouse I-beam in front of the ## code and type suitable text such as `Page` *before it (not forgetting a* [Space]*).*

Also, from the Insert menu, you can insert the date and/or time – this will appear properly when printed, or during a screen show (it just shows as // or :: in the various views), giving the current time and date (not the date of insertion, or editing – such a date would have to be entered as straightforward text).

You may have other ideas about customising the Notes Master. Try them out. Use all the same methods of creating and formatting graphic objects that have already been discussed with Slides.

Then switch back to one of the Notes pages, to see the effect.

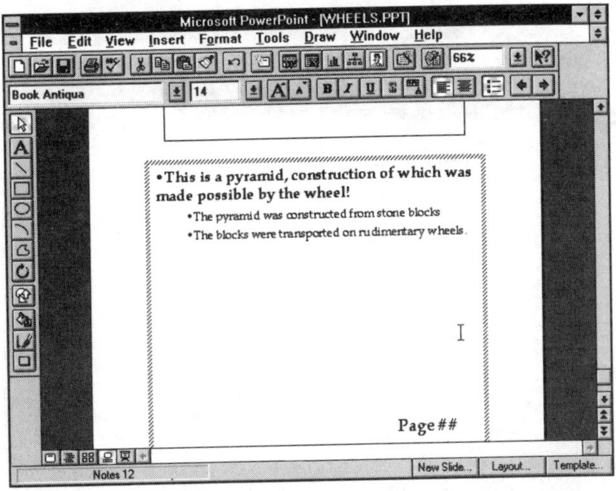

Remember, the page numbers will appear as ## codes on the Notes pages at first. When you come to print out the notes, or view the screenshow they will have proper page numbers.

In the slide above, you can see that some text has been added, as Second Level text. Do this by typing the text, then increasing the indent level ('demoting the text') by either of the following methods:

- click (promotes again)
- by dragging the bullet (or where the bullet would be!) – you should find that the mouse pointer changes to ✥

Try this on the notes you have started.

Text layout

You have already seen that the position of the title, body object and any background objects are set in the Slide Master. The Slide Master also includes text layout formatting.

Switch to the Slide Master.

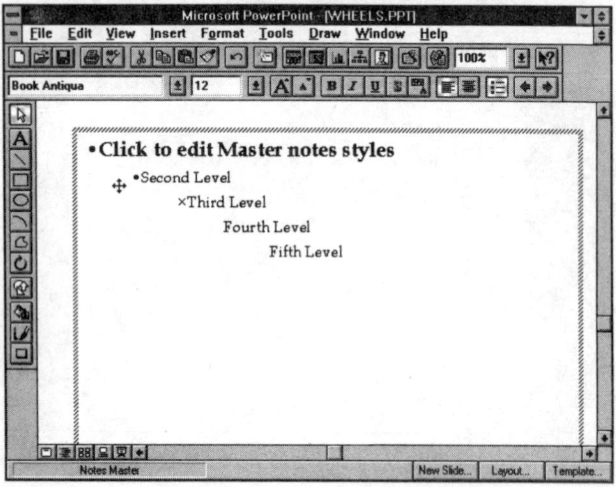

The different levels of points are shown indented. How might you alter this indenting?

Select the text area and choose View Ruler.

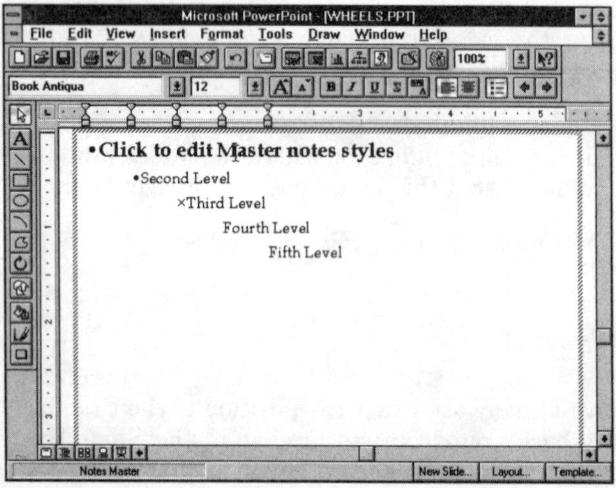

Provided you have the body object selected, the Ruler at the top displays a set of indent markers which correspond to the indent positions of the different levels of bullet that will be used.

You may recognise these indent marker symbols from word-processor rulers. Dragging an indent marker along the Ruler changes the position at which the corresponding text or bullet symbol lies.

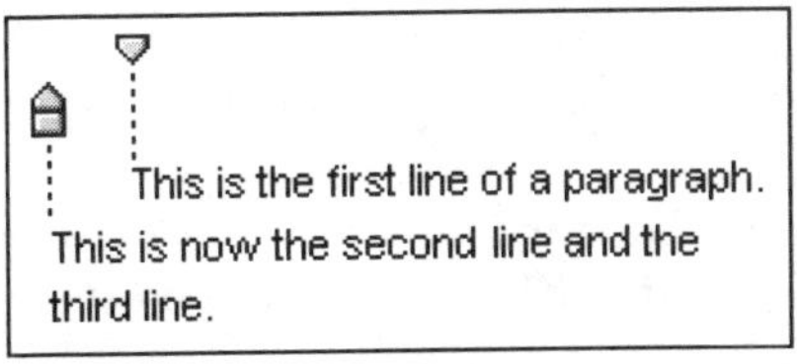

Experiment with dragging the different types of markers, and notice which ones control the different aspects of a bullet point.

You should discover that the markers come in pairs: an upper triangle determines the first line indent, and a lower triangle controls the position of the start of any text which wraps to further lines. The rectangle below moves them as a pair (an upper plus a lower triangle together):

Change the indent positions for the first and second level bullet points and watch the effect on the Master text.

When you have an arrangement you like, switch back to the slides and see the effect this has on the sets of bullet points.

When working on a particular slide, you may decide to View the Ruler that controls the indents for just that slide, and even to set up a different set of indent positions. This is done in the same way that you have just seen.

At this point, you may decide to hide the Rulers again (use View Ruler).

Summary: Notes

- Notes View allows you to enter text that can be printed with the slides, either for your own or your audience's benefit.
- The indenting of notes is controlled by the use of Tab and Shift Tab
- The Notes Master (accessed by Shift – clicking ) is used to set up master styles and positions for notes.

16

PRINTING

This chapter covers:

- Slide Setup
- Printing from PowerPoint
- Print options
- Selecting a printer

Although many PowerPoint presentations are used as screen shows, it can also be useful to print out the slides, for instance on to acetate for OHP use, or even on to ordinary paper for signs and posters. In any case, you need to be familiar with the printing procedure to print out Notes, Handouts and Outlines.

Slide layout

Before you actually print, you will sometimes need to change the orientation and other aspects of the Notes pages and/or the slides. The Slide Setup dialog can be used to specify the orientation and paper size.

From the File menu, choose Slide Setup...

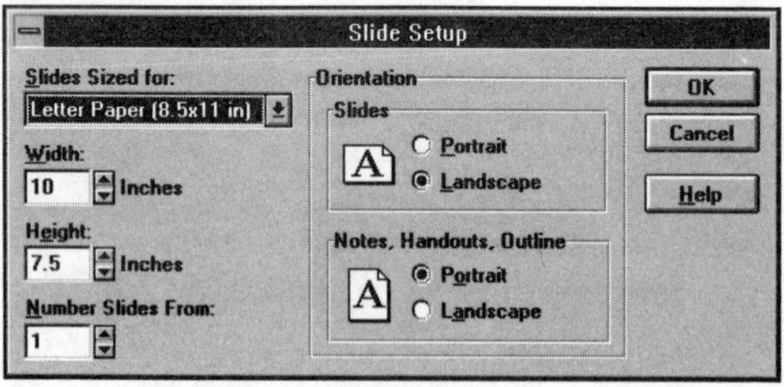

The Slide Sized For list allows you to choose the paper size to which your slides should be printed, or the screen size ratio if they are only to be shown on screen. You can specify a custom size for the slides by altering the values in the Width and Height boxes.

In the centre you can specify which orientation you would like for slides (separately) and other views. The values in the Width and Height boxes change appropriately to reflect this choice. The small page illustration gives a visual indication of the orientation choice.

At lower left you can specify a start value for numbering the slides of the presentation. For example, in a three-slide presentation with a 'Number Slides From' setting of 5 the slides will be numbered as 5, 6 and 7 respectively.

Change the orientation for the slides to Landscape and click OK

Now look through the slides and notice the impact of changing the paper orientation – text is reshaped and reformatted adequately but graphics are distorted. The moral of this may be: think about page size and orientation before spending a lot of time on your design and visual effects.

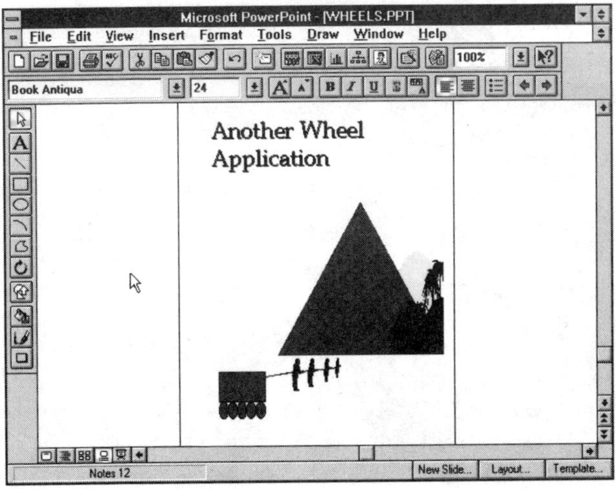

Change the slide orientation back to Landscape from File Slide Setup...

Printing

Choose File Print...

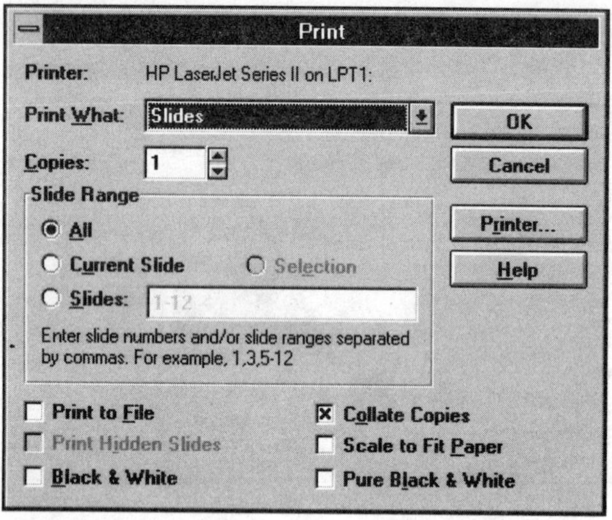

The Print What list

The Print What list allows you to choose which component of the presentation is to be printed. The list contains options for slides/notes and so on:

- Slides – just prints the slides.
- Notes Pages – prints the notes that you worked with in the previous chapter.
- Handouts – sheets with several (2, 3 or 6) thumbnail copies of slides per sheet (economical with paper, but not always doing justice to your graphics).
- Outline View – prints only the main text (titles and bullets) of the presentation, in Outline View.

> *Slides (With Builds) may be offered: if you have specified that your slides should have bullet points building up one at a time (see a later chapter) then you may want to print multiple versions of each slide, each one with one more bullet point showing.*

Print selected slides

The Print Range allows you to specify exactly which slides to print. ◉ All will print the entire presentation. ◉ Current Slide will print only the current slide. ◉ Slides From and To will print the range of slides specified. For example, to print slides 5 to 8 in a ten slide presentation, you would choose ◉ Slides and put 5 in the From box and 8 in the To box. To print from the beginning of the presentation up to a particular slide, you would enter a value only into the To box. To print from a particular slide to the end of the presentation, you would enter a value only in the From box.

Ensure that ◉ All is chosen for the Print Range.

Further options

There are a number of further options at the bottom of the dialog:

Print to file

Checking the Print to File option will send the instruction for printing your presentation to a disk file rather than to the printer. The output file can then be sent to someone else for output (e.g. for higher quality printing or for making colour 35mm slides).

Print hidden slides

This will be available if you have set any slides to be hidden. Hidden slides are those which you can choose whether to show whilst running a Slide Show (more on this later).

Black & white

With Black & White checked, all lines and text will print as black and any colours in the presentation will not print at all (i.e. white). A border is drawn around any unfilled shapes unless they have text attached to them. This is very useful when sending colour presentations to black and white printers or when coloured presentations lack acceptable clarity or readability.

Collate copies

If you want to print a presentation several times and have each complete presentation finish printing before the next one starts (thus avoiding the need to collate them by hand), check this checkbox. If you simply want the pages to come out of the printer as quickly as possible (and don't mind collating by hand), leave this option off. (The difference is speed can be very great – it can be well worth the effort of collating by hand – your decision will depend on the printer and the amount of graphical output).

> *When printing, the operation that takes the most time is having the printer interpret the printing instructions from PowerPoint. If you can reduce the amount of interpretation, printing will be faster. When Collate Copies is on, the printer will have to interpret the instructions for a particular page of output several times, e.g. in printing a presentation ten times collated, the printer interprets slide 1 ten times. With Collate Copies off, the printer interprets the instructions once for each page and simply prints that page the required number of times (for the ten copies above, uncollated printing will interpret slide 1 just once).*

Scale to fit paper

Turn on Scale to Fit Paper when a presentation must be printed on paper of a different size than was called for by the presentation formatting. However, the effect may be to distort the slide slightly.

Pure black & white

This is similar to Black & White (discussed above). When this option is checked, all colour fills are shown in white, all text and lines appear in black, and a border appears around any filled object. Additionally any pictures are shown in greyscales.

This differs from Black & White mainly because with Pure Black & White fills are always rendered as white, whereas with Black & White fills may be rendered as black-and-white patterns.

Ensure that Print to File is off, then set the other options as you see fit.

Printer selection

At the top of the Print dialog is a reminder of the printer to which output will be sent. The printer can be changed in the Print Setup dialog, reached by clicking Printer...

Click Printer...

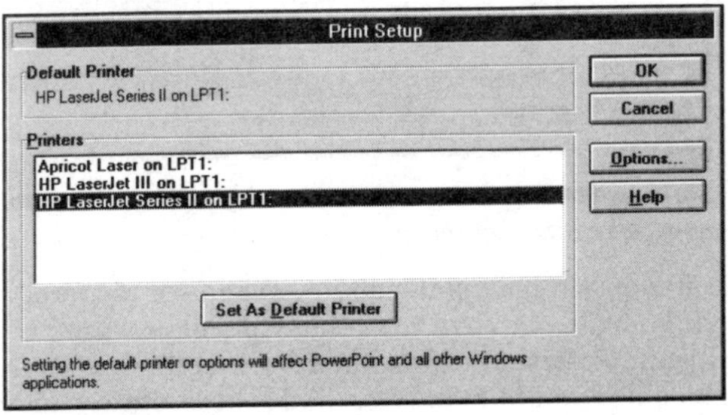

This dialog allows you to choose different printer for output of slides, notes, handouts and outlines. For example, you could print slides to a colour printer but when you come to print out a set of notes you would send them to a cheaper black & white printer.

At the top of this dialog you can see which printer is set as the default.

If you prefer to send the next printing to a different printer, either select that printer from the lower list and click the Set As Default button or double-click the printer of your choice.

Select an appropriate printer (if you have a choice!)

Printer options

Clicking Options... from within the printer dialog takes you to the printer dialog specific to your type of printer. For example:

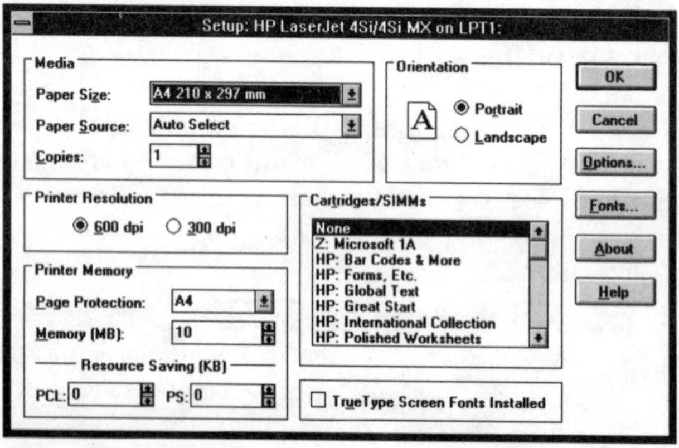

Beware that choices you make here may affect printing from any other Windows application.

One useful option here is the ability to change the Paper Source – for example, if you have a two-bin with plain paper in the upper tray and acetate in the lower tray. Careful choice from this dialog enables you to print your slides on acetate and the Outline on plain paper, without ever leaving your desk.

Cancel *the options dialog (if you need to) and* Close *the printer dialog.*

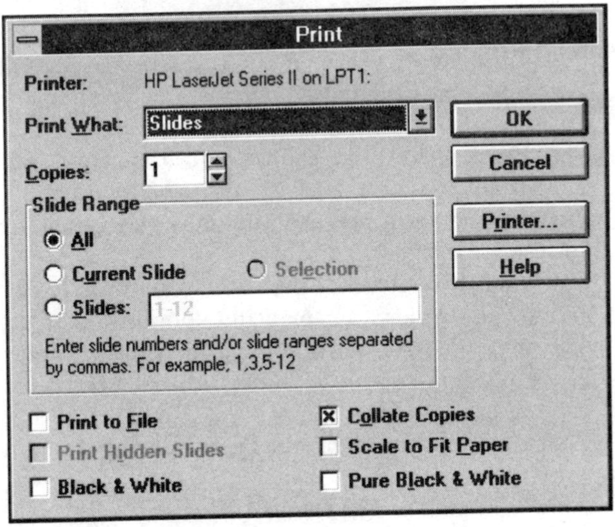

This returns you to the Print dialog.

Click OK *to print the Slides.*

Printing to a colour printer, while it can produce excellent results, can also be expensive. If your presentation needs to be checked, it is often worth printing a draft copy first in black and white for approval before running off the final copy in colour.

Summary: Printing

- The Slide Setup dialog controls the orientation of printing, and allows selection of paper size.
- The Print What list allows you to choose which component of the presentation is to be printed.
- Print output for a presentation may be in slide, note, outline view or handout form.
- Choosing File Print... presents you with a dialog giving a choice of printing options, including printing hidden slides and printing collated copies.
- When producing 35 mm slides through a third-party, use the print to file option.
- There are special controls for rendering black and white print.
- Some options are printer specific.

17

— OUTLINE VIEW —

This chapter covers:

- The benefits of Outline View
- Creating a new presentation in outline view
- Exporting presentation text to Word
- Using the spell checker

Rearranging the text material in outline view

Click ▤ *to switch to Outline View for* `WHEELS.PPT`

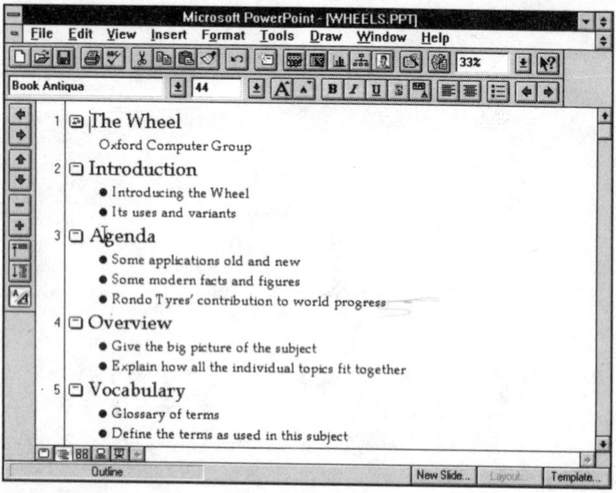

The Outline View allows you to see the main text content of a presentation so that you can work on the overall structure of the presentation without worrying about visual style or graphics. Importantly, you can quickly build up and/or restructure a slide show with point and click techniques – while the slide sorter allows moving entire slides, outline view allows blocks of text to be moved.

What you see

Along the left side of the screen are slide numbers and slide icons representing the slides of the presentation. Slide icons come in two forms: ▭ and ▣, the latter simply indicates that a slide that contains objects that are not visible in this view (e.g. graphic objects).

Double-click the slide number or slide icon for the 'gears' slide:

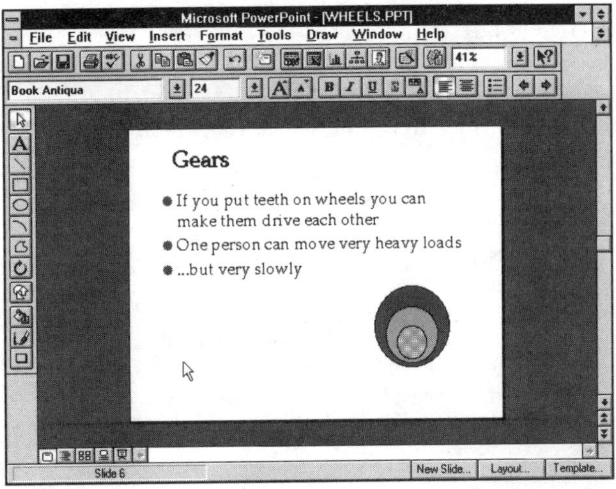

This slide appears in Slide View and there is indeed a graphic object on this slide – which may not match yours.

> *If the graphic object had been added to the Slide Master rather than the slide itself, the slide icon would not indicate a graphic (and of course it would have appeared on every slide).*

Click [Outline View button] *to return to Outline View.*

The Title text for each slide appears to the right of each slide icon. Arranged hierarchically below the title for each slide is the text from the body object. All this text can be edited here or in Slide View – it is the same text just shown in a different way. The text in Outline View is displayed as formatted in the Title and Body Objects although without colour or shadow.

Affecting the view

The way the presentation outline is displayed can be changed by using two new buttons that appear in the Toolbar (usually at the left hand side of the screen) when in Outline View.

Slide titles only

You can show only the titles of the slides by clicking [icon] This is particularly useful when you are manipulating a large presentation.

Click [icon] to see titles only.

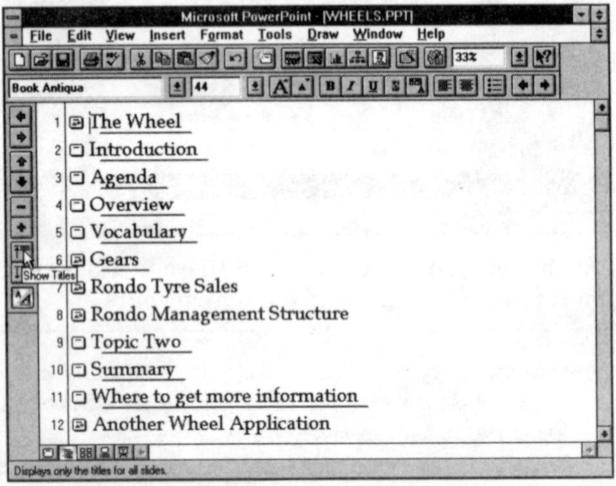

The button shows as depressed in the Toolbar. The Show All button [icon] allows you to reveal all of the text again.

Click [icon] to see all the text.

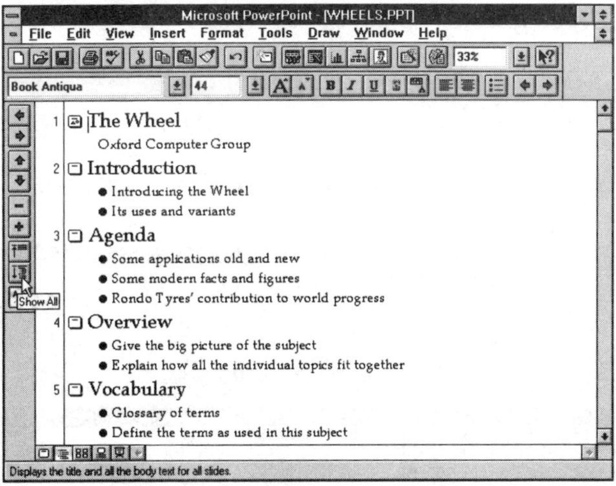

Draft text

You can also modify Outline View to show the outline without any formatting. You may find this useful if certain text is small or is elaborately formatted.

Click [button] to see the outline without formatting.

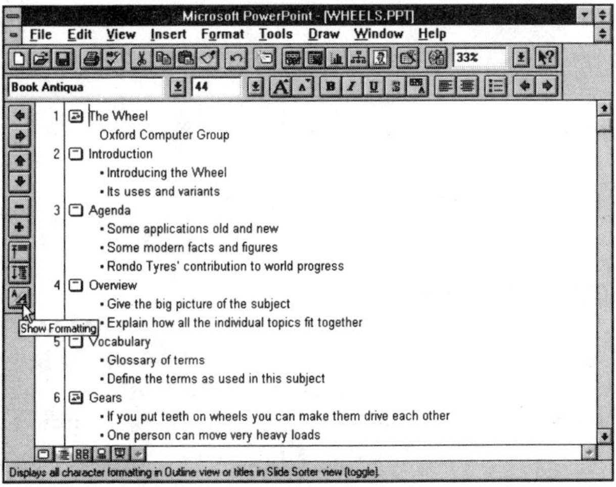

All text appears in a simple, easy-to-read font.

Click to see the formatting again.

Collapsing and expanding slides

If you are creating a long presentation with a lot of text, it may be useful to collapse some slides to their titles (but not all, as above).

Click a slide and click to collapse it.

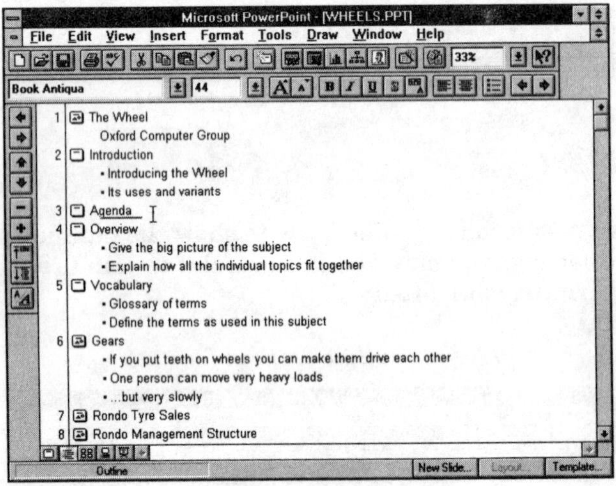

A collapsed slide may be expanded using

Click to see the text on the slide.

Two-column slides

The display of these in Outline View can be misleading. Only the first column of text is displayed by the Outliner. This is because the second column of text is treated as a graphic text object (you would even notice that slide icon is).

Selecting parts of the outline

There are several distinct parts of an outline that you may want to select. Letters, words or series of either can be selected in the usual way by dragging the I-beam over the text to be selected or by holding down Shift and moving the insertion point with the arrow keys ↑, ↓ and so on. Such manual methods can be slow, however, so there are other methods available to select a family (i.e. a paragraph and all its subordinate paragraphs), a simple paragraph, groups of contiguous paragraphs and words. (In what follows, remember that a 'double-click and drag' involves double-clicking on something and holding the mouse button down on the second click, then dragging.)

Select a bullet point on Slide 3.

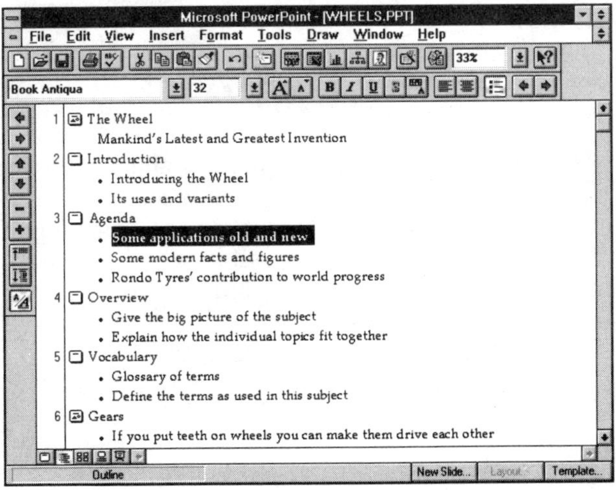

The demote ➡ and promote ⬅ tools can be used to indent and unindent the selected paragraphs by one heading level. Junior sub-points will be demoted or promoted automatically when these tools are applied to a main point. Formatting will be adjusted accordingly (following the defaults set out in the Slide Master).

Demote the selected bullet point, using the ➡ tool.

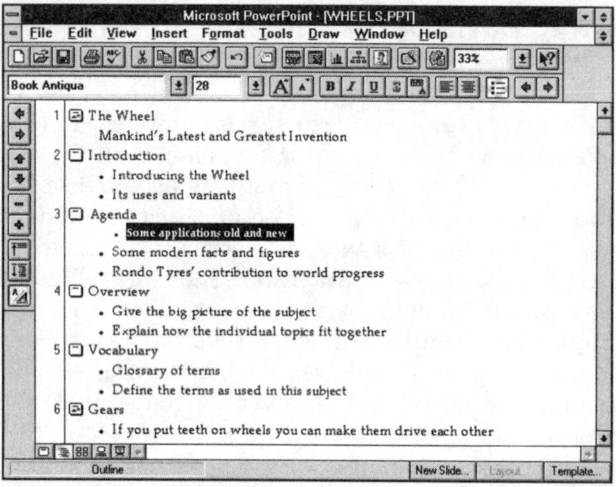

The keyboard method for this task is to hold down [Shift] [Alt] while using the [←] and [→] keys.

Promote and demote the selected bullet point, using the keyboard.

Similar techniques can be used to move a point up or down in a sequence. You can either drag with the mouse (dragging the slide icon) or use the [↑] and [↓] tools on the Outlining Toolbar. As well as moving a point within a slide, it is possible to move it onto another slide (by dragging the bullet).

Drag the selected bullet point:

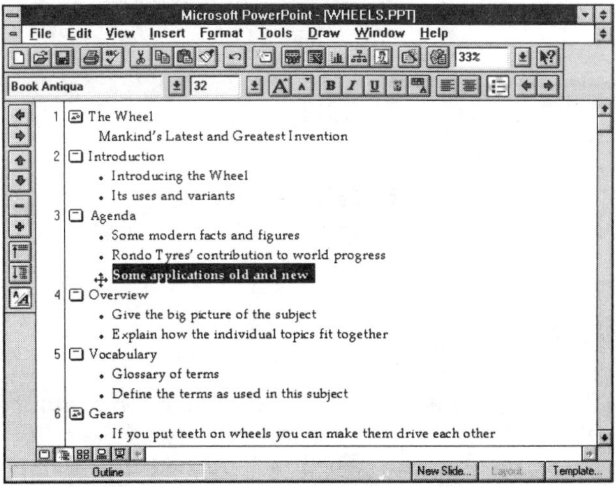

Entire slides may be deleted, by selecting the slide and pressing the delete key. This action is undone by selecting Undo on the Edit menu, as usual.

It would be wise to save WHEELS.PPT *using* [save button] *before experimenting - possibly under a new name.*

You may like to experiment now with deleting a slide and using Edit / Undo to restore it.

— Rearranging points in slide view —

Many of the re-ordering, demoting and promoting techniques you have seen in Outline View also apply in Slide View. However, you will not be able to drag a bullet points from one slide onto another in Slide View.

Switch to Slide View and practise changing the order of bullet points, demoting and promoting using the outlining tools and using the mouse.

Close WHEELS.PPT *e.g. by pressing* Ctrl F4 *or taking the Close option from the File menu.*

Save it if you wish to keep recent changes.

PowerPoint and Word

Report it

It may be useful to save an outline of your presentation in a form that Word can read. To do this click the 'Report It' tool on the Standard Toolbar. Word is launched and a dialog box giving a choice of file formats may appear. If it does, accept Word's choice, which should be RTF (Rich Text Format).

You might like to try this if you have Microsoft Word available.

The outline will now be saved in a temporary file and appear as text in the Word window. Slide title, main bullet points and minor bullet points will appear as text with a series of different styles, namely Heading1, Heading2 and Heading3, etc. It is now possible to edit the outline using Word commands. You may then save the outline of your presentation as a Word 6 file, perhaps with a view to developing a more detailed report or wordy document using the presentation outline as a basis.

Present it

The reverse situation occurs when you have the first draft of ideas for a presentation created in Word. Provided the standard heading styles or Tab has been used in Word, the outline can easily be exported to PowerPoint for working up into a full presentation.

Starting in Word, set out your ideas and use the standard styles Heading1, Heading2, Heading3, etc. Heading levels 1 to

5 will be converted to corresponding outline levels in PowerPoint (i.e. text with the style Heading1 will become slide titles, text with the style Heading2 will become main bullet points, text with the style Heading3 will become sub-points, and so on). However, although Word supports heading styles down to level 9, PowerPoint only has levels 1 to 5, so text with Word styles Heading6 ...9 will appear on the slide show as body text.

The Present It macro (choose Tools Macro, select PresentIt and click Run) will create a text file based on your outline, with filename extension `.RTF`. This can later be read in PowerPoint and used as the basis for a presentation. You may of course choose to make further changes in PowerPoint in the usual way – text formatting, adding graphics and so on.

When you want to open the `.RTF` file in PowerPoint, use  to display the File Open dialog. Choose Outlines from the List Files of Type: list box. You will now be able to see files with .DOC and .RTF extensions instead of those with .PPT extensions in the file name list box.

Creating a new presentation using Outline View

You can create new presentations from scratch in Outline View. This is often a helpful way of getting your thoughts onto 'paper' (or in this case a PC) and ordering them, without getting distracted by graphics, layout, etc.

The technique is simply to type the titles and bullet points into a blank outline, moving, promoting or demoting them as necessary.

To remind you: while typing in the new titles and points there are two useful keyboard equivalents of which you should be aware.

- Enter will create a new paragraph at the same level as the current paragraph (i.e. title or bullet points)

- Ctrl Enter will create a new title if pressed when the current paragraph is a bullet point; it will create a new bullet point if the current line is a title.

These keyboard equivalents are illustrated in the instructions that follow. As usual, only press Enter or other keys where shown.

- Create a new presentation and choose Blank Presentation.

Click OK to move on to the New Slide dialog, choose 'Bulleted List' and OK again to see the first slide.

Switch to Outline View (if necessary).

You will see a blank outline with one untitled slide icon.

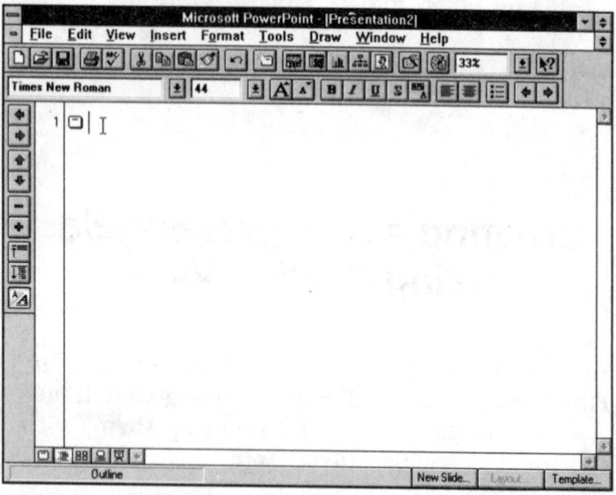

Type the name of the first slide as follows:

```
New Advertising Campaign
```

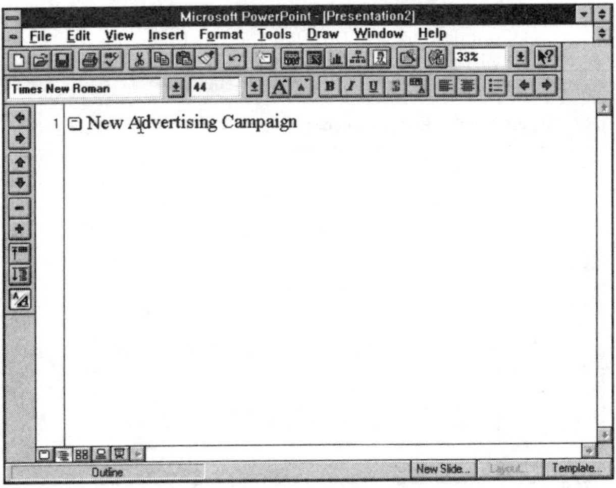

Now to add a few bullet points for the first slide. As was mentioned above, if the current paragraph (i.e. the paragraph currently containing the insertion point) is a slide title and you press Ctrl Enter you create a new bullet point.

Press Ctrl Enter *to create a bullet point.*

Type the text of the bullet point as follows:

Emphasis on 'Discovery' and new product or feature.

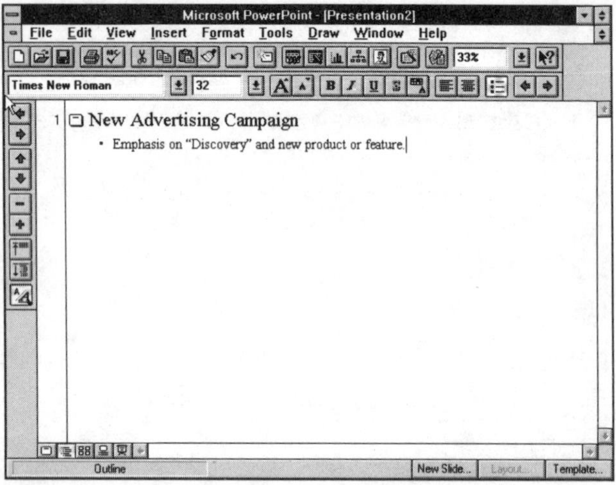

You may desire a few more bullet points for the first slide. Enter will create new bullet points.

Type the following (including the deliberate spelling mistake):

Enter

Must be humerous Enter

Cartoons

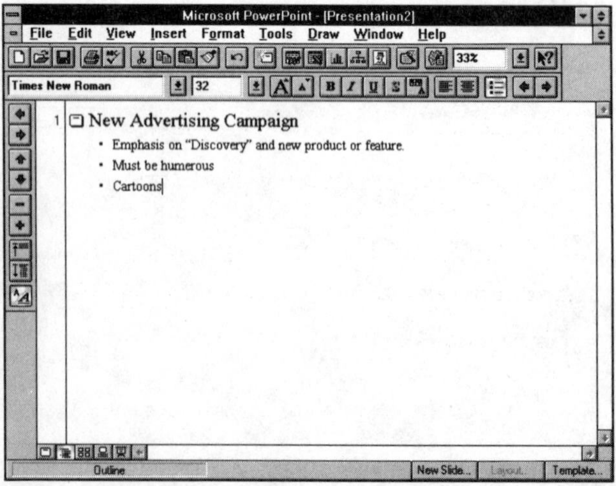

Perhaps you now need another slide – Ctrl Enter will do this for you.

Press Ctrl Enter *and then type the title for the new slide as follows:*

Caveperson Discovers Drag and Drop

To create the bullet points for this new slide, type:

Ctrl Enter

Use of non-sexist language Enter

Drag and Drop is an important Windows feature

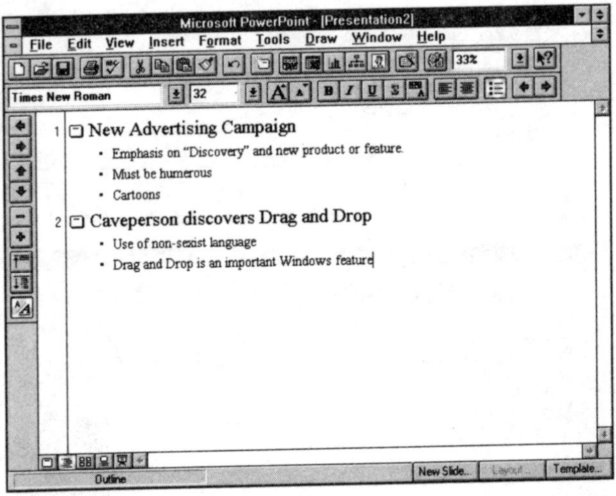

To complete the presentation add three more slides and bullet points as shown below (using Enter *and* Ctrl Enter *as appropriate).*

Interior Decorator Tries out Cut and Paste

- **Cut and Paste is not new but is extremely important**
- **Common across most Windows products**

Santa Experiments with Windows

IntelliSense

- Enough said ...
- No gag needed for this one

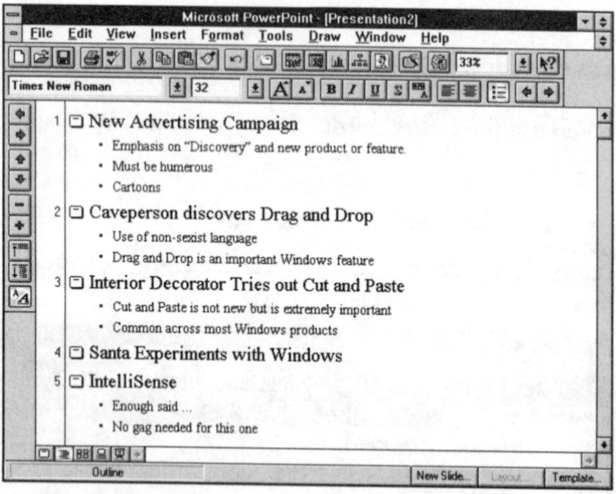

Switch to Slide View and then change to Slide 1.

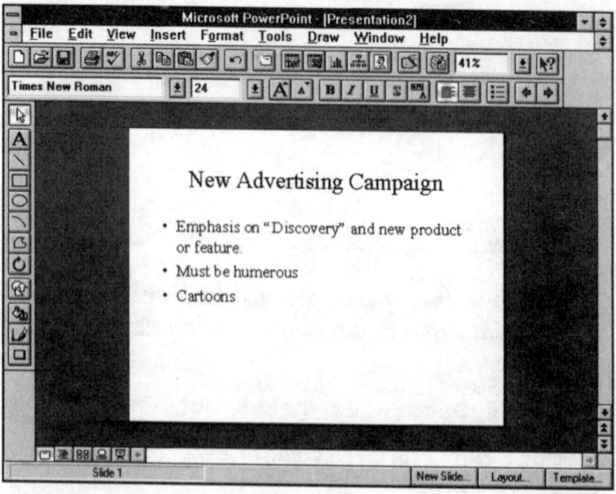

Run the slide show (click).

The spell checker

There may not be much text in your presentation, compared with the average word-processed document, but if the slides are to be presented in front of people you wish to influence it is especially important that there are no spelling mistakes. Many people may not mind (or even notice!), but a proportion of your audience will be totally distracted by a spelling mistake. PowerPoint's speller checks not only the Slide text but Notes text and even the words attached to any drawn objects.

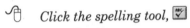

The spell checker is launched by clicking the spelling tool, or pressing . It will check words found after the insertion point for those that do not match entries in the dictionary. You can add other correct words to a custom dictionary for your own needs.

Click the spelling tool,

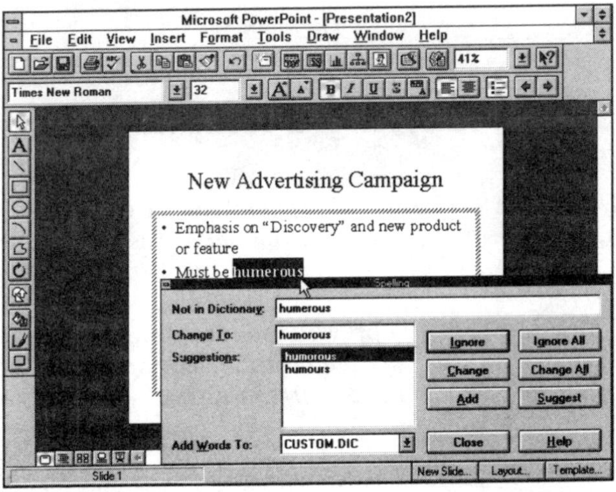

Any (supposedly) mis-spelt word will appear in the Not in Dictionary text box, where it can be edited ('humerous' above). This should not usually be necessary, as the spell checker offers you a number of suggestions. The most obvious will appear in the Change To text box (i.e. 'humerus' above, in this case wrong). You can accept this by clicking [Change]

Otherwise you can select one of the other words offered in the Suggestions list box (in the case above you should choose 'humorous' from the list).

Make sure 'humorous' is selected, then click [Change].

Continue checking the presentation, clicking [Ignore] *or* [Change] *as appropriate.*

Other correct words, perhaps technical terms or proper nouns special to your own work, can be added to the custom dictionary. By default, this is the same custom dictionary that other Microsoft applications use, so if you have been using for instance Word's Speller you may already have a good collection of your own special words in the custom dictionary.

Beware that you do not inadvertently add wrongly-spelt words to the custom dictionary!

Applying a template

The design can be improved by applying a template. This is done using the [Template...] button found in the bottom right of screen.

Click [Template...] *to apply a new template (remember that you can preview the templates before applying one). For example,* CONFETIC.PPT *from the* CLROVRHD *directory:*

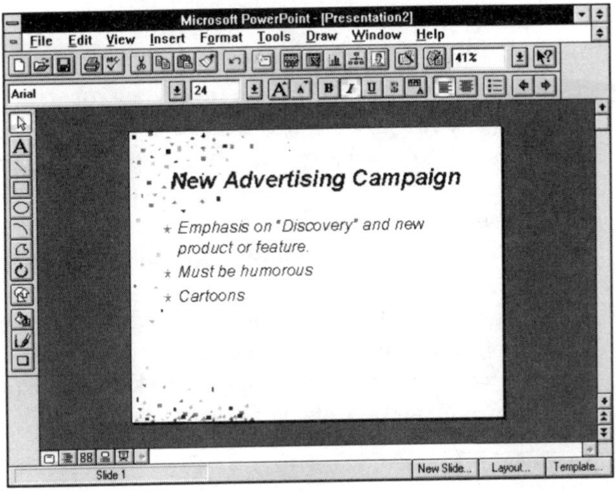

The names of the templates are 8-letter contractions supposed to indicate what they look like. In this case CONFETIC.PPT has a sprinkle of confetti in colour on the left of the slide. Similarly the directory name - CLROVRHD - indicates that the templates it contains are designed for use as colour overheads. BWOVRHD, naturally, contains templates for black and white overheads, and the templates in SLDSHOW are specially designed for use with slide shows.

Change to Slide 1, if necessary, and run the slide show again.

Save the presentation as `ADVERT.PPT` *and close the presentation.*

Summary: Outline View

- Outline view gives you an overview of the text content of your presentation.
- Slide headings only or the full slide text can be viewed (excluding any 'graphic' text). Formatting can be seen or hidden, for clarity.
- Slide text can be promoted, demoted and easily moved in outline view.
- The presentation text can be exported to Word using the Report It tool (and Word outlines imported).
- PowerPoint ships with a spell-checker that allows you to proof the text of the presentation.

18

MANAGING & RUNNING SLIDE SHOWS

This chapter covers:

- Finding existing slideshows and slide text
- Rearranging the slides by Drag & Drop
- Transition between slides.
- Slides time rehearsals.
- How to hide slides to suit a particular audience.

Finding Existing Work

We will take a few moments here to mention features that cannot be covered fully.

File Find

Open the file WHEELS.PPT *if necessary (remember that it may be one of the four Most Recently Used filenames on the File menu).*

It won't always be as easy as that to find a slideshow.

Take the Find File... option from the File menu:

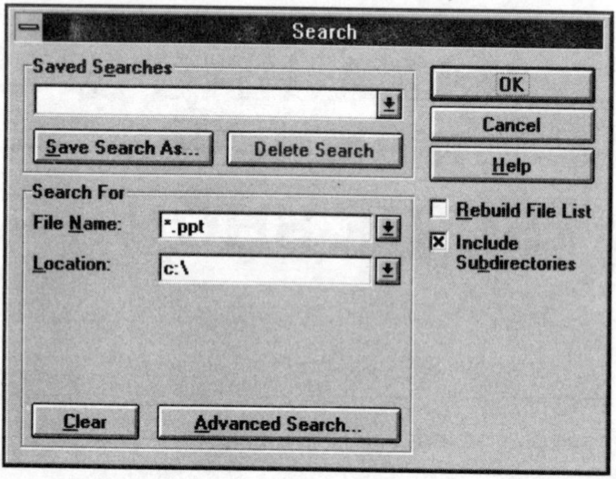

We cannot cover all the options here, but searching for all .PPT files on a particular drive (including subdirectories) will often be all you need (if you wish this to be a fresh file list, not including anything found in previous searches, you should also check the box for Rebuild File List).

On clicking OK (and after a delay):

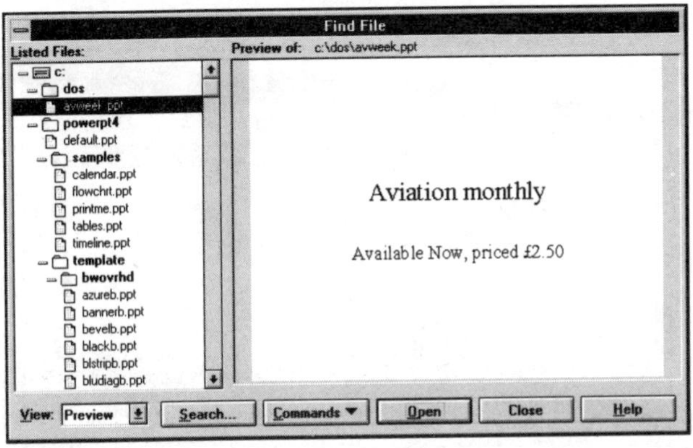

You can preview the first slide, and open a presentation, or simply close the dialog. There are other commands available:

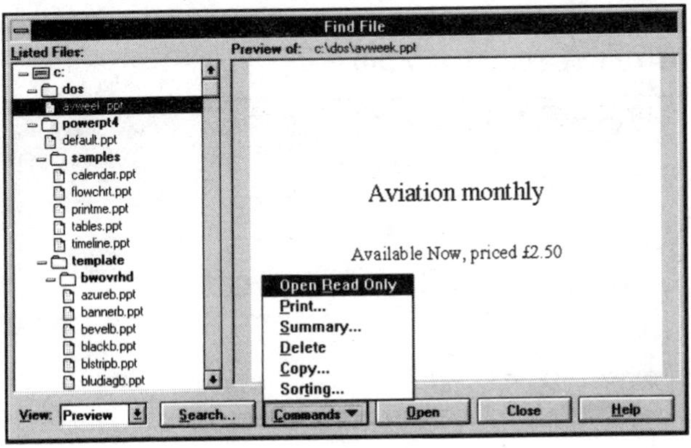

Notice in particular that you can delete unwanted files.

From the original Search dialog, you can go to the advanced search dialog:

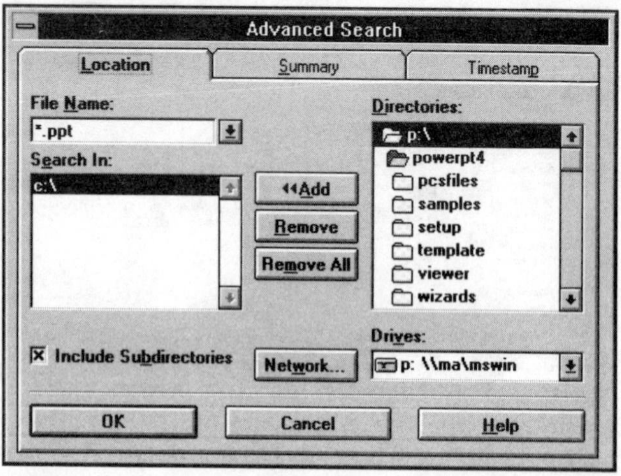

From here you can add a series of paths to be included in the search. From the summary tab:

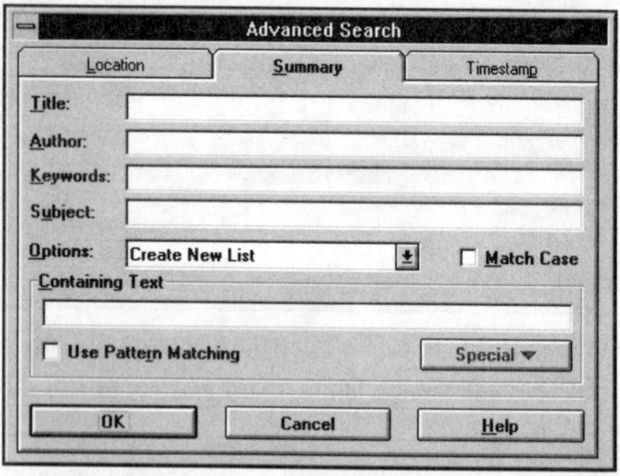

you can enter any information stored in the summary dialog for your presentation, or even search for any text in the presentation (much slower as it involves reading the entire presentation). From the Timestamp tab:

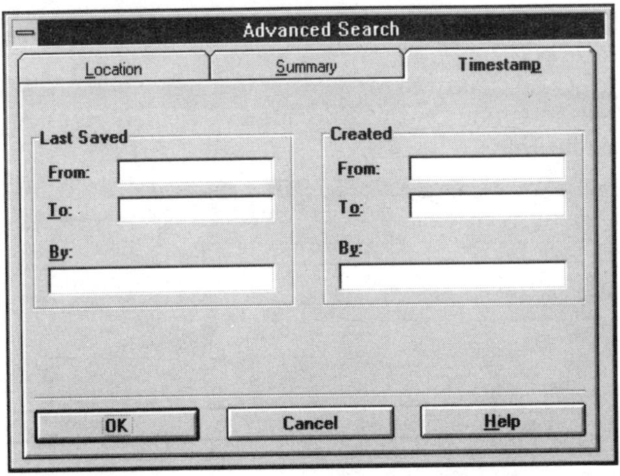

you can search on the basis of when, and by whom, your presentations were created or last saved.

Find and Replace

It may be that, having found your presentation, you wish to find a slide with some particular word or words. The Find option on the Edit menu (with shortcut Ctrl F) is provided for this. It is trivially easy to use, and searches any slide text, and then the masters.

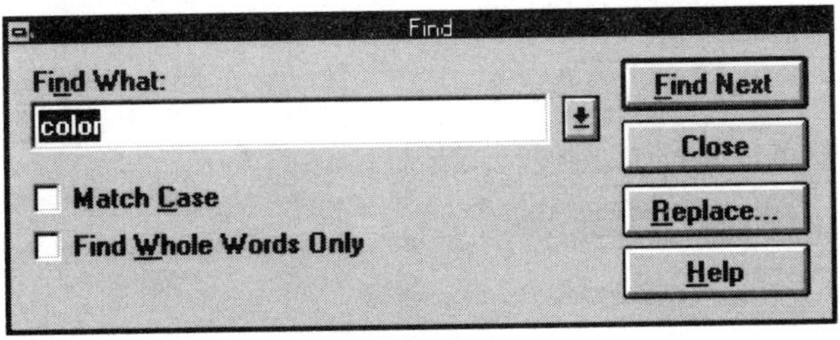

There is a checkbox to indicate that you wish to Find Whole Words Only (e.g. 'the' as a word rather than as part of 'theatre'), and another to indicate that you wish to Match Case (e.g. find 'Mark' not just 'mark'). You can experiment by searching for any text in your presentation.

Sometimes you may wish to replace a word, or words, with another in a systematic manner – perhaps swapping a name for another because you are presenting to a new audience or client. The Replace option on the Edit menu (with shortcut Ctrl H) is provided for this.

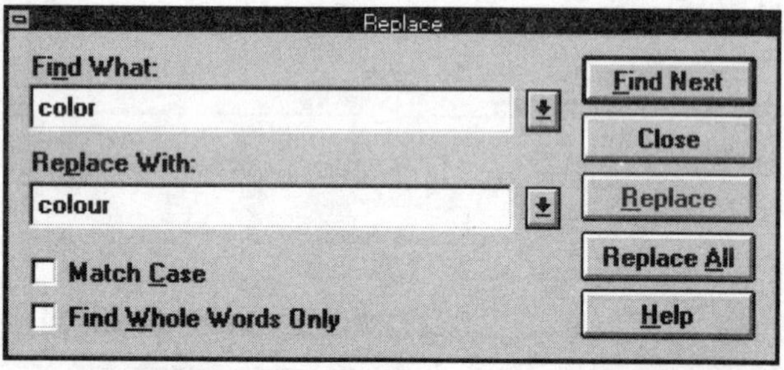

Again it is very easy to use, but watch out not to be too systematic, for instance: imagine replacing 'The federation of computer operators' (throughout a presentation) with the 'The federation of truck operators' (by replacing 'computer' with 'trucks'). Any unconnected use of 'computer' would be replaced by 'truck', regardless of context!

'Blank' Slides

You will add some special features which will make the show more interesting if it is to be presented as a screen show.

If necessary, switch to Slide Sorter View.

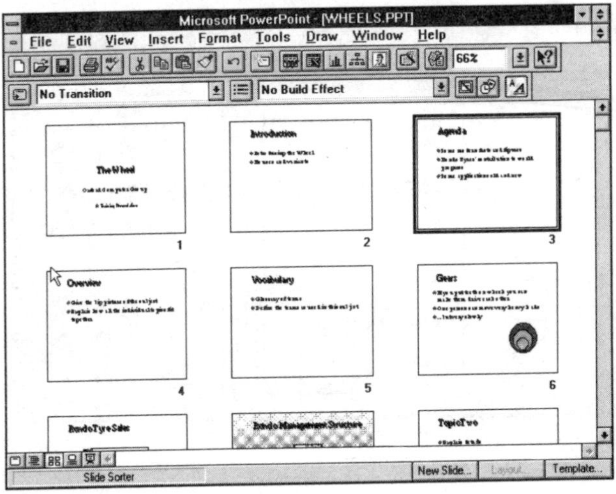

Perform any final rearranging of your slides

Sometimes you may want a pause in a slide show. Whilst there are keyboard methods for this (B for black, W for white), if you are using a mouse and you know where the pause is to come you can insert a black or white slide (or one that has the background objects but no text). In any case it is a good tip to include a black or white slide at the end of your presentation (or again, one that has the background but no text) – it gives a nice smooth finish.

Add a blank slide with background only as the very last slide: to do this, insert a new slide, choose 'Blank slide' from the AutoLayout list. When you've inserted it, move it to the end of the presentation.

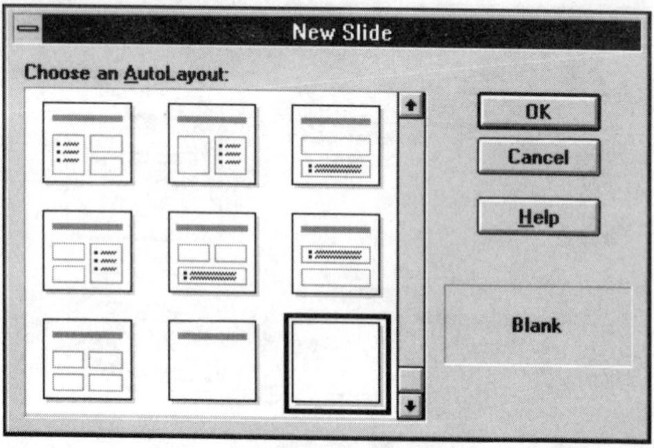

Transitions and Timing

The change from one slide to the next can seem very abrupt. PowerPoint provides different methods of transition from one slide to another. If you set a transition for a particular slide, this affects the way this slide is drawn on the screen.

Click the first slide to select it then click

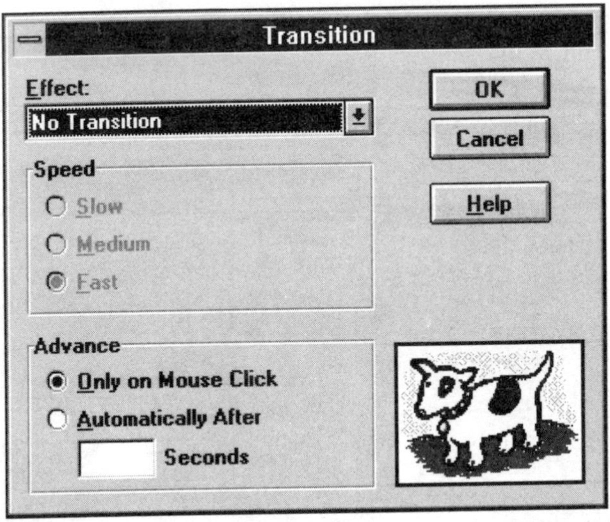

In the Transition dialog you can preview the way each transition effect looks when applied to a sample picture in the dialog ('Spot' the dog). You can also choose whether you want slides to advance automatically, after a specified time interval, or to advance only when the mouse is clicked (or other keyboard method is used). The dog is simply a picture with which to demonstrate the effect of the transition you choose.

Pull down the list of Effects and select one.

When you have seen the effect demonstrated, use ↓ to browse through the rest of the list and see what each effect looks like.

Finally, choose one effect and click OK

Depending on the speed of your computer and the complexity of your presentation, you may decide not to use Slow or Medium speed options for transitions – anything less than Fast can look terrible in a real slide show!

You will have noticed that there is an option to advance automatically after so many seconds – so automatically timed shows can be put together.

A transition icon appears below Slide One. Having seen the demonstrations in the Transition dialog, you may decide to apply other transitions to the remaining slides by selecting the slide and using the drop-down list of transitions on the Slide Sorter toolbar.

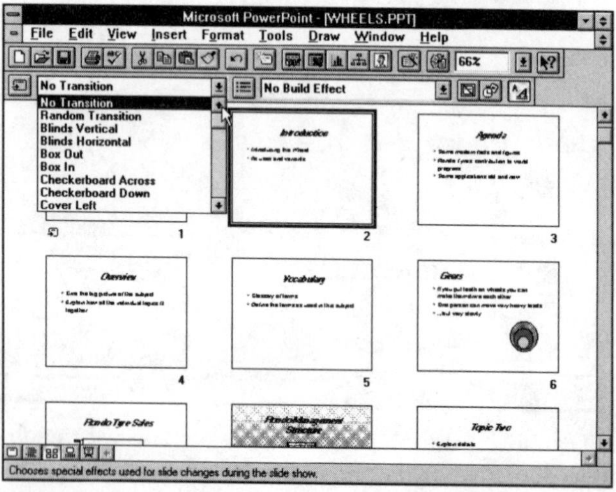

An easy way to preview the transition that you have set for a slide is to click the transition icon just below the slide.

A slide show on screen

When you have set transitions for several (or all) of the slides, these will be used in the on-screen slide show.

Start the Slide Show using

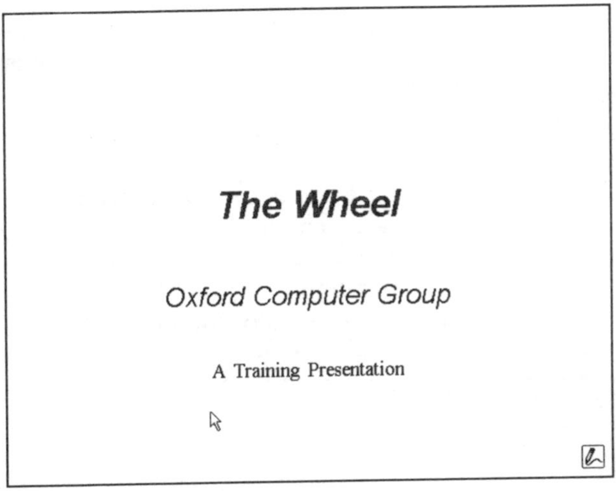
The Wheel
Oxford Computer Group
A Training Presentation

Click the left mouse button to advance to the next slide.

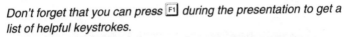

Don't forget that you can press F1 *during the presentation to get a list of helpful keystrokes.*

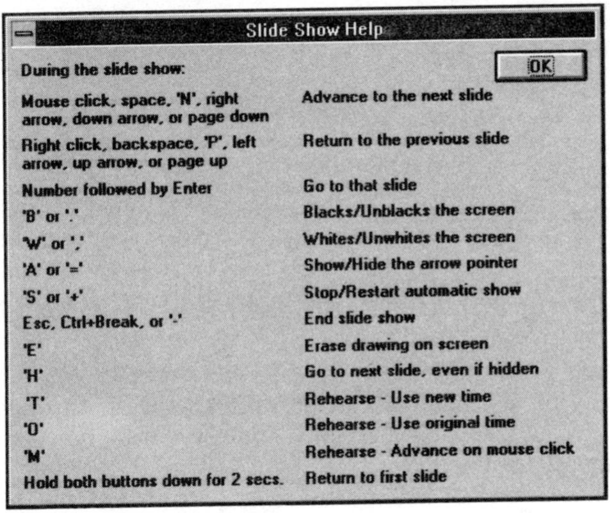
Slide Show Help
OK
During the slide show:
Mouse click, space, 'N', right arrow, down arrow, or page down
Advance to the next slide
Right click, backspace, 'P', left arrow, up arrow, or page up
Return to the previous slide
Number followed by Enter
Go to that slide
'B' or '.'
Blacks/Unblacks the screen
'W' or ','
Whites/Unwhites the screen
'A' or '='
Show/Hide the arrow pointer
'S' or '+'
Stop/Restart automatic show
Esc, Ctrl+Break, or '-'
End slide show
'E'
Erase drawing on screen
'H'
Go to next slide, even if hidden
'T'
Rehearse - Use new time
'O'
Rehearse - Use original time
'M'
Rehearse - Advance on mouse click
Hold both buttons down for 2 secs.
Return to first slide

If the show is very complex, you may wish to jump to a particular slide – perhaps in response to a detailed question from the audience. Do this by typing the number of the desired slide, then Enter.

If you are likely to need to jump between slides in this way, keep a list of the slides titles and numbers (compiled in Outline View) on the desk in front of you.

Remember that you can use the mouse pointer for emphasis to 'scribble' temporarily on a slide – first wiggle the mouse a bit and use it to click the pencil/mouse icon at the bottom right of the slide which has now appeared, then draw over the part of the slide to emphasise by holding down the left mouse button. Press E to erase the highlighter markings. Click the pencil/mouse icon again to finish drawing, allowing you to continue the presentation using the mouse.

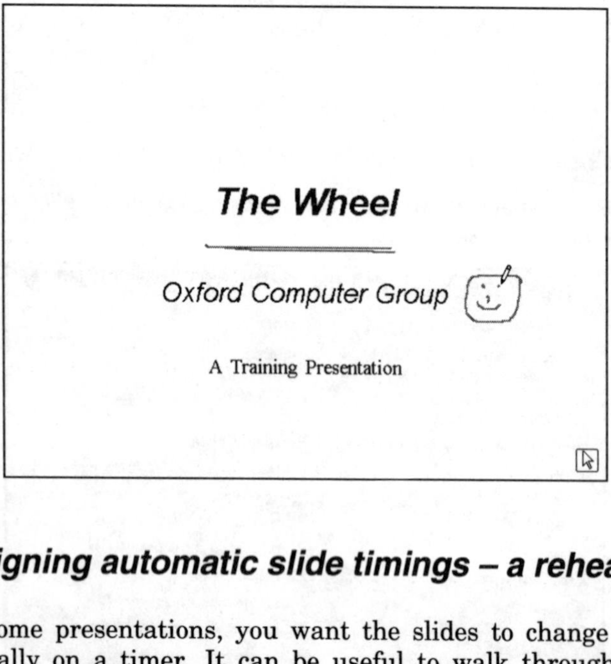

Assigning automatic slide timings – a rehearsal

For some presentations, you want the slides to change automatically on a timer. It can be useful to walk through your presentation, watching the slides and estimating how long each slide should be displayed.

Click to start the slide show rehearsal.

The first slide appears as in a slide show, and when the slide is fully drawn a button appears, carrying a digital clock. When you feel enough time has elapsed for the audience to read and understand the slide, or for you to finish presenting the information on it, you click the clock button to assign the time to that slide and move on to the next.

Let the presentation run through and set new timings for each slide.

When you have set a time for each slide, you are invited to save the new timings (you should do so unless they were completely wrong), and you are informed of the total duration of the presentation.

You should find that the number of seconds recorded for viewing a particular slide appears underneath the slide, together with any transition indicator.

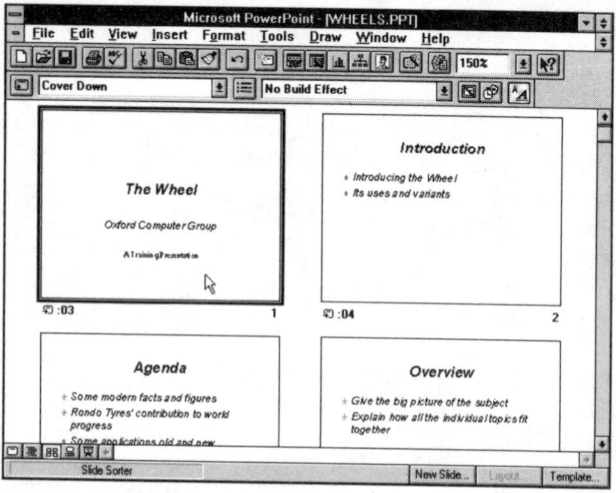

After setting times, it is important that you change an option setting in the Slide Show dialog, so that the timings which you have just recorded are in fact used when the show is run. This dialog includes other useful features.

From the View menu, choose Slide Show.

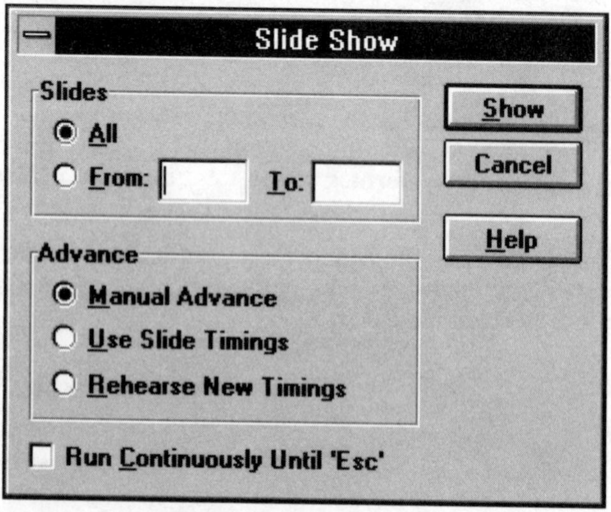

Here you must choose the option to Use Slide Timings. After this, the automatic slide timings will be used whenever you run a slide show using . Notice that you could also specify that only part of the presentation be run, by entering a range of slide numbers.

Another important feature here is the Run Continuously until Esc checkbox. With the option, PowerPoint will keep on re-running the show until you interrupt it by pressing [Esc]. You could use this feature if you were setting up a presentation for an open day or exhibition. The slide show would repeat itself all day while your important clients watch (you hope). In this case you would probably disconnect the keyboard and mouse.

Try this – check ☒ Run Continuously, click [OK] *and watch! If you get bored, press* [Esc]

Hidden Slides

Some slides may be included in a presentation, although they carry fine detail which may not interest all audiences. You might decide to make these Hidden slides, so that they are usually skipped but you as the presenter can decide to show them if needed.

Select one suitable slide, and click 

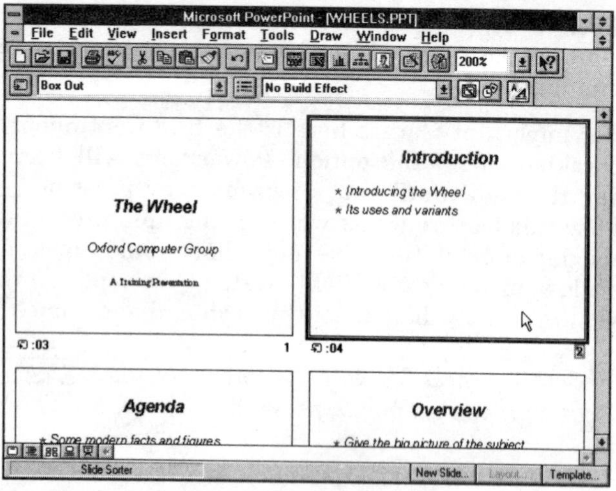

A hidden slide icon appears under the selected slide. When you run the slide show and reach this slide, if you decide you want to include it after all just move the mouse a little to expose the hidden slide icon in the bottom right corner of the screen and click the new icon to show the hidden slide.

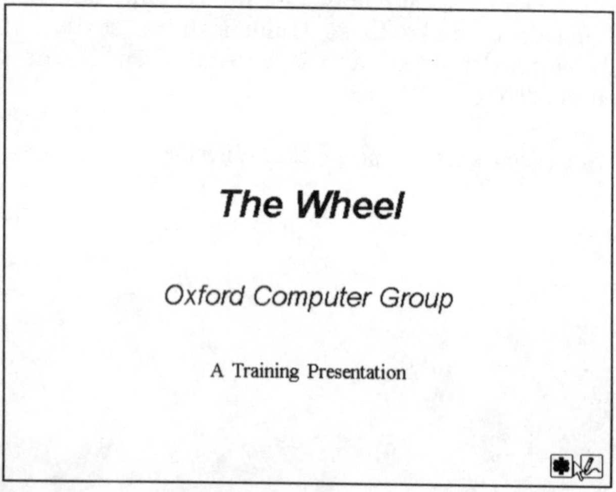

Try this. Run the Slide Show, advance to the slide before the hidden slide, move the mouse slightly and click the hidden slide icon.

Building Bullet Points

A slide with a number of bullet points may have more impact if the bullet points appear one at a time. This is known as building the bullet points. Some presenters prefer to use this feature if they want the audience to concentrate on one point without reading ahead to other points which they haven't discussed yet.

You will adapt the Agenda slide to present the topics one at a time.

Click the Agenda slide, then click

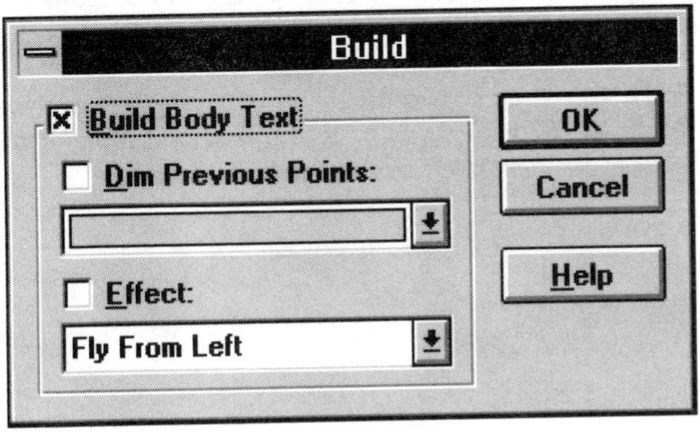

Make sure the checkbox to Build body text is checked.

Another option is for previous points to be shown in another colour after you have discussed them, thereby emphasising the current point:

Check Dim Previous Points and choose a colour from the drop-down list.

You may also want the new points to appear with an effect – something like a transition (discussed earlier) applied to just one bullet point. These are listed in the Effects drop-down list.

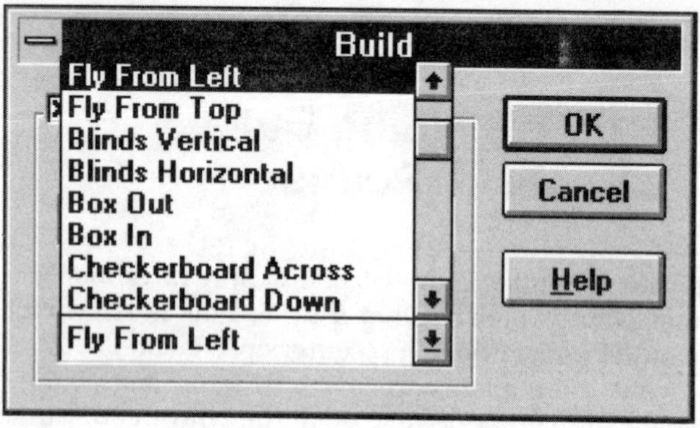

If desired, check Effect and choose an effect from the list. Click OK

You may now want to re-run the slide timing rehearsal, to assign timings to the arrival of each of the bullet points in this build slide.

When you have added all the special effects you want, run the final slide show using , trying out some of the control keystrokes listed earlier.

Finally, save and close `WHEELS.PPT`

Summary: Slide Sorter and Slide Show Views

- You can rearrange the slides by dragging & dropping whole slides when in  view.
- Using a 'blank' slide can be a useful pause.
- Using a blank slide at the end can give a more graceful conclusion than finishing by returning straight to PowerPoint.
- PowerPoint provides different methods of transition from one slide to another.
- A build effect, emphasising certain points, can also be applied, using .
- Slide display times can be rehearsed and the slides displayed for fixed periods of time only.
- Slides can be hidden, so that a presentation can be tailored to suit a particular audience with minimal changes. To show these slides, click the hidden slide icon during the slide show.

APPENDIX 1: KEYSTROKES

In this appendix, you revise some useful keystrokes:

- Ctrl A means hold down Ctrl then press A
- Function keys are written as F1 to F10

Although there are mouse-driven ways to do everything in PowerPoint, some people prefer keyboard methods. Here are some of the most useful keystrokes. For a full listing refer to Appendix C in the Microsoft PowerPoint User Guide.

General shortcuts	
Ctrl Z	Undo
Ctrl X	Cut
Ctrl C	Copy
Ctrl V	Paste

Selecting and editing text	
Ctrl A	Select All
Double-click	Select Word
Triple-click	Select Paragraph
F2	Swaps between editing text and selecting the text placeholder
F7	Spelling
Ctrl Alt E	Gives accented é (also for íáú)

Different views	
Ctrl Alt O	Outline View
Ctrl Alt P	Slide Sorter View
Ctrl Alt N	Slide View

Working in slide view	
Tab	At the start of a line in Slide View, Tab will demote the line (in Outline View will work wherever in line)
Shift Alt with ↑ ↓ ← or →	will move bullet point up or down and to promote or demote it
Ctrl M	New slide
Ctrl Shift M	New slide, with no AutoLayout dialog

Slide Show View

Possibly the most useful key in this view is F1, the standard Windows help key. Whilst in Slide Show View, F1 presents the following dialog, helpfully listing all the pertinent keystrokes:

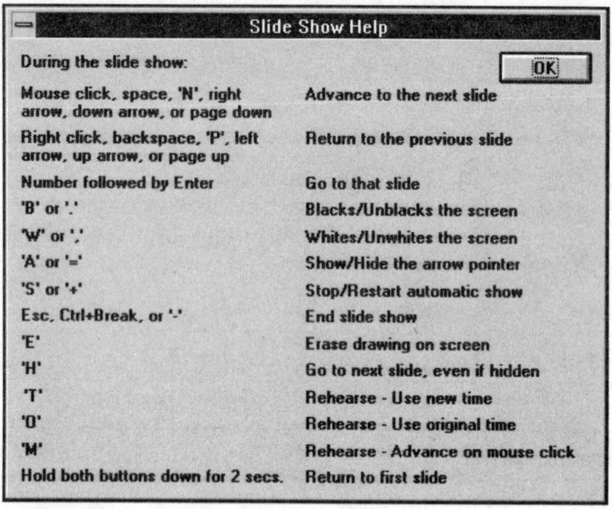
Slide Show Help
During the slide show:
OK
Mouse click, space, 'N', right arrow, down arrow, or page down
Advance to the next slide
Right click, backspace, 'P', left arrow, up arrow, or page up
Return to the previous slide
Number followed by Enter
Go to that slide
'B' or '.'
Blacks/Unblacks the screen
'W' or ','
Whites/Unwhites the screen
'A' or '='
Show/Hide the arrow pointer
'S' or '+'
Stop/Restart automatic show
Esc, Ctrl+Break, or '-'
End slide show
'E'
Erase drawing on screen
'H'
Go to next slide, even if hidden
'T'
Rehearse - Use new time
'O'
Rehearse - Use original time
'M'
Rehearse - Advance on mouse click
Hold both buttons down for 2 secs.
Return to first slide

APPENDIX 2: INSTALLING POWERPOINT

This appendix covers:

- The system hardware requirements for running PowerPoint
- The software requirements for running PowerPoint
- The process for installing PowerPoint on a stand-alone machine
- Typical, Custom, and Laptop installation types and the minimum system requirement for each
- Locations for storing PowerPoint files

System requirements

In order to be able to run PowerPoint 4, your computer must meet certain minimum hardware and software requirements. Computers which do not reach these standards will not be powerful enough to run PowerPoint 4, although you may find that they would be able to run earlier versions of this package.

The minimum hardware your machine must have is as follows:

- An IBM PC or compatible, with an 80386, i486, Pentium or more powerful processor
- An EGA monitor, or some higher resolution compatible with Microsoft Windows
- 4 MB of memory
- A hard disk with at least 5MB free (for a minimum installation of PowerPoint only)

The Minimum software requirements are:

- MS-DOS operating system version 3.1 or later
- Any of the following versions of Microsoft Windows:
    - Windows 3.1 or later
    - Windows for Workgroups 3.1 or later
    - Windows for Pen Computing
    - Windows NT 3.1 or later

The installation process

In this section, the method for installing PowerPoint on a normal, stand-alone computer is considered. It is possible to set up PowerPoint to run on a network, but that is beyond the scope of this book, and you are referred to the manual that comes with the software for more information on that.

Installing PowerPoint is a relatively simple process: the installation disks come with an automated installation program; all you have to do is make a few simple choices along the way. The installation process is conducted from within Windows. With Disk 1 of the set in drive A, it can be started:

- In File Manager, by double-clicking on `SETUP.EXE`
- In Program Manager or File Manager by choosing File Run, then typing `A:\SETUP`

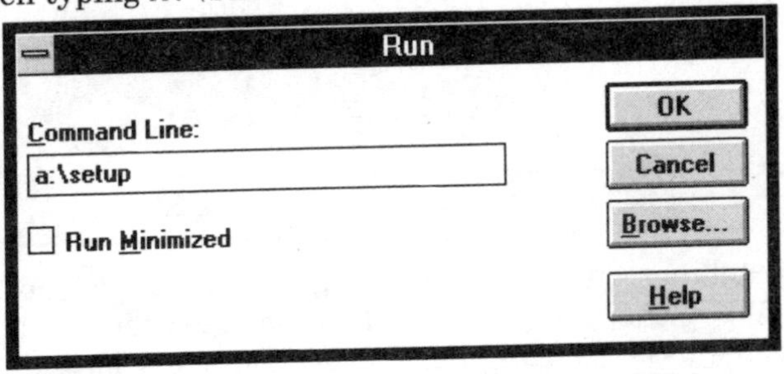

After checking your system, the screen will eventually show this:

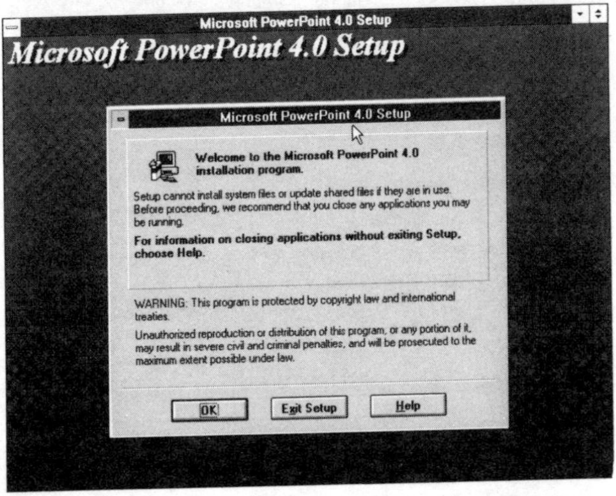

You are now running the setup program. After other screens of information, (and which you get depends on whether you have installed PowerPoint on your machine before,) you will arrive at the following screen:

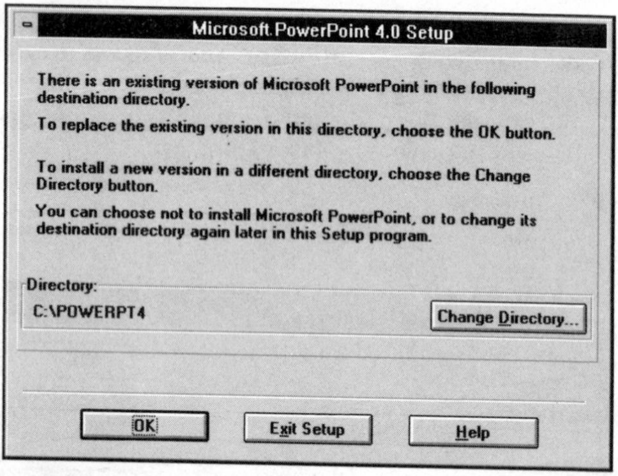

This is telling you where it is going to put most of the PowerPoint files. Generally, you should not need to change this, but it is possible to do so using the Change Directory button. Otherwise, use OK to proceed with the installation.

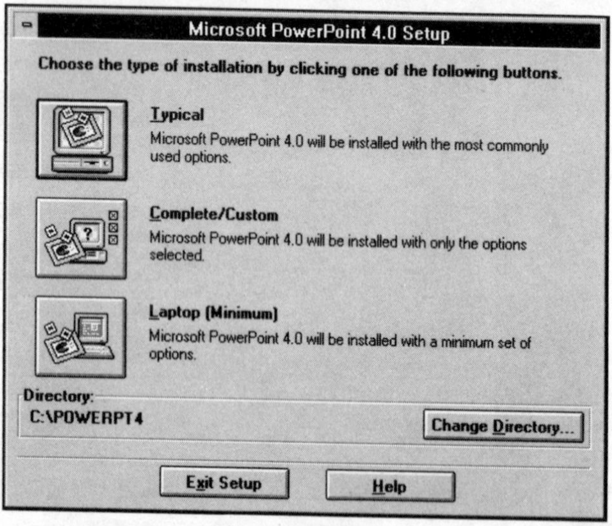

PowerPoint offers you three different levels of installation: Typical, Complete/Custom, and Laptop.

- Typical installation installs those parts of PowerPoint used by the typical user. For every-day use of PowerPoint, and for the things covered in this book, a typical installation would be sufficient. This form of installation will require 18MB free space on the hard disk of your computer.

- Complete/Custom allows you to pick which parts of PowerPoint you install. If you need to limit the amount of space taken up by PowerPoint, you may want to use this facility to pick exactly those features you require. A complete installation of PowerPoint requires 31MB of hard disk space.
- Laptop installation is a minimum installation–only those files deemed virtually essential to PowerPoint are installed on your machine. Since laptops usually have less hard disk space than other PCs, this minimum installation might be appropriate. A laptop installation requires 5MB of hard disk space.

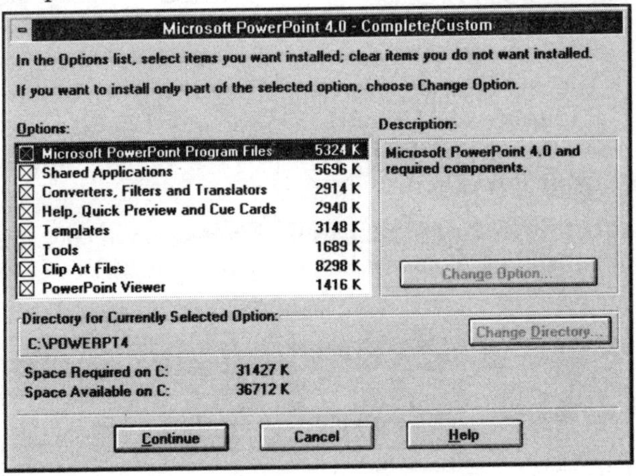

On choosing a Custom/Complete installation, the next screen will allow you to specify which parts of PowerPoint you want to install. By clicking on an option, you toggle between including it and excluding it. Towards the bottom of the dialog, there is a display of how much space the chosen installation will require, and how much is available.

Having moved on from this dialog, you are now asked which Group in Program Manager you want the PowerPoint icons to appear in. After a few miscellaneous questions, the installation process begins.

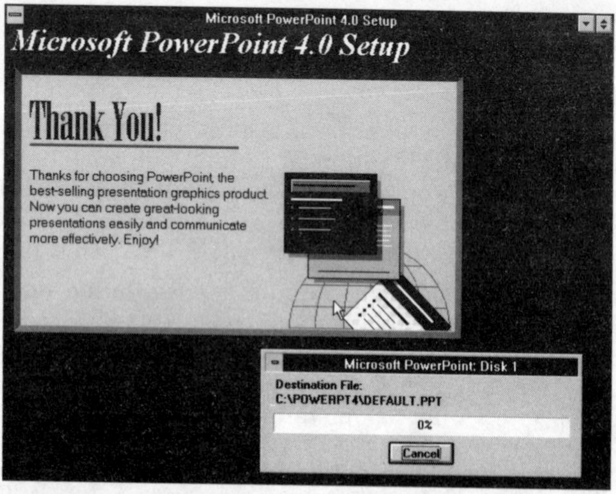

A dialog appears in the corner of the screen, showing how far through the installation process you are, and what file is currently being processed. Information screens, like the one shown here in the top left of the screen, will occasionally appear, telling you about PowerPoint.

When all of the required files from this disk have been installed onto the hard disk, you will be prompted to insert the next disk in the series:

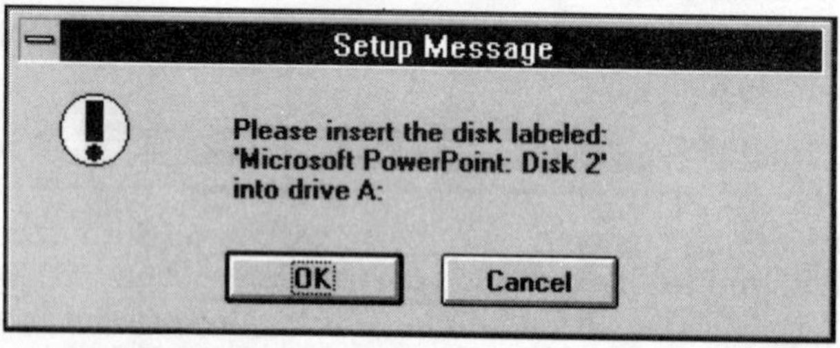

Replace the disk in Drive A with the next disk in the series, then click OK. Continue in this manner until you have completed the installation.

INDEX

Oliver an... ...apmans'

DATA PROC... ...SING

... Cert. Ed.,

...turer at The Hatfield ... the author of "Computer Science" and "...puter Studies", published by DP Publications.

SEVENTH EDITION

D.P. PUBLICATIONS LTD
12 Romsey Road,
Eastleigh,
Hants.
SO5 4AL
1986

ACKNOWLEDGEMENTS

The Authors wish to express their thanks to the following:

Institute of Chartered Accountants in England and Wales (ICA)
Chartered Association of Certified Accountants (ACA)
Institute of Cost and Management Accountants (ICMA)
Association of Accounting Technicians (AAT)
Society of Company and Commercial Accountants (SCCA)
Institute of Data Processing Management (IDPM)
for permission to reproduce past examination questions.

The Authors wish to express their thanks to the following for permission to reproduce pictures and diagrams.
(Separate acknowledgements are included with each picture and diagram):

IBM United Kingdom Ltd.	Digital Equipment Corporation (DEC)
International Computers Ltd.	MICOM-Borer Ltd.
Rediffusion Computers Ltd.	Feedback Data Ltd.
NCR Ltd.	Norsk Data

Van Nostrand Reinhold Company Ltd., for permission to use the illustrations at Fig. 8.1 which is taken from Chapin: COMPUTERS – A SYSTEMS APPROACH published by Van Nostrand Reinhold Coy, copyright 1971 by Ned Chapin.

First Edition		1972
Second Edition		1973
Reprinted	Feb.	1975
Third Edition		1975
Reprinted	Feb.	1976
Fourth Edition		1979
Reprinted	Nov.	1979
Reprinted	April	1980
Fifth Edition		1981
Reprinted		1982
Sixth Edition		1983
Reprinted		1984
Reprinted		1985
Seventh Edition		1986

ISBN 0 905435 63 X

Printed by Guernsey Press Co. Ltd.,
PO Box 57
Braye Road, Vale
Guernsey, Channel Islands

Preface

AIM OF THE MANUAL.

1. The primary aim of the manual is to provide a simplified approach to the understanding of data processing. It is intended for those with little or no knowledge of the subject.

It covers the Data Processing syllabus requirements of:–

The Chartered Association of Certified Accountants:
Paper 1.5 "Numerical Analysis and Data Processing"
Paper 2.7 "Systems Analysis and Design"

The Association of Accounting Technicians:
Paper 6 "Elements of Information Systems"
Paper 11 "Analysis and Design of Information Systems"

The Institute of Cost and Management Accountants:
Paper 7 "Information Technology Management"

It also covers large parts of other syllabuses which have a Data Processing requirement. These include The Institute of Data Processing Management, BTEC, The Institute of Chartered Secretaries and Administrators, Institute of Administrative Management.

NEED.

2. All business personnel, management staff and accountants need to have a good knowledge of DP techniques. In recent years there have been major developments in Information Technology (IT) ie. the technologies associated with the creation, manipulation, storage and communication of information; principally computing, telecommunications and electronics. These developments have given rise not only to the rapid evolution of DP techniques but to the greater integration of data processing techniques with other activities in organisations. These developments all create an even greater need for business and management professionals to have a knowledge of DP and its related Information Technology. This need is reflected in the broadening of Data Processing examination syllabi, when they are updated, and in the introduction of examinations with titles such as "Information Technology Management" and "Business Information Technology".

3. A vast number of books have been written on the various aspects of Data Processing and Information Technology. Most of them tend to be of a technical nature, aimed at technically minded people. Others are so brief and introductory as to be of little practical value and very few are suited to study by students of business and accountancy. The need as seen by the authors was for a manual covering *all* aspects of Data Processing and the relevant aspects of Information Technology *written specifically* for business and accountancy students.

APPROACH.

4. The manual has been designed for independent study but is well suited for use in conjunction with tuition at Colleges etc. Great efforts have been made to present a simplified and standardised layout.

END OF CHAPTER.

5. At the end of chapters is found:-

a. Summary of chapter.

b. Points to note. These are used for purposes of emphasis and clarification.

c. Questions and Answers. Their use is explained in Appendix 4.

APPENDICES.

6. Use has been made of appendices and the students should note carefully the purpose of each one:-

a. Appendix 1. Contains outline answers to questions set at the end of chapters.

e. Appendix 2. Contains questions *without* answers for use in conjunction with classroom tuition. The questions, taken from recent papers of the ICA, ACA, ICMA, AAT, SCCA and IDPM, are grouped according to the Parts of the Manual.

b. Appendix 3. Contains detail which has been excluded from the main text in the interest of clarity.

f. Appendix 4. Contains notes on: using the questions and answers; effective study; examination technique.

HOW TO USE THE MANUAL.

7. Students are advised to read the manual chapter by chapter since subsequent work often builds upon topics covered earlier.

8. The subject of DP is spread over many separate parts and it is inevitable that certain questions will remain unanswered as the student proceeds. The pieces should fit together as progress is made through the manual.

9. Students are advised to view the machinery described in this manual at first hand. Failing this try to get hold of manufacturers' "glossies" and visit your library and find a book of illustrations.

SUGGESTIONS AND CRITICISM.

10. The authors would welcome any suggestions or criticism from students or lecturers.

Note to the 7th Edition.

The material in the text has been extensively revised and brought up to date in order to give the reader an up to date account of modern data processing. At the same time the opportunity has been taken to respond to suggestions and criticisms received by the authors. The text contains new material on **Information Technology, Data Communications, Expert Systems, Spreadsheets** and the **Data Protection Act** together with many new diagrams and photographs of modern DP equipment. Examination Questions and Answers have been updated and obsolete material has been removed.

C.S. French
March 1986

Contents

APPENDICES

Introduction To Data Processing

1. This Part introduces you to the subject of Data Processing (DP), and outlines general aspects which are common to *all* methods of data processing ie. manual, mechanical and electronic.

2. You will find the introduction more relevant and easier to follow if you bear in mind the following general points.

3. Broadly speaking, organisations strive to achieve certain goals for the benefit of their owners or clients. These goals may be expressed in terms of objectives such as increasing revenue, avoiding cost, or improving services. Such objectives will need to be met within various financial constraints, and within the limitations of available resources.

4. In order to reach its objectives an organisation must be able to plan ahead, and control and coordinate its activities. For this it depends upon the provision and communication of information. This requirement is met, at least in part, by the *"Data Processing System"* within the organisation.

5. The Data Processing System is therefore an important part of an organisation and *data* handled by the DP System is itself a valuable resource because of the benefits which are obtained from its use.

1 Introduction to Data Processing

INTRODUCTION

1. This chapter introduces you to data processing by, first of all, explaining the differences between "data" and "information". Common factors determining the methods of data processing are introduced. The stages of data processing, are explained and illustrated. A useful representation of a data processing system is also explained and illustrated. Then the concepts of transactions and batching are introduced.

Finally, an overview of the manual is provided to guide your way through the manual. A minimum of prior knowledge is assumed of the reader although many readers may already be familiar with some of the examples given.

2. a. **'Data'** is the term used to describe basic **facts** about the activities of a business. For example, the number of hours worked by any employee on a particular machine; his rate of pay, the amount and type of materials consumed in a particular process; the number of tons of finished product produced in a day or week.

   b. **Information** is obtained by assembling items of data into a meaningful form. eg. a payroll, efficiency reports etc.

   c. Information can range from a simple routine operating report up to that required by top management to make strategic decisions, although the distinction is not important as far as an understanding of DP is concerned.

3. **Data processing** (DP) is the term given to the process of collecting all items of data together to produce meaningful information.

The methods of data processing vary from those which are almost entirely manual to those which rely on the use of large electronic computers. In practice most data processing nowadays will involve the use of some mechanical or electronic aid such as calculators, which increase in sophistication year by year.

4. There still exist those data processing systems which make use of electro-mechanical devices but the advent of versatile micro-computers has hastened their demise.

5. Note that prior to the introduction of mechanical, and later electronic methods of processing large volumes of data, the term "data processing" was rarely used. Now that the use of computers has become

widespread, the term is almost invariably associated in people's minds with Electronic Data Processing (EDP).

EXAMPLES OF INFORMATION AND DATA.

6. The following examples (common to almost all businesses) are explained in relation to the information required and the data needed to obtain that information. The examples have been deliberately selected because they are those with which you can (hopefully) readily identify and use as a yardstick throughout your studies:

a. **Payroll.** Large and small companies have to pay their employees and the information needs are, at least, the payslip (to show the employee how much he or she has earned and the reasons for deductions etc.), a company record of the payslip details (payroll) and analysis for accounting purposes (total tax deducted etc). If the employees are paid in cash (as opposed to cheque/direct credit to their bank accounts) then a coin analysis may be needed for the bank. For management control purposes, analysis of labour hours into various categories such as idle time, sickness and absence can be produced.

The 'data' from which the information is derived is likely to have come from some form of time records, eg. time sheets, and recorded details of employees, eg. tax codes.

b. **Invoice.** Companies selling goods on credit produce an invoice setting out the details of the sale. These include the customer's name and address, customer's order number, the date of the sale, and the quantity, price, description and value of the goods sold. This invoice (information) is needed to record the customer's indebtedness. The customer order details and seller's details of goods provided the 'data' from which it is compiled.

c. **Statement of Account.** Following on from the invoice example, a summary of all the invoices and payments made by the customer in a month, in the form of a 'statement', is produced and sent to the customer to show the amount still owing. The Statement of Account is the 'Information' coming from invoices and cash receipts (data).

FACTORS DETERMINING THE METHODS OF DATA PROCESSING.

7. Common factors determining the methods of data processing can be explained under the following headings:-

a. Size and type of business.

b. Timing aspects.
c. Link between applications.

SIZE AND TYPE OF BUSINESS

8. With each of the examples given, the method of producing the information will largely depend on the size and type of business. In a very small company a single person may be able to have the time to produce all the information required, but as the volume of business increases more people and aids, in the form of calculators and small computers, may be employed. Large volumes of data and information will require the use of large computers.

9. In some companies the payroll will be a matter of simply paying a member of staff the same amount each month, whilst in others a complex payment by results system will have to be coped with. Similarly, invoicing may be simply a matter of, virtually, copying from the customer's order, or it may require complex discount calculations. Simple situations indicate the need for fewer people and aids to produce the information and complex situations indicate the need for more people and aids.

TIMING ASPECTS

10. Some information requirements are less time critical than others. For example, the Payroll and Statements may only be produced once a month, whereas the invoices may be produced (in certain companies) virtually all the time, ie. as a customer collects the goods. The timing requirements for information will have considerable bearing on the methods and equipment needed to provide it.

LINK BETWEEN APPLICATIONS.

11. Where data is needed for more than one information requirement, a different method of processing it may be suggested. For example, an item sold may not only need to be used in the production of the invoice but also be needed to amend the recorded stock position. A manual system would require separate operations to satisfy the requirements, whereas a computer system would include the automatic use of data in both applications. This ability of computer systems to perform a variety of processing operations on a single "pool" of data contrasts sharply with manual systems. In manual systems the data being used by one individual becomes inaccessible to another individual.

DP STAGES.

12. Whatever method, or combination of methods, is used it will be seen that data will pass through the same **basic stages** in the processing cycle. An example is given of the production of a payroll which is simplified for the purpose of illustration but which none the less bring out the salient points.

13. Payroll Example

Stage i. Details of hours worked by each employee **(data)** is recorded on a Time Sheet **(source document).** All Time Sheets are forwarded to the wages office. The source documents will be sorted into the sequence required by the payroll.

ii. The data is then checked for correctness and validity and some form of copying **(transcription)** onto another document (eg. summary sheet) may take place. The source documents are then temporarily stored.

iii. The source documents now accumulated for the complete pay period (probably a week in our example) are used for the next stage which is the actual calculation process.

iv. Details of gross pay, tax, insurance and net pay are arrived at. Reference is made to data held in Tax Tables, in tables of rates of pay and in employee records. The latter must be brought up to date eg. Pay to Date details.

v. Individual pay slips, a summarised pay roll and coin analysis are produced **(information).**

14. Each of these stages is identified by a name Viz:

i. **Origination** – of data
ii. **Preparation** – getting the data ready
iii. **Input** – the act of passing the data to the processing stage.
iv. **Processing** – all that is necessary to arrive at the net pay etc., and to keep data up to date (eg. data in employee records).
v. **Output** – the production of the end product.
(See Fig. 1.1)

Note
a. How data is transmitted from **stage** to **stage.**
b. Use made of temporary storage after preparation.
c. The reference to **stored data** (tax tables, rates of pay and employee records) during the processing stage.

d. Controls will be part of the whole procedure eg. checking Time Sheets.

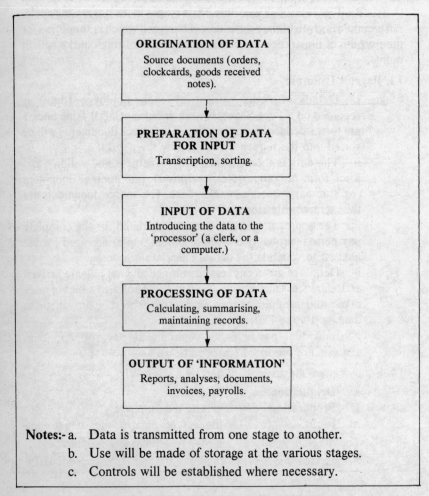

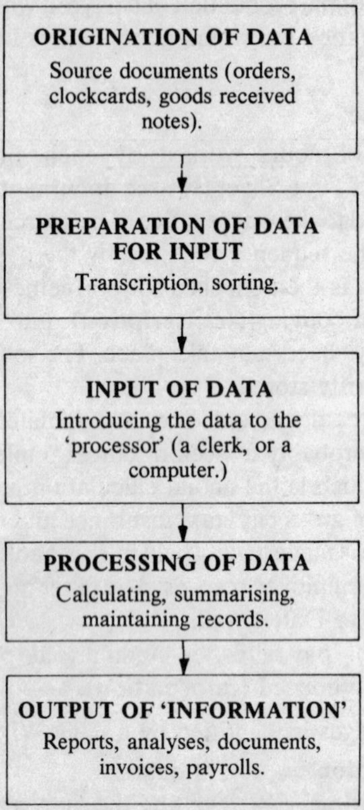
ORIGINATION OF DATA
Source documents (orders, clockcards, goods received notes).
PREPARATION OF DATA FOR INPUT
Transcription, sorting.
INPUT OF DATA
Introducing the data to the 'processor' (a clerk, or a computer.)
PROCESSING OF DATA
Calculating, summarising, maintaining records.
OUTPUT OF 'INFORMATION'
Reports, analyses, documents, invoices, payrolls.

Notes:- a. Data is transmitted from one stage to another.
b. Use will be made of storage at the various stages.
c. Controls will be established where necessary.

FIG 1.1 DATA PROCESSING STAGES

DP MODEL

15. Having seen a general view of the data processing stages (Fig. 1.1), we now turn to a general view of the Data Processing System. In essence **all** DP systems consist of the four basic interrelated elements illustrated in fig. 1.2. This *representation* may be referred to as a "model" of the Data Processing system. It may also be called a "logical model" to emphasise the fact that it is not representing physical features.

16. This concept of a "model" goes rather deeper and is more useful than this simple illustration suggests. For example the data within the DP system may be viewed as part of the DP model, in that it *represents* or reflects the state of affairs. eg. the current balance represents the state of a customers account.

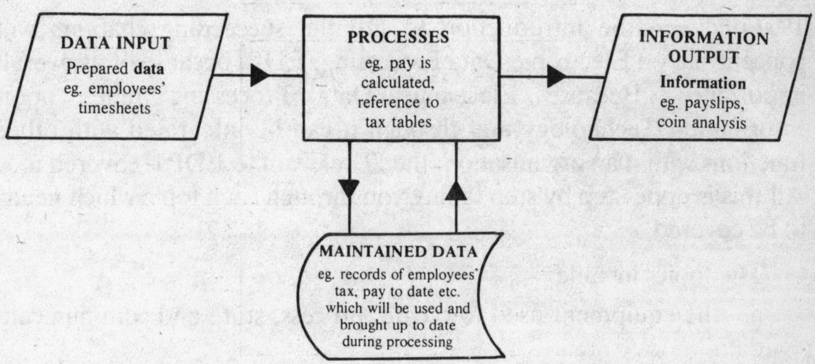

Note

a. The 4 elements of this model:-
   i. DATA INPUT
   ii. PROCESSES
   iii. INFORMATION OUTPUT
   iv. MAINTAINED DATA

b. The diagram shows a "logical" structure (ie. non-physical).

c. For the meaning of symbols see NCC symbols in appendix 3.2).

FIG. 1.2. THE LOGICAL MODEL OF A DATA PROCESSING SYSTEM.

TRANSACTIONS AND BATCHES.

17. The units of data for processing, such as individual customer orders or individual timesheets, are called **transactions.** Incidently, the act of processing such a unit of data is also called a transaction but the context should make it clear which meaning is intended. According to the determining factors (paragraphs 7-11), transactions may either be processed singly or in **batches.** A batch is merely a number of transactions (eg. in the form of source documents) accumulated together and *processed* as a single unit.

18. Batching introduces a time-lag into the processing cycle but also introduces some useful controls eg. checking that a batch contains the required number of documents helps to detect and correct document loss.

OVERVIEW OF MANUAL.

19. Following the introduction to DP the succeeding chapters will concentrate on Electronic Data Processing (EDP) because of its overall importance. Because Electronic Data Processing relies upon Information Technology and through it can be integrated with other functions within an organisation, the IT relevant to EDP is covered too. All this is done step by step taking you through each topic which needs to be covered.

The topics include:

a. the equipment used to create, process, store and communicate data.

b. the methods needed to exploit the equipment effectively.

c. the role of specialists such as systems analysts and programmers and the tools and techniques they use in designing and implementing systems.

d. the identification, with the aid of examples, of what makes an appropriate application for EDP.

e. the management of DP and its related IT.

20. It must be stressed that many questions will come to your mind as you progress with your studies, many of which will not be answered until you have completed them.

Much thought has gone into the layout and sequence of chapters. You would be well advised to study them in the order presented.

SUMMARY.

21. a. "Data" are the basic facts about the activities of a business.

b. "Information" is data assembled into a useful form.

c. Data processing stages are:- origination, preparation, input, processing and output.

d. A number of factors determine the methods of data processing.

e. A DP system may be represented as a "logical model".

f. Data may be processed singly or in batches.

POINTS TO NOTE.

22. a. The data processing stages are sometimes referred to collectively as the data processing 'cycle', because of the way the stages are repeated.

b. The data processing stages and the concept of batching are common to all methods of DP ie. whether manual, mechanical, or electronic.

c. The terms 'procedure' and 'system' tend to be used synonomously, eg. payroll 'procedure', or payroll 'system'.

d. Strictly speaking, the term 'Data Processing' means any data processing operation, regardless of the method used. To many people, however, it is virtually synonymous with computer processing eg. a company advertising for a D.P. Manager wants someone to run its computer installation, not its office.

e. The end product of data processing is information irrespective of the data processing facilities (eg. accounting machine or computer) used to produce that information. Throughout any study of data processing, therefore, you need to be constantly aware of the necessity for good presentation of information.

QUESTIONS.

1. Distinguish between 'data' and 'information'.

2. Define 'Data Processing'.

3. Outline possible advantages and disadvantages in batching some documents for processing.

Answers to 'end-of-chapter' questions begin on page 416.

Data Processing's place in Information Technology (IT)

1. From chapter 1 we have seen that Data Processing is the collection and manipulation of items of data to produce meaningful information. For many years the methods of Data Processing have involved electronic means, principally the computer. Any modern study of Data Processing must therefore look at Electronic Data Processing (EDP) in detail. However, EDP must be seen in context as one of a number of important areas of Information Technology (IT).

2. Definition. Information Technology is the technology which supports activities involving the creation, storage, manipulation and communication of information, together with their related methods, management and application.

3. Although EDP is part of IT it is not sensible to think of EDP as being in a watertight compartment and therefore it is important for the Data Processing student to be aware not only of EDP but of other areas of IT. This Part introduces EDP and places it in its IT context.

3. The material introduced here will be covered in greater detail in later parts of the manual.

4. Your study of EDP will involve:

a. Understanding the basic elements which make up the computer system, which is at the heart of EDP. You are not expected to be a computer technologist and the material will only be taken to the depth indicated in the preface to this manual.

b. Understanding of the basic elements of IT systems, also to an appropriate depth.

c. Knowledge of how management can best use compuers and other IT equipment to provide better information and to increase profitability.

d. The problems posed to management by IT, especially those posed by EDP.

2 Introduction to EDP

INTRODUCTION.

1. Some form of electronic computer based data processing system is to be found in almost all except the smallest company. Thus it is necessary to concentrate our effort into gaining an understanding of what lies behind such systems.

2. Where manual methods of DP are still in use, they frequently form part of an Electronic Data Processing system and involve the use of simple electronic aids such as calculators. Since to call such methods "manual" is misleading, we will refer to them as "conventional methods".

3. This chapter introduces the basic ideas and terminology of Electronic Data Processing and explains the relationship between electronic methods and conventional methods.

THE RELATIONSHIP BETWEEN ELECTRONIC METHODS AND CONVENTIONAL METHODS

4. The basic principles of conventional methods of DP and EDP are essentially the same. Thus the reader with prior knowledge of conventional data processing can immediately start applying that knowledge to EDP. The computer is merely substituted for manual aids or human labour. The same DP activities take place, but now we are using electronic computers to produce the results (the invoices or payroll etc.). Notice that the computer will not take over *all* of the steps in a given procedure eg. the data may first be collected or recorded by conventional methods.

5. In practice, the computerisation of a data processing system entails more than just the automation of parts of the existing system by means of computers. Analysis of an organisation's information requirements may show that the requirements will be better served by a newly designed and implemented system with the virtues of both the manual and computerised elements.

6. What is involved in an EDP system and how does it differ from conventional methods? In order to answer these questions imagine a simple invoicing application.

a. The customers' records are held in a *magnetic* storage device such as a 'magnetic disk' or 'magnetic tape' (details later). Note that no longer do we have a *visible* record as with the conventional methods. Similarly the records of our items of stock are held in magnetic form.

b. When orders are received it is now the *computer system* which is going to process them, but the computer cannot accept them on the pieces of paper the clerk was accustomed to, so we have to convert the source documents into a *machine-sensible* form, eg. by keying in data at a special keyboard device, or by using machine readable documents. (details later)

c. We will have written down all the steps involved in the invoicing procedure and translated those to be carried out by the computer into the language of the computer. So we now have the sequence of steps in computer language to enable the computer to produce our invoices for us.

d. We have:-

i. Computer and associated machinery.
ii. Master records (Customer) in magnetic form.
iii. Master records (Stock) in magnetic form.
iv. Reference records in magnetic form.
v. Transactions (Orders) in by keyboard device or by machine readable forms.
vi. Procedure in computer language.

e. The computer now processes the transactions against the particular customer records and stock item records involved, and produces invoices on approrpriate stationery using a printer.

CURRENT EDP PRACTICE.

7. Until the late 1970's the vast majority of EDP activities within most organisations were almost invariably concentrated in specialist DP departments. This was largely a consequence of the cost of computers systems and their specialist staff, and the need to achieve economies of scale. However, conventional DP activities on a small scale, which did not require expensive computer equipment, were often distributed within the various departments of the organisation.

8. In the 1980s it has become increasingly common to find departments within organisations which have their own small microcomputer based business computer systems operating quite autonamously of the Data Processing department. These small computers are often used for a variety of tasks not all of which might be classified as Data Processing. In addition, the use of other forms of computerised equipment has become widespread particularly in the areas of office automation and telecommunications.

9. This new technology has been able to establish itself because technological innovations have reduced costs to a point where it can compete with conventional methods. The key feature of the new technology is its ability to deal with **information** in one form or another. More recently the trend has been towards using ways of interconnecting the various types of equipment so as to integrate their functions and manage them more effectively. Thus we see modern EDP taking place not only in specialist DP departments but also being integrated more into the activities of other departments.

10. Definition. Information Technology (IT) is the technology which supports activities involving the creation, storage, manipulation and communication of information, (principally computing, electronics and electronic communications) together with their related methods, management, and applications. Clearly such an all embracing term is open to a number of interpretations according to the context in which it is used.

11. The relationship of EDP to IT is a particularly interesting one. Although EDP is essentially one of a number of important application areas of IT (others include telecommunications, television and computerised manufacture) it is often the EDP specialists in organisations who are best placed to take on the management of IT because they have already come to terms with IT in their own area of responsibility. Thus the management of EDP is increasingly being associated with the management of all IT. In the long run "Business IT" may come to mean much the same as EDP, just as DP is now often taken to mean EDP.

TERMINOLOGY.

12. Notice the following basic terminology used in EDP:

a. **Hardware** is the term used to describe IT equipment, especially that of a computer system.

b. **Program.** A program is a set of instructions written in the language of the computer. A program is used to make the computer perform a specific task such as producing a payroll. (Note the spelling "program" not "programme".)

c. **Systems Analysis.** Before the hardware for an EDP system can be purchased or the programs written the requirements of the system have to be investigated, the facts gathered and analysed, and the design specified. This activity is called SYSTEMS ANALYSIS (OR SYSTEMS ANALYSIS AND DESIGN (SAD)).

d. **Input.** Data entering an EDP system is its input. The transactions (orders) were the input in the invoicing application. (2.6)

e. **Output.** The information produced by an EDP system is its output. The invoice in our example was the output.

There are other terms but these will be explained later. Notice that all the items above are found in other methods of data processing but with different labels. Try not to be put off by this terminology – try to see what is behind each term.

SUMMARY.

13. a. EDP methods of data processing substitute a computer for more conventional machinery, although the system is usually redesigned in order to make maximum use of the computer.

b. Records are no longer in a visible form. They are in a magnetic form.

c. Procedures are translated into a machine-sensible form to be 'obeyed' by the computer (Program).

POINTS TO NOTE.

14. a. Note the spelling of program.

b. Note the concept of the internally stored program; this sets the computer apart from other methods of data processing.

c. In Data Processing we are careful to distinguish between data and information because to do so can be useful.

QUESTIONS.

1. Define these terms:

a. Electronic Data Processing.

b. Information Technology.

3 Introduction to Computers and other IT equipment

INTRODUCTION.

1. Having been introduced to EDP in the previous chapter we will have our first look at the COMPUTER itself, the types found, purposes for which they are used and the basic elements that go to make one. Then we will take a look at other Information Technology used in conjunction with the computer for EDP.

TYPES OF COMPUTER

2. Details of the various types of computer, and equipment associated with them, will be given in later chapters. For the time being the following general classification should prove sufficient.

BASIC TYPES

3. a. **Digital.** So called because it functions by taking discrete numbers and performing mathematic calculations on them and is the type used in commercial *data processing.*

b. **Analog.** This type of computer measures physical magnitudes such as temperature, pressure etc. A slide-rule and car speedometer are examples of analog devices. Analog computers are used for scientific and engineering purposes. They are *not* concerned with commercial data processing and therefore not required to be studied.

PURPOSE.

4. a. **Special purpose.** These, as the name suggests, are computers designed for a particular job only; to solve problems of a restricted nature. Examples are computers designed for air traffic control or weapons guidance systems.

b. **General purpose.** Computers designed to solve a wide variety of problems are called general purpose machines. Within the limitations imposed by their particular design capabilities, they can be adapted to perform particular tasks or solve problems by means of specially written programs.

The computers described in this manual will be GENERAL PURPOSE DIGITAL computers, with occasional references to computers used for specialist DP applications.

FURTHER CLASSIFICATION

5. The following terms are used to describe different types of computers:-

a. A **main-frame** computer is a medium or large machine, which keeps its records on magnetic files.

b. A **mini-computer** is a small machine which has, however, all the characteristics of the main-frame. Note that there is no clear dividing line between the smaller main-frames and the larger minis. The distinctive features are not technical, but small size and price.

c. A **micro-computer** is the smallest machine in the range of computers and is the latest to be developed. There is little practical difference between the smaller mini-computers and the larger micro-computers.

d. A **Personal Computer (PC)** is a micro-computer designed primarily for independent use by an individual at work or in the home. (See fig. 3.0)

e. A **Word Processor** is a *special purpose* computer used in the production of office documents, letters, contracts, etc.

NB. A general purpose computer can run a Word Processing program and hence temporarily become special purpose.

COMPUTER GENERATIONS.

6. The first *electronic* computers were produced in the 1940s. Since then a series of radical breakthroughs in electronics has occured. With each major breakthrough, the computers based upon the older form of electronics have been replaced by a new **"generation"** of computers based upon the newer form of electronics. These "generations" are classified as follows:-

a. **First Generation.** Early computers using electronic value. (circa 1940s).

b. **Second Generation.** More reliable computers using transistors which replaced the first generation. (circa 1950s).

c. **Third Generation.** More powerful, reliable and compact computers using simple integrated circuits. (circa 1960s and early 1970s).

d. **Fourth Generation.** The computers in use today, and which contain more sophisticated micro-electronic devices.

e. **Fifth Generation.** There are many predictions that by the end of this century computers will have been developed which will be able to converse with people in a human like manner and which will be

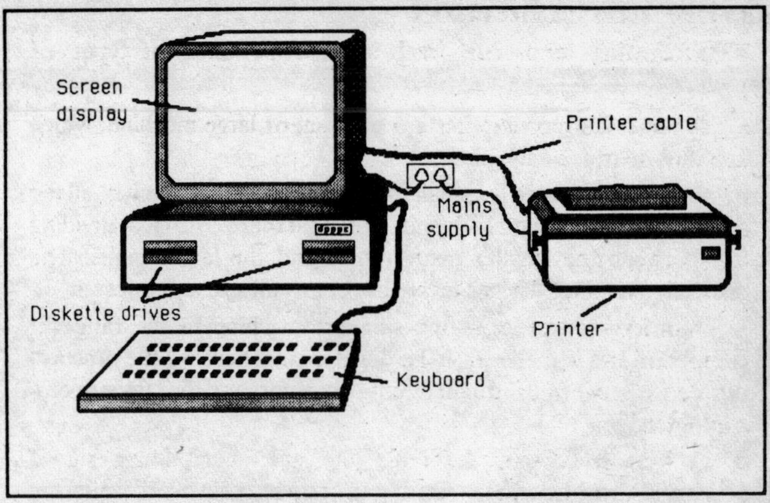

FIG. 3.0. A TYPICAL PERSONAL COMPUTER (PC)

able to mimic human senses, manual skills and intelligence. The term "Fifth Generation" is often used to describe such computers.

BASIC ELEMENTS (FUNCTIONS) OF A COMPUTER SYSTEM.

7. The basic elements or functions which make up a computer system are no different to those found in conventional methods of data processing and are as follows:-

a. Input.

b. Storage.

c. Control.

d. Computing/Processing.

e. Output.

8. Brief description of each element.

a. **Input.** As indicated earlier in 2.6b, a computer cannot accept data in forms customary to human communication. It is necessary therefore, to present data to the computer in a way which provides easy conversion into its own electronic pulse based forms. This is commonly achieved by typing the data into keyboard devices which convert it into *machine-sensible* forms. In some cases machine readable documents or media are produced as part of the input process. Data finally enters *storage*.

b. **Storage.** Data and instructions enter *main* storage, and are held

NCR 16-bit Personal Computer Moder NCR PC4i
(Picture courtesy NCR Ltd)

until needed to be worked on. The *instructions* dictate action to be taken on the *data.* Results of action will be held until they are required for output. Main storage is supplemented by less costly *auxiliary* or backing storage for mass storage purposes. Backing storage serves an important role in holding 'maintained data'. (Fig. 1.2)

c. **Control.** Each computer has a control unit which fetches instructions from main storage, *interprets* them, and issues the necessary *signals* to the components making up the system. It directs all *hardware* operations necessary in obeying instructions.

d. **Computing/processing.** Instructions are obeyed and the necessary arithmetic operations etc are carried out on the data. The section that does this is called the Arithmetic-Logical Unit (ALU). In addition to arithmetic it also performs so-called "logical" operations. These operations take place at incredibly high speeds eg. 1 million numbers may be totalled in one second.

e. **Output.** Results are taken from main storage and fed to an output *device.* This can be a printer, in which case the information is automatically converted to a *printed form.*

9. The elements are produced in chart form in fig. 3.1. Compare fig. 3.1 with the logical model of a DP System fig. 1.2 and you will see how computers are well suited to DP applications.

10. Notice particularly the following points in Fig. 3.1.

a. **Data flow** is as follows:

i. Data flows from the input devices into *main storage* ready to be processed and the results of processing flow from main storage to the output devices.

ii. Data flows from main storage to the ALU. The ALU performs operations on the data thus generating results which flow back to main storage.

iii. Data in main storage which is not needed for the time being may be passed to auxiliary storage from where it subsequently may be brought back to main storage when needed for processing.

iv. Instructions (essentially a special form of data) flow from main storage to the control unit which interprets them and causes the required hardware operations to take place.

b. **Commands flow** from the control unit to the other elements of the computer system and are distinct from data flow.

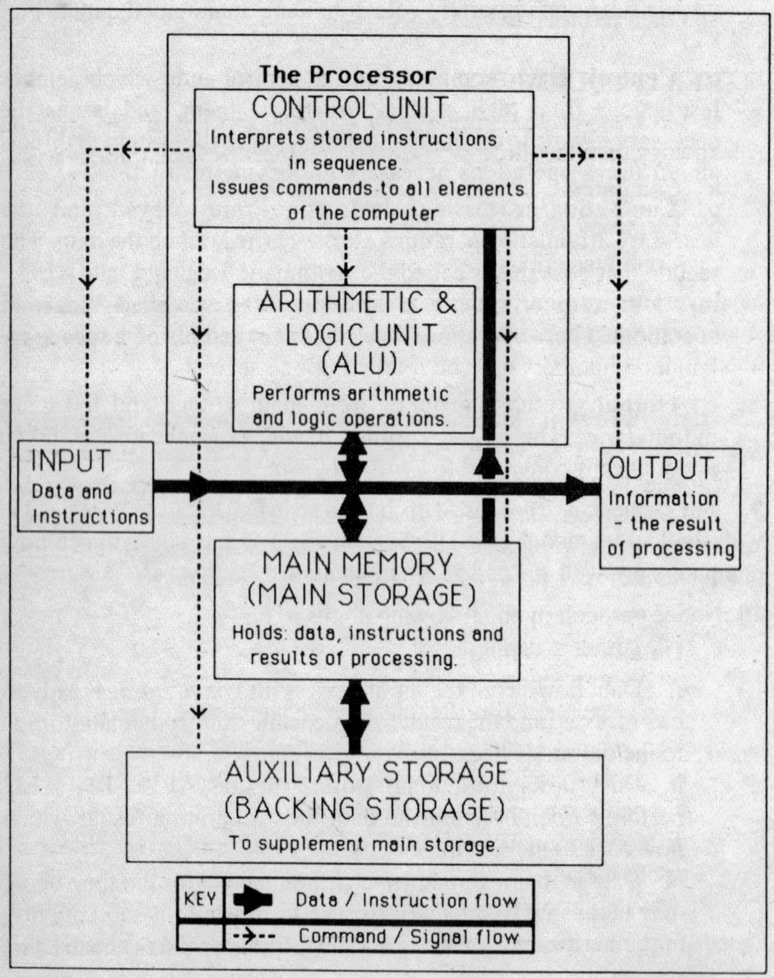

FIG. 3.1. THE ELEMENTS OF A COMPUTER SYSTEM

c. The arithmetic and logic unit (ALU) and control unit combine to form THE PROCESSOR.

d. Data held on backing storage may be input to main memory during processing, used, brought up to date using newly input data and then returned to backing storage.

OTHER IT EQUIPMENT.

11. If we look at the purely technological aspects of Information Technology then the three most important areas of development are:

a. Computers

b. Electronics

c. Communications.

However, we are merely interested in the ways in which combinations of these technologies can be used to satisfy various kinds of information need.

12. Many different kinds of data are handled by Information Technology, eg. text, voice and picture. The established technologies, each able to handle one or more kind of data, such as telephone, telex, TV and computers, have been developed in recent years so that their functions can be integrated and they may be combined together into single IT systems. Thus in any one IT system we may find:

a. Information in these forms:

i. Text (eg. financial reports, contracts and letters).

ii. Picture (eg. printed diagram or video display).

iii. Voice (eg. Recorded message or synthesised sound).

b. Various means of transmitting the data, for example:

i. private telephone exchanges handling voice and data.

ii. public data communication services.

iii. conventional or optical fibre cable transmission on private or public circuits.

iv. satelite communication.

Details of the hardware used and its DP applications will be covered in later chapters.

SUMMARY

13. a. Most computers used for data processing are general purpose digital computers.

b. Computers may be classified as:-

i. Digital or analog.

ii. Special purpose or general purpose.
iii. Mainframe, mini-computer or micro-computer.
iv. 1st, 2nd, 3rd or 4th generation.

c. The basic elements (functions) of a computer system are:
i. Input.
ii. Storage
iii. Control.
iv. Computing/Processing.
v. Output.

d. The main technologies of Information Technology are:
i. Computers.
ii. Electronics.
iii. Communications.

e. IT systems create, store, manipulate and communicate data in a variety of forms in order to satisfy information needs.

POINTS TO NOTE

14. a. The elements of a computer system are readily applied to the general model of a DP system.

b. Computers are able to perform repetitive tasks accurately on large volumes of data with the minimum of manual intervention. By exploiting these abilities to process and maintain data, to provide required information, EDP has gained a considerable advantage over conventional DP methods.

c. The computers used for DP today are mostly fourth generation general purpose digital computers, which may be mainframes, mini-computers or micro-computers.

d. The terms "Central Processing Unit (CPU)" and "Central Processor" are sometimes used instead of "Processor". Beware of these terms, however, because they have in the past also been used to refer to the processor plus main memory. Their use in this text has been avoided as far as possible because of this possible ambiguity.

e. The various technologies associated with IT are often said to be **converging technologies** because they are being developed so that their functions may be integrated.

QUESTIONS.

1. *What is a Personal Computer?*
2. *Describe the flow of data and commands in a computer system.*

Hardware

1. Hardware is the name given to all the physical devices found in a computer system. The converse is 'Software' which is the term given to the programs which are required to put life into the Hardware.

2. Chapter 4 gives an overview of this Part by introducing hardware and its uses.

3. **Input devices** are described in chapter 5. These devices either accept data at a keyboard and then convert the data into machine-sensible form or they accept data which has already been created in machine sensible form (eg. a machine readable document).

4. **Output devices** are described in chapter 6. They are used to produce the data in a humanly sensible form (or in a machine sensible form for later re-input).

5. **Main Storage** is described in chapter 7. Main Storage holds data and programs currently in use.

6. **Auxiliary Storage devices** are described in chapter 8. They are used to provide mass storage of data/records.

7. **The Architecture of Micro, Mini and Mainframe Computers** is described in chapter 9. The chapter starts by describing how the Processor works and then goes on to describe the hardware features of typical microcomputers, minicomputers and mainframe computers.

8. **Communications Equipment and Systems Interconnection** is described in chapter 10. The chapter deals with hardware from other areas of IT and shows how computers can be connected together, and to other electronic equipment, to form completely integrated IT systems.

9. The reader may benefit from this Part by first reading it through to gain an *overall picture,* skipping any difficult detail, and then referring back to this Part, when necessary, later.

4 An Overview of Hardware

INTRODUCTION.

1. The purpose of this chapter is to provide an overview of hardware, in order to prepare you for the subsequent chapters which go into more detail.

2. Common types of hardware are introduced by the use of suitable examples.

3. The main headings under which hardware is discussed in this chapter are:

a. The Silicon Chip.

b. Data Storage.

c. Backing Storage.

d. Data entry.

e. Data transmission and networks.

f. Output.

4. Although the basic uses of hardware are mentioned in this chapter, a full discussion of its uses is deliberately excluded, because a full knowledge of hardware capabilities and limitations must precede any evaluation of which hardware is best suited to a particular application. The *uses* will become clear after you have come to the Parts on "Systems Analysis and Design" and "Applications."

THE SILICON CHIP.

5. Although the Control Unit, ALU and Main Memory of the computer carry out different functions (fig. 3.1), from a hardware viewpoint the basic components of these elements of a modern computer are very similar. This similarity arises from common manufacturing processes.

6. The complex circuits found in these elements of the computer are manufactured from a single minute sliced wafers of silicon crystal. Such devices are called **"silicon chips"** or **"semi-conductor devices"** (see fig. 4.1).

7. Microprocessors. A microprocessor is an entire small computer processor manufactured on a single chip. Computers built around such devices are called **"microcomputers"**, or more correctly **"microcomputer based systems"**.

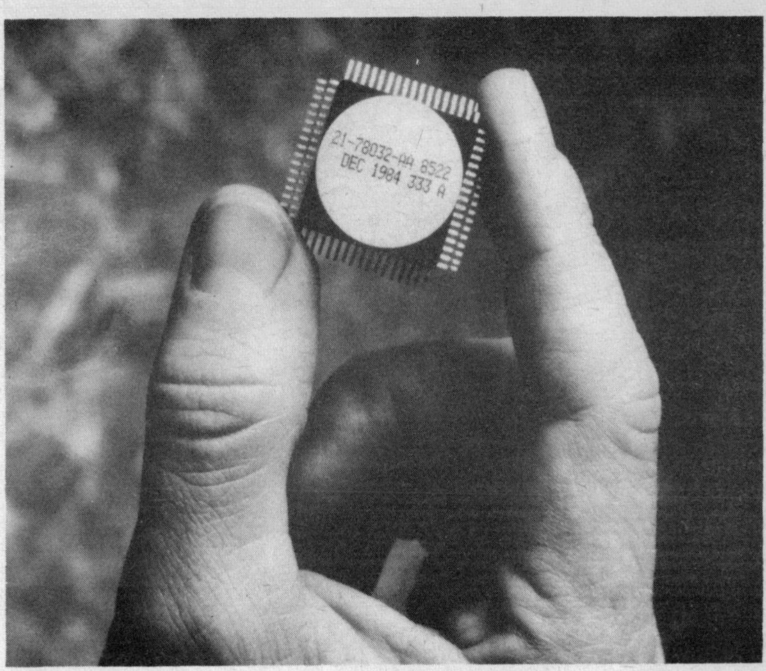

The 78032 VLSI Chip – the heart of Digital Equipment's new addition to the
VAX range, the MicroVAX II.
The following are trademarkes of Digital Equipment Corporation:
VAX, MicroVAX.
(Picture courtesy of Digital Equipment Corporation (DEC))

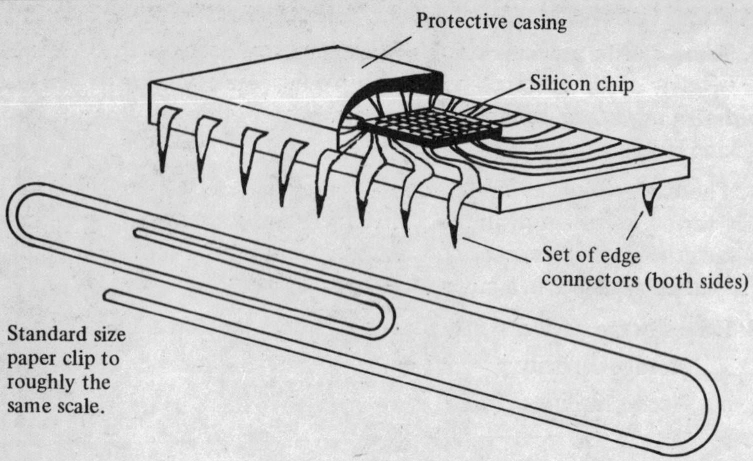

FIG. 4.1. A COMPUTER COMPONENT CONTAINING A SILICON CHIP.

8. The first micro-processor was produced in 1972 by the Intel corporation.

9. Most micro-processors do not contain main storage which is normally produced on separate silicon chips.

10. Semi-conductor memory is the name given to main storage manufactured on silicon chips.

11. The most common types of semi-conductor memory are **"volatile"** which means that all data is lost if the power supply is removed.

12. Main features. The semi-conductor devices within the computer have the following features:-

a. Their operation is wholly electronic, and consequently they are very fast and reliable.

b. Despite the complexity of these devices, modern manufacturing methods have enabled them to be produced at costs which represent only minor portions of the total costs of whole computer systems. e.g. In a micro-computer costing £2000, the micro-processor may only have cost £10.

c. These devices are highly miniaturised. This feature may be exploited in order to provide computer hardware which can be accommodated comfortably in the office or home.

DATA STORAGE.

13. Some specific aspects of data storage have just been discussed under the heading of the silicon chip, but now we turn our attention to *general hardware aspects of data storage* applicable to both main storage and backing storage.

14. There are several different types of hardware used for data storage. This variety stems from the fact that there are a number of physical characteristics which must be considered in deciding the appropriateness of a particular device in a given situation.

15. Data storage devices will be discussed under these headings:-

a. Storage capacity.

b. Access facilities.

c. Size.

d. Robustness.

e. Relative costs.

16. Storage capacity. Storage capacities may be expressed and compared in terms of the number of **'characters'** stored (A character is a symbol such as a letter (A-Z), or digit (0-9), or special symbols such as +, −, £ etc). For example, *main storage* of a small computer may be expressed in terms of tens of thousands of characters whereas *backing storage* of a larger computer may be expressed in terms of tens of millions of characters.

17. Access facilities. Broadly speaking, the two main factors are:-

a. Mode of access.

b. Speed of access.

18. For the time being an everyday example will provide a basic distinction between mode of access and speed of access. You may 'access' data (ie. get facts) from this book in two modes:-

a. *Serially,* by reading through from the first page to the last,

or b. *directly* by using the index to go straight to the data you need.

19. The first alternative is more efficient if you require most or all of the facts, but the latter is faster if you only want a few facts. If you require to have the *immediate* recall of facts, then you may need to use your own memory, instead of the book, as your 'data storage medium'.

20. These ideas will be related to particular items of hardware later.

21. Size. Despite major strides in miniaturisation, (the components within modern chips are more densely packed than the cells of the human brain), some backing storage devices and media remain undesirably bulky. Most backing storage devices have some electro-mechanical parts which contribute to their bulk. When data is to be stored for long periods with minimal access the most compact backing storage media are favoured because of the value of saving space.

22. Compared with normal paper based data storage, as in the form of rows of filing cabinets, computer storage methods are all incredibly more compact.

23. Robustness. Compared with paper based storage, computer data storage may appear to be less robust. Such a view is based upon the fact that most computer storage media may only be used in carefully controlled environments. In practical terms this is seldom a serious problem for DP applications, since the "office environment" is one which is suitable for most computer hardware.

24. Relative Costs. There are big differences in costs between the various types of computer storage. Awareness of the various alternatives allows the most economical alternative to be selected in a given situation. Conversely, if the storage requirements have not been properly specified, an unduly expensive alternative may be selected unnecessarily.

BACKING STORAGE.

25. The main backing storage media in use today are:

a. Magnetic Disk (hard or floppy).

b. Magnetic Tape.

These media will be described in detail in later chapters. Magnetic Disks are flat rotating circular plates coated with magnetic material. (ie. Disks). Some magnetic disks are rigid and called **hard disks,** others are *flexible* and are called **floppy disks** or **diskettes.** Hard disks are more expensive but are faster more reliable and bigger.

26. Disks provide direct data access (4.18).

27. Magnetic tapes are similar in principle to the tapes used domestically for audio or video recording. Tape is a serial medium (4.18) and is mainly used as a "backup" or archiving medium. Tape is also used as an input medium because data on other media may be converted onto magnetic tape prior to input in order to give faster input.

28. Magnetic Media Problems. The common forms of backing storage media in use today are similar in principle to the medium of the domestic tape of cassette recorders. Consequently they are susceptible to stray magnetic fields and to dust.

29. There are some advantages associated with these features of magnetic media. For example, whereas confidential data on paper may prove difficult to dispose of, magnetic media are not directly readable by humans and may be wiped clear magnetically.

DATA ENTRY.

30. There are problems associated with entering data into computers because humans communicate less quickly than computers and in a different way ie. by speech, writing etc. A computer's internal communication is based upon codes formed from high frequency electronic pulses.

31. The basic problems are overcome by using devices which can encode our data into a form which is usable by the computer.

Modern methods fall into three broad categories:-

a. Keyboard entry.

b. Document reading.

c. Data capture.

32. Keyboard entry. One typical keyboard input device is the **VDU** (Visual Display Unit). See fig. 4.2.

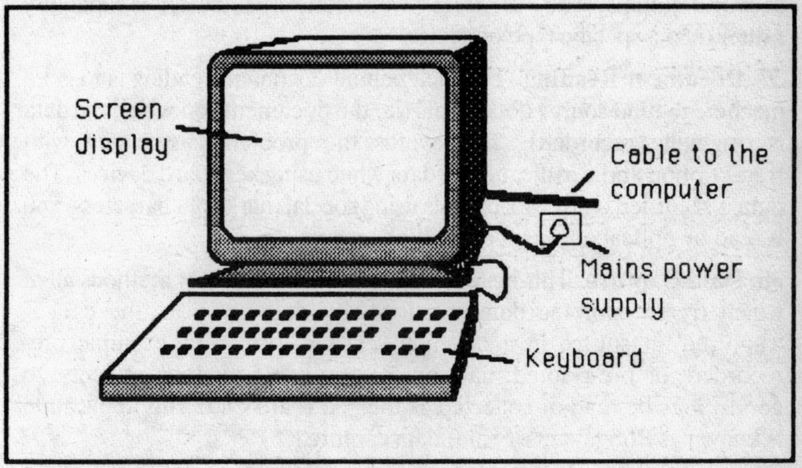

FIG. 4.2. A VDU TERMINAL

33. The VDU is really two devices in one; one for input, one for output. Data is fed in via a keyboard, which is like a typewriter keyboard, and is both passed into the computer and displayed on the screen. The VDU can also receive and display messages from the computer.

34. There are many different types of VDU but the two main ways of using VDUs are:

a. To connect the VDU directly to the computer. This is known as **on-line** data entry. Any device used for on-line data entry in this manner is called a **terminal.**

b. To use the VDU in conjunction with some other data entry system in order to prepare data on a fast and reliable input medium. A popular modern example of this is the **key-to-floppy-disk** or **key-to-diskette** system. These are microcomputer based systems which take in data from the VDU and store it on floppy disks. At some later stage the floppy disks are used for input to the main computer.

35. In both the cases just given the data can be *checked and corrected as it is being input* and no non-reusable medium is being wasted.

36. It has become common in recent years to use microcomputers as terminals in addition to any other tasks they do. PCs (3.5d) are often used for this purpose. Indeed, the PC may also be able to process some of the data and thus relieve the load on the main computer to which it is connected. A terminal with such capabilities, ie. able to act not only as a terminal but to do some processing itself, is normally called a **"work station".** The more sophisticated VDUs often have the ability to serve as work stations. Thus the term "work station" indicates a capability rather than a specific type of device.

37. Document Reading. The idea behind document reading is to get a machine to read source documents (ie. the documents on which the data is originally recorded). This avoids the problems associated with transcription and vertification of data when using keyboard devices. The data is recorded on the documents using special marks or characters, and is read by optical or magnetic reading techniques.

38. Data Capture. This heading covers a wide variety of methods all of which try to combine data creation with data entry ie. the data is 'captured' at source in a machine sensible form. For example pre-recorded, or pre-printed, data on some suitable medium attached to goods, may be read or collected as the goods are sold. This application is known as **PoS** (Point of Sale) data capture.

39. A further very different example of data capture is **audio input** either by means of a microphone or via a telephone. Such devices may be fitted to a work station in addition to the normal keyboard.

DATA TRANSMISSION AND NETWORKS

40. Used in a general sense the term 'data transmission' refers to the movement of data from one location to another. Data in a physical form such as documents can be moved by despatching through the post, by using a car or van or by employing a courier service.

41. In DP 'Data transmission' is usually understood to mean the movement of data by telecommunications systems. It is possible by this means to link a number of remote terminals to a central computer. Data and information can be transmitted between the computer and the terminals in both directions. The use of telecommunications facilities makes possible much faster transmission.

42. The basic components of a data transmission system are:

a. a central computer
b. terminal devices
c. a telecommunications link between a. and b. (see fig. 4.3).

43. Special equipment is needed to provide the communications link. In fig. 4.3 the devices called MODEMS are able to send data along and receive data from a telephone circuit so that the terminal can be used in exactly the same way it could be if connected directly to the computer by a short piece of cable when in fact the terminal could be in another city or country.

44. When they were first introduced the basic data transmission systems, like the one just described, were regarded as another part of the data entry system. It took no time at all to recognise and exploit the possibilities of *two way* point-to-point transmission.

45. Many organisations set up their own *local private systems.* British Telecom (BT) (Formerly part of the Post Office) set up *public services* in the UK with the trade name DATEL.

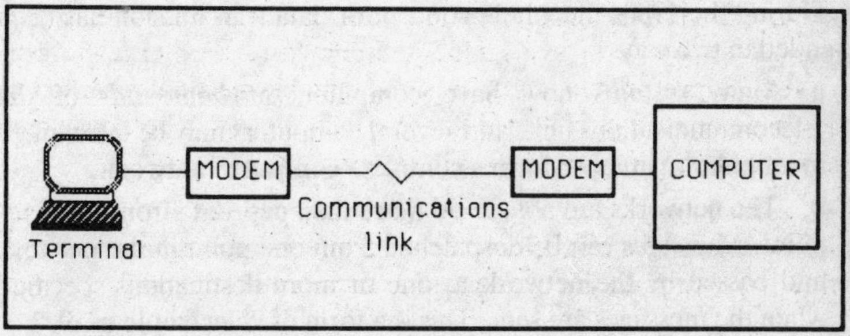

FIG. 4.3. POINT-TO-POINT DATA COMMUNICATIONS

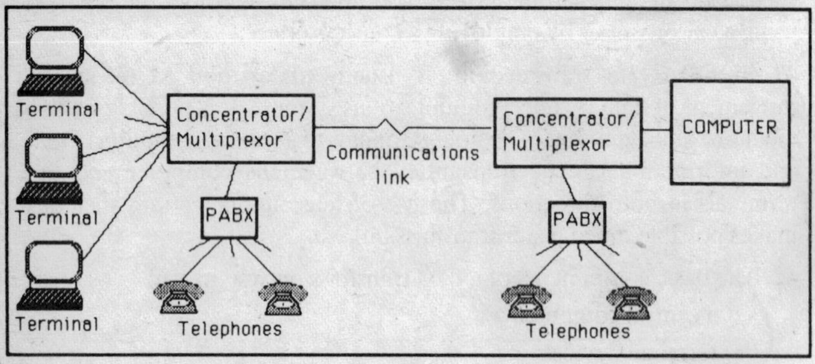

FIG. 4.4. DATA COMMUNICATIONS LINKS

46. Fig. 4.4 provides an example of a more advanced form of communications link but still based upon the same basic idea shown in fig. 4.3. The devices called **concentrators** are able to use one communications link to the computer for a number of terminals which are close to one another, ie. the data to and from the set of terminals is *concentrated* into a single data stream. The method of using one single communications link to carry a number of separate signals is known as **multiplexing** and hence the device is called a **multiplexor.**

47. Another feature of fig. 4.4 is the use of the same communications link for telephone messages. The telephones are connected to the concentrator/multiplexor via a **PABX** (Private Automatic Branch Exchange). There are many different types of PABX but the significant point to note is the integration of two technologies; computer and telecommunications.

48. During the 1980s the whole concept of data transmission has been extended in two ways:

a. Many systems now have computers at *both ends* of the telecommunications link, and several computers may be interlinked in a similar manner to form a complete **computer network.**

b. The networks are able to do more than pass data from point-to-point. **Messages** can be despatched from one point in the network and passed by the network to one or more destinations specified when the messages are sent. This is a form of **"electronic mail."**

49. There are local, national and international networks in current use, and most major networks are interconnected.

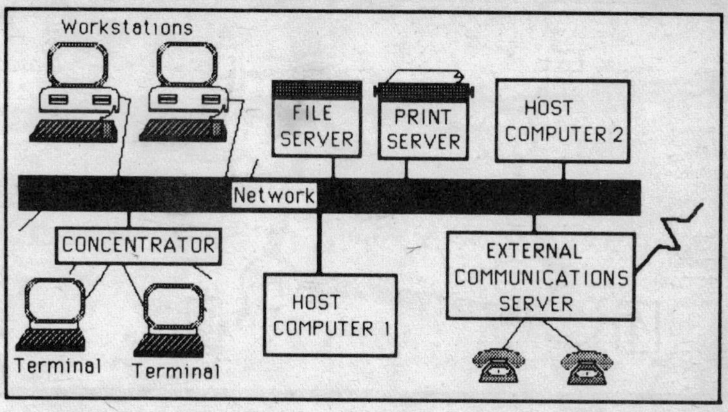

FIG. 4.5. LOCAL AREA NETWORK

50. In fig. 4.5 there is an example of a **Local Area Network (LAN)** as may be used on a single site within an organisation. The purpose of the LAN is to *connect* a variety of pieces of equipment by means of a shared link in order to allow their intercommunication. The terminals and workstations in fig. 4.5 are able to connect to either one of two "host" computers at will. The network also has a **file server** and a **print server.** The former is a special computer which provides a form of auxiliary storage which can be used by any other computer on the network and the latter is a special computer which can receive data from other computers on the network and print it. There is also an **external communications server** on the LAN which enables communication between equipment on the network and systems elsewhere by means like those described in 4.44 – 4.47.

51. LANs cannot be used over long distances. Instead **Long Haul Networks (LHNs)** are used. The feature of a typical LHN are shown in outline in fig. 4.6. Computers at separate locations each have their own connection to the network. The point of connection is often called a **gateway.** When the network is used for electronic mail the gateway connection normally takes the form of some kind of **IMP (Interface Message Processor)** which has the ability to receive, store and forward messages. The communications links between IMPs can take a variety of forms such as cable, optical fibre or satelite transmission.

52. Data transmission equipment has also been exploited as part of local or national **information retrieval systems.** For example in the UK, BT offer a computer based service connected to users by telephone links. Its trade name is "PRESTEL" and is one example of a **'Viewdata'** system. More details will be covered in later chapters.

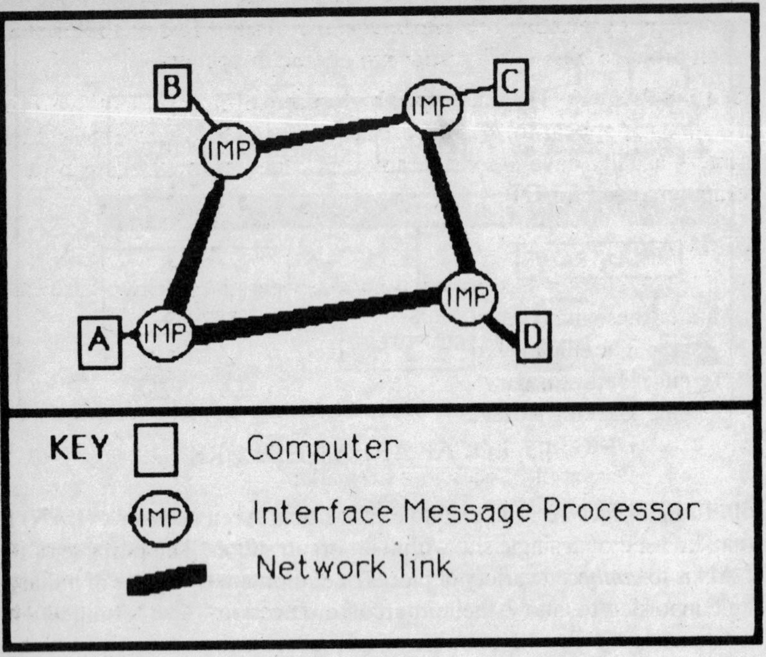

FIG. 4.6. LONG HAUL NETWORK

OUTPUT.

53. At the present time most information produced by computers is output in the form of printed paper documetns, reports etc. Over the last few years an increase in the number of computer systems being used for "on-line" information retrieval has meant that considerable volumes of data are displayed on VDU screens instead of being produced in printed form.

54. In both these cases the information is expressed in terms of characters, (4.16) but in the long term more information may be provided in the form of **images** (ie. pictures or diagrams).

55. Quite apart from a number of valuable innovations over many years, the development of output devices has been largely concerned with trying to find ways of improving the speeds, costs and reliability of printers. Print quality and quietness have been additional aims for some printer applications.

56. The two main types of printer currently in use are:

a. character printers

b. line printers.

57. Character Printers are low speed printers which mimic the action of typewriters by printing *one character at a time.* Most of the printers which produce high quality print are character printers.

58. Line Printers. The majority of high speed printers *print whole lines at a time* (or appear to) and are consequently called *line printers.* Line printers usually have a considerable work load on mini or mainframe computers used for DP.

SUMMARY.

59. a. The chapter has provided an overview of computer hardware under these main headings.

i. The silicon chip.
ii. Data storage.
iii. Backing storage.
iv. Data entry.
v. Data transmission and networks.
vi. Output.

b. General characteristics have been introduced, with examples, so that when you encounter details of particular hardware in later chapters, you will have some basic criteria by which to evaluate them.

POINTS TO NOTE.

60. a. In Data Processing, the interest in hardware only extends as far as understanding those features of hardware which determine its uses and limitations.

b. Note the difference between "on-line" ie. connected to the computer and under its control, and "off-line" ie. away from the computer.

QUESTIONS.

1. a. What is meant by the term semi-conductor devices?

b. Give three features of semi-conductor devices.

2. Explain the term "data transmission".

5 Input Devices and Media

INTRODUCTION.

1. The following devices and the media associated with them will be described:-

a. Keyboard devices
   i. VDUs
   ii. Terminal typewriters
   iii. Consoles

b. Document readers – documents with characters/marks in special formats.
   i. Optical readers
   ii. Magnetic ink readers

c. Data Capture devices
   i. Direct input devices
   ii. Data loggers/recorders

d. Magnetic media and storage devices
   i. Magnetic tape unit – magnetic tape
   ii. Floppy disk unit – floppy disk (diskette)

Some of these devices can be used for *both* input and output. In this chapter they will be regarded purely in their input role, except where the input and output operations are inextricably linked, as in the case of the VDU.

KEYBOARD DEVICES.

2. Visual Display Unit (VDU). (as introduced in 4.32) There are many different types of VDU in use today. Only the more common features and variants will be described.

3. *Features*

a. It is a dual purpose device with a keyboard for data input and a cathode ray tube display for output. The latter is similar to a TV screen.

b. The keyboard resembles the QWERTY typewriter, keyboard, but usually has several additional keys which are used to control and edit the display.

c. Characters (4.16) are displayed on the screen in a manner which resembles printed text. A typical full screen display is 24 rows by 80 columns (ie. 1920 characters).

d. The display can normally be generated in two different modes:-
i. **Scrolling mode** in which lines appear at the bottom and move up the screen rather like credits on a movie screen.
ii. **Paging mode** in which one complete screen full is replaced by another rather like a slide projector display.

e. Most VDUs, have features which allow particular parts of the display to be highlighted or contrasted eg.
i. Inverse (Reverse) video ie. black on white instead of white on black.
ii. Blinking displays.
iii. Two levels of brightness.
iv. Colour – on the more expensive models.

f. Cursor controls. A cursor is a small character-sized symbol displayed on the screen, which can be moved about the screen both vertically and horizontally by means of special keys on the keyboard. During data input, the display may resemble a blank form. In this case data may be entered by first moving the cursor to a space on the 'form' and then typing in the data. Further keys may allow the data to be edited or corrected.

g. Inbuilt microprocessors. The numerous internal functions of almost all modern VDUs are controlled by inbuilt microprocessors. The more expensive models are often called **intelligent terminals.** These devices are sometimes capable of limited amounts of processing, and with further enhancements these devices can often be turned into small microcomputer systems in their own right. As was indicated in 4.36 an advanced VDU or a Personal Computer able to not only act as a terminal but also able to do some processing itself is normally called a **work station.** Fig. 5.0 shows a Personal Computer being used as a work station to which a variety of input devices have been attached.

h. **Mice & joysticks.** (fig. 5.0). These devices have a variety of uses as alternatives to the keyboard. In simple cases they can be used to move the cursor about the screen. As the mouse is moved about the desktop the cursor moves about the screen. A button on top of the mouse can be pressed when the desired position is reached. The motion of the mouse is sensed by a rolling ball which is mounted in the underside of the mouse and in contact with the desktop. The joystick can be moved left, right, up or down to move the cursor and also has a button used like that on the mouse.

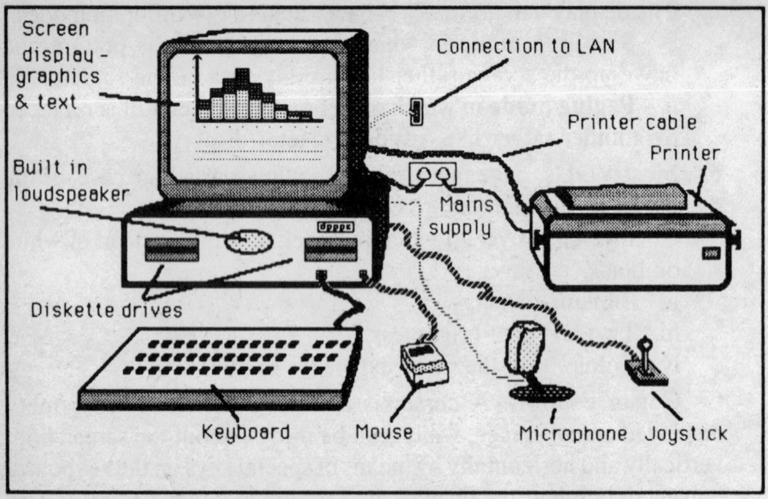

FIG. 5.0. PERSONAL COMPUTER WITH
A SELECTION OF INPUT AND OUTPUT DEVICES.

4. Variations on the VDU.

a. **Graphics Versions.** Some VDUs have high quality displays which can be used for line drawings, draftsmens drawings etc.

b. **Light Pens.** A special pen used in conjunction with a graphics VDU. The VDU can detect the location of light shining on the screen by means of special hardware and software. This is a design aid which simplifies input of details of positions on the screen.

c. **Touch Terminals.** An alternative to the light-pen. The VDU can detect when a point on the screen is touched.

d. **Voice Data Entry (VDE).** Additional circuitry plus a microphone is added to the VDU. The unit can be switched to "learn" a number of words, typically less than 200, which it achieves by recording a "sound pattern" for each word typed in. When the unit is switched to input it displays and inputs any word which it recognises. These units are particularly suitable for people wishing to use a few words again in situations where their hands are not free to use a keyboard eg. people in laboratories, invalids etc.

An IBM 3277 model 2 Information Display Station and Light Pen. Picture courtesy of IBM.

A pad and puck used as an attachment to a VDU for non-keyboard data entry

5. Terminal Typewriters. A Terminal typewriter is also a dual-purpose device. It has a keyboard for data input and a small printer for output. It closely resembles a modern electric typewriter, hence its name.

6. *Features.*

a. The keyboard resembles the QWERTY typewriter keyboard, but usually has several additional keys which are used for device control.

b. The printer is usually a character printer (4.57). Details will be covered in the next chapter.

7. As is the case of VDUs, terminal typewriters may be used either as terminals or as part of some other data entry system (see 4.34).

8. Consoles. A **console** is a device which is being used for communication between the *operator* (ie. the person responsible for operating the computer) and the program which is controlling the computer. (This special program is often called the **monitor.**) Terminal typewriters and VDUs can both be used as consoles, although the use of a terminal typewriter is usually prefered because of the permanent printed record which they produce.

9. Control messages are keyed in by the operator (eg. the next task required) and acted upon by the program. Messages can also be typed by the monitor for action by the operator (eg. indicating that a 'run' has finished). All messages are printed by the typewriter. Note that the input in this case consists of *operating messages* for controlling the system.

10. Note that when a terminal is used it is sometimes necessary to be able to communicate control messages as well as data and information. The terminal may therefore be able to perform *console* functions.

DOCUMENT READERS.

11. Optical Readers and Documents. There are two basic methods of Optical Document Reading:

a. **Optical Character Recognition (OCR).**

b. **Optical Mark Recognition (OMR).**

These two methods are often used in conjunction with one another, and have much in common. Their common and distinguishing features are covered in the next few paragraphs.

12. Features of an Optical Reader.

a. It has a document feed hopper and several stackers including a stacker for "rejected" documents.

b. Reading of documents prepared in optical characters or marks is accomplished as follows:

i. **Characters.** A scanning device recognises each character by the amount of reflected light (ie. OCR) (see fig. 5.1).

ii. **Marks.** A mark in a particular position on the document will trigger off a response. It is the *position* of the mark that is converted to a value by the Reader. (ie. OMR) (see fig. 5.2).

c. Documents may be read at up to 10,000 A4 documents per hour.

13. Features of a document.

a. Documents are printed in a stylised form (by printers etc fitted with a special type-face) which can be recognised by a machine. The stylised print is also recognisable to the human eye. Printing must be on specified areas on the document.

b. Some documents incorporate optical marks. Pre-determined positions on the document are given values. A mark made in a position using a pencil is read by the reader.

c. Good quality printing and paper are vital.

d. Documents require to be undamaged for accurate reading.

e. Sizes of documents, and scanning area, may be limited.

14. Magnetic Ink Reader and Documents. The method of reading these documents is known as **Magnetic Ink Character Recognition (MICR).**

15. *Features of Magnetic Ink Readers.*

a. Documents are passed through a strong magnetic field causing the iron oxide in the ink encoded characters, to become magnetised. Documents are then passed under a read head when a current flows, at a strength according to the size of the magnetized area (ie. characters are recognised by a magnetic pattern).

b. Documents can be read at up to 2,400 per minute.

0 1 2 3 4 5 6 7 8 9
A B C D E F G H I J
K L M N O P Q R S T
U V W X Y Z

0123456789
ABCDEFGHIJ
KLMNOPQRST
UVWXYZ
abcdefghij
klmnopqrst
uvwxyz

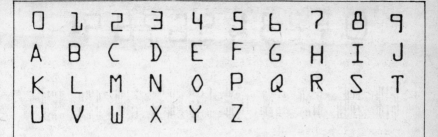

FIG. 5.1. SPECIMEN CHARACTERS FROM TWO COMMON OCR CHARACTER SETS.
[UPPER SET : OCR-A LOWER SET : OCR-B]

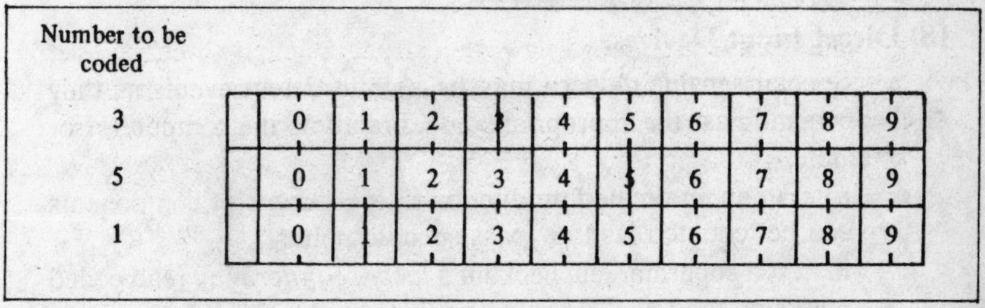

FIG. 5.2. A MARKED DOCUMENT READY FOR OMR.

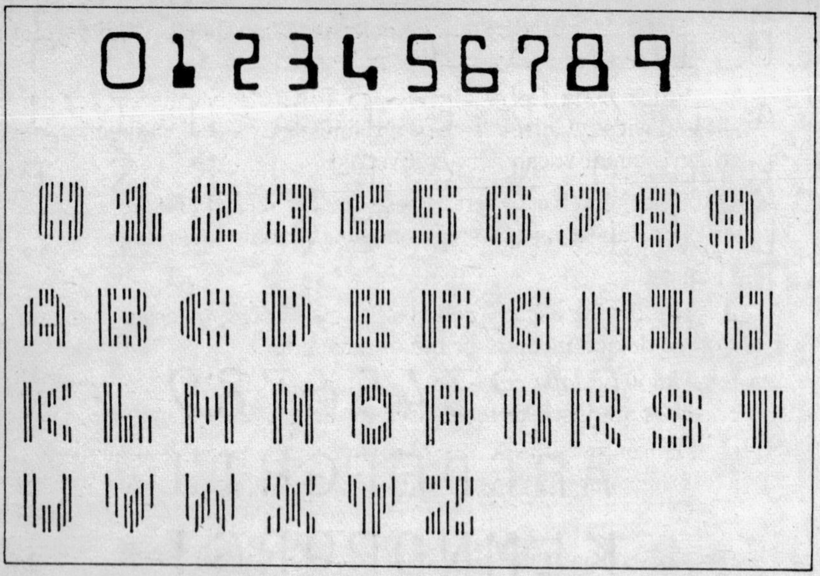

FIG. 5.3. SPECIMEN CHARACTERS FROM TWO COMMON MICR CHARACTER SETS.
[UPPER SET : E13B LOWER SET : CMC7]

16. *Features of documents.*

a. The quality of printing needs to be very high.

b. The characters are printed in a highly distinctive type style using ink containing particles of iron oxide which gives the required magnetic property. (see Fig. 5.3).

DATA CAPTURE DEVICES

17. These devices are mostly special purpose devices intended for use in particular applications. Common, special and typical examples are described in the next few paragraphs.

18. Direct Input Devices.

a. Special sensing devices may be able to detect events as they happen and pass the appropriate data directly to the computer. For example.

i. On an automated production line, products or components can be 'counted' as they pass specific points.

ii. At a supermarket checkout a *laser scanner* may read coded marks on food packets as the packets pass by on the conveyor.

This data is used by the computerised till to generate a till receipt and maintain records of stock levels.

b. **Voice Data Entry Devices.** (5.4d) Data can be spoken into these devices. Currently they are limited to a few applications in which a small vocabulary is involved.

19. Data Loggers/Recorders. These devices record and store data at source. The data is input to the computer at some later stage.

20. *Features.*

a. The device usually contains its own microprocessor and data storage device/medium or radio transmitter.

b. *Magnetic tape cassettes* are often used for data storage. The cassettes are just like those used for domestic audio systems.

c. Data entry to the device is usually by means of a small keyboard, like a calculator keyboard, and/or by some special reading attachment.

21. A basic device, using only a keyboard for data entry, and able to transmit data, is effectively a portable terminal.

22. Popular attachments to both portable and static devices are the *light-pen wands* and *magnetic wands.* These attachments resemble pens at the end of a length of electrical flex. They can read specially coded data in the form of either optical marks/characters, or magnetic codes, which have previously been recoded on strips of suitable material. A common version is the *bar-code reader.* (see Fig. 5.4).

10 0116971 0

FIG. 5.4. A BAR-CODED STRIP READABLE BY A LIGHT-PEN WAND.

MAGNETIC MEDIA STORAGE DEVICES.

23. Under this heading we will consider:-

a. Magnetic tape unit – magnetic tape.

b. Floppy disk unit – floppy disk (diskette).

These devices and media may also be used for data storage or output.

24. It should be noted that magnetic tapes and floppy disks normally come to have input data on them for one of three reasons:-

a. The data has been entered at some other device (eg. VDU) and encoded on the tape of diskette by some suitable hardware.

b. The data has been converted from a slow medium to enable faster input.

c. The data has previously been output by a computer. eg. in order to transfer data from one computer to another.

25. Magnetic Tape Unit and Magnetic Tape. The main magnetic tape medium is half inch reel-to-reel tape. Two lesser alternatives are magnetic tape cassette and magnetic-tape cartridge. The following description deals mainly with ½" reel-to-reel versions.

26. *Features of the Tape Unit.*

a. It holds the magnetic tape reel and also a second reel for 'taking up' the tape (similar in concept to a tape recorder). (See Fig. 5.5).

b. It has a 'read head' for 'reading' the information stored on the tape, ie. for transferring data from the tape into main storage.

c. The tape moves past the read head at up to 200 inches per second.

27. *Features of the Magnetic Tape.*

a. It is ½" wide and 300, 600, 1200, 2400 or 3600 feet long.

b. It has a plastic base, coated with magnetisable material on *one* side.

c. Data is stored in tracks. There are 7 or 9 tracks (depending upon the tape unit) which run the length of the tape. The data is coded so that one CHARACTER is recorded across the 7 or 9 tracks. (See Fig. 5.6 which illustrates 7 track tape).

d. An aluminium strip, called a 'load point marker', marks the physical beginning of the tape for recording purposes; (the first 20 ft. or so is not used, apart from threading into the unit). Similarly the physical end of the tape is marked by an 'end of reel marker' (the *last* 20 ft. or so is not used for recording).

e. The *density* of recording can *vary* between 200–6,250 characters to the inch.

f. The tape is re-usable ie. can be overwritten (as can tape used with tape recorders) – 20,000 – 50,000 passes are possible.

g. It has a practical storage capacity of 40 million characters (approx) per reel.

IBM 2401 Magnetic Tape Units

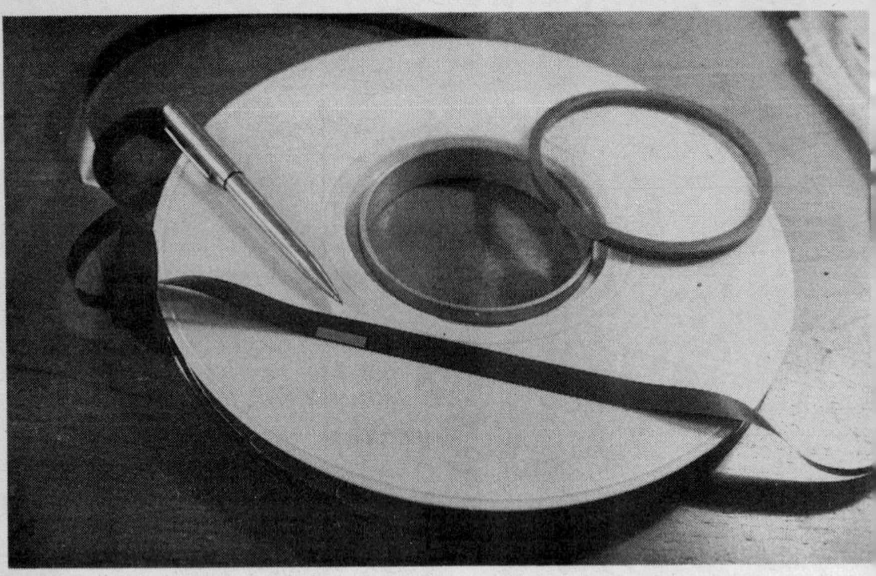

A magnetic tape (reverse side) with a write permit ring visible and removed from the back of the tape.

The pen tip is pointing to the 'Load point marker' at the start of the tape.

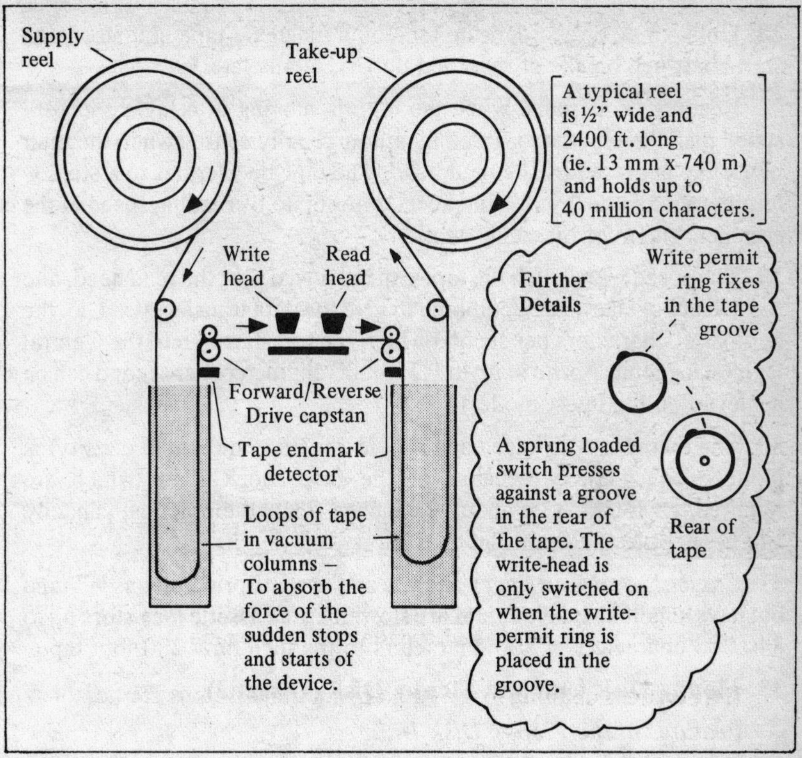

FIG. 5.5. MAIN FEATURES OF A MAGNETIC TAPE UNIT.

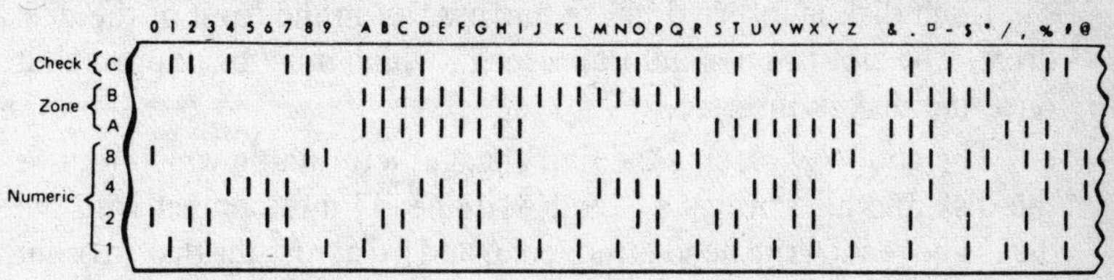

N.B. The vertical marks on the tape in this figure represent invisible "spots" of magnetism on the tape which have been magnetised in one of two possible directions. Those spots magnetised in the opposite direction are not shown. There are seven spots of magnetism across the tape, one in each of the channels 1, 2, 3, 4, A, B & C, for each character recorded. The set of spots across the tape for a single character constitute a "frame".

FIG. 5.6. MAGNETIC TAPE CODING.
(Courtesy IBM UK Ltd.)

28. Unlike a tape recorder, the tape on a magnetic tape unit stops and starts between blocks of recorded data. (Details later).

Reading takes place when the tape is moving at a high, *constant* speed past the read head. Reading automatically ceases when the inter block gap is sensed by the read head. The tape decelerates to a stop on termination of one "read" and accelerates up to its reading speed at the commencement of the next "read".

29. The speed with which the tape can be moved past the read head, and the density of characters, combine to give the data transfer speed, ie. the number of characters per second which are transferred into the Central Processing Unit. A *rate* of up to 1,250,000 characters per second can be achieved on the latest models.

30. The theoretical storage capacity (ie. length x maximum density) is reduced considerably because of the Inter-Block Gaps which are required, each taking up about .75 inches. Thus the practical capacity can be as little as 20 million characters.

31. *Cassettes and Cartridges* operate on the same principles as ½" tape but have smaller capacities and are slower. eg. a cassette may store up to 340,000 characters at 800 characters to the inch on a 280 foot tape.

33. Floppy Disk Unit and Floppy Disk (Diskette).

Features of the Floppy Disk Unit.

a. Most floppy disk units are *dual drive* units, ie. able to hold two separate floppy disks at a time.

b. Each disk is inserted into a narrow slot in the front of the disk drive. The slot has a small flap over it, which must be clipped shut once the disk is inserted.

c. The action of closing the flap engages a turntable which rotates the disk and also brings a "read/write head" into contact with the disk. The read/write head is moved to and fro across the disk in order to either record data on the disk surface (a "write"), or 'read' back data which has previously been recorded.

d. Floppy disks rotate at 360 rpm.

e. Floppy Disk Units are sometimes incorporated physically into the VDU associated with the system.

34. *Features of the floppy disk.*

a. A pliable disc permanently sealed within a rigid, smoothly lined, protective plastic envelope. (see fig. 5.7).

b. Data is stored on tracks.

c. The two most common size are 8" and 5¼".

d. Storage capacities range from 60 thousand characters to 1¼ million characters.

Label
■ Represents exposed disk surface
Index hold. Used to locate start of data recording on each track.
Security tag holes which can be covered by tape. Used when needed to stop recorded data being accidentally lost. This serves the same function as a magnetic tape write permit ring. (On some disks adding the tape protects the disk – a less sound practice).
Spindle hole surrounded by surface gripped by spindle clamp in order to rotate the disk.
The read/write head presses against this slot supported by a pressure pad below and moves across the slot from track to track rather like the arm on a record player.

A Floppy Disk in its protective envelope. Typical sizes 5¼" square or 8" square.

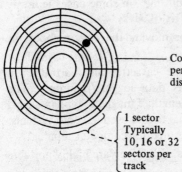

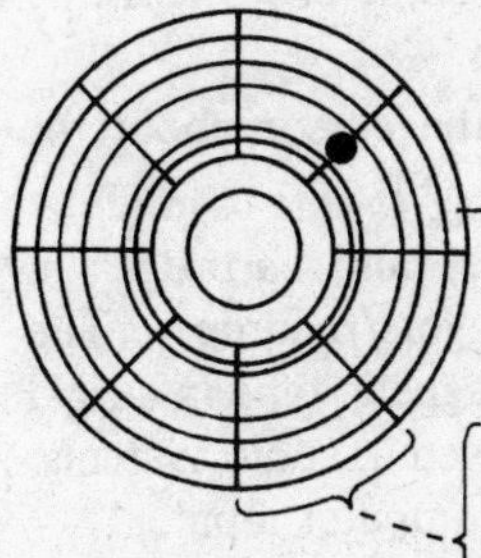
Concentric tracks (invisible). Typically 77 per side on 8" disks and 40 per side on 5¼" disks but there are many common variations.
1 sector Typically 10, 16 or 32 sectors per track

NB
The data from each sector can be read into main storage without having to first read data from inner or outer tracks ie. **direct access** not **serial access.**

A Floppy Disk

Storage capacity.

"Single sided" disks only use one surface for data recording.

"Double side" disks use both recording surfaces.

Techniques can be exploited to double the data storage capacity of each track ie. the choice is between "single density" or "double density".

The typical capacity of a single sided single density floppy disk is 125 thousand character (5¼") or 250 thousand characters (8"). Figures for double sided double density floppy disks are four times those for single sided single density.

FIG. 5.7. FLOPPY DISK (DISKETTE) DETAILS.

SUMMARY.

35. The features of the *main* hardware units and media, for transfering data into the computer, have been covered. They are:-

a. Visual Display Unit (VDU).
b. Terminal Typewriter.
c. Optical reader – Documents.
d. Magnetic ink reader – Documents.
e. Direct input devices.
f. Data loggers/recorders.
g. Magnetic tape unit – Magnetic tape.
h. Floppy disk unit – Floppy disk (Diskette).

POINTS TO NOTE.

36. a. Only the units in 35a-35d handle data in forms which are both machine *and* human sensible.

b. The actions of the input devices are under the control of the computer's processor because the devices are "on-line" to the computer when being used for input purposes. Note however that these devices may also be used "off-line" in some cases ie. away from the computer.

c. Some VDUs have devices for moving the cursor about the screen. e.g. "joysticks".

d. Note the use of magnetic tape cassettes and cartridges in conjunction with devices such as data loggers/recorders. The cassette and cartridge use a short length of magnetic tape in a rigid plastic case. The cassette is identical to that used in audio systems. The cartridge is similar but more suited for computer input.

The advantage of these devices is that they are highly portable and inexpensive.

QUESTIONS.

1. *What is a "work station"?*
2. *Describe the main features of a floppy disk (diskette).*

6 Output Devices and Media

INTRODUCTION.

1. The following devices and media will be described:-

a. Printers – Single sheet or continuous stationery.

b. Terminals – VDU or Terminal typewriter.

c. Microform recorder – Microfilm or Microfiche.

d. Magnetic tape unit – Magnetic tape.

e. Floppy-disk-unit – Floppy disk (diskette).

f. Others.

PRINTERS.

2. A basic classification of printers is:

a. **Character Printers** which print one character at a time.

b. **Line Printers** which print whole lines at a time.

c. **Page Printers** (also called **Image Printers**) which print whole pages at a time.

3. Print Speeds tend to be expressed in terms of cps (characters per second) or lpm (lines per minute). Printers may be classified as

a. **Low speed** (10 cps to approx 300 lpm) – usually character printers.

b. **High speed** (Typically 300 lpm – 3000 lpm) – usually line printers or page printers.

4. Basic Methods of producing print.

a. **Impact or Non-Impact printing.** Impact printers *hit* inked ribbons against paper whereas non-impact printers use other methods of printing eg. Thermal or electrostatic. Most impact printers are noisy.

b. **Shaped or Dot-Matrix printing.** The difference is explained in Fig. 6.1. A dot matrix can also be used to produce a whole **picture** or **image,** (2c) similar in principle, but superior in quality, to the minute pattern of dots in a newspaper picture.

LOW SPEED PRINTERS.

5. Dot matrix impact character printers. These are the most popular and widely used low speed printers. They are often loosely refered to as **"dot matrix printers".**

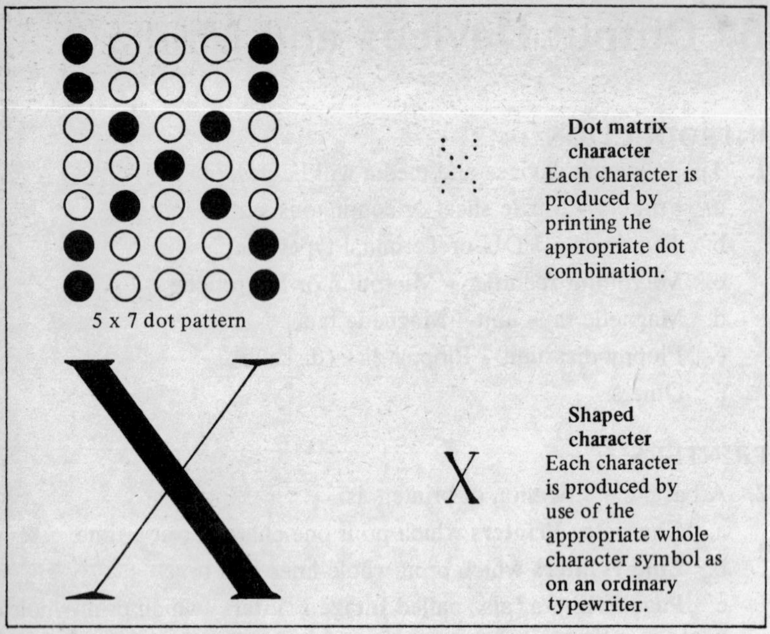

5 x 7 dot pattern
Dot matrix character
Each character is produced by printing the appropriate dot combination.
X
Shaped character
Each character is produced by use of the appropriate whole character symbol as on an ordinary typewriter.

FIG. 6.1. SHAPED AND DOT MATRIX CHARACTER.

6. *Features.*

a. As with all character printers the device mimics the action of a typewriter by printing single characters at a time in lines across the stationery. The print is produced by a small 'print head' which move to and fro across the page, stopping momentarily in each character position to strike a print ribbon against the stationery with an array of wires.

b. According to the number of wires in the print head, the character matrix may be 7×5, 7×7, 9×7, 9×9. The more dots the better the image.

c. Line widths are typically 80, 120, 132 or 160 characters across.

d. Speeds are typically from 30 cps to 200 cps.

e. Multiple print copies may be produced by the use of carboned paper (eg. 4-6 copies using NCR paper).

f. Some higher quality versions have:-

- i. Inbuilt alternative character sets.
- ii. Very good print quality.
- iii. Features for producing graphs, pictures, and even colour by means of multiple print ribbons.

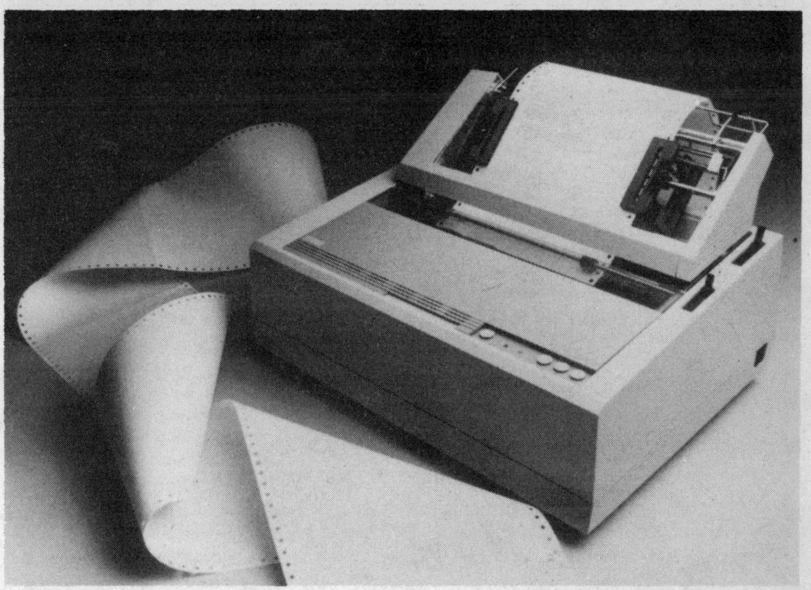

The LQP03 letter quality printer from Digital Equipment which includes a full-character 130-petal daisy wheel.
(Picture courtesy of Digital Equipment Corporation (DEC))

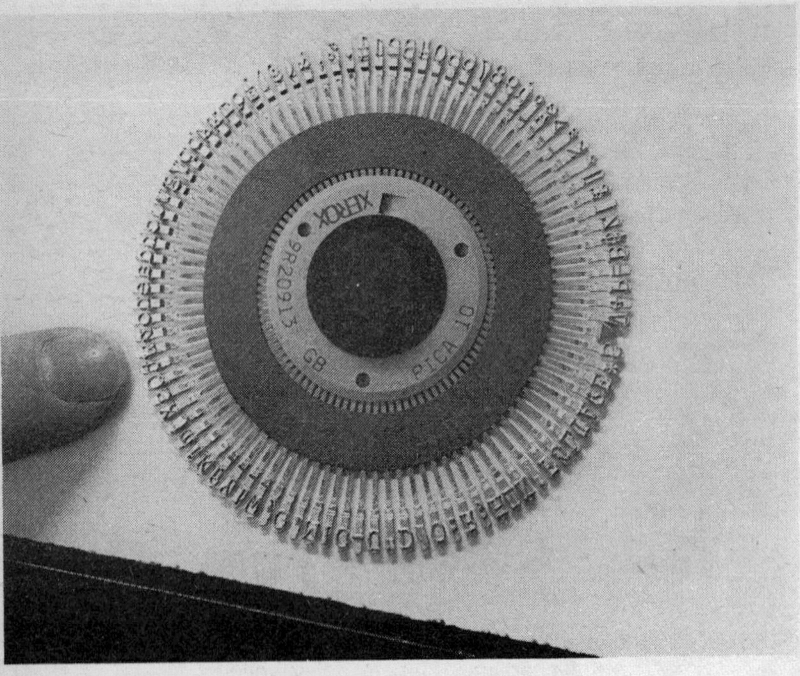

A daisy wheel.

7. Daisywheel Printers. Another popular type of low speed printer which is favoured when high print quality is demanded.

8. *Features.*

a. An impact shaped character printer.

b. These printers are filled with *exchangeable* print heads called **daisywheels.** (See Fig. 6.2). To print each character the wheel is rotated and the appropriate spoke is struck against an inked ribbon.

c. Speed typically 45 cps.

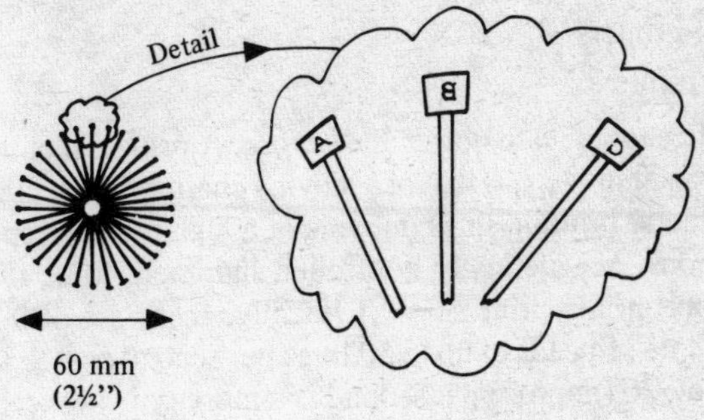

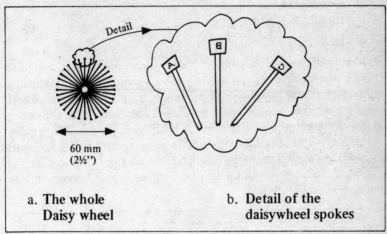

a. **The whole Daisy wheel**

b. **Detail of the daisywheel spokes**

FIG. 6.2.

d. Similar to dot matrix printers in terms of page size and multiple copy printing.

9. Other low speed printers. There are many other low speed printers too numerous to mention. Two others worth a mention are:-

a. **Thermal Printers.** These are non-impact character matrix printers which print onto special paper using a heated print head. They are very quiet and this gives them a big advantage for some applications.

b. **Inkjet Printers.** These are non impact character matrix printers which fire ink droplets onto the paper by using an "electrostatic field". They too are very quiet but are not so widely used at present.

HIGH SPEED PRINTERS.

10. There are two basic types of high speed printers:-

a. Line Printers.

b. Page Printers.

Both types operate with continuous stationery.

11. Line printers. These are impact shaped-character printers which as their name suggest print whole lines at a time. There are three main types:

a. Drum printers.

b. Chain printers.

c. Band printers.

12. It will suffice to indicate how *b* and *c* work. A principle of operation typical of the faster models, is that of a moving chain, with the links being engraved character printing slugs, moving at a high constant speed past printing positions. Magnetically controlled hammers force *the paper* against the appropriate print slugs. Typically, there are 120 printing positions to a 'line'. Speeds of up to 50 lines per second *can* be achieved although, as yet, 20 (approx) per second is a more typical speed. Using continuous stationery with interleaved carbons, up to 7 copies can be obtained. (See Fig. 6.3).

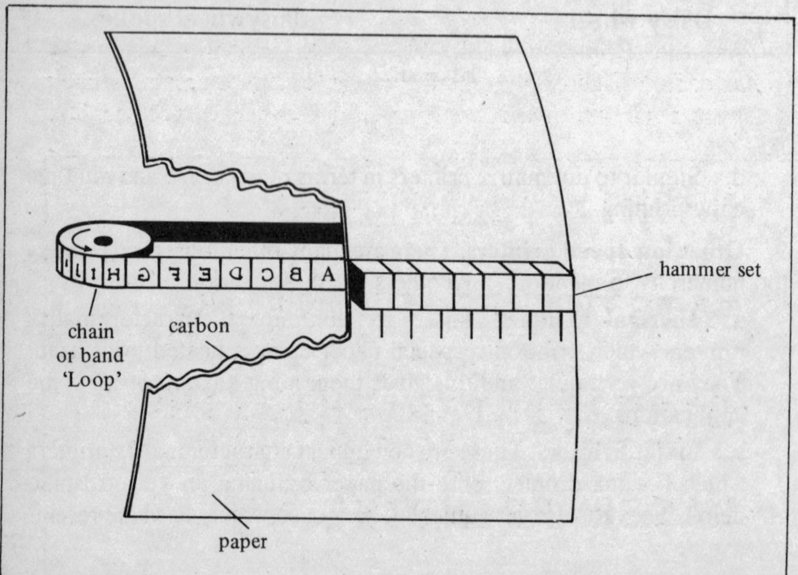

FIG. 6.3. A CHAIN OR BAND PRINTER.

The band printer works in a similar manner to the chain printer but the bands, which are made of steel, may be exchanged quite readily to provide a variety of character sets.

13. Page Printers. The printers print an *"image"* of a whole page at a time. The image may consist of conventional print, diagrams, pictures, or a combination of these thus making pre-printed stationery unnecessary.

14. According to technical features given emphasis in particular designs, these printers are also known as **Optical printers, Laser printers** or **Xerographic printers.**

15. An electroncially controlled laser beam marks out an electrostatic image on the rotating surface of a photoconductive drum. Ink toner is attracted onto the electrostatic pattern on the surface of the drum. The toner is then transferred onto the stationery as the stationery comes into contact with the drum.

16. A typical laser printer will print 146 pages per minute. When printing at a normal 6 lines per inch vertically, this represents a speed of 10,500 lpm but with smaller spacing speeds of up to 30,000 lines per minute may be achieved on some models. Lower speed, lower price laser printers are also available which are able to produce high quality printing at speeds of up to 500 lines per minute.

PRINT QUALITY

17. Comparing Print Quality. A *rough* comparison of print quality may be obtained from Figure 6.4. It should be noted that the diagram is a copy of a copy and that *some* matrix printers rival daisywheels in print quality.

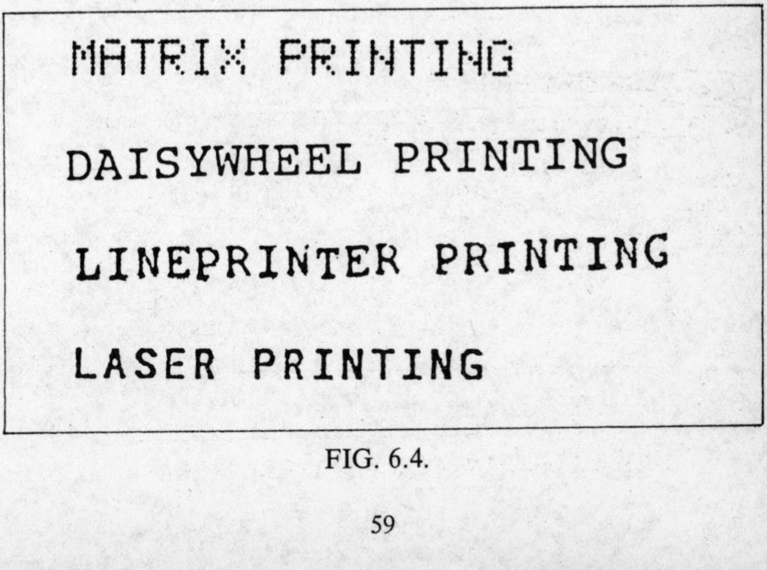

FIG. 6.4.

The LN03 desk-top laser printer from Digital Equipment Corporation.
(Picture courtesy of Digital Equipment Corporation (DEC))

TERMINALS.

18. A terminal is a device which allows output to be provided at a point remote from the computer. The two methods commonly used are:

a. Visual Display Unit (VDU).

b. Terminal typewriter.

The devices also deal with input, and are described in 5.2-5.6.

19. Most terminal typewriters incorporate matrix or daisy-wheel impact printers.

20. The one feature of many terminals or work stations not discussed in any detail in 5.2 – 5.6 was **Computer Graphics.** A wide variety of pictures, diagrams, graphs, line drawings animated cartoons etc. can be produced on computer output devices and the general term for all such forms of output is **computer graphics.** The two basic methods of producing graphical images are:

a. Block based images.

b. Pixel based images.

21. Block based images are simple and effective. The basic building *blocks* are **graphics characters** which the device can display or print in addition to the ordinary alphabetic and numeric characters (see fig. 6.5). The graphics characters available vary from device to device. One standard form of block based image is that used on the British TV ceefax and oracle services.

22. Pixel based images are of a higher quality than block based images. The principle is basically the same as that used for simple dot matrix character printing (fig. 6.1) ie. the image is built up from an appropriate combination of dots. To achieve this the whole VDU screen is organised into rows and columns of individual "dot" positions called pixels. On a black and white screen each pixel can simply either be on (black) or off (white) (see fig. 6.5). On a colour screen each pixel may comprise a cluster of red, green and blue primary coloured dots which can be on and off in different combinations.

23. The more pixels there are, the more detail can be represented, ie. the higher the **resolution.** A screen with more than 30,000 pixels will normally be classified as a **high resolution graphics (HRG)** screen and will be capable of representing reasonably smooth curves and accurate drawings. Specialist graphics terminals are available, however, with more than 700,000 pixels.

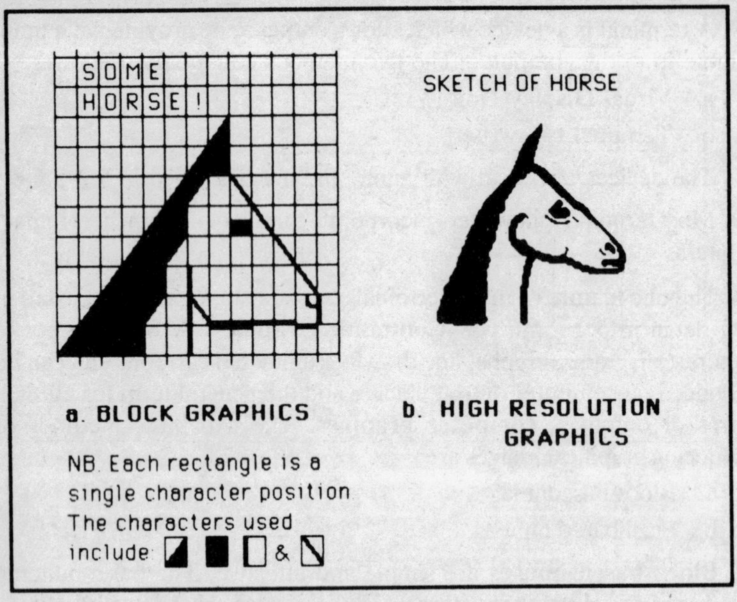

FIG. 6.5. COMPUTER GRAPHICS

24. Many graphics workstations provide software which allows pictures to be created by the use of devices such as mice (5.3h). For example, by holding down the button on the mouse while moving the mouse across the desk top a line may be drawn across the screen. The graphics facilities can also be used to allow the user of the device to operate it in simpler and more visually interesting ways. For example, alternative operations available to the user may be represented by simple graphical images called **icons** which the user can select by means of a mouse. A pointer on the screen is moved by using the mouse so that the pointer is above the required icon. The mouse button is then clicked to select the operation represented by the icon (see fig. 6.6).

MICROFORM RECORDERS AND MICROFORMS.

25. Microforms are photographically reduced documents on films. There are two types:

a. **Microfilm** – 16 mm roll film.

b. **Microfiche** – sheet film 105mm × 148mm.

Both types are produced in the same manner.

26. Output is written onto magnetic tape, which is then fed into a machine called a microform recorder which reads the magnetic tape and

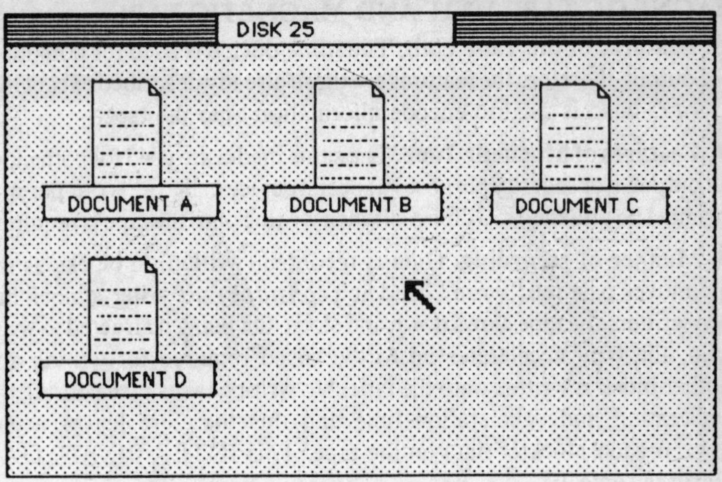

The figure shows a simple screen display of the contents of a diskette. Four documents, A, B, C and D are available for inspection. A particular document can be selected by moving the arrow over it by means of the mouse and then clicking the mouse's button.

Each document is represented by its own named icon.

FIG. 6.6. A GRAPHICAL DISPLAY USING ICONS AND A MOUSE.

copies the data onto microforms. The information can subsequently be inspected by using a viewer which projects onto a screen. Full-size copies can be printed if required. This technique is useful when large volumes of information are used internally, since economies can be made in stationery costs and storage space. It is usually referred to as COM (Computer Output on Microfilm/Microfiche).

27. Storage Capacities.

a. A typical 16mm roll will hold the equivalent of 3,000 A4 pages.

b. *One* typical microfiche will hold the equivalent of about 98 A4 pages.

MAGNETIC TAPE UNIT AND MAGNETIC TAPE.

28. Features of the Tape Unit. The *same* device is used for both input *and* output, therefore the features are those already described except that a"*write*"-head is used to encode information onto the tape.

29. Features of Magnetic Tape. The same media are used for both input and output. For security purposes a special device called a "write-permit" ring must be attached to a tape reel when writing onto the tape is required.

30. Manner of recording. Data is recorded (written) in blocks as the tape moves past the "write" head at a *constant* rate. After a block has been written, the tape slows down and stops. On being instructed to write again, the tape accelerates up to the speed required for writing and another block is written onto the tape. No writing takes place during the acceleration and deceleration time and this therefore leaves a gap between each block of data on the tape. This INTER BLOCK GAP measures some ¾".

FLOPPY DISK UNIT AND FLOPPY DISK (DISKETTE)

31. The *same* devices and media are used for both input *and* output. Details were given in 5.33.

32. It should be noted that the most common reason for producing output on magnetic tape or floppy disk is to enable subsequent re-input to the same computer, or to some other computer.

OTHER OUTPUT DEVICES AND MEDIA.

33. Graph Plotters. These devices are able to 'draw' diagrams or graphs by using a special pen control mechanism. They are mostly used for scientific or engineering purposes but are occasionally used in data processing.

34. Speech Output. In principle, spoken output should be an extremely useful medium. Unfortunately the devices currently available produce unnatural sounds and are limited to a few specialist applications. The situation is likely to improve over the next few years.

SUMMARY.

35. The *features* of the *main* hardware units and media for the output of data from the processor have been covered. They are:-

a. Printers – Single sheet or continuous stationery.

b. Terminals – VDU or terminal typewriter.

c. Microform recorder – Microfilm or Microfiche.

d. Magnetic tape unit – Magnetic tape.

e. Floppy disk unit – Floppy disk (diskette).

f. Others.

POINTS TO NOTE.

36. a. Line printers can print in *Optical Character Recognition* form, ie. allowing later re-input without further transcription.

b. Some matrix printers can be used to produce bar-coded strips eg. for use as stock labels.

QUESTIONS

1. Outline the possible advantages and disadvantages in using a VDU for output.

2. The data processing manager of a large computer installation is concerned about the high volume of printout from the installation's two printers and the subsequent paper storage problems in the user departments. As a consequence he is considering the use of 'Computer output on microform', COM, (Microfilm or Microfiche).

Explain what is meant by COM and the difference between microfilm and microfiche. give the advantages and disadvantages of the systems. (ICMA)

3. Explain the terms:

a. Computer graphics.

b. Pixel.

c. icon.

d. mouse.

7 Main Storage

INTRODUCTION.

1. Main storage plays a vital role in the operation of the central processor. It is wholly electronic and in close proximity to the rest of the processor. Therefore any data within main memory is almost instantly accessible to the processor. For this reason main memory is also called **Immediate Access Storage** (IAS), but is also called **internal storage** or **main memory.**

FUNCTION.

2. Main storage holds the program instructions and the data being processed. It will also store the intermediate results of processing awaiting transfer to the output devices.

PHYSICAL FEATURES.

3. Main storage in modern computers is constructed from semi-conductor memory chips (4.10). Features of the basic types of semi-conductor memory are covered here.

4. The most common type of semi-conductor memory is called **RAM** (**R**andom **A**ccess **M**emory). RAM is *volatile* ie. data is lost when the power supply is removed. A non volatile alternative to RAM is ROM (**R**ead **O**nly **M**emory), in which all contents are permanently set during manufacture.

5. Uses.

6. a. **ROM** usually forms a small proportion of main storage, and is used to store vital data and programs which need to be held within main storage *at all times.*

b. **RAM** usually forms the major proportion of main storage, and is used to store data and programs *temporarily* during those times when they are needed in main memory. It is constantly being re-used for different data items or programs as required.

REPRESENTATION OF DATA.

7. You have seen that data is represented in magnetic tape by "spots" of magnetism each magnetised in one of two possible directions (fig. 5.6). Inside the computer, data is represented electronically by storage cells which are either charged or discharged. In RAM the cells may be charged and discharged at will, and can thus be re-used to store different data items. In ROM the cells are *permanently* set to one state or the other.

THE BINARY SYSTEM.

8. As has just been indicated computer storage is based upon the two-state concept (eg. charged *or* discharged), and use is made of a numbering system which has TWO as its base – the BINARY system. Remember this is a *digital* computer.

9. Binary Representation of numbers. The basic points which you need to be aware of are detailed here:-

a. *All* numbering systems are based on *two* concepts:-
   i. Absolute value.
   ii. Positional value.

b. The decimal system has absolute values 0 to 9
and positional values allied to powers of 10

c. The binary system has absolute values 0 to 1
and positional values allied to powers of 2

EXAMPLE 1: The number '26' in *decimal* is made up thus:-

POSITIONAL VALUES	10^3 (1000)	10^2 (100)	10^1 (10)	10^0 (1)		10^1	10^0
Digit 6 in position 10^0				6	$= 6 \times 10^0 =$		6
Digit 2 in position 10^1			2		$= 2 \times 10^1 =$	2	0

= **DECIMAL** 26

EXAMPLE 2: The number 26 in *binary* is made up thus:-

POSITIONAL VALUES	2^4 (16)	2^3 (8)	2^2 (4)	2^1 (2)	2^0 (1)		2^4	2^3	2^2	2^1	2^0
Digit 0 in position 2^0					0	$= 0 \times 2^0$					0
Digit 1 in position 2^1				1		$= 1 \times 2^1$				1	0
Digit 0 in position 2^2			0			$= 0 \times 2^2$			0	0	0
Digit 1 in position 2^3		1				$= 1 \times 2^3$		1	0	0	0
Digit 1 in position 2^4	1					$= 1 \times 2^4$	1	0	0	0	0

= **BINARY** 1 1 0 1 0

Notes:

a. The 1's and 0's making up a binary number are referred to as *B*inary Dig*its* or BITS. Thus the number 26 is composed of 5 BITS.

b. Inside the computer's storage a '1' would be represented by an electronic "cell" in a chip being in an electrically charged state (or ON) and a 'O' by an electronic "cell" in a chip being in an electrically discharged state.

10. Binary Codes. Most computers nowadays use a derivation of the "pure" binary notation just described, in what may be called "Binary Coded" representations of data. These methods use a *fixed* number of binary digits **(bits),** in fact the basis for most systems is the use of the *just* 4 binary positional values only. Each *decimal digit* may be represented by four bits. (See Fig. 7.1).

DECIMAL VALUE	BINARY (PURE)	BINARY-CODED DECIMAL (assuming a 6 BIT CODE)		
0	0000			001010
1	0001			000001
2	0010			000010
3	0011			000011
4	0100			000100
5	0101			000101
6	0110			000110
7	0111			000111
8	1000			001000
9	1001			001001
10	1010		000001	001010
11	1011		000001	000001
22	10110		000010	000010
26	11010		000010	000110
34	100010		000011	000100
47	101111		000100	000111
90	1011010		001001	001010
631	1001110111	000110	000011	000001

FIG. 7.1. SELECTED EXAMPLES OF DECIMAL, BINARY AND BINARY-CODED DECIMAL CODES.

11. In order to accommodate 26 letters of the alphabet, and a certain number of "special" characters (ie. full stops, commas etc.) further bits are added to make a total of 6, 7 or 8 bits according to the coding system used.

12. The three most commonly used codes are:

a. **ASCII** (American Standard Code for Information Interchange).

A set of 128 characters is represented by this code. Most of the characters are used for normal printing purpose (see fig. 7.2) but a few characters are not printable and are used to control the hardware used in printing characters or transmitting them, eg. the Delete character included at the end of the table. The code shown in fig. 7.2 is actually the British version of the printable characters because the "£" character has been substituted for the "#" character which is present in the standard American version as is normal for British Data Processing applications.

BINARY CODE	ASCII CHARACTER	BINARY CODE	ASCII CHARACTER	BINARY CODE	ASCII CHARACTER
0010 0000	.	0011 0000	0	0100 0000	@
0010 0001	!	0011 0001	1	0100 0001	A
0010 0010	"	0011 0010	2	0100 0010	B
0010 0011	£	0011 0011	3	0100 0011	C
0010 0100	$	0011 0100	4	0100 0100	D
0010 0101	%	0011 0101	5	0100 0101	E
0010 0110	&	0011 0110	6	0100 0110	F
0010 0111	'	0011 0111	7	0100 0111	G
0010 1000	(	0011 1000	8	0100 1000	H
0010 1001	)	0011 1001	9	0100 1001	I
0010 1010	*	0011 1010	:	0100 1010	J
0010 1011	+	0011 1011	;	0100 1011	K
0010 1100	,	0011 1100	<	0100 1100	L
0010 1101	–	0011 1101	=	0100 1101	M
0010 1110	.	0011 1110	>	0100 1110	N
0010 1111	/	0011 1111	?	0100 1111	O

BINARY CODE	ASCII CHARACTER	BINARY CODE	ASCII CHARACTER	BINARY CODE	ASCII CHARACTER
0101 0000	P	0110 0000	\	0111 0000	p
0101 0001	Q	0110 0001	a	0111 0001	q
0101 0010	R	0110 0010	b	0111 0010	r
0101 0011	S	0110 0011	c	0111 0011	s
0101 0100	T	0110 0100	d	0111 0100	t
0101 0101	U	0110 0101	e	0111 0101	u
0101 0110	V	0110 0110	f	0111 0110	v
0101 0111	W	0110 0111	g	0111 0111	w
0101 1000	X	0110 1000	h	0111 1000	x
0101 1001	Y	0110 1001	i	0111 1001	y
0101 1010	Z	0110 1010	j	0111 1010	z
0101 1011	[	0110 1011	k	0111 1011	{
0101 1100	\	0110 1100	l	0111 1100	¦
0101 1101	]	0110 1101	m	0111 1101	}
0101 1110	^	0110 1110	n	0111 1110	~
0101 1111	_	0110 1111	o	0111 1111	del

FIG. 7.2. THE ASCII CHARACTER SET

b. **BCD** (BINARY CODED DECIMAL) – a 6-bit code (see Fig. 7.3a).

This code is by far the least common of the three listed here.

c. **EBCDIC** (Extended Binary Coded Decimal Interchange Code) -an 8-bit code. (Sometimes called 8-bit ASCII) (see Fig. 7.3b).

This code is very widely used on large computers especially by IBM.

ALPHA CHARACTER	BINARY CODE	ALPHA CHARACTER	BINARY CODE	ALPHA CHARACTER	BINARY CODE
A	11 0001	J	10 0001	–	–
B	11 0010	K	10 0010	S	01 0010
C	11 0011	L	10 0011	T	01 0011
D	11 0100	M	10 0100	U	01 0100
E	11 0101	N	10 0101	V	01 0101
F	11 0110	O	10 0110	W	01 0110
G	11 0111	P	10 0111	X	01 0111
H	11 1000	Q	10 1000	Y	01 1000
I	11 1001	R	10 1001	Z	01 1001

a. REPRESENTATION OF CHARACTERS IN BCD.

ALPHA CHARACTER	BINARY CODE	ALPHA CHARACTER	BINARY CODE	ALPHA CHARACTER	BINARY CODE
A	1100 0001	J	1101 0001	–	–
B	1100 0010	K	1101 0010	S	1110 0010
C	1100 0011	L	1101 0011	T	1110 0011
D	1100 0100	M	1101 0100	U	1110 0100
E	1100 0101	N	1101 0101	V	1110 0101
F	1100 0110	O	1101 0110	W	1110 0110
G	1100 0111	P	1101 0111	X	1110 0111
H	1100 1000	Q	1101 1000	Y	1110 1000
I	1100 1001	R	1101 1001	Z	1110 1001

b. REPRESENTATION OF CHARACTERS IN EBCDIC.

FIG. 7.3.

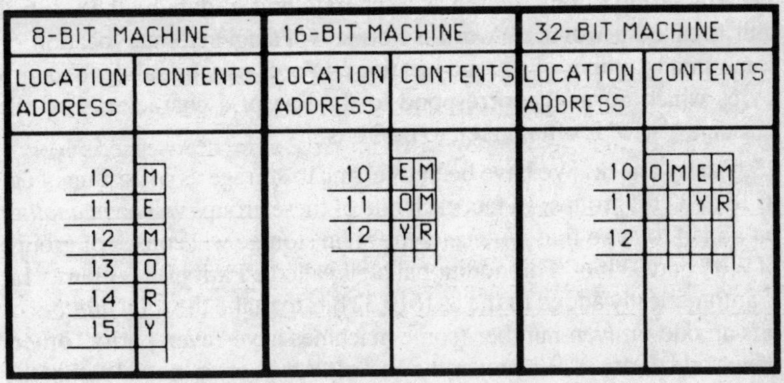
8-BIT MACHINE
16-BIT MACHINE
32-BIT MACHINE
LOCATION ADDRESS
CONTENTS
LOCATION ADDRESS
CONTENTS
LOCATION ADDRESS
CONTENTS
10 M
11 E
12 M
13 O
14 R
15 Y
10 E M
11 O M
12 Y R
10 O M E M
11 Y R
12

FIG. 7.4. ALTERNATIVE STORAGE DESIGNS

ALTERNATIVE STORAGE DESIGNS.

13. Since bits need to be grouped together, in order to represent numbers or characters, main storage is organised that way. There are numerous ways in which this is done in practice but the basic ideas should be covered in sufficient detail by the following examples:

a. In the smaller microcomputers bits are grouped together 8 at a time, ie. in semi-conductor memory the storage cells in RAM or ROM are constructed using groups of 8 cells. Each group of 8-bits is a separate entity called a **storage location** and can be addressed by the Control Unit. Every storage location has its own unique address called its **location address** and can be addressed independently in this way. A single storage location is large enough to hold one ASCII character, one BCD character, EBCDIC character or two BCD numeric values. Microcomputer using this method of storage are often referred to as 8-bit microcomputers. (see Fig. 7.4).

b. On larger microcomputers and smaller minicomputers the storage locations are normally at least 12 bits long. A common size for a memory location is 16-bits and computers with memory locations of this size are called 16-bit computers. A single storage location on a 16-bit computer will be able to hold two characters (eg. ASCII or EBCDIC) and will normally *"pack"* characters two to a location for that reason (see Fig. 7.4). Such computers usually have facilities for accessing the right half and left half of each word separately in order to handle individual characters.

c. 32-bit storage locations are found on the larger minicomputers and smaller mainframe computers. Such computers normally have a variety of ways of accessing all or part of each memory location.

14. Any group of bits treated as a separate unit of data by the Control unit is called a **word.** A word is normally a single storage location or some small number of storage locations. Words may be subdivided into **bytes** which normally correspond to the size of a character. For this reason a "byte" is often taken to be 8 bits.

15. Parity check. We have been referring to storage as consisting of eg. 8, 16 or 32 bit groups. In fact each one of these groups will have *another* bit added to it, so that *physically* the main storage will consist of groups of 7, 17 and 33 bits. This additional bit is called a Parity Bit. A parity bit is automatically added to the 8, 16 or 32 bits to make the total *number* of bits an odd or even number (some machines have "even parity" others have "odd parity"). Whenever the character byte etc is moved within the computer, a check is automatically made on the *number* of bits at the receiving end. This is to ensure no bit is "lost" in transmission. Thus in odd parity machines (ie. the total number of bits (including parity-bit) in every character adds up to an odd number) if an even number of bits were counted on the receiving end it indicates that the machine is malfunctioning. See Fig. 7.5 which has adopted the "odd" parity system.

Note: Small computers do not always incorporate parity checking systems which can bring their reliability into question in some situations.

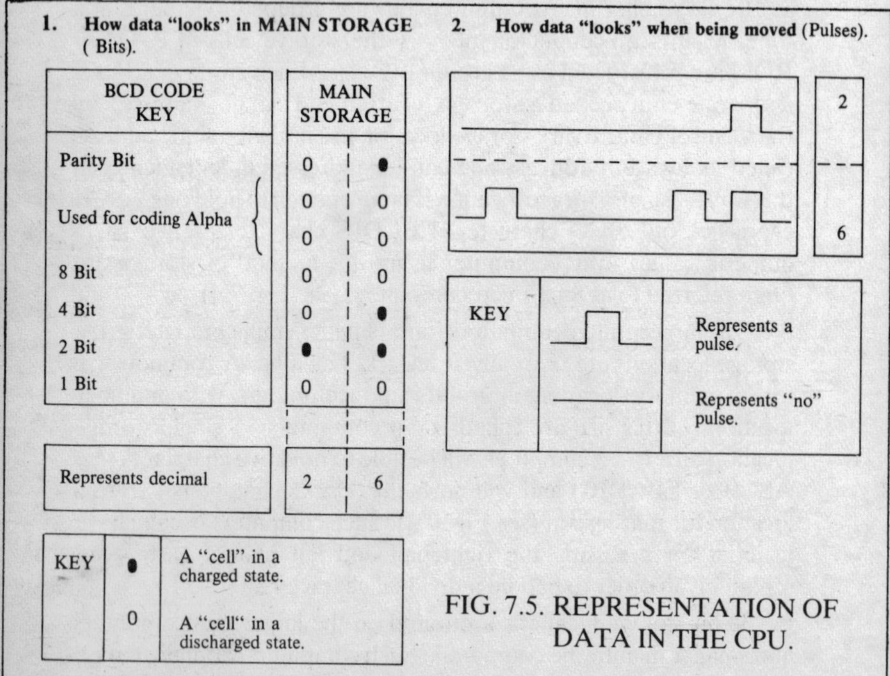

FIG. 7.5. REPRESENTATION OF DATA IN THE CPU.

16. How main storage operates. Once data is *read* into storage from an input unit it remains there (ie. the particular cells are charged or discharged) until it is replaced by other data. Data read into the same locations will destroy what was there previously (rather like the latest recording you make on your tape recorder will destroy the previous one). As internal storage is limited and only used for holding data currently worked on, the *contents* of the storage locations will be continually changing. Storage locations can in some ways be regarded as pigeon holes in a mail room. Each pigeon hole (storage location) is addressable and will contain different data depending on what was last put in it.

ACCESS TIME.

17. Each item of data stored in main storage whether stored as characters, bytes or words is accessible to the control unit on a completely random basis. The speed with which this access is made is so fast as to be called *immediate.* eg. accessible in less than one millionth of one second.

STORAGE CAPACITY.

18. Storage sizes are sometimes expressed in terms of 'K' ($K = 2^{10} = 1024$). eg. a typical 8-bit microcomputer may have a main storage capacity of 32K bytes. Larger capacities are sometimes expressed in terms of **megabytes** (mega for a million).

SUMMARY.

19. a. Main storage is wholly electronic, and consequently very fast and reliable.

b. Data is almost instantly accessible to the processor when held in main storage.

c. Data *must* be transferred to main storage before it can be processed by the processor. Programs *must* be transferred to main storage before they may be executed.

d. Semi-conductor memory (RAM and ROM) are most commonly used in main storage.

e. The 'Character', 'Byte' or 'Word' storage location has been likened to pigeon holes. The *contents* of the locations will continually change.

f. Data may be represented in the form of binary codes. Three common code conventions are.

i. BCD
ii. ASCII
iii. EBCDIC.

POINTS TO NOTE.

20. a. Although other *types* of main storage exist, the concepts are basically the same, ie. they possess the ability to address individual locations which can contain characters or numbers.

b. A common manufacturing process used to produce semi-conductor devices such as memory chips is known as MOS (Metal-Oxide Semi-conductor) technology. MOS memory is therefore the main replacement of core storage.

c. Pure binary number representations (Fig. 7.1) associated with a word of 32 bits would have as many leading 0's as were required to make up the number of bits to 32.

QUESTIONS.

1. Explain the following terms as they relate to the representation of data in a computer:

a. bit
b. byte
c. binary coded decimal
d. word.
(ACA)

2. Explain the basic difference between an 8-bit computer and a 16-bit computer.

8 Auxiliary or Backing Storage

INTRODUCTION.

1. Ideally, all data for processing should be stored in main storage so that all internal operations can be carried out at maximum speed. As it is, main storage is relatively expensive and is therefore only used for storing the necessary instructions and the data currently being operated on. Auxiliary storage is provided for the mass storage of programs and files, ie. those programs and files not currently being operated on but which will be transferred to the main storage when required.

2. Although data in the form of files held on auxiliary storage is not immediately accessible, as it would be if held in main storage, it is never the less within the computer system. It can therefore serve an important purpose as part of a pool of maintained and accessible data.

3. There are many media for auxiliary storage. The *main* media are described here, most are in magnetic form:

a. Magnetic tape unit – magnetic tape.

b. Magnetic disk unit – magnetic disk.

c. Magnetics diskette unit – magnetic diskette (floppy disk).

d. Optical disk unit – optical disk.

e. Solid state storage devices.

f. Mass storage devices and media.

g. Other auxiliary storage devices and media.

MAGNETIC TAPE UNIT AND MAGNETIC TAPE.

4. In addition to its role as an input/output medium, magnetic tape is also used as an auxiliary storage medium. The devices and media have already been explained.

NB. Tape cassettes and tape cartridges are smaller versions which work on broadly similar principles, but the tapes are narrower and are held in small plastic cases.

EXCHANGEABLE MAGNETIC DISK UNIT AND MAGNETIC DISK PACK.

5. a. **Features of an Exchangeable Disk Unit.**

i. The disk unit is the device in which the disk pack is placed. The disk*pack* is placed into the *unit* and connects with the drive mechanism.

ii. Once the pack is loaded into the unit the read/write

mechanism, located inside the unit, positions itself over the first track of each surface. The mechanism consists of a number of arms at the ends of which there is a read/write head for each surface. All arms are fixed together and all move together as one when accessing a surface on the disk pack. See Fig. 8.1.

iii. The disk when loaded is driven at a high number of revolutions (several thousand) per minute and access can only be made to its surfaces when the disk revolves.

b. **Features of an Exchangeable Disk Pack.**

i. Disks are of a size and shape similar to a long playing record.

ii. The surfaces of each disk are of a magnetisable material (except the outer-most surfaces of a pack which are purely protective). Thus there are 10 recording surfaces in a 6 disk pack and 20 in an 11 disk pack.

iii. Each surface is divided into a number of *concentric tracks* (typically 200).

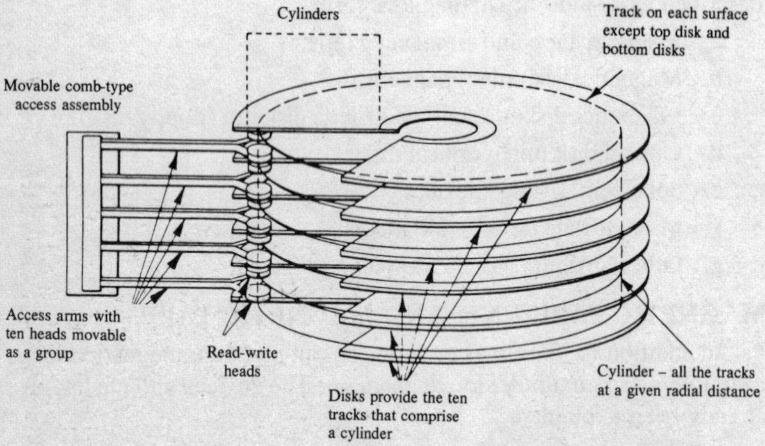

FIG. 8.1. MAGNETIC DISK.

d. The disks within a *pack* are inseparable ie. the pack, of either 6 or 11 disks, is *always* used as a single unit.

e. The latest models of disk pack can store 200 million characters. Disks with a capacity of 30 to 60 million characters are now common.

Exchangeable Disk – Magnetic Tape Units in background (ICL)

FIXED MAGNETIC DISK UNIT AND MAGNETIC DISK.

6. a. **Features of a Fixed Disk Unit.**

i. The unit houses a number of non-removeable disks.

ii. It has read/write heads, either located on the end of 'arms' (as with exchangeable disks) or serving each track (as with the magnetic drum).

iii. It has a motor that rotates the drive at a high constant rate but because of its size, the speed will be slower than that of exchangeable disk units.

b. **Features of a Fixed Disk.**

The older systems are generally *larger* than disks in an exchangeable disk pack. Some modern computers use a single fixed disk which is the same size as the exchangeable disk, for storing programs.

WINCHESTER DISKS.

7. "Winchester" technology disks were developed by IBM just a few years ago in order to overcome some problems associated with established disk technology. Winchester disks are fixed disks in hermetically sealed disk units and have robust mechanical features. They have toughened surfaces, and read/write heads which move even closer to the disk surface. The heads actually 'land' on the disks surface when the disk finally stops! They can operate in adverse environments which are dusty or humid, have greater reliability and also have greater storage capacities in comparison with the earlier technology disks of the same size.

MAGNETIC DISKETTE UNIT AND MAGNETIC DISKETTE (FLOPPY DISK)

8. In addition to its role as an input/output medium, magnetic diskette is also used as an auxiliary storage medium. However, its use for this purpose is usually limited to small microcomputer based systems. The devices and media have already been explained.

9. One variation on the diskette which has become popular in recent years is the **microfloppy** disk. These are normally 3¼ inches in diameter and are used on a variety of small microcomputer based systems and workstations eg. the Apple Macintosh or the ACT Apricot. They are generally regarded as an improvement over the normal 8 inches and 5¼ inch diskettes because of these features (see Fig. 8.2):

a. They have a more rugged plastic cover which keeps the whole disk surface covered and protected when not in use.

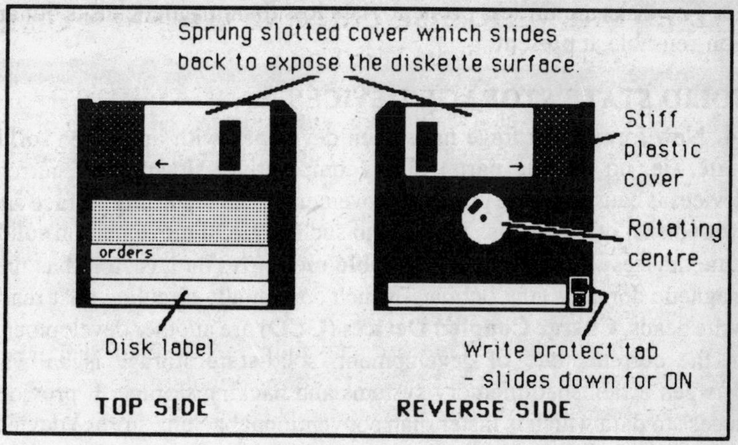

FIG. 8.2. 3¼" MICROFLOPPY DISK

b. The cover has a slot giving the disk drive heads access to the disk which is automatically slid open while the diskette is inserted into the drive but otherwise is held closed against dust and dirt by a tiny spring.

c. The microfloppies have storage capacities comparable with those of their larger counterparts and are thus more space efficient.

OPTICAL DISK UNIT AND OPTICAL DISK.

10. These devices and media have been under development for many years but have only recently become available as marketable products. They work on a similar principle to that used for the domestic compact disc which has become very popular as a replacement for the LP record.

11. Features of the Disk Unit.

a. The device is similar in appearance to a fixed magnetic disk unit but data is written onto the disk by burning a permanent pattern into the surface of the disk by means of a high precision laser beam.

b. Data is read back by using the laser at lower intensity and detecting the pattern of light reflected from the beam by the surface of the disk.

12. Features of the Disk.

A typical disk has a surface of 40,000 tracks each divided into 25 sectors and a total capacity of a staggering one gigabyte (ie. 1000 million characters).

13. The disks are far less prone to data loss than magnetic disks but are non-reusable at present.

SOLID STATE STORAGE DEVICES

14. New forms of storage have been developed with are called **solid-state.** (ie. no moving parts). The (comparative) slowness of current devices is caused by the physical movement of the recording surface and (with disks) of the heads. There is no such physical movement in solid-state devices. For example, in **'bubble memories'** data is stored as tiny magnetic domains (the bubbles) which continually circulate past read/write heads. **Charge Coupled Devices (CCD)** are another development. In the current state of development, solid-state storage is halfway between established memory systems and backing storage. It provides access to data which is faster than conventional backing storage devices but slower than memory. On the other hand, it has a capacity higher than memory but lower than backing storage.

15. Solid state backing storage has for some time looked poised to supersede disk storage, but so far it has not been able to compete in terms of cost.

MASS STORAGE DEVICES AND MEDIA.

16. Some large corporations and government agencies have a need for vast data storage capacities. This need can be met by mass storage devices. These devices are "automated libraries" of disk and tape cartridges. The total capacity of such a system may be as much as 500 billion bytes! Further detail is not merited.

OTHER AUXILIARY STORAGE DEVICES AND MEDIA.

17. There are many other forms of auxiliary storage in use today, many of them aimed at specialist uses. One worth mentioning because from its name it is easy to confuse with the microfloppy, is the **microdrive** developed by Sinclair Research Limited for use on home computers. The microdrive does not use a disk but uses a long loop of magnetic tape held in a special cartridge.

18. RAM disks (also called silicon disks) are popular on personal computers and workstations. They are not disks at all in fact. Rather, they are RAM memory being used as if it was a diskette. The advantage is fast performance but any data to be kept must be copied onto a magnetic disk before the computer is switched off because RAM disks are volatile. Thus the uses of RAM disks are limited.

SUMMARY.

19. a. Auxiliary storage is used, as its name suggests, to supplement main storage.

b. The Physical features *only* have been discussed.

c. The main auxiliary storage media is mainly in *magnetic* form.

d. The main hardware devices and media for Auxiliary Storage are:-

i. Magnetic tape unit – Magnetic tape.
ii. Magnetic disk unit – Magnetic disk.
iii. Magnetic diskette unit – Magnetic diskette (floppy disk).
iv. Optical disk unit – Optical disk.
v. Solid state storage media.
vi. Mass storage devices and media.
vii. Other auxiliary storage devices and media. The comparative performance of backing storage media/devices is shown in the table on page 82.

POINTS TO NOTE.

20. a. Note the terms "on-line" and "off-line". "On-line" means being accessible to and under the control of, the processor. Conversely, "off-line" means *not* accessible to, or under the control of, the processor. Thus, *fixed* magnetic disks are *permanently* "on-line"; a magnetic tape reel or an exchangeable magnetic disk pack is "on-line" when placed in its respective units, but "off-line" when stored away from the computer; terminals, *wherever* their physical location, are said to be "on-line" when directly linked to the processor.

b. On exchangeable disks, the read/write heads serving each *surface* will be positioned over the *same relative track* on *each surface* because the arms on which they are fixed move simultaneously.

c. In any answer involving magnetic disks, you should concentrate on the *exchangeable* disk as this is the most commonly used.

d. The devices and media have been separated for ease of explanation. It should be noted however that in the case of *fixed* disk, the media are permanently fixed to the device, and therefore they are not talked of as being separate.

e. Auxiliary storage is also referred to as *backing storage.*

f. Input, output and storage devices are referred to collectively as peripheral devices.

g. Some disk packs are produced in side loading version containing just one or two platters. They are normally called **disk cartridges.**

Devices and Medium	Typical Access Times	Typical Storage Capacities	Typical Transfer Rates	Types of Stoage SAS (Serial Access Storage) DAS (Direct Access Storage)	Where Used as a Backing Storage Medium (see earlier notes on input/output)
1. Magnetic tape Cassette or tape Cartridge.	[A search is required – several minutes).]	Up to 145,000 ch (cartridge 256,000 ch).	10–3,000 cps (cartridge 3,000 cps).	SAS	Used on small microcomputer based systems. Cartridge used on small minicomputers sometimes.
2. Floppy-disk (Diskette).	260 ms	180 k bytes to 1.25 M bytes.	24,000 cps.	DAS	Used on microcomputer based systems.
3. Magnetic Tape.	[A search is required – several minutes.]	40 M bytes.	160,000 cps.	SAS	Used on minicomputer and mainframe computer systems.
4. Magnetic Disk (Hard Disk) (Exchangeable) (See notes below).	60 ms	60 M bytes.	312,000 cps.	DAS	Used on minicomputer and mainframe computer systems.
5. Optical Disk	60 ms	1,000 M bytes.	320,000 cps.	DAS	Used on minicomputers and mainframe computers.

Some removable Winchester disks are available in cartridge form.

h. Simplified versions of magnetic tape or cartridge units known as **"streamers"** may be used to create "backup copies" from Winchester disks.

QUESTIONS.

1. *Describe a microfloppy disk and explain any advantages which it may have over a 5¼" diskette.*

2. *Why is storage divided into main storage and backing storage?*

9 The Architecture of Micro, Mini and Mainframe Computers

INTRODUCTION.

1. Just as the basic elements of a human dwelling (kitchen, bedroom, bathroom etc.) are constructed and combined in ways which depend upon the type of dwelling required (flat, detached house, mansion etc.), so the basic hardware elements of a computer system are constructed and combined into "architectural forms" which depend upon the type of computer required. The computer counterpart to the single dwelling (eg. the detached house) is a "stand alone machine" with a single processor and no connection to any other computer. This chapter starts by describing the basic features of an individual processor, including the function and operation of its elements.

2. Human dwellings are often combined into larger structures (eg. terraced houses, blocks of flats etc.) and likewise individual computers are frequently combined into large systems with multiple processors (eg. "distributed systems"). This chapter gives a description of the hardware features of the various types of modern computer system.

BASIC FEATURES OF THE PROCESSOR.

3. The diagram of the elements of a computer system (Fig. 3.1) shows the processor as consisting of two parts:-

a. The control unit.

b. The arithmetic and logic unit.

4. The function of the processor is to control the sequence of operations, to give commands to all parts of the computer system, and to carry out the necessary processing.

5. The processor controls the input of data into main storage, processes the data, passes the results to main storage and then sends the results from main storage to output devices of various types.

6. All movements within the processor are wholly *electronic,* which is also true of main storage but not of other hardware.

CONTROL UNIT.

7. Functions. The Control Unit has been likened to the conductor of an orchestra, because of the co-ordinating and controlling function it carries out. It is the nerve centre of the computer, controlling all hardware operations, ie. those of the input-output units, storage and of the processor itself.

8. How it operates. It fetches the requisite instruction from main storage, *stores* it in a number of special registers, *interprets* the instruction and causes the instruction *to be executed* by giving signals (or commands) to the appropriate hardware devices.

ARITHMETIC AND LOGIC UNIT (ALU).

9. Function. The ALU has two main functions:-

a. It carries out the arithmetic, ie. add, subtract, multiply, divide.

b. It also performs certain "logical" operations, eg. the comparison of two numbers to determine which is the greater.

10. How it operates.

a. The various factors to be processed are taken from main storage as directed by the Control Unit, and stored in its registers. They are then added etc. together and the results placed back in main storage. Basically most computers only "add". Subtraction is achieved by "complementing and adding". Division is carried out by successive complementing, adding (ie. = to subtraction) and shifting. Multiplication is achieved by shifting and adding.

b. Logical operations are virtually the same arithmetical process, but the results (say of subtracting one number from another) will determine different courses of action to be taken by the Control Unit. This gives the computer its decision taking ability.

SYSTEM ARCHITECTURE.

11. Although the basic elements of the computer are essentially the same for almost all digital computers, there are variations in construction which reflect the differing ways in which computers are used. As indicated in the introduction the style of construction and organisation of the many parts of a computer are its "architecture".

12. In order to recognise the characteristics of the different types of modern computer systems, and to understand how these systems are used, some basic features of computer architecture must be understood.

13. Modular Construction. The principles of modular construction were established in the 1960s and have been developed through to the present day. Broadly speaking, modules are standard components which can be combined together in a variety of ways.

14. Busses. Busses provide a standardised way of interconnecting modules. Just as the ring main electrical circuit in a house has standard sockets into which a variety of electrical appliances may be plugged, a bus has slots with multiple electrical contacts into which modular components can be placed.

15. Busses are used to convey power, data and control signals.

ARCHITECTURE OF A MICRO COMPUTER SYSTEM.

16. In order to illustrate the concepts just introduced, the architecture of a small computer system is shown here (Fig. 9.1). A typical configuration of a micro-computer based system is shown in the diagram. Provided that sufficient slots are present in the bus, other units can be plugged in eg. a Winchester disk drive may be added.

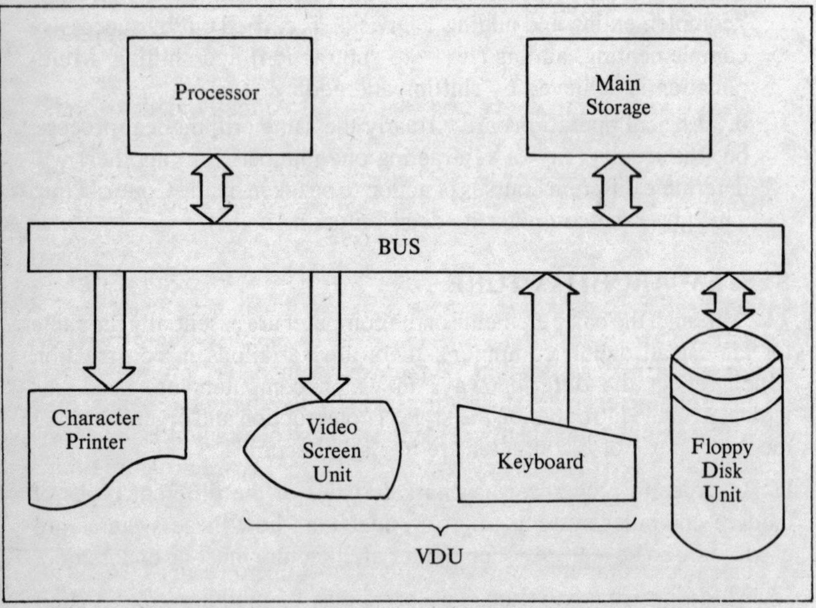

FIG. 9.1. SIMPLIFIED TYPICAL ARCHITECTURE OF A SMALL MICRO COMPUTER BASED SYSTEM.

17. Memory Organisation. In a small system like that shown in Fig. 9.1 the main storage may be organised as shown in Fig. 9.2.

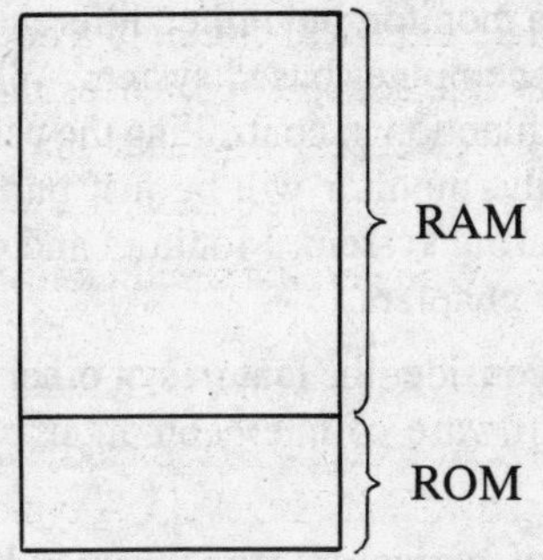

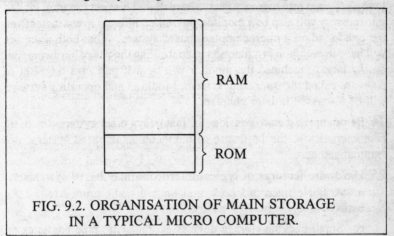

FIG. 9.2. ORGANISATION OF MAIN STORAGE IN A TYPICAL MICRO COMPUTER.

18. Firmware. Programs held in ROM are called **firmware.** They are stored permanently in the ROM and are ready for use when the computer is switched on.

19. When a microcomputer is switched on it is normally made to start executing the instructions held in ROM. This either takes place automatically as part of switching on, or sometimes a "boot" button has to be pressed too. This is known as a "booting up the system".

20. On small microcomputer based systems like the one shown in figure 9.1 the firmware ROM normally contains a special program called a **monitor** which starts being executed on switchon and "boot up". Monitors differ greatly from one machine to another but a typical monitor will display a "prompt" on the video screen. (A "prompt" may be a single character eg. "*" to let the user know the computer is ready for input). The monitor may then accept interpret and obey a limited number of commands typed in at the keyboard. eg. "L" for Load a program from the floppy disk (or maybe from a tape cassette) or "X" to execute a program once it has been loaded.

21. Some microcomputers may have much more firmware in ROM even to the extent of being able to accept "interpret" and execute programs written in a programming language such as BASIC. The microcomputer is then said to have BASIC in ROM.

22. Further details of monitors and the interpretation and execution of languages such as BASIC will be given in later chapters.

23. On larger computers such as mini computers and main-frames a boot operation may cause a special "loader program" in firmware ROM to load a program into memory from a hard disk. This first program loaded into memory will also be a monitor, but rather different in character from the one found on a microcomputer based system. What both monitors will have in common is a function in controlling the use of hardware, but on the larger machines the monitor will be just part of a large set of software called the **operating system.** Monitors and operating systems will be discussed in later chapters.

24. Before moving on to consider the features of other systems the basic characteristics of the hardware of microcomputer based systems are summarised here.

25. Hardware features of typical microcomputer based systems:-

a. A single microprocessor and limited main storage (eg. 128K bytes).

b. Small backing storage devices eg. magnetic tape cassettes on very small machines, dual floppy disks on the majority of machines, and small Winchester disks on the larger models.

c. Low speed printers eg. dot matrix or daisywheel character printers.

d. *Usually* a single VDU, occasionally as many as six or eight VDU's.

NB. In some machines several items may be built into a single cabinet eg. the VDU may also house the processor and disk drives.

THE ARCHITECTURE OF MINI AND MAIN FRAME COMPUTER SYSTEMS.

26. The smaller mini-computer systems can be indistinguishable from the larger micro-computer based systems. However, a typical mini-computer has noticably different features from a microcomputer and is essentially a scaled down version of its 'big brother' the main frame computer.

27. Hardware features of a typical minicomputer systems:-

a. Medium size processor and main storage. ie. sufficient to handle the data processing needs of a number of terminals (eg. 1 Megabyte of main storage).

b. Hard disk storage, and magnetic tape storage in some cases.

c. Line printer. eg. 300 lpm versions.

d. Multiple terminals. eg. 20 VDUs or more.

28. It is also difficult to draw a line of demarcation between the larger mini-computers and small main frame computers. The hardware in a main frame may be similar to the hardware in a mini-computer, but there is usually much more of it eg.

a. Very large processors with massive amounts of main storage eg. hundreds of megabytes.

b. Large number of magnetic disk and tape units.

c. High speed line printers eg. 2000 lpm.

d. The ability to support large numbers of terminals eg. 100 or more VDUs.

29. Front End Processors (FEPs). Many main frame computers incorporate minicomputers which are used to handle input and output from various terminals, thus relieving the main computer of some tasks associated with input and output. The minicomputer being used for this purpose is called a Front End Processor (FEP).

30. The front end processor may not only deal with terminals close to the main computer it may also deal with *remote* terminals which are situated at the end of data transmission lines.

MULTI-PROCESSOR SYSTEMS.

31. Traditionally, multi-processor systems have been very large computers with two or more main processors and large main storage which has been wholly or partially shared. This arrangement not only serves to handle a large processing load but also provides backup in the case of breakdown. (ie. if one processor fails the system can continue to operate). Such systems are called **multi-processing systems** (see Fig. 9.3).

32. In recent years other ways of exploiting a multiple number of processors within a single system have been devised. At the lower end of the system size range it is common to have individual microcomputers which contain several microprocessors, eg. one for the processing, one to handle the screen graphics, one inside the diskette drive, and so on. On larger systems a number of autonamous or semi-autonamous computers may be interconnected in a network to form a single distributed system. However, the subject of distributed systems and networks is rather too large to be discussed within this chapter and has therefore been left for separate discussion in the next chapter.

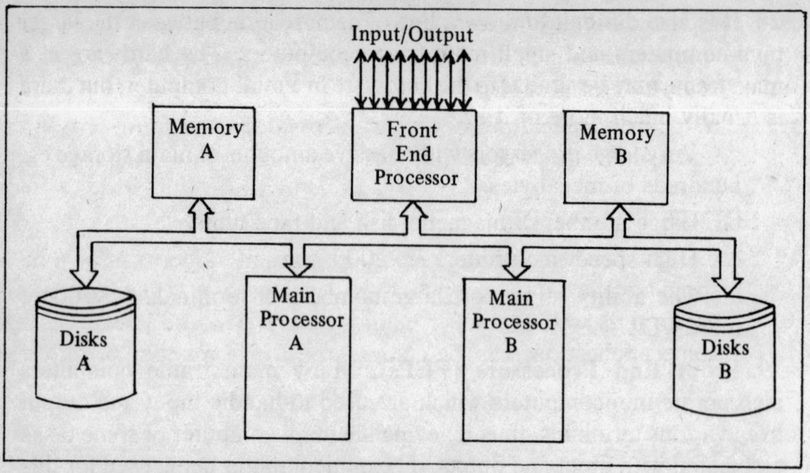

FIG. 9.3. A MULTIPROCESSING SYSTEM WITH FRONT END PROCESSOR AND DUPLICATED DISK STORAGE AND MEMORY.

NEWER ARCHITECTURAL FEATURES.

33. Cache Memories. These are high speed RAMs which work at speeds which match the processor. They are used to hold data which has recently been accessed from disk in anticipation of its use in the near future. Subsequent accesses if they occur will be fast because the disk will not require accessing again. The least accessed data in cache memory is replaced by newly accessed data.

34. Content Addressable Storage (CAS). This storage works in a different way from normal storage. Suppose that each word in memory can hold 4 characters and that location 200 contains "FRED". In normal storage the address, 200 would be used to load "FRED". In content addressable memory "FRED" would be passed along a data bus and the memory would pass 200 back indicating the location of "FRED". Thus a paragraph of stored text could be retrieved by supplying a word contained in the paragraph. CAS is very useful for rapid data selection or retrieval but is expensive at present.

SUMMARY.

35. a. The processor has no mechanically moving parts. Electronic pulses moving at nearly the speed of light are used in data representation.

b. Control Unit and the Arithmetic and Logic Unit are the constituent parts of the processor.

c. Modern computer "architecture" is characterised by *modular components* which are linked together in a building block fashion, often by means of *busses.*

d. Hardware features of typical micro-computers, mini-computers and main frames were described.

POINTS TO NOTE.

36. a. The fact that some larger micro-computers perform as well as some smaller mini-computers and some larger mini-computers perform as well as smaller main frames is just one indication that some applications can be computerised in a number of different ways.

QUESTIONS.

1. What are the essential differences between mainframe, mini and micro-computers? Give examples where each would be used to the best advantage. (IDPM Part 1)

10 Communications Equipment and Systems Interconnection

INTRODUCTION.

1. This chapter describes the basic types of hardware used for communication between computer systems and also describes the ways in which the interconnections may be made. Descriptions of other forms of communication equipment are included where their uses include IT applications areas related to data processing. The chapter starts with traditional forms of communication based upon the telephone system and then goes on to discuss more modern techniques including computer networks. Applications of this technology and specialist communication services are not included here but are described in chapter 18.

2. Some of the basic features of data communications systems were introduced in 4.40 – 4.52 by means of a variety of typical examples. Here we will go through the different types of system in turn in more detail.

TRADITIONAL METHODS.

3. Of the two long established methods of telecommunications, telephone and telex the one which has for a long time been used for a variety of forms of data transmission is the telephone system.

4. It will prove useful to remind ourselves of some of the familiar and significant features of the telephone system. Two key features are:

a. It is **circuit switching** system, ie. when a call is placed a circuit is established by the switching equipment in the exchange and then the circuit is maintained for the duration of the call.

b. The electrical signal transmitted is the direct **analog** of the sound at the receiver, albeit of a quality far short of hi-fi!

5. The simplest forms of data transmission involve the connection of terminals to a computer via a telephone line. In order to use the telephone link the *digital* signals of the terminal and computer must be converted into *analog* form in order to be transmitted along the telephone line. This can be done by a device called a **MODEM,** short for **MOD**ulator – **DEM**odulator, (see Fig. 10.1). The modem plugs directly into the telephone wall socket in the home, office or computer room.

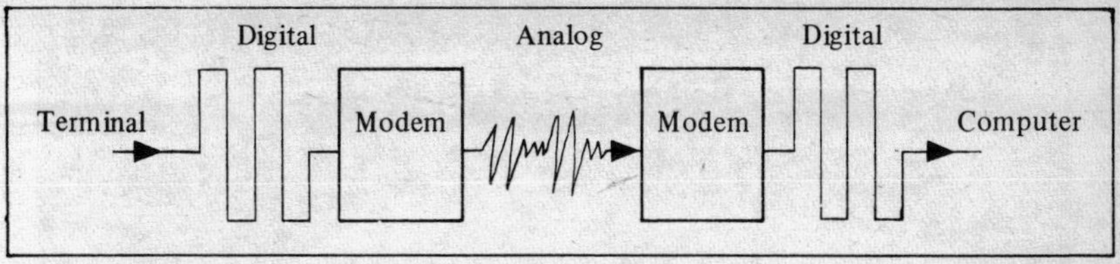

FIG. 10.1. DATA TRANSMISSION AND THE USE OF MODEMS.

6. In the absense of a modem in the vicinity of the terminal a portable device known as an **acoustic coupler** may be used instead (see Fig. 10.2). Modern acoustic couplers are very compact and can be very handy to use in conjuction with portable microcomputers or data collection devices. However, they tend to be slightly more error prone than modems.

7. A standard domestic telephone line used in conjunction with these simple devices is normally able to transmit data quite reliably at speeds up to about 30 characters per second. With relatively modest upgrading of the equipment and telephone line used it is possible to push the speeds up to approximately 120 characters per second.

8. Data transmission is not confined to the public telephone system. A private telephone system may be used too. Also, it is possible to set up permanently wired data transmission lines instead of dial-up lines. These lines, which are often leased or rented, can be set up to transmit data at much higher speeds than can be achieved over the standard telephone line, over 1000 characters per second in some cases.

9. Data transmission lines tend to be quite costly in comparison with the equipment used so there is a considerable advantage in using a technique called **multiplexing** which makes it possible for the same line to be used for a number of separate signals at the same time. Signals are transmitted

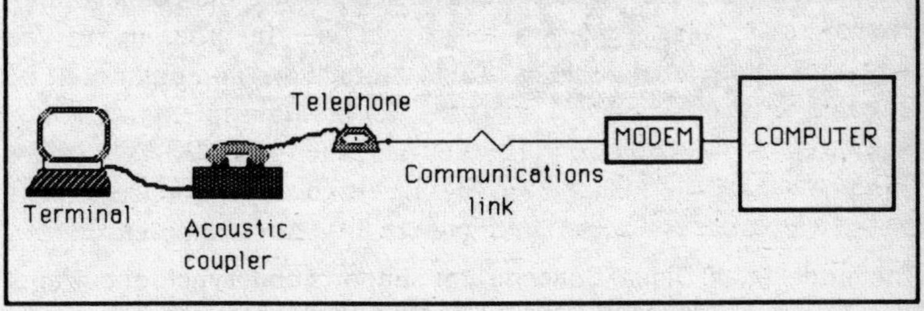

FIG. 10.2. A COMMUNICATIONS LINK.

The model M760 TDM for attachment to 48K or 64K Kilostream links
(Digital Multiplexor picture courtesy MICOM-Borer Ltd)

The model M790 Digital Concentrator supports both synchronous and asynchronous traffic simultaneously.
(Picture courtesy MICOM-Borer Ltd)

by a device called a **Multiplexor** and received by a device called a **demultiplexor.** There are many methods of multiplexing. One form of multiplexing involves a device known as a **concentrator** which is typically used to connect a number of slow terminals in close proximity to a single transmission line. (See Fig. 4.4) Data items are normally transmitted to or from the terminals concentrator at irregular intervals and so the terminals to which they belong are identified by identification numbers transmitted with the data items.

CHARACTERISTICS OF DATA TRANSMISSION LINES.

10. A data transmission link is normally called a **channel.** One very important characteristic of a channel is its capacity to carry data. This capacity is directly related to the range of frequencies with which it is possible to transmit bits along the channel, a characteristic known as the **bandwidth** of the channel. Channels with broader bandwidth, called **broadband** or **wideband** channels, have greater transmission capacities.

11. The actual rate of data flow, ie. **"data transfer rate",** is often expressed in terms of the number of bits transmitted per second, or alternatively a unit called the **baud** which in simple cases is the same as the number of bits per second. It normally takes between 8 and 10 bits to transmit an individual character depending upon the method of transmission. So, for example, a 300 baud line will typically carry about 30 characters per second. Maximum data transfer rates vary according to the medium used. A **coaxial cable,** as used for a TV aerial can carry up to 140 million bits per second, equivalent to about 2000 telephone lines, whereas an **optical fibre** can carry data at rates in excess of 500 million characters per second.

12. Transmission along a channel is possible in three modes:

a. **Simplex.** Transmission is possible in only one direction.

b. **Half Duplex.** Transmission is possible in both directions, but not simultaneously.

c. **Duplex.** Transmission is possible in both directions simultaneously.

13. There are two alternative ways of transmitting the data:

a. **Asynchronous transmission.** The characters are transmitted singly at will at irregular intervals in time. This method is well suited to conversational interactions and is the one most often used for transmission on standard telephone lines at low baud rates.

b. **Synchronous transmission.** Prepared sets of characters are transmitted together as blocks at fixed rates. This method is more efficient at transmitting large quantities of data and is the one most often used at high baud rates.

14. All data transmissions have to be controlled by some kind of convention adopted between the sender and the receiver, just as the two way radio operators used "roger", "over" and "out". These conventions are called data transmission **protocols.**

DIGITAL COMMUNICATIONS.

15. When considering the traditional telephone based data transmission methods we saw that an important feature of these systems was the use of analog transmissions, ie. the signals varied continuously in accordance with the sound waves to be transmitted. In digital transmissions the signals are at discrete levels corresponding to particular binary states, HIGH and LOW say. Digital transmissions are clearly more directly related to the binary based data representations used in computers and are also superior to analog transmissions on a number of technical grounds. Therefore, digital transmission systems have been developed in recent years as alternatives to the traditional analog telephone systems.

16. Although these systems are designed primarily for data transmission they can also transmit speech if the signals are converted into digital form. This conversion is often handled by a **PABX** (Private Automatic Branch Exchange).

17. There are a number of different digital transmission systems in existence. One example, is the British Telecom Kilostream service which has facilities to transfer data at rates up to 64 thousand bits per second. Fig. 10.3 shows a number of typical applications of this equipment using the products by MICOM-Borer Ltd.

MESSAGE SWITCHING AND PACKET SWITCHING.

18. The traditional telephone circuits and modern digital circuit just described have one feature in common. They are both employ fixed lines or circuit switching (10.4). In the case of circuit switching the data path has to be set up end-to-end *before* any transmission takes place and must be maintained throughout the duration of the call even if there are gaps in data transmission. Thus the system has some inherent delays and inefficiencies. Two alternatives to circuit switching which attempt to overcome its deficiencies are **message switching** and **packet switching.**

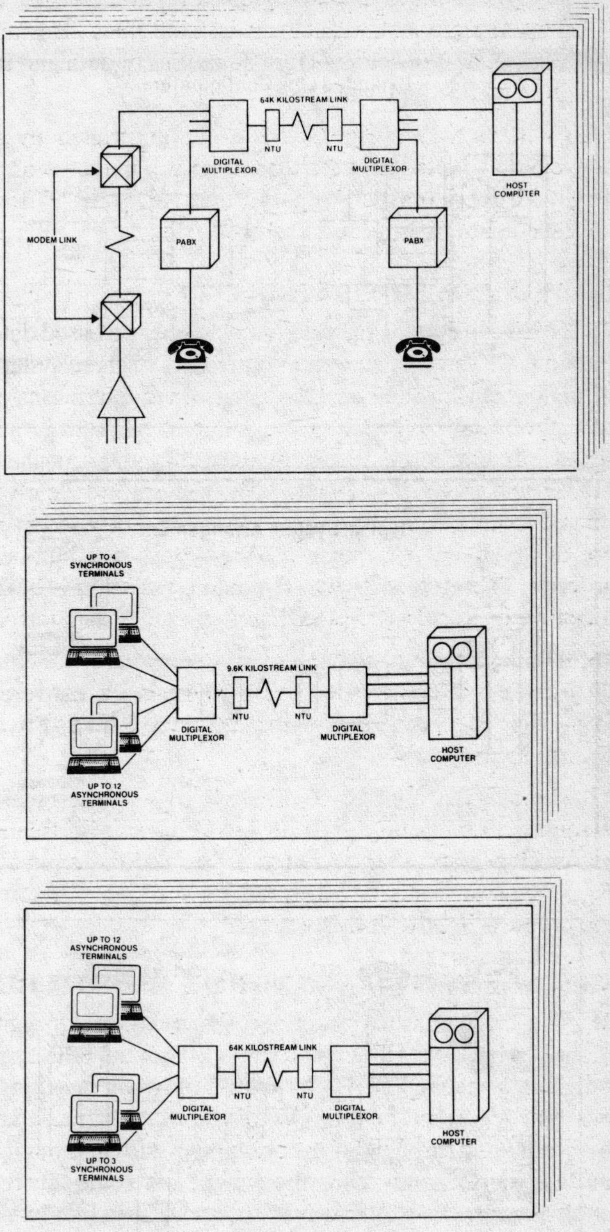

FIG. 10.3.

(Picture Courtesy MICOM-Borer Ltd.)

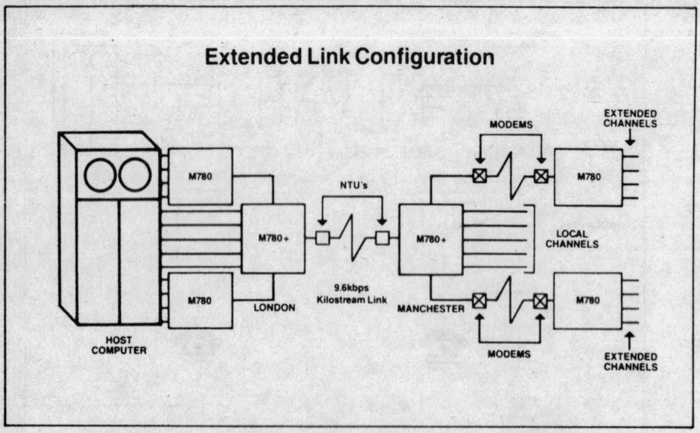
Extended Link Configuration
MODEMS
EXTENDED CHANNELS
M780
NTU's
M780+
M780+
M780
LOCAL CHANNELS
M780
LONDON
9.6kbps Kilostream Link
MANCHESTER
M780
HOST COMPUTER
MODEMS
EXTENDED CHANNELS

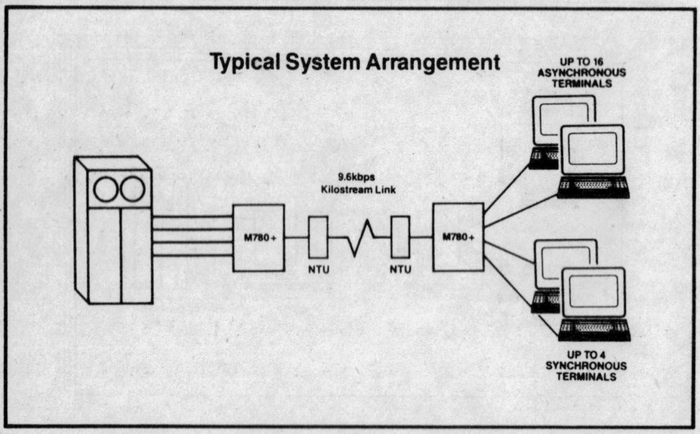
Typical System Arrangement
UP TO 16 ASYNCHRONOUS TERMINALS
9.6kbps Kilostream Link
M780+
NTU
NTU
M780+
UP TO 4 SYNCHRONOUS TERMINALS

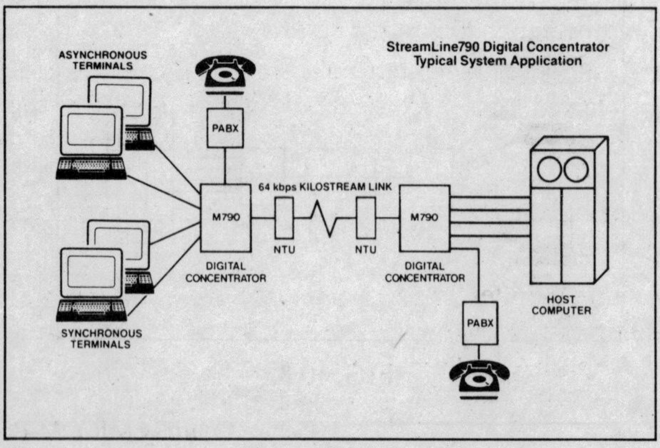
ASYNCHRONOUS TERMINALS
StreamLine790 Digital Concentrator Typical System Application
PABX
64 kbps KILOSTREAM LINK
M790
NTU
NTU
M790
DIGITAL CONCENTRATOR
DIGITAL CONCENTRATOR
SYNCHRONOUS TERMINALS
PABX
HOST COMPUTER

FIG. 10.3 (cont)

19. In a simple message switching circuit the transmission is done in stages with the content of the whole transmission, ie. the message, being sent along separate and successive sections of the circuit in turn. At the beginning and end of each section there is computerised unit called an **IMP** (Interface Message Processor) which is able to receive, store and forward the message to the destination to which it is electronically addressed. This is a form of **store and forward** system and has some inherent delay in it because of the need to assemble the whole message before transmission occurs at each stage.

20. A rather more versatile alternative is the packet switching system. A packet consists of details of the sender, the intended destination 'address', a small portion of a message and other data used for control purposes. Each packet is transmitted in the same way as a whole message in a message switching system. The packet itself enters and exits the circuit via a device called a **PAD** (Packet Assembler/Disassembler).

21. Packet switching does not suffer from the inherent delay of message switching and also make more flexible and efficient use of the transmission circuit because it only establishes each link for as long as it needs it to transmit each packet. The lack of delays means that packet switching systems may be used for conversational modes of transmission as well as for bulk data transmission. All these features aid economy.

22. The individual links, both in message switching systems and packet switching systems, tended to use digital transmission techniques.

COMPUTER NETWORKS AND DISTRIBUTED SYSTEMS.

23. An interconnected set of two or more computers may be called a **"computer network".** However, if the computers in the network operate together as a single unit which to the user appears as a single computer, albeit physically dispersed, then the complete system is more accurately described as a **distributed system.**

Therefore, although, *any* interconnected set of computers is often conveniently referred to as a "computer network" the use of the term often implies an interconnected set of *independent* computers and not a distributed system. However, it may be useful when considering a distributed system to be able to recognise the particular type of network on which it is based.

24. Networks used to interconnect computers in a single room, rooms within a building or building on one site are normally called **Local Area Networks (LANs).** LANs normally transmit data in a digital form using media such as coaxial cable or multi-stranded cable.

25. The networks which interconnect computers on separate sites, separate cities or even separate countries are called **Long Haul Networks (LHNs)** or **Wide Area Networks (WANs).** LHNs tend to use packet switching methods or message switching methods and exploit optical fibre media and satelite transmissions in many cases.

BASIC ADVANTAGES OF USING NETWORKS.

26. There are many possible advantages in using networks. The basic ones are:

a. The sharing of resources (eg. computers & staff) and information.

b. The provision of local facilities without the loss of central control.

c. The even distribution of work, processing loads etc.

d. Shared risk and mutual support.

e. Improved and more economic communication facilities in general, eg. including voice communication.

STANDARDS FOR NETWORKS.

27. Communication between interconnected computer systems is a complex activity which takes place at a number of different levels. At the lowest level there is the physical transmission of signals and at the highest level there may be communication of messages in everyday language.

28. In an attempt to form a basis for standardising such interconnections the International Standards Organisation (**ISO**) has devised a standard based upon a set of seven distinct levels or layers of communication. This model is known as the reference Model for Open System Interconnection, or **OSI** for short. Separate standard are gradually being established to cover each of the separate layers. Work on standardising the lower levels is largely complete. It includes a series of standards numbered X1, X2, X3 . . . etc. developed by the **CCITT** (Consultative Committee for International Telephone and Telegraphy) of which X25, for example, is a standard for packet switching.

NETWORK STRUCTURES.

29. A number of standard network structures are shown in Fig. 10.4. The individual circles in Fig. 10.4 represent computers connected to the network in the case of LANs and represent IMPs to which computers are connected in the case of LHNs.

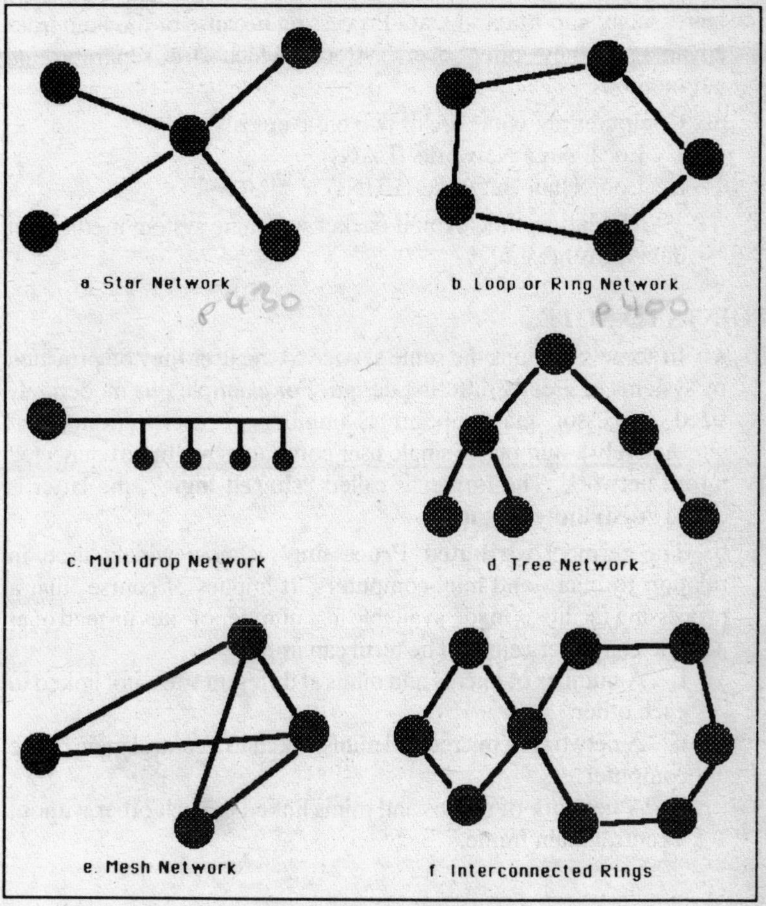

FIG. 10.4. NETWORK STRUCTURES.

SUMMARY.

30. a. The long established methods of data communication are based upon the telephone system and employ circuit switching methods and analog transmissions.

b. Digital data transmission is technically superior to analog transmissions, akin to the data representations used in computers and is gradually replacing traditional analog methods.

c. Message switching and packet switching offer advantages over circuit switching systems.

d. Computer networks and distributed systems are becoming increasingly important in Data Processing because of the numerous advantages they offer over systems which are separate and autonomous.

e. Computer networks are of two basic kinds:

i. Local Area Networks (LANs).

ii. Long Haul Networks (LHNs).

The latter often exploit packet switching system methods of data transmission.

POINTS TO NOTE.

31. a. In some situations the same service to the user may be provided by systems of greatly differing design. For example *one* moderately sized processor may support a number of user terminals *or* alternatively a number of single user computers might be connected into a network. The former is called **"shared logic"**, the latter is called **"distributed logic"**.

b. The term **'Distributed Processing'** is now widely used in relation to micro and mini-computers. It implies of course, that a processing facility is made available at a number of sites instead of at a single computer centre. The term can imply:-

i. A number of micros and minis at different sites, not linked to each other.

ii. A network of micros and minis linked to a central main frame computer.

iii. A network of micros and minis linked to each other without a central main frame.

QUESTIONS.

1. What are the main purposes of the following hardware items – give an account of the mode of operation of each of the hardware units:

i. MODEM

ii. Diskette

iii. VDU

iv. Write permit ring
(IDPM Part I)

2. *Explain any FIVE of the following terms used in data communication systems indicating their relevance to systems, and where applicable describe the hardware needed:*

   a. *LAN*
   b. *Band*
   c. *Multidrop Lines*
   d. *Star Network*
   e. *Asynchronous transmission*
   f. *Modem*
   g. *Acoustic coupler*

   (IDPM Part II)

3. *Explain the advantages which a packet switching system has over a conventional circuit switching system.*

Computer Files

1. Files can be considered to be the framework around which data processing revolves. ie. maintained data and input data are organised into files.

2. Chapter 11 sets out the concepts of magnetic files. Chapter 12 describes the methods of organising a file on magnetic *tape* and how access is made to the records in such a file. Chapter 13 does the same with regard to magnetic *disk*.

3. In the interests of clarity only two magnetic storage devices are used as a basis for discussing computer files. These are:-

a. Magnetic tape – Serial Access Storage (SAS)

b. Magnetic disk (Hard of Floppy) – Direct Access Storage (DAS).

4. The *general* principles discussed with regard to magnetic *tape* or magnetic *disk* can be applied to other media according to whether the media are SAS media or DAS media.

11 General Concepts

INTRODUCTION.

1. The purpose of this chapter is to look at the general concepts which lie behind the subject of computer files before going on to discuss the different methods of organising them. The term "file" in EDP is used to describe *a collection of related records.* It should be recognised that all discussions of "files" which follow is to be considered in an *EDP context.*

2. Purpose. A file holds data which is required for providing information. Some files are processed at regular intervals to provide this information (eg. payroll file) and others will hold data which is required at irregular intervals (eg. a file containing prices of items).

3. There are two common ways of viewing files:-

a. **Logical files.** A "logical file" is a file viewed in terms of *what* data items its records contain and *what* processing operations may be performed upon the file. The user of the file will normally adopt such a view.

b. **Physical files.** A "physical file" is a file viewed in terms of *how* the data is stored on a storage device such as a magnetic disk and *how* the processing operations are made possible.

4. A logical file can usually give rise to a number of alternative physical file implementations. These alternatives are considered in later chapters.

ELEMENTS OF A COMPUTER FILE.

5. A file consists of a number of *records.* Each record is made up of a number of *fields* and each field consists of a number of *characters.*

a. **Character.** A character is the smallest element in a file and can be alphabetic or numeric.

b. **Field.** An item of data within a *record* is called a field – it is made up of a number of *characters,* eg. a name, a date, or an amount.

c. **Record.** A record is made up of a number of related fields, eg. a customer record, or an employee payroll record. See Fig. 11.1.

CLOCK NUMBER	EMPLOYEE'S NAME	DATE OF BIRTH	SEX	GRADE	HOURLY RATE
1201	P J JOHNS	06 12 45	F	4	300

Characters Field

Notes: 1. Clock number is the Key field. (11.11)
2. Grade is coded.
2. Hourly rate is expressed in pence.

FIG. 11.1. PAYROLL RECORD (PART ONLY).

ALTERNATIVE TERMINOLOGY.

6. The terminology of paragraph 5 (ie. record, field and character) is firmly established as a means of describing the characteristics of files in general situations. However, the use of this terminology can lead to excessive attention being directed toward physical details, such as how many characters there should be in a field. Such issues can divert attention from matters of high priority, such as what fields should be recorded in order to meet the information needs of the user. To overcome this difficulty, two alternative sets of terms have been developed, one set for physical files, the other set for logical files. They are:-

a. **For physical files**
   i. Physical Record.
   ii. Field.
   iii. Character (a physical feature).

b. **For logical files.**
   i. Logical Record – of an "entity".
   ii. Data item – "attributes" of the "entity".

7. Entities are things (eg. objects, people, events etc.) about which there is a need to record data eg. an item of stock, an employee, a financial transaction etc. The individual properties of the entity, about which data is recorded, are its **"attributes"** eg. the attributes of an invoice (entity) will include the "name"; "address"; "customer order number"; "quantity"; "price"; "description".

A logical record is created for each entity occurrence and the logical record contains one **data item** for each **occurrence** of the entity's attributes. eg. the "customers name" would be a data item and there would be **one** only in the logical record. Whereas the attribute "quantity" would have as many data items as there are entries on the invoice.

8. The relationship between the various terms used is summarized in the following table:-

Things about which there is a need to record data	Entities	–	each entity has a number of *attributes*
How the data is recorded	Logical records (1 per entity occurrence)	–	each logical record contains a number of *data items*
Physical details of how the data is recorded	Physical record (1 or more per logical record)	–	each Physical record contains a number of *fields.*

TYPES OF FILES.

9. a. **Master file.** These are files of a fairly permanent nature eg. customer leger, payroll, inventory, etc. A feature to note is the regular *updating* of these files to show a current position. For example customers' orders will be processed increasing the "balance owing" figure on a customer ledger record. It is seen therefore that master records will contain both data of a static nature, eg. a customer name and address, and data which, by its nature will change *each time* a transaction occurs, eg. the "balance" figure already mentioned.

b. **Movement file.** Also called Transaction file. This is made up of the various transactions created from the source documents. In a sales ledger application the file will contain all the orders received at a particular time. This file will be used to update the *master* file. As soon as it has been used for this purpose it is no longer required. It will therefore have a very short life, because it will be replaced by a file containing the *next* batch of orders.

c. **Reference file.** A file with a reasonable amount of permanency. Examples of data used for reference purposes are price lists, tables of rates of pay, names and addresses.

ACCESS TO FILES.

10. Key field. Once having created files of data in magnetic form one must have the means of access to particular records within those files. In *general* terms this is usually done by giving each record a "key" field and the record will be recognised or identified by that particular key. Examples of key fields are:-

a. Customer number in a customer ledger record.

b. Stock code number in a stock record.

c. Employee clock number in a payroll record.

11. Not only does the key field assist in accessing records but the records themselves can, if required, be *sorted* into the sequence indicated by the key.

STORAGE DEVICES.

12. Mention is made here of the two storage devices which will be considered in connection with the storage of files. (ie. Physical Files).

a. **Magnetic tape.** The significant feature with regard to its use as a storage medium is the fact that it is a serial access medium. (4.18)

b. **Magnetic disk.** This device on the other hand is a direct access medium (4.18) and therefore has a distinct advantage over tape in this respect.

NB. This advantage is reflected in the fact that disk is the major medium used for on-line storage.

13. These characteristics will loom large in our considerations about files in the chapters that follow. Note then that they are inherent in the *physical* make up of the devices and will clearly influence the *type* of files stored on each one, and how the files can be *organised* and *accessed.*

PROCESSING ACTIVITIES.

14. We will need to have access to particular records in the files in order to process them. The major processing activities are given below:-

a. **Updating.** When data on the master record is changed to reflect a current position, eg. updating a customer ledger record with new orders. Note that the old data on the record is replaced by the new data.

b. **Referencing.** When access is made to a particular record to ascertain what is contained therein, eg. reference is made to a "prices" file during an invoicing run. Note that this does *not* involve any alteration to the record itself.

c. **File maintenance.** New records must be added to a file and records need to be deleted. Prices change, and the file must be altered. Customer's addresses also change and new addresses have to be inserted to bring the file up to date. These particular activities come under the heading of "maintaining" the file. File maintenance can be carried out as a separate run but the insertion and deletion of records is sometimes *combined* with Updating.

d. **File enquiry or interrogation.** This is similar in concept to referencing. It involves the need to ascertain a piece of information from, say, a master record. For example, a customer may query a Statement sent to him. A "file enquiry" will get the data in dispute from the record so that the query may be settled.

FIXED/VARIABLE LENGTH RECORDS.

15. The question whether to use records of a fixed or variable length is one which usually does not have to be considered in manual/mechanical methods. It is a major issue in the design of physical files in computer systems.

a. **Fixed.** Every record in the file will be of the same fixed number of fields and characters and will never vary in size.

b. **Variable.** This means that not *all* records in the file will be of the same size. This could be for two reasons:-

i. Some records could have more *fields* than others. In an invoicing application for example (assuming a 6 character field to represent "total amount for each invoice") we would add a new field to a customer record for each invoice. So a customer's record would vary in *size* according to the *number* of invoices he had been sent.

ii. Fields *themselves* could vary in size. A simple example is the "name and address" field because it varies widely in size.

16. It should be noted however that in the examples at 15b a fixed length record *could* be used. In 15bi. the record could be designed in the first instance to accommodate a fixed number of *possible* invoices. This means the records with less than the fixed number of invoices would contain blank fields. Similarly in 15bii. the field could be made large enough to accommodate the *largest* name and address. Again records with names and addresses of a smaller number of characters would contain blanks.

17. Fixed length records make it easy for the programmer because he is dealing with a known quantity of characters each time. On the other hand they result in less efficient utilisation of storage. Variable length records mean difficulties for the programmer but better utilisation of storage.

HIT RATE.

18. This is the term used to described the rate of processing of master files in terms of active records. For example if 1,000 transactions are processed each day against a master file of 10,000 records, then the hit rate is said to be 10%.

SUMMARY.

19. a. A file is a collection of *related* records.

b. A file is made up of **records,** which are made up of **fields,** which are made up of **characters.**

c. It is often advantageous to distinguish between physical files and logical files.

d. Fields within logical records are normally called **"data items"** (or just **"items").**

e. A record is recognised or identified by the record KEY.

f. Files can be broadly classified as, master files, movement (or transaction) files, and reference files.

g. The physical nature of the storage device will have a direct bearing on the way files are organised on it, and also on the method of access.

h. Four processing activities are: Updating, Referencing, File Maintenance and File Enquiry or Interrogation.

i. Referencing is usually carried out during updating and is incidental to it.

j. Files can consist of records of fixed length or variable length. The decision on which is adopted is a question of programming ease v storage utilisation.

POINTS TO NOTE.

20. a. The meaning given to "file" in EDP eg. a collection of "transactions" is just as much a "file" in EDP as is a "master" file.

b. Magnetic tape is a serial medium, disk is a direct access medium.

c. A file may be described in terms of its **"structure"** and in terms of its **organisation.** Its *structure* is determined by which data items are included in records and how the data items are grouped within records. Its *organisation* is determined by how the records are arranged within the file.

QUESTIONS.

1. *a. Give your definition of the word 'file' as it is used in the context of data processing.*

b. Distinguish between a master file and a transaction (or movement) file and explain the relationship between them.

c. List FIVE factors to be considered in determining how a master file should be organised. (ACA)

12 Magnetic Tape

INTRODUCTION.

1. Before tackling this chapter revise 5.25–5.27 which describes the physical attributes of tape itself (in the form of reels) and the "reading" and "writing" devices called the Tape Unit. File organisation is the arrangement of records within a particular file. We start from the point where the individual physical record layout has already been designed ie. the file "structure has already been decided?" How do we organise our many hundreds, or even thousands of such records (eg. customer records) on magnetic tape? When we wish to access one or more of the records how do we do it? This chapter sets out to explain how these things are done.

WRITING ON TAPE.

2. Records are "written" in the first place from main storage onto the tape by the CPU. Each record is written onto tape in response to a "write instruction". This process will be repeated until all the required records are written onto the tape ie. until the file is complete. Fig. 12.1 illustrates what the tape will look like in diagrammatic form.

Cust. 1	Inter Record Gap	Cust. 2	Inter Record Gap	Cust. 3	Inter Record Gap	Cust. 4			

FIG. 12.1. DIAGRAM ILLUSTRATING RECORDS ON MAGNETIC TAPE.

Notice the inter-record gap (IRG) which is caused by the tape slowing down at the conclusion of one "write" and accelerating at the beginning of the next.

READING FROM TAPE.

3. Having created (ie. written) a file of records onto tape, we will later need to *process* the file. To do this, we take the reel of tape and mount it on to a tape unit. Records are now "read" *from* the tape into main storage. Each record is read in response to a "read instruction". Notice that when "reading", the tape automatically stops when the IRG is sensed.

FILE ORGANISATION.

4. Organisation of a file on tape is simply a matter of placing the records one after the other onto the tape. There are two possible arrangements of files:-

a. **Serial.** When records are written onto tape *without* there being any relationship between the record keys. *Unsorted* transaction records would form such a file.

b. **Sequential.** When records are written onto tape in *sequence* according to the record keys. Examples of sequential files are:-

i. **Master** files.
ii. **Sorted** transaction files.

ACCESS.

5. a. **Serial files.** The only way to access a serial file on tape is SERIALLY. This simply means to say that each record is read from the tape into main storage one after the other in the order they occur on the tape.

b. **Sequential** files. The method of access used is still SERIAL but of course the file is now in sequence, and for this reason the term SEQUENTIAL is often used in describing serial access of a sequential tape file. It is important to note that to process (eg. update) a sequential master tape file, the transaction file must *also* be in the sequence of the master file. Access is achieved by first reading the transaction file and then reading the master file until the matching record (using the record keys) is found. Note therefore that if the record required is the twentieth record on the file, in order to get it into storage to process it, the computer will first have to read in *all* nineteen preceding records.

NB. These limited methods of organisation and access have lead to tape becoming very much less common than disk as an on-line medium for the storage of master files. Tape continues as a major storage medium for other purposes such as off-line data storage and backup.

UPDATING THE FILES.

6. a. Because of the design of the tape unit it is not possible to write records back to the same position on the tape from which they have been read. The method of updating a tape file therefore is to form a *new* master file on a *new* reel of tape each time the updating process is carried out.

b. Updating a master file held on tape entails the following:-

i. Transaction file and master file must be in the same sequence.

ii. A transaction record is read into main storage.

iii. A master record is read into main storage and written straight out again on a new reel if it does not match the transaction. Successive records from the master file are read (and written) until the record matching the transaction is located.

iv. The master record is then updated in storage and written out in sequence on the new reel.

The four steps are repeated until all the master records for which there is a transaction record have been updated. The result is the creation of a *new* reel of tape containing the records that did not change plus the records that have been updated. The new reel will be used on the next updating run. (See Fig. 12.2)

FILE MAINTENANCE.

7. File maintenance is the term used to describe the following:-

a. Removing or adding records to the magnetic file.

b. Amending static data contained in a record eg. customer name or address, prices of stock items following a general price change.

The term generally applies to master files.

8. Removing a record entails leaving it off the carried forward tape reel, while adding records entails writing the new record onto the C/F tape reel in its correct sequence. Variable length records present no problems because there are no constraints on the size of records which can be written onto tape.

FILE LABELS.

9. In addition to its own particular 'logical' records (ie. the customer or payroll records) each *tape file* will generally have two records which serve organisational requirements. They are written onto the tape in magnetic form as are the logical records. These two records are usually referred to as LABELS. One comes at the beginning of the file and the other at the end.

a. **Header label.** This is the first and its main function is to identify the file. It will contain the following data:-

i. A specified field to identify the particular record as a label.

ii. File name – eg. PAYROLL; LEDGER; STOCK.

iii. Date written.

DAY 1

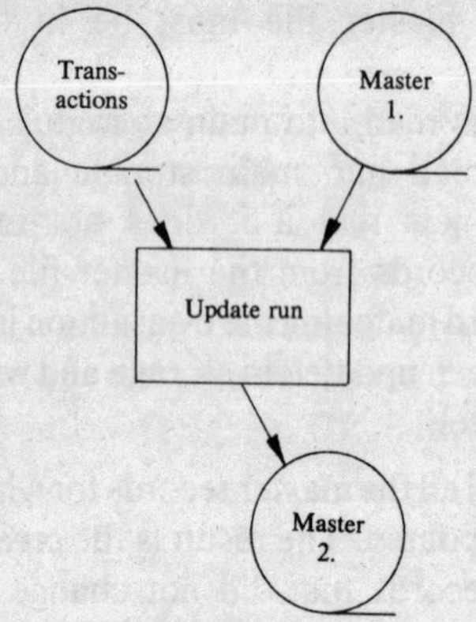

Note:

1. **Master 1** "gives birth" to Son M2.
2. Therefore M1 is said to be 'Father Tape' and M2 the 'Son Tape'.

DAY 2

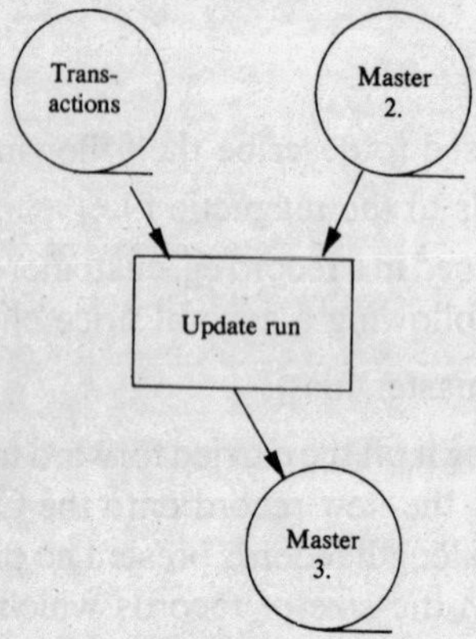

Note:

1. M2 from Day 1 is now the input Master. M2 now gives birth to a Son M3.
2. The position is now:-
M1 is the Grandfather tape.
M2 the Father tape.
M3 the Son tape.

This can be carried on ad infinitum but there will be a definite policy with regards to how *many* generation are kept; Grandfather – Father – Son should be adequate. If an accident should befall M3 on Day 3's Update run then no matter, we can recreate it by doing Day 2's Run again. The keeping of the Master and appropriate Transaction files ensure security of the system's files. Notice as new 'generations' are born the oldest tapes are re-used. The old information they contain is overwritten.

FIG. 12.2. FILE SECURITY ON TAPE – THE FATHER-SON CONCEPT.

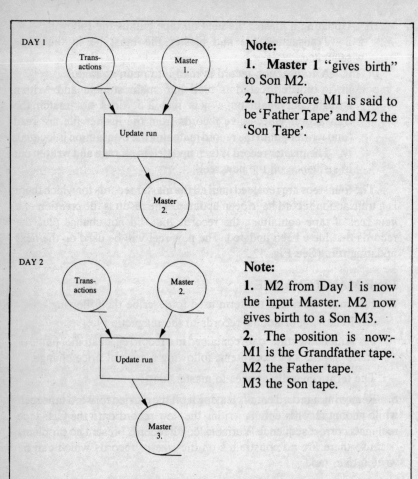

iv. Purge date – being the date from which the information on the particular tape reel is no longer required and from which the reel can be re-used.

This label will be checked by the Program before the file is processed to ensure the correct tape reel has been mounted.

b. **Trailer label.** This will come at the end of the file and will contain the following data:-

i. A specific field to identify the particular record as a label.

ii. A count of the number of records on the file. This will be checked against the total accumulated by the Program during processing.

iii. Reel number if the file takes up more than one reel of tape.

CONTROL TOTALS.

10. Mention is made here of one further type of record found on tape files – one which will contain control totals, eg. financial totals. Such a record will follow the Trailer Label.

BLOCKING OF RECORDS.

11. The gaps created between each record on tape represent wasted space but more importantly they represent unproductive *time* spent by the tape unit in slowing down and accelerating in between each write and read operation. In order to reduce the number of IRGs and thus speed up the *total* time taken to process a tape file the technique of blocking records is adopted. Thus a single "read" or "write" instruction will cause a number of records to be read or written. See Fig. 12.3.

SUMMARY.

12. a. An inter block gap is created after each block is *written* on tape.

b. When the tape is being read the IBG terminates the "read" operation (ie. the transfer of the data in that particular block).

c. Tape is a serial medium and can only be accessed serially.

d. Updating is achieved by creating a physically different file each time.

e. File maintenance involves adding and deleting records and the amendment of static data contained in records.

f. Labels are provided for control/organisational purposes.

g. **A diagram showing the components of a tape file** is shown in Fig. 12.4.

TAPE 1 "SINGLE RECORD" BLOCKS

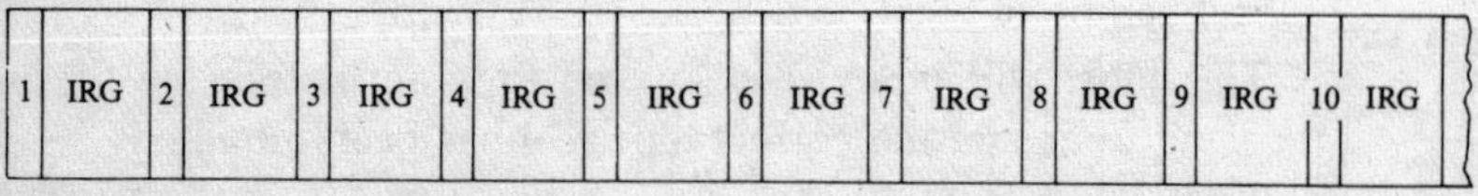

TAPE 2 "6 RECORD"BLOCKS

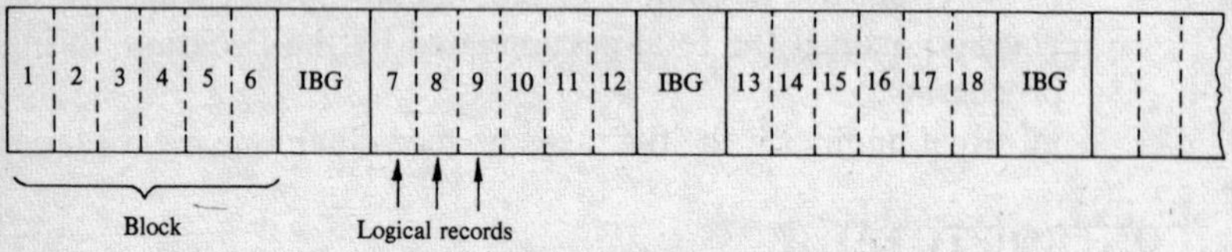

Note:

1. The saving in the *overall* input/output time. Each IRG (IBG) represents time *wasted.* Tape 2 cuts out 15 IRGs (17 are required in tape 1 for 18 records) representing a *very significant* speed up in the process of transferring records to main storage.

2. The saving in *space* used on tape, although the saving in time is more important.

3. The number of records comprising a block is known as the *blocking factor.*

4. The block is the *physical* unit of transfer between the tape and internal storage and the IRG is now referred to as the IBG.

5. The Block may be called a **physical record.**

6. The individual records making up the block are known as the **logical records.**

7. The size of each block will depend on:-

a. The size of the logical records.

b. The size of internal storage available for input/output purposes.

FIG. 12.3. BLOCKING RECORDS ON MAGNETIC TAPE.

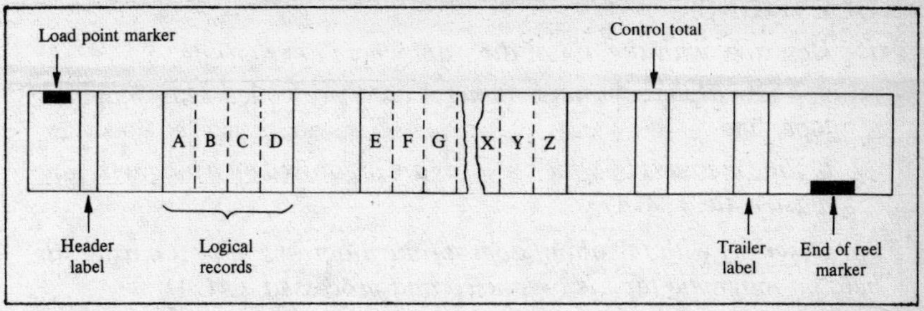

FIG. 12.4. DIAGRAM ILLUSTRATING COMPONENTS OF A TAPE FILE.

POINTS TO NOTE.

13. a. Note the amount of data transfer *time* saved by blocking records together on tape. (Fig. 12.3).

b. When we talk of "transferring" or "reading" from tape, this really means *copying* it from tape because the data is still *there* on the tape. This concept holds good *whatever* the medium in computers.

c. Data can also be written onto tape "off-line" ie. by a Magnetic Tape Encoder, (15.9), and by transferring from another medium to tape eg. from punched cards to tape (done by means of a special type of tape unit linked to a card reader). Transaction files are generally associated with these methods of "preparing" tape.

d. The size of blocks is limited by the amount of main storage available for the input/output area.

e. Tape labels are *magnetic* labels for use by the computer program.

f. The expression "reading the master/transaction file" really means in effect "reading *one* block into main storage". A separate "read" instruction is required for each block on tape to be "read" into main storage.

g. The use of the term "generation" in connection with master files (Fig. 12.2).

h. Magnetic tape is *not* normally used as a storage medium for master files undergoing processing, but is frequently used for "backup copies" of all kinds of files.

i. Some tape units may be operated in a mode in which data is transferred between the tape and main storage in a continuous stream for "backup" or "recovery" purposes. This is known as **streaming.**

QUESTIONS.

1. *Describe, with the aid of diagram where appropriate.*

   a. how alphabetic and numeric data are coded onto magnetic tape, and

   b. the methods by which records are organised on a magnetic tape master file. (ACA)

2. *Describe, with the aid of appropriate diagrams, how a master file held on magnetic tape is organised and processed. (ACA)*

3. *In relation to Magnetic Tape, briefly explain the following terms:-*

Magnetic Storage	*Content of frames*	*Parity*
Records	*Blocking*	*Inter Block Gap*
Header record	*Trailer record*	*Write protect*
Read after write		

(IDPM Part 1)

13 Magnetic Disk

INTRODUCTION.

1. The exchangeable type disk will be used as a basis for this chapter because it is most often used in practice. Hard disks are the main file processing medium on mini and mainframe computers, and floppy disks are the main file processing medium on microcomputers. The principles covered by this chapter are applicable to both hard and floppy disks. Any relevant differences will be highlighted when appropriate.

2. You should be thoroughly conversant with the relevant hardware described in 5.33–5.34 and 8.5–8.9 before going on with this chapter, which is concerned with the organisation of files on disk and how files are accessed.

WRITING ON DISK.

3. Records are "written" onto a disk as the disk pack revolves at a constant speed within its disk unit. Each record is written in response to a "write" instruction. Data goes from main storage through a read-write head onto a track on the disk surface. Records are recorded one after the other one each track.

NB. All references to "records" in this chapter should be taken to mean "Physical records" unless otherwise stated.

READING FROM DISK.

4. In order to process files stored on disk the disk pack must first be loaded into a disk unit. Records are read from the disk as it revolves at a constant speed. Each record is read in response to a "read" instruction. Data goes from the disk to the main storage through the read-write head already mentioned. Both reading and writing of data are accomplished at a fixed number (thousands) of characters per second.

5. We will take for our discussion on file organisation, a "6 disk" disk pack, meaning it has ten usable surfaces (the outer two are not used for recording purposes). But before describing how files are organised let us look first at the basic underlying concepts.

CYLINDER CONCEPT.

6. Consult Fig. 8.1 where the disk pack is illustrated and note the following:

i. There are *ten* recording surfaces. Each surface has 200 tracks.
ii. There is a read-write head for *each* surface on the disk pack.
iii. *All* the read-write arms are fixed to *one* mechanism and are like a comb.
iv. When the "access" mechanism moves all ten read-write heads move *in unison* across the disk surfaces.
v. Whenever the access mechanism comes to rest *each* read-write head will be positioned on the *equivalent* track on *each* of the ten surfaces.
vi. For *one* movement of the access mechanism access is possible to *ten* tracks of data.

7. In the case of a floppy disk the situation is essentially the same but simpler. (Fig. 5.7) There is just *one* recording surface on a "single sided" floppy disk and *two* recording surfaces on a "double sided" floppy disk. The other significant differences are in terms of capacity and speed.

8. Use is made of the physical features already described when organising the storage of records on disk. Records are written onto the disk starting with track 1 on surface 1, then track 1 on surface 2, then track 1 on surface 3 and so on to track 1 on surface 10. One can see that conceptually the ten tracks of data can be regarded as forming a CYLINDER.

9. Data is written onto successive cylinders, involving *one* movement only of the access mechanism for each cylinder. When access is made to the stored records it will be advantageous, in terms of keeping access mechanism movement to a minimum, to deal with a cylinder of records at a time.

10. Conceptually the disk can be regarded as consisting of 200 CYLINDERS. Cylinder 1 comprises track 1 on each of 10 surfaces; cylinder 2 comprises track 2 of each of the 10 surfaces and so on to cylinder 200 which comprises track 200 on each of the 10 surfaces. This CYLINDER CONCEPT is fundamental to an understanding of how records are organised on disks. An alternative term for cylinder is SEEK AREA, ie. the amount of data which is available to the read-write heads as a result of one movement of SEEK of the access mechanism.

HARD SECTORED DISKS AND SOFT SECTORED DISKS.

11. The tracks on a disk are sub divided into **sectors** (see Fig. 13.1). There are two alternative design strategies for the division of tracks into sectors. One is called **soft sectoring,** the other is called **hard sectoring.** In either case *whole* sectors of data are transferred between the disk and main storage.

NB. A disk said to have "no sectors" is effectively a soft sectored disk.

12. A soft sectored disk has sectors which may be varied in length, up to some maximum value which is never more than the size of a complete track. Sector size and position is *soft*ware controlled, hence the term "soft sectored".

13. A *hard sectored* disk has sectors of fixed length. There may be anything from 8 to 128 sectors per track. Sector size and position is predetermined by hardware, hence the term "hard sectored".

14. You may compare a sector with a physical record or block on magnetic tape (Fig. 12.3). In fact it is common to use "sector" and "block" as synonyms. However, in the case of hard sectored disks, blocks may be grouped together into larger units called "buckets" or "logical blocks". It is therefore prudent to call a sector a "physical block" so as to avoid any possible ambiguity.

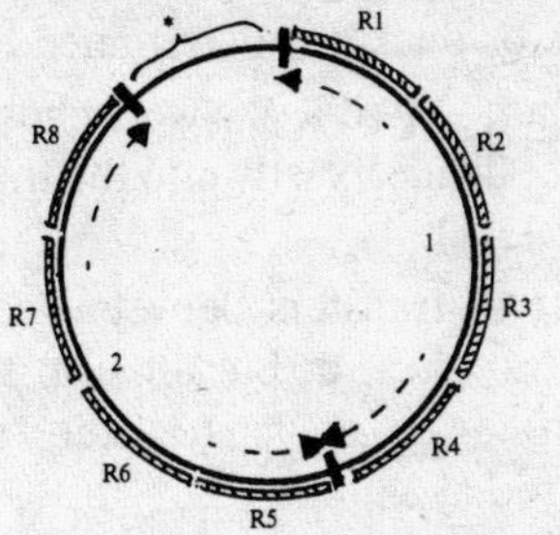

a. A Soft Sectored Disk.

The start of each track is marked physically by a notch or hole. The start of each sector is marked by special data recorded there.

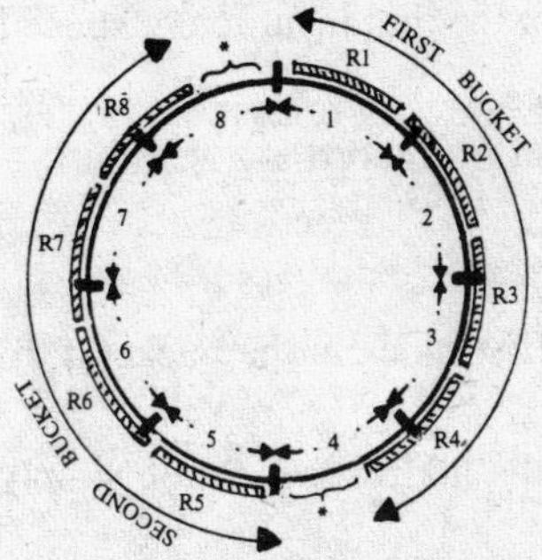

b. A Hard Sectored Disk.

The start of each track and sector is marked physically by a notch or hole. There may also be recorded marks as on the soft sectored disk.

Key

SECTORS (ie. BLOCKS)
ARE NUMBERED 1, 2, 3 . . .
LOGICAL RECORDS:
ARE NUMBERED R1, R2, R3, . . .

* INDICATES WASTED STORAGE SPACE.

Note

Reading a bucket is treated as a single read operation, although in reality it is a sequence of hard sector reads.

FIG. 13.1. BLOCKING RECORDS ON MAGNETIC DISK.

BASIC ADDRESS CONCEPTS.

15. As the disk is a direct access device a record can be accessed independently of other records. To enable the disk to locate a record, the record must have some form of ADDRESS. The whole area of each disk can be sub-divided to enable this to be accomplished.

a. **Cylinder.** The major subdivision as we have seen is the cylinder.

b. **Track.** Each cylinder is comprised of a number of tracks (10 in our quoted example).

c. **Block.** The smallest addressable part of a disk is a block (ie. a sector). This forms the unit of transfer between the disk and main storage.

d. **Bucket.** When the block size is fixed (ie. when the disk is hard sectored) a number of blocks (ie. sectors) are grouped to form a larger unit of transfer. This unit is called a bucket or logical block.

16. The block or the bucket is therefore the unit of input/output on disk. As on magnetic tape, records will be combined together to form one of these units. The optimum size for a block or bucket is determined by:

a. the need to optimise fillage of a track – eg. if a size were chosen for a variable length block which did not divide exactly into the track size, space would be wasted. (See Fig. 13.1).

b. the need to minimise the number of transfers between main storage and disk storage. The larger the block or bucket size, the more records will be brought into main storage at each transfer. (eg. in Fig. 13.1a, four records are transferred at a time).

c. the need to economise in the use of main storage. A large block or bucket may occupy so much main storage that insufficient space is left for other data and programs.

17. In basic hardware terms, the address of a record is given thus:-

a. cylinder number

b. track number

c. block number (which will be the first block in the bucket if this concept applies).

NB. On a single sided floppy disk the address would be simply

a. "track" number }
b. block number. } (ie. one of a number of concentric tracks).

Thus the address 1900403 indicates

a. cylinder 190

b. track 4

c. block 3.

ACCESS TIME.

18. Access time *on disk* is the time interval between the moment the command is given to transfer data from disk to main storage and the moment this transfer is completed. It is made up of three components:-

a. **Seek time.** This is the time it takes the access mechanism to position itself at the appropriate cylinder.

b. **Rotational delay.** This is the time taken for the bucket to come round and position itself under the read-write head. On average this will be the time taken for half a revolution of the disk pack. This average is called the **'latency'** of the disk.

c. **Data transfer time.** This is the total time taken to *read* the contents of the bucket into main storage.

19. Access time will vary mainly according to the position of the *access mechanism* at the time the command is given. For example if the access mechanism is already positioned at cylinder 1 and the record required happens to be in cylinder 1 no movement of the access mechanism is required. If, however, the record required is in cylinder 200, the access mechanism has to move right across the surface of the disk. Once the bucket has arrived at the read-write head, the transfer of data to storage begins. *Speed of transfer* of data to main storage is very fast and is a constant rate of so many thousand characters per second. A hard disk will operate at speeds roughly 10 times faster than a floppy disk.

FILE ORGANISATION.

20. There are four basic methods of organising files on disk:-

a. **Serial.** Exactly as for tape. Records are placed onto the disk one after the other with no regard for sequence.

b. **Sequential.** Again as for tape; records are written onto the disk but in a defined sequence according to the record keys.

c. **Indexed sequential.** Records are stored in sequence as for 20b but with one important difference – an *index* is provided to enable individual records to be located.

d. **Random.** Records are actually placed onto the disk "at random", that is to say there is no *obvious* relationship between the records as with 20b and c. A mathematical formula is derived which when applied to each record key, generates as an answer, a bucket address (as illustrated in para 17). The record is then placed onto the disk at this address. (eg. one possible formula might be: given key = 37073. Divide by 193 giving 190 remainder 403. (Address is taken as cylinder 190, track 4, block 3).

ACCESS.

21. a. **Serial files.** As for tape the only way to access a serially organised file is SERIALLY.

b. **Sequential files.** As for tape also, in fact the comments under 11.5b apply equally to sequentially organised files on disk.

c. **Indexed sequential files.** There are three methods of access:

i. **Sequential.** This is almost the same as in b above; the complete file is read in sequential order using the index. The method is used when the hit rate is high. The method makes minimal use of the index, minimises head movement and processes *all* records in eack block in a single read. Any transaction file must be pre-sorted into the sequence of the master file.

ii. **Selective Sequential.** Again the transaction file must be pre-sorted into the same sequence as the master file. The transaction file is processed against the master file and *only* those master records for which there is a transaction are selected. Notice that the access mechanism is going forward in an ordered progression (never backtracking) because both files are in the same sequence. This minimises head movement and saves processing time. This method is suitable when the hit rate is low, as only those records for which there is a transaction are accessed.

iii. **Random.** Transactions are processed in a sequence which is not that of the master file. The transactions may be in another sequence, or may be unsequenced. In contrast to the selective sequential method, the access mechanism will move *not* in an ordered progression but back and forth along the file. This method is used when transactions are processed immediately – ie. there is not time to assemble files and sort them to sequence. It is also used when updating two files simultaneously. For example, a transaction file of orders might be used to update a stock file *and* a customer file during the same run. If the order file was sorted to customer sequence, the customer file would be updated on a *selected sequential* basis and the stock file on a random basis. (Examples will be given in later chapters).

d. **Random files.** Generally speaking the method of access to random files is RANDOM. The transaction record keys will be put through the *same* mathematical formula as were the keys of the master records thus creating the appropriate bucket address. The transactions in random order are then processed against the master file, the bucket address providing the address of the record required.

METHODS OF ADDRESSING.

22. For direct access one must be able to "address" (locate) each record whenever one wants to process it. The main methods of obtaining the appropriate address are as follows:-

a. **Index.** The record keys are listed with the appropriate disk address. The incoming transaction record key is used to locate the disk address of the master record in the index. This address is then used to locate the appropriate master record. We referred to this method in para 21c.

b. **Address generation.** This is another method which has been mentioned earlier in para. 21d. The record keys are applied to a mathematical formula which has been designed to generate a disk hardware address. The formula is very difficult to design and you need not worry about it. The master records are placed on the disk at the addresses generated. Access is afterwards obtained by generating the disk address for each transaction.

c. **Record key = disk address.** It would be convenient if we could use the actual disk hardware address as our record key. Our transaction record keys would then also be the appropriate disk addresses and thus no preliminary action such as searching an index or address generation would be required in order to access the appropriate master records. This is not a very practical method, however, and has very limited application.

NB. Files organised as in 22b and 22c are said to be "self indexing".

UPDATING DISK FILES.

23. As individual records on disks are addressable, it is possible to *write back* an up-dated record to the same place from which it was read. The effect is therefore to *overwrite* the original master record with the new or updated master record. This method of updating is called **"Updating in place"** or **"overlay".** Note the sequence of steps involved:-

a. The transaction record is read into main storage.

b. The appropriate master record is located on disk and is read into main storage.

c. The master record is updated in main storage.

d. The master record (now in updated form) is written from main storage to its original location, overwriting the record in its *pre-*updated form.

24. a. The method described can only be used when the *address* of the record is *known;* ie. when a file is organised Indexed Sequentially or Randomly.

b. Files organised on a Serial or Sequential basis are processed in the same way as magnetic tape files ie. a physically different carry forward master file will be created each time the file is processed. Such a new file could be written onto a different disk pack or perhaps on a different area of the same disk pack.

25. The Grandfather-son method of file security cannot be applied to "update in place". A common alternative is shown in an example in Fig. 13.2.

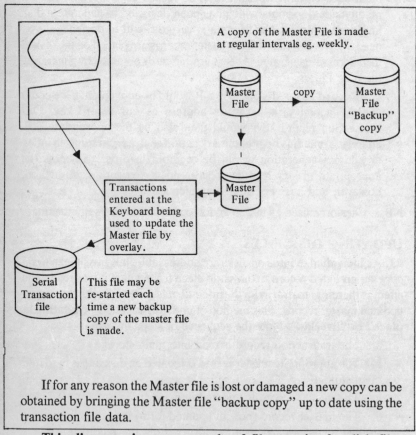

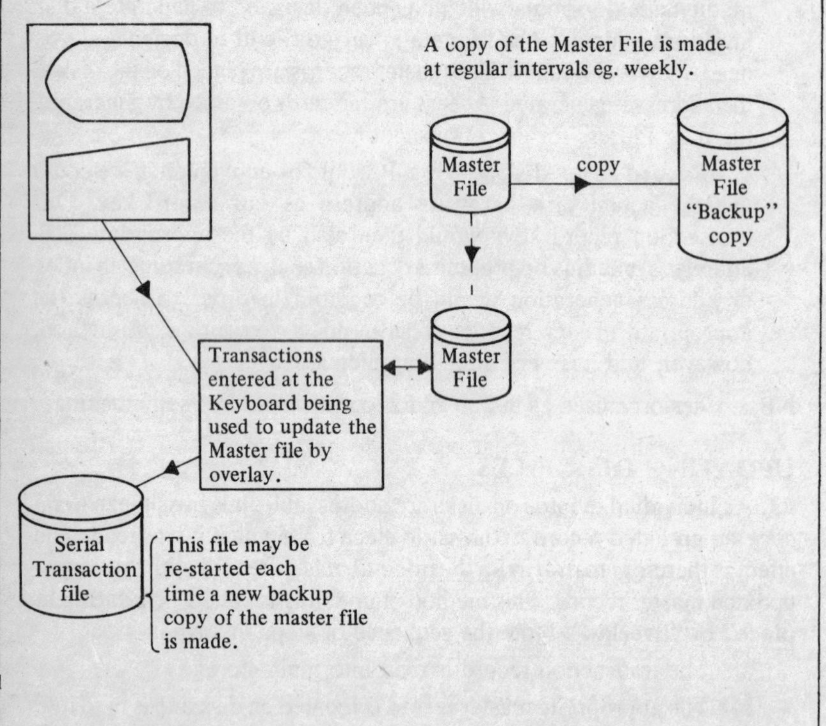

A copy of the Master File is made at regular intervals eg. weekly.
Master File
copy
Master File "Backup" copy
Master File
Transactions entered at the Keyboard being used to update the Master file by overlay.
Serial Transaction file
This file may be re-started each time a new backup copy of the master file is made.

If for any reason the Master file is lost or damaged a new copy can be obtained by bringing the Master file "backup copy" up to date using the transaction file data.

This diagram gives an example of file security for disk files updated by overlay.

FIG. 13.2.

FILE MAINTENANCE – DISK FILES.

26. a. If disk files are organised and processed in the same manner as magnetic tapes then the remarks made in the previous chapter apply.

b. Disk files which are updated using the "overlay" method present certain problems:

i. When new records are to be inserted it may not be possible to put them, there and then, in sequence on the file.

ii. Similarly if during the process of *updating* a variable record it were to be made longer, it may not be possible to write it back to the disk in its original place, unless of course sufficient space had been allowed for such expansion.

c. To cater for such circumstances, an OVERFLOW area is usually included in the disk file and such records as those referred to above are placed in this area temporarily and an indication of their whereabouts placed on the main part of the file (usually called the HOME area).

d. Records which are to be removed from the file have a deletion marker placed on them during a file maintenance run.

FILE REORGANISATION.

27. As a result of the foregoing the number of records in the overflow area will increase. As a consequence the time taken to locate such a record will involve first seeking the home track and then the overflow track.

Periodically it will be necessary to reorganise the file. This will entail rewriting the file onto a new disk pack:-

i. Putting the records that are in the overflow area in the home area in the proper sequence.

ii. Leaving off the records which have a deletion marker on them.

iii. Rewriting any index which is associated with the file.

OTHER ORGANISATION AND ACCESS METHODS.

28. The methods of file organisation and access described so far are closely related to the physical features of the disk. It is now common practice for much of this detail to be "hidden" from programmers or users of the system. Instead the operating system (9.23) handles the physical levels of organisation and access, and provides standard *logical file* organisation and access models.

29. Some examples of logical file organisation.

a. **Sequential files.** A programmer need merely regard the file as a sequence of records, and need have no concern for their physical location. A program instruction to read the next record will result in the appropriate record being transferred into memory ie. the programmers "view" may just be like this:-

R1	R2	R3	R4	R5	R6 etc.

R1. . . .R6 are logical records.

b. **Direct Files.** These are files which provide fast and efficient direct access. ie. they are normally *random files* with *one* of a number of appropriate addressing methods. A common type of direct file is the **Relative File.** The logical organisation of a relative file is like this:-

R1	R2	R3	R4	R5	R6 etc.
1	2	3	4	5	6

R1. . .R6 are *logical records* with *logical keys* 1. . .6.

A relative file may be accessed sequentially or randomly.

c. **Index Sequential Files.** Logical versions of index sequential files are simpler than their physical counterparts, in that logical keys are used, instead of disk addresses, and details of overflow are hidden from the programmer. The accessing methods are the same as those given in 21c.

OTHER 'DIRECT ACCESS' MEDIA.

30. The ability to access records independently of others within the file, ie. at random or *directly* has resulted in the term *direct access* devices being given to those devices able to offer this facility. The Optical disk unit is another direct access device.

LABELS/CONTROL TOTALS.

31. Header and trailer labels and control totals – akin to those used on magnetic tape – will be used on disk files also.

SUMMARY.

32. a. Conceptually the disk is regarded as being composed of so many concentric CYLINDERS.

b. Disk is an addressable medium and therefore specific records can be accessed leaving the rest of the file undisturbed.

c. Organisation on disk is by cylinder, track, and bucket (or block).

d. Access time on disk consists of three components, seek time, rotational delay, and data transfer time.

e. The overlay or "in place" method of updating *can be* used on disk.

f. Methods of file organisation on disk are:
   i. Serial.
   ii. Sequential (with or without an index).
   iii. Random.

g. Methods of access to disk files are:-
   i. Serial (for serial and sequential files).
   ii. Selective sequential (for indexed sequential files).
   iii. Sequential (for indexed sequential files).
   iv. Random (for random and indexed sequential files).

h. File maintenance on disk raises problems:-
   i. When inserting new records.
   ii. When updating variable length records.

i. Special overflow areas are designated on disk to take new records and over-length records temporarily.

j. A periodic file reorganisation run is required with disk files to place records residing temporarily in overflow area into their correct sequence in the file and to leave off "deleted" records. Any index also has to be reconstructed during this run.

k. A summary of normally accepted methods of File Organisation on disk and associated methods of access is given at Fig. 13.3.

FILE ORGANISATION METHOD	METHOD OF ACCESS
1. Serial } (Sequential)	Serial } (Sequential)
2. Sequential } (Sequential)	Serial (Sequential) } (Sequential)
3. Indexed Sequential	a. Sequential b. Selective sequential c. Random (Direct)
4. Random (Direct or Relative)	Random (Direct)

FIG. 13.3.

NB. Terms in parentheses are alternative terms normally used at a logical level.

POINTS TO NOTE.

33. a. The expression "the disk" has been used in this chapter. It is probably more correct to use the slightly more verbose expression "the disk pack".

b. "Seek area" or "cylinder" constitutes the amount of data available at any one time to the read-write heads, for only one movement of the access mechanism. Note however that data can only be read or written from *one* read-write head at any one time.

c. Although it is a direct access device, the disk is very often used without making use of the particular characteristic of direct access for reasons which will be stated later.

d. Updating in place (overlay) is generally adopted in conjunction with *fixed* length records.

e. The methods of file organisation and access were dealt with separately in the text for clarity. They are however very much related.

f. If you are asked a question about "File Organisation" the chances are you will be required to talk about the whole subject including, of course, access.

g. Although dealt with separately in the interests of clarity File Maintenance and File Reorganisation are closely related and should both be included in an examination answer on either subject.

h. It is desirable to have a disk overflow area on the *same* cylinder as the home area. If the overflow area is on a different cylinder then the access mechanism has to move *twice* for one access; once to the home area and then to the overflow area. The second movement is not required if the home area and the overflow area are on the same cylinder.

i. Note the implication of an overflow area during the Sequential access of an Indexed Sequential file on DISK. Access is made to every record in their *logical* sequence, which may *not* be the same as the *physical* sequence because some of the records will be residing temporarily in an overflow area.

j. Details of file processing methods will be covered in later chapters.

k. The basic methods of file organisation on disk (13.21) may also be used to build more complicated methods of file organisation. Two methods of note are:

i. **Inverted File Organisation** in which secondary indexes are formed and maintained which enable direct access to the file by other fields in addition to the key field.

ii. **Hierarchical File Organisation** in which the file consists of primary records each with a pointer to repeating groups of sub-records, eg. primary invoice records with order-item sub-records.

QUESTIONS.

1. *What factors would govern the choice of storage media?*

2. *Explain the basic principles relating to the organisation of data on a disk pack and describe the indexed sequential method of file organisation. (ACA)*

3. *A computer is sometimes described as having five basic elements. Other descriptions divide storage into two categories, internal and external, so making a total of six basic elements.*

Describe briefly the two categories of storage and explain fully the purposes which they serve. (ACA)

4. a. *Describe magnetic disc storage.*

   b. *Briefly outline the data storage and access methods which are possible on disc.*
   (IDPM Part 1)

Data Communication and Controls

1. The data which is required to be processed by the computer must be presented to it in a *machine-sensible* form. Therein lies the basic problem since most data *originates* in a form which is *far* from machine sensible. Thus a painful error-prone process of transcription must be undergone before the data is suitable for input to the computer.

2. The process of data collection involves getting the original data to the "processing centre", transcribing it, sometimes converting it from one medium to another, and finally getting it into the computer. This process involves a great many people, machines and much expense.

3. A number of advances have been made in recent years, towards automating the data collection process so as to bypass or reduce the problems. This Part will consider both traditional and modern methods.

4. Chapter 14 traces the various stages through which data travels before being used for processing against master files. Chapter 15 describes the various methods/media used for the collection of data. Chapter 16 discusses the factors which influence the choice of a particular method/medium. Chapter 17 examines the subject of system controls both in connection with data collection and computer processing. Chapter 18 looks at the services provided and applications supported by Data Communications and Networks.

14 Data Collection Stages

INTRODUCTION.

1. Data can originate in many forms but the computer can only accept it in a machine-sensible form (ie. the language of the particular input device). The process involved in getting the data from its point of origin to the computer in a form suitable for processing against master files is called Data Collection. This chapter outlines the stages involved in this process.

2. Before dealing with the individual stages of data collection it should be noted that data collection *starts* at the source of the raw data and *ends* when valid data is within the computer in a form ready for processing. (eg. as a valid sorted transaction file).

STAGES IN DATA COLLECTION.

3. a. Data creation. eg. on clerically prepared source documents.

b. Transmission of data.

c. Data preparation. ie. Transcription and verification.

d. Possible conversion from one medium (eg. diskette) to another (eg. magnetic tape).

e. Input of data to the computer for validation.

f. Sorting.

g. Control – all stages must be controlled.

4. Not all data will go through every stage and the sequence could vary in some applications. A high proportion of input data starts its life in the form of a manually scribed or typewritten document and would have to go through all the stages. However, efforts have been made to reduce the number of stages. Progress has been made in preparing the source document itself in a machine-sensible form so that it may be used as input to the computer without the need for transcription. In practice the method/medium adopted will depend on factors such as cost, type of application, etc. This will be discussed further in chapter 16.

STAGES EXPLAINED.

5. a. **Data Creation.** There are two basic alternatives, the first of which is the traditional method:-

i. **Source Documents.** A great deal of data still originates in the form of clerically prepared source documents.

ii. **Data Capture.** Data is produced in a machine sensible form at source and is read directly by a suitable device eg. a bar code reader.

b. **Data transmission.** This can mean different things according to the method/medium of data collection adopted.

i. If the computer is located at a central point, the documents will be physically "transmitted" ie. by the post office or a courier to the central point. (eg. posting batches of source documents).

ii. It is also possible for data to be transmitted by means of telegraph lines to the central computer in which case no source documents would be involved in the transmission process. (eg. transmitting data captured at source).

c. **Data preparation.** This is the term given to the *transcription* of data from the source document to a machine-sensible medium. There are two parts; the original transcription itself and the verification process that follows.

NB. Data Capture eliminates the need for transcription.

d. **Media conversion.** Very often data is prepared in a particular medium and converted to another medium for faster input to the computer, eg. data might be prepared on diskette, or captured onto cassette, and then converted to magnetic tape for input.

e. **Input.** The data, now in magnetic form, is subjected to validity checks by computer program before it is used for processing against the appropriate master file.

f. **Sorting.** This stage is required to re-arrange the data into the sequence required for processing eg. into the sequence of the master file. (This is a practical necessity for efficient batch processing of sequential files).

g. **Control.** This is not a *stage* as such, because control is applied throughout the *whole* data collection.

DATA COLLECTION MEDIA/METHODS IN OUTLINE.

6. a. Source document keyed directly into diskette (key-to-diskette) from some documents.

b. Source data keyed directly onto magnetic tape (Key-to-Tape) from a source document.

c. Source data keyed onto magnetic tape but via a disk (Key-to-Disk) from a source document.

d. Portable encoding devices.

e. The source document itself prepared in machine-sensible form using Character Recognition techniques.

f. Source data captured in 'Tags'.

g. Use of Plastic Badges or Data Carriers.

h. Creation of data or input as a by-product of another operation.

i. On-line transmission of data from source.

SUMMARY.

7. a. Data collection is the process of getting data in a form suitable for processing against master files.

POINTS TO NOTE.

8. a. Many traditional methods require data preparation, eg. Key-to-Disk, key-to-tape etc.

b. Many modern methods collect data in machine sensible form thereby eliminating data preparation eg. Character recognition, source document capture etc.

15 Methods and Media

INTRODUCTION.

1. This chapter explains the various media/methods used in the data collection process. We will go through them one by one in the order previously indicated.

2. In earlier chapters we concentrated on devices and media. Now we consider the whole data entry process.

KEY-TO-DISKETTE.

3. We start with key-to-diskette systems because they represent a major modern method of data entry.

4. The simplest key-to-diskette system is a stand alone workstation consisting of a high quality VDU with inbuilt dual diskette units and microprocessor. (Fig. 15.1a).

5. The workstation operates under the control of its own programs which format the screen like a document, verify and validate input data, and transfer the data onto diskette. Programs for dealing with different source documents may be held on diskette and loaded by the workstation user when required.

6. The workstations are compact, robust, reliable, portable and operate autonomously. They therefore enable distributed data entry (close to the source of the data) together with a simple means of transfering data to a central computer.

7. Larger systems often include local printers to provide hard copy (ie. on paper) of the disk input (eg. for audit trail purposes), and electronic data transmission facilities (Fig. 15.1b). The largest systems normally form part of a distributed data processing system in which workstations are multi-purpose devices and facilities for data storage and transmission are varied and flexible. eg. a workstation may act as an interactive terminal to the main computer, or large volumes of data on diskette may be converted to magnetic tape for faster bulk input. (Fig. 15.1c).

8. The systems just described represent the new generation in a line of developments intended to lead to the total replacement of punched card systems. Methods which represent earlier attempts are Key-to-tape, and Key-to-disk.

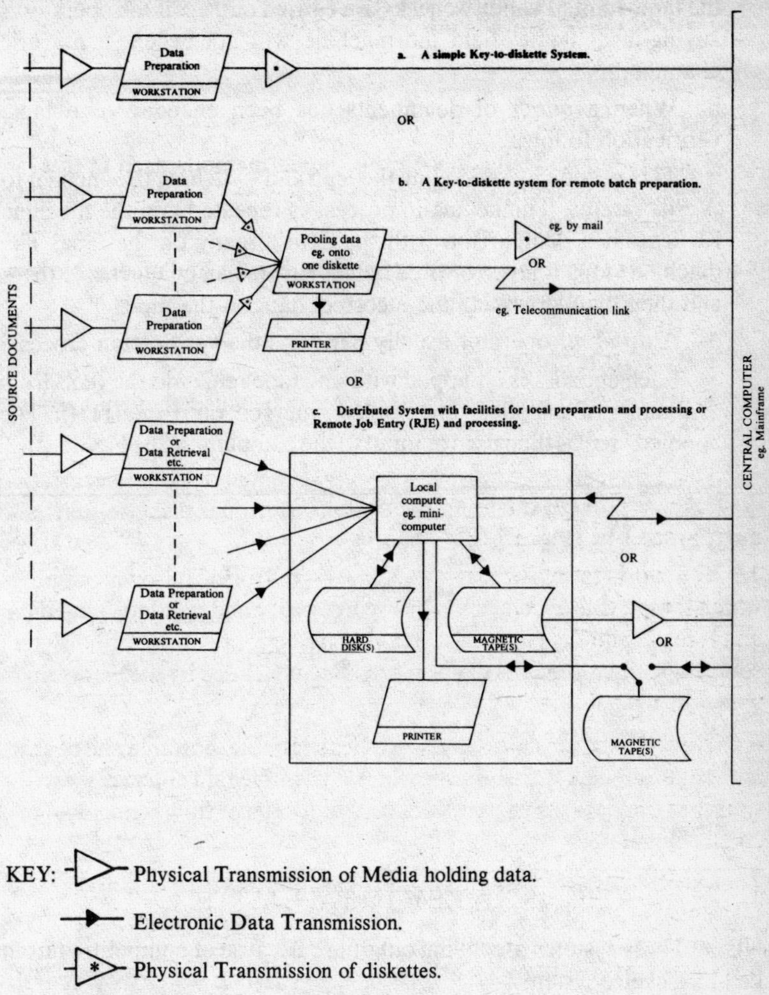

NB. WORKSTATIONS may be eg. microprocessor based VDU with integral dual diskette units.

FIG. 15.1. SOME TYPICAL DATA ENTRY SYSTEMS.

KEY-TO-TAPE.

9. This involves the use of a machine called a Magnetic Tape Encoder. The machine consists of a keyboard, a small electronic memory, and a reel of magnetic tape which is removable. The steps involved are as:

a. Data from a source document is keyed by an operator on to the tape reel via the encoder's 'memory'. Before passing from memory to the tape, limited validity checks are carried out, eg. if the operator is keying-in a 'name' field the machine will not accept a numeric character.

b. When a *batch* of documents has been encoded onto tape, verification follows.

c. This is done by re-loading the tape and switching the encoder to 'Verify' status. The keying-in process is repeated and the machine carries out a comparison with the data already on the tape. The machine stops if an error is detected. Errors can be corrected there and then by *overwriting* the incorrect data on the tape.

d. A *different* operator usually performs the verification process.

e. Each encoder is equipped with one tape reel, and the reels from a *number* of encoders are pooled (merged onto *one* reel). The "pooled" reel is then used as input to the computer. (See Fig. 15.2).

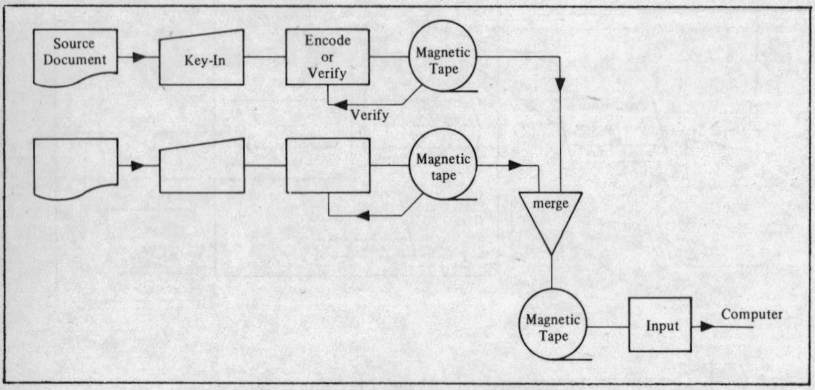

FIG. 15.2. A KEY-TO-TAPE SYSTEM.

NB. These systems are falling out of use because of competition from key-to-diskette systems.

KEY-TO-DISK.

10. These are complete "systems" consisting of a number (between 5-60 depending on model) of Key Stations linked directly to a mini computer (processor). The processor itself consists of a small memory, an arithmetic logic unit, and a control unit. Directly linked to the processor is a disk unit and a tape unit. All the key stations and the processor will generally be located together in one room. The system operates as follows:-

a. Data from a source document is keyed in at a key station by an operator. Data is automatically formatted and stored on the disk under control of a program in the processor. (The program is changed for each different type of application ie. payroll, invoice etc).

b. Verification is done by a different operator who keys in the same data from the source documents. This is compared with the data already residing on disk and errors can be corrected there and then. Data to be verified is identified by batch numbers.

c. On instructions keyed in by the supervisor via a console typewriter completed batches are written from disk to a magnetic tape reel which is taken to the computer and used as input.

d. A limited amount of sorting and validation is carried out by the system.

e. Each key station be used for both keying and verification.

f. Control totals are automatically assembled by the processor. (See Fig. 15.3).

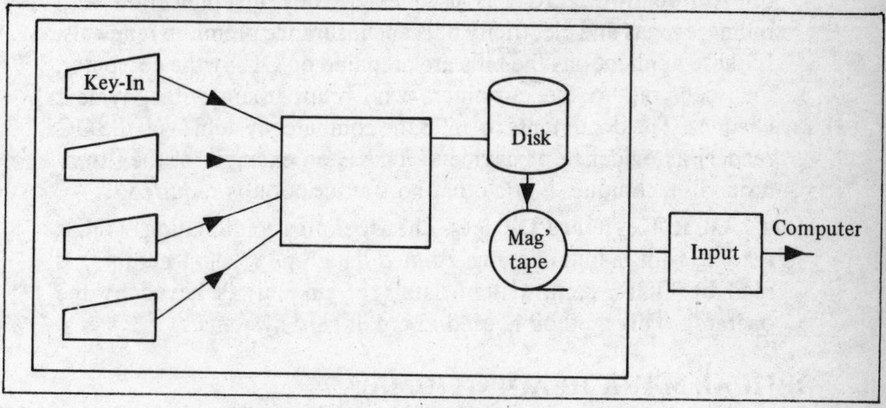

FIG. 15.3. A KEY-TO-DISK SYSTEM.

PORTABLE ENCODING DEVICES.

11. Portable encoding devices are now in common use eg. data loggers (5.19). Note that these devices often employ magnetic cassettes or cartridges for storage purposes.

CHARACTER RECOGNITION.

12. The methods described so far have been concerned with turning data *into* a machine-sensible form as a pre-requisite to input. By using Optical Character Recognition (OCR) and Magnetic Ink Character Recognition (MICR) techniques, the source documents *themselves* are prepared in a machine-sensible form and thus *eliminate* the transcription stage. Notice however that such characters can *also* be recognised by the human eye. (See Fig. 5.1 and 5.3).

OPTICAL CHARACTER RECOGNITION (OCR).

13. a. **Technique explained.**

i. Alphabetic and numeric characters are created in a particular type style which can be "read" by special machines (5.12). The characters look so nearly like 'normal' print that they can *also* be read by humans.

ii. Characters are *created* by a variety of machines (eg. line printers, typewriters, cash registers etc.) fitted with the special type-face.

iii. The special optical character reading machines *can* be linked to a computer, in which case the data is read from the document into the processor.

b. **Applications.** OCR is used extensively in connection with billing, eg. gas and electricity bills and insurance premium renewals. In these applications the bills are prepared on OC by the computer, then sent out to the customers who return them with payment cheques. The documents re-enter the computer system (via. the OC reader) as evidence of payment. This is an example of the "turn-around" technique. Notice that no transcription is required.

c. **OCR/Keyboard Devices.** These permit a combination of OCR reading with manual keying. Printed data (eg. account number) is read by OCR; hand-written data (eg. amount) is keyed by the operator. This method is used in credit card systems.

OPTICAL MARK READING (OMR).

14. a. **Technique explained.** Mark reading is discussed here because it is often used in conjunction with OCR although it must be pointed out that it is a technique in *itself*. Positions on a document are given certain values. These positions when 'marked' with a pencil are interpreted by a machine. Notice it is the 'position' that the machine interprets and which has a predetermined value.

b. **Application.** Meter reader documents are a good example of the use of OMR in conjunction with OCR. The computer prints out the document for each customer (containing name, address, *last* reading etc.) in OC. The meter reader records the current reading in the form of 'marks' on the same document. The document re-enters the computer system (via a reader which reads OC *and* OM) and is processed (ie. results in a bill being sent to the customer). Note that this is another example of a "turnaround" document. (See Fig. 15.4).

MAGNETIC INK CHARACTER RECOGNITION (MICR).

15. a. **Technique explained.** Numeric characters are created in a highly stylised type, by special encoding machines using magnetic ink. Documents encoded thus are 'read' by special machines (5.14).

b. **Application.** One major application is in Banking (look at your own cheque book) although some local authorities use it for payment of rates by instalments. Cheques are encoded at the bottom with account number, branch code, and cheque number *before* being given to the customer (ie. pre-encoded). When the cheques are received *from* the customers the bottom line is completed by encoding the *amount* of the cheque (ie. post-encoded). Thus all the details necessary for processing are now encoded in MIC and the cheque enters the computer system via a magnetic ink character reader to be processed.

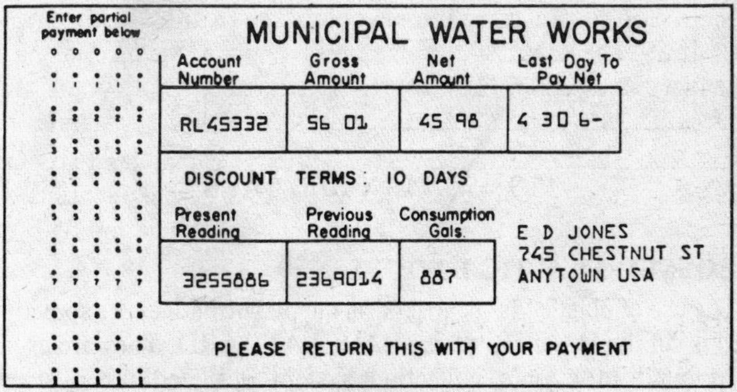
Enter partial payment below

MUNICIPAL WATER WORKS

Account Number	Gross Amount	Net Amount	Last Day To Pay Net
RL45332	56 01	45 98	4 30 6-

DISCOUNT TERMS: 10 DAYS

Present Reading	Previous Reading	Consumption Gals.
3255886	2369014	887

E D JONES
745 CHESTNUT ST
ANYTOWN USA

PLEASE RETURN THIS WITH YOUR PAYMENT

FIG. 15.4. TURNAROUND DOCUMENT (OCR/OMR).
(Courtesy IBM UK Ltd.)

PUNCHED TAGS.

16. The use of tags as a data collection technique is usually associated with clothing retailing applications although they are also used to some extent in other applications.

a. Small cardboard tags are miniature punched cards.

b. Using a special code, data such as price of garment, type and size, and branch/dept are *punched* into the tag, by a machine. Certain of the data is also *printed* on the tag.

c. Tags are affixed to the garment before sale and are *removed* at the point of sale. At the end of the day's trading each store will send its tags (representing the day's sales) in a container to the Data Processing Centre.

d. At the centre the tags are *converted* to more conventional diskette or magnetic tape for input to the computer system.

e. Note that data is "captured" at the source (point of sale) in a machine-sensible form and thus needs no transcription and can be processed straight-away by the machine. (See Fig. 15.5).

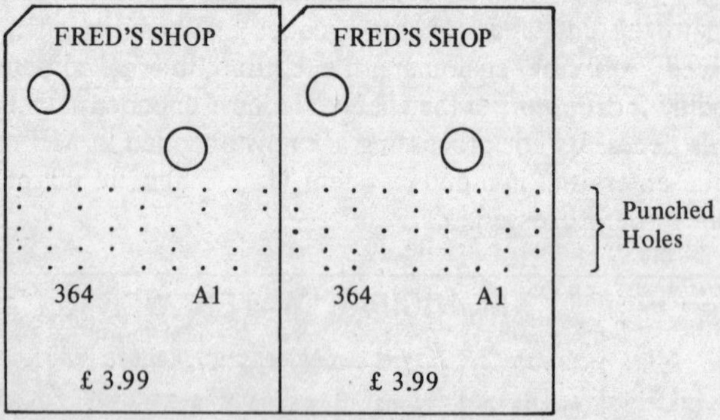

FIG. 15.5. PUNCHED TAGS.

EMBOSSED PLASTIC BADGES.

17. The use of plastic 'data carriers' as the plastic badges are sometimes called is similar in concept to the BARCLAYCARD. They are usually incorporated in a data collection system designed for a specific application. They are in use as Shop Floor data collection systems. Three elements make up such a system:-

a. **A plastic card.** This is embossed with both machine and human-sensible data. These cards can carry a variety of data according to the application. There may be a set of two or three cards. The first will contain the identification details of an operative eg. number, machine etc. The second will contain details of a job eg. number of units etc.

b. **A data recorder.** To record a job the operative inserts the cards into the recorder and presses a lever. The data is automatically transcribed into a card (similar to a punched card). Also produced is a flimsy copy for immediate control purposes. Most recorders have facilities for manual insertion of variable data, eg. items of production are recorded by *setting keys* on the machine.

c. **Converter.** This machine accepts the output (the card) from the data recorder and converts it into a medium acceptable as computer input eg. magnetic tape.

Note that the data finally captured at the conversion stage is then processed by a computer to produce the necessary information eg. production figures etc. The system described is an off-line system of data collection but the data recorder can be linked *direct* to a computer to give an on-line system of data collection.

BAR-CODED AND MAGNETIC STRIPS.

18. Data can be recorded on small strips which are read optically or magnetically. Optical reading is done by using printed 'bar codes'; ie. alternating lines and spaces which represent data in binary (see Fig. 5.4). Magnetic reading depends on a strip of magnetic tape on which data has been encoded. The data are read by a 'light-pen' which is passed over the strip. Portable devices are available which also include a key-board. An example of their use is in stock recording; the light-pen is used to read the stock code from a strip attached to the shelf, and the quantity is keyed manually. The data are recorded on a magnetic tape cassette. This technique is also used at check-out points in super-markets. Goods have a strip attached and stock code and price are read by the light-pen. The data thus collected are used to prepare a receipt automatically, and are also recorded for stock control purposes.

BY-PRODUCT.

19. All the systems describe up to now have been designed specifically with data colleciton in mind but data can very often be collected as a by-product of some other operation. Two good examples of this are found with the operation of accounting machines and cash registers:-

a. **Accounting machines.** Paper tape punches are attached to the accounting machine thus collecting immediately in machine-sensible form, sales statistics (invoicing application) stock figures (stock ledger) etc. The data is thus in a form suitable for computer processing.

b. **Cash registers.** These are fitted with tally roll printers or magnetic tape cassette units. A mass of statistical data is captured at source without any intermediate operation. The rolls of tape etc. are forwarded to the Data Processing Centre for input to a computer.

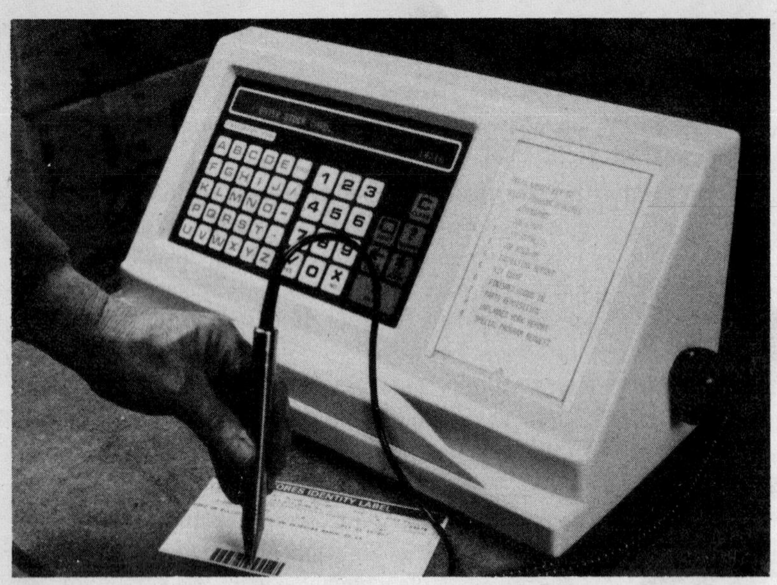

Feedback model 490 Multi-Function Industrial Terminal with Slot Bar Code Reader and Feedback 479 Wand attachment
(Picture courtesy Feedback Data Ltd)

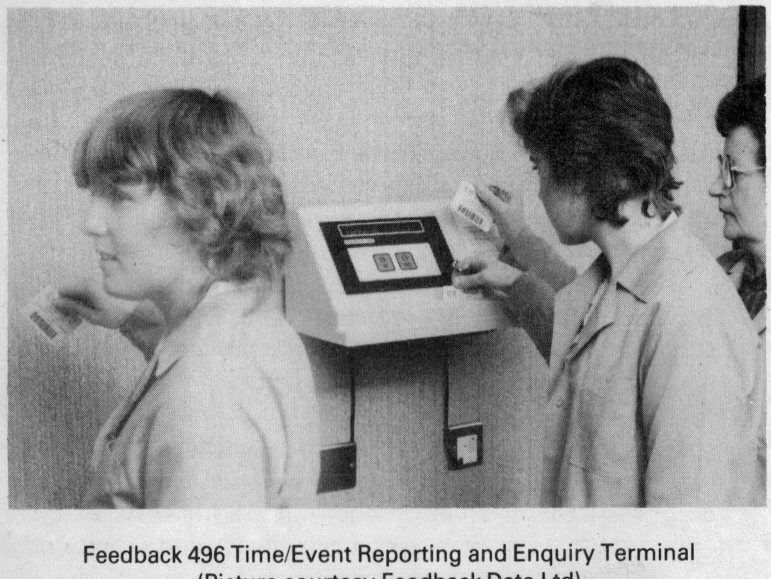

Feedback 496 Time/Event Reporting and Enquiry Terminal
(Picture courtesy Feedback Data Ltd)

ON-LINE SYSTEMS.

20. a. The ultimate in data collection is to have the computer linked *directly* to the source of the data. If this is *not* feasible then the next best thing is to 'capture' the data as near as possible to its source and feed it to the computer with little delay.

b. Such methods involve the use of data transmission equipment. The computer is linked to the terminal point (the source of data or near) by a telecommunication line and data is transmitted over the line to the computer system.

c. Data enters the terminal either by keying in via a keyboard or is transmitted using a paper tape attachment or some other medium (data having been transcribed from the source document previously).

d. On-line methods obviate the need for physical transportation of source documents to the processing point. There is also less delay in producing processed information especially if the data link provides for two-way transmission of data (ie. from terminal to computer and computer to terminal).

e. Such systems can involve large capital outlay on the necessary equipment which is usually justified in terms of speed of access to computer files and quicker feed-back of information.

DIRECT DATA ENTRY (DDE).

21. A Direct Data Entry Station consists of a Visual Display Unit with a keyboard. Data is keyed by the operator, checked, displayed on the screen and then entered for processing.

A DDE station can also be used to interrogate the computer files. The technique is particularly common with the smaller computer systems, but may be used in any configuration.

POINT-OF-SALE TERMINALS.

22. The Point-of-Sale Terminal **(PoS)** is essentially an electronic cash register which is linked to a computer, or which records data onto cassette or cartridge (15.19b).

In its simplest form, it may simply transmit the details of a transaction to the computer for processing.

The more complex terminals can communicate with the computer for such purposes as checking the credit position of a customer, obtaining prices from file and ascertaining availability of stock.

The terminal usually includes a keyboard for manual entry of data. A bar code reader may also be provided, typically to read stock codes.

Signature Verification System for NCR PC

SIRRES is a Signature Recording and Retrieval System which enables specimen signatures to be stored on computer and called up immediately on a terminal screen for comparison with that being presented.

It consists of an electronic camera kit to photograph the signature, software which runs on an NCR Decision Mate V personal computer to encode and transmit the signature to a central NCR I-series computer for storage. The signature is retrieved and displayed on the Decision Mate V screen.

(Picture courtesy NCR Ltd)

IBM 3660 Supermarket System illustrating Bar Coding and a Point of Sale Terminal (POS)

SUMMARY.

23. a. Data collection is accomplished in stages from source document through to actual processing against master files.

POINTS TO NOTE.

24. a. **Terminology.**

i. **Data collection.** The process of getting data to the computer in a machine-sensible form for processing.

ii. **Data capture.** Sometimes used as a substitute term for data collection but more specifically refers to data 'captured' in a machine-sensible form at its *source.*

b. **Differences between Key-to-tape and Key-to-disk.**

i. Key-to-tape uses *separate* machines (called encoders) and individual tapes have to be pooled for input.

ii. Key-to-disk. All key stations are *linked* to a processor and have *simultaneous* access to disk for entry of data. Data is transferred by the processor after verification to one tape reel under control of a supervisor.

iii. *No* operator handling of separate tapes is involved in Key-to-disk.

c. Note how smaller key-to-diskette systems are similar to key-to-tape and larger key-to-diskette systems are similar to key-to-disk.

d. **Key-to-tape.** The process of getting data from the source document to tape is referred to as 'ENCODING'.

e. **Punched tags.** A major manufacturer of systems based on punched tags is KIMBALL and thus you may find that they are referred to as KIMBALL TAGS.

f. Note how *on-line systems* speed up response time.

QUESTIONS.

1. a. What are the usual stages in data collection prior to the updating of a master file?

b. Describe the key-to-disk method of data preparation. (ACA)

2. Define and give TWO examples of the use of each of the following:
MICR Bar Marking
OCR Badge Readers
(IDPM Part 1)

16 Choice of Method and Media

INTRODUCTION.

1. The selection of the best method of data collection is often the biggest single problem faced by the computer user, because of the high costs involved and the other problems described. This chapter deals with the factors which influence the choice.

FACTORS.

2. The choice of data collection method/medium may be influenced by the following factors:-

a. **Appropriateness.**

i. **Magnetic Tape** is an established method of input. It is re-usable, and can be input at high speeds. Moreover, key-to-tape systems provide a method of data collection with facilities for checking and control as the data are keyed, plus reducing the need for verification. *Magnetic tape cassettes* and *cartridges* are also growing in importance, being cheap and easily transportable. Input speeds are not as high as with ½" magnetic tape.

ii. **Magnetic diskettes** (floppy disks) are of major importance as input media. Like magnetic tape, they are re-usable and advanced equipment is available for their preparation. They are compact and relatively cheap.

iii. **Character Recognition.**

(a) **MICR** is largely confined to banking. It was developed in response to the need to cope with large volumes of documents (in particular, cheques) beyond the scope of conventional methods (eg. diskettes). It is a very reliable but expensive method.

(b) **OCR** is more versatile than MICR and less expensive. It is suited to those applications which use a turnaround system such as billing in gas and electricity where volumes are too high for conventional methods. It is limited to applications in which a 'turn-around' document can be used – eg. a bill printed by the computer, part of which is returned with the payment.

(c) **OMR** is very simple and inexpensive. The forms can however be prepared only by people who have been trained in the method.

All character recognition techniques suffer from the possible disadvantage of requiring a standardised document acceptable to the document reader.

iv. **Direct Data Entry** is a very simple and convenient method, but is not suitable for large amounts of data.

v. **Terminals** provide a very fast means of data collection. They may also provide a fast means of output direct to the point of use. But costs are increased by the need to provide terminals at a number of different points and the use of data transmission.

vi. **Special Media** such as plastic badges, perforated tags and bar-coded strips reduce costs, but are essentially tailored to particular types of application.

b. **Cost.** This must be an overriding factor. The elements of cost are:-

i. **Operators.** (probably the biggest).

ii. **Machinery.** (capital and running costs).

iii. **Buildings.** Floor space and environmental requirements.

iv. **Recording media.** Punched tags and printed media are not re-usable. Magnetic media are re-usable but do eventually wear out.

c. **Time.** This can be quite fundamental in the choice of method/medium and is very much linked with cost because the quicker the response required the more it generally costs to get that response.

On-line systems will cut down this delay; so will methods like OCR which prepare source documents in a machine-sensible form.

d. **Accuracy.** This is linked with a. and f., and is a big headache in data collection. Input must be 'clean' otherwise it is rejected and delays occur. Errors at the preparation stage also are costly. Substitution of the machine for the human is the answer in general terms.

e. **Volume.** Some methods will not be able to cope with high volumes of source data within a reasonable time scale.

f. **Confidence.** It is very important that a system has a record of success. This is probably why more dated methods, like key-to-tape, take time to fall out of use. OCR and key-to-diskette have gained ground, and will grow in importance.

g. **Input medium.** The choice of input medium is very much tied up with data collection. Often it will be an integral part of data collection eg. on-line systems. Key-to-disk methods have the advantage of collecting data on what is a fast input medium. These two examples are enough to demonstrate the way in which input medium is a prime consideration when looking at the collection of data.

SUMMARY.

3. a. Data collection is a costly, time consuming, and, in many cases, cumbersome process. Therefore methods of reducing cost and/or of reducing the time involved must be worthwhile.

b. Remember the factors which influence choice of system:-
   i. Appropriateness or suitability.
   ii. Cost.
   iii. Time.
   iv. Accuracy.
   v. Volume.
   vi. Confidence.

c. Magnetic media are important for data collection as well as for storage.

d. Specialist methods such as kimball tags and plastic badges are in the minority but are important in their particular fields.

POINTS TO NOTE.

4. a. Note that data preparation is a part of the data collection process.

b. Data is often captured/prepared in one machine-sensible medium and converted to another before input to computer.

c. OCR/MICR "readers" can be of the type that are used off-line or on-line to the computer. The off-line readers may be linked to a magnetic tape unit so that the optical character/magnetic ink documents can be converted to tape for much faster input.

QUESTIONS.

1. What do you consider to be the advantages and disadvantages of the various methods/media of data collection?

17 System Controls

INTRODUCTION.

1. This chapter is concerned with controls within a DP system. The objects of control are:

a. To ensure that all data are processed.

b. To preserve the integrity of maintained data.

c. To detect, correct and re-process all errors.

d. To prevent and detect fraud.

The different controls are dealt with under the following headings:

a. Manual controls – applied to documents prior to computer processing.

b. Data preparation controls.

c. Validation checks.

d. Batch controls.

e. File controls.

DESIGN CONSIDERATIONS.

2. Controls are a major consideration of the systems designer. They must be designed into the system and thoroughly tested. Failure to build in adequate control has caused many expensive system failures.

3. The need for controls must be clearly defined at the outset to enable the appropriate action to be taken to provide them. User staff and auditors should be fully consulted.

IMPORTANCE OF CONTROL.

4. Control must be instituted as early as possible in the system. The quality of input data is of vital importance to the accuracy of output. Everything possible must be done to ensure that data are complete and accurate before input to the computer.

TYPES OF ERROR.

5. The systems designer must provide for the following types of error:

a. Missing source documents.

b. Source documents on which entries are omitted, illegible or dubious.

c. Transcription errors (eg. errors in copying data from one form to another).

d. Data preparation errors (eg. errors made when preparing diskettes).

e. Program faults.

f. Machine faults.

Note:
Machine faults are far less common in practice than is often supposed. Modern computers are self-checking to a very considerable extent (eg. parity) and usually signal any internal failure. The machine is very often blamed for what are really faults in systems design or programming.

MANUAL CONTROLS.

6. Even in advanced DP systems, considerable checking of source documents is often necessary. Such checks may be:

a. **Scrutiny** to detect:
   i. missing entries.
   ii. illegible entries.
   iii. illogical or unlikely entries.

b. **Reference** of the document to a file to verify entries.

c. **Re-calculating** to check calculations made on the document.

DATA COLLECTION CONTROLS.

7. The collection of data for processing involves transcribing it into a form suitable for machine processing. There is a very real possibility of error at this stage, and control must be imposed to prevent or detect transcription errors. The type of control depends on the method of data collection used.

a. **Magnetic Tape.** The basic control is to repeat the keyboarding operation, the second stage being known as verification.

b. **Character Recognition.** With these techniques, accuracy depends on the character reader detecting any doubtful character or mark. Some readers provide facilities for display of the character and its immediate manual correction by the operator. Otherwise, the document is rejected by the machine.

c. **On-line systems.** These depend on the data being printed (by a type-writer) or displayed (by a VDU) and checked by the operator before being released for processing.

VALIDATION CHECKS.

8. A computer cannot notice errors in the data being processed in the way that a clerk or machine operator does. Validation checks are an attempt to build into the computer program powers of judgement so that incorrect items of data are detected and reported. These checks can be made at two stages:

a. **Input.** When data is first input to the computer, different checks can be applied to prevent errors going forward for processing. For this reason, the first computer run is often referred to as VALIDATION or DATA VET.

b. **Updating.** Further checking is possible when the data input are matched with master files. The consistency of transactions with master file records can be checked by the program. It is possible to perform checks of this type during the Validation Run if the master file is on-line at the time.

9. The following are the main types of validation check which may be used.

a. **Presence.** Data are checked to ensure that all necessary fields are present.

b. **Size.** Fields are checked to ensure that they contain the correct number of characters.

c. **Range.** Numbers or codes are checked to ensure that they are within the permissible range (eg. costs codes within the series allocated).

d. **Character check.** Fields are checked to ensure that they contain only characters of the correct type (eg. that there are no letters in a numeric field).

e. **Format.** Fields are checked to ensure that the format is correct (eg. that a part number contains the correct number of alphabetic and numeric characters in the correct sequence).

f. **Reasonableness.** Quantities are checked to ensure that they are not abnormally high or low (eg. that the amount of a certain type of goods ordered is "reasonable").

g. **Check Digits.** Use of a check digit enables a number to be self-checking. It is calculated using a mathematical formula and then becomes part of the number. (See Appendix 3.1). When the number is input to the computer, the Validation Program performs the same calculation on the number as was performed when the check digit was generated in the first place. This will ensure the number is correct, eg. no digits have been transposed.

The checks described above are usually applied during the first processing run. When input data are matched with master files, further checks may be made. These are:

a. **New records.** If a complete new record is input for insertion into the master file, a check is made to see that a record with the same key number is not already present.

b. **Deleted records.** If input indicates that a record is to be deleted from the file, an error is reported if the record is not present on the file.

c. **Consistency.** Before the master file record is amended, a check may be made to ensure that the new data is consistent with data already stored in the record (eg. before updating a payroll record with overtime payments, the record would be checked to ensure that the employee was not a salaried member of staff not entitled to overtime).

BATCH CONTROLS.

10. Batch controls are fundamental to most computer-based accounting systems. The stages of batch control in a computer-based system are:-

a. **Batching.** At an early stage in processing, documents are arranged in batches by being placed in a wallet or folder, or clipped together. The number of documents in a batch may be standard (eg. 50) or may represent a convenient group (eg. one day's orders from one sales office). A *batch cover note* is attached to the batch.

b. **Numbering.** Each batch is allocated a unique number, which is entered on the batch cover note.

c. **Batch registers.** Each department or section responsible for processing the batch records its receipt and despatch in a register. It is thus possible to check that all batches have been received and dealt with, and to trace any batch which gets lost or delayed.

d. **Batch totals.** Control totals are obtained for each batch, usually using a desk adding or calculating machine. The control totals comprise:

   i. the number of documents in the batch,

   ii. totals of the fields which it is required to control (eg. total value of invoices; total value of overtime payments; total quantities or orders).

These totals are entered on the batch cover note.

e. **Data preparation.** When input is prepared, the batch totals are included. (eg. if key-to-diskette is used, batch totals are typed in first and checked against the entered data).

f. **Reconciliation.** When the input data are read by the Validation program, batch totals are reconciled. The input items are accumulated and the total agreed to the input batch control total. If the two totals do not agree, an error is reported. The report shows the two totals, the difference, and may provide a listing of all the items in the batch. The batch does not go forward for processing; it is re-input after the error has been found and corrected.

g. **Hash totals.** Batch totals are usually used to control the number of forms processed and the quantitites they contain. It is also possible to apply the technique to numbers such as customer or payroll numbers. When batch totals are obtained the numbers are also added and entered on the batch cover note. The totals are input and reconciled in the way just described. Since the totals are meaningless and useful only for control, they are called "hash" or "nonsense" totals.

FILE CONTROLS.

11. It is essential to ensure that data are not only input correctly, but also maintained correctly and processed correctly right through the system. It is also necessary to ensure that data in master files are not corrupted by machine or program failures.

The necessary safeguards are provided by *file control totals.* At the end of each file, there is a special block (sometimes blocks) which holds the total value of the items stored in the file. For example, the net total of the balances, and account of the number of records. When the file is processed, totals are accumulated from each record. At the end of the run, these totals are compared with those in the file control block. Any difference between the two totals indicates some error in processing or some corruption of data in the file.

File control totals are derived from batch totals, and the following paragraphs explain how this is done.

a. **Transaction files.** When batch totals have been reconciled, data are written onto a magnetic file for further processing. By adding all the correct batch totals for the run, a control total for the transaction file is obtained. This total is used to ensure that the transaction file is correctly processed during subsequent runs, and that all transactions are processed when the master file is updated.

b. **Master files.** When the master file is updated from the transaction file, the processing of the transaction file is controlled as described above. The control totals in the master file are then adjusted by the amount of the transactions which have been inserted into it. Subsequent runs of the master file are reconciled to the control total.

c. **Clerical control.** It is possible to maintain an independent control on computer processing. Records are kept of the batch totals and are added to provide a run total, ie. the total value of transactions passed to the DP department for processing. When the computer outputs are received the control totals printed by the machine can be reconciled to the original batch figures. Adjustments have to be made, of course, for individual items rejected by the computer because they fail validity checks.

EXAMPLE – PURCHASE INVOICE PROCESSING SYSTEM.

12. The operation of these controls is illustrated by the example which follows (Fig. 17.1) of a Purchase Invoice Processing System. Note that the system has been simplified for the sake of clarity. On the left, a system flowchart shows the main processing stages. On the right, the controls imposed at each stage are explained.

COST OF CONTROL.

13. The cost of control should be measured against the cost of *not* having it. It is possible to have too much control as well as too little. The inability of the computer to detect by itself faults in programs or data should always be kept in mind. Controls should be designed in relation to the consequences of an error going undetected, and after investigations into the types of error likely to occur. Controls should be inserted into the system at the point where they give maximum benefit. It is often necessary to adjust controls (particularly validity checks) in the light of practical experience.

SUMMARY.

14. a. Controls need to be designed into a system carefully.

b. Controls are considered under the following headings:
   - i. Manual
   - ii. Data preparation
   - iii. Validation checks
   - iv. Batch controls
   - v. File controls

c. Control is costly. Consideration should be given to what *should* be controlled rather than what *can* be controlled.

SYSTEM FLOWCHART

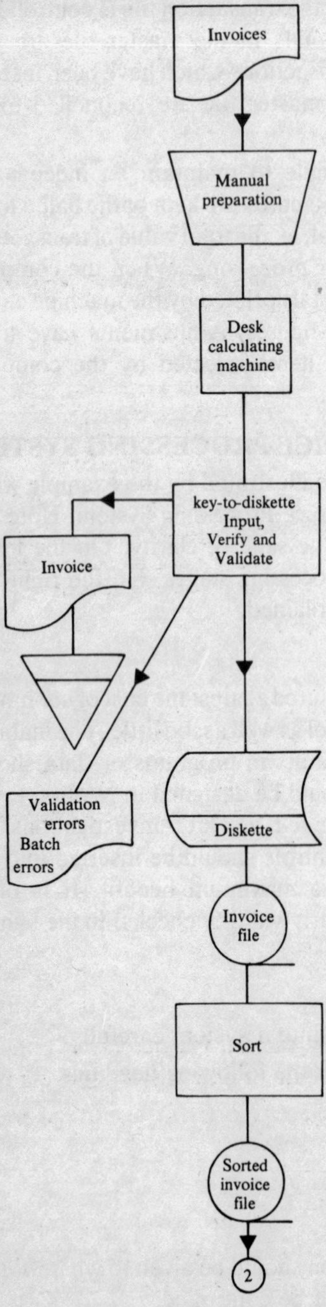

PROCESSING AND CONTROL STAGES

Receipts
Invoices received from suppliers

Manual preparation
1. Supplier number verified by reference to supplier file.
2. Invoice checked against purchase order and goods received note.
3. Invoice scrutinised for legibility.
4. Invoices arranged in batches.
5. Batch Cover note attached and numbered.

Desk calculating machine
1. Invoice calculations checked (quantity x price, discount)
2. Batch totals obtained for
   a. number of invoices.
   b. value of invoices.

Input and verification
1. Key in
   a. invoice details
   b. batch totals
2. Data verified.
3. Errors corrected.

Validation
1. Validation checks (eg)
   a. all fields keyed in correctly.
   b. supplier number (check digit)
   c. invoice value (reasonable)
2. Batch control totals reconciled.
3. Valid data copied to magnetic tape (Invoice File).
4. Invalid data reported (subsequent re-processing and re-input not shown).
5. Batch control totals accumulated to provide file control total.

Sort
1. Invoice details sorted to supplier sequence (sorted invoice file).
2. File control total copied onto new file.

. . . continued

continued . . .

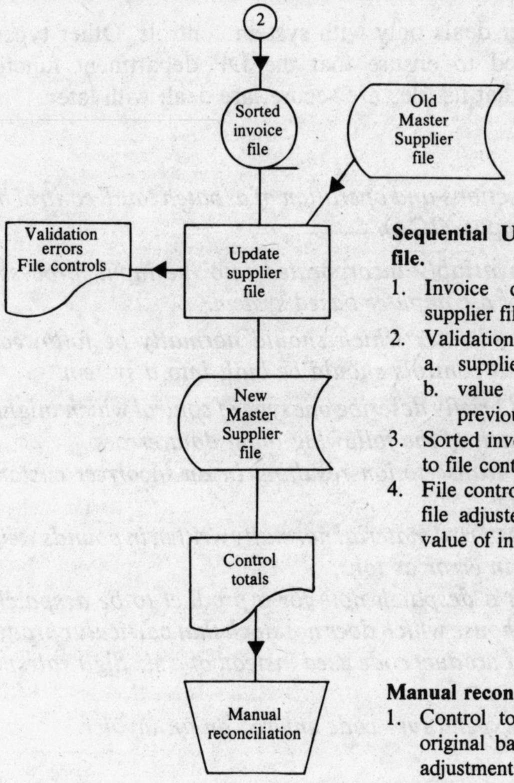

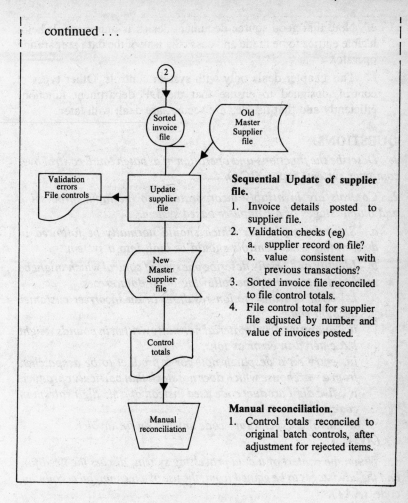

Sequential Update of supplier file.

1. Invoice details posted to supplier file.
2. Validation checks (eg)
   a. supplier record on file?
   b. value consistent with previous transactions?
3. Sorted invoice file reconciled to file control totals.
4. File control total for supplier file adjusted by number and value of invoices posted.

Manual reconciliation.

1. Control totals reconciled to original batch controls, after adjustment for rejected items.

FIG. 17.1.

POINTS TO NOTE.

15. a. Note the importance of detecting an error as quickly as possible so that it may be put right and the data re-enter the system quickly.

b. Long delays are caused by rejected input. It has to 'go round again' and this can cause days of delay.

c. The unit of control for input is usually the batch.

d. Note the use of the check digit. Its use preserves the integrity of the numeric field and when used in conjunction with the record key it ensures a transaction is processed against the correct master record.

e. Note that good source document design is important. It helps legible entries to be made and eases the task of the data preparation operator.

f. This chapter deals only with system controls. Other types of control, designed to ensure that the DP department functions efficiently and that its files are secure, are dealt with later.

QUESTIONS.

1. Describe the functions and operation of a 'batch total' control over computer systems input. (ICA).

2. Controls are invariably incorporated into the input, processing and output stages of a computer-based system.

a. State the guidelines which should normally be followed in determining what controls should be built into a system.

b. Identify and briefly describe one type of control which might be used to detect each of the following input data errors:

i. error of transcription resulting in an incorrect customer account code;

ii. quantity of raw material normally written in pounds weight but entered in error as tons;

iii. entry on a despatch note for a product to be despatched from a warehouse which does not stock that particular product;

iv. five digit product code used instead of a six digit salesman code;

v. invalid expenditure code entered on an invoice.

(ACA).

3. Within the context of a data processing system, discuss the need for, and the advantages to be gained from, the use of a meaningful accounting code. (AAT).

4. What data preparation and data validation checks may be applied to input data to assist in ensuring that the data is reliable for processing? Give full details of each method described. (IDPM Part 1).

18 Data Communications and Networks

INTRODUCTION.

1. In chapter 10 we examined the hardware aspects of data communications and system interconnections. In this chapter we complete the picture by looking at the way the hardware is used in data communications and network services.

2. We start by examining the various public services currently available for data communications and networks. The private services are examined next but since they are broadly comparable with the public services they are discussed briefly. Finally Electronic Mail is described because of its growing use in both LANs and LHNs.

PUBLIC SERVICES.

3. In the UK the principal public data communication and network services are provided by **British Telecom (BT).** However, BT is no longer a state owned company operating a monopoly. It has been privatised and now has competition for some services from other companies, eg. Mercury Communications. Of the different types of services available the majority are still based upon the ordinary telegraph and telephone circuits, which are capable of carrying data as well as speech. However, the whole industry is going through a period of rapid change and there is every indication that the current situation may change significantly within a few years.

4. System X is indicative of the changes under way. It is a digital telephone exchange system developed by BT which is currently being installed across the whole country and is due for completion in 1992. It will provide better exchange facilities than those available at present and will also provide higher performance data transmission facilities on its standard lines. When it is completed the MODEM will be obsolete.

5. The long established BT services for standard point-to-point data transmission have the trade name **DATEL** with each individual service being identified by its own number – DATEL 200, 600, 1200, 2400, 4800 etc. The number corresponds to the transmission speed in bits per second (bps). Asynchronous transmission methods (10.13) are used for transmission speeds up to 1200 bps and synchronous transmissions are used at speeds of 1200 bpi or greater. Much higher speeds can be provided, up to 48,000 bps by using wideband circuits (10.10).

6. The DATEL services make provision for the use of public lines and privately leased lines. The latter tend to be used by organisations with significant amounts of data to transmit.

7. TELEX (short for telegraph exchange) is another well established service. It is a public dial-up switched circuit system with over 80,000 users in the UK and over a million world wide. The transmitter/receiver at each subscriber point of connection is a teleprinter, similar to a computer console typewriter.

8. A newer form of TELEX service has been developed in recent years. It is called **TELETEX** (a name easily confused with **Teletext** – to be described later). Teletex terminals are able to transmit low resolution graphics pictures as well as text. The teletex service is still under development. There are proposals to make available a higher level teletex service which transmitts high quality pictures compatible with FAX (see below).

9. Facsimile Transmission (FAX for short) is another service which has grown in importance in recent years. Pictures and diagrams may be transmitted from place to place using FAX terminals connected to a standard telephone line. A typical FAX terminal looks like a small desktop electrostatic photocopier. Indeed, it scans and prints pictures using the same principles. Of course, it has a number of features not found on a photocopier to enable the transmission and reception of data. A basic FAX terminal is able to transmit or receive A4 size documents but many machines have facilities for automatic dialing, multiple polling, call reservation and the transmission of documents of various standard sizes. Lines with speeds greater than 2400 bps are preferable for these devices. Then a whole document can be transmitted within a few minutes.

10. PRESTEL is a computer based information service available from BT over the telephone line with the aid PRESTEL terminals. Prestel is an example of **viewdata** which also has the international name **videotex.** Viewdata systems can be either public or private. An example of a public viewdata service, like PRESTEL, is shown in Fig. 18.1. The viewdata terminals, like those used on PRESTEL, are plugged into standard telephone sockets. In the home a telephone set may be used to display the information, provided it has been fitted with a special adaptor and keypad.

11. PRESTEL has been described as an "electronic encyclopedia for the home" but its main success has probably been in various business applications. There are currently over 60,000 PRESTEL users and over

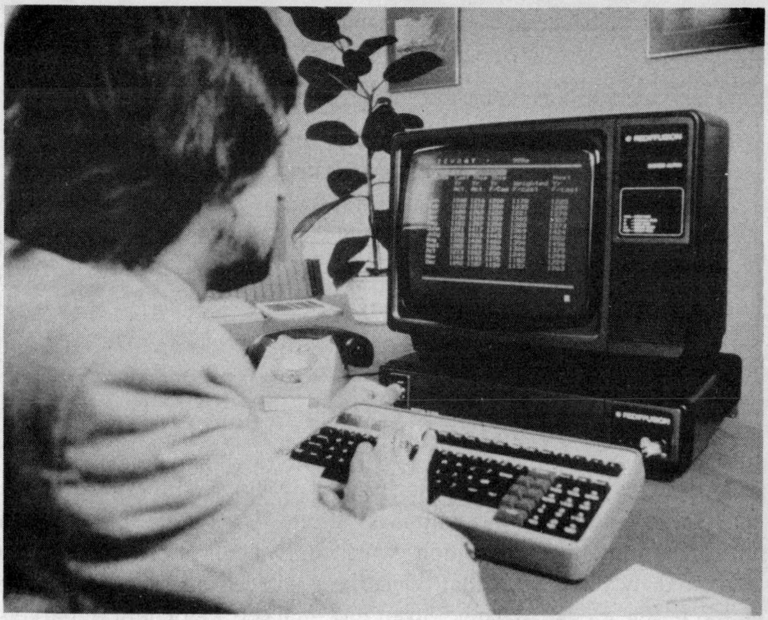

A "System Alpha Model 1 Teleputer" Terminal for use with private Videotex and British Telecom's Prestel.
Picture by courtesy of Rediffusion Computers Ltd.

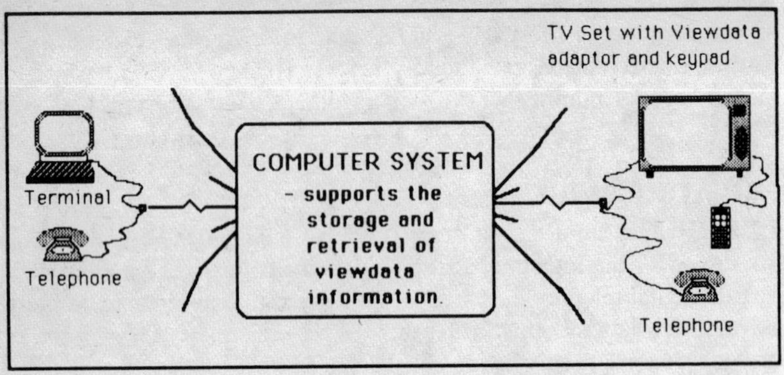

FIG. 18.1. A VIEWDATA SYSTEM.

1,200 sources of information being used to provide PRESTEL with over 300,000 "frames" of information. A "frame" is a screen sized page of information. The information which has been most successfully exploited by business is that concerning subjects such as the money markets, the stock exchange, insurance markets, agricultural markets and travel information. Users pay a standard rental plus call charges and a charge for each page viewed. Some pages may be viewed freely others may cost several pence to view for a few minutes. Organisations may purchase frame space in order to provide information to PRESTEL users. The information is fed via a PRESTEL terminal. PRESTEL is a two-way service so a user wishing to respond to information given (eg. surveys, services or advertisements) is able to do so.

12. Do not confuse **viewdata** with **teletext,** which is also a computer based information system, and which has some features in common with viewdata. The important difference is that whereas viewdata is a two-way system, teletext is a receive-only system. Teletext services are provided by the BBC (*Ceefax*) and ITV (*Oracle*). In teletext the "frames" of information are transmitted together with the TV signals using spare bandwidth. Provided the set has been fitted with a teletext adaptor it is able to decode the signals and display the frames of information on the TV screen. A hand held control pad allows individual numbered frames of information to be selected. The methods used by viewdata and teletext for displaying frames of information are compatible with one another.

13. PSS is a packet switching system (10.20) provided by BT and operating in a network linking major cities. The PSS network has links with other major networks including several in Europe and North

America. Many companies have become major users of this service since its introduction in the early eighties and it is likely to expand even further. Each connection to the PSS network is called a PSS gateway and has an account number which is rather like a telephone number only longer.

PRIVATE SERVICES.

14. The Public Services just described have their private counterparts. So, just as BT has introduced System X, many companies have installed private digital telephone exchanges. There are also companies running private viewdata systems. For example, several travel tour operators provide a viewdata service for travel agent.

15. An important trend in recent years has been the move towards integrating the various kinds of services used within the organisation. For example, if a building is to be rewired so as to provide lines from a central computer to workstations in offices it is possible to install one single digital transmission circuit containing a PABX (10.16) which is able to handle both the data communications and the telephone communications. Even greater integrations of services can be achieved if LANs are used (10.24). Devices used for viewdata or FAX can be interconnected with the main computer system, or even Personal Computers, so as to form one large information system. In such a system orders collected by a private viewdata system can be automatically processed along with those collected by more conventional means or perhaps by a member of the sales staff equiped with a portable personal computer.

ELECTRONIC MAIL.

16. As its name suggests **Electronic Mail** has some features comparable with those of the postal service. These features are given here in outline:

a. Each user has a "mailbox" which is accessed via a computer terminal or workstation within the system by entering an account number and password. Messages are drawn to the users attention when entering the system, for example, by displaying message headings on the screen.

b. When a message is sent it consists of two parts:

   i. A header which specifies the address of who it is to be sent to and the address of who it is from. The address may merely be another account number in simple cases.

   ii. The text of the message.

c. The mailing system provides computerised ways of preparing, and editing the text of the message.

d. The mailing system also provides computerised ways of selecting messages to be read and then displaying them, saving them, deleting them, forwarding them or replying to them as required.

17. Electronic mail is an increasingly common facility to be found on LANs. On some LANs one computer may specialise in handling the electronic mail. Such a computer is called a "mail server". Users on the LAN always communicate with the mail server when dealing with mail. On other systems each computer takes a share of the work in processing the electronic mail.

18. Electronic mail on LHNs is transmitted using message switching systems or packet switching systems. There are already a number of private Electronic Mail systems which exploit public packet switching systems. The sender's computer and receiver's computer do the work of assembling the message, making the transmission and disassembling the message. BT intend to launch a public electronic mail system which will probably make use of their existing PSS system.

SUMMARY.

19. The following services have been discussed:

a. Digital telephone systems such as System X.
b. The BT DATEL service.
c. TELEX and TELETEX.
d. Facsimile Transmission (FAX).
e. Viewdata (videotex) and BT's PRESTEL.
f. Teletext (BBC's Ceefax and ITV's Oracle).
g. The BT packet switching system (PSS).
h. Electronic Mail.

POINTS TO NOTE.

20. Each of the services described is important in its own right in terms of its uses in Data Processing but it is when these separate systems are integrated into a single IT system that they can have a particularly significant effect on the way in which Data Processing activities are carried out.

QUESTIONS.

1. What are the main problems that can arise in capturing raw data for use within a computer system? What solutions would you propose? (ICMA).

2. a. *Explain the term "data communications".*

   b. *Describe examples of traditional data communications equipment used for point-to-point communications.*

3. *Explain the difference between teletex and teletext.*

4. *Describe a public viewdata service.*

System Description and Programming

1. When a new computer system is to be developed, it becomes necessary to express the requirements in a number of ways. The requirements must initially be expressed in terms that the user can understand and agree to. Ultimately these requirements will be presented to the computer in a form of a set of instructions which the machine can obey, ie. a program. Any associated manual procedures must also be specified.

2. Over many years various methods have been developed to enable the clear and unambiguous expression of requirements and procedures. This Part looks at the these methods in detail.

3. In chapter 19 a number of methods of specifying processing requirements and procedures are illustrated.

4. Chapter 20 explains how to produce decision tables and decision trees.

5. The remaining two chapters in this Part deal with programming principles and practices, and programming languages.

6. These definitions are given here in order to aid the understanding of the following chapters:-

a. **Program.** A program is a series of *instructions* assembled to enable the computer to carry out a specified procedure.

b. **Programming.** The process of taking the steps in a procedure and putting them in the coded "language" of the computer is called "Programming".

c. The *computer* program comprises a large number of the steps necessary to carry out a procedure (eg. sales ledger) and is placed into main storage whenever the particular procedure is to be carried out. Once in main storage the sequence of instructions is carried out *automatically* until the last customer's record has been processed.

19 Specifying Processing Requirements and Procedures

INTRODUCTION.

1. The first half of this chapter deals with the *traditional* methods of specifying a data processing system ie. by the use of Flowcharts. Flowcharts were widely used in the past and are still important from an examination point of view. The second half of this chapter introduces modern methods which have superseded flowcharts in most circumstances. Some specialised methods eg. the use of decision tables, have been left for full discussion in later chapters.

THE NEED FOR THE METHODS.

2. The general model of a DP system (Fig. 1.2) highlights the fact that in essence all a DP system does is perform processing operations on input data, or stored data, to produce information. The prospective *user* of a new DP system will tend to view the proposed system in those terms (eg. "I want to feed in the hours worked and get back a payroll cash analysis, among other things"). However, such requirements must be expressed in precise and clearly defined terms to ensure that when the system is developed it does what it is intended to do.

3. Computer specialists need to be able to analyse the user's information requirements, design suitable solutions, implement new DP systems and then maintain the systems. To do all this they need a number of "tools" for the job.

4. Different "tools" are used at different stages in the work. For example, the "Systems Analyst", whose job it is to analyse the user requirements, must be able to express the requirements in terms that the user can understand and ratify, and must also be able to express the requirements in terms which aid the design process (we will see how charts and diagrams can be effective tools for this). At a later stage a programmer will need to break down design specifications of processing functions into simple well controlled operations on data. Well proven and efficient methods are needed at all stages.

FLOWCHARTS.

5. Flowcharts are a traditional means of showing, in diagrammatic form, the sequence of steps in a system and the relationship between them. Various *types* of flowchart are described here.

TYPES OF FLOWCHART.

6. We will consider flowcharts under four headings:-

a. Blockcharts (or diagrams).
b. Systems flowcharts.
c. Procedure flowcharts.
d. Program flowcharts.

BLOCK CHARTS.

7. The block chart (or diagram) shows the sequence of the main procedures in a system and can be regarded as the simplest form of flowchart. The object of such a chart is to give the broad picture only and it will contain no detail of *how* each procedure is carried out. See Fig. 19.1.

SYSTEMS FLOWCHARTS.

8. The systems flowchart shows in more detail the procedures outlined in the block diagram. It provides a picture of the processing operations in the system. The systems flowchart is concerned with the complete system (not just the part the computer plays in it) and will therefore include both clerical and computer operations. (The symbols are shown in Appendix 3.2).

9. Because of the additional detail involved in constructing systems flowcharts they sometimes take up more than one standard sheet of paper. This is overcome by dividing up the flowchart, and linking the various parts by means of connector symbols. (Examples will be given in chapters 24 and 25).

10. The common System Flowchart symbols are shown in appendix 3.2. Use of specific symbols for input, storage etc may be useful if it is important to show the physical details of a particular design, but generally speaking the NCC symbols are preferable because they highlight the logical (ie. non-physical) features and therefore avoid hiding the important data flows of the design in unnecessary physical details of a particular implementaiton.

PROCEDURE FLOWCHARTS.

11. These charts are in tabular form and normally contain NCC symbols (Appx. 3.2). They are often employed to describe an existing manual system which is a candidate for computerisation and act as an aid to problem analysis. The following example takes a *written* description of a manual sales ledger system and shows the corresponding procedure flowchart.

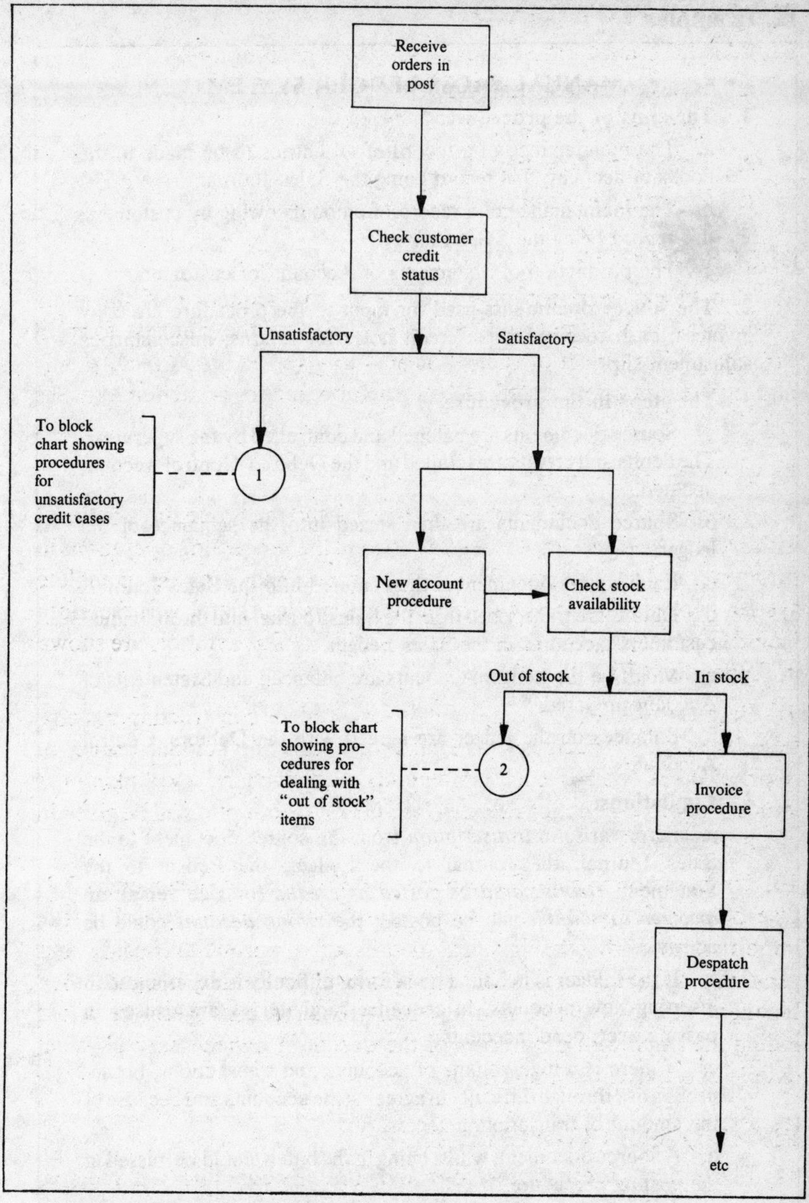

FIG. 19.1. A BLOCK CHART SHOWING THE MAIN CLERICAL PROCEDURES FOR DEALING WITH A CREDIT ORDER.

12. Example.

MANUAL SALES LEDGER SYSTEM

1. The aims of the procedure.

a. The maintenance of a record of all entries to be made to the books of account; this record being the Sales Journal.

b. The maintenance of a record of amounts owing by customers; this record being the Sales Ledger.

c. The production of Statements of Account for customers.

2. The source documents used for input to the procedure are copy invoices; cash received slips; credit notes for returns; miscellaneous adjustment slips.

3. The steps in the procedure.

a. Source documents are batched and controlled by the supervisor. The debits and credits are totalled and the Debtors' Control Account updated.

b. Source documents are then sorted into the sequence of the ledger.

c. Each source document is then entered into the Sales Journal.

d. Details are transcribed from the Sales Journal into the individual customers' accounts in the Sales Ledger.

e. Monthly, the Ledger Accounts are balanced and Statements of Account prepared.

f. Balances on the ledger are agreed with the Debtors' Control Account.

4. Limitations.

a. Errors arise in *transcription* from the source document to the Sales Journal; the Journal to the Ledger; the Ledger to the Statement. *Debits could be posted as credits* (or vice versa); an *incorrect amount* could be posted; the *wrong account* could be adjusted.

b. If the Ledger is in bound book form, difficulty is experienced in inserting new accounts, in sequence, and delays are caused in passing over 'dead' accounts.

c. If there is a high volume of accounts and transactions, bottlenecks arise through difficulty in agreeing the accounts and because of the amount of transcription necessary.

d. A source document, whilst being in the batch, could be missed in the posting procedure.

NB. This example provides more than a mere description of the procedures, because in investigating an existing system it is essential always to record all its features and limitations. Without such details the System Analyst could easily retain old faults in the new design.

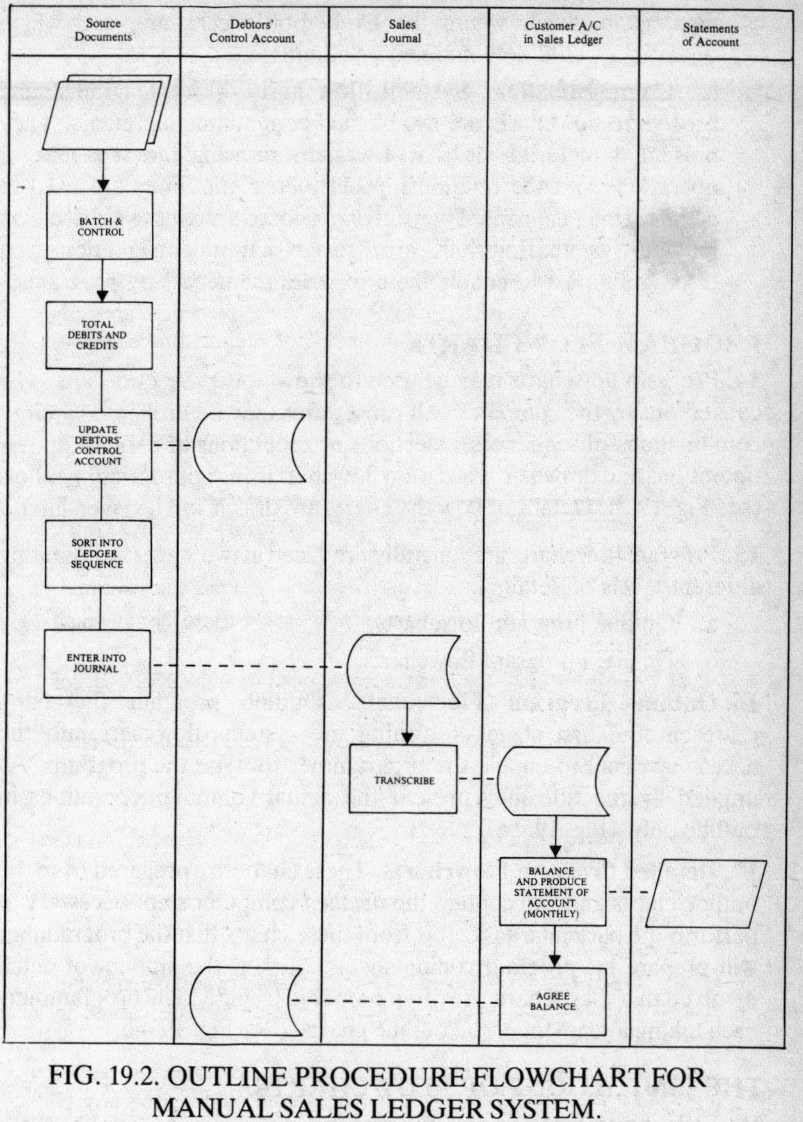

FIG. 19.2. OUTLINE PROCEDURE FLOWCHART FOR MANUAL SALES LEDGER SYSTEM.

USES.

13. Procedure charts, block charts and system flowcharts are used by systems analysts during the recording and design stages. They serve two main purposes:-

a. **Analysis.** By putting down the many operations involved in a system in the form of a flowchart the analyst obtains a better idea of what is involved, where the likely bottlenecks are, and which operations could be combined or eliminated.

b. **Communication.** Systems flowcharts, block diagrams, and procedure flowcharts are established communication media. They present a pictorial view of a system showing the sequence of operations and the relationship between them. They are used to acquaint management of present or proposed systems to aid decision making. Systems flowcharts are also part of the documentation given to programmers to enable them to write the necessary programs.

PROGRAM FLOWCHARTS.

14. Program flowcharts may be used to show *how* procedures are to be carried out by the *computer*. All procedures may be broken down into combinations of sequences, selections or repetitions of basic computer operations and drawn on a program flowchart using appropriate symbols (see Fig. 19.3). Details of how the charts are drawn will be given later.

15. Program flowcharts are generally produced in two stages representing different levels of details:-

a. Outline program flowcharts.

b. Detailed program flowcharts.

16. Outline Program Flowcharts. Outline program flowcharts represent the first stage of turning the systems flowchart into the necessary detail to enable the programmer to write the programs. As implied by the title they present the actual computer operations in outline only. (Fig. 19.4 a.)

17. Detailed Program Flowcharts. These charts are prepared from the outline charts and will contain the *detailed* computer steps necessary to perform the particular task. It is from these charts that the programmer will prepare his program coding sheets. Such is the amount of detail involved that these charts are often prepared by individual programmers each taking a segment of the outline charts. (See Fig. 19.4 b.)

THE LIMITATIONS OF FLOWCHARTS.

18. Flowcharts were originally introduced as aids to a systematic process of analysing problems and developing suitable computer based solutions. In recent years flowcharts have been heavily criticised as being cumbersome and inefficient tools for the job. Newer alternatives have been introduced and widely adopted.

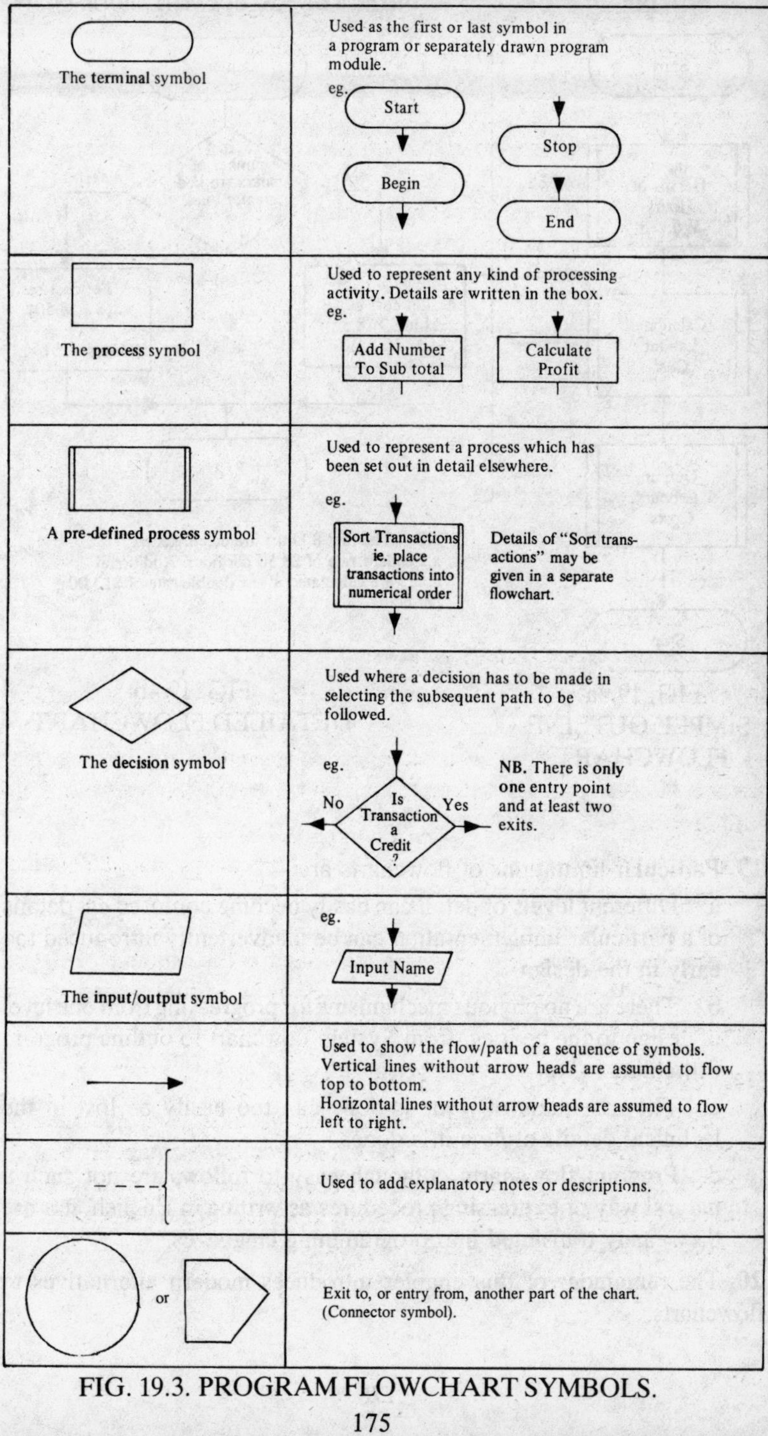

FIG. 19.3. PROGRAM FLOWCHART SYMBOLS.

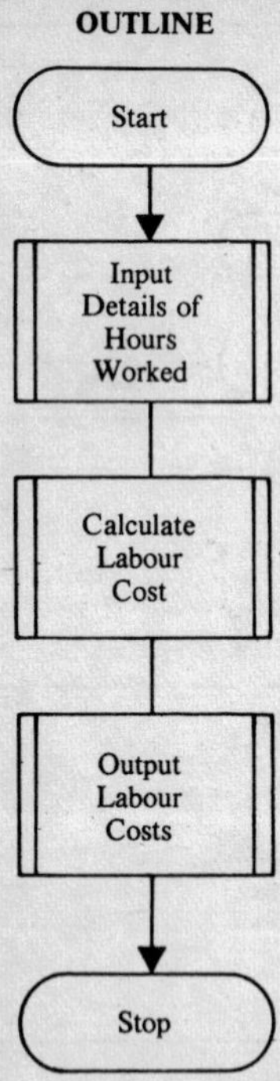

FIG. 19.4a.
SIMPLE OUTLINE FLOWCHART.

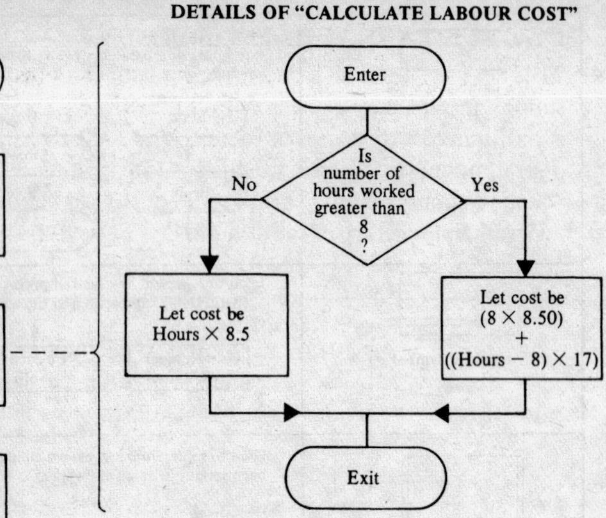

NB. The first 8 hours are calculated at a standard rate of £8.50 per hour. Additional hours are calculated at the double rate of £17.00 per hour.

FIG. 19.4b.
DETAILED FLOWCHART.

19. Particular limitations of flowcharts are:-

a. Different levels of detail can easily become confused eg. details of a particular implementation can be inadvertently introduced too early in the design.

b. There are no obvious mechanisms for progressing from one level of design to the next eg. from System flowchart to outline program flowchart.

c. The essentials of *what* is done can too easily be lost in the technical details of *how* it is done.

d. Program flowcharts, although easy to follow, are not such a natural way of expressing procedures as writing in English, nor are they easily translated into programming languages.

20. The remainder of this chapter introduces modern alternatives to flowcharts.

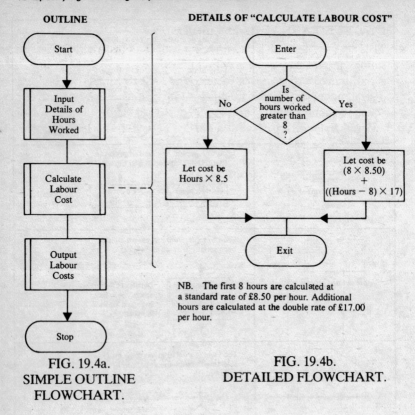

DATA FLOW DIAGRAMS (DFDs).

21. These are used in modern methods of Systems Analysis. They are simple, in that they use a convention with few symbols and rules, and avoid unnecessary technical detail. They aid the analyst in building a logical model of the system which is free of unnecessary detail, and in which the important data flows stand out. They aid the user in providing an intelligible picture of the system. See Figs. 19.5 and 19.6.

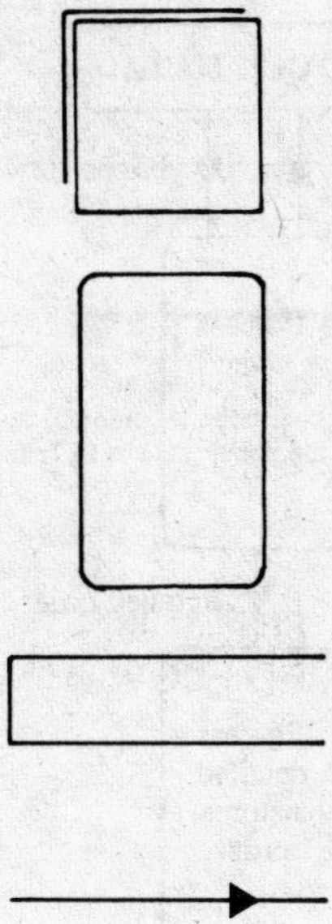

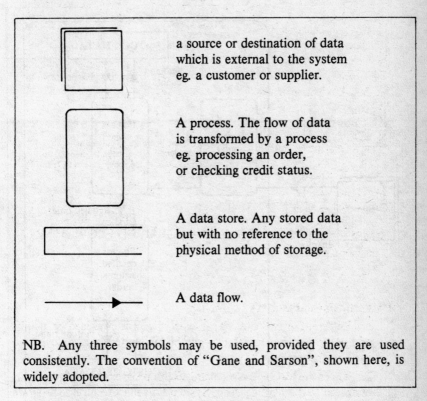

a source or destination of data which is external to the system eg. a customer or supplier.

A process. The flow of data is transformed by a process eg. processing an order, or checking credit status.

A data store. Any stored data but with no reference to the physical method of storage.

A data flow.

NB. Any three symbols may be used, provided they are used consistently. The convention of "Gane and Sarson", shown here, is widely adopted.

FIG. 19.5. DATA FLOW DIAGRAM BASIC CONVENTIONS.

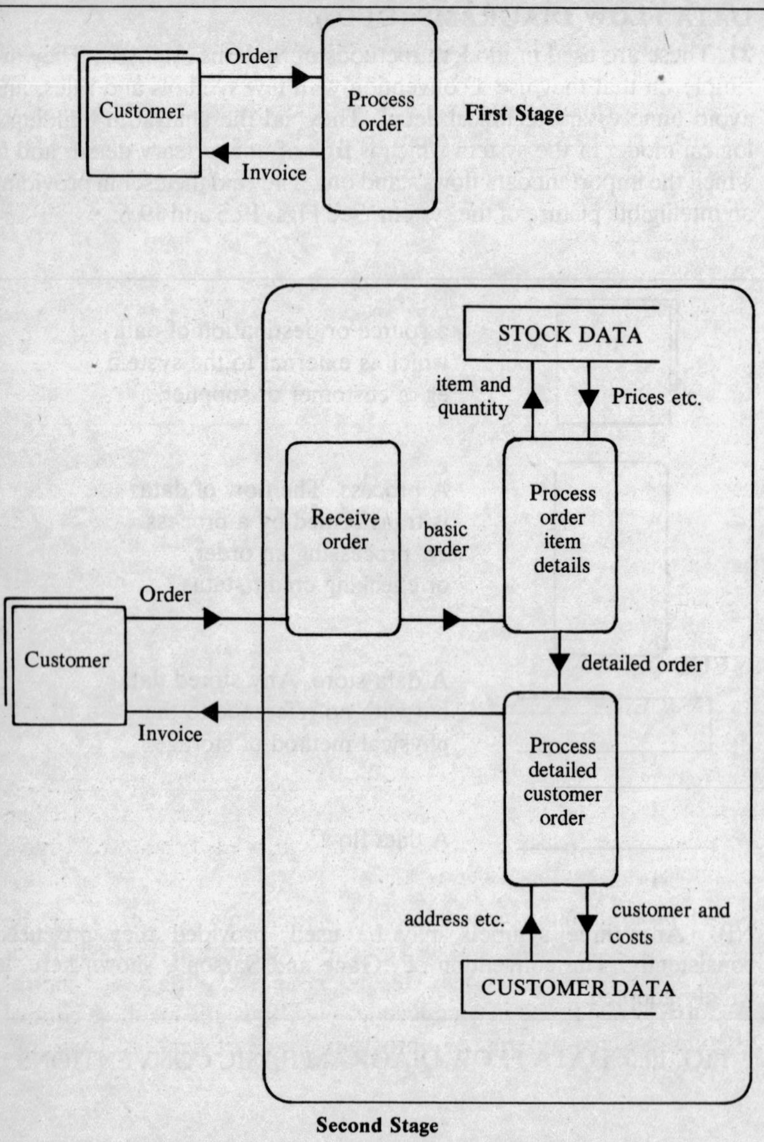

NB. Processes are expanded at each stage. Exception details (eg. out of stock items) are omitted at early stages.

FIG. 19.6. DATA FLOW DIAGRAM OF AN ORDER PROCESSING SYSTEM.

STRUCTURE DIAGRAMS.

22. Computer systems are frequently required to produce information in some "structured" form, eg. as a report. Some "structured" data, eg. files, will normally be processed in order to produce the required information. **Structure diagrams** are used to describe the structure of the data, and from the structure diagrams the appropriate processing procedures may be produced, normally with the aid of additional structure diagrams.

23. One popular programming methodology based upon this approach is known as "Jackson Structured Programming" (JSP), after its founder M.A. Jackson.

24. Data and programs are described in terms of three basic components:

a. Sequences.

b. Selections.

c. Repetitions.

25. Structure diagrams are built from these components working from top to bottom. Each line is *read from left to right* and expands the previous line into more detail. (See Fig. 19.7).

PSEUDOCODE.

26. Pseudocode is a modern alternative to the program flowchart, but without the limitations of the flowchart (para. 19).

27. Pseudocode is half way between English and a programming language. It is based upon a few simple grammatical constructions which avoid the ambiguities of English but which can be easily converted into a computer programming language.

28. All programming procedures, no matter how complex, may be reduced to a combination of controlled sequences, selections or repetitions of basic operations. This fact gives rise to the basic "control structures" to be found in pseudocode. Fig. 19.8 explains these control structures by cross reference to program flowchart symbols. (Also see Fig. 19.9).

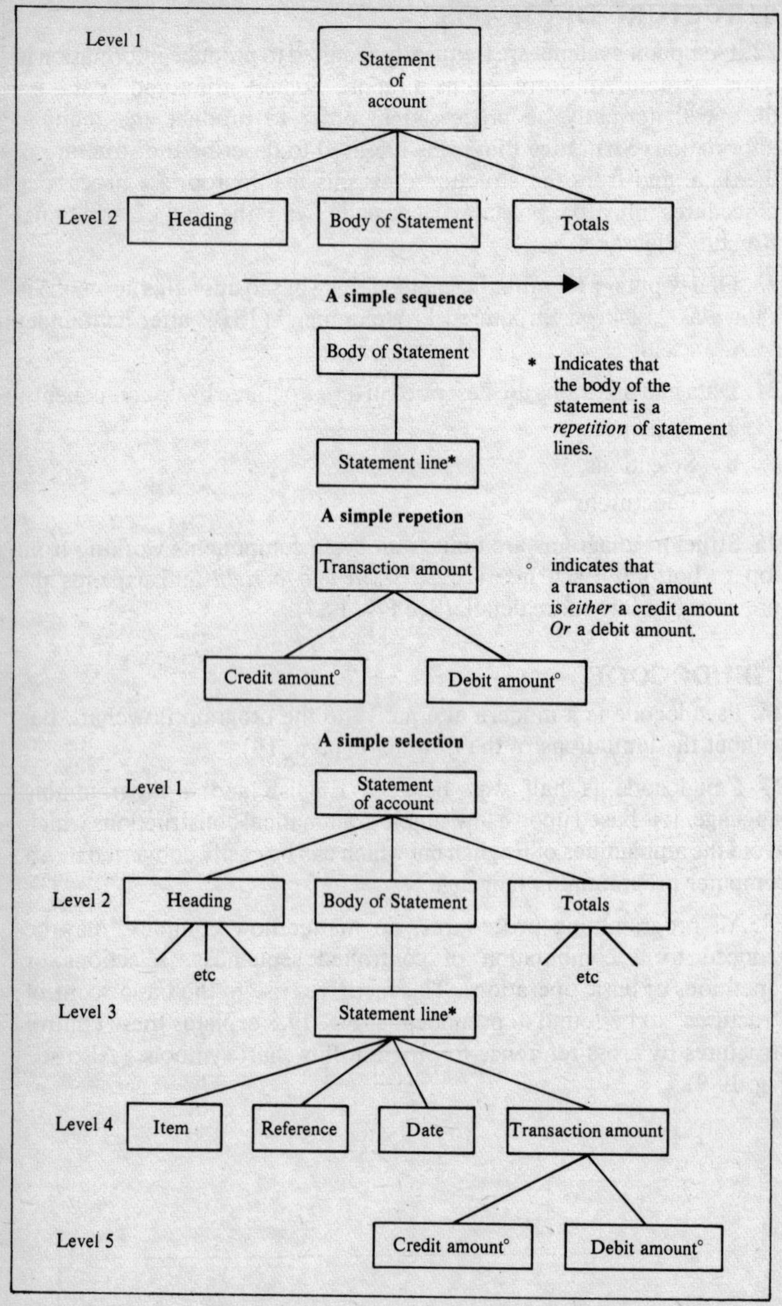

FIG. 19.7. STRUCTURE DIAGRAM EXAMPLES.

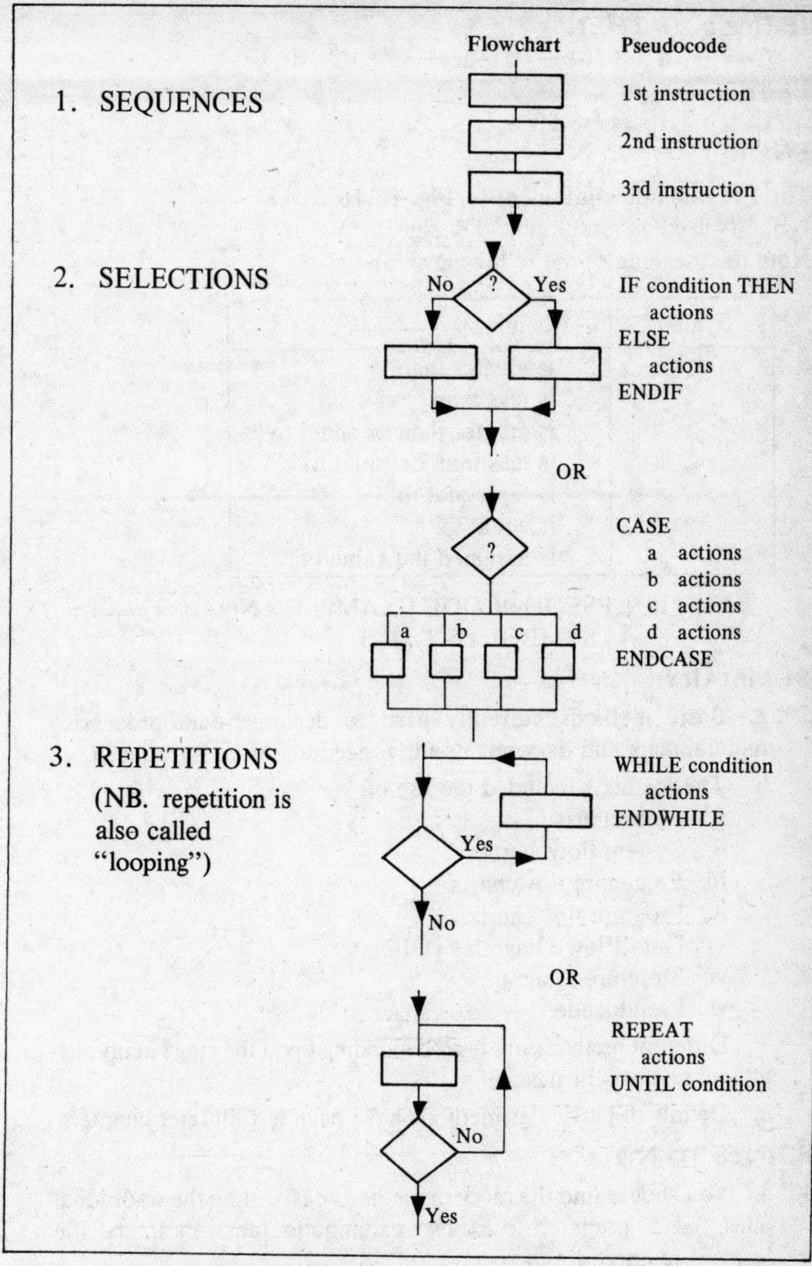

FIG. 19.8. PROGRAM CONTROL STRUCTURES.

```
IF Hours > 8 THEN
   Cost ← (8 * 8.50) + ((Hours −8) * 17)
ELSE
   Cost ← Hours * 8.50
ENDIF
```

The Pseudocode equivalent to Fig. 18.4b.
NB. * is used as a multiplication sign.
Note the meaning of the following symbols.

Symbol	Meaning
>	"is greater than"
<	"is less than"
⩾	"is greater than or equal to"
⩽	"is less than or equal to"
<>	"is not equal to"
=	"is equal to"
←	"is assigned the value of"

FIG. 19.9. PSEUDOCODE EXAMPLE AND SYMBOL DETAILS.

SUMMARY.

29. a. Basic methods currently used to describe data processing requirements and data processing procedures were introduced.

b. The methods included the use of:

i. Blockcharts.
ii. System flowcharts.
iii. Procedure flowcharts.
iv. Program flowcharts.
v. Data Flow Diagrams (DFDs).
vi. Structure Diagrams.
vii. Pseudocode.

c. Different methods are used depending upon the stage in investigation, analysis or design.

d. Details of particular methods have been left till later chapters.

POINTS TO NOTE.

30. a. You should find the modern methods easier than the traditional ones, but be prepared to express examination answers in specific forms if required to do so.

QUESTIONS.

1. State four limitations of program flowcharts. Suggest one alternative to flowcharts.

20 Decision Tables and Decision Trees

INTRODUCTION.

1. In considering a particular problem it is sometimes difficult to see all the possible factors involved and how they interact. Decision tables are used to analyse a problem. The conditions applying in the particular problem are set out, and the actions to be taken, as a result of any combination of the conditions arising, are shown. Decision trees are a graphical representations of decision tables. Their purpose is to aid the construction of decision tables.

2. Decision tables and trees are means of expressing process logic. They may therefore be used in conjunction with, or in place of, flowcharts or pseudocode.

3. This chapter begins with a very simple example of a commercial situation involving conditions and actions. The example is then used in the succeeding paragraphs to illustrate the concepts of decision tables and trees.

EXAMPLE 1.

4. A clerk, in assessing the amount of discount allowed on a customer's order is required to comply with the following policy:-

'Any order of £500 or more received from a credit worthy customer attracts discount of 5%, and, similarly, orders of less than £500 attract discount of 3%. Other circumstances must be referred to the supervisor for a decision'.

Now see this policy illustrated in the form of a decision tree at Fig. 20.1, and as a decision table at Fig. 20.2.

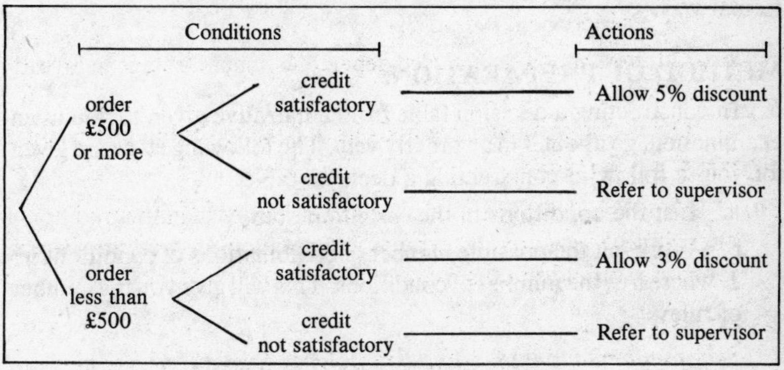

FIG. 20.1. A DECISION TREE..

CONDITIONS	RULES 1	2	3	4
Is order £500 or more?	Y	Y	N	N
Is credit satsifactory?	Y	N	Y	N
ACTIONS				
Allow discount of 3%			x	
Allow discount of 5%	x			
Refer to Supervisor		x		x

KEY		
	Y	YES
	N	NO

FIG. 20.2. A DECISION TABLE.

FORMAT.

5. Decision tables have a standardised format and are comprised of four sections (separated by double lines):-

a. **Condition stub.** This section contains a list of all possible conditions which could apply in a particular problem eg. "order of £500 or more", "satisfactory credit".

b. **Condition entry.** This section contains the different *combinations* of the conditions, each combination being given a number termed a 'Rule'.

c. **Action stub.** This section contains a list of the possible actions which could apply for any given combination of conditions, eg. give discount of "3%", "5%", "refer to supervisor".

d. **Action entry.** This section shows the actions to be taken for each combination of conditions.

NB. The decision tree contains the same information but in a less formal way.

METHOD OF PREPARATION.

6. In constructing a decision table from a narrative given to you in an examination, go about it in an orderly way. The following steps are given for you to follow in constructing a decision table.

a. List the conditions in the *condition* stub.

b. Work out the possible number of combinations of conditions ie. 2^n where n = the number of conditions. This will give you the number of rules.

In the worked example, there are 2 conditions, thus 2^2 (2×2) = 4 possible combinations (rules).

c. Rule up sufficient columns in the condition entry section for the number of combinations, ie. 4.

d. When entering 'Y' or 'N' the combinations must be *unique* (ie. no two columns must be alike). The 'halve' rule is applied to each row of condition rules as follows:-

i. **Row 1.** Y's are inserted for half the number of rules (2 in our case) then N's are inserted for the other half.

ii. **Row 2.** Alternate the Y's and N's, the groups being half the size of those in Row 1. (The group size in our example is 2 therefore the second row size will be 1 ie. Y, N, Y, N).

In an example where there are more than two rows, the halve rule is contined for the other rows.

e. Enter the action stub.

f. Follow down each rule and mark in the appropriate action to be taken.

NB. The decision tree is drawn from left to right. Each question is filled in the same order as the corresponding decision stub entry.

EXAMPLE 2.

7. The unit price of a particular product is £15 if less than 10 are purchased, £14 if between 10 and 49 are purchased, and £13.80 if 50 or more are purchased. If the customer also has preferred customer status then the purchase is subject to a discount of 10%.

This policy is illustrated in the form of a decision table in Fig. 19.3 which is arrived at by setting out all 16 rules and then eliminating impossible cases leaving just the six shown.

SUMMARY.

8. a. Decision tables are of standardised format and are used in conjunction with, or in place of, flowcharts.

Decision tables are divided into four sections:-

CONDITION STUB	CONDITION ENTRY
ACTION STUB	ACTION ENTRY

CONDITIONS	RULES					
	1	2	3	4	5	6
order < 10	Y	Y	N	N	N	N
10 ⩽ order < 50	N	N	Y	Y	N	N
50 ⩽ order	N	N	N	N	Y	Y
Preferred Customer	Y	N	N	Y	N	N
ACTIONS						
charge £15 per item		x				
charge £13.5 per item	x					
charge £14 per item				x		
charge £12.6 per item			x			
charge £13.80 per item						x
charge £12.42 per item					x	

FIG. 20.3.

POINTS TO NOTE.

9. a. The form of decision table dealt with is called LIMITED ENTRY because the *conditions* and *actions* are *limited* to the condition/action *stub* respectively. EXTENDED ENTRY tables are ones showing a *part* only of the condition/action in the *stub* with the balance in the *entry* eg. in the action *stub* of Fig. 19.2 the first two actions could be combined as "allow discount" and in the action *entry* "3%" and "5%" shown in place of the crosses.

Limited entry format and extended entry format can both be used in a single table for individual conditions or actions. Where a table contains *both* types of format it is called a MIXED ENTRY decision table.

b. When one type of format is used in preference to another depends on particular circumstances. In general terms, extended entry and mixed entry tables use fewer conditions and actions and are thus more compact, but are not so easily checked for completeness as are limited entry tables.

c. It is possible to present processing requirements to the computer in the form of decision tables, instead of programs, provided a special item of software called a "decision table processor" is available. Although some decision table processors have been available for a number of years they have not been widely adopted.

QUESTIONS.

1. When invoicing customers, the invoice clerk has to work out the discounts allowable on each order. Any order over £200 attracts a "bulk" discount of 7½%. A customer within the trade is allowed 15%. There is also a special 5% allowed for any customer who has been ordering regularly for over 2 years.

a. construct:-

i. A flowchart.

ii. A decision table.

to illustrate the management's policy.

b. State the possible advantages and disadvantages of using:-

i. Flowcharts.

ii. Decision tables.

2. A company wishes to grade its employees in accordance with a new grading structure given below:

Grade 'A' employees must satisfy at least **two** *of the following requirements:*

a. they must possess acceptable academic qualifications;

b. they must have completed a training programme;

c. they must have the commendation of their departmental head.

Failure to achieve a Grade 'A' rating automatically means a grading of 'B'.

However, if employees qualify for Grade 'A' ratings but have not received their heads' commendations they are classed as 'Grade 'A' under review' and referred to the Personnel Officer for further investigation.

Employees who are classed as Grade 'B' but who have obtained their heads' commendations are classed as 'Grade 'B' provisional' and are required to undertake further training.

You are required to:

a. Prepare a limited entry decision table describing the grading system;

b. discuss the advantages and disadvantages of decision tables compared with flowcharts.

(ICMA)

21 Programming Principles and Practices

INTRODUCTION.

1. Programming principles and practices are determined by recognised programming aims and the need for good programming methods. This chapter uses a simple programming exercise to illustrate these various aspects of programming.

2. The chapter is primarily concerned with *program writing.* Details of program execution are left till later chapters. The reader should note the difference between *program writing,* which is a once only task and the *machine's execution* of a program which occurs every time the program is placed in main storage ie. whenever there is a requirement for "running" it on the machine.

THE IMPORTANCE OF GOOD PROGRAMMING METHODS.

3. Today, great reliance is placed upon computers for all kinds of applications, including banking, insurance, public and private administration, national defence, and so on. Computers are only machines and will slavishly follow the program instructions given them.

4. The costs of programming have risen because the shortages of skilled personnel, as required for programming, have pushed up labour costs, whereas the costs of hardware have fallen because of technical innovation and increased automation. It is a false economy to reduce programming standards in order to achieve greater programmer output, because of potentially damaging effects of errors, high correction and maintenance costs and difficulties experienced in transfering sub-standard programs from one computer to another.

5. The need for good quality programming is greater than ever, but there is also a need to reduce programming costs. Experience has shown that it pays to put greater effort into program **design** rather than into trying to get a badly designed program to work. The longer an error goes undetected the more costly it is to correct and so the early stages of program design are **very** important.

PROGRAMMING AIMS.

6. These are summarised as follows:-

a. **Reliability.** ie. the program can be depended upon always to do what it is supposed to do.

b. **Maintainability.** ie. the program will be easy to change or modify when the need arises.

c. **Portability.** ie. the program will be transferable to a different computer with a minimum of modification.

d. **Readability.** ie. the program will be easy for a programmer to read and understand (this can aid a, b and c).

e. **Performance.** ie. the program causes the tasks to be done quickly and efficiently.

f. **Storage saving.** ie. the program is not allowed to be unnecessarily long.

Some of these aims are in conflict with others eg. c and f.

PROGRAMMING EXERCISE.

7. This exercise illustrates program writing.

8. Requirement. A simple program is required which will aid the checking of credit and debit totals in batches of cash transactions. A batch of 10 transactions (cash and adjustments) is to be input at a VDU keyboard. When all 10 transactions have been input, the total credit and total debit are to be displayed on the VDU screen.

9. System Flowchart. A system flowchart for this problem is shown in Fig. 21.1.

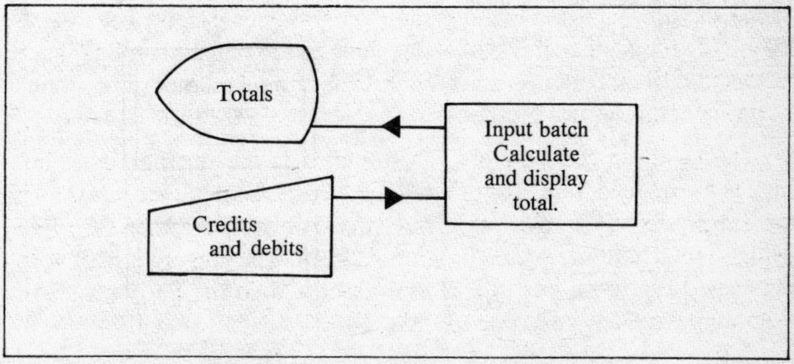

FIG. 21.1.

10. Planning the method of solution. There are a number of possible solutions, even for this simple problem eg.:-

a. **Method A.**
Input all the numbers.
Calculate the totals.
Print the totals.

b. **Method B.**
Input the numbers, adding to the totals as each number is input.
Print the totals.

Method A has the advantage of separating out the different operations. Method B will be more instructure to consider first so it is adopted for this example.

11. Developing the method using suitable aids. The two main aspects to consider are:

a. The operations to be performed on the data.

b. The way the operations are to be combined into sequences, selections or repetitions.

12. Step 1. In outline method B can be represented as in Fig. 21.2. Please note that *pseudocode is strongly recommended to you* in preference to flowcharts as a means of developing your solution. The flowcharts are given so that you can easily express solutions in flowchart form if required to do so.

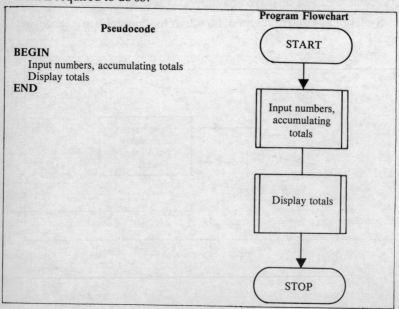

Pseudocode

```
BEGIN
   Input numbers, accumulating totals
   Display totals
END
```

Program Flowchart

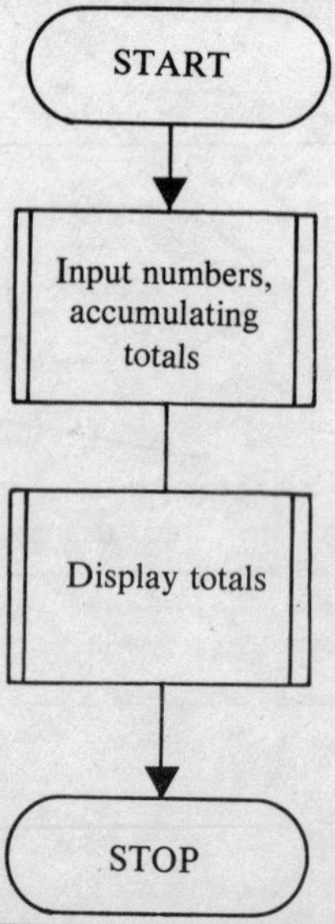

FIG. 21.2.

13. Step 2. We now fill in the next level of detail. "Input numbers, accumulating totals" needs further consideration. At this step it helps to make a comparison with this method and the use of a pocket calculator. With a pocket calculator we can add up a set of numbers by *first* clearing the display and then *repeatedly* adding one number to the "total" at a time. Here we do something very similar except we have two totals, one for credits, the other for debits.

14. In this particular problem there are 10 transactions which must be counted as they are entered.

15. Data Considerations. The data items used in the program can now be identified. They are:

a. **Numerical constants** [Numbers of fixed value identified by name]

   i. Number-in-batch (Having the value 10 in this case)

b. **Numerical Variables** [Numbers identified by name but of changing value]

   i. Credit–total.
   ii. Debit–total.
   iii. Transaction–amount.
   iv. Transactions–counted.

c. **Character Variables** [Characters identified by name but of changing value]

   i. Transaction type ('C' for Credit or 'D' for Debit)

16. The details of the stage can now be written (Fig. 21.3).

Pseudocode

NB. Comments are enclosed within braces thus:- {*comment*}

```
BEGIN
  {Set up constant}
  Number-in-batch        ← 10

  {Set up initial values}
  Credit-total           ← 0
  Debit-total            ← 0
  Transactions-counted   ← 0

  {Input Numbers, accumulate totals}
  WHILE Transaction-counted < Number-in-batch

      Input Transaction-amount, Transaction-type
      {Add one to transactions-counted}
      Transactions-counted ← Transactions-counted + 1
      Update-totals
  ENDWHILE
  Display-totals
END
```

Flowchart

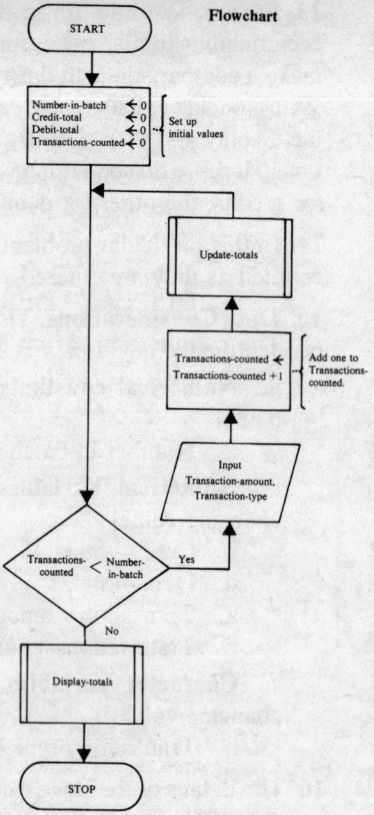

FIG. 21.3.

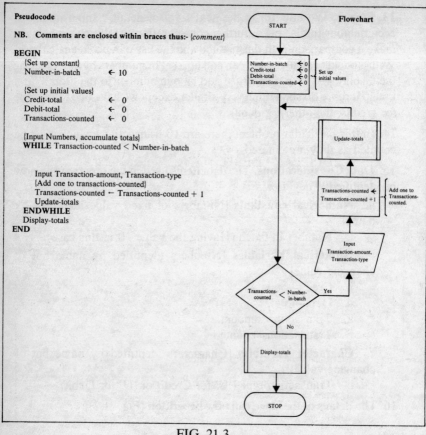

17. Step 3. The next level of detail can now be added ie. details of "Update-totals" and "Display-totals".

a. "Update-totals" involves a *selection* of a credit update or a debit update. See Fig. 21.4.

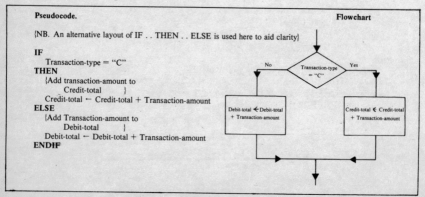

Pseudocode.

{NB. An alternative layout of IF . . THEN . . ELSE is used here to aid clarity}

```
IF
   Transaction-type = "C"
THEN
   {Add transaction-amount to
        Credit-total        }
   Credit-total ← Credit-total + Transaction-amount
ELSE
   {Add Transaction-amount to
        Debit-total         }
   Debit-total ← Debit-total + Transaction-amount
ENDIF
```

Flowchart

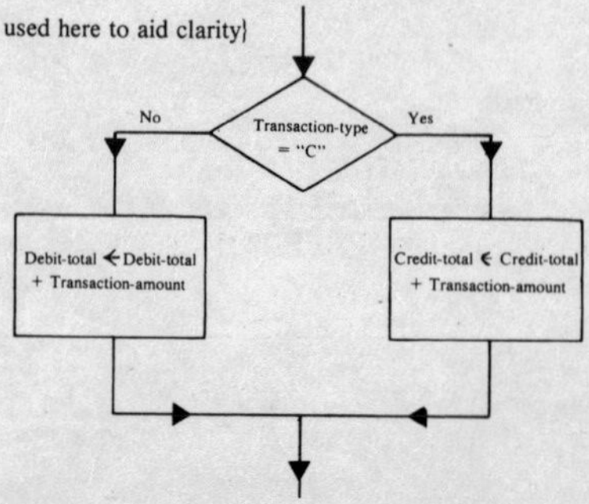

FIG. 21.4.

b. "Display-totals" involves displaying the value of the credit-total and the value of the debit-total. For the displayed values to have meaning, and hence provide information, some comments will need to be output with the data. The instruction:-

DISPLAY "CREDIT TOTAL", Credit-total

means display *literally* what is inside the quotation marks followed by the *value associated with* Credit-total. Thus "Display-totals" consists of:

DISPLAY "CREDIT TOTAL", Credit-total
DISPLAY "DEBIT TOTAL", Debit-total

18. The complete program is shown in pseudocode in Fig. 21.5. The reader may wish to draw the corresponding flowchart as an exercise.

```
BEGIN
  {Set up constant}
  Number-in-batch          ← 10

  {Set up initial values}
  Credit-total             ← 0
  Debit-total              ← 0
  Transactions-counted     ← 0

  {Input Numbers, accumulate totals}
  WHILE
    Transactions-counted < Number-in-batch

    Input Transaction-amount, Transaction-type
    {Add one to transactions-counted}
    Transactions-counted ← Transactions-counted + 1
    {Update-totals}
    IF
      Transaction-type = "C"
    THEN
      {Add Transaction-amount to
            Credit-total            }

      Credit-total ← Credit-total + Transaction-amount
    ELSE
      {Add Transaction-amount to
            Debit-total             }

      Debit-total ← Debit-total + Transaction-amount

    ENDIF
  ENDWHILE
  Display "CREDIT TOTAL", Credit-total
  Display "DEBIT TOTAL", Debit-total
END
```

FIG. 21.5.

19. Writing the instructions in a programming language. As an example the pseudocode of Fig. 21.5 is shown transcribed into the computer programming language BASIC in Fig. 21.6 BASIC has been used for the example because of its widespread use. The use of BASIC here, in no way implies that BASIC is particularly suitable as a data processing language. Therefore the reader should neither spend time studying the fine detail of this example nor consider it necessary to learn BASIC in order to understand Data Processing.

20. Transcribing the instructions into "machine-sensible" form. Programs are input to the computer in the same way as data. Details of exactly how the computer interprets the program instructions and executes them are left to a later chapter. Initially the program is executed using test data to check that it works correctly.

21. Testing the program. The program needs to be tested to ensure that it has been written and transcribed correctly, and does what it is supposed to do. Test data is carefully selected for this purpose. For example the program just described would need to be tested with a set of transactions including debits *and* credits so that *all* input, processing and output alternatives were tested.

22. Documentation includes such things as a statement of the problem, flowcharts, pseudocode, test data and results, user instructions etc. Documentation is a byproduct of the program writing process which aids maintenance or modification of the program during its lifetime. Things such as comments or remarks in programs, and meaningful data names, are forms of self documentation.

PROGRAM STRUCTURE.

23. There are two aspects to program structure:

a. **Code level structure.**

b. **Program level structure.**

It is easier to examine them in that order but program level structure is the more important of the two.

24. In Fig. 19.8 it was shown how the basic operations within a program may be organised and combined using standard control structures such as While. .Endwhile, If. .then. .else and Repeat. .until. This is code level structure, ie. the organisation and combination of individual fragments of code using standard control structures.

25. In the early stages of programming the main **operations on data** within the program must be identified and combined using the standard control structures. This is program level structure, ie. the organisation

```
100  REM  PROGRAM EXAMPLE.
110  REM  AUTHOR C S FRENCH.
120  REM
130  REM    THIS PROGRAM INPUTS A BATCH
140  REM    OF TEN CASH TRANSACTIONS AND
150  REM    PRODUCES TOTALS FOR THE
160  REM    CREDITS AND DEBITS.
170  REM
180  REM  CONSTANTS
190  REM    N : NUMBER IN BATCH
200       LET : N = 10
210  REM  VARIABLES
220  REM    C : CREDIT TOTAL
230  REM    D : DEBIT TOTAL
240  REM    T : TRANSACTIONS COUNTED
250  REM    A : TRANSACTION AMOUNT
260  REM    T$: TRANSACTION TYPE
270  REM
280  REM  BEGIN
290  REM      SET UP INITIAL VALUES
300           LET C = 0
310           LET D = 0
320           LET T = 0
330  REM
340  REM      WHILE
350  REM               TRANSACTIONS-COUNTED
360  REM          < NUMBER-IN-BATCH
370               IF T > = N THEN 610
380  REM
390  REM          INPUT TRANSACTION AMOUNT
400  REM          AND TRANSACTION TYPE
410               PRINT "TRANSACTION AMOUNT";
420               INPUT A
430               PRINT "TRANSACTION TYPE (C OR D)";
440               INPUT T$
450  REM          NOTE PROGRAM DOES NOT CHECK FOR
460  REM         INVALID T$ INPUTS
470  REM
480  REM          ADD 1 TO TRANSACTIONS COUNTED
490               LET T = T + 1
500  REM
510  REM          UPDATE TOTALS
520               IF T$ = "C" THEN 570
530  REM                 DEBIT
540                      LET D = D + A
555               GOTO 590
560  REM                 CREDIT
570                      LET C = C + A
580  REM        ENDIF
590             GOTO 370
600  REM        ENDWHILE
610             PRINT "CREDIT TOTAL"; C
620             PRINT "DEBIT TOTAL"; D
630       END
```

NB. Lines starting with REM are merely **rem**arks for the programmers benefit.

FIG. 21.6.

and combination of the main operations on the data using standard control structures.

26. Structured Programming is the name given to program writing which employs such program structuring techniques. However, the term is often used very loosely to mean anything from happening to use standard control structures in a program to using very systematic design methods employing both code level structures and program level structures.

27. The **operations on data** mentioned in paragraph 25 take the form of **subprograms** (also called **subroutines** or **procedures**). A subprogram is a *named* component of a program which performs some *well defined operation on data.* A subprogram is almost like a separate self contained program except that the main program, of which it is a component, controls its operation. Data is "passed to" the subprogram by the main program. The subprogram performs the required operations. Then, results are "passed back" to the main program by the subprogram. This may be compared with a manual procedure, eg. where an unsorted batch of transactions is *passed* to a clerk who sorts the transactions into order, creates a control total, and then *passes* them back.

28. The items of data passed to and from the subprogram are called its **parameters.** Once a subprogram's name, parameters and operations on the parameters have been specified it can be written as if it were an independent program. Clearly, this is very useful when producing very large programs because it not only means that the task can be broken down into smaller more manageable sub-tasks it also means that the sub-tasks can be divided between a number of programmers. This is the basis of a popular programming method called **stepwise refinement.**

29. When using the method of **stepwise refinement** the whole programming problem is analysed and the main subprograms are identified and specified. The **top level** of the program design is then completed by specifying these subprograms and the program level structure at the top level. The next step involves taking these subprograms and completing the same process again on each of them, ie. identifying the subprograms and control structures from which they can be constructed. This process continues again at each level until the subprograms are so small that they can be written using simple code.

30. At each stage in the stepwise refinement process the individual subprograms are tested separately, which makes it much easier to find and correct errors than would be if all the testing was left to the end. Of course, the completed program has to be tested too.

31. In paragraph 10 "method A" lent itself to the method of stepwise refinement better than "method B" because it allowed the program to be broken down into three separate and easily defined subprograms. To complete the first stage in stepwise refinement we must complete the task of specifying the subprograms and selecting the control structures.

32. The top level of the program is shown in outline in Fig. 21.7. There are three subprograms called "Input-Transactions", "Calculate-Totals" and "Print-Totals" which are arranged into a simple control **sequence** enclosed between BEGIN and END. The direction in which the parameters are passed (IN or OUT) is indicated in the parameter description. The set of ten transactions are passed as a parameter which is a single data item called an ARRAY.

```
BEGIN
  Input-Transactions  (
                         OUT : ARRAY OF TRANSACTIONS
                      )
    (*
       This procedure obtains the details of ten transactions from the user and then
       passes them OUT to the main program as a parameter which is an array of
       ten records.
    *)

  Calculate-Totals    (
                         IN  : ARRAY OF TRANSACTIONS
                         OUT : CREDIT TOTAL
                         OUT : DEBIT TOTAL
                      )
    (*
       This procedure is passed IN the array of ten transaction records as a
       parameter, calculates the totals and passes OUT the credit totals and debit
       totals as parameters.
    *)

  Print-Totals  (
                   IN : CREDIT TOTAL
                   IN : DEBIT TOTAL
                )
    (*
       This procedure is passed IN the credit totals and debit totals as parameters
       and displays them on the screen.
    *)
END
```

NB. This example uses an extended form of pseudocode in which:

i. The parameters of the subprograms are represented between parentheses "(" and ")" after the subprogram name.

ii. Comments specifying what the subprograms do are enclosed between the symbols "(*" and "*)".

FIG. 21.7. OUTLINE TOP LEVEL PROGRAM DESIGN.

STAGES OF PROGRAMMING.

33. In the process of producing the necessary instructions making up a program, the following stages can be recognised:-

a. Understanding the problem.

b. Planning the method of solution.

c. Developing the method using suitable methods and notations, eg. stepwise refinement and pseudocode.

d. Writing the instructions in a programming language.

e. Transcribing the instructions into "machine-sensible" form.

f. Testing the subprograms separately and the program as a whole.

g. Documenting all the work involved in producing the program.

34. If during testing the program an error is discovered then *it is important to go back to earlier stages* in order to correct the error. If the error comes from misunderstanding the problem it will probably be better to start again from the beginning. An outline of what happens at each programming stage now follows.

35. Understanding the problem. The programmer needs to know exactly what the program is required to do and normally works from a detailed "System Specification" (dealt with later) which lays down the *inputs, processing,* and *outputs* required.

36. Planning the method of solution. Depending upon the extent of the task, the program preparation may be shared amongst many programmers. Such cooperation requires an overall plan. Large programs may require each programmer to write a separate part of the program. These separate parts are often called modules or segments. The modules may be prepared and tested separately, then linked together to be tested as a whole.

37. Developing the method by using suitable methods and notations. Modern approaches to programming recognise the fact that complicated problems can be solved most easily if they are broken down into simpler more manageable tasks in a step by step fashion. At each step the problem is broken down further and consideration of details is put off as long as possible. This general approach is known as **Top Down Programming by Stepwise Refinement.**

38. Writing the instructions in a programming language. This may be regarded as the last step in Stepwise Refinement. The instructions written in pseudocode (or given in a flowchart) are written in a programming language. There are different types of programming "languages" and details will be given in the next chapter. Programs are sometimes written on special-forms called "Coding Sheets."

39. Transcribing instructions into "machine-sensible" form. In order to input the program to the computer the program instructions on the Coding Sheets must either be copied onto an input medium eg. diskette or typed directly into the computer eg. via a VDU Keyboard.

40. Testing the subprogram separately and the program as a whole. Once a subprogram or program has been written it is subjected to various tests to check that it has been written out and transcribed correctly, and does what it is supposed to do. These tests invariably reveal errors which have to be corrected. This can be quite a lengthy, and expensive process. Careful and thorough design in the early stages of programming will help to minimise these errors. The later an error is discovered the more expensive and troublesome it will be to get rid of.

41. Documentation. It is very important that the work of the programmer in producing a finished program is fully documented. This documentation will include a statement of the problem (System Specification), flowcharts, pseudocode tables, coding sheets, test data and results, technical details, details and instruction for the user etc. Producing these documents should be done as part of each stage in programming and not as an afterthought. If this is done the documentation will aid the programmer in programming and good documentation will aid the maintenance of a program during its lifetime. Some programs have very long lives. For example some programs written during the 1960's are still in use today, although they may have been subjected to *regular maintenance* eg. modification or bringing up to date.

SOFTWARE ENGINEERING.

42. Although almost anyone can write a simple program in a language like BASIC, just as any reasonably competent individual may be able to erect a shed in the garden, the production of larger programs to suitable standard of reliability maintainability etc. require professional methods. The shed builder is hardly a civil engineer! The adoption of systematic methods and engineering principles to the specification, design, implementation and testing of programs, including the management of such activities, has in recent years been given the name **Software Engineering.** Although it may be argued that Software Engineering is no more than a new name for good programming principles and practices it is nevertheless a useful term to use when wishing to indicate that what is meant is professional software development to industrial standards rather than amateur code writing.

COMPUTER STAFF.

43. Is is easier to see programming in context if at this stage we give some consideration to the work of the staff involved. An outline of the work is given in the following paragraphs. Greater detail will be given in a later chapter.

44. Systems Analyst. The main jobs of the analyst are:-

a. To examine the feasibility of potential computer applications.

b. Analysis of existing systems with a view to their application to a computer.

c. Design of computer-based systems, their implementation, and review.

45. It is very likely that systems analysts would work in project teams with a senior analyst in charge.

46. Programmers. Following the design process the job of programming begins. The programmer:-

a. Encodes the procedures detailed by the analyst in a language suitable for the specified computer.

b. Will liaise very closely with the analyst and the user to ensure logical correctness of programs.

47. Programmers also frequently work in project teams.

SUMMARY.

48. a. Good programming methods are important for economic and other reasons.

b. Programming aims include:
   - i. Reliability.
   - ii. Maintainability.
   - iii. Portability.
   - iv. Readability.
   - v. Performance.
   - vi. Storage saving.

c. Programming takes place in stages.

d. Modern programming methodologies have been developed with particular regard for programming aims b i to b iv above.

e. Structured programming and subprograms were introduced.

f. The work of computer staff has been introduced.

POINTS TO NOTE.

49. a. Good programs only come from good program design and good program design only comes from giving sufficient thought and effort in the early stages of programming.

b. The programmer cannot solve a programming problem satisfactorily if the problem has not been properly stated.

c. Subprograms are also sometimes called "subroutines" or "procedures".

d. One subprogram may be called upon several times, in different places within the same program.

QUESTIONS.

1. Use pseudocode to represent the management policy given in question 1 chapter 20.

2. A key-to-diskette system is to be used for the entry of orders received by a mail order business. What validation checks might be applied to the order details?

3. In the preparation of a program from program specification to operational running, certain essential tasks have to be completed by the programmer.

List and explain the main stages of the work undertaken by a programmer in achieving an operation program. (ACA)

4. **You are required,** *in the context of computer programming, to explain the following terms and to give an example of each:*

a. loop;

b. conditional branch;

c. sub-routine;

d. unconditional branch;

e. literal.

(ICMA)

22 Programming Languages and Applications Generators.

INTRODUCTION.

1. The earliest computer programs were written in the actual language of the computer. Nowadays however, the programmer writes his programs in a programming language which is relatively easy to learn and this program is translated into the language of the machine before being used for operational purposes. This translation is done by the computer.

2. The purposes of this chapter is to learn about the various types of programming language of which there are three:

a. Machine language itself.

b. Low level languages.

c. High level languages.

3. Is is **not** necessary for the reader to learn a machine or low level language in order to understand data processing. High level languages merit more attention, but an understanding of pseudocode, together with an understanding of the details given in this chapter, should be sufficient for examinations in data processing.

MACHINE LANGUAGE.

4. The basic features of machine language are illustrated here by means of a simple example. Part of a program is considered in which the larger of two numbers is determined. The procedure is first expressed in pseudocode:-

```
IF
    First-number > Second-number
THEN
    Larger ← First-number
ELSE
    Larger ← Second-number
ENDIF
```

NB. This pseudocode is very similar to the way in which the procedure would be stated in some high level languages.

FIG. 22.1.

5. Fig. 22.2. shows the machine language version of the program shown in Fig. 22.1, together with the low level language version. Some further details are given in Appx. 3.3 for the benefit of those readers who have a particular interest.

LOW LEVEL LANGUAGE	MACHINE LANGUAGE [in a 16 bit machine (7.13)]	
. BEGIN	LOCATION ADDRESS	CONTENTS (BINARY)
FNO :	0	value of first number
SNO :	1	value of second number
LNO :	2	value of larger number
LDA FNO	3	0000000000000000
SUB SNO	4	0011000000000001
JAG FGT	5	1010000000001001
LDA SNO	6	0000000000000001
STA LNO	7	0001000000000010
JPU EIF	8	0110000000001011
FGT : LDA FNO	9	0000000000000000
STA LNO	10	0001000000000010
EIF : HLT	11	1110000000000000
. END	12	etc.

INSTRUCTION FORMATS.

1. Each machine language instruction is made up of an "operation code" and one or more "operands".

a. **Operation code.** The operation code is that part of the instruction which indicates to the computer what action is to be taken eg. add, move, read etc. When the instruction is fetched by the control unit the code will be identified and the necessary circuitry activated. The number of unique operations a particular computer is capable of performing is wired into the machine when it is built. In this example the lefthand four bits are used for the operation code. eg. in location 4 the operation code is "0011" for subtract.

b. **Operand/s.** The operand is that part of the instruction which indicates the *address* of data to be worked on or identification "address" of an input/output or storage device. In this example the righthand 12 bits are used for the operand eg. in location 4 the operand code is "000000000001" ie. address "1".

Many modern computers have *two or more operands*. Multiple operands reduces the *number of* individual instructions required to complete a given task.

2. The low level language instructions correspond to machine language instructions. They each have an optional label, an operation code and an operand eg. In this example "FGT : LDA FNO" has the label "FGT" followed by the operation "LDA" followed by "FNO", an address.

FIG. 22.2.

MACHINE EXECUTION.

6. In order to follow through the discussion of machine language to its natural conclusion the following details of machine execution are presented here:-

a. The instructions are automatically executed in the sequence in which they occur in main storage.

b. When its turn comes, each instruction is *fetched* from main storage by the control unit (Fig. 3.1) and placed in a register. Then the control unit interprets the instruction and causes its execution by controlling the actions of the appropriate hardware.

c. Some instructions prompt the control unit to switch to some other point in the instruction sequence for the next *fetch,* and thereby give a mechanism for selecting or repeating particular sequences of instructions.

d. There are five basic types of machine instruction:

i. Input/Output – which control the transfer of data between peripherals and the processor.

ii. Arithmetic – which perform additions, subtractions etc.

iii. Branch – which control repetitions and selections (see c).

iv. Logic – which match and compare data items.

v. Data handling – which move and manipulate data.

7. Writing in machine language is a tedious business and not done nowadays except on very few small computers. Just consider what it entails for the programmer.

a. All the machine's operation codes have to be memorised.

b. He would need to assign all memory addresses and keep a very careful track on them.

c. Instructions have to be written as they will eventually be obeyed, *in sequence.* Thus any insertions or deletions would entail the *relocation* of all succeeding instructions.

d. Subsequent revision of a completed program would be so impracticable as to almost require a complete *rewrite.*

8. The whole process is very time-consuming and inefficient.

LOW LEVEL LANGUAGES.

9. The first step towards easing the lot of the programmer came with the introduction of SYMBOLIC or low level languages.

10. Features of low level languages.

a. Mnemonic codes are used in place of the operation code part of the instructions eg. SUB for Subtract (see Fig. 22.2) which are fairly easy to remember.

b. Symbolic addresses are used in place of actual machine addresses. These would be appropriate to the particular application, eg. "GROSPAY" being a symbolic address in a payroll program. The symbol is chosen by the programmer and used consistently to refer to one particular item of data. (eg. in Fig. 22.2 "FNO" is a symbolic address for First Number).

11. This symbolic language made program writing so much easier for the programmer but clearly a program written in this form is *not* acceptable to the machine. Thus the symbolically written program has to be *translated* into machine language before being used operationally.

12. The translation process is actually done by the *computer* itself by means of a special translating program written and supplied by the manufacturer.

13. Terminology.

a. **Assembly.** The term used to describe the translation process ie. the production in machine code form of a program written in a symbolic language.

b. **Assembler program.** The manufacturer's specially written program (sometimes referred to as a processor) which the computer uses to produce a machine language program from a program written in symbolic language.

c. **Source program.** The name given to the program written in symbolic language.

d. **Object program.** The name given to the program in machine language produced by the assembly process.

14. The assembler:-

a. Translates symbolic operation codes into machine code, and symbolic addressed into actual machine addresses.

b. Includes the necessary linkage for closed sub-routines. (See Appx. 3.3).

c. Allocates areas of main storage.

d. Will indicate invalid source language instructions.

e. Produces the object program on disk or tape.

f. Produces a printed *listing* of the object program together with comments. Notice that *one* symbolic instruction is translated into *one* machine instruction (ie. one for one) which is one feature which distinguishes a low level language from a high level language. (See Fig. 22.3).

15. Macro instructions. Notice that low level languages made program writing easier but the programmer had still to write out *every* single instruction in the source language. A macro instruction is a *single* instruction written as part of the assembly language which, when assembled, will generate *many* machine code instructions. These groups of instructions perform common sequences of instructions such as input/output operations and a whole library of 'Macros' (some written by the manufacturer, some by the user) will be kept on magnetic media. During the assembly process the macro instruction causes the group of instructions to be "called" from the library (which will be available during assembly) to form part of the object program. You can almost regard them as sub-routines (open sub-routines). (See Appx. 3.4).

HIGH LEVEL LANGUAGES.

16. Although they constitute a great advance on machine coding, low level languages have their limitations:

a. With the exception of macros, the assembly process produces machine instructions on a ONE for ONE basis and therefore program writing is still a relatively time-consuming business for the programmer.

b. Although the ability to write programs using symbols eases the job of programmer, the low level languages still suffer from being very much *machine-oriented.* By this is meant they conform to the logic of a particular machine, therefore the programmer has still to have a great deal of knowledge of the detailed workings of the particular machine. Notice that every family of computers will have its *own* particular low level language.

17. A breakthrough came with the development of HIGH LEVEL LANGUAGES. These languages move away from machine dependence and are generally more problem oriented. Source programs are written in statements almost akin to English, a great advance on the use of mere symbols.

18. Features of high level languages.

a. They have an extensive vocabulary of words, symbols and sentences.

b. Programs are written in the language and whole statements are translated into *many* (sometimes hundreds) of machine code instructions.

c. Libraries of macros and sub-routines can be incorporated.

d. As they are problem *oriented* the programmer is able to work at least to some extent independently of the machine.

e. A set of rules must be obeyed when writing the source program (akin to rules of grammar in writing English if you like).

19. Terminology.

a. **Compilation.** Term used to describe the translation process.

b. **Compiler.** The manufacturer's specially written program which translates (or "compiles") source language program.

c. **Source/object programs.** Exactly the same as for low level languages.

20. The compiler:-

a. Translates the source program statements into machine code.

b. Includes linkage for closed sub-routines.

c. Allocates areas of main storage.

d. Produces the object program on disk or magnetic tape.

e. Produces a printed copy (listing) of the source and object programs.

f. Produces a list of errors found during compilation eg. the use of 'words' or statements not included in language vocabulary; or violation of the rules of syntax. (See Fig. 22.3).

TYPES OF HIGH LEVEL LANGUAGE.

21. Five main types are:-

a. Commercial languages.

b. Scientific languages.

c. Special purpose languages.

d. Command languages for operating systems.

e. Multipurpose languages.

COMMERCIAL LANGUAGES.

22. These are your concern and the most well known of them is COBOL (Common Business Oriented Language). There are others but you should concentrate on this one for examination purposes. A detailed knowledge is not required but these paragraphs should be enough for your purposes.

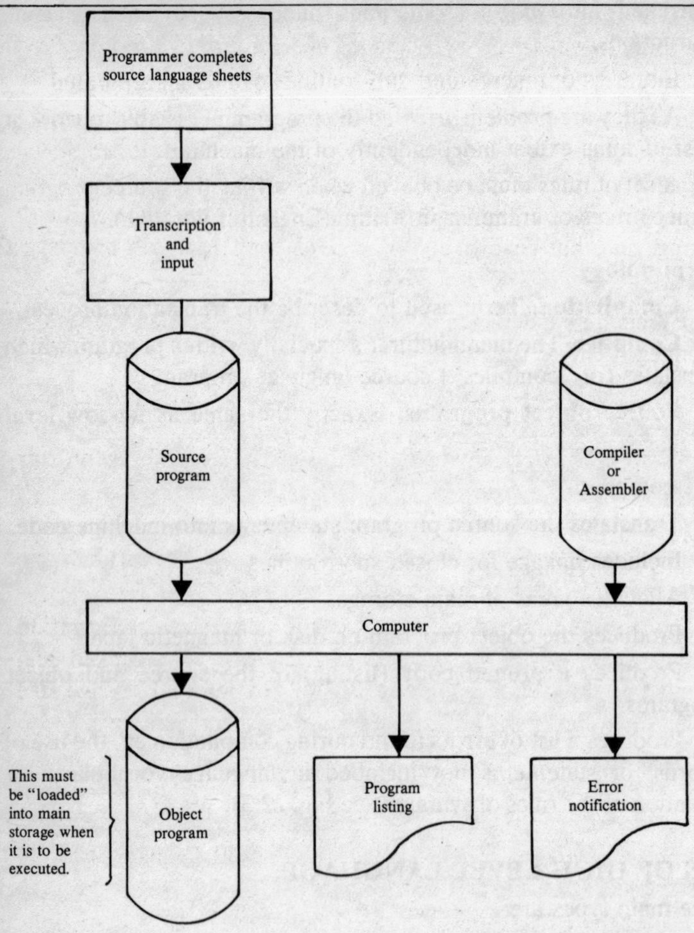

Note:

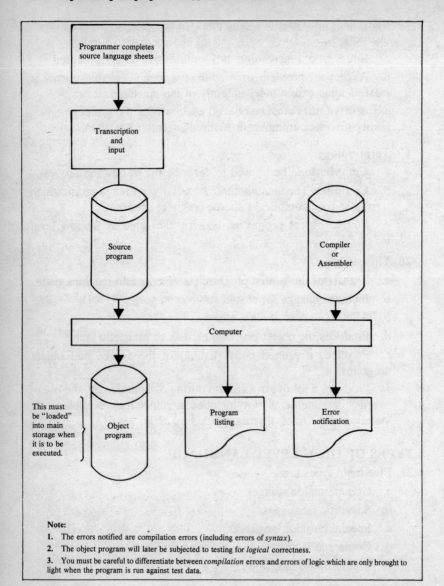

1. The errors notified are compilation errors (including errors of *syntax*).
2. The object program will later be subjected to testing for *logical* correctness.
3. You must be careful to differentiate between *compilation* errors and errors of logic which are only brought to light when the program is run against test data.

FIG. 22.3. PROCEDURE TO PRODUCE OBJECT PROGRAM.

23. COBOL is a good example of a PROBLEM-ORIENTED language. In other words its vocabulary reflects the type of *problem* to be solved rather than the type of *computer* on which the object program will be used.

24. It was intended that any program written in COBOL could be compiled and within reason, run on any computer. This has not worked out in practice, however, and each manufacturer has his own version of the language *and* thus his own compiler. This applies to most high level languages.

Some "machine independent" versions are now available on small computers eg. "CIS-COBOL".

25. COBOL is a *high level language* developed for *commercial* use. The *source program* is written using *statements* in a stylised but a readable form of English. Every *Cobol* program is made up of *four divisions:-*

a. **Identification division.** This contains the title of the program for identification purposes. It may also contain the date on which the program was written and the name of the author.

b. **Environment division.** Specifies the particular configuration (hardware) on which the object program will be compiled and executed eg. Model of machine (IBM 4341), internal storage size needed for running the object program, peripheral units etc.

c. **Data division.** All items of data to be used in writing the program are listed and identified. Names or labels are given for each *file* and any *records* or *fields* which are referred to later. Record/field *sizes* and *contents* (eg. whether alpha or numeric) are also specified. Working storage areas are defined.

d. **Procedure division.** Contains the program instructions necessary to solve the particular problem indicated in the program flowchart. These are to be in the form of statements written in a type of English and which conform to the rules of the language. (Cobol language). The statements written must use the data labels as defined in divisions 2 and 3. The compiler will report any inconsistencies. Also used are RESERVED WORDS which can only be used in a specific context because they convey a special meaning to the compiler. (Misuse of these words is reported by the compiler).

e. **Illustration of reserved words.**

"ADD TAX TO GRADPENS".

ADD . . . . . TO are reserved words indicating to the compiler that two items of data must be added together.

"TAX" and "GRADPENS" are labels of two items of data defined in the Data Division.

f. **Examples of COBOL Statements.**
(The statements are in block capitals; explanatory notes in small letters).

i. **Peripheral Instructions.**
OPEN INPUT-PAY-FILE. (prepares a file for processing)
READ PAY-FILE AT END GO TO FIN. (reads file into memory)
READ CARD-FILE AT END GO TO FIN. (reads input file)
WRITE PAY-LINE AFTER ADVANCING ONE LINE. (print after throwing paper).

ii. **Arithmetic Instructions.**
MULTIPLY HOURS BY RATE GIVING BASICPAY.
ADD BONUS TO BASIC PAY GIVING GROSSPAY.
SUBTRACT INCTAX FROM GROSSPAY GIVING NETPAY.

iii. **Branch Instructions.**
GO TO PENSION-RTN. (unconditional branch)
IF GROSS-PAY GREATER THAN 100 GO TO EXCEPTION-RTN. (conditional branch).

g. **Data Handling Instruction.**
MOVE DEDUCTIONS TO DATAC. (transfers a field to working store).

SCIENTIFIC LANGUAGES.

26. The most well known:-

a. ALGOL (**Alg**orithmic **O**riented **L**anguage). Used for scientific and engineering purposes and has particularly powerful mathematic facilities. (ALGOL 68 is a more recent extensive version).

b. FORTRAN (**For**mula **Tran**slation) mainly used for engineering applications but also of scientific use.

27. Features of these languages.

a. Extensive arithmetic computational ability.

b. Large library of inbuilt mathematical function.

c. Ability to handle mathematical expressions and procedures.

d. Array handling facilities.

SPECIAL PURPOSE LANGUAGES.

28. These are languages intended to be 'tailor made' for a particular type of problem, eg. Machine Control, Wages, Simulation, Control of Experiments. Examples are:

a. **CSL** which is a Simulation Language.

b. **Coral-16, IRTB** (Industrial Real-time Basic) and **RTL/2** which are used for real-time applications such as Process Control, ie. the direct control of physical processes, eg. Chemical plants and Power Stations.

c. **Ada** a relatively new language for real-time and some general purpose applications.

d. **Modula and Modula-2** This language is rather like an extended form of **Pascal** (see later) and is primarily especially suited to computer systems development work.

e. **QUEL** (**QUE**ry **L**anguage) and **QBE** (**Q**uery **B**y **E**xample) are examples of database query languages. (Further details in chapter 26).

COMMAND LANGUAGES FOR OPERATING SYSTEMS.

29. These are languages used to control the operation of the computer. The required facilities will be apparent after you have read chapter 28.

MULTIPURPOSE LANGUAGES.

30. These are languages which are intended to cope with a number of different types of application areas, eg. business and scientific. Examples are discussed below.

31. PL/1 was introduced by IBM as a language intended for use for business **and** scientific applications. It has been a very successful language except for the fact that its comprehensive multipurpose facilities have made it too large for use on small machines such as microcomputers and some other manufacturers have been reluctant to adopt it.

32. BASIC (**B**eginners **A**llpurpose **S**ymbolic **I**nstruction **C**ode). BASIC was created in 1964 by J. G. Kemmeny and T. E. Kurtz at Dartmouth College USA. The language was originally designed as a simplified version of FORTRAN for use in teaching programming. From those simple beginnings the language has grown to become a very popular multi-purpose language available on a wide variety of machines but particularly microcomputers and minicomputers. Today more commercial programs are being written in BASIC than are being written in COBOL, although BASIC is still behind COBOL in terms of the volume of commercial code already in existence.

33. Early versions of BASIC, and sadly many versions in use on small computers today, deserve strong criticism for having features which encourage bad programming methods. However, some newer versions such as the product "True-BASIC" devised by T. E. Kurtz and based upon the latest ANSI standard are very significantly better.

34. Other languages which are regarded as multi-purpose languages include **Pascal,** and **Modula** which are both languages designed by N. Wirth and have features which support structured programming methods more readily than many of the older languages such as COBOL or FORTRAN. Pascal and Modula are effectively their own pseudocode.

OTHER FORMS OF HIGH LEVEL LANGUAGE.

35. The language described so far in this chapter may be described as **procedural languages** because they describe **how** the computational procedures are to be carried out. There are radically different approaches to programming, however, which make use of languages which are non-procedural in that they assert **what** the required result is rather than how it is done. The details of *how* are actually handled as part of the language translation process. Two basic approaches to this assertional style of programming are:

a. **Logic Programming** for which one popular language is **Prolog.**

b. **Functional Programming** for which there are many languages available today including **LISP, ML** and **Hope.**

APPLICATIONS GENERATORS.

36. Applications generators have been in existence for many years but in their more modern forms they are often called **Fourth Generation Languages** because their supporters claim that they offer more cost effective alternatives to the high level languages such as COBOL associated with the era of 3rd Generation Computers.

37. A good applications generator may be regarded as being a very high level language which provides simple and powerful ways for the user to do such things as:

a. define data records.

b. define report or screen layouts.

c. select combinations of standard processing operations.

d. handle simple queries.

This may be achieved by presenting the user with a set of options to chose from. Thus the applications generator is usually tailoring a generalised piece of software to a particular application. There are different types of applications generators for different types of DP problems.

38. One popular applications generator is Panasophic's GENER/OL which may be used on IBM mainframes. There are numerous applications generators available for minicomputers and minicomputers many of which are useful but which often greatly overstate their capabilities!

SUMMARY.

39. a.

LANGUAGE	TRANSLATOR	INSTRUCTIONS GENERATED	ORIENTATION
Machine	None	N/A	N/A
Low level (symbolic)	Assembler	1 for 1 (+ macros)	Machine
High level	Compiler	Many for 1 statement	Problem

b. i. Low level languages are designed with particular machines in mind.

ii. High level languages are generally problem oriented.

POINTS TO NOTE.

40. a. As terminology is not completely universal, a little thought will help you decide what the examiner wants.

b. "Translator" is the *general* term for both the assembler *and* compiler and you can use it as such.

c. The word "Processor" is sometimes used instead of translator but "Processor" is used with two different meanings:-

i. Here it refers to a Software Program.

ii. It is also an abbreviation for "Central Processing Unit' which of course is a hardware device.

d. If you get a question on languages generally and not a specific comparison of high and low level languages then base your answer on *high level* languages.

e. Note the use of the world *library:*

i. Meaning a *place* (room) where tapes/disks are kept.

ii. A collection of macros or sub-routines or other programs kept on a magnetic device such as disk or tape.

f. Be prepared, in examination questions, for terms like "Assembler Language" meaning Low Level Language.

g. Applications Generators (Also called Fourth Generations Languages) are growing in importance as alternatives to conventional high level languages for many DP applications.

QUESTIONS.

1. What are the advantages and disadvantages of high level languages?

2. What is Software?
Write brief notes on two of the following:-

a. Sub-routines.

b. Loops.

c. Compiler.
(ICMA)

3. a. What are the characteristics of, and what advantages are claimed for High Level programming languages?

b. Outline, with the aid of a diagram, how a program written in a High Level language becomes a machine code program ready for operational use. (ACA)

4. a. Briefly list the main distinguishing features of high level programming languages.

b. Describe and indicate the purpose of the four divisions of a COBOL program. Illustrate your answer with a simple example of a statement which might be used in each division. (ACA)

File Processing and Database Systems

1. The processing of files is of major importance in DP. This Part discusses the subject in detail.

2. In order to understand file processing it is necessary to first have some prior knowledge of both storage devices and media, and programming which is why the subject matter of this Part could not be introduced earlier in this book.

3. Chapter 23 is an introduction to file processing and explains the basic principles methods and concepts.

4. Chapter 24 describes traditional sequential file processing and makes particular reference to batch processing and magnetic tape.

5. Chapter 25 describes non-sequential file processing with particular reference to magnetic disk. It describes more advanced batch processing methods and introduces the ideas of transaction processing.

6. The methods of chapters 23, 24 and 25 may be described as *conventional file processing*. In chapter 26 some problems of conventional file processing methods are identified and possible solutions are presented in the form of data bases and integrated systems.

23 Introduction to File Processing

INTRODUCTION.

1. In one sense computerised data processing *is* file processing ie. in practical terms data processing almost invariably involves the processing of files.

2. The recognition of this characteristic of computerised data processing highlights some important points:-

a. File processing methods must be understood in order to understand the methods of modern DP.

b. Understanding the fundamental purposes of file processing leads to a clearer understanding of the purposes of DP systems.

3. This chapter considers these two points in an introductory way. It builds on the material presented in the Part on Computer Files and prepares the way for the more detailed treatment given in the remaining chapters in this Part of the book.

DP MODELS.

4. The concept of a "Logical model" was introduced in chapter 1 (Fig. 1.2).

5. The maintained data within the DP system should correspond to what is happening outside the DP system. For example, in the case of a Stock Masterfile we need the stored values of numbers of items in stock to correspond to the actual number of goods in the warehouse. Take the example of the master file storing details of our own bank current account, we require that the balance corresponds to the actual balance of payments or withdrawals. Of course we may be prepared to accept some delay between the time changes happen and the time the master file reflects them.

6. Since every data processing system is required to provide timely, accurate and appropriate information about the real state of affairs, there is a fundamental requirement for the state of the data processing system to *correspond to* the real state of affairs ie. the data processing "model" must be valid. We now consider how this requirement is met.

RELATING THE SYSTEM TO THE DP MODEL.

7. For the sake of simplicity consider a DP system which deals with just one of the many functions within a given organisation eg. a stock control system.

8. Details about individual stock items may be stored as logical records in a stock master file. ie. a stock item is an "entity" (11.7). One "attribute" (11.7) of the stock item entity will be the number of items in stock.

9. Events taking place in the organisation will change the actual stock. The master file must be made to reflect these changes so that the required information about stock can be produced from it.

10. Events such as the introduction of new stock items, or the discontinuation of existing items, correspond to the *insertion* or *deletion* of entities in the master file.

11. Events such as the delivery of items to replenish stock, or the removal of items as they are sold, correspond to *"Debiting"* or *"Crediting"* the attribute value of the number of items in stock.

12. Events such as price increases to stock items correspond to *changing* an attribute value of stock item price.

13. From the cases just considered the following basic file processing activities can be identified:-

a. Insertions and Deletions } File maintenance
b. Changes
c. Debits and Credits } File update

In fact these activities are typical of most file processing applications. The reader should be able to see the parallels in other applications eg. We may open or close an account, change a client's address and credit or debit the client's account.

14. Although file updating and file maintenance are different file processing activities they are sometimes combined together for convenience. The term "master file update" is often used loosely to mean both update and maintenance and in the remainder of this Part the same meaning will apply.

15. Transactions. Relevant details of events need to be recorded and input to provide the data needed to update the master file. Since data is recorded about the events, the events are entities too. In traditional file terminology these entities are called transactions.

16. There are two basic strategies for processing transactions against the master file:-

a. Transaction processing – ie. processing each transaction as it occurs.

b. Batch processing – ie. collecting transaction together over some interval of time and then processing the whole batch.

17. One method of processing is no better than the other. It is a matter of "horses for courses". Details of the different methods of file processing will be discussed in the chapter following this one. The relative advantages and disadvantages of the different methods will be included in the discussion.

INFORMATION RETRIEVAL.

18. Master files may also be processed merely to provide information ie. without the maintained data being altered in any way. There may, however, be a need to manipulate data in such cases.

19. The file processing activities involved in data retrieval may be broadly classified as:-

a. Searching.

b. Selecting.

c. Sorting.

d. Summarising.

20. Searching. A query about an individual account or about a particular stock item may require looking through a master file to find the appropriate record or records.

21. Selecting. In producing a report it may be necessary to select records in a particular category and use details of their attributes. eg. producing a report of accounts exceeding their credit limit or of stock items out of stock etc.

22. Sorting. Having selected records they may provide more information if rearranged into an appropriate sequence eg. descending size of credit excess or in alphabetic sequence of stock supplier.

23. Summarising. Totals of selected items may provide sufficient information in many cases eg. total number of accounts exceeding limits or total value of stock on order.

24. Appropriate details of these processing methods will be given in the remaining chapters of this Part.

SUMMARY.

25. a. File processing is of major importance in data processing.

b. Data Processing systems model the real state of affairs and thereby serve as a source of information about the parts of an organisation to which they are applied.

c. File processing activities keep maintained data up to date and provide appropriate information as and when required.

POINTS TO NOTE.

26. a. In recent years file processing activities concerned with information retrieval have become at least as important as the traditional, repetitive, computational, processing activities such as payroll production.

24 Sequential File Processing

INTRODUCTION.

1. In earlier chapters the basic ideas concerning files, storage media and processing requirements were introduced. In this chapter those ideas are applied to sequential file processing.

2. Sequential file processing is an important feature of the simpler and long established methods of batch processing. Such methods were established when magnetic tape was the main file processing medium. Today, the same methods continue to be used but with magnetic disk as the usual choice of storage medium.

3. The chapter contains two examples. The first is used to explain how a sequential master file is updated. The second example is more general and typifies sequential file processing using magnetic tape. The example is followed by a discussion of the advantages and limitations of magnetic tape as a file storage medium.

4. In order to see sequential file processing in context, as part of batch processing, batch processing is explained before considering the first example.

BATCH PROCESSING EXPLAINED.

5. The majority of commercial computer applications are involved in batch processing. Transactions are accumulated into batches of suitable sizes, then each batch is sorted and processed. The concept is not new, in fact it is *also* adopted in most manual and mechanised systems of data processing. By its very nature a batch processing system will involve a degree of "delay". Generally, the result of processing a particular *item* of data will not be known until the results of the *batch* are known.

EXAMPLE – UPDATING A SEQUENTIAL MASTER FILE.

6. This example illustrates the basic principles involved in the update of a sequential master file, by dealing with the update of a simple stock master file.

7. Each item of stock is an entity about which data is recorded in one logical record. Each logical record is identified by its own unique key (its stock number). At any one time only some of the set of available keys will be *allocated* to stock items. eg. if an account number is a key some account numbers are not allocated.

8. It will aid a clearer understanding of the master file update if we think of the master file as the *complete* sequence of available keys, although only some keys will be allocated to stock items at any one time. The *status* of a key, ie. allocated or not allocated, is signified by the fact that only allocated keys have records physically present within the master file.

9. Processing operations. There are different types of transactions, and each transaction corresponds to a particular operation on a master file record. The status of the key will determine whether or not the operation is a valid one in a particular situation. The possible combinations of valid and invalid operations are shown in the following table:-

		TRANSACTION TYPE				
		INSERT NEW RECORD	DELETE EXISTING RECORD	CHANGE EXISTING RECORD	CREDIT EXISTING RECORD	DEBIT EXISTING RECORD
Key Status Prior To Processing The Transaction	Allocated	×	✓	✓	✓	✓
	Not Allocated	✓	×	×	×	×

Key: ✓ : a valid operation.
X : an invalid operation.

eg. "Insert new record" is **not** a valid transaction if the key is already allocated ie. present. Similarly "Delete existing record" is **not** valid if the key is not allocated.

FIG. 24.1.

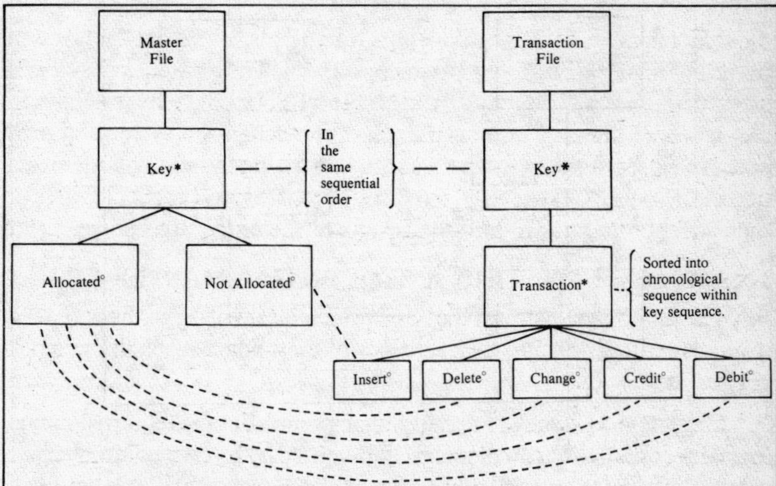

NB. ----- indicates valid operations.
Note: Some master keys may not have any corresponding transactions.

FIG. 24.2. STRUCTURE DIAGRAMS FOR THE TWO FILES USED IN THE UPDATE

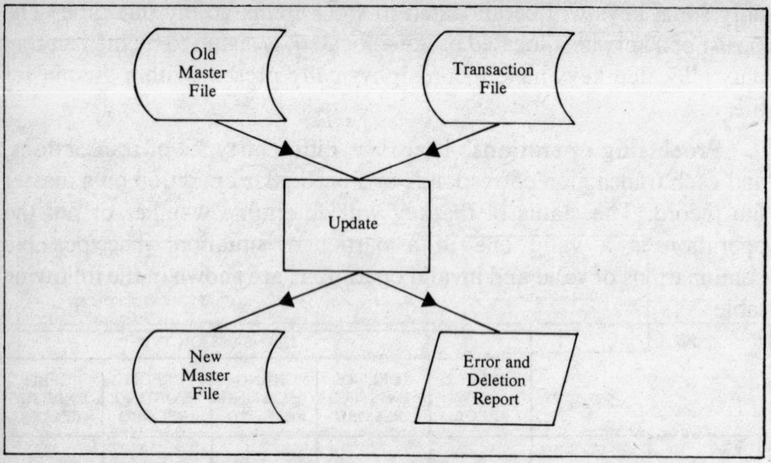

FIG. 24.3. SEQUENTIAL MASTER FILE UPDATE – SYSTEM FLOWCHART.

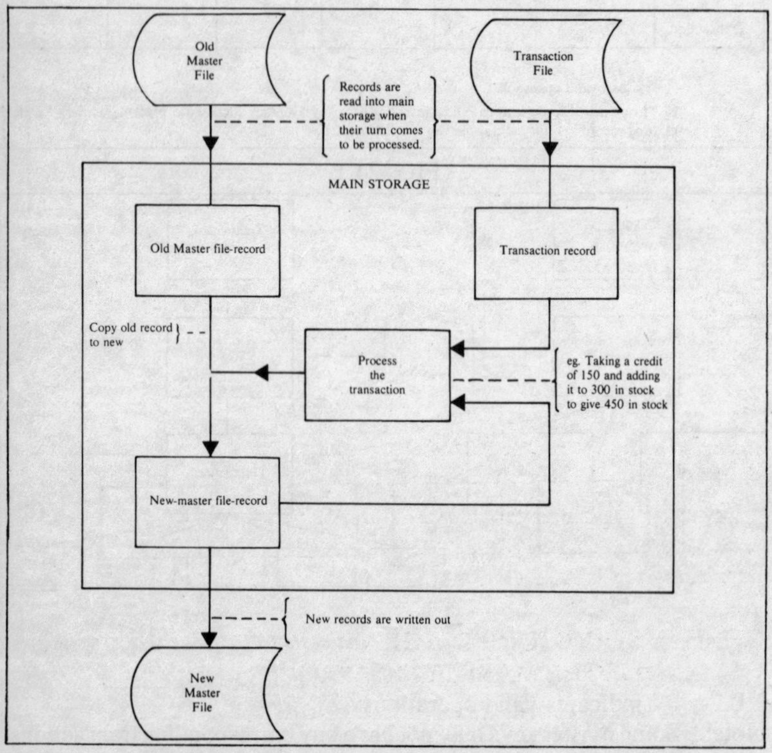

FIG. 24.4. THE FLOW OF DATA DURING A SEQUENTIAL FILE UPDATE.

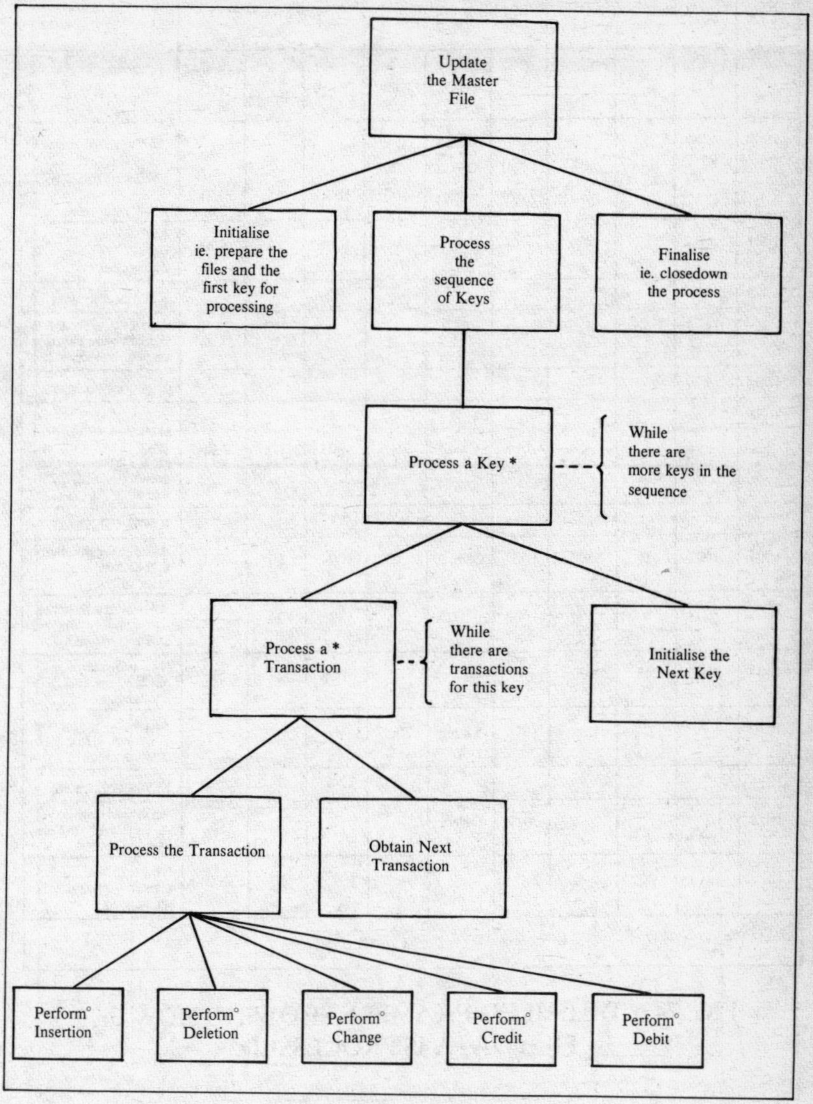

FIG. 24.5. A STRUCTURE DIAGRAM GIVING AN OVERVIEW OF THE MASTER FILE PROCESSING.

Key	Oldmaster File Records			Transaction File Records			New Master File Records			Comment
	Key	Item Price	Number in Stock	Key	Type	Value	Key	Item Price	Number in Stock	
1000	1000	15	300	1000 1000 1000	Credit Credit Debit	150 200 300	1000	15	350	The number in stock takes the successive values 300, 450, 650, 350, as credits and debits are made
1001	1001	25	450				1001	25	450	No transaction, so master record is unchanged
1002										Key not allocated
1003	1003	20	250	1003	Delete					Master record is deleted by not writing to new master
1004										Key not allocated
1005				1005 1005	Insert Credit	30 250	1005	30	250	A new master record is created with an item price of 30 and zero stock. Stock is then credited with 250 items.
1006										Key not allocated.
1007	1007	15	300	1007	Change	20	1007	20	300	Assume for simplicity that change applies to price only.
1008	1008	30	350	1008	Insert	35	1008	30	350	An invalid transaction – cannot insert existing record
1009	1009	25	400				1009	25	400	No transaction, so master record is unchanged.
1010				1010	Debit	200				An invalid transaction – cannot debit non existent stock.
1011										Key not allocated.
1012				1012	Delete					An invalid transaction – can only delete existing record
1013	1013	30	200				1013	30	200	No transaction, so master record is unchanged.
.... etc .... And so on										

FIG. 24.6. DETAILED EXAMPLE SHOWING HOW THE FILE DATA IS PROCESSED.

```
BEGIN  {Main Program}
        {Initialisation}
        Open-files
        Read-old-master-file
        Read-transaction-file
        The-key-to-process ← Min(Old-master-key,Transaction-key)
                                {ie the smaller of the two is
                                 assigned to The-key-to-be-processed}
        Initialise-the-key-to-be-processed
                WHILE The-key-to-be-processed <> Sentinel
                        {ie While there is a key to process}
                        WHILE Transaction-Key = The-key-to-process
                                {ie While there is a transaction
                                 for this key}
                                Process-the-transaction
                                Read-transaction-file
                        ENDWHILE
                        IF Key-is-allocated THEN
                                Write-new-master-record
                        ENDIF
                        The-key-to-process ← Min(Old-master-key,Transaction-key)
                        Initialise-the-key-to-process
                ENDWHILE
        Close-files
END


{Details of procedures given above}

PROCEDURE (Read-old-master-file)
        { This procedure reads the next record from the master
        file. If the end of file has been reached then this
        procedure will assign a "Sentinel" to the
        old master key. A sentinel is a high value signifying
        the end of a sequence of number. In this case the
        sentinel value of the key will be 9999.
        }

PROCEDURE (Read-transaction-file)
        {This procedure will be the same as "Read-old-master-file"
        except that it applies to the transaction file and its keys.
        }

PROCEDURE (Initialise-the-key-to-process)

BEGIN
        IF The-key-to-process <> Sentinel THEN
                IF The-key-to-process = Old-master-key THEN
                        Key-allocated ← TRUE
                        New-master-record ← Old-master-record
                        Read-old-master-record
                ELSE
                        Key-allocated ← FALSE
                ENDIF
        ENDIF
END
```

continued. . .

. . .continued

```
PROCEDURE (Process-the-transaction)

{NB. There are 5 types of transaction}
BEGIN

        CASE Transaction-type
                INSERT:
                        IF Key-allocated = FALSE THEN
                                {Copy details from transaction
                                to new master}
                                Key-allocated ← TRUE
                        ELSE
                                {Print error -record already exists}
                        ENDIF
                DELETE:
                        IF Key-allocated = TRUE THEN
                                Key-allocated ← FALSE
                                {Write to deletion report}
                        ELSE
                                {Print error -record does not exist}
                        ENDIF
                CHANGE:
                        IF Key-allocated = TRUE THEN
                                {Make changes to new master}
                        ELSE
                                {Print error -record does not exist}
                        ENDIF
                CREDIT:
                        IF Key-allocated = TRUE THEN
                                {Add transaction amount to new master record value}
                        ELSE
                                {Print error -record does not exist}
                        ENDIF
                DEBIT:
                        IF Key-allocated = TRUE THEN
                                {Subtract transaction amount from new master record value}
                        ELSE
                                {Print error -record does not exist}
                        ENDIF
        ENDCASE
END
```

FIG. 24.7. MASTER FILE UPDATE.

10. Batched Transactions. Batches of transactions of different types are accumulated together into a transaction file. The means by which these transactions are entered into the system have been covered in earlier chapters.

11. In the case of a sequential master file update, the transaction file is *sorted* into the same key sequence as the master file prior to processing. This enables the processing to be carried out in an orderly and efficient manner.

12. Within one transaction file there are likely to be multiple transaction records with particular key values eg. several debits from the same stock item. The sequence in which these transactions are processed should correspond to the chronological sequence of events which created them eg. new stock must be introduced before it is removed, and similarly a key must be allocated before stock is debited from its record.

13. The way in which transaction file and master file are related by key sequence is shown in Fig. 24.2.

14. The update. An overview of the update is provided by Fig. 24.3. Fig. 24.4 gives a further level of detail by showing how only one key is processed at a time, so that only a limited number of records need be present in main storage at any one time.

15. The procedure is given in outline in the structure diagram (Fig. 24.5) and in greater detail, in pseudocode, in Fig. 24.7. The procedure shown in these two diagrams may be easier to understand if read in conjunction with Fig. 24.6.

EXAMPLE 2 – MULTIPLE FILE UPDATES.

16. This example, which deals with order processing, shows batch processing involving the update of two master files. The method typifies batch processing using magnetic tape. The reasons why *magnetic disk is normally used in preference to magnetic tape* will be given later.

17. The following Systems Flowcharts should be studied in conjunction with the notes that follow them.

FILE UPDATES USING MAGNETIC TAPE.

This chart illustrates the computer runs necessary to update the stock and customer files and to produce invoices. Orders are entered at a VDU and the stock file (held in stock number sequence) and customer file (held in customer number sequence) are stored on magnetic tape.

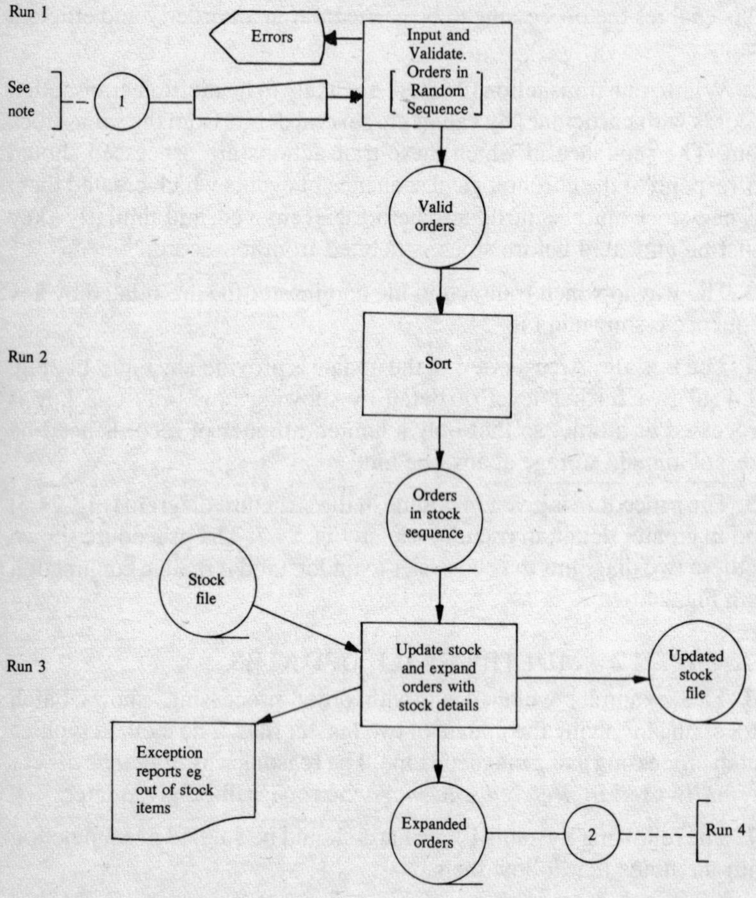

Note:

Connector symbol 1 shows the link between this part of the systems flowchart and another part of the chart which contains the clerical procedures involved in preparing the documents for input.

FIG. 24.8.

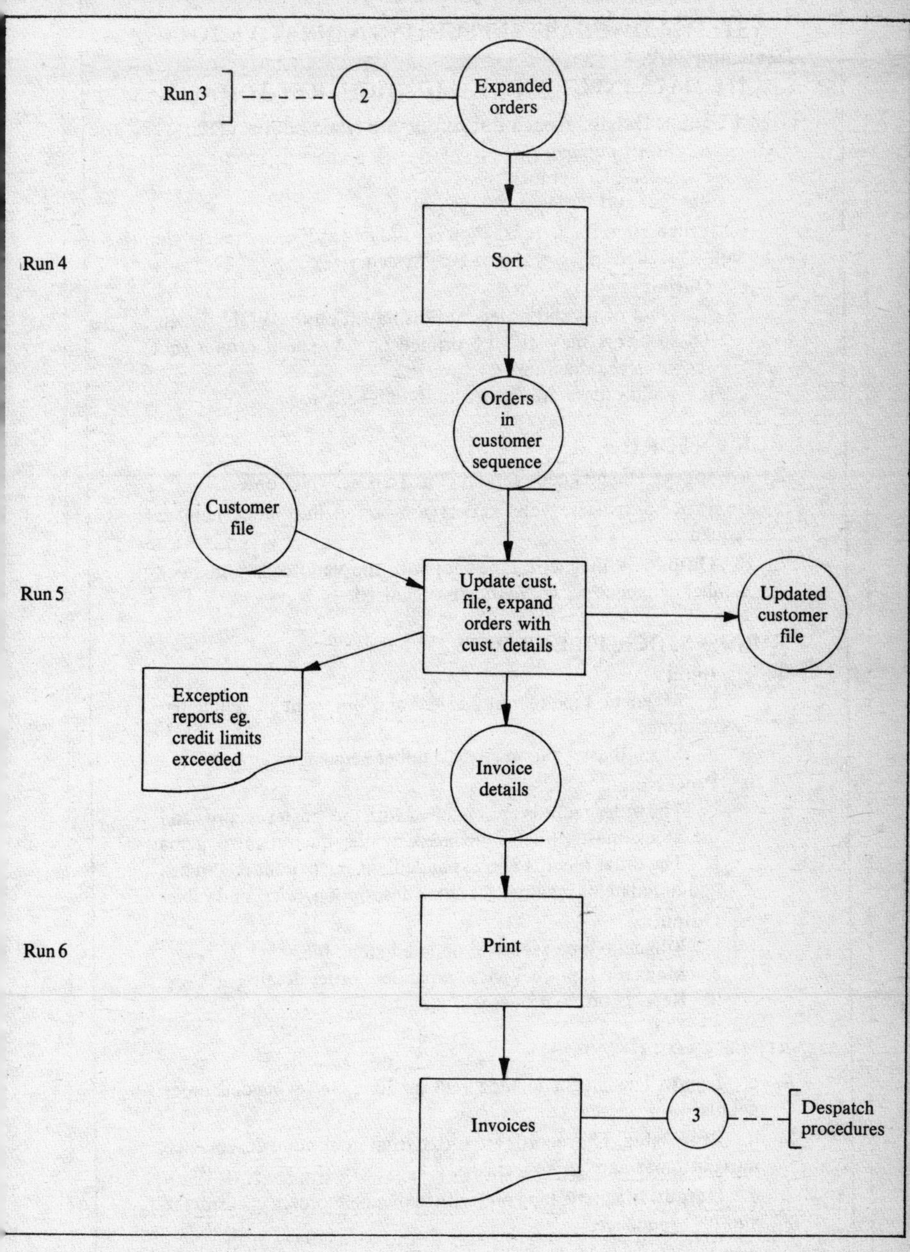
Run 3
2
Expanded orders
Run 4
Sort
Orders in customer sequence
Customer file
Run 5
Update cust. file, expand orders with cust. details
Updated customer file
Exception reports eg. credit limits exceeded
Invoice details
Run 6
Print
Invoices
3
Despatch procedures

FIG. 24.9.

SYSTEM FLOWCHART SUPPORTING NARRATIVE TO FIG. 24.8 and 24.9.

RUN 1 DATA INPUT AND VALIDATION (KEY-TO-TAPE).

1. a. **Input** Details of each transaction are typed in at a VDU:-

i. Stock number.
ii. Customer number.
iii. Quantity ordered.

b. **Processing.** Each transaction is validated as it is entered. ie. the data is "vetted" by the key-to-tape system.

c. **Output**

i. Data of invalid orders are displayed on the VDU screen. These errors may also be printed on low speed printer (not shown in the diagram).
ii. Valid orders are written onto *magnetic tape.*

RUN 2 – SORT.

2. a. **Input.** The magnetic tape reel at 1c.ii. ie. valid orders.

b. **Processing.** The valid orders are sorted into stock number sequence.

c. **Output.** A magnetic tape reel with the valid orders in stock number sequence ie. *sequentially* organised.

RUN 3 – STOCK FILE UPDATE.

3. a. **Input.**

i. Magnetic tape reel at 2c. ie. valid orders in stock number sequence.
ii. Stock master file in stock number sequence.

b. **Processing.**

i. The order records are matched with the master records and the stock master file is updated by the quantities of items
ii. The order records are 'expanded', ie. each order record has additional fields included for stock description, price, and value.

c. **Output.**

i. Magnetic tape reel with updated stock file.
ii. Magnetic tape reel with 'expanded' order details.
iii. Reports on "out of stock" items.

RUN 4 – SORT.

4. a. **Input.** The magnetic tape reel at 3c.ii., ie. expanded order details.

b. **Processing.** The records are sorted from stock number sequence into customer number sequence.

c. **Output.** Magnetic tape reel with 'expanded' orders in *customer number* sequence.

FIG. 24.10.

RUN 5 – CUSTOMER FILE UPDATE.

5. a. **Input.**

i. the magentic tape reel at 4c.

ii. Customer master file in customer number sequence.

b. **Processing.**

i. The order records are matched with the customer master records and the invoice amount calculated. The customer master records are updated by the value of the invoices.

ii. Name and address details are extracted from master records.

c. **Output.**

i. Magnetic tape reel with updated customer file.

ii. Magnetic tape reel with invoice details.

iii. Reports on credit limits being exceeded (etc.)

RUN 6 – PRINT OUTPUT.

6. a. **Input.** The magnetic tape reel at 5c.ii. ie. invoice details.

b. **Processing.** The invoices are printed.

c. **Output.** Printed invoices on the line printer.

Notes:

1. The use of tape as the storage medium requires that each transaction file and appropriate master *must* be in the same sequence in order to carry out processing.

2. Consequently there is need for much sorting and re-sorting of the transaction file.

3. Two updating runs were required (ie. Updating the stock file and the customer file) and a sort was necessary before each.

4. Not all the information required could be obtained in one RUN and thus 6 separate runs were necessary to produce the final output.

5. a. If an order is found to be unacceptable on Run 5 (for reasons of "credit" for instance) then the stock file shows a false position. The order will have been recorded during Run 3, thus reducing the balance of the particular produce. Notice that all subsequent orders for that product on Run 4 will be processed in the light of the stock having been depleted by the amount involved; a situation which in fact does not exist as Run 5 shows.

b. The stock file is "put right" on the next run by means of a "receipt" transaction (ie. an adjustment voucher).

FIG. 24.11.

MAGNETIC TAPE.

18. Having just considered an example in which magnetic tape was shown in use for file processing, this is an appropriate point for us to discuss the advantages and limitations of tape as a storage medium.

19. Advantages of tape.

a. It is relatively cheap. (eg. approx' £10 per reel vs approx £250 per disk pack).

b. It has high capacity enabling it to store the largest files.

c. The data transfer speed is fairly high.

d. It requires no complicated systems software for its operation.

e. Industrial standards govern the way data is normally recorded on tape. This ensures compatibility between different computers and therefore allows bulk off-line data transfers between systems.

20. Limitations of tape.

a. The major limitation of tape lies in the fact that it is a *serial* non-addressable medium and many of the other limitations spring from this.

b. As tape is a serial medium all transaction files must be in the sequence of the appropriate master file. This involves a great deal of *unproductive* time spent in sorting and re-sorting input data.

c. Updating a master tape file involves reading and writing the complete file however small the transaction file may be. Notice that when the batches are very small (ie. the hit-rate (10.19) is low) – this will involve a high proportion of *redundant processing* (ie. the reading and writing of the inactive records).

d. Because tape is a non-addressable medium a particular record cannot be accessed directly. Information required from a particular record is *not available* until the whole batch has been processed.

e. Several runs are required to produce output and this may result in some files not reflecting a *true up to date position* at a given moment (Fig. 24.11 Note 5).

21. These limitations have caused the steady decline of tape as an on-line storage medium, although tape is still of major importance for off-line storage eg. backup and data entry. Magnetic tape is still used in some applications where there is a high hit-rate, where "delay" as such is of no consequence, and where a direct access facility is not required. Examples of such applications are payroll which requires processing only once a week and files of historical data which are only required periodically.

SUMMARY.

22. a. Batch processing was explained.

b. A detailed example of the updating of a sequential master file was given.

c. Multiple file updates were explained by example.

d. The advantages and limitations of tape as a file processing medium were explained.

POINTS TO NOTE.

23. a. Tape is no longer an important on-line storage medium because it is a serial access medium.

b. Tape is very important as a low cost high volume off-line storage medium.

QUESTIONS.

1. Draw a program flowchart to update a stock master file held on a magnetic disk in item reference order. The input to update the master file includes receipts and issues and is held on magnetic tape which has been sorted by a previous program into the following sequences:-

Item reference:
Receipts;
Issues.

The control totals are the only items to be printed by this program. (ICMA)

25 Non-Sequential File Processing

INTRODUCTION.

1. The previous chapter introduced sequential file processing by the use of examples which explained the basic methods and which typified the use of magnetic tape. In this chapter we will see how the advantages of magnetic disk over magnetic tape make it possible to use disk for a wide variety of file processing activities including more sophisticated forms of batch processing. Several examples are used to illustrate the points that are made.

MAGNETIC DISK.

2. Disk is a direct access storage medium and therefore overcomes the major limitation of tape. This gives it a very real advantage over tape in this respect. Disk does require the use of systems software, although this is not a serious problem with the current range of computers. It has a higher data transfer speed than most models of tape and effectively has a greater storage capacity. The cost of disk is much higher than that of tape but it is a cost users seem willing to pay for the benefits of its use.

3. Not all the limitations of tape are overcome by the use of disk. However the facility of direct access will help to solve some of the problems and help to alleviate others. We will now reconsider the limitations of tape in the same order as previously outlined (24:20) and see how the use of disk helps overcome them.

a. The question of access has been covered already and disk does overcome this limitation completely.

b. Despite the fact that disk provides a direct access facility it is often expedient to sort a transaction file into the sequence of the master file. For example an Indexed Sequential File processed Selective Sequentially makes use of direct access while involving the access mechanism in *no* back-tracking. If the same file were processed in a random manner (ie. using an unsorted transaction file) a great deal more time would be spent by the access mechanism in moving to and fro across the face of the disk. The first method involves sorting time and seek time, the second involves no sorting but considerably more seek time. Individual circumstances will indicate the method to be used.

c. If a very large file with a low hit-rate is stored on disk then the direct access capability makes it possible to access *only* those records requiring updating, thus eliminating the redundant processing which occurs with tape.

d. Requests for information can be answered quickly. File Enquiry (as it is called) is accomplished by linking a terminal (possibly a Visual Display Unit – VDU) to the CPU. A request for information can be answered by displaying the contents of a particular record on the VDU. This could be done while the enquirer (a customer) is waiting at the other end of a telephone. Notice that using a multiprogrammed computer (ie. one that runs more than one program at a time), file enquiries can be answered during the running of another program eg. an updating program. (An example will be given later).

e. In the example in Fig. 25.1 the use of disk storage solves the problem of a file not reflecting a true situation. The stock file is stored on disk and access is made to it at the *same time* as the customer file. Thus the two runs are combined and all the data required is available at the same time. The underlying principle is important because it represents a significant advance on tape processing.

Notice that the "delay" problem is *still* present, because it is inherent in the batch processing system itself.

4. Most small system use either floppy disks or small hand disks and can exploit the direct access capabilities of disks. However, few small systems can provide simultaneous file access by multiple programs as just described in d. although it is becoming more common on 16 bit micro-computers.

FILE UPDATES USING MAGNETIC DISK.

This chart shows the computer runs necessary to update the stock and customer files and to produce invoices. Orders are entered at a VDU and the stock file (held in stock number sequence) and customer files (held in customer number sequence) are stored on magnetic disk.

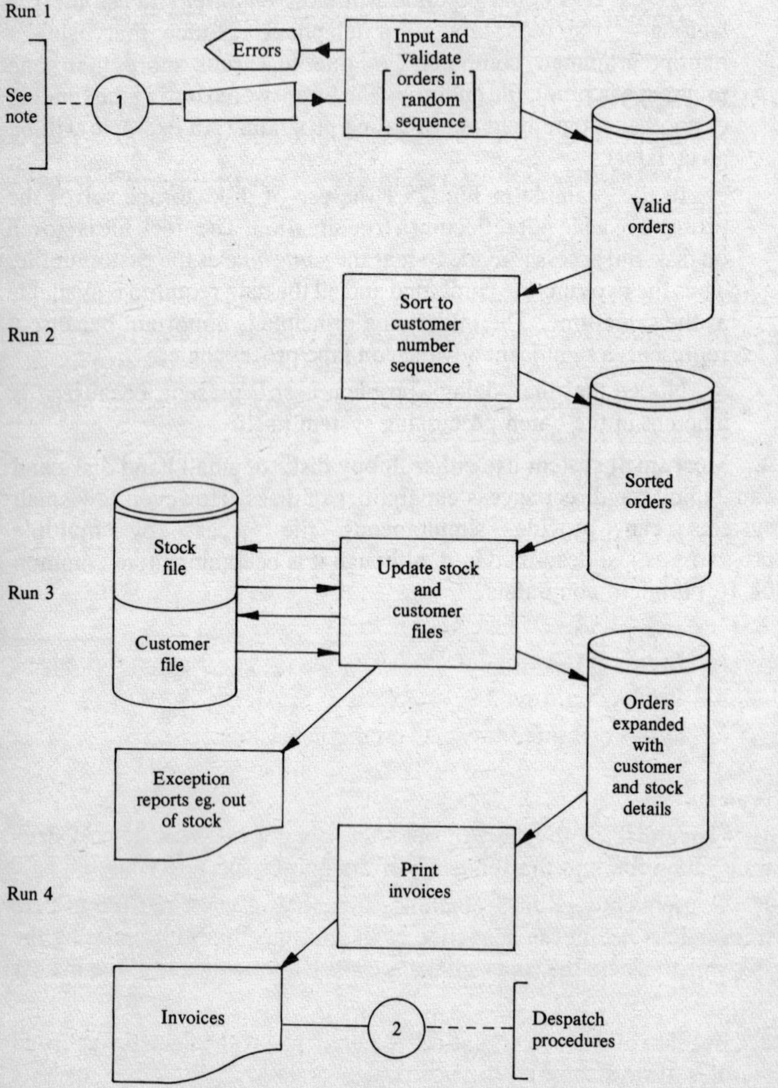

FIG. 25.1.

SYSTEMS FLOWCHART DISK PROCESSING – SUPPORTING NARRATIVE.

RUN 1 – DATA VALIDATION.

a. **Input.** See Fig. 24.10 para 1a.

b. **Processing.** See Fig. 24.10 para 1b.

c. **Output.** Onto disk instead of tape, otherwise the same as shown in Fig. 24.10.

RUN 2 – SORT.

a. **Input.** The magnetic disk used for output in Run 1.

b. **Processing.** Sorting of valid orders into customer number sequence.

c. **Output.** Onto disk.

RUN 3 – UPDATE OF STOCK AND CUSTOMER FILES.

a. **Input.** The magnetic disk used for output in Run 2.

b. **Processing.** Access to the customer file is by the Selective Sequential method and to the stock file by the Random method. Invoice values are calculated.

c. **Output.**

i. Mangetic disk with details of invoices.

ii. Exception reports.

NB. For file security details see Fig. 12.2.

RUN 4 – PRINT OUTPUT.

a. **Input.** Invoice details.

b. **Processing.** Invoices are printed.

c. **Output.** Printed invoices on the lineprinter.

Notes:

1. Using disk as the storage medium it is not *essential* to sort each transaction file into the sequence of the master file.

2. Consequently, Run 3 combines updating of customer file (where transactions *are* in the sequence of the master file) with updating the stock files (where the transactions are *not* in the sequence of the master file).

3. Because of this, fewer runs are required than with magnetic tape, and the files always show a *true* position.

FIG. 25.2.

MULTI-USER SIMULTANEOUS FILE PROCESSING.

This chart shows the simultaneous processing of two files and file enquiry in a multi-user, multi-programming system.

1. It is a multi-programming system because more than one program is running. In this example one program is the update program (as in Fig. 25.1 run 3), another is the file enquiry program.

2. The stock file and customer file are each being processed by both programs so simultaneous file processing is taking place.

3. This required direct access storage and a file organsion method which supports random access.

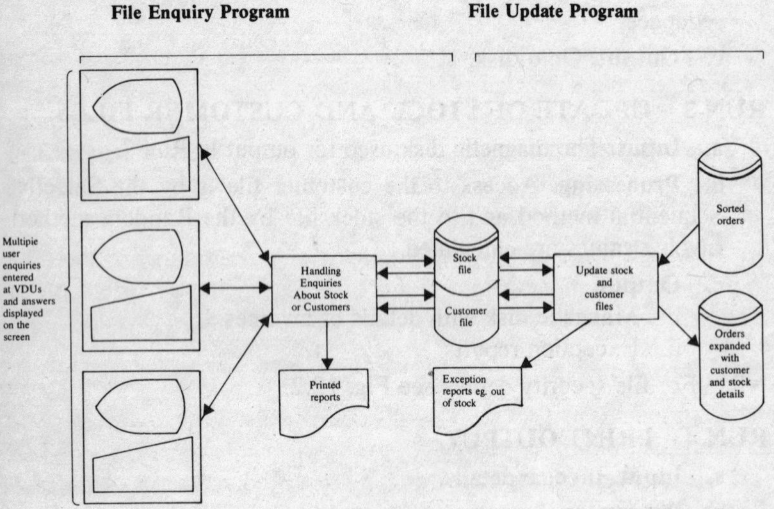

FIG. 25.3.

PROCESSING APPLICATIONS USING DISK STORAGE.

5. a. **File enquiry.** This has been mentioned already. The information required must be stored on a DAS medium. Random access would be necessary in this particular application in order to be able to deal with any enquiry as it arose.

b. **Random access.** Building Societies and Insurance Companies have extremely large files with a very low hit-rate. Random access is used in view of the small size batches, thus saving the vast amount of redundant processing of inactive records which would be required with tape. Such files stored on tape can take some six hours to process completely, which will give you an idea of the problem.

c. **Simultaneous processing of files.** A customer file and stock file can be processed together provided the stock file is on a DAS medium.

6. So far we have considered the concept of batch processing purely in terms of computer processing and have seen how the use of disk storage can overcome many of the limitations of tape. We now want to extend our considerations to include the link with data collection so that we can see a more complete picture.

LINK WITH DATA COLLECTION.

7. For many years the delay spoken of earlier in terms of batch processing was *aggravated* by the time it took for data to pass through all the stages of data collection (14.3) prior to processing. Newer methods of data collection have helped to reduce data collection times. The change to key-to-disk eliminated media conversion. The use of OCR/MICR eliminated the transcription process.

8. Although these methods of data collection add delay to the time cycle of the system, nevertheless this time lag is perfectly acceptable to many users, which is why this form of DP is still widely used.

ON-LINE PROCESSING.

9. The methods just discussed tend to involve some *physical* transportation of data or *manual intervention* in the data collection process. The data source itself can be linked directly to the computer in which case there is no manual intervention and the whole process is automatic. This "on-line data entry" may take place by means of data transmission equipment or as part of a distributed system. By one means or another data arrives at the main computer where the processing is to take place.

10. On receipt at the main computer, the data (which may be coming from hundreds of remote terminals), is at once stored on disk and after a suitable interval, is sorted and then processed (involving data validation, updating and production of output). Notice that in essence all we have done is to dramatically speed up the process of data collection. The batch processing concept *still applies.*

11. The advantage of "on-line" processing is that data is less out of date when it arrives in the computer. As a result, files reflect a much more up to date, a much more *real* picture of a particular set of circumstances.

Furthermore, the results of processing are available more quickly as they can be fed back to the same terminal if need be. Additionally the remote terminal can also be used for enquiries which arise at the source.

12. The major Clearing Banks have an on-line system of processing coupled with File Enquiry. This is a good example to quote in an examination answer.

13. It should be realised that on-line systems of batch processing are much more costly than the conventional method involving transporting the data by post. However the advantages lie in the time saved and the availability of more up to date information.

TRANSACTION PROCESSING.

14. We have just seen how the time lag in batch processing systems can be reduced by the use of various data colleciton techniques and more especially by the use of the techniques of on-line processing (coupled with the use of DAS). Most businesses *do not* require their files of data to be right "up to date" at all times and gear their activities to a time-cycle which is acceptable.

15. There are situations, however, which require any data that arises to be immediately processed and the relevant file updated because any action taken must be based on the *true current* circumstances. Such a processing system is said to be working in REAL-TIME. Real-time processing is the processing of data so quickly that the results are available to influence the activity currently taking place. Decisions are continually being made on the very latest information available because files are kept permanently up to date.

16. You could say that a single transaction becomes the batch, which is processed *on demand.* Thus the process of input, validation, updating and output must be gone through just as with batch processing but for *each* transaction as and when it occurs. This real-time processing of individual transactions is known as **"Transaction Processing"**.

17. Transaction processing is just one kind of real-time processing. Other kinds of real-time processing are those concerned with the control of physical systems such as chemical plants or power stations.

18. Further details of transaction processing and its applications will be given in later chapters.

SUMMARY.

19. a. The various non-sequential file processing methods have been illustrated by example.

b. A direct access storage device such as disk is essential for these processing methods.

c. *On-line processing of batches* and *transaction processing* have been explained.

POINTS TO NOTE.

20. a. Note how DAS makes possible file enquiry and on-line systems.

QUESTIONS.

1. a. Draw a system flowchart showing the **main** *programs which would typically be required in a computer-based stock control system.*

b. Give, and briefly explain:

i. **Five** *examples of transaction or amendment data which would normally be input into such a system,*

ii. **Five** *examples of the kind of reports you would expect the system to produce, also indicating their frequency.*

(ACA)

2. a. Explain the following terms as they relate to the organisation and processing of files held on magnetic disks:

i. cylinder,

ii. overflow.

b. What advantages do disk have over magnetic tapes as file storage media?

(ACA)

26 Database Systems

INTRODUCTION.

1. When organisations first began to use computers, they naturally adopted a piece-meal approach. One system at a time was studied, re-designed and transferred to the computer. This approach was necessitated by the difficulties experienced in using a new and powerful management tool. It has the drawback, however, of producing a number of separate systems, each with its own program suite, its own files, and its own inputs and outputs. The main criticisms of this approach are that:

a. The computer-based systems, being self-contained, do not represent the way in which the organisation really works – ie. as a complex set of inter-locking and inter-dependent systems.

b. Systems communicate with each other outside the computer. This proliferates inputs and outputs and creates delays. For example, input of a customer order to an order processing system might create an output of an invoice set, which in turn would have to be converted back into input for activating the sales accounting system. Similarly, if the order reduced stock levels to the re-order point, another output would be created which would then have to be input to the production control and/or the purchasing system.

c. Information obtained from a series of separate files is less valuable because it does not give the complete picture. For example, the sales manager reviewing outstanding orders from customers has to get information about stocks from another file.

d. Data may be duplicated in two or more files, creating unnecessary maintenance and the risk of inconsistency.

INTEGRATED FILE SYSTEMS.

2. Integrated files systems represent an approach to solving the problems just described, by conventional means. In an integrated file system the data is pooled into a set of inter-locking and inter-dependent files which are accessible by a number of different users.

3. When a transaction enters an integrated file system *all* the appropriate files are updated. The features of an integrated system are shown in Fig. 26.1.

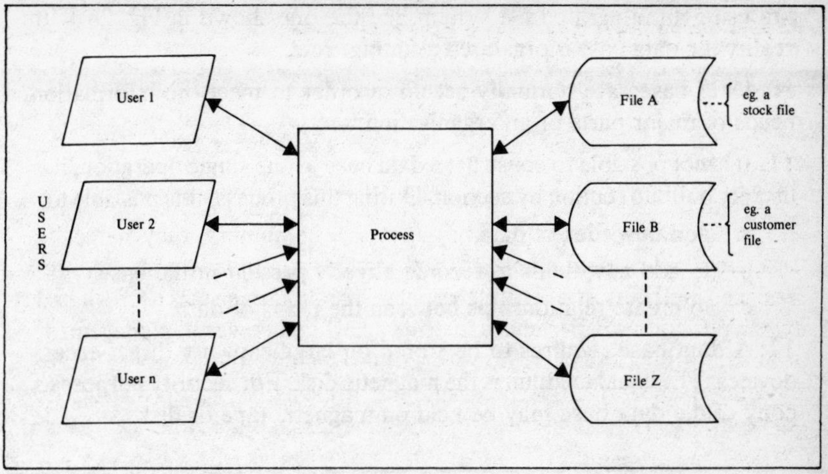

FIG. 26.1. AN INTEGRATED FILE SYSTEM.

4. A large number of integrated file systems are in use today. Many of them have been tailor made to meet the requirements of particular organisations.

5. Integrated file systems do not provide a satisfactory answer to all the criticism mentioned in paragraph 1 however. They tend to suffer from the problems caused by *data duplication* (1d) and from the fact that the task of maintaining the data is shared between the programs which access and maintain the data and therefore lacks proper central control.

NB. The idea of integrating the *processing functions* will be returned to later in this chapter.

DATA BASES.

6. Data bases represent a radically different approach to solving the problems discussed so far in this chapter.

7. Data Base Definition. A data base is a single organised collection of structured data, stored with a minimum of duplication of data items so as to provide a consistent and controlled pool of data. This data is common to all users of the system but is independent of programs which use the data.

8. The independence of the data base and programs using it means that one can be changed without changing the other.

9. The users of a data base may find it convenient to imagine that they are using an integrated file system like the one shown in Fig. 26.1. In reality the data base is organised as in Fig. 26.2.

10. Data bases are normally set up in order to meet the information needs of major parts of an organisation.

11. It is not possible to construct a data base in one single operation, it is usually built up section by section. During this process, it is possible to:-

a. add new files of data.

b. to add new fields to records already present in the base.

c. to create relationships between the items of data.

12. A data base requires to be stored on large-capacity direct-access devices. The usual medium is the magnetic disk. For security purposes a copy of the data base may be held on magnetic tape or disk.

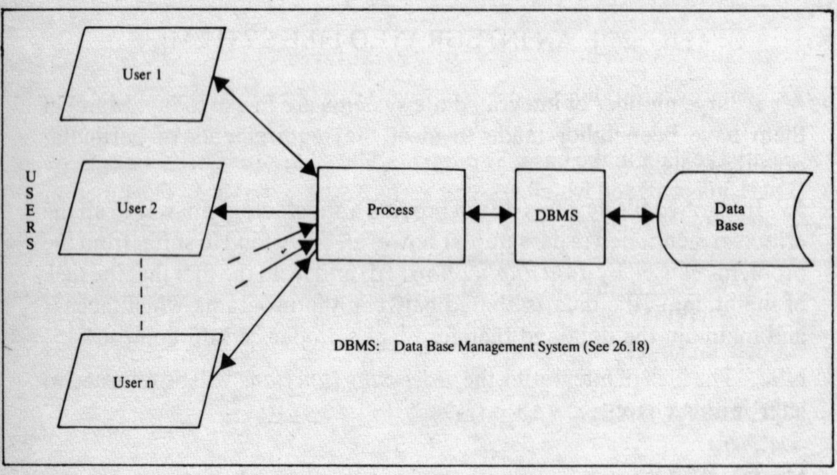

FIG. 26.2. AN OUTLINE VIEW OF A DATA BASE SYSTEM.

13. It is often *wrongly stated* that there is no duplication of data in a data base. Data may be duplicated, but it is important to realise that duplications are minimised and controlled. This is referred to as *"controlled redundancy"*.

14. When new sets of data are added, it is often found that some of the required data is already stored for other purposes.

The data base is maintained by a 'single input'. This means that just as there is little duplication of data, there is also no duplication of inputs.

One transaction will cause all the necessary changes to be made to the data.

The data items in the base are 'linked' or 'chained' to each other so that any required relationship between different items of data can be established. As the base is expanded, or as user requirements change, these relationships can be changed and new relationships can be established.

15. The user is unaware of the structure of the data base. The Data Base Management System (see 18) provides the user with the services needed and handles the technicalities of maintaining and using the data.

COMMUNICATING WITH THE DATA BASE.

16. Some data bases have their own computer languages associated with them which allow the user to access and retrieve data at a terminal. Other data bases are only accessed via languages such as COBOL, to which extra facilities has been added for this purpose.

17. Data descriptions must be standardised. For this reason, a **Data Description Language (DDL)** is provided which *must* be used to specify the data in the base. Similarly, a **Data Manipulation Language (DML)** is provided which must be used to access the data. The function of these two languages may be compared to the Data and Procedure Divisions of a COBOL program, although their scope is wider and the degree of standardisation much higher. As indicated by the previous paragraph DDLs and DMLs may be either free standing or embedded in another language.

THE DATA BASE MANAGEMENT SYSTEMS (DBMS).

18. The Data Base Management System is a *complex software system* which constructs, expands and maintains the data base. It also provides the interface between the user and the data in the base.

The DBMS allocates storage to data. It maintains indices so that any required data can be retrieved, and so that separate items of data in the base can be cross-referenced. As mentioned above, the structure of a data base is dynamic and can be changed as needed.

19. The DBMS maintains the data in the base by:-

a. adding new records,

b. deleting 'dead' records,

c. amending records.

In addition to these functions (which are performed by any file maintenance program) it can expand the base by adding new sets of records or new data to existing records.

20. The DBMS provides an interface with user programs. These may be written in a number of different programming languages. However, the programmer need not be familiar with the structure of the base because the data his program requires is retrieved by the DBMS.

21. The DBMS provides facilities for different types of file processing. It can:-

a. process a complete file (serially or sequentially)

b. process required records (selective sequential or random)

c. retrieve individual records.

It can also, as has been explained above, retrieve related records or related data within records.

22. The DBMS also has the function of providing security for the data in the base. The main aspects of this are:-

a. protecting data against unauthorised access

b. safeguarding data against corruption

c. providing recovery and restart facilities after a hardware or software failure.

The DBMS keeps statistics of the use made of the data in the base. This allows redundant data to be removed. It also allows data which is frequently used to be kept in a readily accessible form so that time is saved.

23. Data Dictionary. The DBMS makes use of descriptions of data items provided by the DDL. This "data about data" is called a **data dictionary.**

THE DATA BASE ADMINISTRATOR (DBA).

24. The importance of a data base is such that a special manager is often appointed, sometimes with a staff. His functions are described below.

He must have a sound knowledge of the structure of the data base and of the DBMS. He must also be thoroughly conversant with the organisation, its systems, and the information needs of the managers.

25. He is responsible for ensuring that:-

a. the data in the base meets the information needs of the organisation.

b. that the facilities for retrieving data and for structuring reports are appropriate to the needs of the organisation.

26. He is responsible for the following documentation:-

a. The data dictionary.

b. Manuals for users describing the facilities the data base offers and how to make use of those facilities.

27. Another function is to supervise the addition of new data. For this purpose, he will have to liaise with the managers who use the data, and the systems analysts and programmers who develop the systems.

Security of the data base is also the responsibility of the Administrator, and in the future, requirements of privacy.

The Administrator is also responsible for periodic appraisal of the data held in the base to ensure that it is complete, accurate and not duplicated.

EXAMPLE OF A DATA BASE.

28. There are at present few organisations who have a really comprehensive data base. An example is given here of a data base used by a major computer manufacturer.

29. The data base comprises:-

a. Records of customers who have purchased or rent the manufacturers computer equipment.

b. Records of the different items of equipment ie. processors, peripherals and other devices.

c. Records of spare parts showing the location where they are stored and the quantity held.

d. Records of customer engineers responsible for maintenance and repairs.

30. The uses made of the data base are too numerous to list completely, but a selection does give some idea of the facilities which a data base can provide:-

a. **Accounting.** Customers are billed for maintenance and rental charges. Any change in configuration automatically causes the customer charges to be amended (the 'single input' principle).

b. **Spares.** The database is used to control stocks of spares. It can also be used to find the location of a spare part nearest to the installation which requires it.

c. **Modifications.** If a modification to a particular item of equipment is needed, all installations in which it is present can be quickly identified.

d. **Engineering Services.** The data base shows which customers are served by which engineer (an example of the 'linking' or cross-referencing of records). Engineers can be allocated to cover absence or sickness or to assist at an installation which is in trouble. The records show which types of equipment the engineers are qualified to service.

ADVANTAGES OF A DATA BASE.

31. The following are the advantages of a data base:-

a. Information supplied to managers is more valuable because it is based on a comprehensive collection of data instead of files which contain only the data needed for one application.

b. As well as routine reports, it is possible to obtain *ad hoc* reports to meet particular requirements.

c. There is an obvious economic advantage in not duplicating data. In addition, erorrs due to discrepancies between two files are eliminated.

d. The amount of input preparation needed is minimised by the 'single input' principle.

e. A great deal of programming time is saved because the DBMS handles the construction and processing of files and the retrieval of data.

f. The use of integrated systems is greatly facilitated.

INTEGRATED SYSTEMS..

32. The data base represents the integration of the data/ information of an organisation. Associated with this concept is the integration of the systems which use the data. As has been seen, the development of separate systems increases the amount of external communication (inputs and outputs) between systems and is also likely to duplicate programming effort.

33. The concept is best illustrated by an example of three systems which are often integrated: order processing, sales accounting and stock control.

a. The basic input to the system is that of a customer order.

b. On input, the order is validated in the normal way. It is then

i. checked against the customer record to ensure that the credit position is satisfactory, and

ii. checked against the stock file to ensure that the stock is available.

c. After the order has passed these checks, the files are updated. The stock level is reduced by the amount ordered. An invoice is generated, and the customer record is updated.

d. The documentation is distributed as necessary; eg. the invoice is sent to the customer and the copies for despatch procedure sent to the warehouse.

e. If the supply of the order causes the stock level to fall below the re-order level, a report is printed indicating that replenishment of stock is necessary.

f. Subsequently, the monthly statement for the customer would be produced.

34. This example obviously represents only a small part of the total activities of the company. Possible future developments would be:

a. In a manufacturing organisation, input of a customer order would generate the necessary works order. This would be the 'input' to the production scheduling system, which would in turn generate the Bill of Materials.

b. The Bill of Materials would be 'input' to the Stock Control system. The necessary stocks would be allocated. If purchases were necessary, an input to the Purchasing system would be generated.

c. Subsequent receipt of the invoice from the supplier would cause another input to the Purchase Accounting system, resulting in checking of the invoice, notification of queries and eventual payment of the suppliers.

d. The Production Scheduling system would allocate the necessary machines and labour, using and updating Plant and Personnel files.

e. At the due date, the Production Scheduling system would activate the Production Control system. Progress of the job through the factory would be controlled and actual inputs from the factory floor would be received to monitor progress.

On completion of the order, the documentation would be produced and the Customer file updated with details of the invoice.

35. It will be realised of course that a number of new files would have to be added to the data-base to make this possible – resource files of plant and labour, supplier file, work-in-progress etc.

At the time of writing the above is somewhat futuristic, as very few organisations have constructed a *comprehensive* data base and *fully* integrated their systems. A gradual approach, building up the data base section by section and adding new systems one at a time is obviously desirable. There is really nothing difficult to understand in the concept; the approach is simply to move into the computer *all* the files, *all* the systems and *all* the communications between them, instead of using the computer for only the more straightforward work and linking the computer-based systems externally.

FILE MANAGEMENT SYSTEMS.

36. A number of software products have appeared on the market in recent years which appear to offer *some* of the features of data bases on even the smaller computers. These products, some of which claim to be "data base packages" are usually more correctly called "File Management System".

37. Typical file management systems usually have rudimentary DDLs and DMLs which allow the user to set up and maintain a few files with a minimum of programming effort or skill. Facilities are often included which allow limited but extremely useful data retrieval functions such as sorting and selecting.

38. A file management system may therefore be thought of rather loosely as a "computerised filing cabinet".

SUMMARY.

39. a. The development of separate systems with their own files is simple but does not make the best use of resources. Integrated files, data bases, and integrated systems are more difficult to instal, but have many advantages.

b. A data base is a comprehensive, consistent, controlled and coordinated collection of structured data items.

c. A **Data Base Management System (DBMS)** is a software system which constructs, maintains and processes a data base.

d. Communication with the data base is via the **Data Description Language (DDL)** and **Data Manipulation Language (DML).**

e. The **data dictionary** holds "data about data" in the data base.

f. **A Data Base Administrator (DBA)**is the manager responsible for that data base.

g. Integrated systems are a natural corollary to data bases.

POINTS TO NOTE.

40. a. Another term you may come across is 'data bank'. This has a slightly different meaning to 'data base'. An organisation constructing a data base will put into it only data that it expects to use – for obvious reasons of economy. A 'data bank' on the other hand is designed to contain any data that *may* be required – just as a librarian has to keep stocks of books, *some* of which may never be referred to. An example of a data bank is a file of legal cases; they all have to be there because enquiries cannot be predicted, but some may never be inspected.

b. The integrated system extends data base to include *all* information flows in a business and automates as many 'decisions' as possible to produce a comprehensive management information system.

c. The computer is being increasingly used as the centre of a *communications network.* Many organisations are replacing the traditional, centralised methods of data collection with terminal devices linked to a central machine. The flows of data (inwards) and information (outwards) are greatly accelerated, and there is considerable improvement in communication and control.

d. Integrated file systems are integrated systems without the use of data bases.

QUESTIONS.

1. a. Explain the term 'data base' and how the operation of a data processing system using a data base differs from one using conventional file structures.

b. What advantages are to be gained from using a data base system?

c. What are the essential design features which should be incorporated into the system? (ICMA)

2. Some computer installations, particularly the larger, more sophisticated ones, are using databases in which to store the organisation's data.

You are required to:

a. define a database;

b. list and explain briefly **five** *of the advantages claimed for a well-designed database;*

c. *explain briefly* **three** *of the major problems associated with the implementation and operation of a comprehensive database;*

d. *distinguish between the logical and physical structure of data.*

(ICMA)

Software

1. Definition. Software is the expression used (in contrast to *hardware*) to describe *all* programs which are used in a particular computer installation.

2. There are numerous types of software, so the whole of chapter 27 is used to provide a detailed classification of the different types and a description of each type.

3. Operating systems are such an important type of software that the whole of chapter 28 is used to provide a discussion of them.

27 Software Types

INTRODUCTION.

1. This chapter explains the differences between the various types of software and describes each type.

TYPES OF SOFTWARE.

2. The two basic types of software are:-

a. System software.

b. Applications software.

3. System Software. The user of a computer has at his disposal a large amount of software provided by the manufacturer. Much of this software will be programs which contribute to the control and performance of the computer system. Such programs are given the collective name system software. Any one of these programs is a **systems program,** eg. compilers (22.9) and DBMs (26.18) are systems programs.

4. Applications Software. Applications programs may be provided by the computer manufacturer or supplier but in many cases the users produce their own applications programs called **user programs.** (eg. payroll programs, stock control programs etc.) A single applications program is often called a **job.** Sometimes a job may be divided into smaller units called **tasks.** A job may comprise program + data. Most applications programs can only work if used in conjunction with the appropriate systems programs.

5. Further sub-division. A more detailed sub-division of 2a and 2b is as follows:-

a. Operating systems and control programs b. Translators c. Utilities and service programs d. Data Base Management Systems (DBMSs)	System Software
e. User applications programs f. Applications packages.	Applications Software

6. The remainder of this chapter discusses software under headings which correspond to this classification.

OPERATING SYSTEMS AND CONTROL PROGRAMS.

7. Computers are required to give efficient and reliable service without the need for continual intervention by the user. This requirement suggests that computers should monitor and control their own operation where possible. **Control programs** are the means by which this is achieved. A control program controls the way in which hardware is used.

8. Under many circumstances at least two programs are within main storage. One may be an applications program the other will be a control program which monitors, aids and controls the applications program.

9. On small computer systems such as microcomputers the control program may also accept commands typed in by the user. Such a control program is often called a **monitor.**

10. On larger computer systems it is common for only part of the monitor to remain in main storage. Other parts of the monitor are brought into memory when required ie. there are "resident" and "transient" parts to the monitor.

11. The resident part of the monitor on large systems is often called the **Executive** or **Supervisor Program.**

12. The executive is one of a suite of control programs which are able to allow a number of applications programs to run concurrently and in sequence without the intervention of the user. Such a suite of control programs is called an operating system, but a more precise definition is now given.

13. An **operating system** is a suite of programs which takes over the operation of the computer to the extent of being able to allow a number of programs to be run on the computer without human intervention by an operator.

14. The reader should now be aware of what operating systems and control programs are, and how they relate to other software. Further details are left for discussion in the next chapter.

TRANSLATORS.

15. A translator is a program which converts statements written in one language into statements in another language. Two types of translator have already been introduced but there are three basic types of translator:-

a. Assemblers (22.13).
b. Compilers (22.19).
c. Interpreters.

16. Assemblers and Compilers have already been explained. Interpreters are most easily understood by comparing them with compilers.

17. Both compilers and interpreters are commonly used for the translation of high level language programs but they perform the translation in two completely different ways.

The **compiler** translates the *whole* of the high level language source program into a machine code object program prior to the object program being loaded into main memory and executed. Contrast this with the **interpreter** which deals with the source program *one instruction at a time,* completely translating *and* executing each instruction before it goes onto the next.

18. If a **compiler** is used, the same program need only be translated once. Thereafter, the object program can be loaded directly into main storage and executed.

19. If an **interpreter** is used, the source program will be translated everytime the program is executed. Executions carried out in this way may be ten times slower than the execution of the equivalent object programs!

20. Despite their apparent inefficiency interpreters are widely used, particularly for the programming language BASIC on small computers, because they are easier to use than compilers.

21. Interpreters also have other uses eg. for dealing with user or operator commands to operating systems.

22. Cross Compilers and Cross Assemblers. Cross Compilers and Cross Assemblers are translators which are used on one computer in order to produce object programs for use on a second computer. Usually the computer used for the translation is a mini-computer or main frame and the object program is used on a microcomputer.

23. Two other items of software which are included here for convenience are:-

a. **Generators.** From a given specification this program will *generate* a *program* which, when run, will produce a defined output from a given input. A good example is a generator which will generate a program which, when run, will produce reports to 'given' formats and from specified input data. (Application Generator were discussed in 23.36).

b. **Simulation/emulation.** When a user buys a new computer he is very often faced with the job of rewriting existing programs in the language of the new machine. As a *temporary expedient* the *existing* programs are run on the *new* machine in conjunction with another program known as a *simulator.* This is itself read into main storage and takes each instruction of the existing program in turn and translates it into equivalent codes of the new machine. The process is called *simulation.* Note that *both* programs have to be accommodated in main storage when being executed.

Sometimes a special *hardware* device is used in addition to a simulator. This can be 'plugged' in to the computer and virtually modifies its circuitry. When simulation is aided by this particular hardware it is referred to as EMULATION.

UTILITIES AND SERVICE PROGRAMS.

24. Utilities, also called service programs, are systems programs which provide a useful service to the user of the computer by providing facilities for performing common tasks of a routine nature.

25. Common types of utility programs are:-

a. Sort.

b. Editors.

c. File copying.

d. Dump.

e. File maintenance.

f. Tracing and debugging.

26. Sort. This is a program designed to arrange records into a predetermined sequence. A good example of the requirement for this service program is the need for sorting transaction files into the sequence of the master file before carrying out updating. Sorting is done by reference to a record key.

a. **Parameters required.** It is a *generalised* program which must be *"specialised"* as it were, before use; this is accomplished by supplying the program with parameters which will be different for each application. Such parameters are:-

i. Key – size and number (if more than one).

ii. Record size (length).

iii. Peripheral units available for the sorting process, ie. number of tape units, disk units, etc. which can be made available to the program.

iv. Required sequence (ascending order of numeric or alphabetic keys etc).

b. **How accomplished.** Sorting is generally accomplished in *two phases:-*

i. **String generation phase** during which records are read from the unsorted input file into main storage, formed into small groups, (records are in sequence within groups) and written as sequenced groups or *strings* onto other output tapes/disks.

ii. **String merging phase** during which the strings are read into main storage, *merged* into larger groups (records are in sequence within groups), and written out. The process is repeated until the whole file is in one sequence.

Each repetition of the string merging phase is called a *pass*. The length of strings generated will depend on the size of records, the number of records, and the amount of RAM available in main storage.

27. Editors are used at a terminal and provide facilities for the creation or amendment of programs. The editing may be done by the use of a series of commands or special edit keys on the keyboard. If for example a source program needs correction because it has failed to compile properly, an editor may be used to make the necessary changes.

28. File copying. (also called media conversion) This is a program which simply copies data from one medium to another, eg. from disk to tape.

29. Dump. The term 'dump' means "copy the contents of main storage onto an output device". This program is useful when an error occurs during the running of application programs. The printed "picture" of main storage will contain information helpful to the programmer when trying to locate the error. It is also used in conjuction with a CHECKPOINT/RESTART program. This program stops at various intervals during the running of an application program and dumps the contents of main storage. If required, the Checkpoint/Restart program can get the application program back to the last checkpoint and restart it with the conditions exactly as they were at the time.

NB. "Dump" is sometimes used to mean "copy the contents of on-line storage onto an off-line medium" eg. dumping magnetic disk onto magnetic tape for backup purposes.

30. File maintenance. A program designed to carry out the process of insertion/deletion of records in any files. It can also make amendments to the standing data contained in records. File maintenance may also include such tasks as the reorganisation of index sequential files on disk.

31. Tracing and debugging. Used in conjunction with the testing of application programs on the computer. Tracing involves dumping internal storage after obeying specified instructions so that the cycle of operations can be traced and errors located. Debugging is the term given to the process of locating and eliminating errors from a program.

NB. Well written and tested programs will tend to be more reliable and will therefore require less debugging than badly written programs.

DATA BASE MANAGEMENT SYSTEMS (DBMSs).

32. These were described in the previous chapter and need no further discussion.

USER APPLICATIONS PROGRAMS.

33. User applications programs are programs written by the user in order to perform specific jobs for the user. Such programs are written in a variety of programming languages according to circumstances, but all should be written in a systematic way such as that indicated in 21.23.

34. For many applications it is necessary to produce sets of programs which are used in conjunction with one another and which may also be used in conjunction with service programs such as sort utilities.

35. For some applications it may be necessary to compare available software or hardware before writing the applications software. For example, the user may wish to compare the performance of two different COBOL compilers. Such a comparison may be made using a bench mark.

36. Benchmarks. A benchmark is a standard program, or assembly of programs used to evaluate hardware or software. For example, a benchmark might be used to:

a. compare the performance of two or more different computers on identical tasks.

b. ascertain if the configuration provided by a manufacturer performs according to his claims.

c. assess the comparative performance of two Operating Systems.

APPLICATION PACKAGES.

37. These are similar in concept to service programs except that application packages are generalised programs for solving *business* problems as opposed to programs for carrying out computer systems tasks.

38. Many users have the same type of problem to put onto a computer and thus manufacturers and specialist software writers have written standard programs to solve these problems and sell them to the many users who want them. Examples are Stock Control, Sales Invoicing, Network Analysis.

39. Applications packages are of major importance to small computer system users who do not have the necessary resources or expertise to produce their own software.

40. Advantages of packages.

a. The main advantage is the saving of programming effort and expense on the part of the user. Development costs are effectively shared between the users.

b. The user gets a well tried and tested program which he is able to use with confidence.

c. Relatively quick implementation results from the use of packages.

41. Practical considerations.

a. Many users' systems will differ in some detailed area especially if there is a relationship between applications, as there is for example between labour cost analysis and payroll.

b. A solution would be for the user to modify his system to suit the package but this has its problems.

c. Some users may decide arbitrarily to design a system to suit the package.

d. Some software houses built packages on the *modular* principle and thus are able to combine the various modules to suit a particular user's requirement.

e. The question of cost must not be ignored and will be reflected in the service provided by the supplier of the package.

f. A number of Trade Associations etc. have sponsored the writing of packages for particular industries. The Motor Manufacturers Association have set up packages for their dealers.

g. Thorough research should be made into the reliability of the package and the particular software house offering it for sale. It is a good idea to ask current users of the package about their experience.

h. A program maintenance agreement should be sought where changes to the package are likely, eg. a payroll package could be affected by government legislation.

42. How the package is supplied. A package normally consists of:

a. A program (or suite of programs) actually written onto a suitable medium eg. magnetic tape, disk or floppy disk.

b. Documentation which specifies:
   i. how to set up the package
   ii. how to use the package
   iii. necessary technical details.

43. Any software which the user buys is likely to be supplied in a similar form to that just described. Suppliers tend to provide no more than the necessary technical detail in order to protect their trade secrets.

SUMMARY.

44. a. Software falls into two main categories:-
   i. System software.
   ii. Applications software.

b. A further sub-division of software is as follows:-
   i. Operating system and control programs which ensure efficient hardware use with a minimum of human intervention.
   ii. Translators which translate from one language to another.
   ii. Utilities and service programs which perform routine tasks for the user.
   iv. Data Base Management Systems which maintain data bases.
   v. User applications programs which are written by the user for a specific purpose.
   vi. Applications packages which are purchased by the user for a particular application.

POINTS TO NOTE.

45. a. Time spent in running systems software is really non-productive from an organisational stand point.

b. The operating system (especially the executive part) can be regarded as a "Program which controls Programs".

c. The paragraphs on Generators and Simulation were included under Translating Programs for convenience only; they should not be included in a discussion of Translating Programs in an examination answer.

QUESTIONS.

1. You company is installing a computer.

Describe the types of software which you would expect a computer manufacturer to provide with his hardware and explain what purpose each serves. (ICMA)

28 Operating Systems

INTRODUCTION.

1. The concept and basic purpose of an operating system was introduced in the previous chapter (27.7). This chapter explains the purposes, facilities and functions of operating systems and also describes various types of operating system.

WHY OPERATING SYSTEMS WERE ORIGINALLY DEVELOPED.

2. Over many years the increased processing speed of the *central processing unit* and its massive problem-solving capability brought about the need for more sophisticated means of *operating* computers. *Problems* encountered on the early generations were:-

a. **Set-up time.** Required as each job was put onto machine and during which time the computer was completely *idle.* For example, changing tape reels on tape units, changing stationery on a printer, etc.

b. **Manual intervention.** This was necessary in order to investigate error conditions and to initiate corrective action. Again the machine would lie idle while this was being done.

c. **Imbalance between processor and peripherals.** This meant that the central processor was lying idle for "long" periods of time during the operation of peripheral units.

3. When analysed it can be seen that in a computer system comprising *many* units only a *small part* is "in action" performing a specific task at any *one* point in time. What is required is a "super controller" to ensure that the vast facilities are used to optimum advantage. It became clear that the job could only be undertaken by some form of *internally stored program.* This became known as an *operating system.*

DEFINITION.

4. An operating system is a *suite* of programs which has taken over many of the functions once performed by human operators. The sophistication and speeds of modern computers is beyond the capability of human operators to control without the aid of an operating system.

5. For a more precise definition of an operating system see 27.13.

BASIC ORGANISATION.

6. Part of the operating system remains in main storage *permanently* during the running of the computer. This part is called the EXECUTIVE (or Supervisor) and as the name suggests is the "controlling" part of the operating system. It controls the running of all other programs. The remainder of the operating system programs are stored on a direct access storage device (preferably) from which any particular one will be "called' into main storage by Executive when required.

7. On small computers the operating system takes the form of a rudimentary control program normally called a **monitor.** (27.9).

8. On many very small microcomputers the monitor is stored permanently in ROM and starts execution the moment the computer turns on. A message is usually displayed on the VDU screen by the monitor to signify it is ready to accept commands which the user may type in at a keyboard.

9. On most other modern computers the monitor or executive is not in main storage when the machine is switched on. The system must be "booted up". This often involves pressing special "boot buttons" or switches which cause the hardware to load the monitor or executive into main storage from a predetermined position on a disk.

FUNCTIONS AND OPERATION.

10. Functions of an Operating System.

a. Scheduling and loading of jobs in order to provide for continuous processing.

b. Control over selection and operation of input/output devices and file handling.

c. Calling into main storage of programs and sub-routines as and when required.

d. Passing of control from one job (program) to another under a system of priority when more than one application program occupies main storage.

e. Provision of error correction routines.

f. Furnishing a complete record of all that happens during processing (usually in the form of a typewritten log).

g. Communication with the computer operator usually by means of the console typewriter.

11. Examples of programs provided by the operating system and to which the application programs branch (under control of Executive) are:-

a. The reading and writing of records and, where necessary, blocking and de-blocking.

b. Peripheral control, eg. back-spacing tape reels, advancing paper in the printer.

c. Opening and closing files, ie. checking file labels and purge dates.

12. Many jobs can be stacked on devices and instructions as to priority (if any) of operation given to the Operating System. After the initial start given by the operator the processing of the various jobs will continue automatically with instructions being given by Executive via the console typewriter concerning the changing of tape reels or disk packs.

13. If a particular application program requires a great deal of use of the printer, Executive will cause this output to be put onto *disk* during the running of the program.

Then later as a *separate* job, it will automatically perform the transfer from disk to printer. This second run is usually carried out as a background job to another main application program. This particular technque is called output SPOOLING (Simultaneous Peripheral Operations On-Line). (See Fig. 28.1).

14. Notice that an Operating System must have hardware *reserved* for *its* programs. Some of the Operating Systems for the latest computers require a large amount of main storage, a number of disk drives, and the use of consoles and printers. The use of some storage may be EXCLUSIVE whilst the use of the printer may be SHARED with applications programs.

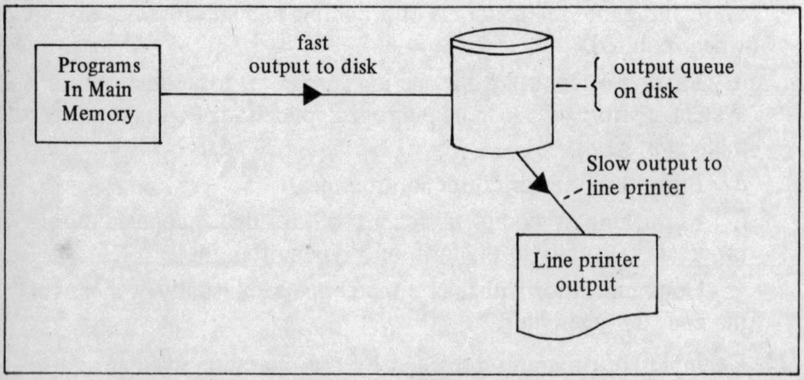

FIG. 28.1. SPOOLING.

BUFFERING.

15. Buffering serves as a good example of how an operating system is able to make efficient utilisation of hardware.

16. The differing speeds of the various items of hardware cause problems of under utilisation of devices waiting to be used. Take, for example, the difference in speed between a document reader and the processor. To read a document takes anything between 30 and 60 milliseconds, which is a thousand times slower than the speed with which data can be moved within the processor. A simple example is given to illustrate the problem, followed by the *partial* solution as a result of 'Buffering'.

17. Example. Suppose 2000 documents need to be input and the details on the document printed out on a line printer (one print line being used for each document read). The document reader operates at 1000 documents per minute and the printer at 500 lines per minute. The processing cycle and time required, would be as illustrated at Fig. 28.2.

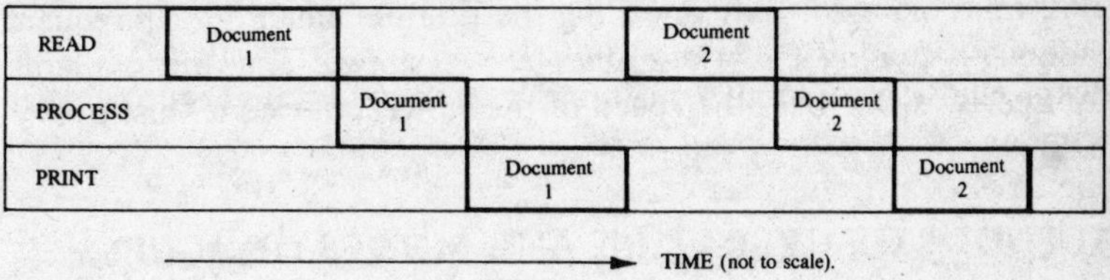

FIG. 28.2.

Total time required:-

READ	$= 2000 \times \frac{1}{1000} =$		2 MINUTES
PROCESS	NEGLIGIBLE		–
PRINT	$2000 \times \frac{1}{500} =$		4 MINUTES
		TOTAL	6 MINUTES

18. It should be recognised that whilst a document is being *processed,* both the document reader, and printer, are idle. Similarly, when a document is being read, the processor and printer are idle, and when a line is being printed, the processor and reader are idle.

19. Solution. Buffering is the name given to the technique of transferring data into temporary storage, prior to *processing* or *output.* This enables the *simultaneous operation of devices* as illustrated at Fig. 28.3.

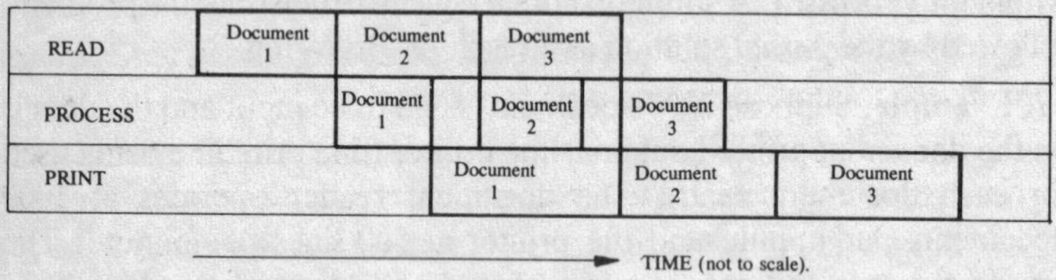

FIG. 28.3.

Total time required:- After reading the first document all subsequent reading, processing and printing can be overlapped. Thus the total time required is a little over the speed of the slowest device ie. just over *4* minutes.

METHODS OF OPERATION AND MODES OF ACCESS.

20. Operating systems are often described in terms of the methods by which they *operate the system* and the modes of system access they provide. The common alternatives are introduced here. More detail will be given in the following paragraphs where necessary.

a. **Multiprocessing.** This is the name for the situation which occurs if two or more processors are present in a computer system and sharing some or all of the same memory. In such cases two programs may be processed at the same instant. In the remainder of this discussion assume just one processor is used unless otherwise stated.

b. **Multiprogramming.** This occurs when more than one program in main storage is being processed **apparently** at the same time. This is accomplished by the programs taking turns at short bursts of processing time.

c. **Batch processing.** The job (program + data) is not processed until fully input. The jobs are entered and stored on a disk in a **batch queue** and then run one or more at a time under the control of the operating system. A job may wait in a batch queue for minutes or hours depending on the work load. No amendments are possible during processing.

d. **Remote job entry** refers to batch processing where jobs are entered at a terminal remote from the computer, and transmitted in to the computer.

e. **Interactive Computing.** this occurs if the computer and terminal user may communicate with each other.

f. **Conversational mode.** This is Interactive computer operation where the response to the users message is immediate.

g. **Multi-access.** This occurs if the computer allows interactive facilities to more than one user at a time.

h. **Time-sharing.** Processor time is divided into small units called **time slices** and shared in turn between users to provide multi-access.

i. **Real-time system.** A real time system is a computer system which is capable of processing data so quickly that the results are available to influence the activity currently taking place. There is often a need for multiprocessing and a front end processor in these systems.

MULTIPROGRAMMING.

21. Computer programs, if looked at in basic terms, can be seen to perform nothing more than a repetition of three steps:-

a. **Input** – reading into main storage from a peripheral device.

b. **Computing** – using the processor.

c. **Output** – writing out from main storage to a peripheral device.

22. In the very earliest of computers only *one* of the three steps could be performed at any one time and the processor was idle during input and output operations. The imbalance between processor and peripherals was improved with the concept of SIMULTANEITY, ie. the simultaneous operation of two or more peripherals (28.19).

23. Nevertheless, developments along these lines were only concerned with processing one program in the computer at a time. In order to utilise the considerable processing power of the processor more effectively a way was found to have *more* than one program in main storage at any one time. These programs *share* the processor between them.

24. Programs generally will use various proportions of input/output (peripheral) time and computing (processor) time.

a. Programs which use a *lot* of peripheral time and very *little* processor time are referred to as being PERIPHERAL BOUND (a good example is the media conversion program which does hardly any computing at all).

b. Programs which require *great* use of the processor and relatively little of peripherals are said to be PROCESSOR BOUND.

25. The ideal situation is to have one or more of each type of program in main store *at any one* time so that while one is carrying out an input/output operation under another is using the processor. In this way the imbalance between the processor and peripherals is reduced and a balance between computing time and I/O time is achieved.

26. Multiprogramming. This term is used to describe the technique of having *more* than one program in main storage at any one time and *apparently* being processed at the same time. The Executive program will transfer control from one program to another so that when one is using the processor another is making use of peripherals. Skilful inter-leaving of programs increases utilisation of the processor.

27. Partitions. In order to achieve this *sharing* of the main storage, it is regarded as being divided into PARTITIONS. Each program will occupy a partition.

28. Interrupt. The control program (Executive) has the ability to *interrupt* a particular program to pass control to another. It is this power which enables the inter-leaving of programs. The applications program can request resources via interrupts. the interrupt concept is fundamental to the proper working of a multiprogrammed computer.

TIME-SHARING.

29. From the way in which multi-programming has just been described it should be clear how it can improve the throughput of batch jobs. When multi-access interactive users are to use a system, the multi-programming must take place under a strategy which gives each user both a fair share of processor time and conversational facilities. Time-sharing serves this purpose.

30. In a time-sharing system a clock is used to divide up processor time into "time-slices" and these time-slices are shared between the users in an appropriate way.

31. A typical time-slice lasts less than one hundredth of one second. At each pulse of the clock the user program currently being executed has its execution suspended. (The user will probably not be aware of this because time-slices happen so frequently that within a second execution is likely to be resumed). Then the operating system checks the status of each user, in strict sequence, to see whether the user requires processor time. Some may not. For example, they may have paused during typing for some reason. Once the operating system finds a user requiring processor time, that user's program is allowed to continue execution for the duration of the time-slice.

32. When the end of the sequence of users is reached, the operating system returns to the start of the sequence and repeats the sequence again. This is known as **polling** in a **round-robin.**

TYPES OF OPERATING SYSTEM.

33. Single program systems. The majority of small micro-computer based systems have **monitors** (27.9) which allow a single user to operate the machine in an interactive conversational mode but normally only allow one user program to be in main storage and processed at a time. ie. there is no multi-programming of user programs.

34. There are a number of well established operating systems which fall into this category. Apart from those operating systems which are specific to particular manufactures machines there are some which are available on a wide variety of different machines. CP/M (Control Program for Microcomputers) produced by Digital Research is a good example.

35. Simple Batch Systems. These are systems which provide multi-programming of batch programs but have few facilities for interaction or multi-access. Many commerical computer systems in use during the 60's and early 70's were of this type.

36. Multi-access and Time-sharing Systems. The majority of operating systems fall into this category, but there is a wide range of complexity in such systems.

37. On the larger micro-computers and smaller minicomputers there are a number of operating systems which are available for use on a variety of machines produced by different manufacturers. One such operating system which is gaining in popularity is UNIX which was developed by Bell Laboratories in the USA.

38. On large minicomputers and main frames, operating systems are normally specific to the particular machine and manufacturer.

39. Real-Time Systems. The operating system has to cater for the type of real-time system being used. The three types are given here in order of increasing response time.

a. A more complex multi-access time sharing system where each user has a largely independent choice of system facilities eg. each using a different language.

b. Commercial Real-time systems in which there is essentially one job such as handling booking and the multi-access user has a clerical rather than programming function. These systems often make use of extensive data bases.

c. **Process Control Systems** eg. a system to control the operation of a chemical factory plant. Response to changes must be as fast as possible and reliability is essential.

40. Our primary interest in DP is type (a) and (b) just described. These systems not only have more complex operating system but also have more sophisticated hardware. One feature worthy of a separate mention is **virtual storage.**

VIRTUAL STORAGE.

41. In order to execute a program it has to be loaded into main storage. Hitherto the *whole* program has been loaded into storage. Thus a program size is governed by the amount of main storage available to it.

Note however that only a small part of the program is 'active' at any point in time – the remainder is *inactive* but still occupies valuable main storage.

This particular circumstances has been exploited by a special programming technique in which programs are divided up into small segments or "pages". During processing pages are called into main storage for execution as required.

The programmer is no longer limited by the size of main storage because only the segments of his program occupy it at any time. He can regard the disk capacity as his *virtual* storage.

The technique also facilitates multi-programming

SUMMARY.

42. a. Operating systems were originally developed to take over the functions performed by the human operator.

b. The modern operating system is a "program which controls programs" and is an essential part of the system.

c. The "intelligent part" of the operating system is the executive which remains permanently in main storage.

d. The operating system carries out a variety of functions to schedule, control and monitor the use of hardware by software.

e. Differing speeds of various hardware items are catered for by techniques such as spooling and buffering.

f. The features of operating systems can be classified in a variety of ways according to methods of operation or modes of access.

g. Multi-programming and Time-sharing are two important methods exploited by many different types of operating systems.

POINTS TO NOTE.

43. a. The size and sophistication of an operating system will match the requirements of the overall computer system. At its simplest the operating system will be required to do little more than control the operation of the input/output and storage devices. Other computer systems will require the operating system to cope with such things as the simultaneous processing of many programs and checkpoint/restart procedures.

b. Buffering enables better utilisation of equipment and faster throughput.

c. Buffering is *one* method of overcoming the difference in speeds of hardware devices.

d. SPOOLING. The term also applies to the conversion of *input* transactions from Document/Disk etc, such operations being carried out in a multi-programmed computer as "background" jobs. In this case it is called *Input* Spooling.

e. 'Simultaneity' is the name given to a computer's ability to carry out the simultaneous operation of more than one device.

f. Partitions in multiprogrammed computers are not physical but organisational (conceptual), ie. respective sizes of partitions can change according to new requirements.

g. Multiprogramming is a TECHNIQUE *not* an item of software. It has been included in this chapter because of its close association with Operating Systems. (You can't have multiprogramming *without* an operating system to control it).

h. You *can* have a computer operating system in a single programmed computer.

i. That part of the operating system which remains permanently in main store (ie. Executive) is said to be "RESIDENT", the rest of the operating system is "TRANSIENT".

QUESTIONS.

1. Define multi-programming. Discuss the hardware and software facilities necessary to facilitate multi-programming. (ICMA)

Systems Analysis and Design

1. System Analysis may be defined as the methods of determining how best to use computers, with other resources, to perform tasks which meet the information needs of an organisation.

2. The use of the word "analysis" in the term is therefore misleading because "analysing" is only *one* of the activities which are generally regarded as coming under the heading "Systems Analysis".

3. Systems Analysis consists of a series of stages forming part of what is often called the "System Life Cycle".

Life Cycle Stages:-

a. Preliminary Survey/Study.

b. Feasibility Study.

c. Investigation and Fast Recording.

d. Analysis.

e. Design.

f. Implementation.

g. Maintenance and Review.

(Stages c–g: Main Stages in Systems Analysis and the work of the "Systems Analyst")

4. An overview of the system life cycle is given in chapter 29.

5. System Analysis originally developed as a branch of Organisation and Methods (O & M), but is now a more major activity because of the increased use of computers. The development of Systems Analysis from O & M is discussed in chapter 30.

6. The subsequent chapters in this Part deal with the details of the stages in Systems Analysis.

29 The System Life Cycle

INTRODUCTION.

1. New computer systems frequently replace existing manual systems, and the new systems may themselves be replaced after sometime. The process of replacing the old system by the new happens in a series of stages and the whole process is called the **"system life cycle"**.

2. This chapter provides an overview of the system life cycle. The individual stages in the life cycle are described in detail in subsequent chapters.

THE LIFE CYCLE IN OUTLINE.

3. Fig. 29.1 shows the major stages in the system life cycle.

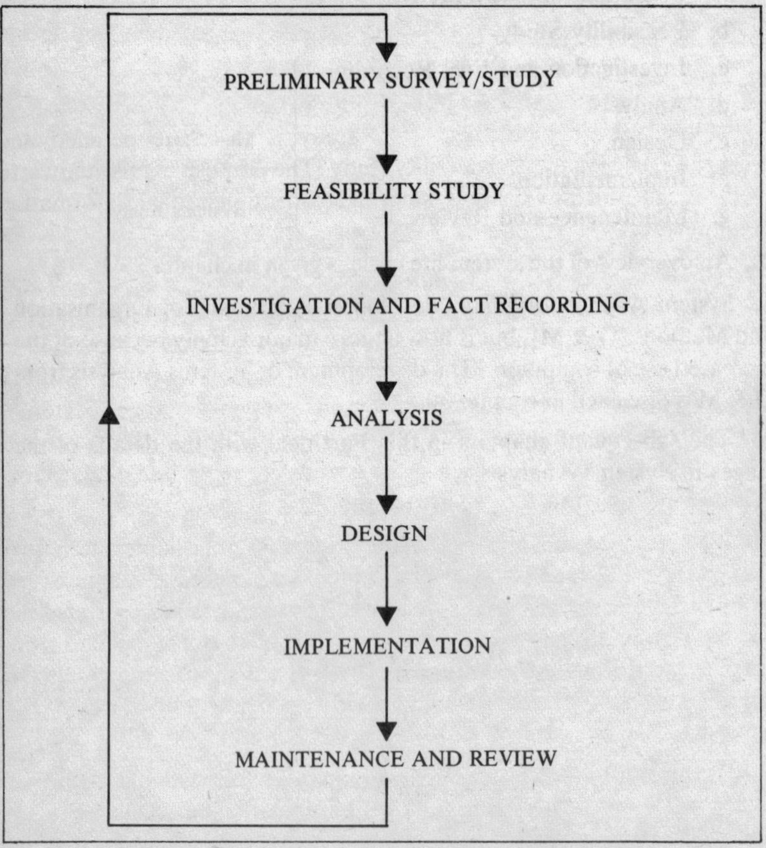

FIG. 29.1. THE SYSTEM LIFE CYCLE.

4. The start of a new system life cycle is normally the result of some *"trigger"* such as the perception of a business need, failures or limitations of the existing system causing dissatisfaction, or heightened awareness of modern developments. Whatever the reason it is management who will initiate the selection of a project for preliminary study or investigation.

5. Preliminary Survey/Study. The purpose of this survey is to establish whether there is a need for a new system and if so to specify the objectives of the system.

6. Feasibility Study. The purpose of the feasibility study is to investigate the project in sufficient depth to be able to provide information which either justifies the development of the new system or shows why the project should not continue.

7. The findings of the feasibility study are presented to management in the form of a report which will make appropriate recommendation. If the report finds in favour of the project then senior management may decide to move to the next stage.

8. Investigation and Fact Recording. At this stage in the life cycle a detailed study is conducted. This study is far more detailed and comprehensive than the feasibility study. The purpose of this study is to fully understand the existing system and to identify the basic information requirements.

9. Analysis. Analysis of the full description of the existing system *and* of the objectives of the proposed system should lead to a **full specification of the user's requirements.** This **Requirements Specification** can be examined and approved before system design is embarked upon. In recent years greater emphasis has been placed upon this stage because of former expensive and frustrating experiences of designs which failed to meet requirement. The earlier in the system life cycle that a mistake is discovered the less costly it is to correct.

10. Design. The analysis may lead to a number of possible alternative designs. For example different combinations of manual and computerised elements may be considered. Once one alternative has been selected the purpose of the design stage is to work from the requirements specification to produce a **System Specification.** The system specification will be a detailed set of documents which provide details of all features of the system.

11. Implementation. Implementation involves following the detail set out in the system specification. Two particularly important tasks are programming and staff training. It is worth observing in passing that the programming task has its own "life cycle" in the form of the various stages in programming ie. analysis and design occur at many different levels.

12. Maintenance and Review. Once a system is implemented and in full operation it is examined to see if it has met the objectives set out in the original specification. Unforseen problems may need to be overcome and that may involve returning to earlier stages in the cycle to take corrective action. From time to time the requirements of the organisation will change and the system will have to be examined to see if it can cope with the changes. At some stage the system life cycle will be repeated again and yet again.

AREAS OF RESPONSIBILITY.

13. Different types of staff are responsible for different stages in the life cycle. For example the early stages will have a significant involvement by senior management, the middle stages will be the responsibility of "Systems Analysts" and a stage such as implementation will give major responsibility to programmers.

14. In the remainder of this Part those activities which are primarily the responsibility of the system analyst will be discussed. The responsibility of programmers have already been discussed in earlier chapters. Some further details of the early stages in the system life cycle will be dealt with in the Part on "Management of EDP".

SUMMARY.

15. a. The system life cycle is the series of stages involved in replacing an old system by a new one.

b. The life cycle stages are:
   - i. Preliminary Survey/Study – initiated by management.
   - ii. Feasibility Study.
   - iii. Investigation and fact recording.
   - iv. Analysis.
   - v. Design.
   - vi. Implementation.
   - vii. Maintenance and Review.

c. Some form of documentation accompanies all stages in the cycle. The following documentation is of particular importance:-
   - i. Feasibility study report.
   - ii. User requirements specification.
   - iii. System specification.

POINTS TO NOTE.

16. a. "System Analysis" takes place at all stages in the life cycle not just the analysis stage.

30 The Development of Systems Analysis Methods

INTRODUCTION.

1. Systems Analysis developed as a specialised branch of Organisation and Method (O & M), which is a general approach to solving procedural problems.

2. Initially, Systems Analysis merely adopted and adapted the methodology of O & M to computerised systems. Within a few years increases in the levels of computerisation and the thrust of innovation resulted in the initiative for developments in methodology being taken over by Systems Analysts. In more recent years the methods which of necessity had to be developed in order to create complex computer systems have taken the methodology of Systems Analysis still further away from its O & M origins.

3. This chapter draws attention to these developments by comparing modern Systems Analysis with O & M. The chapter also shows how System Analysis is organised.

ORGANISATION AND METHOD.

4. Definition. Organisation and Methods (O & M) can be defined as the *systematic* analysis of *selected* procedural problems in order to produce alternatives which will be more suitable, technically and economically.

5. Link with Work Study. The concept of the scientific approach to data processing activities developed from *Work Study* techniques used on the factory floor. In fact, the terms *Work Study in the Office* and *Work Simplification* have been used synonomously with the term O & M.

The Work Study approach includes not only finding the best *method* of carrying out data processing activities, but also setting *time standards* for completion of the work (through work measurement).

Techniques of work measurement used on the factory floor can be very precise because of the routine repetitive nature of the work. Much data processing work is *not* so readily suited to *precise* measurement, and less precise standards are often set.

STAGES OF O & M.

6. An O & M study consists of the following stages, which are comparable to stages in the system life cycle described in the previous chapter:-

a. **Investigation.**
   i. Confirmation of the terms of reference.
   ii. Obtaining all the relevant facts.
   iii. Recording.

b. **Analysis** (of all the facts as recorded).

c. **Design** (of alternative systems).

d. **Implementation** (of the new system) and *Review.*

7. As the stages of O & M and Systems Analysis are so closely related, duplication of content within this Part is avoided by giving the O & M stages in outline in this chapter and giving detailed descriptions under the corresponding heading within the discussion of Systems Analysis.

8. Terms of reference. The objectives of the assignment must be clearly established by management and must include any constraints with regard to areas of investigation. Upon the extent of the objectives will depend the *length of study* and the *number of people* involved.

It is the responsibility of management, not of the O & M team, to define the objectives of a study. Examples of assignments undertaken by an O & M team are as follows:-

a. "To investigate the need for and the best method of, checking purchase invoices."

   Notice that this is concerned with a single *operation* within a whole procedure.

b. "To find the most economical method of producing sales invoices."

   This particular assignment finds itself with wider terms of reference, ie. it is concerned with a whole *procedure.*

c. "To suggest alternatives to the present stock control/materials procurement/accounts payable procedures."

   The scope of this assignment is wider still because it deals with many procedures which by their nature may be linked together.

9. Fact finding. Detailed fact finding is required. The aim is to find out exactly who does the work in what manner, where, and at what time.

10. Fact recording. During the fact finding stage, unless the investigator has formulated a plan for the keeping of notes of the facts, he will end up with a mass of notes on all areas, which will be difficult to examine.

A good practice is to sectionalise notes into *areas* of investigation (eg. by *department* or *operation*) or by *type* of information (eg. organisation charts, interviews, forms, etc.). Use should be made of *procedure flow charts* and *work charts,* examples of which are shown in Fig. 30.1.

Charts are used to give a pictorial representation of a procedure, departments' or operators' work etc, to aid analysis. There are no *standard* work charts, but the following are examples of those used.

1. Movement chart (or string diagram). This is used to show the movement of clerks or documents and is constructed by lines drawn, or string pinned, on a planned layout of the work area.

2. Process chart. This is used to portray the *operations* to be carried out, the *flow of work,* and the *distance between points of operation.*

It is constructed by listing the operations (filing, copying, sorting etc.) down the left hand side and *standard symbols* used to pictorially represent those operations (eg □ = filed; '0' = operation).

3. Operation chart. This shows what is done and gives a comparative record of productive and idle time of an operator and machine:-

OPERATION	TIME	OPERATOR	TYPEWRITER
Making tea	0915	✓	×
Typing	1000	✓	✓
Idle	1030	×	×
Taking dictation	1100	✓	×

4. Procedure flow chart. This shows the flow of multiple copy forms:-

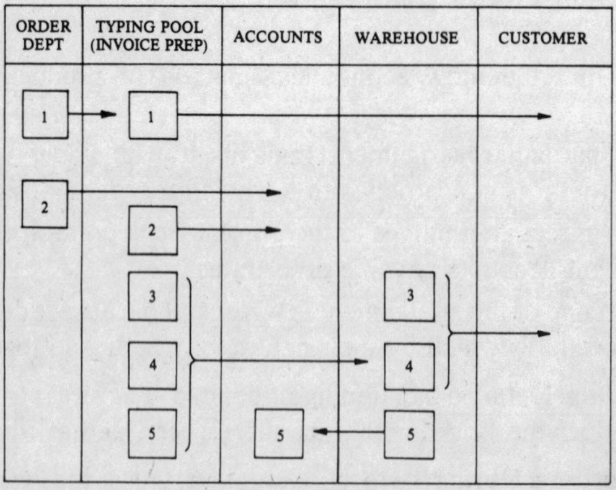

FIG.30.1. WORK CHARTS.

11. Analysis. During the previous stage, or even before he starts investigating, the investigator may form ideas about possible solutions to the problem. The analysis stage is an important *separate* stage between investigation and design. Its aim is to make sure that every aspect is critically examined and that *all feasible alternatives* are eventually produced.

12. Design. This is the stage of an O & M assignment in which the O & M specialist must use his creative abilities in producing all feasible alternatives. Ideas will already have formed in his mind during the analysis stage and these will not be formalised.

13. The design aspects of O & M are, in principle, the same as those of systems analysis. The difference lies in interpreting the needs of a system using conventional methods rather than computer methods.

14. Implementation. This stage follows on from design and involves the coordinating and controlling of the steps necessary to ensure the *agreed* design becomes operational. The amount of work involved varies with the complexity of the procedures adopted but will involve training of staff, ordering of equipment and forms, and production of procedure manuals.

15. Review. It must be ensured that the new methods have been adopted as prescribed and are in fact working according to plan. The results of checking will be used as feed-back for future exercises.

SIMILARITIES AND DIFFERENCES BETWEEN SYSTEMS ANALYSIS AND O & M.

16. O & M represents a general approach to solving procedural problems and therefore considers all possible solutions. However, those problems which require the use of computers for their solution have tended to become the concern of a specialist offshoot of O & M. This specialisation is called Systems Analysis and is dealt with as a separate Part because of the special nature of computers themselves.

17. The major difference between systems analysis and O & M is the difference between the *general* and the *specific.* O & M is the general approach to solving procedural problems whilst systems analysis applies this approach specifically towards computer solutions. The following would seem to arise out of this basic difference:-

a. **Length and breadth of studies.** Generally, O & M assignments are shorter and do not cover such a wide area as systems analysis assignments.

i. **Length of studies.** Computers are only able to carry out the operations for which they have been programmed. Thus *every* detail must be catered for in advance by the analyst and built into the Systems Specification from which the final programs are prepared, and this can be a very lengthy process indeed. Many of the O & M assignments, on the other hand, are concerned with manually executed procedures, and many minor steps can be left to the discretion of the clerk or supervisor. They would therefore tend to take much less time to conduct.

ii. **Breadth of studies.** Systems analysis is generally involved with complete *systems* whereas O & M is often involved merely with a *step* in a *procedure.*

b. **Organisational changes.** Wide organisational changes are generally necessary to gain full benefit from the introduction of computers. Organisational disruption is normally on a far lesser scale as a result of O & M assignments.

c. **Personnel.**

i. **Technical knowledge.** Systems analysts specialise in the capabilities and limitations of computers. They must understand programming techniques and languages to be able to communicate requirements to programmers, and must keep abreast of the rapid developments in hardware and software. O & M officers, with computer aspects taken out of their hands, specialise in conventional methods of data processing.

ii. **Business knowledge.** Systems analysts need a good knowledge of the many application areas in which they become involved to be able to recognise, and aid the re-definition of, management information requirements.

iii. **Ability to communicate.** The systems analyst is involved with people in many departments during any study. There is a natural suspicion of computers and a resistance to the changes that must accompany them. In these circumstances communications skills are a vital factor in the systems analyst's success.

d. **Effect of mistakes.** The consequences of mistakes made in the applications of computers are bound to be more far reaching than those made using conventional methods. These effects will be in terms of both *cost* and the *organisation* generally.

DEVELOPMENTS IN SYSTEMS ANALYSIS METHODOLOGY.

18. For many years the main differences between Systems Analysis and O & M were most noticeable in the contrasting methods of design. (See para. 13). However, computers may be utilised to provide complex systems which have no conventional counterpart. As has been explained in chapter 26 these complex systems can integrate organisational functions and pool organisational data into data bases.

19. The scale and complexity of these systems posed problems to the conventional methods of analysis and so newer methods were devised. Advances in the analysis and design of data base gave rise to a number of new formal methods of analysis which have proved successful and become more widely applicable throughout Systems Analysis.

20. It is not necessary for you to learn the practical details of Analysis but you should be aware that a variety of methods exist. Their significance may be expressed by saying that Systems Analysis is now, if anything, more of a Science than an Art.

21. The stage has been reached at which it may be more accurate to described O & M as a branch of Systems Analysis rather than Systems Analysis as a branch of O & M.

ORGANISATION OF SYSTEMS ANALYSIS.

22. The requirements of people engaged in systems analysis, ie. wide *technical knowledge, business knowledge,* and *experience,* are not normally found in one individual. Thus teams of analysts are generally formed and operate on specified assignments. Specialisation within the team will result in junior analysts doing the fact finding and recording, with more senior analysts designing and implementing. The way they may fit into organisation structure of a business is shown at Fig. 30.2.

SUMMARY.

23. Systems Analysis developed as a branch of O & M but now the roles are reversed.

24. Systems analysis may be defined as the methods of determining how best to use computers, with other resources, to perform tasks which meet the information needs of an organisation.

25. a. O & M is the scientific approach to solving procedural problems.

b. The terms of reference for an investigation must be established

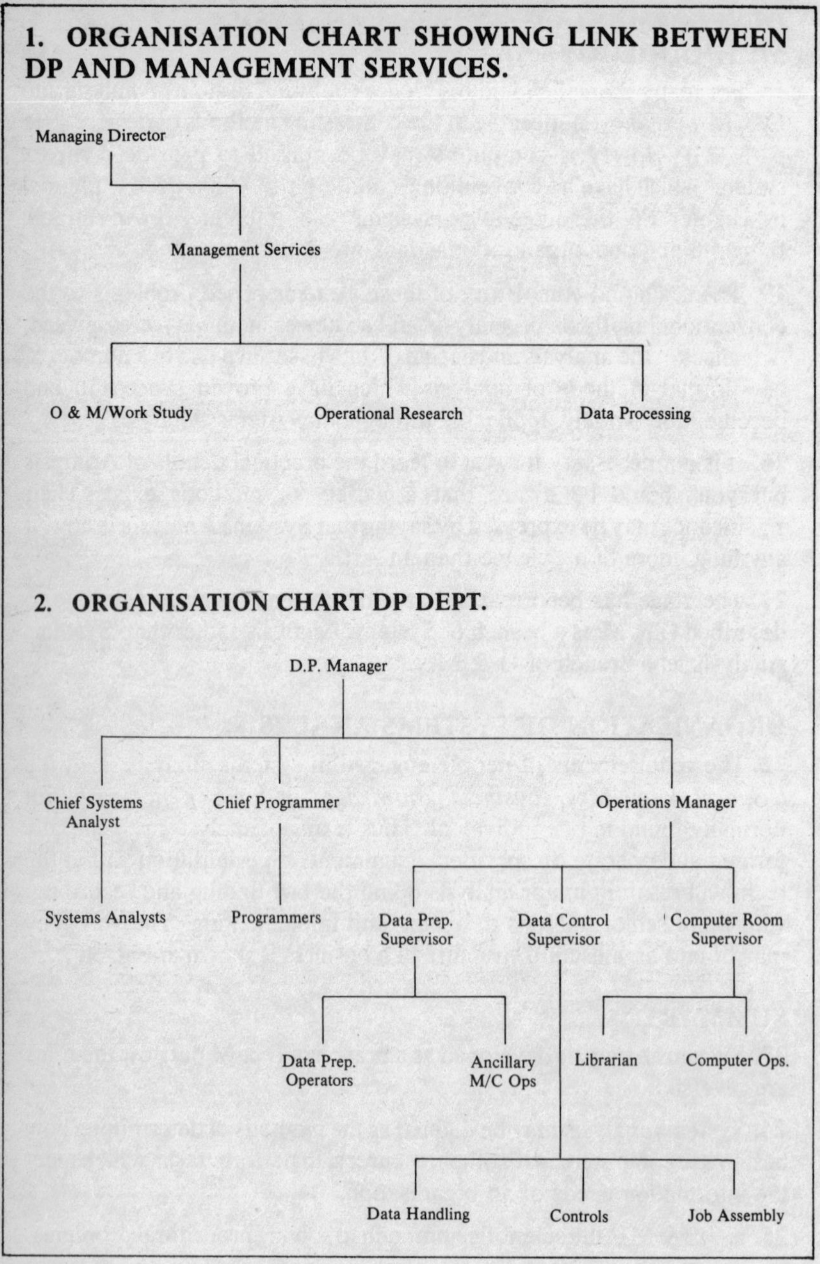
1. ORGANISATION CHART SHOWING LINK BETWEEN DP AND MANAGEMENT SERVICES.
Managing Director
Management Services
O & M/Work Study
Operational Research
Data Processing
2. ORGANISATION CHART DP DEPT.
D.P. Manager
Chief Systems Analyst
Chief Programmer
Operations Manager
Systems Analysts
Programmers
Data Prep. Supervisor
Data Control Supervisor
Computer Room Supervisor
Data Prep. Operators
Ancillary M/C Ops
Librarian
Computer Ops.
Data Handling
Controls
Job Assembly

FIG. 30.2.

by management, not the O & M team (although the team could well *advise* management).

c. O & M stages are:-
   i. Investigation.
   ii. Analysis.
   iii. Design.
   iv. Implementation and review.

d. The standards set, through work measurement, will be appropriate to the nature of the work. (See Appx. 3.5).

e. Controls are established to ensure compliance with standards set.

26. The stages of Systems Analysis have been developed from the stages of O & M but are more formal in their methods.

POINTS TO NOTE.

27. The terms of reference for an O & M study must be clearly set out. If a study takes place with no clear objectives, side tracking will occur and no positive results will be achieved.

28. In considering the difference between O & M and systems analysis the following points should be borne in mind:-

a. The approach in a systems analysis assignment is similar to that adopted in an O & M assignment.

b. The "O & M officer" will specialise in the capabilities and limitations of *conventional methods* of data processing whilst the "Systems Analyst" will specialise in the capabilities and limitations of *computerised* data processing.

c. Both the O & M officer and systems analyst should, however, have open minds and be prepared, when considering alternative designs for a new system, to consider a solution in terms of the other's specialisation.

31 Investigation and Analysis

INTRODUCTION.

1. The items to be covered in this chapter are the confirmation of the terms of reference, the fact finding and recording, and the analysis of the recorded facts to produce a requirements specification.

TERMS OF REFERENCE.

2. It is of the utmost importance that clear objectives are laid down by management. If analysts are allowed to set their own objectives, then these may not accord with the overall company objectives. Before the analyst begins his task, he should, therefore, confirm the terms of reference. The *number of analysts required,* and the *length* and *breadth* of the assignment will depend, to a great extent, upon the objectives set. For example if the objective were "to reduce the turn-round time for orders from one *week* to a *day"* a completely new system would perhaps need to be designed requiring many analysts, taking a long time and having wide effects on the organisation. Conversely, the objective "to reduce the number of clerks in the accounts department" may require a straight transfer of existing procedures to a visible record computer or magnetic tape computer involving fewer analysts, shorter time and little organisational disruption.

FACT FINDING.

3. It is essential to gather all the facts about a current system to ensure that all *strengths* and *weaknesses* are discovered. Thus, when a new system is designed, as many of the weaknesses as possible are eliminated, whilst retaining the strengths.

4. There are four main techniques available, those used depending upon the particular circumstances:-

a. **Interviewing.** This is probably the most widely used technique and the most productive. Interviewing is an art not readily acquired. During interviews facts about what is happening come to light, together with the opinions of the interviewee regarding weaknesses in the system. The personal contacts are important in getting the cooperation of the people involved, and in giving them the feeling of having made a substantial contribution towards the design of the new procedure. It is vital to gain the confidence of the individuals concerned at this stage in order for all the facts to be gathered.

b. **Questionnaires.** The second technique is the use of questionnaires. They save the time of the interviewer but are difficult to design and are generally considered irksome to complete. They are particularly useful when a little information is required from a great number of people. Moreover when the study involves many different geographical locations they may be the only practicable method of gathering facts.

c. **Observation.** This is best employed in conjunction with other techniques and carried out after the observer has an understanding of the procedures involved. Only then will he be able to spot irregularities and generally apply a "seeing" eye to the job.

d. **Record inspection.** The study of organisation charts, procedure manuals and statistics, can reveal much useful information about a procedure. However, a close study of the forms currently being used should give the best guide to current practice which may, or may not, accord with the original requirements.

FACT RECORDING.

5. As discussed under O & M (30.10) the sectionalising of notes should be practised. The charts used in O & M would also be used in systems analysis. In addition use will be made of decision tables and flow charts. The flow charts will reflect the varying degree of detail required. These two forms of recording are particularly suited because of the "YES/NO" type of situation met in solving computer problems.

6. Note that at this stage no attempt is made at analysis or design since the existing system must be fully understood first.

ANALYSIS.

7. At this point, the analyst has gathered all the facts which are relative to the objectives set and has grouped them into a form suitable for analysis. The analysis stage is an important intermediate stage between investigation and design. The analyst must examine all the facts he has gathered in order to make a proper assessment of the existing system. He must resist the temptation to include ideas in the new system which have not been fully worked out. The aim of this stage is to ensure that *all* feasible alternatives are eventually produced. The present system must be criticised against the Principles of Procedure (see below), after which the strengths and weaknesses of the system should be apparent.

8. Principles of procedure (also used in O & M) The present system may be criticised against the principles of procedure:-

a. **Purpose.** Are the purposes being satisfied? Are they still *necessary?* Could they be achieved in *any other way?*

b. **Economical.** Is it economical? Benefits should be related to the cost of producing them. Are there more economical methods?

c. **Work flow.** Are the work flows satisfactory?

d. **Specialisation/simplification/standardisation.** Are the three S's being practised? Is the work capable of being carried out by machine? Can the complex procedures be simplified? Are standard practices observed?

e. **Flexibility.** Is the system flexible? What will be the effect on the system of a big increase or decrease in the volumes to be processed?

f. **Exception principle.** Is the principle of exception being observed? Factors requiring action should be highlighted and not submerged in a mass of routine detail.

g. **Reliability.** How reliable is the procedure? What provision is there for such events as staff sickness, machine breakdown? Could more up to date equipment be justified?

h. **Form.** Is the information being produced in the form best suited to the recipient? Is there a need for a hard copy?

i. **Existing system.** If a change is made, what equipment and other facilities currently being used could be incorporated in the new procedure?

j. **Continuous control.** What types of errors are occurring? Are the controls satisfactory? What other types of controls could be used?

k. **Time.** Is the information being produced in time for meaningful action to be taken?

9. Requirement Specification. An important aim of the analysis is to produce a **Requirements Specification.** In recent years methods have been developed so that the Requirements Specification contains a description of the required system in an *implementation free* form which is intelligible to the user.

10. A Systems Analyst, with sound business knowledge, will discuss the Requirements Specification with the user. This analyst, aided by the Requirements Specification, will have the important task of bridging the gap between the business user and the technical designer.

11. At the end of these discussions the Requirements Specification should be in an accepted form, estimates for alternative designs should be prepared, and the decision to proceed with a particular design can be made.

12. Conceptual Models. Within the documentation of the Requirements Specification is a **system definition** also expressed in an *implementation free* way ie. free of the constraints of any particular design alternative. Such a system definition is called a **"conceptual model"**, a term originally used in data base design.

13. Don't be put of by the name because a conceptual model has three very natural components:-

a. a *data model* which defines the data requirements in terms of entities, attributes and relationships. (eg. an entity such as an order contains attributes such as quantities required and has a relationship with other entities such as customers).

b. a *process model* which defines the processing requirements in terms of events and operations. (eg. the event of an order arriving gives rise to operations such as the update of stock data and production of invoices).

c. a *system model* which defines functional areas and their interrelationship (eg. one functional area may deal with the reception of an order and then pass it to another functional area which processes the order).

14. The methods for constructing the conceptual model are too specialised for inclusion in this book although the models themselves are easy to understand. For example, data flow diagrams (Fig. 19.6) may be used to represent system models.

15. It should be clear by now that the Requirements Specification should present a clear, thorough and unambiguous description of WHAT the system is required to do and should NOT fall into the trap of ruling out possible design alternatives by specifying HOW the system should be designed and implemented. However, there are bound to be some limitations on the kinds of design which can be considered and some very specific and essential features about the design may be known right from the start. For example, there may be specific limitations on the budget available, the accommodation which can be used or the timescale in which events must happen. Also, it may be essential that the new system makes use of or is compatible with some existing equipment. Such information belongs in the Requirements Specification along with the implementation free descriptions which may be regarded as the "high level" features of the design.

SUMMARY.

16. The terms of reference of an assignment must be clearly laid down.

17. Fact finding, recording, and examination, are necessary to discover the strengths and weaknesses of the area under investigation.

18. The analysis stage is important because of the need to ensure that

a. the requirements are *fully* understood and correctly specified.

b. *all* feasible design alternatives are contemplated.

It is an important breathing space between investigation and design.

19. There is a tendency, in practice, for some analysts to neglect the analysis stage and to go ahead with the design of a new system based on a pre-conceived notion that he has held from the beginning. In this way the system produced may be neither what is required nor the most feasible alternative. The mandatory production of a Requirements Specification guards against such bad practices.

POINTS TO NOTE.

20. a. Methods of analysis have been developed greatly over recent years. It is not necessary for you to learn these methods but you should be aware of their importance in improving the quality and effectiveness of Systems Analysis.

b. Improvements to the analysis stage have an impact on the design stage. The designer starts from a much stronger position if he has a Requirements Specification.

QUESTIONS.

1. Even if the objectives of an assignment indicate the need for a completely new system, it is still important to critically examine the present system. Why do you think this is so?

2. An important aspect of System Analysis is the 'fact finding' stage of a systems investigation. Depending on the circumstances and the system being studied, several different methods of fact finding may be used.

You are required to:

a. state **three** *methods of fact finding;*

b. give their advantages and disadvantages and the circumstances in which each might be used.

(ICMA)

32 Systems Design

INTRODUCTION.

1. It is during the design stage that the systems analyst is called upon to use his creative abilities. The implementation free nature of key elements of the Requirements Specification means that *all* feasible alternative designs are open to consideration. By applying judgement, skill and knowledge the analyst can interpret the Requirements Specification to create one or more **System Specifications** (or System Definitions). A System Specification provides *detailed* documentation of the new system, ie. it gives the detail of a particular implementation, unlike the Requirements Specification which is free of unnecessary prescription of the design. A System Specification requires acceptance by management just as the Requirements Specification does.

2. This chapter deals with the elements of design and the sequence in which they are carried out. Design criteria are then dealt with and are followed by a description of a System Specification.

AN ALTERNATIVE APPROACH.

3. Before embarking upon the elements of design we should first consider an important alternative to the design process just outlined, namely, the use of ready made systems with standard applications packages or applications generators. For many small organisations, and small departments in large organisations, the development of a one-off system tailored to the organisation's particular requirements is out of the question for economic reasons, however desirable it may be in principle. Therefore, the system design task is not so much one of developing the elements of design from the Requirements Specification as a task of examining standard hardware and software packages to see if anything is available which can meet the requirements, and if so, seeing how they can meet the requirements and which of the alternatives is most suitable.

4. If this alternative approach is adopted the design task does not disappear but merely takes a different and simplified form. The considerations to be covered in this chapter still apply but in the context of selecting from the design alternatives made available by the standard package or packages. These considerations take place in conjunction with those concerned with selecting a package (see 27.37 – 27.43 & 26.36 – 26.38). This approach to design is the one most commonly adopted where microcomputers are used for the final system.

DESIGN ELEMENTS.

5. The design of a new system can be conveniently divided into the following elements:-

a. Outputs.
b. Inputs.
c. Files.
d. Procedures.

6. Outputs. It is necessary to consider what is required from the system before deciding how to set about producing it. These requirements will have become clear as the project progressed. The analyst will need to consider form, types, volumes, and frequency of reports and documents. Choice of output media will also have to be made.

7. Inputs. Consideration of input will be influenced greatly by the needs of output, eg. the necessity for quick response from the system would determine the need for an on-line type of input. Consideration would be given to:-

a. Data collection methods, and validation.
b. Types of input media available.
c. Volumes of input documents.
d. Design of input layouts.

8. Files. This element is very much linked to input and output. Input is processed against the files to produce the necessary output. Considerations involved in designing files are:-

a. Storage media.
b. Method of file organisation and access.
c. File security.
d. Record layouts.

9. Procedures. Procedures are the steps which unify the whole process, which link everything together to produce the desired output. These will involve both computer and clerical procedures. They will start with the origination of the source document and end with the output document being distributed. The design of the computer programs will constitute a major task in itself.

10. Because of their importance in the design of a new procedure the aspects of form design the design of quantitative reports and internal check are dealt with in some little detail. (NB. This is a traditional O & M activity too).

11. Forms design.

a. **Introduction.** The design of forms and the design of procedures are very much linked. The completion of a form may be the first operation of a procedure (eg. compilation of an order form); a by-product of an operation within a procedure (eg. a receipt, as a by-product of posting to the cash book, in machine accounting); the end product of a procedure (eg. reports to management); or the form may be completed at various stages within a procedure (eg. invoice sets).

Whether the requirements of the form dictate the procedure, or the steps in the procedure dictate the design of the form, is determined by individual circumstances. Very often, the justification of expensive machines brings in its wake the need for redesign of forms to fit the procedure.

b. **Aim.** The aim is to keep forms to the minimum consistent with serving the needs of the system.

c. **Features of design.**

i. **Sizes.** The use of *standard* size forms should be used, as it is more economic to do so, and *handling, filing,* and *copying* are simplified.

ii. **Types of paper.** The quality of paper used should be appropriate to requirements. Consideration should be given to such things as frequency of handling, storage needs, conditions under which forms are completed, and prestige requirements.

iii. **Identification.** There should be a brief, self explanatory title; copies should be identified by different colours or bold symbols; serial numbering may be required for internal check purposes.

iv. **Common information.** If two forms are used in conjunction with each other, the common information should be in the same sequence and postion.

v. **Vertical spacing.** There should be adequate space for each item of entry (eg. an invoice should have enough spaces to cover the normal number of items ordered). If a typewriter is being used in recording data on a form, consideration must be given to the normal vertical spacing requirements of the machine.

vi. **Columns.** The length of column headings should be tailored to the width required by the information to be entered in the column.

vii. **Pre-printing.** As much as possible of the common detail should be pre-printed, leaving only variable data to be entered.

viii. **Clarity.** There should be overall simplicity of instructions. Material of a similar nature should be grouped together. A logical sequence for completion should be followed and unambiguous wording should be used. The size of the print should make for ease of reading.

ix. **Miscellaneous.** There may be a requirement for perforation for subsequent bursting or pre-punched holes for subsequent filing.

x. **Multi part sets.** Where more than one document is to be raised at the same time, consideration should be given to the method employed in carrying the image through all copies eg. carbon; no carbon required paper; carbon patches, etc.

12. Design of Quantitative Reports.

a. **General.**

i. The date rendered, and the period of time to which the report relates, should be shown.

ii. The report should have a reference number, show the names of persons rendering and receiving it, and have an apt, concise title.

iii. The quality and size of paper, the spacing and the sequence, should be such as to aid completion and subsequent use.

b. **Principle of exception.** Due emphasis must be given to facts according to their degree of importance, allowing managers to focus attention on deviations from plans.

c. **Comparative figures** should be shown to highlight trends or show relative value (eg. previous period : current period and profit : capital employed).

d. **Conciseness.** facts and figures should be presented in a concise fashion (eg. use of a summary).

e. **Units employed** should be clearly indicated (eg. £'s, lbs, cwts).

f. **Language.** The knowledge of the recipient must be borne in mind to avoid jargon.

g. **Co-ordination of statistics.** There must be co-ordination in the use of basic data (eg. sales being based on orders received *or* on goods despatched).

h. **Method of presentation.** The use of graphical methods, as alternatives to listings of figures, should be considered.

i. **Timing.** Submission of reports should be as frequent as required according to the decision to be taken.

j. **Accuracy.** Reports should be as accurate as possible subject to purpose, clarity, cost and speed of presentation.

k. **Relevance.** Reports should only include information on areas controllable by the recipient.

FAULTS AND WEAKNESSES IN REPORT DESIGN.

13. a. **Completeness.** A weakness is that a decision may be taken on incomplete information. It may be that the information is necessarily incomplete ie. unquantifiable information is also required for a decision. It may also be that the subjective summarisation of reports at lower levels of management results in the exclusion of important information.

b. **Pertinence.** Many reports are sent 'just for interest' and whilst there is a need for certain information, outside the direct control of an individual, to be sent for co-ordination and co-operation purposes, the volume should be kept to a minimum to allow concentration on essentials. Reports should be reviewed regularly to ensure that they are still serving a useful purpose.

c. **Method of presentation.** Quantifiable reports tend to become standard in presentation and can lose their impact. To maintain effectiveness, thought should be given to changes in the method of presentation (eg. changing a listing of figures to graphical presentation).

d. **Timing and frequency.** Many reports are produced at an uneconomic cost through unnecessary speed and frequency of presentation. A cost-to-benefit analysis must be made of reports, to ensure that the speed and frequency of presentation are justified by the action to be taken on them.

The effectiveness of pertinent information depends upon the form and timing of its presentation. Persons given the responsibility of compiling reports must be trained to ensure that raw data becomes effective information.

NB. The end product of data processing is information irrespective of the data processing facilities used to produce that information. Throughout any study of data processing, therefore, you need to be constantly aware of the necessity for good presentation of information.

14. Internal check. (NB. These considerations also apply to O & M).

a. **Definition.** The arrangement of procedures and systems, and the *allocation of duties* so that there is an automatic check on what is being done.

b. **Principle.** No one person should be placed in the position of having responsibility for *all aspects* of a business transaction. Thus the work flow is so arranged that the work of one person, or section, is independently checked by some other person or section.

c. **Purposes achieved.**

i. The possibility of fraud and error is reduced.
ii. The responsibility for errors is determinable.
iii. Supervision is assisted (because of the built-in checks).
iv. The work of internal and external auditors is reduced.

d. **Examples of the operation of internal check.**

i. The serial numbering of forms.
ii. The requirement for two signatures on cheques.
iii. The use of control accounts.

DESIGN METHOD AND DESIGN SEQUENCE.

15. Over the last ten years or so a number of design methodologies have become established, each with its own set of dedicated supporter.

16. The advocates of each of these methodologies naturally proclaim the advantages of their methods over the alternatives. Terms such as "structured", "hierarchical", "top-down", and others are used to label the different approaches to design.

17. What all these design methodologies have in common is a recognition that large problems, such as those found in design, can only be tackled effectively if they are broken down into smaller, more manageable tasks in some systematic way. The same ideas were first put into practice with considerable success in program writing, where terms such as "Structured" and "Top-down" suffer less ambiguity.

18. Without going into unnecessary detail about any particular method it is still possible to identify the following design sequence:

a. The system is described at a logical level in terms of *what* it will do in the context of a particular design. ie. a combination of design elements (para 3) will be put together in a way which can meet the requirements in general terms.

b. The "logical model" is refined in a series of steps in which successive detail is added. Some steps may be re-traced as the emerging design is evaluated. Considerations of physical details are postponed as long as possible, because, for example, it is senseless to design a report document before it is decided exactly what the report should contain.

c. Finally the physical detail is added to the logical detail so that the design shows not only *what* the system should do but also exactly *how* it should do it.

CRITERIA FOR DESIGN.

19. Purpose. The purpose must be to meet the demands of the Requirements Specification, and for that matter, the objectives which were agreed at the beginning of the project. At one time, and still in some organisations, a Requirements Specification was not produced at the end of the analysis stage and so the System Specification had to serve both purposes.

20. Some of the criteria outlined in the following paragraphs may be applied to the Requirements Specification. Where the criteria do apply it is a clear indication of the economic benefits of the Requirement Specification in catching errors earlier and saving inappropriate design effort and costs.

21. Economical. The costs and benefits of the new system should be compared with those of the existing system. This is not easy to do because of the difficulty of quantifying benefits such as "better or more" information. It is important however that the attempt be made.

22. Work flows. The best work flows must be attained. This includes methods of transmitting data to and from the computer, the number of runs required, file organisation, the requirements of internal check, and the link with clerical procedures.

23. Specialisation, simplification and standardisation. The benefits to be derived from the practice of the "three S's" are well known. The analyst will have them in mind throughout the design stage.

24. Flexibility. Points to be considered here are:-

a. **Integration of procedures.** Systems should be designed with possible integration of procedures in mind. This is particularly important as the centralised nature of computer processing makes possible the integration of many procedures carried out independently under conventional methods.

b. **Modularity of hardware.** It is important when choosing the hardware to ensure that it is capable of being expanded (units added) when the need arises.

c. **Peak periods/treatment of exceptions.** The system can be designed to cope with peak period processing; an alternative arrangement is to use a bureau for the unusually high loads. Similarly, exceptional items (ie. those not recurring frequently) could be designed into the system but it may be more convenient to have them dealt with separately by conventional methods.

25. Exception principle. The principle of exception should be incorporated in the design of the new system, so that only deviations from plan are reported for management's attention. In a stock control system, for example, warnings would be given of slow moving stocks. The analyst must ensure that only *necessary* output is produced.

26. Reliability. The reliability of all the hardware and software must be considered. The analyst must ensure that facilities required for the new system have a proven record of reliability. Maintenance requirements, the expected life of the hardware, and the back up facilities (in case of breakdown) must be considered.

27. Form. Data must be presented to the computer in a machine sensible form. The analyst must consider all the methods of input and try to reduce the steps necessary between origination of data and its input. If output from one run is used as the input to another, the ideal medium for the subsequent input should be used. When output is required in a humanly legible form, choice of method of presentation is important. Methods available are visual display, printed copy, graphical, etc, and the needs of the person receiving the output will determine which one is appropriate.

28. Existing system. Consideration must be given to the existing staff, procedures, equipment, forms, etc, in the design of any new system. For example, if punched card input is currently being operated, the procedures already exist for transferring the source data into a machine sensible form although it may well not be incorporated into the design of a new computer system.

29. Continuous control. As the majority of steps are carried out automatically, there is an even greater need for care in internal check. Audit trails (43.17) must be laid to the satisfaction of the auditors. Controls such as those described in Chapter 17 should be incorporated.

30. Time. The analyst must design the system to satisfy time requirements. Speeds of equipment, modes of access and processing methods must be considered. The length of the processing cycle is a most important consideration. The presentation of source data to the computer and the production of output documents will be subject to strict time constraints.

SYSTEMS SPECIFICATION (OR DEFINITION).

31. The Systems Specification is the detailed documentation of the proposed new system. It serves two main purposes:-

a. **Communication.** It serves as a means of communicating all that is required to be known to all interested parties; as follows:-

i. **Management** for final approval.

ii. **Programmers** to enable them to write the programs necessary for implementation.

iii. **Operating staff,** detailing all necessary operating procedures.

iv. **Users,** as they will ultimately be responsible for running the new system. They must therefore be fully aware of the contents of the Specification and their agreement is essential.

b. **Record.** A permanent record of the system in detail is necessary for control. It will be used for evaluations, modification, and training purposes.

It is of particular importance to have the system well documented as those analysts who took part in its design go on to other projects, or perhaps change employment.

32. Different persons require to know only *parts* of the whole specification (eg. programmers need to know the runs required and the file layouts, but will not need to know the timings for data preparation or numbers of staff required etc.) The specification is also produced at different stages of design ie. *in outline* for top management, *in detail* for lowest levels. The specification is sectionalised to enable only the appropriate parts to be sent to the interested parties.

33. Contents. The following are the main items to be found in a Systems Specification.

a. **Preliminary information.** This comprises contents, lists, names of recipients of particular sections, names of those having authority to change files, programs, etc.

b. **Objectives of the system.** A brief statement is given of the aims indicating the departments and the main procedures involved. The benefits arising from implementation are also stated.

c. **Systems description.** This will detail all procedures both clerical and computer using flowcharts where applicable.

d. **Detailed specification** of:-

i. Input files.
ii. Output files.
iii. Master files.
} with specimen layouts.

iv. Source documents.
v. Output documents.
} with specimen copies of each document.

Supporting narrative would accompany each item. Methods of file organisation and modes of access are detailed.

e. **Program specification.** This contains:

i. Details of inputs, outputs and processes for each program run.

ii. Test data and expected results.

iii. Stop/start, file checking, error checking procedures.

iv. Controls.

v. Relationship between procedures and computer runs.

f. **Implementation procedures.**

i. Detailed timetable (using networks or other scientific aids).

ii. Details of conversion procedure.

iii. Change-over procedures, including systems testing.

g. **Equipment.** All equipment including ancillary equipment necessary and maintenance arrangements.

h. **User department instructions.** These relate to the input to the system (ie. times for forwarding source documents) the output from the system (ie. dealing with documents, and control totals etc).

SUMMARY.

34. The design stage is the creative stage in systems analysis, all feasible design alternatives should be considered.

35. The systems analyst can use the Requirement Specification as the criteria against which he can judge his designs.

36. The Systems Specification is important as a means of communication and a record of the detailed design.

POINTS TO NOTE.

37. a. Terminology is not universal. For example a "System Specification" may also be called a "Requirement Specification". This is seldom a practical difficulty because the context normally prevents any ambiguity.

b. The terms *'specification'* and *'definition'* are used synonomously.

c. The Systems Specification acts as the *acceptance* of the design of the new system by all levels of management.

d. In reading this chapter on design, students should realise that much of the detail involved has been described under the appropriate headings eg. data collection computer files, etc. etc.

e. An alternative approach to System Design, particularly relevant to small organisations, is the design of the system around available applications packages.

QUESTIONS.

1. What are the factors which govern choice of output media and device?

2. A computer has been installed in your company. You were involved in the design of the cost control information that will be provided by the computer.

List the shop floor "labour" control information that you have specified.

Draft one of the relevant output documents produced by the computer (ICMA).

3. An important factor in the efficient operation of any data processing system, whether manual, mechanised or computer based, is the design of the forms used.

What are the major principles of good form design? Illustrate your answer, where appropriate. (ICMA)

33 Implementation Review and Maintenance

INTRODUCTION.

1. Implementation follows on from the detailed design stage. This involves the co-ordination of the efforts of the *user* department and the data processing department in getting the new system into operation. A Co-ordinating Committee is sometimes formed for this purpose, having as its members the managers of the departments concerned and a representative from the DP department. The analyst responsible for the design of the new system will be an important member because of his thorough knowledge of the system.

2. Planning for the implementation will have begun early in the design stage. Details will have been stipulated in the Systems Specification.

They would cover the following:-

a. Training of staff.

b. Programming.

c. System testing.

d. Master File conversion.

e. Changeover procedures.

f. Review and Maintenance.

TRAINING OF STAFF.

3. The amount of training required for various categories of personnel will depend upon the complexity of the system and the skills presently available. The systems analyst would be required to ensure that all persons involved with the new system were capable of making it an operational success. The following aids would be used, as appropriate:-

a. **Handbooks.** These will be produced as part of/or development from, the Systems Specification.

b. **Courses.** Either full-time or part-time courses, often run by the computer manufacturers.

c. **Lectures.** General background knowledge, or knowledge of specific areas, could be covered by means of lecture.

PROGRAMMING.

4. The programmer must design programs which conform to the requirements set out in the system specification (32.29). The stages in programming have already been discussed in chapter 21.

SYSTEM TESTING.

5. There is a need to ensure both that the individual programs have been written *correctly* and that the *system* as a whole will work, ie. the link between the programs in a suite. There must also be co-ordination with *clerical* procedures involved. To this end the systems analyst must provide the necessary test data as follows:-

a. **Program testing.** The systems analyst will need to supply test data designed to ensure that all possible contingencies (as specified in the Systems Specification) have in fact been catered for by the programmer. *Expected results* of the test must be worked out beforehand for comparison purposes.

b. **Procedure testing.** The aim of procedure testing will be to ensure that the *whole system* fits together as planned. This will involve the clerical procedures which precede input; the actual machine processes themselves; and the output procedures which follow. Overall timings and the ability of staff to handle the anticipated volumes will all be under scrutiny.

MASTER FILE CONVERSION.

6. It is necessary to convert the existing master files into a magnetic form. The *stages* of file conversion will depend on the method currently used for keeping the files (eg. manually; in box files) but are likely to be:-

a. Production of control totals, by adding machine.

b. Transcription of all 'standing' data (such as account number, address etc.) to a special input document designed for ease of data entry.

c. Insertion of all *new* data required onto input document eg. account numbers where none were used previously.

d. Transcription of data from documents to magnetic media. This can be a major task in the case of large manual system. Extra staff may need to be drafted in.

e. Verification of transcribed data.

f. Data is then used as input to a 'file creation run'. A specially written computer program produces the master records in the required format.

g. Printing out of files for comparison with old files.

h. Printing out of control totals for agreement with pre-lists.

i. At a date immediately prior to changeover, variable data is inserted in master files. (eg. *balance* on accounts).

CHANGEOVER PROCEDURES.

7. There are two *basic* methods of changing over to a new system:-

a. **Parallel.**

b. **Direct.**

8. Parallel. The old and new systems are run concurrently, using the same inputs. The outputs are compared and reasons for differences resolved. Outputs from the old system continue to be distributed until the new system has proved satisfactory. At this point the old system is discontinued and the new one takes its place.

9. Direct. The old system is discontinued altogether and the new system becomes operational immediately.

A variation of *either* of the two basic methods is the so-called 'pilot' changeover.

A 'pilot' changeover would involve the changing over of *part* of the system, either in *parallel* or *directly.*

10. The features of the various methods of changeover are:-

a. **Parallel.**

i. It is a costly method because of the amount of duplication involved.

ii. This method would mean the employment of extra staff or overtime working for existing staff. This can create difficulties over the period of the changeover.

iii. It is only possible where the outputs from old and new systems are easy to reconcile, and where the systems are similar.

iv. Its use does give management the facility of fully testing the next system whilst still retaining the existing system.

b. **Direct.**

i. If the new system bears no resemblance to the old then a direct changeover is probably inevitable.

ii. There must be complete confidence in the new system's reliability and accuracy before the method is used.

c. **Pilot.**

i. Use of the variation of the two main methods is possible when part of the system can be treated as a separate entity, eg. a department or branch might be computerised before the undertaking as a whole.

REVIEW AND MAINTENANCE.

11. Once the system has become operational it will need to be examined to see if it has met its objectives. For example the costs and benefits will be compared with the estimates produced at the systems inception. This particular activity is often known as *"post audit"*.

12. The system will also need to be reviewed and maintained periodically for the following reasons:-

a. To deal with unforeseen problems arising in operation. eg. programs may need to be modified to deal with unforseen circumstances.

b. To confirm that the planned objectives are being met and to take action if they are not.

c. To ensure that the system is able to cope with the changing requirements of business.

13. The results of a systems review would be used in future systems analysis assignments.

SUMMARY.

14. a. Implementation is concerned with the *co-ordinating* and *controlling* of the activities necessary to put the new system into operation.

b. *Staff training, programming, testing, file conversion, change-over,* review and maintenance are the stages in implementation.

c. The systems analyst is needed at this stage because of his knowledge of the designed system and its implications.

POINTS TO NOTE.

15. a. Note the difference between program testing and procedure testing.

b. The responsibility for program testing lies with the programmers who will be required to provide evidence of testing.

c. The Part you have just read is entitled Systems Analysis because the term is generally used to describe the particular activities detailed in its chapters. In practical terms, however, the various stages will be undertaken as part of the System Life Cycle and a systems study carried out on the instructions of top management. You will be given further details of the system life cycle in chapter 38.

QUESTIONS.

1. What are the features of the various methods of changeover?

2. *What do you understand by the following terms:-*
   a. *Source program;*
   b. *Object program?*

Give an account of how these two kinds of program are related and explain the steps in preparing a fully tested object program. (ICMA)

3. *A company with 700 employees and labour cost analysed over 80 headings has decided to use a standard "package" program to process its payrolls and provide labour cost analysis.*
   a. *What is a package program and what are the advantages of using one?*
   b. *Describe briefly the steps you would take to organise the transfer of the necessary records to the computer files. ICMA*

4. *An O & M exercise is to be undertaken by your company prior to the introduction of a computer.*

Describe the stages into which the O & M exercise would be sub-divided assuming that any proposals made will be implemented. (ICMA)

5. a. *What are the constituent parts which go to make up a typical systems analyst's assignment?*
   b. *Describe briefly the analyst's function in three of such constituent parts. (ICA)*

6. *What information would you expect to find in a well-prepared systems specification? (ICA)*

7. *The monthly accounting routines of a computer based company include one in which suppliers' authorised invoices and credit notes are used:*
   i. *to update the trade creditors file,*
   ii. *to update the cost allocation file, and*
   iii. *in the case of cost allocation 910 (plant and machinery) to update the plant register file.*

All input relates to existing records on file. Master files are maintained on tape.

You are required to draw a computer systems flowchart in respect of the above routine, indicating the computer runs required and giving brief notes for each process.

Control totals only are required in respect of i. and ii. but for iii. a print out of each movement for the month, with descriptive narrative is required. (ICA)

8. *Explain how a systems analyst investigates a business system. (ACA)*

9. *Outline the main stages in the development of a systems project and briefly describe the work carried out by the systems analyst at each stage. (ACA)*

Applications

1. This Part brings together the areas of DP you have studied by discussing specific applications areas in which a computer is put to work.

34 Application Areas

INTRODUCTION.

1. The purpose of this chapter is to focus attention on the areas where computers are employed. In doing so we will concentrate on the underlying principles rather than the details of the procedures themselves many of which have been dealt with elsewhere in the manual. First of all however we will consider the criteria for using computers.

CRITERIA FOR USING COMPUTERS.

2. The following are the criteria by which to judge an application's possible suitability to the use of computers:-

a. **Volume.** The computer is particularly suited to handling large amounts of data.

b. **Accuracy.** The need for a high degree of accuracy is satisfied by the computer and its consistency can be relied upon.

c. **Repetitiveness.** Processing cycles that repeat themselves over and over again are ideally suited to computers. Once programmed the computer happily goes on and on automatically performing as many cycles as required.

d. **Complexity.** The computer can perform the most complex calculations. As long as the application can be programmed then the computer can provide the answers required.

e. **Speed.** Computers work at phenomenal speeds. This, combined with the ability to access records directly and from remote locations, enables them to respond very quickly to a given situation.

f. **Common data.** One item of input data can effect several *different* procedures. For example a customer's order for a particular stock could involve production of an invoice, updating of the customer's record, updating the stock record, and initiating a re-order for the stock item. The many files involved can all be stored in one physical location and accessed together so that a decision is made in the light of all the information. Contrast a manual system where the item of data will go through many separate independent procedures.

3. It is usually the combination of two or more of the criteria listed which will indicate the suitability of an application to computer use. The criteria that have been described will be used by those who carry out the

Preliminary Survey (29.5) in order to judge the suitability of applications for computerisation.

4. Technological innovations over the last ten years or so have not only increased the range of technically feasible applications, they have reduced costs so that computers provide a cost effective solution to a far wider range of problems than they did before.

APPLICATION AREAS.

5. In general terms one can consider the application areas under two headings:-

a. Routine administrative, or clerical.

b. Management.

The earliest computers concentrated on the clerical applications such as payroll and order processing, but today there is an awareness of the power of the computer in many other areas notably management information and office automation.

ROUTINE APPLICATIONS.

6. Some of these you will have already met elsewhere in the manual:-

7. a. **Payroll.** This was invariably one of the first applications to be put onto the computer by a user. It is a well defined procedure sometimes involving complex piece rate and bonus calculations. Much of the data could also be used for labour cost control.

b. **Order processing.** This can satisfy nearly all the criteria. Notice the data common to stock recording, sales ledger, and invoicing.

8. Although these and similar applications may be considered as routine tasks a great deal of the data is of use in aiding planning and control. Also there is a definite link between production, purchasing, sales, etc, and the computer applications should reflect this link. For this reason the routine and the control applications would ideally be part of an *integrated* system.

9. Many organisations have taken the levels of computerisation of routine tasks to very advanced states, thereby increasing their efficiency and expanding their spheres of activity. The clearing banks are a notable example. They first computerised cheque clearing in the late 1950s. Now they have extended banking concepts with the aid of computers to create on-line cash dispensers and credit transfer facilities which may lead to a distant goal of the "cashless society".

10. The price paid for such advances is total reliance on computer systems.

11. Office Automation. Office automation involves the substantial use of computers, in conjunction with other electronic equipment, to automate the basic secretarial and clerical task of the office. It is the *routine* nature of a large amount of office work that makes office automation a likely candidate for automation, and reduced equipment costs now make it cost effective.

12. Basic office automation consists of Word Processors connected to one another and to a corporate computer by means of a local network (10.24).

13. Word Processing. The term 'Word Processing' has developed from the use of micro or mini computing equipment to produce documents such as standard letters, accounts, contracts, estimates etc. Special purpose software enables a document to be displayed on the VDU as it is typed in at the keyboard. A completed document can be transferred to the printer any number of times and/or recorded on disk for future use. Some basic typing functions, eg. carriage return, are taken over to speed up the process and a wide range of additional keyboard functions make it possible to edit and re-edit documents simply – thus removing the need for correcting fluids and/or re-typing. Other facilities include machine generated page numbers, indexes etc. or generating a list of individually headed letters using standard paragraphs and a list of names and addresses stored on disk. Whilst the name *'Word Processor'* has been given to a machine dedicated to this type of work, which usually requires a quality printer, increasingly the smaller office uses a micro computer for *all* data processing work, including word processing.

MANAGEMENT.

14. A company needs information on which to base decisions concerning the current operations and future plans. It requires this information to be timely and accurate. Examples of the use of computers in the area of **management control** are now given:-

a. **Stock control.** The computer is able to process data quickly, making available information on stock levels, slow moving items or trends in demand. A central computer can link together widely separated warehouses, thus treating them as one vast stockholding. Customer orders can be satisfied from an alternative warehouse should an item not be available in the local area. Used in this way the

Digital Equipment's DECmate III word processor.
"DECmate" is a trademark of Digital Equipment Corporation.
(Picture courtesy of Digital Equipment Corporation (DEC))

computer enables stockholdings to be kept to a minimum, thus releasing cash for other purposes.

b. **Production control.** This is an extremely complex area especially in batch production factories. Production must be able to respond quickly to changes in demand and other circumstances. To do so requires the provision of up to date information which is accurate and timely. On-line systems such as Plastic Badges help to get the data from the shopfloor quickly enough to influence current events. Machine loading, materials control, batch size calculation, and machine utilisation are all things which a computer can make more efficient because of its ability to make complex calculations and sift vast amounts of data speedily and accurately. Sophisticated computerised control systems must be capable of assessing the effect on production of the continuing happenings which are the everyday lot of the production manager.

c. **Labour control.** Much of the information used in the control of labour can be obtained from the payroll and personnel records applications. Ideally they will all be part of an integrated system. An analysis of labour hours into various categories such as idle time, sickness, and absence, can aid forecasting future requirements. Departmental and sectional summaries help to highlight these problems on a wider basis. Actual performance is measured against budgeted performance. Daily reports for the shop floor manager aid control of routine operations. Reports of a more general nature will aid overall manpower utilisation.

d. **Network Analysis.** This technique is used for the planning and control of large complex projects. Examples are the building of a factory, the installation of new plant and the manufacture of an aircraft or ship. The model (which requires the careful preparation of large amounts of base data) shows each stage in the project and its dependence on other stages. For example, when new plant is being installed, it cannot be moved in until the site has been prepared, and this in turn cannot take place until the old machines have been removed. When the necessary data has been supplied, the program produces a plan which management can use. A great advantage of the technique is that the plan can be quickly modified by the program in the light of actual progress, and revised plans produced at short notice to allow for delays. The program also indicates the *critical path,* ie. the series of interdependent activities which will take longest to complete and which, if delayed, will hold up the whole project. Resources can then be concentrated on these activities.

e. **Linear Programming.** This technique is used to find the optimum solution (ie. that which maximises profits or minimise costs) from a large number of possible alternatives. Examples are the optimisation of product mix and the minimisation of transport costs. Again, a considerable amount of accurate base data has to be supplied to construct a model. The methods used are not dealt with in detail here; the key point to note is that the computer has the storage capacity and the speed to calculate and evaluate *every* conceivable solution and thus to find the best one. The manager, if dependent on human resources, cannot possibly do this; the timing required to make the necessary calculations would be prohibitive. He would have to depend on his experience and perhaps instinct.

f. **Financial Modelling.** A model is constructed of the companies finances – its resources, its income and its expenditure. It is possible by using the model to *simulate* the effects of different policies. For example, the likely results of different investment policies can be forecast, and external factors such as the national growth rate and the trend in national incomes can be introduced to see what effects they will have. It is possible by a series of computer runs, with variations of the basic assumptions on each one, to obtain a forecast of the likely effects of alternative policies. The usefulness of the computer lies in its high speed, which enables it to simulate in a few hours events which will actually occur over many years. The technique is of great use to the manager in enabling him to evaluate the results of different decisions which he can make.

15. Management Support Tools. The examples given in the previous paragraph are typical of the uses of computers for large scale specialist problems. The software is normally set up and run by specialists who provide management with the results. In contrast with this approach is the direct use of a computer by management in a way which, in many respects, is an extension of the pocket calculator idea. In other words, the manager uses his own personal computer as a specialist management tool.

SPREADSHEETS.

16. An extremely popular and simple tool of the kind just mentioned is the **spreadsheet** of which there are many versions. One of the earliest spreadsheets was the software package called "Visicalc" produced by Visicorp inc. for use on microcomputers. Newer, more advanced versions have since been produced by Visicorp and its competitors. The spreadsheet is a direct extension of the pocket calculator in that it does calculations not just on single values, as is the case with a pocket calculator, but on whole rows and columns.

17. A simple example is shown in Figures 34.1 – 34.3. The complete spreadsheet is shown in Fig. 34.1. It shows some estimates relating to a painting and decorating job. You will notice that the spreadsheet comprises a grid of numbered rows and lettered columns. Each grid position is called a cell and can contain either text or numerical values. It is possible to define formulae by which values in some cells can be calculated from values in other cells. When using the spreadsheet package on the computer the user sees only part of the spreadsheet. The section of the screen displaying part of the spreadsheet is called a window. In addition to the window the user also sees a display of details about the status of one cell currently being edited. A cell is selected for editing by moving the cursor about the screen until it is at that cells position. (see Fig. 34.2).

18. Having done the basic calculation the user can then carry out enquiries of the "what if?" variety such as "what if I mark up the material costs by 10%?" Various kinds of data manipulation are possible:

a. Inserting, deleting or copying rows and columns.
b. Changing the spreadsheet layout or the precision of calculations.
c. Printing the spreadsheet or saving a copy on disk for future use.
d. Performing comprehensive computation using mathematical functions and formulae.

With these functions the spreadsheet can be used for a wide variety of problems: job, cost or production estimation; balance sheets and statements; simple forcasting; asset depreciation.

MORE ADVANCED PACKAGES.

19. Rather more advanced than the simple spreadsheet packages are the **integrated packages** which aid in such things as financial planning or statistical analysis. One example of such a package is "TREND", supplied by Planalysis which has facilities for model building, calculation, printing, graphical display and so on. These packages *support* the decision making processes by taking away the routine calculations and manipulations but do not go so far as recommending courses of action. For that, it is necessary to make use of a system which has some characteristics which we normally associate with human intelligence. Such systems are already in use. They are called **Expert Systems** or **Intelligent Knowledge Based Systems (IKBSs).**

Col> Row+	:A	:B	:C	:D	
1:		CUSTOMER:	F Bloggs	ESTIMATE	
2:					
3:	MATERIALS	UNIT-COST	QUANTITY	TOTAL COST	
4:					
5:	White Gloss (Small)	2.00	0.00	0.00	B5 ×C5
6:	White Gloss (Large)	3.50	2.00	7.00	B6 ×C6
7:	Coloured Gloss (Small)	2.50	3.00	7.50	B7 ×C7
8:	Coloured Gloss (Large)	4.00	1.00	4.00	B8 ×C8
9:	White Emulsion (Small)	2.50	0.00	0.00	B9 ×C9
10:	White Emulsion (Large)	4.50	1.00	4.50	B10×C10
11:	Coloured Emulsion (Small)	3.00	0.00	0.00	B11×C11
12:	Coloured Emulsion (Large)	5.50	3.00	16.50	B12×C12
13:	Cleaning Materials	3.00	1.00	3.00	B13×C13
14:				———	
15:				42.50	Sum of
16:				———	D5 to D13
17:					
18:	LABOUR	HOURS	RATE	TOTAL COST	
19:	Jim Brusher	35.00	10.00	350.00	B19×C19
20:					
21:			GRAND	———	
22:			TOTAL	392.50	D15+D19
23:				———	

Note: a. If the values in columns B and C are changed then all other values can be recalculated automatically by using a recalculate command.

b. Since recalculation is so easy it is possible to handle "what if" questions such as "what if material costs rise by 5%?"

FIG. 34.1. THE COMPLETE SPREADSHEET SHOWING HOW VALUES ARE CALCULATED.

Col>	:A	:B	:C	:D
Row+				
1:		CUSTOMER:	F Bloggs	ESTIMATE
2:				
3:	MATERIALS	UNIT-COST	QUANTITY	TOTAL COST
4:				
5:	White Gloss (Small)	2.00	0.00	0.00
6:	White Gloss (Large)	3.50	2.00	7.00
7:	Coloured Gloss (Small)	2.50	3.00	7.50
8:	Coloured Gloss (Large)	4.00	1.00	4.00
9:	White Emulsion (Small)	2.50	0.00	0.00
10:	White Emulsion (Large)	4.50	1.00	> 4.50 <

Cell

PRESENT CELL POSITION: D10

CELL TYPE: numeric
CELL CONTENTS: +B10*+C10
CELL VALUE: 4.50

ENTER COMMAND OR VALUE: ————

Note: a. Cell positions are specified like map grid references (Column letter, Row number) eg. D10.

b. A cell can contain numerical values or text. eg. cell A3 contains the text "MATERIALS", and cell D10 contains the value 4.50.

c. Numeric values can be either entered directly **OR** calculated from other values, eg. values in column B & C have been entered directly but values in column D are calculated by multiplying unit-costs by quantity. Formulae for calculating values are typed in in the same way as values.

d. Commands to save or print the display can be typed in too.

FIG. 34.2. A SPREADSHEET DISPLAY SHOWING A WINDOW OF COLUMNS A–D AND ROWS 1–10.

	CUSTOMER:	F. Bloggs	ESTIMATE
MATERIALS	UNIT-COST	QUANTITY	TOTAL COST
White Gloss (Small)	2.00	0.00	0.00
White Gloss (Large)	3.50	2.00	7.00
Coloured Gloss (Small)	2.50	3.00	7.50
Coloured Gloss (Large)	4.00	1.00	4.00
White Emulsion (Small)	2.50	0.00	0.00
White Emulsion (Large)	4.50	1.00	4.50
Coloured Emulsion (Small)	3.00	0.00	0.00
Coloured Emulsion (Large)	5.50	3.00	16.50
Cleaning Materials	3.00	1.00	3.00
			42.50
LABOUR	HOURS	RATE	TOTAL COST
Jim Brusher	35.00	10.00	350.00
		GRAND TOTAL	392.50

FIG. 34.3. HOW THE SPREADSHEET OF FIG.
APPEARS WHEN PRINTED.

EXPERT SYSTEMS.

20. An **Expert Systems** is a specialised computer package which can perform the function of a human expert. Some of the first expert systems to gain widespread publicity were those used for medical diagnosis. A medical consultant, assisted by his staff, took part in a lengthy exercise in which both the knowledge base required and the decision making procedures were transferred to the computer. Subsequently, the computer was able to ask the same questions and draw the same conclusions from the answers as the consultant so that a relatively junior doctor, aided by the computer, could be as expert as the consultant!

21. In Data Processing there are many possible applications for Expert Systems, for example, company law, investment, financial planning and personnel. Products are gradually appearing on the market.

Testing NCR Automated Teller Machines
At NCR's manufacturing plant in Dundee, a robot continuously makes withdrawals and other service requests from the ATMs (Automated Teller Machines), putting them through the equivalent of several years transactions to ensure reliability.
(Picture courtesy NCR Ltd)

22. Expert systems normally have the following features (a law Expert System will be used to provide examples):

a. An organised base of knowledge – often in the form of a database (eg. Acts of parliament and Case law.)

b. A user interface able to support diagnostic or similar discussions with the user. (eg. To enable the user to pose legal problems or to check the legality of an intended action.)

c. A facility to hold details of the status of the current consultation. (eg. The user, in consulting the Expert System, may have to go through a lengthy question and answer session and the system has to keep track of the state of the questioning.)

d. An Inference Engine, ie. software which can use the knowledge base and current status of the consultation to either formulate further questions for the user or draw conclusions about what actions to recommend to the user. (eg. a mechanism for formulating and sequencing appropriate questions about the users legal problem.)

e. A knowledge acquisition system, ie. a facility to update the knowledge base. It is via the knowledge acquisition system that the human expert is able to endow knowledge to the expert system. (eg. a suitable system for entering the relevant facts about company law.)

23. Although these basic components are bound to vary from one discipline to another (eg. the knowledge base for Company law is very different from the knowledge base for Personnel Management) the basic structure is the same. Therefore, an established method for developing an Expert Systems is to build the particular Expert System required from a standard non application-specific basic system called a shell. It is possible to purchase a complete Expert Systems or merely a shell from which an Expert System can be created.

24. The user of the expert system sits at a terminal or workstation and takes part in a question and answer session in which data about the problem is typed in. At various stages during the session, or maybe just at the end, the system makes an assessment of the problem and recommends action to be taken.

25. Expert System packages are not confined to Large Computers. Several are available on Personal Computers, eg. Business Information Techniques "Parys" system which is used as an aid in Personnel Management.

CHANGES IN THE SPREAD OF APPLICATIONS.

26. Computers have been successfully applied to many new areas of work in the last few years. Notable examples are:-

a. Office automation (see paragraphs 11–13).

b. CAD/CAM (Computer Aided Design/Computer Aided Manufacture).

c. The use of micro-computer based systems in small firms and offices.

27. Details of CAD/CAM are outside the scope of this book but the introduction of such things as industrial robots may be viewed as a natural extension to systems which already deal with production control and stock control.

28. The advent of micro-computer based system has meant that applications such as payroll and stock control, which could only be economically computerised in organisations of some size, can now be usefully introduced into very small firms.

CONCLUSION.

29. Many of the procedures, and techniques are possible without a computer but it is the speed and accuracy with which the computer carries them out that makes it such an invaluable tool of management.

SUMMARY.

30. a. The criteria for using a computer are, volume, accuracy, repetitiveness, complexity, speed, and the use of common data.

b. Computers can be applied successfully to administrative tasks and to the production of management control information.

c. Spreadsheets and Expert Systems have been discussed.

POINTS TO NOTE.

31. a. Not all applications have been dealt with – other applications have been dealt with elsewhere.

QUESTIONS.

1. At the conclusion of a computer feasibility study you are writing a report to your managing director explaining your choice of storage method.

List the advantages of:-

a. Magnetic disk storage.

b. Magnetic tape storage.

and give three examples of files for which each method is best suited. (ICMA)

2. The Managing Director of your company has just attended a seminar on computers and data processing during which he heard a brief reference to 'spreadsheets' and 'spreadsheet packages'. On his return he has asked you, as an accountant attached to the DP department, to explain these terms.

You are required to describe:

a. *spreadsheets and spreadsheet packages;*

b. *the typical facilities provided by a spreadsheet package;*

c. *an accounting application of such a package.*
(ICMA)

Computer Systems

1. This Part looks at complex computer systems and how they are used.
2. Chapter 35 deals with Micro-computers and Mini-computers.
3. Chapter 36 deals with larger computer systems.

35 Micro-computers and Mini-computers

INTRODUCTION.

1. The basic hardware features of micro-computers and mini-computers were described in chapter 9 (9.25–9.27). This chapter considers the use of these computers and examines where they fit in the overall picture of computer applications.

MICRO-COMPUTERS.

2. The processing capability of the larger micro-computers is comparable to that of many main frames of the 1960s. This fact should emphasise the major role which these small machines can play if properly utilised.

3. Software. The system software available on these systems may be rather limited but this limitation is more than compensated for by the wide range of software applications packages which are available.

4. System Software usually comprises a simple interactive monitor (27.9) and a limited choice of programming languages eg. BASIC, PASCAL and assemblers.

5. Software Packages are available for a wide range of applications including:-

a. payroll
b. stock control
c. order processing invoicing and sales ledger
d. production control
e. job costing
f. information storage and retrieval
g. word processing
etc.

6. A number of well established software suppliers produce software packages which can be made to run on a wide variety of machines produced by different manufactures eg. Micropro's WORDSTAR package for word processing and Visicorp's VISICALC package for financial modelling.

7. Dual-purpose. Many micro-computers are able to meet a dual purpose:

a. They may be used as "stand-alone" machines. ie. working autonomously for a particular purpose.

b. They may be used as "workstations" within a distributed data processing system.

This enables such machines to deal not only with data processing which is only of 'local' interest but also with corporate data processing.

8. Advantages of a microcomputer include:-

a. Cost – a full configuration for less than £4,000.

b. Cheap software packages arising out of the large volume sales.

c. Just plugs into the nearest mains socket.

d. User-friendly "menu driven" programs mean that there is no need to employ specialist staff, the computer can be operated by general clerical staff.

e. Brings E.D.P. within the budget of even the very smallest organisations.

f. Allows a large organisation to implement distributed processing with each department possessing its own independent processing facilities.

9. Disadvantages include:-

a. Limited file store and memory capacity.

b. Smaller systems often lack languages other than BASIC.

c. Purchased software is often of a poor quality.

d. Too often purchased by non-specialists who are too easily convinced by salesmen.

e. Can lead to several departments duplicating the same procedures.

NB. 16 bit micro-computers with hard disks overcome 9a, and 9b is a problem of hobbyist machines rather than small business machines.

MINI-COMPUTERS.

10. The hardware of a typical mini-computer system was described in 9.28.

11. Whereas the typical micro-computer is designed as a single user system (eg. with 1 VDU) the larger micro-computers and typical mini-computers are multi-use systems.

Norsk Data ND-100 Satellite Series 16-bit Minicomputer.
(Picture courtesy Norsk Data Ltd)

12. A user with an apparent need for multiple micro-computers at one particular location may be able to meet the same need with the single mini-computer.

13. Software. There is far more system software available on most mini-computers than there is on the typical micro-computer, but perhaps surprisingly there is not always such a good choice of applications software.

14. System Software on mini-computers has been developed over many years and had its origins in the fast key-to-disk system. Many single-use systems are in use but the typical mini-computer has a time-sharing operating system plus some communications facilities. The latter reflect the fact that mini-computers frequently form part of a distributed system.

15. The choice of programming languages on mini-computers is usually better than that available on micro-computers and is very similar to that available on most main frames.

16. Software package are available for use on most mini-computers but they do not have the same importance that they have with micro-computers. The reasons are simply that the production of applications software for mini-computers has tended to take place using the same methods as those used for main frame computers. That is, software is often written *by the user or for the user* in order to meet his specific requirements rather than to meet the needs of some general market.

17. This situation is changing however, as many packages first written for micro-computers have since been converted and extended to run on larger systems.

18. The applications dealt with by mini-computers include all those listed earlier under the heading of micro-computers but also include such things as:-

a. Retailing eg. Point-of-Sales systems.

b. Banking.

c. Life assurance.

d. Stock Exchange dealing.

etc.

19. Multi-purpose. Mini-computers may be used for several different purposes:-

a. As "stand alone" machines (often multi-user).

b. As the central host computer in a small distributed system eg. with a number of micro-computers acting as "intelligent terminals".

c. As the second tier in a larger scale distributed system eg. acting as a local host to a number of micro-computers but also connected to some central corporate mainframe.

20. Relative advantages and disadvantages of mini-computers compared with other computers.

a. They are more expensive than a typical microcomputer but much less expensive than a main frame.

b. They have system software which is broadly comparable to that found on main frames but they do not always have the same wide choice of applications packages found on micro-computers.

c. They have greater file storage and memory capacities than most micro-computers and can cope with all but the largest data processing problems.

d. Their multi-user and communications facilities make them well suited to the integration of local data processing activities and the provision of distributed processing facilities.

GENERAL CONSIDERATIONS.

21. System Support. Generally speaking, smaller organisations buying micro and mini-computers will not be able to economically justify the employment of the DP specialists required in main frame installations. The supplier must therefore either be able to offer suitable applications packages or be willing to get more involved in program writing for the user. The latter is seldom an economic alternative in the case of micro-computers because the full development cost must be borne by the one user. The supplier will also be expected to provide considerable support for the user.

22. To understand the market situation, it is important to realise that many micros and minis are sold in what is called the OEM market, ie. Original Equipment Manufacturer. That is to say, they are sold not to the eventual user but to another manufactuer who incorporates them into a larger system. Many manufacturers of micros and minis are wholly or partly dependent on this type of business. It was the decision of some of them to provide peripherals and software and to sell direct to the end user that created the recent explosion in 'mini' and now 'micro' sales.

SUMMARY.

23. a. There is no difference in principle between a 'micro' or 'mini' and the larger computer.

b. Machines described as 'micros' or 'minis' vary widely in specification and price.

c. Essentially, the 'micro' or 'mini' is a smaller, cheaper, slower machine which is however acquiring an increasing degree of sophistication.

d. Although the typical micro-computer is noticeably different from the typical mini-computer, the larger micro-computers and smaller minis are indistinguishable for most practical purposes. In answering examination questions, concentrate on typical features first and then mention any overlap.

e. 'Micros' and 'minis' play an important part in computer networks.

f. Software is usually supplied by the manufacturer as part of a complete system.

g. Applications cover a very wide range, and include all conventional accounting tasks.

h. The micro-computer is even smaller and cheaper than the 'mini'.

POINTS TO NOTE.

24. a. Single user micro-computers are often called "Personal Computers" because of their use by individuals either at work, or at home as a hobby.

QUESTIONS.

1. a. Construct the systems flow charts to show the processing runs for a nominal ledger system.

b. i. specify the input and indicate which input could probably be automatically provided by other computer systems.

ii. List the validation checks you would apply to the input.

(ICMA)

36 Large Computer Systems

INTRODUCTION.

1. This chapter illustrates the use of large computer systems by providing a discussion of two applications:-

a. an airline booking system (a Real-time system).

b. a system used by a large corporate organisation.

2. The first application is specialised whereas the second application considers the typical general purpose large system. Refer back to Real-time systems (28.39) before you continue.

APPLICATION 1.

3. Airline booking system. Records of seat availability on all its planes will be kept by an airline on a central computer. The computer is linked via terminals to a world-wide system of agents. Each agent can gain access to the flight records and within seconds make a reservation in respect of a particular flight. This reservation is recorded *immediately* so that the next enquiry for that flight (following even microseconds after the previous reservation) finds that particular seat or seats reserved. Notice the computer records reflect an accurate picture of the airline's seating load at all times because there is no time lag worth mentioning. The computer would then output information for the production of the customer's ticket and flight instructions, on confirmation on the booking by the customer. (see Fig. 36.1).

4. Each booking is a separate transaction which is processed immediately ie. not batched. This is, therefore, a *transaction processing system.*

FEATURES OF REAL-TIME.

5. Response time. The service given by a real-time processing system can be measured in terms of *response time.* This is the time taken by the system to respond to an input, eg. the time interval between the presssing of the last key by the operator of a VDU and the display of the required (updated) information.

6. "Traffic" pattern. An important feature of real-time is the 'traffic' pattern, ie. the *volumes* of data being input, the *times* at which they are input, the *types* of input and the *places* at which they are input.

7. **Reliability.** Because real-time systems operate automatically an extremely high standard of system reliability is required.

a. **Program protection.** Many programs will occupy main storage simultaneously and the integrity of each program must be protected.

b. **File security.** Duplicate files will probably need to be kept and in addition their contents will be dumped at intervals. These measures will aid re-construction should the need arise. (Note the duplicate database in Fig. 36.1).

c. **Stand-by machinery.** In the airline application two CPUs would be required, one of which is operational and the other a stand-by machine. In the event of failure the stand-by machine would automatically come into use. (Again refer to Fig. 36.1).

d. **Security.** Confidentiality of information held on magnetic storage is achieved by the use of special code numbers allowing access to certain files only by certain people.

HARDWARE, SOFTWARE CONSIDERATIONS.

8. Implicit in the operation of real-time systems described are:

a. A large main storage requirement to accommodate systems software and application programs. Also required will be an area to use as buffers for queueing of messages.

b. Direct access storage of large capacity as backing storage.

c. A sophisticated operating system to handle the many different operations being handled simultaneously.

d. A data communication system linking the many terminals with the CPU.

COST.

9. Real-time systems are usually specially designed for a particular application and are extremely costly. Cost will vary with the service one wishes the system to provide. The better the service (ie. the shorter the response time generally) then the more costly it becomes in terms of hardware and software etc.

APPLICATION 2.

10. **Systems used by large corporate organisations.** Such systems are required to meet the diverse information needs within the organisations.

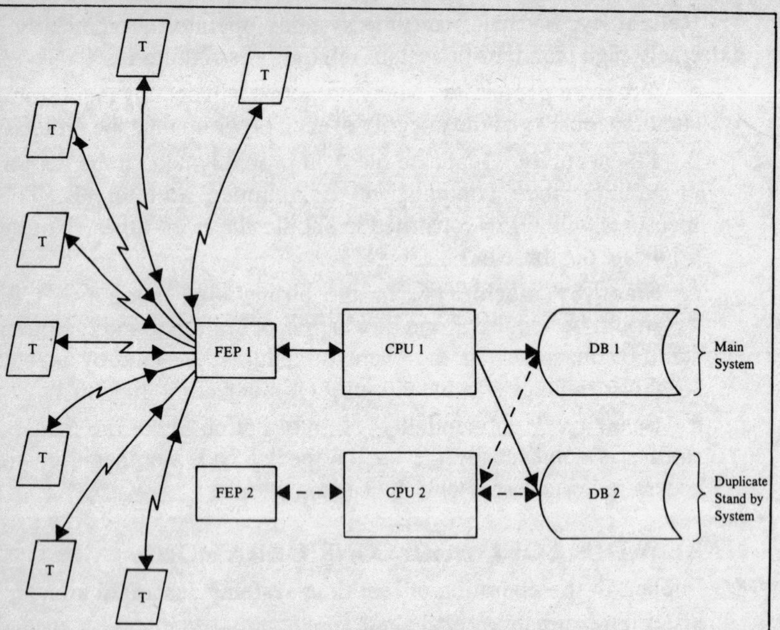

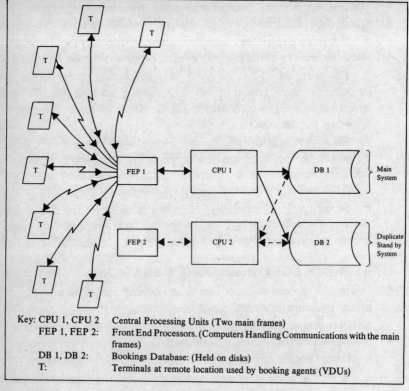

Key: CPU 1, CPU 2 — Central Processing Units (Two main frames)
FEP 1, FEP 2: — Front End Processors. (Computers Handling Communications with the main frames)
DB 1, DB 2: — Bookings Database: (Held on disks)
T: — Terminals at remote location used by booking agents (VDUs)

FIG. 36.1. A REAL-TIME AIRLINE BOOKING SYSTEM.

11. Depending upon the type of organisation any number of the following functions of the organisation may be supported by the computer system:-

a. Top level management.
b. Finance and accounting.
c. Manufacturing.
d. Marketing.
e. Purchasing, stocking and distributing (ie. logistics).
f. Personnel.
g. Administration.

12. Levels of computer support vary from function to function but particularly distinctive levels are:-

a. Automation of basic clerical procedures such as those found in ordering, invoicing, payroll production and bookings. Batch or transaction processing will be used as appropriate.

b. Office automation and communications to support the administrative functions eg. by the use of word processors and electronic mail.

c. Automation of management control operations such as the control of stock, production, materials distribution, accounts and personnel.

d. Automated aids to strategic planning such as financial modelling, linear programming and other analysis methods.

FEATURES OF THESE SYSTEMS.

13. In order to support the processing needs outlined in the previous two paragraphs these systems must be large, versatile, reliable and efficiently organised.

14. Specific features may include:-

a. **Distributed facilities.** For example there may be a mainframe computer at head office acting as host to smaller computers at divisional offices. A divisional office could deal with marketing or production say. A lower level of the distributed system might handle office automation by means of word processors linked to the main computers. (See Fig. 36.2).

b. **Integrated Files or Databases.** The advantages of integrated file processing or databases can be exploited so that, for example, the receipt of orders may *automatically* give rise to, the ordering of materials, the movement of stock, the scheduling of production, the control of production and the distribution of manufactured goods.

c. **Combinations of different processing methods.** Run of the mill stock control and payroll production may take place by batch processing while enquiries, orders, bookings etc. are being handled by transaction processing. Additional processing loads, such as those used for financial modelling, will also be placed upon the system from time to time.

15. The hardware and software features of these systems have comparable complexity to those of the real-time systems mentioned earlier in the chapter. The principal differences are:

a. The distribution of processing, communications and data.

b. The use of many different types of software to support the varied processing needs.

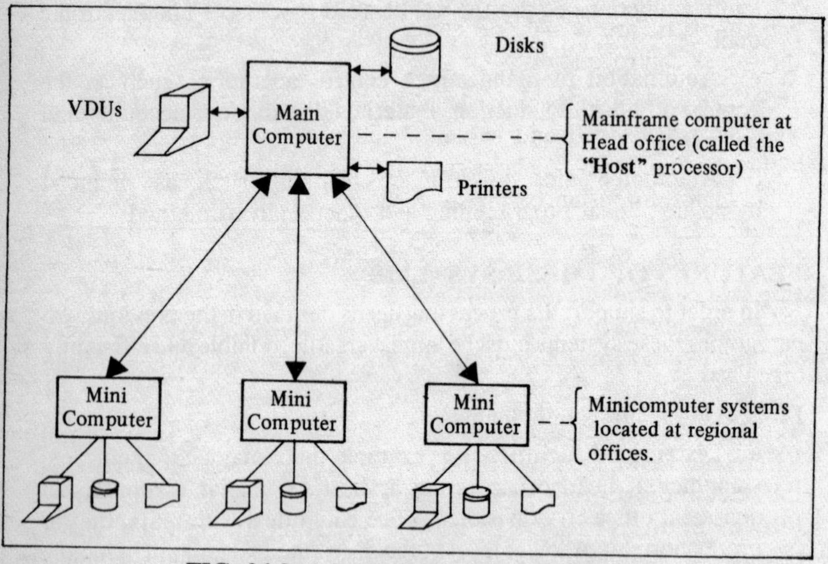

FIG. 36.2. A DISTRIBUTED SYSTEM.

EXAMPLES.

16. An example covering all functions listed in paragraph 11 is provided by a computer system used by a modern manufacturer such as a company which manufactures and sells a wide range of domestic appliances. The distribution of the computer resources (similar to Fig. 36.2) may well reflect the different area of operation. The stocking and distribution of goods to retailers may be supported by one computer system, the purchasing of parts and raw materials by another, the automated production plant by a third system and the finances, accounting, personnel, administration and top level management by a host system at main office. The component systems of such a distributed system will operate particularly effectively if the various operations are properly integrated so that the system works as a whole, rather than as a number of connected units operating autonomously. The term **Computer Integrated Manufacture (CIM)** has been adopted to describe totally computerised manufacturing systems of this kind.

17. There are numerous examples of systems of this kind, each with their own particular variations on the same basic theme depending upon the basic type of the organisation concerned. Thus the financial institutions, insurance companies, banks and building societies are heavily computerised but particularly with regard to financial transactions, personnel, customer accounts and services. On the other hand, organisations in the retail trade, particularly the high street stores and supermarkets, are heavily dependent on large computer systems for their stock control and distribution.

18. When we look at these particular areas more clearly we can see how they have developed and exploited specialist computerised facilities within the framework of a large conventional computer system. The high street banks, for instance, have gone from the computerisation of their cheque clearing system, which started as long ago as 1950, to the inclusion of automatic processing of standing orders and direct debit by the BACS (Bankers' Automatic Clearing Services Ltd) to newer developments such as the Cash Dispenser, ie. the popular machine nestling in a hole in the wall outside the bank and offering a 24 hour service (most of the time!).

19. The next stage of development is likely to be the increased use of **Electronic Fund Transfer (EFT)** which is already well established in the USA where customers at supermarkets and service stations can enter their credit card or bank card into the special till and have the money transferred automatically and instantly. EFT also covers the transfer of funds between banks including international transfers. International transfers are often handled by **The Society for Worldwide Inter-bank Financial Telecommunications (SWIFT).** These systems are more than just computer systems, they are IT systems.

SUMMARY.

20. The applications described in this chapter use large amounts of hardware. The first system must have fast response times in order to satisfy the needs of the users. The second system must strike a balance between response and processing throughput. The airline booking system has essentially one large job to handle but the other system has many different jobs to handle.

21. Real-time involves the processing of data as it arises thus providing records which are permanently up-to-date.

22. Response time, traffic pattern and reliability are major features.

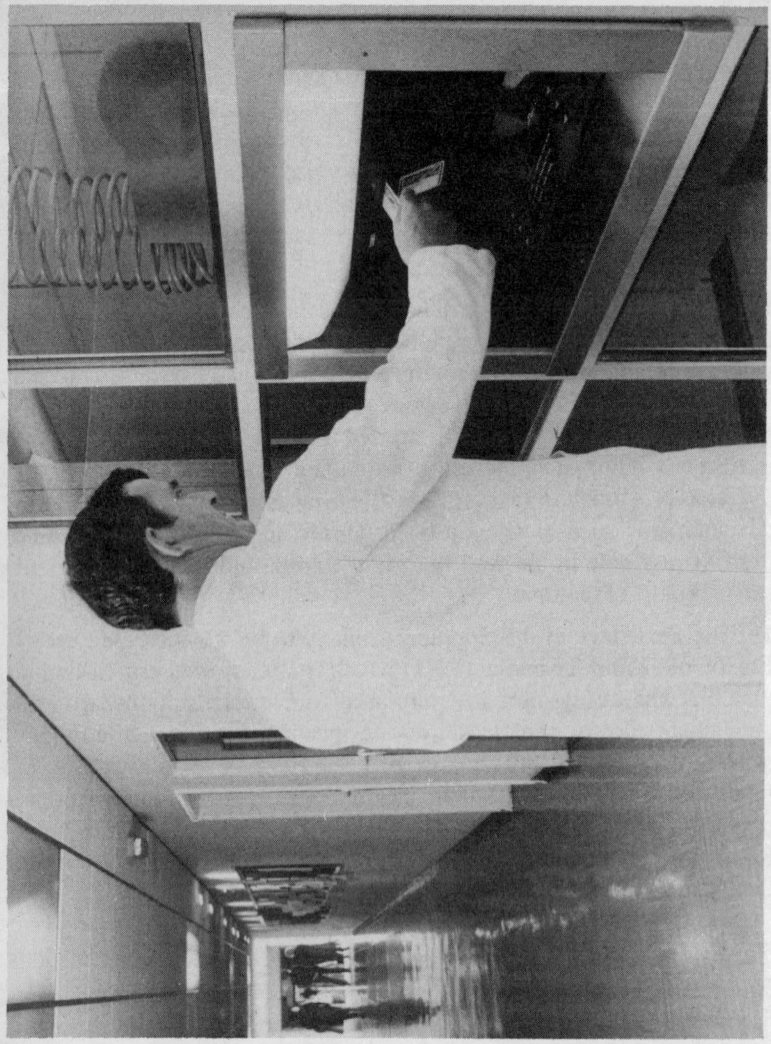

NCR 5080 ATM (Automatic Teller Machine)
Installed at Johnson Wax Ltd Factory for staff use
(Photograph courtesy NCR Ltd)

23. The hardware and software requirements are complex.

24. The system in a large corporate organisation will:-

a. have distributed processing, communications and data.

b. use many different types of software.

c. exploit integrated files or databases.

d. use a variety of processing methods.

POINTS TO NOTE.

25. In the case of a transaction processing system such as the one used by the airline the following points apply:-

a. The accurate assessment of response time and traffic pattern is very difficult but of vital importance, as errors can be very costly in terms of size of CPU, sophistication of software and line capacity. (Unlike batch processing, where overtime or an additional shift might be possible, real-time processing depends upon the system being able to cope at the time required).

Because of the difficulties of accurate assessment, applications are normally implemented on a 'pilot' basis (eg. with the airlines reservations system – no pun intended – a few branch offices would have access initially).

b. The essence of a real-time system is that it should provide an up-to-date (real) picture of events as they occur. Therefore a retrieval system is generally associated with it. It is possibly for this reason that students give undue prominence in examination answers to this latter function, forgetting that they are dealing with a system of *processing* just as they were with batch systems.

26. Other areas where real-time applications of computers are applied are automated process control and production control.

27. There are various interpretations of the term real-time. A system where the time factor is critical is properly called a real-time system.

28. Most large scale organisations are now totally reliant upon systems like the one described in the third example in the chapter.

QUESTIONS.

1. a. What do you understand by the term configuration? Give an example.

b. Explain the term "random access'. Give an example of the application of random access and state in about fifty words why you consider this application is suitable.

c. Explain the terms "on-line" and "off-line". What is the particular advantage of "off-line" output working? (ICMA)

2. *a. What is meant by the term 'real-time processing'?*

   b. Explain the hardware and software facilities which are required for the operation of a real-time system. (ACA)

3. *Distinguish between on-line and real time processing. Give an example of a commercial data processing application where real time processing would be applicable and explain what characteristics make it necessary to consider this type of processing. (ICMA)*

Management of DP Projects and Systems

1. With the knowledge of the various elements that go into making up an EDP system you are now in a position to consider planning the use of computers and the organisation of a DP department.

2. Chapter 37 goes through the various stages from identifying the need for a computer to its installation and implementation of the new system. Chapter 40 describes the various activities that are found in a DP department. Chapter 41 discusses some of the overall problems associated with the introduction of computer methods.

3. Notice that in order to highlight the basic principles the text is broken down into what appear to be well defined areas. In practice however there will be much overlapping.

4. Also included in this Part is a chapter on Computer Service Bureaux and chapters on Control and Audit of Data Processing Activities (Chapters 40–42).

37 Project Management

INTRODUCTION.

1. Good planning is a pre-requisite of any business activity and computer data processing is no exception. This chapter deals with the planning and management of data processing projects by tracing the steps involved in the System Life Cycle (Ch 29).

2. The reader should recognise the fact that in this chapter we are primarily concerned with the management aspects of the system life cycle whereas in chapter 29 to 33 the Systems Analysis aspects were considered.

3. In this chapter the assumption will be made that the company is *not* currently using a computer for the application concerned and that the size of the application is such as to make computerisation have a major impact on the organisation. It should be noted, however, that even for small applications, such as those requiring the use of a single microcomputer, the management task must still be done. Indeed, there is a particular danger when managing the development of many small systems that the development will end up happening in a piecemeal and fragmented way which can subsequently create serious management problems.

PRELIMINARY SURVEY/STUDY.

4. There will come a time when the question of using a computer will arise. As a result, the board will decide to make an initial investigation into the possibility of using one. This will probably be carried out by one or two senior executives and/or consultants.

5. Application areas. More often than not a prima facie case can be made for a computer in a particular application area and it is this which will have prompted the board into carrying out the preliminary survey. There are likely to be other application areas to consider in which case a long term plan (including a list of priorities) will need to be drawn up.

6. Outcome. The preliminary study will determine whether or not to continue investigating the need for a computer. If so, SPECIFIC COMPUTER OBJECTIVES will be drawn up. It is important that the user should both agree and signed the objectives to be met by the system.

STEERING COMMITTEE.

7. When a project is established it is quite common also to establish a *steering committee* for the project. The purpose of this committee is to "keep the project on course" so that it meets its objectives. The membership of the committee comprises management members and senior project staff such as analysts, so that the committee can carry out monitoring, controlling and consultative functions.

FEASIBILITY STUDY.

8. Assuming the project is given the go ahead, a study team will be formed to carry out a study of the application area/s. This study team will be under the direction of the steering committee.

9. Purpose. The purpose of a feasibility study is to provide information in order to justify the use of a computer on three grounds:-

a. Technical.

b. Economic.

c. Social.

10. Study steps. Steps in the study will depend on individual circumstances but generally will include the following:-

a. The study team must be aware of the precise objective of the study.

b. Establish the requirements of the particular system being studied.

c. Make a detailed examination of the system to determine how these requirements are met. This will include details of volumes, information flows, time-scales etc.

d. Note any improvements which can be made in the system as it stands as these may well be implemented at once.

e. Formulate the new design on the basis of the application of computer methods, considering various alternatives:-

i. Processing method (Batch, On-line, Real-time).

ii. Choice of system (Microcomputer, minicomputer, mainframe).

iii. Centralised processing or distributed processing.

iv. Methods of data entry, storage and output.

It must be stressed that the appropriate use of manual methods must not be overlooked.

f. Assess costs of possible new systems (staff, buildings, hardware, software etc.) over the life of the project.

g. Make comparisons with the present system.

h. Consideration of social factors ie. effect on staff relations etc.

i. Make recommendations to the Board in the form of a Feasibility Study Report.

11. Depth. A feasibility study will be carried out in enough depth to enable the Board to make a decision on whether or not to proceed with detailed investigation and analysis. The contents of the report naturally will vary according to circumstances, but the main points on which information should be given are as follows:-

a. **Aims and objectives.** It is important that the aims and objectives be clearly stated. These should have been agreed with the line managers. The areas involved in the study should be defined.

b. **Cost/benefit comparison.** The alternative solutions will be outlined indicating the benefits to be gained from each and the costs involved. Comparisons with present methods will be attempted. Benefits which may accrue are:-

i. More timely information.
ii. Better customer relations.
iii. Improved cash flow.

Costs to be considered are development costs, capital outlay and operating costs.

c. **Outline of proposed system.** This will include details of:

i. Outputs.
ii. Files.
iii. Inputs.
iv. Computer runs.
v. Programs and software.

The amount of detail assembled under each heading would be sufficient to enable a decision to be made between alternative solutions (if more than one is included in the report) and for the effects on existing procedures to be gauged.

d. **Effects on organisation.** The effects of the introduction of new methods and procedures on the organisation, in terms of changes in posts, redundancy, and staff re-training, will be included.

e. **Schedule of requirements.** Details of capital equipment, including costs, must be listed.

f. **Implementation.** The plan for the implementation of the proposed system will include a time-table. Methods of change-over will be stated.

g. **Recommendations.** These will recommend a particular solution which could conceivably be the adoption of conventional methods rather than computer methods to solve the company's problems.

CONSIDERATION OF REPORT.

12. The board will consider the report and will want answers to the following questions:-

a. Do the recommendations meet the objectives?

b. Do they still fit overall company objectives? (Note on 12a and 12b – some studies take so long that the original circumstances could have changed. The study itself could have led to a change in objectives).

c. What is the effect on company profits going to be?

d. What is the effect going to be on company organisation and staff?

e. What are the costs involved and can the capital be obtained?

f. What is the time-scale for implementation?

g. Does it look sufficiently into the future, ie. does the proposal allow for possible future expansion and modification?

13. Decision. The board may well ask for further information in certain areas. After the feasibility study report has been studied in detail a decision has to be taken whether or not to proceed.

DETAILED INVESTIGATION AND ANALYSIS.

14. Assuming that a decision is taken to proceed further, this stage continues the process started with the initial survey and feasibility study. At the end of the investigation and analysis a requirements specification is produced. Details of how it is produced were given in chapter 31.

15. The production of a requirement specification provides the basis for a go/no go decision between the feasibility study report and the full system specification.

CONSIDERATION OF THE REQUIREMENTS SPECIFICATION.

16. The board will expect this report to answer the questions brought forward from their earlier considerations of the feasibility study report. In addition, the all important question "Does this specification give a full and accurate statement of the data processing requirement?" must be satisfactorily answered.

17. Decision. Although the requirements specification is "implementation free" it contains sufficient detail for the main design alternative to be identified. The board can approve the specification and decide whether or not to proceed with one or more designs. A balance has to be struck between the danger of eliminating a design alternative too soon and the cost of producing multiple alternative designs. It is also important when approving the specification to be sure that there is a clear technical (and in the case of outside contract legal) basis for determining whether or not the specification has been satisfied when the system has been implemented.

FACILITY SELECTION.

18. The selection of one of the main design alternatives is effectively a selection of the kind of facilities to be used. For example, manufacturers and suppliers *of particular products* may be selected and asked to submit proposals which indicate how they can meet the requirements. Alternatively, the services of a bureau may be used.

DESIGN.

19. The design stage was described in chapter 32. The out-come of this stage is the ultimate in documentation of the new system, the SYSTEMS SPECIFICATION. This will contain full details of all clerical and computer procedures involved.

20. In the case of complete one-off systems the design stage will involve all the activities described in chapter 31. However, in the case of many smaller systems, the design process may be largely a matter of matching what is available to what is required in order to find an acceptable match.

21. Each system specification is considered, along with any associated proposals from manufacturers or suppliers. After what may be a very long process one of the alternatives is selected and pursued.

22. It may well have been decided to use a bureau in which case the following stages would not necessarily apply.

RESOURCE PLANNING.

23. Whether we are acquiring a VRC, or small, medium or larger size computer system a great deal of detailed planning and preparation now needs to be done in order that the installation of the machine and changeover to the computer-based system are achieved smoothly and efficiently.

24. Changing over to a system based on a VRC or micro-computer does not however have the same far-reaching effect on the organisation as that of a medium sized machine. A medium sized machine is assumed in the following paragraphs.

25. Network. The planning required up to the time of delivery of the machine and then on to the time the system is operational is involved enough to require a *Network.* The time-scale may well be linked to the date of delivery of the computer and this could be from 12–18 months. If there are many applications to be computerised a schedule of priorities will ensure that at least one is ready for the computer soon after it is installed. **Estimation** of the time taken to complete tasks, and hence their related costs, must be done most carefully if any reliance is to be placed upon the network. Estimation is never easy but is improved in the long run by keeping records of times taken to complete various categories of task.

26. Main resources. The main resources requiring management's attention will be:-

a. **Site.** This has to be chosen and prepared.

b. **Building.** A new building is to be erected or an existing one modified.

c. **Environment.** Requirements of the computer regarding humidity, dust control etc will need special attention.

d. **Standby equipment.** Arrangements will need to be made for such equipment, in the event of a failure of the company's computer. Very often these can be made with a bureau.

e. **Staff.** Selection and training. The decision has to be made on whether or not to recruit from within the company. Apart from the particular specialists who cannot be found in the company, it is generally found more satisfactory to recruit from within. At least such people will have a good knowledge of the company. Staff required will include:-

i. Management (DP Manager etc).
ii. Clerical.
iii. Analysts and programmers – a few trained people recruited outside to help train company personnel.
iv. Operators – own personnel probably already employed in company as machine operators of some kind.

The manufacturer will often give assistance with training staff and also provide the temporary assistance of his own specialists.

f. **Finance.** Necessary arrangements will need to be made to ensure the appropriate finance is made available. Detailed budgets will be drawn up for each area and strict control exercised over performance in accordance with budget.

INSTALLATION OF COMPUTER.

27. This will affect only a small number of people. The manufacturer's engineers will be responsible for installation of the machinery in conjunction with the DP Manager or his representative. The machine is tested from an engineering point of view and handed over. The whole operation is usually accomplished in a matter of days.

28. Maintenance. Maintenance of the hardware and software will be the subject of an agreement and will ensure the machine is always in working order and spare parts available when required.

IMPLEMENTATION.

29. This consists of:-

a. Training of staff.
b. Programming.
c. System testing.
d. Master file conversion.
e. Changeover procedures.
f. Review (System Evaluation) and Maintenance.

Many aspects of implementation have already been discussed in chapter 33. Some additional points, regarding planning, are made here.

30. Planning this, the final and critical stage, would have started very early in the planning of the project as a whole. Indeed, quite often this particular stage will have a *Network* of its own. This is the time when the computer system is going to take over from the old system and it is a very worrying time for everybody. There will be disappointments, setbacks and frayed tempers. It is a time of upheaval in the company and the value of good planning will be seen clearly during this period.

PROGRAM WRITING AND TESTING.

31. Programmers will get on with the job of writing the computer programs from the Systems Specification. Individual procedures are programmed and compiled and then tested for logical correctness using "dummy" data. After being tested individually the programs are tested as a complete system.

32. Bureau. A bureau may be used for compiling and testing programs while awaiting delivery of the computer.

33. Program testing. It is the programmers responsibility to ensure that each individual program meets its specification. Suitable test data must be used at each stage in programming. It is important that the programs are also subjected to independent testing.

34. The independent test data should be designed by people *other* than the program writers. The analysts in conjunction with the user department should do this job. This will ensure that every eventuality is designed into the test data pack and thus the programs are subjected to the most rigorous examination. All these eventualities must be considered before the specification is given to the programmer. It must be stressed, however, that the final testing is no substitute for good work practices and methods of **Quality Assurance (QA),** ie. setting and enforcing standards of design, documentation, reliability etc. All the evidence available shows that considerable benefits can be obtained from sound QA.

REVIEW (SYSTEM EVALUATION) AND MAINTENANCE.

35. Once the implementation process is complete and the system is operational there is a tendency to heave a sigh of relief but it is just as important to follow up implementation with an evaluation process to ensure the original objectives are being met. This system evaluation is sometimes called "post audit".

36. It must be a properly mounted operation and its findings will be of help in future projects.

37. The need to keep abreast of new techniques is also important in order that the full benefits can be reaped.

38. In order that the new system continues to run efficiently it must be constantly monitored and maintained. This maintenance is bound to be necessary sooner or later and should be planned for.

SUMMARY.

39. a. The need for planning is vital because of the far-reaching effects of the changes that computers bring about.

b. The stages in planning are:
   - i. Preliminary study.
   - ii. Feasibility study.
   - iii. Consideration of report.
   - iv. Detailed investigation and analysis.
   - v. Consideration of requirements specification.
   - vi. Facility selection.
   - vii. Resource Planning.
   - viii. Installation of the computer.
   - ix. Implementation.
   - x. Review (System Evaluation) and Maintenance.

c. All possible alternatives should be explored in a feasibility study ie. VRC/mechanical, including the possible use of a bureau. A decision to rent, buy or lease must be made.

POINTS TO NOTE.

40. a. The detail concerned with many of the points raised in this chapter has been covered in Systems Analysis (29-33).

b. The various steps do not follow neatly one after the other as in the text but overlap each other to a great extent.

c. A feasibility study may be more correctly termed a justification study.

d. Computer planning should not be geared to one application but should be designed to accommodate future applications when they arise.

e. Note the different stages which involve a SYSTEM STUDY:-

i. Initial study.
ii. Feasibility study.
iii. Detailed requirements study.
iv. Detailed systems study.

f. Each of these studies in e. above (or if you prefer, phases, in what will be a complete study in the end) will be conducted to the *depth* required to make a particular decision.

i. **The initial study** will only be made to the depth required for a decision to be taken on whether or not a prima facie case for a computer can be established.

ii. **The feasibility study** will be in greater depth because it must provide the information which determines whether or not the use of a computer is justified to solve the company's problems.

iii. **The detailed requirements study** will identify the precise data processing requirement in an implementation free way.

iv. **Detailed systems study.** Further detail will be required to identify the precise hardware requirements and then to produce a Systems Specification for approval.

g. You may need to make an assumption in an examination answer about the type of system the computer system is replacing ie. manual, mechanical etc.

h. The term systems study can be applied to any of the four studies referred to in 40e. so be careful in answering an examination question on systems studies to indicate the one you are talking about.

QUESTIONS.

1. *When acquiring an in-house computer system which criteria are considered when deciding between the various manufacturers who have submitted tenders?*

2. *How do the contents of a feasibility study report differ from the Systems Specification?*

3. *What points would you include in the review of a newly implemented computer system?*

4. *The use of a computer is being considered by your company.*

   a. *Commencing with the preliminary survey, list all the steps you would recommend to be taken and briefly describe each of these steps.*

   You are to assume the ultimate purchase of a computer.

   b. *The decision to go ahead is then taken. Summarise the remaining steps concluding with the systems evaluation. (ICMA)*

38 Organisation of Data Processing Activities

INTRODUCTION.

1. In most companies a separate department will be set up to control computer-based data processing activities. The purpose of this chapter is to look at a typical DP department and the people that staff it.

2. In larger companies it is often found as part of a Managment Services Division. Titles given to people who perform the functions of a DP department vary between installations; however, the more commonly used titles are used here. An organisation chart was shown in Fig. 30.2 and should be consulted during the reading of the chapter.

3. There are alternative ways in which DP activities may be organised. For example, staff may be grouped into **project teams,** comprised of different types of specialist, instead of being grouped according to job function.

DP MANAGER.

4. The DP Manager is a key figure in the organisation. His or her job is to ensure that the DP department functions efficiently in the *service* of the company. He or she is responsible for ensuring that the DP needs of the organisation are met within the policy guide lines laid down.

5. He or she must be a good administrator as well as having a sound business knowledge. He or she must also have the knowledge and expertise necessary to enable him or her to control the teams of specialists in the various DP fields.

6. Status. It is important that his or her status be clearly defined especially with regard to right of access to the board.

7. Ideally one would like someone who has previous experience of installing successful systems and his appointment should be made very early on in the planning cycle to enable the company to get the benefit of his or her specialist knowledge and experience. If not recruited from outside the potential DP manager could be found in the Management Services Division.

SYSTEMS ANALYSTS. (See chapters 29-33).

8. The job of the systems analyst has already been described but can be briefly stated as follows:-

a. To examine the feasibility of potential computer applications.

b. Analysis of existing systems with a view to their application to a computer.

c. Design of computer-based systems, their implementation, and review.

9. It is very likely that systems anlaysts would work in project teams with a senior analyst in charge.

10. The chief systems analyst will work very closely with his counterparts in other sections and the DP manager, and will assist in forward planning and overall project control.

PROGRAMMERS. (See chapter 21).

11. Following the design process the job of programming begins. The programmer:-

a. Encodes the procedures detailed by the analyst in a language suitable for the specified computer.

b. Will liaise very closely with the analyst and the user to ensure logical correctness of programs.

12. Specialisation. In a large DP department programmers might specialise in certain areas of programming. These may be:-

a. **Applications.** Applications programmers are the people who write the initial programs for each application.

b. **Maintenance.** Once the programs written by the Applications programmer are operational they are handed over to a Maintenance programmer, whose job it will be to carry out any amendments or improvements that may be necessary. The applications programmer then moves on to fresh fields.

c. **Systems software.** This programmer will specialise in writing "non-application" programs ie. systems software. These programs will supplement those supplied by the manufacturer.

13. In smaller installations, of course, a smaller team of programmers will have to turn their hands to any task that comes along.

OPERATIONS MANAGER.

14. He is responsible to the DP Manager for operation of the computer and ancillary equipment. Also under his control will be:-

a. Data control section.

b. Data preparation.

c. The computer room.
d. Tape and disk library/ies.
e. User technical support.
f. User operations support.

15. His will be the task of scheduling all the various tasks for the computer and ancillary machines. The various sections under this control are dealt with separately.

DATA CONTROL STAFF.

16. These staff are responsible for the co-ordination of all machine processing operations and for ensuring a smooth flow of work through the operations department. In order to explain their work we will trace a particular job through from beginning to end.

17. a. **Source documents** accompanied by control totals are received from the clerical function (outside DP department) and vetted visually.

b. **Control totals** are agreed and documents passed under this control to the Data Preparation Section.

c. **Data preparation** section prepares floppy disks or other media from source documents.

d. Source documents are returned to the clerical function and the floppy disks now represent the input for a particular run (job) eg. "invoice run".

e. **Job assembly** section 'makes up' the run and prepare a Run Authorisation document. This will detail the various tapes/disks required and how the output is to be disposed of. This is then passed to the computer room supervisor.

f. **Tape/disk library.** The librarian will provide all the tape reels and disk packs required for the particular job and will pass them to the computer room itself for the computer to process.

g. On completion of the computer run/s the tapes/disks etc. go back to the library and all the documentation to the Data Control section.

18. Control section now scutinises the control log to ensure all action has been taken correctly and to initiate any possible corrective action indicated. Control totals will be reconciled. These will now include totals of items rejected on the run/s but all totals will need to be reconciled back to those compiled at the beginning of the job.

19. The output is dealt with; invoices for example will be despatched to customers and warehouses etc.

20. All necessary information will be fed back to the user department eg. copies of all output despatched, error lists, control totals.

DATA PREPARATION STAFF.

21. These staff are responsible for:-

a. Preparing floppy disks from source documents or preparation by other means eg. key-to-disk etc.

b. Operation of ancillary machines such as floppy disk units, paper bursters etc.

OPERATOR.

22. The operator handles the hardware in the computer room. The operator also handles the input and output media (eg. placing magnetic tapes onto drives), communicates with the operating system via a console. The operator tries to keep the installation running smoothly by stepping in when things go wrong to correct them immediately.

23. The operators work under the direction of the computer room supervisor.

COMPUTER ROOM SUPERVISOR.

24. The computer room is under the day-to-day control of a supervisor. Only authorised personnel are allowed entry. It is essential that anyone who has participated in the writing of the programs is forbidden for security and audit reasons to interfere with the operational running of those programs.

Fig. 39.1. shows the lay-out of a typical computer room.

TAPE/DISK LIBRARIAN.

25. All tape reels and disk packs used in the installation are stored in a library adjacent to the computer room. The librarian issues tapes/disks to the computer room as per a Run Authorisation document from Data Control.

26. The librarian will maintain a register of all tapes and disks noting the particular generations required for current use. Maximum security is observed and access is strictly limited.

This diagram shows the lay-out of a typical Computer Room. There is a separate room for the assembly of incoming work which contains a number of storage cabinets for stationery etc. and a guillotine/decollator for handling output stationery.

Inside the computer room, the various input/output devices face the console to minimise movement by the operators and to allow the senior operator to see what is going on. The CPU, which the operators never touch, is out of the way at one end. In this example, the library of magnetic tapes and disks is kept in the computer room with a desk for the librarian.

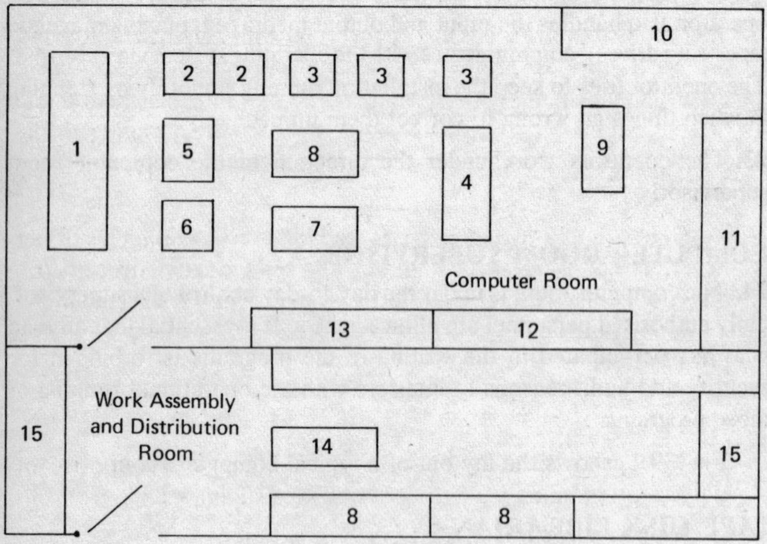

KEY.

1. CPU.
2. Magnetic Tape Drives.
3. Magnetic Disk Drives.
4. Line Printer.
5. Diskette Drives.
6. PABX.
7. Console.
8. Work Tables.
9. Librarian's Desk.
10. Magnetic Disk Cabinet.
11. Magnetic Tape Racks.
12. Diskette Cabinets.
13. Operators and Engineers Manuals.
14. Guillotine/Decollator.
15. Stationery Cupboards.

FIG. 38.1. LAYOUT OF A COMPUTER ROOM.

USER TECHNICAL SUPPORT.

27. With the Data Processing equipment no longer being always concentrated within the DP department and operated by specialists but often being distributed throughout the organisation and being operated by all kinds of staff it is necessary for the DP department to provide the necessary support. Technical support is basically concerned with ensuring that the hardware continues to operate correctly. This includes not only routine tasks of maintenance and cleaning but help in the provision of consumables, such as floppy disks, reconfiguring and upgrading machines, and fault detection and correction. Smaller organisations often rely on their computer supplier for these services.

USER OPERATIONS SUPPORT.

28. Operations support is basically concerned with helping the users of devices such as Workstations, Personal Computers and Word Processors. The help takes the form of assistance in the installation and use of applications packages and interactive software, training in the correct use of devices, media and software, and dealing with problems or queries as they arise.

29. This kind of support is most vital when the user is gaining his or her first experience of using such equipment and serious problems can arise if it is overlooked, for example, if staff are not properly instructed in the care of floppy disks and ways of doing disk backups vital data may be irretrievably lost.

SUMMARY.

30. a. A DP department is headed by a DP Manager and consists of analysts, programmers, operations staff and support staff.

b. Security measures are extremely important:-

i. With regard to magnetic files.

ii. In forbidding unauthorised entry to the computer room and tape library.

POINTS TO NOTE.

31. a. The DP department is responsible for the processing of data but ultimate responsibility for the system itself rests with the user department.

b. Many computer installations work on a shift basis in which case a *shift leader* will act for the operations manager outside "normal" working hours.

QUESTIONS.

1. Much publicity has been given to the impact of computers in business, yet "it is still true that management's real functions remain unchanged".

Discuss this quotation. (ICMA)

2. Draft the organisation chart of a large computer department and outline the main duties of the sections reporting to the operations manager.

To whom do you think the data processing manager should be responsible? Give your reasons. (ACA)

39 Management Considerations

INTRODUCTION.

1. Having some knowledge of the activities of a DP department you are now in a position to understand the management considerations which are the subject of this chapter.

TOP MANAGEMENT INVOLVEMENT.

2. One of the major reasons for the lack of success of so many computer installations can be attributed to the failure of top management to become involved *right from the outset*. The company as a whole must be made aware of the Board's determination to see computerisation succeed, so that full co-operation will be forthcoming all along the line.

3. The need for top management involvement is seen when one considers the issued involved:-

a. High capital investment.

b. Major organisation upheaval.

c. Effects on personnel both managerial and operative.

EDP policy must be formulated as carefully as any other sectional policy and its effect on the long term objectives assessed. Top management knows what information it wants; thus it is up to them to see that the computer provides it.

COMPUTER OBJECTIVES.

4. They must be clearly stated in order that the evaluation process which follows implementation can be meaningful. In particular application areas these can be stated precisely, eg. in stock control "a 15% reduction in stock holdings" and in invoicing "to despatch invoice within 36 hours of despatch of goods".

EDUCATION.

5. a. **Management.** In order for a management to appreciate what the computer can do for the company and what is involved in its introduction, it must have the necessary knowledge. Selected members can be sent on courses and use could be made of the experience of other companies in the EDP field. Company seminars are a good way of communicating the kind of information which management need to be equipped with in order to provide the basis for decision-making.

b. **Staff.** It is very important that staff are fully prepared for what is to come. The computer brings with it new thinking, new disciplines and new methods of working. Training must begin early and everyone made aware of what is required under the new system. Action must be taken to dispel any fears that may precede the coming of the computer. There is a great *human* problem associated with the introduction of computers and it must receive due consideration.

c. **Users. These must be involved from the outset.** The computer is the servant of the user but he must be educated to make the most efficient use of this new management tool. He must be involved with the new system from the analysis stage to ensure that his requirements are designed into the new system. This sense of involvement in the design is important also because he will be responsible for operating the new system eventually.

APPLICATION SELECTION.

6. Applications which give immediate and real benefits should be chosen first. These will be found in the field of management information and control and include:-

a. **Stock control.**

b. **Production planning and control.**

c. **Business forecasting.**

d. **Cash flow analysis.**

What is important is that introduction of EDP methods in these areas can have a major effect on the firm's profitability. Reductions in stock holdings can release badly needed cash. Better production planning can result in more economic batch sizes etc. etc. Administrative applications such as payroll and order processing are important but in themselves don't result in the same dramatic benefits. Priority of application will often be dictated by a firm's particular problems.

The accusation has been made that in the past computers have been nothing more than glorified accounting machines (and very expensive ones at that). The real value of a computer is in its ability to sift large volumes of data quickly and accurately and provide timely and meaningful information on which decisions can be made.

COMPOSITION OF STUDY TEAMS.

7. Teams should be headed by an experienced systems analyst, preferably one who has previous practical experience of a successful project. He should have a number of analysts to do the detailed work.

Also in the team should be a representative of the area being studied. This is important because his detailed knowledge will be required and also the user department must be identified with the project from the outset because it will be responsible for its efficient running eventually. The auditor too will need to be consulted early in the design stage in order to incorporate his particular requirements in the new system. It is essential that the team has sufficient status in order to carry out its task effectively and it must have the backing of top management.

COST OF FEASIBILITY STUDY.

8. This will be one of the factors considered in the Preliminary Survey. Cost will depend on the size of team and length of study but nevertheless it could be quite considerable. The time taken to carry out the study is nearly always underestimated. A time table must be planned but should be flexible. Once the cost of the study has been authorised the study goes ahead. The detailed examination carried out during a feasibility study invariably brings about improvements to the existing system as it stands. It is sometimes found that the cost of the study can be recovered as it were from the savings presented by the elimination of the faults which have been brought to light. Studies vary in length from weeks to many months depending on the objectives set and their complexity.

USE OF CONSULTANTS.

9. Opinions are divided on this question. A survey showed that more firms used outside consultants during the *first* involvement with computers than subsequently. Consultants have much EDP knowledge and experience and if used properly they can be of immense help. However it is vital that the company has someone who himself has enough EDP background to be able to communicate in the consultant's language. The consultant must be given clear terms of reference and management must be prepared to make the necessary decisions the consultant requires during the various stages of his work. It should be remembered however that consultants can only advise, the company must make the decisions based on his advice.

HAVING A COMPUTER ALREADY.

10. Previous chapters were concerned with the situation where a company had no computer and the feasibility study was used as the basis for acquisition. Once a computer is installed and working requests for computerisation of new applications or extension of existing ones will be received in the DP department. Each should be subjected to a preliminary survey and a feasibility study, in order to decide whether or not to put the application on the company's computer. There will come a time when the present hardware will need to be replaced or additional modules purchased. Again the requisite studies will determine the requirement.

SUMMARY.

11. a. Top management involvement and complete identification with computerisation is vital to its success.

b. A complete EDP policy must be evolved and applied.

c. The computer can only be exploited to the full by people who have the requisite knowledge and experience. Thus education and training play a large part in successful computer development.

d. The human problem must not be overlooked.

e. Applications giving the greatest returns should be selected first.

f. Involve line management in study teams.

g. Do not hesitate to use consultants if the requirement arises.

POINTS TO NOTE.

12. a. Do not hesitate to make use of your costing and accountancy knowledge in DP.

QUESTIONS.

1. As a management accountant you are asked to identify the areas of cost of a proposed new computer system. List the major items in those areas.

2. Your company is about to embark on a feasibility study. What do you understand by a feasibility study?

State the main points on which information should be given in a feasibility report. (ICMA)

3. When should a systems survey or study take place? Summarise:

a. the main steps and

b. the work involved: in a systems study.

Assuming that you are a project leader conducting a systems study covering all commercial activities in a company, who would you include in your study team and why? State the industry for which your selection would be suitable. (ICMA)

4. Your company has decided to install a computer. In your capacity as Finance Director draw up a time-table for a seminar to be given to other Board Members.

Explain the steps involved and the individuals who should participate. (ICMA)

5. *It has been said computer based systems are ideally suited to the application of management by exception techniques.*

   a. *State briefly when you think this statement is true and give an example of a specific application of management by exception using a computer.*

   b. *List the factors you would observe to ensure that a management by exception computer system is a viable one. (ICMA)*

6. *'The list of unsuccessful computer installations is a long one and there is no doubt that many organisations are disappointed with the way their computer projects have developed.'*

   What, in your opinion, are the principal reasons for the failure of computer projects? (ACA)

40 Computer Service Bureaux

INTRODUCTION.

1. Bureaux provide a variety of services based upon the operation of computers. They exist to carry out computer data processing services for their customers. Before the introduction of microcomputers, when the only computers available were quite large and expensive, many bureaux concentrated on providing services to organisations which did not have enough DP work to justify the purchase of a computer of their own. Times have changed and now many bureaux have switched their operations towards the microcomputer market.

SERVICES OFFERED.

2. In this list of services it must be remembered that not *all* bureaux offer *all* services, indeed many bureaux will specialise in the provision of particular services.

a. **Data preparation.** Data transcribed onto a variety of media including diskette and magnetic tape. Even preparation of documents in optical characters is carried out by some bureaux. Services can be on an ad hoc basis or of a continuing nature.

b. **Hiring time.** Clients use the bureau's hardware to process their own data using their own programs. Data and programs are sent along and results sent back (or collected). This service is offered on an ad hoc or continuing basis.

c. **Do it yourself.** Customers go along with own data and program and actually use the hardware themselves. Customers must of course provide suitably qualified operators in order to make use of this service, although some bureaux will provide supervisory staff (to be paid for). This is a useful service for program development and testing while a company is awaiting delivery of its computer.

d. **Complete service.** The bureau does everything, initial study, systems design, program writing, testing, and implementation (on its hardware facilities).

e. **Consultancy.** Provision of advice and assistance with any *part* of a customer's DP problems, as opposed to doing everything as in d. Some bureaux hire their specialist staff eg. analysts, programmers, to customers.

f. **Software.** Some bureaux specialise in providing software to suit a particular customer, others provide application packages. Note that these items of software can be used on customer's or bureau's computer.

g. **Time-sharing.** The customer is linked to the bureau's computer by Post Office telephone line and therefore has access to the machine from his own premises. This service is limited to a small number of specialist bureaux.

h. The provision and support of specialist applications software and packages on microcomputers.

REASONS FOR USING BUREAUX.

3. a. **To gain EDP experience.** Staff can familiarise themselves with the type of machinery that the company is about to purchase.

b. **To evaluate hardware/software.** If a bureau has the particular type of machine that a company is considering acquiring then it is possible to evaluate it.

c. **Cost.** Some companies cannot afford a computer of their own. Others with seasonal requirements would find a computer uneconomical to run. Using a bureau, costs are in proportion to use and costly overheads are avoided.

d. **Non-involvement.** There are those who decide to leave the job of EDP to those who have the specialist skills, ie. the bureaux.

e. **Peak loads.** Arrangements will be made by the client for processing of peak loads with which his machine cannot cope.

f. **Program development and testing.** Client will need the use of a machine while awaiting delivery of own computer.

g. **File conversion.** A one-time operation that may be of such magnitude that it can only be done by a bureau. This includes the transcribing of data from the manual files into machine sensible media.

h. **Advice etc.** A client may want advice on how to set up an EDP department, feasibility studies, training staff, etc. A bureau can provide this advice.

i. **Stand-by computer.** The bureau would be under contract to provide processing time in the event of the failure of the client's own machine.

CHARGES.

4. These will vary with type of service, volume of work involved. There will be a contract which should detail the costs clearly. For contract work there could well be a fixed charge plus an amount which will vary with the volume of work carried out each week. It is very important for the user of a bureau to be quite certain about the costs involved *before* selecting a bureau.

CSA.

5. The Computing Services Association lays down a code of conduct and standards of operating for its members. Examples of the areas covered by the Association's rules are security of information, relations with clients and continuity of service.

TYPES OF BUREAUX.

6. Many types of bureaux are to be found including:

a. Independent companies set up for the purpose of providing computer and allied services. Many specialise in particular types of business application.

b. Computer manufacturers run their own bureaux.

c. Then there are companies with spare capacity who offer it to other users; one company actually hires its computer to another company during the night.

d. Polytechnics and Universities are also able to offer some services provided by bureaux. The most common services are consultation and training.

SUMMARY.

7. a. The range of service offered by bureaux is very wide.

b. The situations which bring about the use of a bureau are varied.

POINTS TO NOTE.

8. a. Even if a company uses a bureau to do its processing this does not preclude the need for detailed feasibility study and good design of new systems.

b. Company still needs a DP department (however small) even if a bureau is giving a complete service. There must be a 'link' department between the bureau and the rest of company. Also internal check and audit requirements must be even more stringent.

c. **Computer Time Brokers.** Not strictly a service bureau as such. They provide clients with details of where they can obtain time on a particular computer. Handy in an emergency. They make no charge to the client.

d. Bureaux specialising in the production of software are referred to as **"Software Houses"**.

QUESTIONS.

1. *You have been asked by your managing director to consider the use of a computer service bureau, instead of installing an "in-house" computer.*

   List the advantages and disadvantages of using a service bureau.

(ICMA)

2. *a. Describe the services which may be offered by a large computer bureau.*

   b. Assume that your company's hourly pay-roll is prepared by a bureau. List, with brief explanation:

   i. **Three** *examples of transaction or amendment data which would need to be despatched to the bureau weekly;*

   ii. **Three** *examples of information which would be received back from the bureau.*

   (ACA)

41 Control of Data Processing Activities

INTRODUCTION.

1. Chapter 17 dealt with the controls that should be used to ensure that a particular *system* functions correctly. This chapter deals with control of the organisation and work of the Data Processing Department. This control is established and maintained by setting "standards". Standards ensure that:-

a. work is carried out in a uniform and orderly way.

b. criteria are provided against which the performance of personnel and machines can be measured.

GENERAL.

2. Organisation. There should be complete division of responsibility between the sections described in Chapter 38 with the possible exception of systems analysts and programmers. There should be no overlap of duties between the development and operations staff, and the operations sections should be self-contained! Organisation has become a more complex task in recent years with the increased use of computers by non-specialists throughout the various departments involved with DP equipment.

3. Training. All staff should be fully trained, and the effectiveness of training should be assessed by monitoring performance on the job. It is important to keep training programmes under constant review and to provide additional training so that staff are kept up to date with the latest developments in DP.

4. Scheduling. Schedules of work should be prepared so that:-

a. The various activities of the operations section are co-ordinated.

b. A check can be kept on the progress of systems development.

c. The introduction of a new system is properly co-ordinated between the development and operations functions.

d. Delay can be quickly detected and corrective action taken.

5. Supervision. High standards of supervision should be maintained in all sections.

SYSTEMS ANALYSIS.

6. a. **Consultation.** Management must ensure that users are fully consulted about systems being designed for them, and that their views and criticisms are given due weight.

b. **Evaluation.** All proposals should be fully evaluated, on a quantitative (ie. cost) basis whenever possible.

c. **Documentation.** All systems development work must be fully documented but the following are particularly important:

i. documentation of the existing procedure on completion of the fact finding stage.

ii. documentation of the agreements between user management and the DP department as to the form the new system will take.

iii. the Requirements Specification.

iv. the Systems Specification.

d. **Performance.** It is difficult to measure the work-rate of systems analysts, but some control can be kept by requiring regular (eg. monthly) reports on work done and by regular meetings at which progress is reviewed. In practice, managers often assess performance on the basis of the success (or otherwise) of systems previously developed.

PROGRAMMING.

7. a. **Documentation.** Program documentation must always be complete and up-to-date. Considerable difficulties may otherwise occur when an operational program fails or has to be amended.

b. **Testing.** All programs must be thoroughly tested before being released for operational use. The role of the auditor is especially important.

c. **Performance.** Measurement of the work-rate of programmers is not easy, since the output in terms of number of instructions or statements written may vary with the difficulty of the task. Standards can however be established for:-

i. the style and content of the documentation produced,

ii. the program design method used,

iii. the methods of testing and test plans,

iv. the time required to complete the various stages of program development,

v. the number of instructions statements written,

vi. the number of program errors made,

vii. the amount of program testing time used.

development,

ii. the number of instructions statements written,

iii. the number of program errors made,

iv. the amount of program testing time used.

DATA CONTROL.

8. a. **Documentation.** All work done by the section should be supported by written instructions and job manuals.

b. **Progress.** The section should maintain records to control the punctual receipt of incoming work, its progress through data preparation and computer processing and the eventual distribution of outputs. These records may be in the form of wall-charts so that they are available for inspection by the DP management.

c. **Errors and queries.** Records should be kept of errors and queries raised in the course of processing so that:-

i. correction and re-processing can be controlled.

ii. abnormal error rates can be taken up with the department responsible.

DATA PREPARATION.

9. a. **Documentation.** Manuals or charts should be maintained containing specimen source doucments, indicating what data has to be transcribed.

b. **Performance.** Records should be kept of the output and error rates of each operator and of the section as a whole. Note that with Key-to-Disk systems this can be done by program automatically. Standards can be established for the larger tasks.

c. **Procedures.** Clear-cut procedures should be established and enforced for encoding, verification and error correction (if a separate stage).

d. **Supervision.** Close supervision and high standards of discipline are needed to maintain satisfactory output.

e. **Working conditions.** Good working conditions are essential to maintain output and to promote morale. Particular attention should be paid to:-

i. adequate space

ii. heating and lighting

iii. noise levels.

COMPUTER ROOM.

10. a. **Documentation.** Full Operating Manuals must be provided for every program. Restart procedures should be covered in detail.

b. **Logs.** Records should be kept of computer usage. These are used for:-

i. charging user departments.

ii. controlling machine, operator and software performance.

c. **Operation.**

i. two operators should always be present,

ii. ideally duties should be rotated so that no operator is always responsible for the same run but in practice however this is not always feasible.

d. **Access.** Access to the computer room should be restricted to operating staff. The room should be locked when not manned.

e. **Fire precautions.**

i. there should be an automatic fire-detection system,

ii. adequate fire-fighting appliances should be provided.

f. **Stand-by** arrangements should be made for the use of a "stand-by" machine so that essential work can be done if there is a prolonged breakdown or other mishap. These arrangements should be tested.

Note: This is often a reciprocal arrangement with another user of a similar machine.

TAPE/DISK LIBRARY.

11. The controls dealt with here come under the general heading of FILE SECURITY. It is important to realise that:

a. vital and irreplaceable files may be stored on magnetic tape or disk.

b. reels of tape and disk-packs are physically identical and the risk of confusion is very real.

c. the standard practice of re-using tapes and disk by "over-writing" with new data can, if not properly controlled, result in the loss of files through operator error.

d. magnetic storage media are very easily damaged by an unsuitable environment.

12. a. Every reel of tape of disk-pack must be clearly labelled with a unique reference number.

b. A visual record (eg. a card file or register) must be kept showing the current contents of each tape or disk.

c. Tapes and disks must be stored in an orderly fashion on suitable racks.

SECURITY OF TAPE/DISK FILES.

13. What we are mainly concerned with here is the security of master files. These are very valuable commodities holding as they do such information as is *vital* to the everyday conduct of the company's business. The contents can be damaged or destroyed by erroneous over-writing by machine or program error, or by sheer bad physical handling of the reel or pack.

14. Tape files. The method of file security is linked to the processing method. Remember a physically different c/f file is created on each updating run. The c/f file *and* the transaction records which were used to update it are retained for a period so that if an accident befalls the c/f master we can *recreate* it by processing the transactions that we have retained against the original (b/f) master. See Fig. 12.2. Security is then a simple matter of keeping tapes for a specific number of processing cycles.

15. Disk files.

a. If the same processing method is adopted as for tape then the file security arrangements will be the same.

b. File security of disk files where the overlay or 'in situ' method of updating is adopted is more difficult. There are two methods, sometimes used separately but often used together for maximum security:-

i. One consists of dumping (copying) the disk file onto a tape *before* processing and then at *intervals* to provide back-up should anything happen to the disk pack. Notice the appropriate transaction files are kept also so that processing can be repeated as with tape. (See Fig. 13.2).

ii. During updating, those master records which are updated are dumped onto a tape before and after the particular record has been updated. Thus a 'before and after' copy is held should anything go wrong.

16. Fire. The best safeguard against fire is to store the tape reel or disk pack in a remote section or in a fire proof safe within the computer centre itself.

SOFTWARE PROTECTION.

17. A considerable measure of protection is provided by the Executive/ Supervisor Program of the Operating System. Each file has a standard label block at the beginning which identifies it and contains an "expiry" date before which the file may not be over-written. At the beginning of each run, the label is checked to ensure that:-

i. if *reading* the correct file has been loaded,

ii. if *writing* the expiry date is not later than the current date (which is stored within the machine).

18. The manufacturer provides these checks as part of the standard software, and users must avail themselves of them. Some users build additional checks into their programs.

19. In a multi-programming environment, the Operating System protects files from mutilation by other programs. Each program is restricted to its own files.

WRITE RINGS.

20. A magnetic tape file is read or written during a run, but rarely both. It is possible to prevent accidental over-writing by the use of a "write ring". This is a plastic ring which fits into the back of a reel of tape. If it is *not* fitted, it is impossible for the tape-drive to perform a write, although the tape can be read. Protection can therefore be provided by leaving the ring off. The insertion and removal of these rings is part of standard operating procedures.

CONFIDENTIAL FILES.

21. There are two aspects to the protection of confidential information against unauthorised inspection.

a. If the installation is completely in-house, protection can be provided by conventional methods. Confidential files (eg. payroll) can be kept in locked storage and issued only under proper authority and supervision.

b. The problem becomes much more acute when a number of users have access to a single machine via terminals. Protection is provided by the Operating System. Each user identifies himself by a "password", without which he cannot gain access to the machine at all. He is then restricted to the inspection of authorised files, and this inspection may in turn be restricted to only some of the information in that file. Maximum security in the design of the Operating System is obviously of the utmost importance.

NB. Legal requirements in matters of confidentiality will be covered later in chapter 43 under the heading of Data Protection.

SUMMARY.

22. The following controls and standards are of particular importance:-

a. *Division of responsibility.*

b. *Training.*

c. *Scheduling.*

d. *Supervision and discipline.*

e. *Documentation* – particularly of systems and programs.

f. *Performance measurement* – particularly of data preparation.

g. *File security.*

POINTS TO NOTE.

23. You may be asked *why* documentation is so important. The main reasons are

a. Completion of systems and program documentation acts as an important *control* on the work of the staff responsible.

b. Documentation is important as a means of *communication* within the DP department, and between the DP department and users.

c. It provides a means both of recording *standards,* and of measuring *performance* against those standards.

d. It is a vital safeguard against loss of key staff, whose knowledge may otherwise leave with them.

e. *Records* are essential for the efficient performance of many activities.

24. Many DP departments do not have a good reputation for control, and perhaps for this reason questions on the subject occur frequently in examinations.

25. When using *computer bureaux,* investigations should be made to ensure that its standards and controls are satisfactory. Particular attention should be given to controlling the flow of work to and from the bureau, and to establishing satisfactory communications.

26. An important general aspect of control is **"Data Security"** ie. the control of data to prevent its loss, misuse or disclosure.

27. Closely related to data security is the issue of "Privacy". Privacy is largely a matter of ethics but may influence moral or legal requirements concerning the manner in which data security is implemented. (There is further discussion of this subject in Chapter 44.)

QUESTIONS.

1. Define briefly, and illustrate with an example, where appropriate, any six of the following electronic data processing terms:

Check digit
Limit check
Parity check
Password
Tape mark (reflective spot)
Conversational mode
Batch mode
Turn around document

(ICMA)

2. As the financial controller of your company, one of your responsibilities is the data processing department.

List the procedures and controls necessary to ensure that the department is run efficiently. (ICMA)

3. Benchmark tests are widely used for testing the performance of computers.

What is meant by a benchmark test? In what circumstances are they used and what are their advantages and disadvantages? (ICMA)

4. **Either**

a. i. What dangers are associated with storing information in magnetic form on tapes or on disks?

ii. Describe the safeguards that should be adopted to guard against these dangers and draw a diagram to illustrate one of these safeguards.

Or

b. i. Name three computer output devices, each using a different concept.

ii. Describe the features of each of the three devices named, and give an example of an application in which the use of each is relevant.

(ICMA)

5. A file containing highly confidential information is held on magnetic tape.

Discuss in detail the procedures which should be adopted to:

a. ensure the confidentiality of the data on file;

b. protect the data from loss or damage.

(ICMA)

6. Due to a combination of an inexperienced operator and an electrical fault the main master file of 150,000 policy holders' records was destroyed.

Describe what precautions should have been taken so that the above situation could be retrieved in the case of:

a. a tape based installation;

b. a disk based installation.

(ICMA)

42 Audit of Data Processing Activities

INTRODUCTION.

1. This chapter deals with the audit of computer-based systems and DP departments.

KNOWLEDGE OF ELECTRONIC DATA PROCESSING.

2. The first task of the auditor is to acquire a knowledge of electronic data processing. Without this, he cannot hope to tackle a computer audit successfully. In particular, he should be familiar with:-

a. Organisation and responsibilities of the DP department.

b. Data collection and validation techniques.

c. File organisation and processing techniques.

d. Systems controls.

e. Methods of control of systems development, programming and operational activities.

3. This is a formidable amount of knowledge to master. Some teams of auditors now include members who specialise in this area. This trend is likely to increase as the use of computers spreads and computer systems become more complex and all-embracing.

FILE ORGANISATION AND PROCESSING.

4. The techniques used to organise and process computer files make conventional methods of audit difficult and sometimes impossible to use. The following points are of particular importance to the auditor:-

a. *"Invisible" files.* Files stored on magnetic media cannot be directly inspected in the way that eg. a hand-written ledger can.

b. *"Historical" data.* A complete record of previous transactions is not usually maintained in files. For example, a customer file stored on magnetic tape will often hold details of the last months transactions only, earlier details having been deleted to keep down the length of records.

c. *Sorting.* Source documents are often left in random order; sorting is left until data have been input and the computer can do it. The tracing of source documents can thus be difficult if sufficient attention has not been paid to the audit trail.

DIVISION OF RESPONSIBILITY.

5. Computerisation means the *centralisation* of the processing of many of the applications previously carried out by *different* departments. The traditional safeguard of "division of responsibility" can therefore be eroded. One suite of computer programs may deal with work previously carried out in several different departments. One small team of computer operators may be responsible for the processing of large volumes of work. It is essential that the auditor is aware of the dangers inherent in such a concentration, and of the safeguards that are required.

NATURE OF ERRORS.

6. The type of error which occurs in computer processing undergoes a fundamental change. Computers are usually very reliable and have extensive self-checking facilities; hardware failures which go undetected are rare. Random errors of the type made by clerks (eg. in arithmetic and copying) are almost unknown. On the other hand, a fault in systems design or programming produces *repetitive* errors; in a given set of circumstances the same fault will occur.

7. It follows that much more attention must be paid by the auditor to systems development and testing. If the auditor satisfies himself that the programs are correct and that controls are adequate, less time need be devoted to checking routine operational processing.

INVOLVEMENT IN SYSTEMS DEVELOPMENT.

8. It is essential for the auditor to involve himself in the development of a system. By doing so, he can assure himself that:-

a. The system is properly controlled.

b. Audit requirements are met.

Early involvement (beginning at latest at the stage of system design) is important. Subsequent amendment of the system to meet audit criticisms is expensive and time-consuming.

9. A good working relationship must be established with systems and programming teams. Some explanation of the rights and duties of the auditor will often be needed at first. The auditor must have a sound knowledge of the appropriate control technqiues, and be prepared to specify his own requirements at an early stage.

"AUDITING ROUND THE COMPUTER".

10. One auditing technique concentrates on inputs and outputs to/from the computer and disregards the way in which such results are achieved.

It is adopted for one or two reasons:-

a. The system is such that adequate checks can be made without examination of computer processing.

b. The auditors knowledge of data processing is insufficient for him to carry out an effective audit.

In a fairly simple system, it may be possible to reconcile the outputs without reference to computer processing. For example, payment advices produced by a purchase ledger system may be reconciled with the original invoices by checking batch and file controls and sampling individual payments. This approach becomes however less effective as computer systems become more advanced. For example, in a sales ledger system it will work quite well if the actual value of orders is input. But if the prices are obtained from eg. a stock file it becomes impossible for the auditor to verify the accuracy of invoices and statements without investigation of the computer processing.

TEST PACKS.

11. Another auditing technique depends on the preparation of a set of test data by the auditor. Usually, a number of specimen source documents are prepared and the DP department is asked to process them. Tests are devised to ensure that:-

a. Correct items are properly dealt with.

b. Errors (deliberately inserted by the auditor) are detected and reported.

12. Test packs may be used:-

a. To test a system before it goes 'live'. The successful processing of an audit test may be a pre-requisite of 'going live'.

b. To check that a system is still functioning properly after amendments have been made.

c. In the course of normal operational running, to make sure that no unauthorised alternations have been made.

13. The development of an *effective* test pack is a considerable undertaking and requires detailed knowledge of the system. Once available it may be re-used with little extra effort.

AUDIT PACKAGES.

14. Standard software packages are now available for audit purposes. Properly used, they can save the auditor a great deal of routine work and increase the effectiveness of the audit considerably.

15. The packages are all essentially file-processing programs. The main facilities available are:-

a. Verification of file controls.

b. Verification of individual balances in records.

c. Verification that all necessary data are present in records.

d. Selection of records according to parameters specified by the auditors: eg.
   i. random samples of a given percentage of the file
   ii. data outside specified limits, eg.
      – overdue accounts,
      – non-active records,
      – payments above a certain value.

e. Analysis of file contents: eg.
   i. debts by age or type of customer,
   ii. payments by size or type.
   iii. stock holdings by value.

f. Comparison of two files (reporting any differences) to verify the accuracy of file maintenance.

16. The main considerations in selecting a package are:-

a. Cost.

b. Facilities provided.

c. Ease of use.

d. Efficiency (in terms of machine time needed).

The auditor requires a reasonable amount of computer time to run packages and other tests that he considers necessary.

CONSTRUCTING AN AUDIT TRAIL.

17. The conventional audit trail relies on visible records but because computer processing is carried out electronically and the files themselves are in machine sensible form the trail disappears. It can be constructed to some extent by arranging for print-outs of data and files at intermediate points in processing (ie. between the input of data and the production of outputs). Audit packages may be used for the purpose. Alternatively, the systems designer may be asked to provide for special audit reports, either routinely or on demand. Such reports may be produced for eg:-

a. Exceptional transactions.

b. Random samples.

c. Sections of files (for detailed audit).

d. Intermediate file control totals.

ON-LINE AND REAL-TIME SYSTEMS.

18. These systems increase the difficulties of the auditor, because:-

a. The input of data from a number of remote points is not easily controlled.

b. Source documents are not always readily available for inspection and sometimes may not exist at all (eg. orders taken by telephone).

c. Some control techniques (eg. verification of keyboarding, batch controls) cannot be used.

d. Unauthorised use of the computer or unauthorised inspection of its files may be possible.

e. Immediate processing of transactions through all stages in real-time systems may make an audit trail impossible.

19. It becomes even more important for the auditor to check the system software thoroughly. He must pay particular attention to:-

a. Validity checking of input.

b. Protection against unauthorised inspection of files.

c. Proper identification of terminal users by passwords.

d. Reporting of exceptional or suspicious transactions or enquiries.

20. A useful technique is the monitoring of terminal activities by the central machine. All traffic for a certain period for a selected terminal can be recorded and audited. It is also possible for the auditor to make unannounced visits to terminal locations.

SYSTEMS DEVELOPMENT AND PROGRAMMING.

21. An audit of systems development and programming may be made by:-

a. Inspecting systems and program specifications and program documentation. Systems specifications should be made available to the auditor as a matter of routine.

b. Inspecting system and program tests to ensure that thorough testing has been carried out.

c. Reviewing an operational system to ensure that:-

i. Specified objectives are being achieved.
ii. Costs are not excessive.
iii. Users are satisfied with the service received.
iv. The number of errors is not excessive.

d. Inspecting records of the progress and output of systems analysts and programmers.

OPERATIONAL SECTIONS.

22. The auditor can check the efficiency of operational sections by:-

a. Inspecting records eg:-

i. Computer logs.

ii. Output and error records of the Data Preparation operators.

iii. Work progress and error records kept by the Data Control Section.

b. Verifying the accuracy and punctuality of computer processing with user departments.

c. General observation of standards of discipline, tidiness, punctuality, etc.

CHECK LISTS.

23. Check lists are a useful aid to the auditor who has to deal with a DP department. They consist of comprehensive questionnaires covering all aspects of control. Standard lists are available from eg. The Institute of Chartered Accountants and appear in other auditing publications.

SUMMARY.

24. The auditor must familiarise himself with data processing techniques and the work of the DP department.

25. He must always bear in mind:-

i. the novel features of computer file organisation and processing.

ii. the concentration of responsibility within the DP department.

iii. the repetitive nature of computer system errors.

26. The main audit techniques are:-

i. involvement in systems development

ii. auditing round the computer

iii. test packs

iv. audit packages

v. construction of an audit trail

vi. check lists.

POINTS TO NOTE.

27. If you are using this book to prepare for an auditing paper, do not limit your reading to this chapter. Study also:-

Chapter 17 (Systems Controls)

Chapter 41 (Control of Data Processing Activities)

28. The auditor is not expected to understand programs. He should however have enough knowledge of system and program documentation to be able to scrutinise it intelligently.

The Evolution of Data Processing

1. Throughout the rest of this manual every effort has been made to present the reader with a modern view of data processing. The reader's understanding will be increased by also seeing how data processing took place in the past and why it changed to what it is today. For that reason an account of the evolution of data processing is provided in the following chapter.

43 The Evolution of Data Processing

INTRODUCTION.

1. This chapter outlines developments spreading over a number of years, which have led to a steady movement from manual data processing, through electronic data processing to an increasing number of computerised data processing systems.

2. The reader, having reached this Part of the book, should be able to see the subject matter of earlier chapters in context.

GENERAL DEVELOPMENTS IN EQUIPMENT.

3. The developments which led to the computer systems we have today took place over many years and in a rather piecemeal manner. The next few paragraphs concentrate on practical developments of direct relevance to data processing.

4. One of the early successes in automated data processing was that of Herman Hollerith, who in the 1880's developed a mechanical system for processing the data for the US census. Hollerith's machines processed data which had first to be transcribed into the form of punched cards.

5. The impact of Hollerith's methods was striking. Whereas the census of 1880 on 50 million citizens had taken over 7 years to complete, the census of 1890 on 63 million citizens was completed in just three years!

6. Through Hollerith's example it had been firmly established that machines were able to perform repetitive tasks accurately on large volumes of data, with a minimum of manual intervention. These features of automated data processing can be seen in evidence in the various systems which have been in use since Hollerith's time, right through to the present day.

7. Other early influences are also still apparent. For example, until the 1970's the major medium on which data was encoded for entry into computer systems was the punched card, based upon Hollerith's original design! (See 43.1). Another medium also using punched holes which was popular well into the 1970s was punched paper tape (Fig. 43.2).

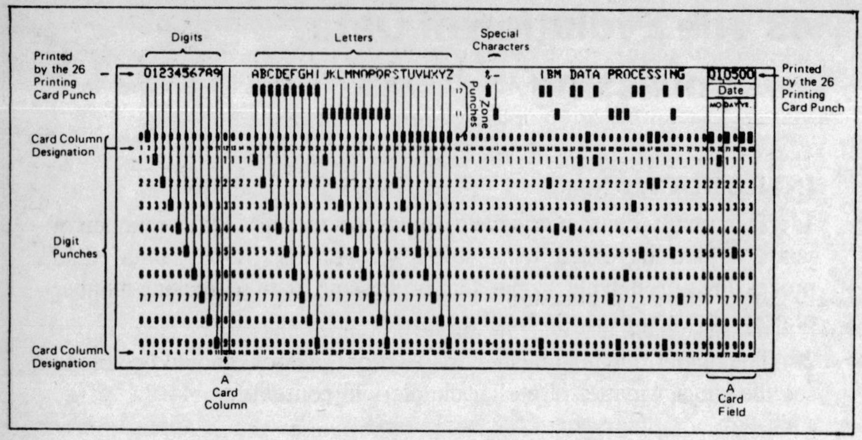

FIG. 43.1. AN 80 COLUMN PUNCHED CARD.
(Figure courtesy IBM (UK) Ltd.)

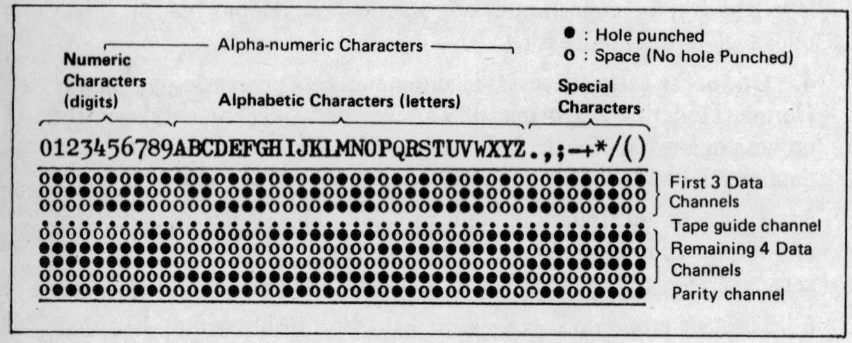

FIG. 43.2. PUNCHED PAPER TAPE.

8. The equipment in use has progressed in stages from being wholly mechanical, through being electro-mechanical, to being almost wholly electronic. Each new stage has brought with it a series of improvements in terms of performance, reliability and cost effectiveness.

9. The first true computers were electronic devices based upon the use of thermonic valves. Among these so called **"First Generation"** computers was the *first commerical computer* "LEO" (Lyon's Electronic Office), produced in 1951.

DEVELOPMENTS IN COMPUTER EQUIPMENT.

10. By the late 1950's the **"Second Generation"** computers had arrived. These computers used transistors instead of valves. The use of transistors reduced size, manufacturing costs and running costs, and improved reliability and processing power. Developments in magnetic storage media and software also took place at about the same time including the introduction of "High level" languages.

11. Further developments in the miniaturisation of electronic circuitry led to Integrated Circuits (ICs), effectively whole circuits on small wafers of crystal. These ICs formed the basis of the **"Third Generation"** computers of the 1960's.

12. The **"third generation"** computers made many computer applications technically feasible for the first time. The second generation computers had firmly established the fact that computers could be used to automate a wide variety of basic clerical procedures but the third generation computers were used to extend the number of applications even further.

13. At this time computers were successfully used for a number of applications which relied upon the computer's direct access storage capabilities. Some applications such as airline booking systems had no direct manual counterpart.

14. Despite these advances, most commercial computer systems were primarily batch processing systems and often lacked any significant data enquiry facilities.

15. A number of limitations held back the greater exploitation of many technically feasible computer applications. These limitations were notably:-

a. the high costs of basic hardware ie. processor, storage devices and input/output devices,

b. the laborious and costly methods of data entry eg. the process of converting data into machine readable forms, the transmission of data etc.,

c. the relative costs of backing storage media compared with conventional paper based methods.

d. the costs of programming.

16. Semi-conductor devices. Throughout the 1960s and into the 1970s the technology which had led to the integrated circuit was developed yet further so that extremely complex circuity could be manufactured on single minute sliced wafers of silicon crystal. Such devices were called **"silicon chips"** or **"semi-conductor devices".** (See Fig. 4.1).

17. By 1972 it was possible to place an entire small computer processor on a single chip. The device was called a **microprocessor.** Computers built around such devices are called **"microcomputers"**, or more correctly, **"microcomputer based systems"**.

18. Other semi-conductor devices were developed specifically for data storage. These *"semi-conductor memories"* rapidly replaced the existing main storage medium which was called **"core store"**. Core store, which is now obsolete, consisted of tiny hand assembled wire meshes on which minute rings of magnetic material (cores) had been threaded.

19. The increased use of semiconductor devices caused hardware costs to fall significantly. Computerisation became the most cost effective solution to a broader range of DP problems particularly in applications requiring smaller computer systems.

20. Data Storage media and methods also improved through the 1960s and 1970s. The two primary media in use, magnetic tape and magnetic disk, benefitted from numerous improvements. Magnetic disk, the more versatile of the two, (12.00, 24.00) became more economically viable. This too, led to more widespread computer applications.

21. Maintained data stored on disks was recognised as an important pooled resource, directly usable for a variety of purposes. The differences in potential between manual DP Systems and EDP Systems were becoming more and more apparent.

DATA ENTRY.

22. The commercial computer systems of the 1960s and early 1970s made extensive use of punched cards as an input medium. There were certain inherent drawbacks associated with using punched cards particularly in connection with laborious, expensive and slow processes of transcription, verification and media conversion.

23. Various attempts to automate this process were attempted with the aim of increasing speeds and reducing costs. They included:-

a. The introduction of data transmission equipment. Various **telecommunication** methods and systems were devised in order to transmit data electronically from remote sites to a central computer. Over the years these systems have developed into superior and more comprehensive national and international networks.

b. Methods of directly encoding data onto fast input media. In order of their introduction these were:-

i. **Key-to-tape systems,** which allowed direct encoding from source documents into magnetic tape. (A reusable medium)

ii. **Key-to-disk systems,** which were really small special purpose computer allowing multiple keyboard data entry from source documents onto disk, and ultimately onto magnetic-tape for input. Key-to-disk systems were quickly adopted for small general purpose work and became the first **"mini computers."**

iii. **Key-to-diskette systems.** Diskettes, also called **"floppy disks"** were an IBM invention intended as a punch card replacement. They have since been adopted as a backing storage medium for small microcomputer based systems.

c. Direct capture of the data at source or on machine-sensible source documents eg. OCR/OMR.

THE CURRENT STATE OF DATA PROCESSING.

24. Technological advances continue to make an even greater number of applications cost effective to computerise. For example office automation has increased dramatically over recent years.

25. Magnetic media costs have fallen relative to paper costs so that computerised filing system are cheaper than conventional systems for many applications. Some predictions imply that magnetic media will be cheaper than paper for all but a few applications within five years.

26. The developments in distributed systems and networks, together with advances in data bases have placed the data processing systems of today into a position to play a far greater role within the organisations they serve. In fact the term "data processing system" appears too narrow for the most modern corporate systems and the term "IT System" is often used instead if other computerised applications including electronic communications are included.

27. There are still many problems to be faced however. Greater reliance on computers calls for greater computer reliability. More applications areas means the need for more software. The more widespread use of computers means the need for systems which are easy for almost anyone to use.

28. Although hardware costs have fallen, software development costs continue to rise. Modern methods of analysis, design and programming attempt to tackle the problem of software cost and produce systems which meet the user's requirements to a high standard of reliability.

29. Considerably more effort will need to be made in solving such problems as those of human/machine communication, the so called "man machine interface".

30. Despite some persistant problems data processing is growing in importance and will probably continue to do so.

SUMMARY.

31. a. DP systems have evolved from manual system to computerised systems through the successive use of three types of equipment:-

i. mechanical aids eg. calculating machines.
ii. electro-mechanical aids eg. accounting machines,
iii. electronic devices eg. pocket calculator or computers.

b. Computers have characteristics which make them eminently suited to a wide variety of DP applications eg.

i. they can repetitively and accurately process data in large volumes with the minimum of manual intervention.
ii. they can maintain 'pools' of data in a controlled fashion which enables the timely provision of information for a variety of purposes.

c. Technical innovations, followed by advances in manufacturing methods, have made the use of computers in data processing not only technically feasible but also cost effective. The range of cost effective applications is broadening all the time.

The Social Aspect

1. In the introduction to the first Part of the manual the reader was asked to bear in mind that data processing systems have an important role to play in enabling the organisation they serve to meet their goals. The reader should, having read this far, be able to see how data processing systems can play such a role. The following chapter returns to a somewhat broader view by looking at data processing, not only within organisation, but within society as a whole.

44 The Social Aspect

INTRODUCTION.

1. The role of computers in society is a large subject to consider and this chapter merely highlights some important issues. Computers are just one example of automation although they have many special features. In a society which relies heavily on all forms of automation and on the automated handling of information, computers are bound to be very important. Issues related to jobs and privacy are particularly significant.

COMPUTERS IN INFORMATION TECHNOLOGY.

2. It is generally recognised that we live in an industrial society in which the efficency of production of wealth depends heavily on various kinds of automation. Computers are special in that they *automate many methods of processing information.* Computers are also playing an ever increasing role in many other forms of automation.

3. Computers, telecommunications equipment, and other technologies associated with automation, come under the general heading of **Information Technology (IT).** Information Technology is having an impact on individuals, organisations and society. Various aspects of this impact will be discussed in the remainder of this chapter. Particular reference will be made to computers, and some key issues, notably privacy and employment.

THE GENERAL BACKGROUND.

4. Prior to industrialisation approximately 90% of the labour force was engaged in agriculture, ie. society was agrarian. Methods of communication were limited and a very small proportion of the labour force was involved with the processing, storage and retrieval of information, which in any case merely involved manual paper based methods or word of mouth.

Industrialisation produced a major shift in the labour force, with the proportion involved in agriculture falling below 10% in the UK. With industrialisation came the beginning of Information Technology and the start of a series of IT developments taking us right up to the present day:- Telegraph, Telephone, Radio/TV, Computers, Microelectronics etc.

5. These new forms of IT, and other developments, produced new forms of work. The larger scale of organisations has given rise to large administrative structures in which there are large numbers of clerical workers and people with technical and managerial skills collectively known as "white collar workers". Computerisation has mainly affected white collar work so far.

6. In addition to changes in the type of work there has been an increase in the number of organisations involved in activities other than manufacture. Some such organisations, for example those in the power industries, contribute to manufacturing and provide a general service. As a result of this change only 25% of the labour force remained in organisations directly involved in the manufacture of goods. For a number of reasons, not particularly related to IT, that 25% has fallen to 20% in the last few years and levels of unemployment have risen.

7. The fact that so few remain in manufacture, although manufacturing continues to generate most wealth, has lead to society today being called "Post Industrial Society".

8. Looking at the whole of the national and international community, and at the way organisations are run, highlights the fact that modern society is heavily dependent on the communication, processing and storage of information. It is claimed by some, that we are moving towards an "Information Society" in which the majority of the labour force will be engaged in Information Processing and the use of "Information Technology".

9. It is a mistake to imagine that technological innovation is what causes such changes. Such changes are the collective result of actions taken by those people able to control and influence the use and distribution of resources, within their own organisations, or within society at large. The uses of resources are determined by the goals which are being pursued.

ORGANISATIONS.

10. The uses of computers in various kinds of organisations have been discussed in a number of earlier chapters. The term "organisation" was used fairly informally. However, it is possible to be more formal in defining what an organisation is and doing so highlight some significant points.

11. An organisation is a human group which has been deliberately constructed with the aim of seeking specific goals. An organisation will be reconstructed, from time to time, so that it can continue to seek its goals effectively.

12. The goals sought will depend on the organisation.

Examples:

a. The owners of commercial organisations may have profit as their goal with themselves as the main beneficaries eg. in private or public companies.

b. The goals of many organisations are to provide a *"services"* to their clients or the general public eg. medical services, schools and colleges.

c. Other organisations have the mutual benefits of their members as goals eg. clubs or trade unions.

13. Any organisation needs to be controlled and coordinated and to be able to plan ahead. To do so it will need information and facilities to communicate.

14. In most organisations, and particularly in large ones, Information Technology can aid in the processing of information and thereby help the organisation to meet its goals. Whether or not an organisation uses such technology will depend on its evaluation of the technology in relation to its own goals.

EVALUATION OF INFORMATION SYSTEMS.

15. There are many methods of evaluating new methods and technologies. In the area of computerisation the main methods are those used in Systems Analysis (chapter 29). A proposed computer system is evaluated in terms of how well it can meet objectives which will enable the organisation to meet goals such as profit, service or optimum use of resources.

16. The results of such evaluations determine whether organisations invest in computers. This in turn promotes or limits technological developments.

17. Large organisations such as government bodies or large corporations can have a major influence in this way. For example the US government attached a high importance to micro-electronics and silicon chip technology because of the goals of providing national defence. That depended on having miniaturised electronic circuitry in rockets, planes etc. The necessary research and development costs were provided from the defence budget.

COMPUTERISATION AND WORK.

18. When computers are introduced into organisations because of the benefits they can provide, it usually affects the work of staff within the organisation. Some jobs are changed, some may be created and some may be lost. This creates a demand for training and retraining.

19. Any loss of jobs due to computerisation can give rise to alarm, particularly at a time of high unemployment. However such job "losses" probably signify yet another shift in the work of the general labour force as has happened many times in the past.

20. Only a very small proportion of the current level of unemployment is directly attributable to new technology. In certain particular applications jobs are likely to be lost, notably:-

a. Some office jobs eg. caused by Word Processing.

b. Factory production where industrial robots may replace production line workers.

21. Whether these job losses will result in permanent unemployment is another matter. It depends on the process of redeployment of labour and labour retraining. It may help to consider an example at this stage.

22. In the USA in the early 1970s there were proposals to introduce bar coded POS equipment into supermarkets. This appeared to be an attractive proposition because a saving of $100 million could be achieved if such equipment was introduced into 5000 stores.

23. Initially there was alarm from the trade unions who predicted 20% job losses by 1975, the date at which implementation was due to be completed.

24. These fears were unfounded for two reasons. Firstly the rate at which the new technology was introduced was much slower which allowed staffing changes to be dealt with by redeployment and natural wastage. By 1979 only 803 stores had equipment installed. Very different from the predicted 5000 by 1975. The trade unions were also able to negotiate an automation deal with their employers. This protected their jobs. The store owners were still able to make large savings by the introduction of the equipment, and to redeploy staff in ventures which improved and extended company activities. (In Britain the banks have also used automation to allow them to redeploy staff in broader and better services).

25. Since these early difficulties were overcome the introduction of the equipment has continued smoothly in the USA and at an increasing rate. In Britain this kind of supermarket automation is only just under way.

PRIVACY AND DATA PROTECTION.

26. Another consequence of higher levels of computerisation is the increase in the use of computer based equipment to store large quantities of data about individuals. Some of this data is of a particularly personal or private nature and there is a natural concern that it should not be misused. There is also concern that individuals may have personal information stored about them without their knowledge or control, and that it may be hard or impossible to find out whether such information is accurate.

27. In 1975 a government white paper considered this issue and in 1976 a committee was set up chaired by Sir Norman Lindop. The idea was that systems dealing with records containing personal details should be controlled.

28. The Lindop report appeared about two years later and was well received. It established a number of principles eg. that stored data should only be used for the purpose for which its use was originally authorised and intended. The report suggested that a **Data Protection Authority (DPA),** should be set up which would enforce codes of conduct for different types of systems.

29. At about the same time, the Council of Europe set up a "Convention for the Protection of Individuals with regard to Automatic Processing of Personal Data". Each country signs twice, once to agree to legislate and the second time when it has legislated. Britain had only signed once by early 1983 and computer organisations such as the BCS (British Computer Society) and CSA (Computer Services Association) have expressed fears that delays could cost the UK dearly in terms of lost international contracts through failure to introduce legislation.

30. Such legislation is the primary responsibility of the Home Office, itself an important user of computer data banks of an unusual kind, eg. those concerned with police records like those held on the Police National Computer at Hendon (North London).

31. A further government white paper appeared early in 1982. It only covered some aspects of data protection. In April 1983 a bill began its passage through Parliament but ran into initial trouble over the issue of confidentiality. The bill was lost when the general election was called but was reintroduced in a slightly modified form becoming an act in 1984.

THE 1984 DATA PROTECTION ACT.

32. The 1984 Data Protection act was intended "to regulate the use of automatically processed information relating to individuals and the provision of services in respect of such information." What is immediately apparent is that the act does not cover manual records. This fact is not only a disappointment to those concerned with freedom of information but may also be a discouragement to the use of computers for some applications.

33. The act defines a number of terms including "Data" (information in a processable form), "Personal Data" (data relating to identifiable living individuals) and "Data Subject" (the living individual concerned).

34. The act requires those using personal data to register with the **Data Protection Registrar.** The end of April 1986 was set as the deadline for initial registrations for existing users.

35. There are a number of general and specific exemptions. These exemptions are the subject of considerable controversy and practical difficulties. At the general level there are exemptions for a number of government departments for reasons stated to be related to national security and covering some aspects of criminal records, immigration, health and social security. More specifically, there are exemptions for work such as word processing, pensions, accounting and payroll. However, these exemptions are rather weak in that if the system under consideration carries out other tasks it may not be exempt. For example, if the payroll system is used for anything more than calculating and paying wages it will not be exempt.

36. An organisation may easily make a genuine mistake in interpreting these rules but will still be liable to criminial prosecution. Therefore, it is not surprising that many organisations have appointed an expert whose sole responsibility is to deal with matters concerned with the act. The title for such a post is normally that of **Data Protection Officer.**

37. In future, it will be important for all staff involved in Data Processing to have an awareness of what the act covers so that they know when to consult a Data Protection Officer for specific advice.

38. The main points covered by the act which need to be born in mind are:

a. Data about individuals which is held for processing must have been obtained fairly for a specific lawful purpose.

b. The data must only be used for the specific purpose and may only be disclosed in accordance with the specific purpose.

c. Data must not be excessive for the purpose but merely adequate and relevant.

d. Data must be accurate, up to date and kept no longer than necessary.

e. The data must be protected and held securely against unauthorised access or loss but must be accessible to data subjects on request.

THE FUTURE.

39. The current rapid rate of computerisation and technical innovation has lead some people to talk of a "micro electronics revolution". To others these changes are merely viewed as another phase in the process of automation which started with the industrial revolution. Either way it seems reasonable to expect change and yet more change in the future.

40. The "fifth generation" supercomputers may well be here by the end of this century if current research and development programmers keep to schedule. Who can say whether these computers will cause delight or dismay? The answers do not rest in the technology.

SUMMARY.

41. a. The place of computers in Information Technology was discussed.

b. The general background to the current state of computerisation in society was given.

c. Organisations were defined and their role in computerisation was discussed.

d. Computerisation and its impact on employment was discussed.

e. Privacy and recent development in data protection were discussed.

f. The future was considered briefly.

POINTS TO NOTE.

42. a. Computerisation is not just a matter of technological innovation and development. It is a process which involves individuals, organisations and society in general.

Case Exercises

1. The case exercises in the following chapter comprise questions on particular applications systems. The questions, which will probably take over an hour to answer, are accompanied by suggested solutions and author's notes.

2. Although the questions have been primarily taken from the examinations set by the ICMA, they should also prove useful to students preparing for other examinations for which this book is used as a text.

45 Case Exercises

INTRODUCTION.

1. The questions given in this chapter are quite long by normal examination standards. In fact an examination candidate would have one hour and twelve minute to devote to producing an answer. The answer would be worth a maximum of 40% of the marks obtainable in the three hour examination.

2. It takes some time to understand these questions and it would be quite reasonable to spend fifteen minutes, or more, in reading the question and planning a solution.

3. You may find it helps you to understand each question better if you try to sketch a systems flowchart on a second reading and if you also underline what appear to be important facts given in the question.

4. Suggested solutions follow each question. Do not be alarmed if your answers are different. Questions of this kind are open to a variety of interpretations. As long as your answer is well thought out and properly takes into account the details given in the question you have little to worry about. However, by comparing your answers with those suggested you should be able to improve the quality of your answers and build up your confidence.

5. In order to be as instructive as possible some non-essential detail has been added to the solutions.

QUESTION 1.

A company manufacturing and selling a range of 200 standard stationery products is planning to employ a mini-computer for its routine administration, accounting procedures, and stock and production activities.

The computer configuration will comprise a processor, 10 megabytes of disk storage, a 150 lines per minute printer and three visual display units.

The first application envisaged is an integrated order processing, finished stock control, sales invoicing and accounting, and sales analysis system.

The majority of orders are received by telephone and will be input interactively on a visual display unit sited in the sales office. Facilities will be provided for the checking of credit status and the determination of product availability.

Each day all orders received up to 4.00 pm will be accumulated and documents printed out before 5.00 pm. These documents will be sent to the despatch department for the packing and despatch of goods the following day.

Despatch data will be input on a visual display unit located in the despatch department. This will update the order position and will generate data for invoicing purposes. Invoices will be produced in batch mode once per day.

In the context of the above, you are required to:

a. identify the transactions which will be required to be input for this system;

b. describe briefly the contents of the main files;

c. list in sequence the processes associated with order input, emphasising the interactive nature of this part of the system;

d. produce system run flowcharts of the batch procedures involved in the production of daily invoices and periodic sales analyses (assume two analyses, one by product within area sequence and one by customer type).

[Parts **(a)** and **(b)** 5 marks each, part **(c)** 10 marks and part **(d)** 20 marks = **40 marks**]
(ICMA)

ANSWER 1.

1. **Author's preliminary notes.**

a. You are only required to produce system run flowcharts for batch procedures but a quick sketch of the systems flowchart of the *whole* system may help your understanding of the question.

b. Since the question mentions an "integrated" system we should envisage a system in which data items should not need to be re-input for each processing procedure.

c. The "interactive" features of ordering require that master files must be kept up to date throughout the day.

d. The "batch" nature of the despatch procedures suggests that products and customer credit committed to orders are held pending until the despatch procedure takes place.

2. **Suggested Solution.**

a. **Required input transaction:-**

i. Customers' orders.
ii. Cancellations or changes to Customers' orders.
iii. Despatch data for orders.

iv. Product receipts, amendments, insertions, deletions and returns.

v. Customer cash receipts, credits, debits, insertions and deletions.

b. **Contents of main files:-**

i. Products Master file:-

Product number
Product description
Total quantity in stock } Difference ie. 'free' stock
Stock allocated to orders } could be stored or calculated.
Unit selling price (ex. VAT) }
VAT rate } Current and Previous
Reorder level
Quantity on order from production.

ii. Customer master file:-

[NB. This single logical file will probably be split into several physical files]

Customer account number
Customer name and address } Alternative addresses for deliveries/invoices
Area code } etc. may be recorded.
Customer type
Credit limit
Current balance excluding non-despatched orders
Current balance including non-despatched orders
date and number of last order { despatched and non-despatched }
order details
details of receipts
etc.

iii. Pending orders file:-

Order number {generated automatically on creation}
Customer account number
Customer address
Total value (ex Vat) (inc Vat)
Product number }
Product description }
Quantity required } Repeated for each product
Unit price {with and without VAT} }
Total selling price {with and without VAT} }

iv. Despatched Orders file – as for pending orders
v. VAT Master file
  Order Number
  Invoice Number
  Customer account number
  VAT amount {at each rate}
  Total amount
vi. Sales analysis file
  Product number
  Invoice number
  Order number
  Customer type
  Area code
  Quantity despatched/returned.

c. **Order input**

i. All orders will be entered via a VDU by a clerk. The majority of orders are telephoned in and it is the handling of these orders which exploits the interactive facilities of the system.

ii. The customers will identify themselves to the clerk by giving their account number and name when they telephone. The customer account number will be keyed in by the clerk. The customer details will then be displayed on the VDU screen so that the clerk can confirm names and addresses and check credit status. If at any stage in creating the order the credit limit is reached the clerk will have to adopt the appropriate credit control procedure eg. reference to a supervisor. The order number will be generated by the computer.

iii. The customer will specify which products are required by reference to a catalog or similar document. The clerk will assist the customer as necessary and will key in the product number. Product details will be displayed on the screen, including the free stock available. The clerk will key in the quantity required unless there is insufficient stock available in which case some appropriate action will be taken eg. order an alternative, or accept order despite the delay.

iv. The customer and products files will be updated to reflect the current state of affairs eg. current balance and allocated stock will require changing.

v. Different screen displays will appear at each stage of order entry according to whether the customer is confirming addresses, enquiring about products, deciding upon quantities required, or asking for unit or total prices.

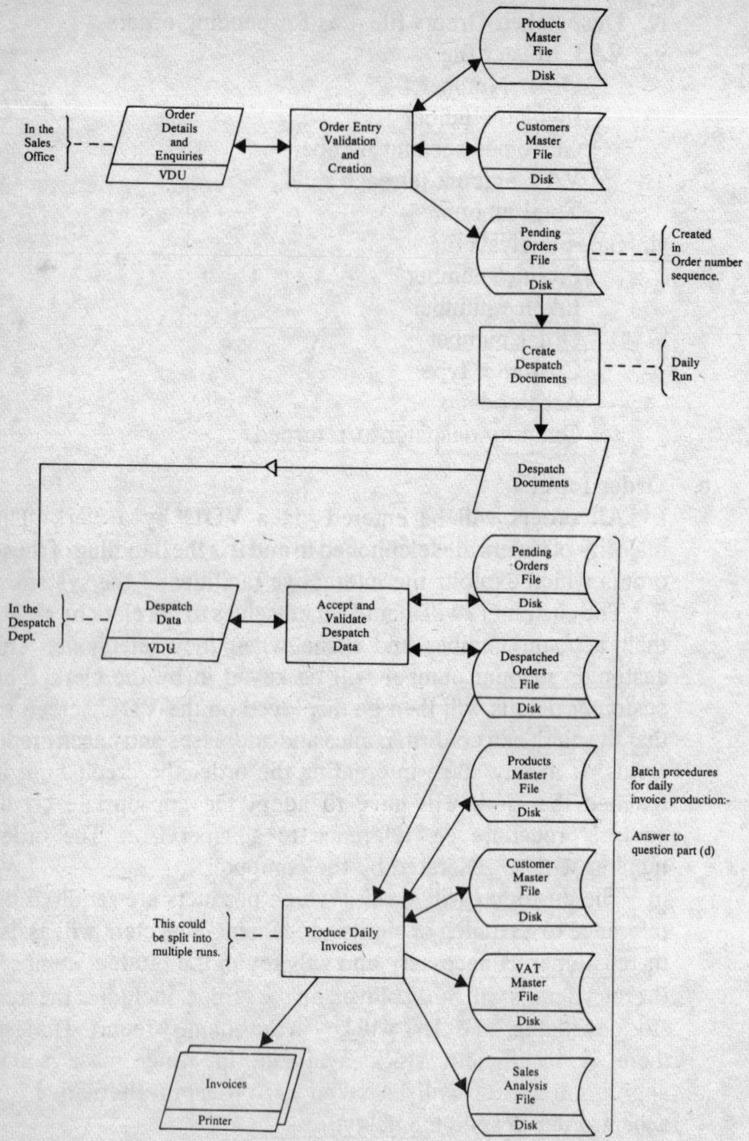

FIG. 45.1. SYSTEMS FLOWCHART FOR ORDERING, DESPATCHING AND INVOICING.

[NB. In the absence of any evidence in the question to the contrary it is assumed that the disks have the capacities, and software necessary for simultaneous file processing.]

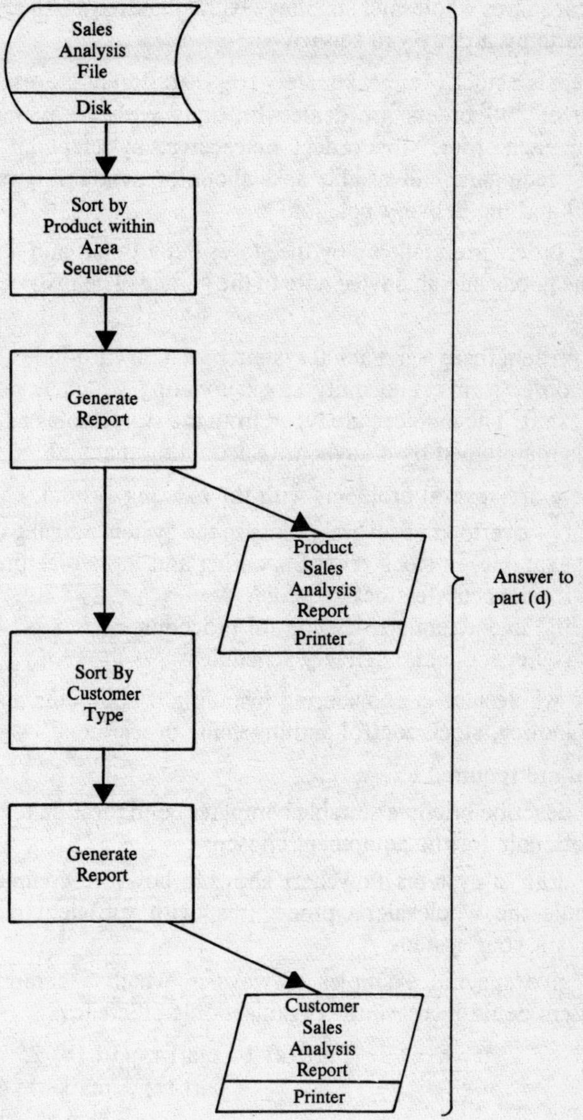

FIG. 45.2. SYSTEMS FLOWCHART FOR SALES ANALYSIS.

QUESTION 2.

A car spares wholesaler supplies several hundred small garages with spare parts by a daily van service.

There is a stock of approximately 10,000 different spare parts and an average of 200 orders are dealt with daily with an average of five items on each order. Most orders are received by telephone and when ordering each garage invariably asks about the availability of the parts required and the delivery position.

The orders are made up by the stores department and a van driver takes the goods and an advice note to the garage. The invoice is sent by post later.

At present there is a manual system based on card-index files, hand written order forms, and daily stock updating which is done by an evening shift. The invoices are typed from the stores notes and the sales ledger is maintained by a keyboard accounting machine.

There are several problems with the existing system, namely:

i. overload at several points in the system causing delays, for example, in stock record updating and in invoice preparation;
ii. inaccurate stock records;
iii. uneconomic stock control procedures;
iv. uneconomic delivery schedules.

The wholesaler is considering installing a computer to deal with order handling, stock control and invoicing procedures.

You are required to:

a. describe briefly a suitable computer configuration together with a rationale for the equipment chosen;

b. draw a systems flowchart showing how the computer would handle the wholesaler's procedures, with sufficient narrative to explain your system;

c. give specific examples of ways in which a computer based system could increase the organisation's efficiency.

[Part **(a)** 10 marks, part **(b)** 25 marks and part **(c)** 5 marks = **40 marks**]
(ICMA)

ANSWER 2.

1. **Author's preliminary notes.** At face value this question may appear somewhat similar to question one, in that it also deals with a stock control

system. However, the question is primarily concerned with how a computer system can be used to replace a manual system and overcome the problems associated with the manual system. A fast, efficient, accurate, reliable and economic computer system is required.

2. Suggested Solution.

a. i. The features of the computer configuration must help to overcome the problems of the existing system. Interactive on-line order entry should be effective in overcoming the problems. Stock records can then be kept up to date. Customers will be able to make orders based upon accurate stock records. Invoicing can be handled efficiently and quickly. Repetitive clerical tasks can be performed by the computer and the computer can be used to generate more economic delivery schedules.

ii. Interactive order entry suggests that VDUs should be used and since an average of 200 orders per day must be entered, which corresponds to 25 orders per hour in an 8 hour day, several VDUs will be needed. Given that other data will also need to be entered 6, or possibly more VDUs may be necessary.

iii. Disks are essential for file storage in an on-line system. The size of the stock file suggests that in order to provide suitable disk storage two or more large disk drives are needed. Having at least two disk drives also makes disk file security more straight forward.

iv. The number of despatch note and invoices required can be produced on a line printer. There may be some merit in having an additional printer, accessible from the stores, which can be used to produce despatch notes as the orders are created.

v. The peripherals and processing functions identified so far suggest that a mini-computer system is required to handle the work. Such a system should have sufficient main storage and a the appropriate system and application software.

b. i. Orders are entered on-line (see answer to question 1). (Fig. 45.3).

ii. The customers' orders may be accumulated during the day (or half day) and then the invoices may be produced by batch processing.

iii. If customers are allocated set delivery routes and a sequence position on the route then the computer can analyse the orders and produce a delivery schedule for the driver.

iv. Routine maintenance of the master files will follow normal practice (see notes on Fig. 45.4).

iv. "Static" customer details are held in the customer master file. Sales details are stored in the sales ledger.
v. (See question 1 answer for typical file contents).

b. **NB.** All files are on disk.

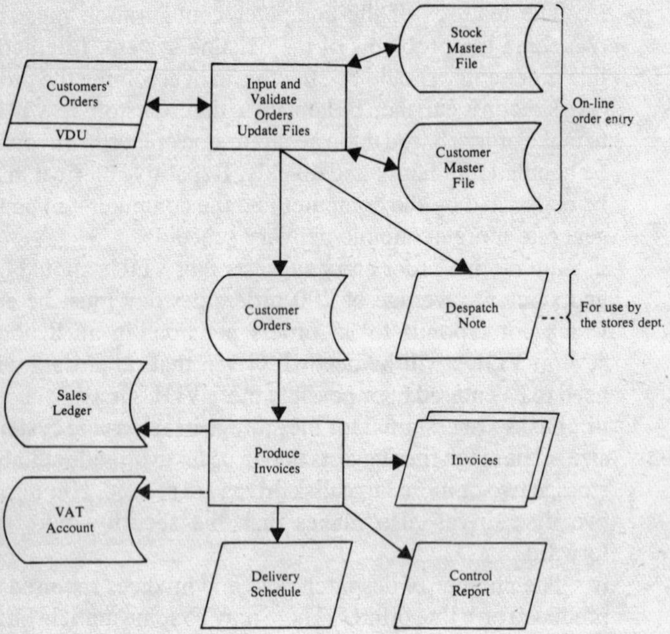

FIG. 45.3. ORDER ENTRY AND INVOICE CREATION.

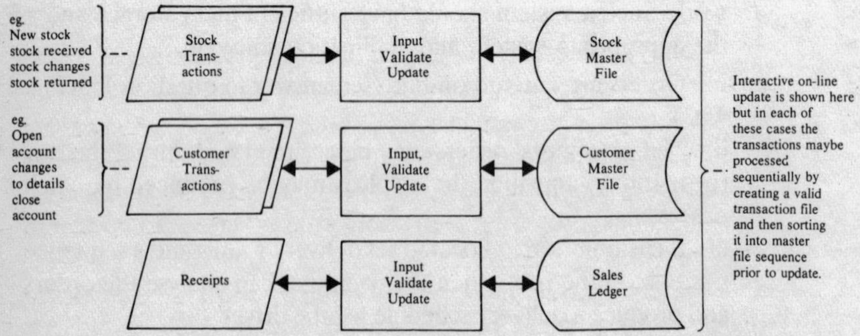

FIG. 45.4. OUTLINE SYSTEM FLOWCHARTS FOR THE REMAINDER OF THE SYSTEM.

c. **Specific examples of increased wholesale efficiency.**

i. There would be fewer problems with customer orders because of the accuracy of stock records.

ii. There would be less chance of lost orders through out of stock items because re-ordering could be prompted as a by-product of processing the stock file.

iii. Overstocking could be detected and remedied more easily.

iv. The automation would free clerical staff for other work.

v. Better credit control would reduce the incidence of bad debts.

vi. Better delivery schedules would reduce transport and labour costs.

vii. The *general benefits* would be increased revenue, reduced costs and improved services.

QUESTION 3.

An insurance company specialises in motor business and operates through a network of approximately 100 brokers.

The company has a medium sized computer with both serial and direct access backing storage, key to disk encoders, and a line printer.

All communications to customers are through the brokers and the company receives amendments, premiums, new risks and all other information by post from the brokers.

The data processing system deals with the following activities:

a. Daily processing of input comprising: new clients, client amendments, payment receipts, file amendments and deletions.

b. Daily print out of renewal reminders in client within broker sequence for those clients with a renewal date 20 working days ahead.

c. Weekly processing of agreed claims; production of claim payments, claims statistics and updating of client files.

d. Weekly print out in client within broker sequence of payments overdue, of part payments and of clients whose insurance has been automatically terminated. An insurance is automatically terminated if a communication has not been received on or before the fourteenth working day after renewal date.

e. Monthly analysis of premiums received and claims made by vehicle category within occupation code within zone code.

f. Monthly analysis of new business, cumulative premium income, claims made, commission due or earned (monthly and cumulative year to date) for each broker.

The major items contained in the main client file are as follows:

Client number
Client name
Client address
Client date of birth
Vehicle make and registration number
Vehicle category
Client occupation code
Insurance category
Voluntary excess
Restrictions on use
Zone
Premium
Premium renewal date
Last premium paid date
Claims record
Broker reference

You are required to:

a. draw a systems run flowchart or flowcharts to deal with the activities specified above: your flowchart(s) must contain sufficient narrative to identify clearly what work is being carried out and in particular the major items contained in any files used other than the client file which is already specified;

b. discuss briefly ways in which the time delays inherent in the existing batch processing system could be eliminated or reduced.

[**(a)** 30, **(b)** 10 = **40 marks**]
(ICMA)

ANSWER 3.

1. Author's preliminary note. In answering this question pay particular attention to where data is stored, when data is entered and when data is used to provide reports. This will help you to identify the main processing activities needed and what other files are needed within the system.

2. Suggested Solution.

a. i. Since "all communications with customers are through brokers" the client master file has been organised as a sequential file in client within broker sequence.

ii. A brokers' master file is considered necessary. Since direct access backing storage is available the brokers file has been organised as an index sequential file. (Processed randomly in Figs. 45.5–45.8 and sequentially in Fig. 45.10).

iii. The brokers' master file contains the following items:-

Brokers reference
Brokers name and address
Number of clients
Number of new clients
Number of clients lost
Premiums received
Number of claims made
Value of claims made

(Number of clients through Value of claims made: This month and year to date.)

iv. The systems flowcharts Fig. 45.5-10 have been annotated so as to reduce the supporting narrative.

v. The clients master file is a sequential file (which may be stored on disk or tape).

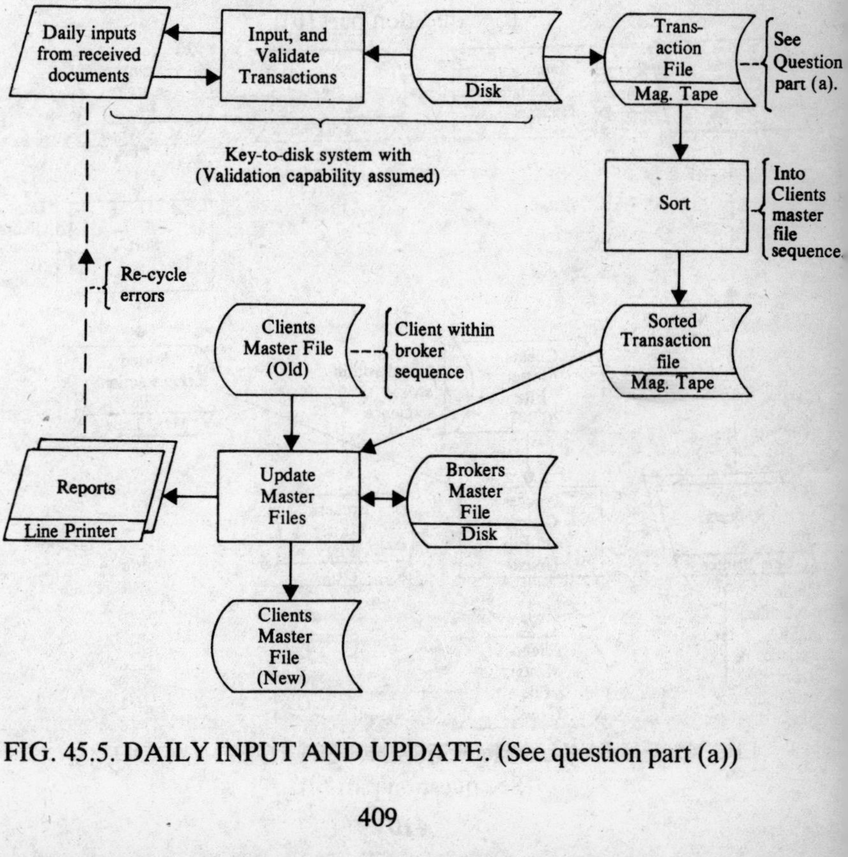

FIG. 45.5. DAILY INPUT AND UPDATE. (See question part (a))

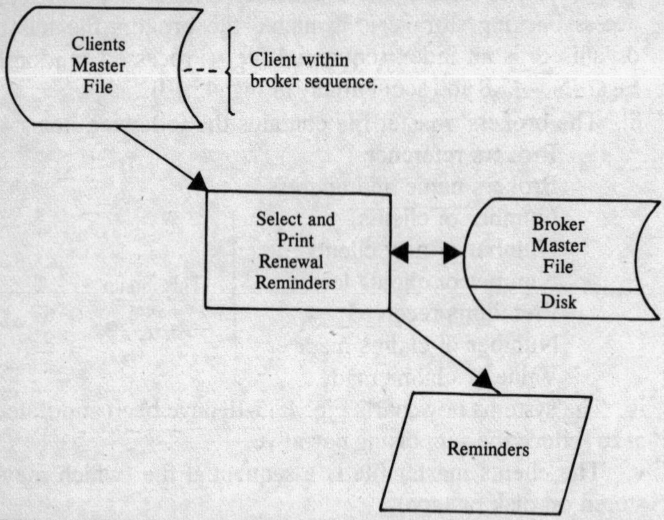

FIG. 45.6. DAILY PRINTOUT OF RENEWAL REMINDERS.
(See question part (b))

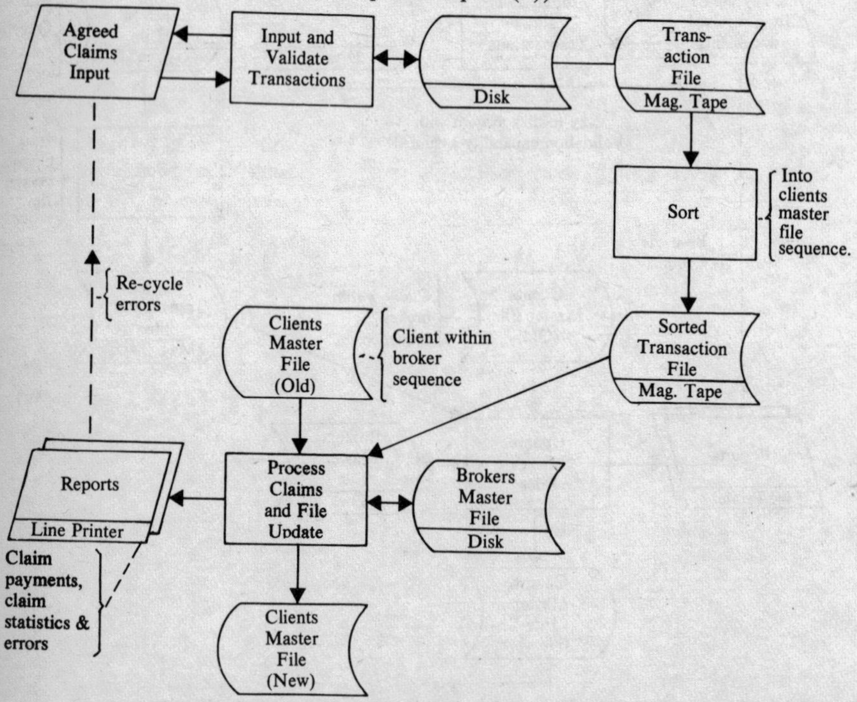

FIG. 45.7. WEEKLY PROCESSING OF AGREED CLAIMS.
(See question part (c))

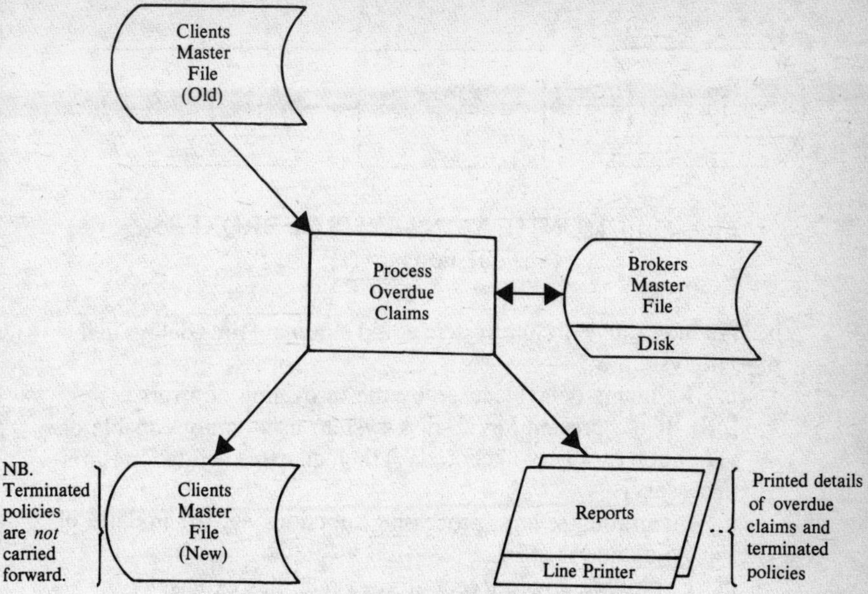

FIG. 45.8. WEEKLY PROCESSING FOR OVERDUE CLAIMS. (See question part (d))

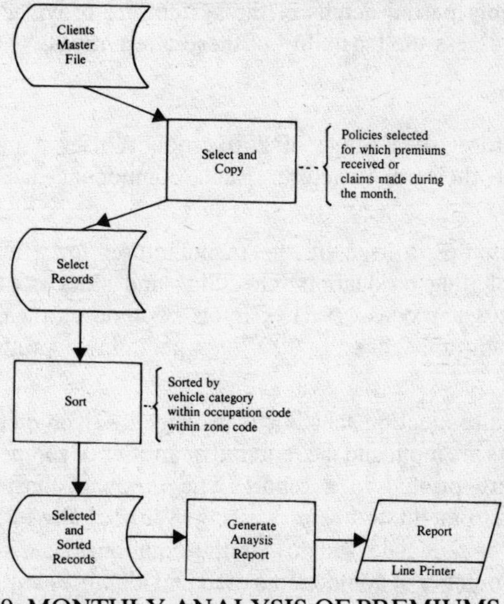

FIG. 45.9. MONTHLY ANALYSIS OF PREMIUMS RECEIVED AND CLAIMS. (See question part (e))

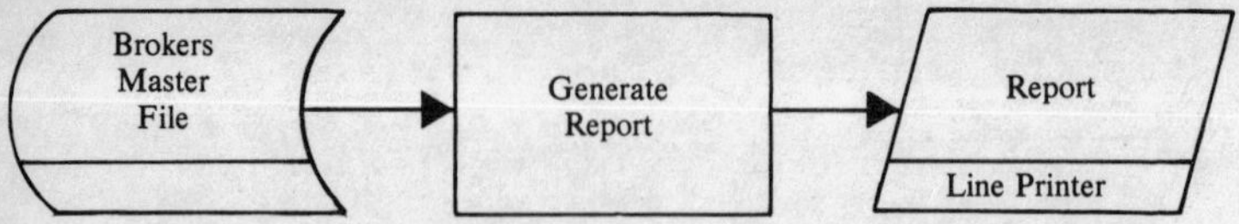

FIG. 45.10. MONTHLY ANALYSIS OF BROKERS.
(See question part (f))

b. An interactive on-line system could eliminate time delays in the present system by:-

i. Reducing delays caused by the re-cycling of errors.

[NB. If the present key-to-disk system used is not capable of validation (not very likely today) then an extra validation run is necessary]

ii. Integrating several processing functions eg. the updates of Fig. 45.5 and Fig. 45.7.

iii. Exploiting direct access storage facilities extensively.

The use of a distributed on-line system with terminals and local printers in brokers offices could be very fast and effective, but this would need a very thorough analysis and design process.

Since only partial details of the system are provided it is not possible to assess the feasibility of these alternatives.

QUESTION 4.

A manufacturer of a range of 200 products uses a number of components for their manufacture. Each component has its own supplier.

A mini-computer is used by the manufacturer for a number of applications including production scheduling and stock control. The system comprises a processor, 512k bytes of main storage, two 60 megabyte exchangeable disks, a 300 lines per minute printer and 6 VDUs.

Each week a production schedule is produced. Given quantities of selected products are input and the required quantities of components for each product are printed in a report. The products master file is structured so as to facilitate this processing. Without any further data entry, a report is produced which lists the components in sequence, details the total number of components used and identifies any products affected by insufficient component stock. Production is changed if necessary. The major items in the components file are as follows:-

Component number
Component description
Supplier code
Unit cost
Quantity in Stock (actual and committed)
Reorder details eg. reorder level
Quantity on order
Quantity used (year to date)

a. Draw systems flowcharts which show how the various processing procedures are carried out. Provide sufficient narrative to explain the system and indicate clearly the major items contained in any files used other than the components file.

b. When component prices change how can the affected products be identified? What changes to the system would make this identification simpler.

c. Suggest possible ways of improving the system.

[Part **(a)** 25 marks, part **(b)** 10 marks and part **(c)** 5 marks = **40 marks**]

ANSWER 4.

1. Author's preliminary notes.

a. Only part of the whole system has been described so this will be reflected in the answer to part (a) of the question.

b. It is the fact that there are many products, each containing many components, which causes the file organisation and processing problems in this application.

2. Suggested Solution.

a. i. The products file "facilitates" the production of the first report and is therefore assumed to have the following structure:-

Product number
Product name
Product description
Product stock details
Product cost {sum of component costs}
Component number } Repeated for each components
Quantity used } in component number sequence.

The file is sequenced on Product number.

ii. The Required products file records will contain these items.

Product number
Quantity to be manufactured.

iii. The Required components file will contain these items:-

Product number Component number Quantity required	One occurence of all three for each product – component pair.

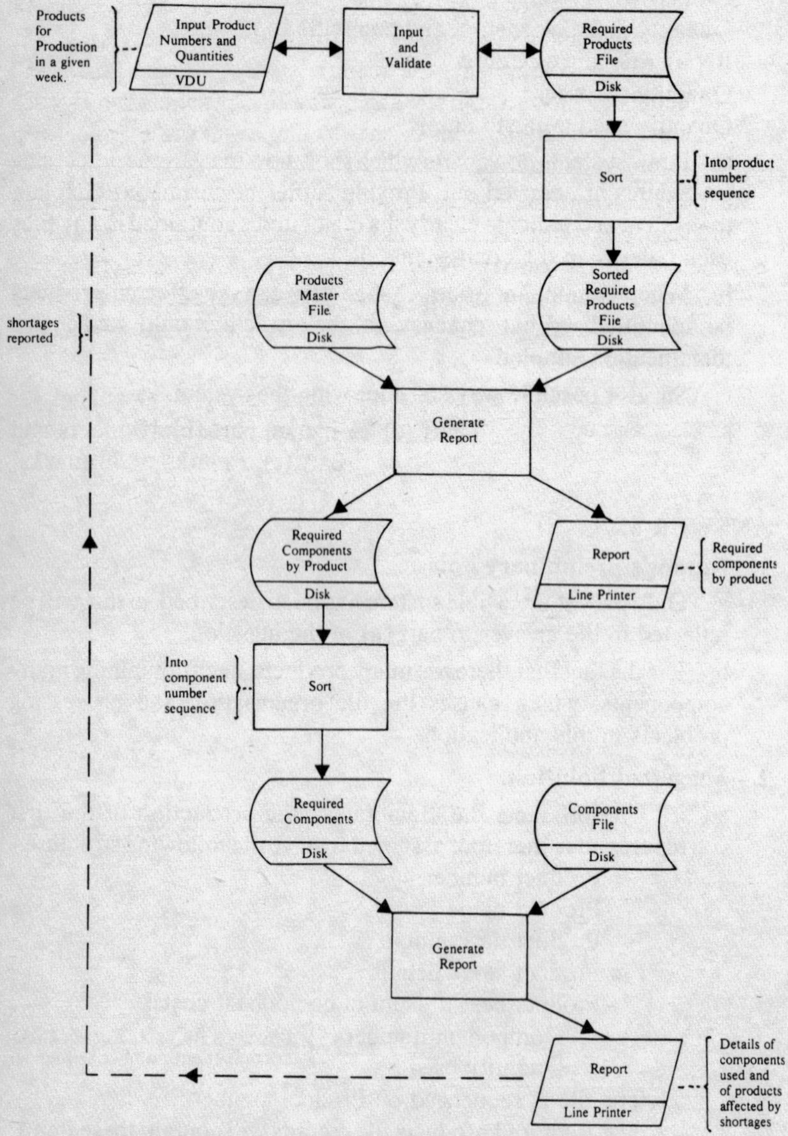

FIG. 45.11. SYSTEMS FLOWCHARTS.
(See question part (a))

b. i. If only a few component costs change then the details can be held in main storage and the products will be updated in a single pass. However, if a large number of component costs are changed a similar sorting procedure to that shown in Fig. 45.11 will be required. ie. product – component pairs must be identified and sorted into the appropriate sequences.

ii. If the components file records each contained "used-on" details of products, in the same way that products file records contains multiple component details, then some processing would be simplified.

c. It is clear that the organisation of the files to facilitate one processing activity can make another processing activity less easy. The solution in answer **(b)ii** leads to replication of data in the products and components file. The system could be improved by the the use of database system which would then support the variety of processing needs more easily.

The use of index files of product-component pairs and simpler product and component files might also be considered.

Appendix 1 Answers to all questions set at end of chapters.

Chapter 1.

ANSWER 1.

(1.2).

ANSWER 2.

(1.3).

ANSWER 3.

Possible advantages of batching.

a. Processing data in batches tends to be more efficient and economical than processing single transactions.

b. Batching provides manageable units for control purposes.

c. Processing can be left until slack times in some cases.

Possible disadvantages of batching.

a. Delays in obtaining information.

b. Correct transactions being delayed still further because of errors in other transactions in the same batch.

c. Uneven loads on the processing facilities.

Chapter 2.

ANSWER 1.

a. Using electronic means to manipulate collected or stored data in order to produce meaningful information.

b. (2.10).

Chapter 3.

ANSWER 1.

(3.5d).

ANSWER 2.

(Fig. 3.1) (3.10).

Chapter 4.

ANSWER 1.

a. (4.6).

b. (4.12).

ANSWER 2.

(4.40 – 4.41).

Chapter 5.

ANSWER 1.

(5.3g).

ANSWER 2.

5.34.

Chapter 6.

ANSWER 1.

Possible advantages.

a. No media costs or discarded paper output.

b. Can be used for characters or graphic display.

c. Fast display for enquiry handling.

Possible disadvantages.

a. Output is temporary and cannot be stored.

b. Possibly unpleasant for the eyes of view for long periods.

c. Only a small part of the information (1 screen full) can be viewed at a time.

ANSWER 2.

(6.25 – 6.27).

Possible advantages.

a. Saves storage space.

b. Saves the expense of printed output, as does a VDU, but has permanence.

c. Cheaper to distribute than bulky paper.

Possible disadvantages.

a. Can only be read by special viewer.

b. Cannot be annotated or corrected by hand.

c. Cost prevents frequent updates.

ANSWER 3.

a. (6.20).
b. (6.22).
c. (6.24).
d. (5.3h).

Chapter 7.

ANSWER 1.

a. 7.10.
b. 7.14.
c. 7.12b.
d. 7.14.

ANSWER 2.

(7.13).

Chapter 8.

ANSWER 1.

(8.9).

ANSWER 2.

(8.1).

Chapter 9.

ANSWER 1.

9.25 – 9.28.

Uses: Microcomputer – Personal Computer, Word processor.
Minicomputer – Small multi-user order processing.
Mainframe – DP applications such as Payroll in a large corporation.

Chapter 10.

ANSWER 1.

i. Data transmission (10.5.)
ii. Data Storage (5.33).
iii. Data input/output (5.2 – 4).
iv. Data security (Fig. 5.5).

ANSWER 2.

a. (10.24).

b. (10.10 – 10.11).

c. (Fig. 10.4) (Fig. 4.5).

d. (Fig. 10.4).

e. (10.13).

f. (10.5).

g. (10.6).

ANSWER 3.

(10.21).

Chapter 11.

ANSWER 1.

a. 10.1.

b. 10.10.

c. 10.11-19 inclusive.

Chapter 12.

ANSWER 1.

a. 12.2, Fig. 5.6.

b. 12.4, Fig. 11.3.

ANSWER 2.

12.1-11 inclusive.

ANSWER 3.

(Fig. 5.6)	(Fig. 5.6)	(7.15 & check channel in Fig. 5.6)
(Fig. 12.3)	(Fig. 12.3)	(Fig. 12.3)
(Fig. 12.4)	(Fig. 12.4)	(Fig. 5.5)

(Read head following and checking the the writehead)

Chapter 13.

ANSWER 1.

The main types of storage are:-

(IAS) Immediate access storage eg. RAM.

(DAS) Direct access storage eg. magnetic disk.

(SAS) Serial access storage eg. magnetic tape.

The tasks that they are best suited to carry out are:-

a. **Immediate access.** Because of its unique electronic properties giving extremely quick access to stored data this type of storage is used as the computer's *main storage.* Access to individual characters/bytes is completely independent of their position in store. It is in the main storage that the programs are held during processing so that their instructions can be executed swiftly. also the particular data currently being worked on is held in main storage. Ideally, IAS would be used for storage of all data because it is fast in operation. This is not practicable because of cost and its use therefore is limited to main storage. Thus some alternative form must be found for storing the files and data which are not immediately required by the program.

b. **Direct access.** One such alternative is DAS. Storage capacity can vary from thousands to hundreds of millions of characters. DAS has the important facility of allowing direct access, that its records can be accessed independently of each other. It is thus suitable for files being processed in a selective manner, also for storing programs and systems software which are required to be called into main storage at any time during the running of an application program. It is an essential requirement for on-line processing or where file-interrogation facilities are needed.

c. **Serial access.** If bulky auxiliary storage is required and the need for random access is not present then the choice may well fall on SAS the most common form of which is magnetic tape. It is also cheaper than RAM disk or drum. Because of its inherent serial nature, access to a record on tape is a function of its position on the tape. Therefore every preceding record on a master file must be read (and written out onto the new tape) before the required record can be located. Nevertheless millions of characters can be stored very cheaply.

CONCLUSION.

IAS is the ideal storage medium but is very expensive. If bulk storage is required combined with facility for random access then the less expensive DAS is indicated. If the limitations of Serial Access are no serious hindrance then the cheapest form of store ie. SAS can be used.

ANSWER 2.

'Basic Principles' 13.1-19 (NOTE. cylinder concept in key).
'Index Sequential' 13.20c, 13.21c.

ANSWER 3.

See answer 1.

Note: Internal Storage (Immediate Access Storage).
External Storage (DAS and SAS)

See also 8.2.

ANSWER 4.

a. 5.33-5.34, 8.5-8.9.

b. 13.21.

Chapter 15.

ANSWER 1.

14.6.
15.12.

ANSWER 2.

MICR – Bank Cheques, Insurance returns.
OCR – Giro Cheques, Billing.
BADGE READERS – Product Pricing for PoS, Employee clock recording.
BAR MARKING – PoS, Library Cards.

Chapter 16.

ANSWER 1.

INTRODUCTION.

1. It *must* be noted that advantages and disadvantages are relative. Also in many cases a user will disregard certain disadvantages of being of no consequences, or will be obliged to adopt a method *despite* its disadvantages. Finally, as has already been pointed out in the text, some methods will be better suited for certain applications than others.

KEY-TO-DISK (Key Processing).

2. Possible advantages.

a. Data is keyed onto magnetic tape which is a fast input medium.

b. A certain amount of validation can be done off-line (to the main computer).

c. Incorporates control totals.

d. There are no cards etc. to be handled by operators (nor tapes for that matter).

e. Error correction is more easily accomplished than with punched cards.

f. Quieter and cleaner (no card dust) than card machine (it is electronic).

g. Only one tape reel involved (compare key-to-tape). Fewer operators may be required than for punched cards or paper tape.

h. Once data has been keyed onto disk verification can be carried out from any of the key-stations.

3. Possible disadvantages.

a. All key stations are linked to *one* processor – if the processor breaks down all key-processing ceases.

b. A relatively high capital outlay needs large volumes of data to justify it.

KEY-TO-TAPE (ENCODING).

4. Possible advantages.

a. Data is encoded direct onto magnetic tape.

b. There is no card handling involved.

c. Error correction is easier than with punched cards.

5. Possible disadvantages.

a. Tapes have to be re-loaded to verify (not with key-to-disk).

b. Tapes have to be pooled before input (not with key-to-disk).

c. Not so flexible as key-to-disk in terms of program capability.

MAGNETIC TAPE CASSETTE.

6. Possible Advantages.

a. Can be prepared as a by-product.

b. Inexpensive.

c. Easily transportable.

7. Possible disadvantages.

a. Slower input than ½″ tape.

b. Smaller capacity of cassette.

KEY-TO-DISKETTE.

8. Possible advantages.

a. Data is encoded directly onto the diskette.

b. There is no card handling involved.

c. Error correction is easy.

d. Diskettes are easily transportable.

9. Possible disadvantages.

a. Diskette needs careful handling.

OCR.

10. Possible advantages.

a. No transcription is required, thus there are no errors in the data preparation stage.

b. Characters are both human and machine-sensible.

c. Documents prepared in OC are suitable for use as turnaround documents.

11. Possible disadvantages.

a. A high standard printing of optical characters is required.

b. High document standards are needed to keep down error rejections.

c. The cost of readers/scanners is relatively high, especially those used on-line to the computer.

MICR.

12. Advantages and disadvantages as for OCR except that print tolerances are much stricter.

Possible disadvantage.

a. Very high degree of accurancy required in forming characters.

PUNCHED TAGS.

13. Possible advantages.

a. Data is captured at source.

b. Data collection is done mainly by machine (handling excluded).

c. Sales attendant's job is simplified as data is already recorded.

14. Possible disadvantages.

a. There are limits to the amount of data which can be stored in tags.

b. Problems arise if (in retailing) goods are marked down in price.

c. Tags are small and present handling problems.

PLASTIC BADGES.

15. Possible advantages.

a. Plastic badges are able to withstand much handling and are suitable for shop floor systems are ordinary employees can operate the machines.

b. The collection system is mechanised.

c. The data recording machines can be linked directly to the computer.

16. Possible disadvantages.

a. Limited scope.

b. The recording machines are operated by the workers themselves.

ON-LINE SYSTEMS.

17. Possible advantages.

a. Transcription can be eliminated.

b. Speeds up entry of data to the computer and return of processed information.

c. Cuts down delays in dealing with error rejections.

18. Possible disadvantage.

a. Cost is considerable.

Chapter 17.

ANSWER 1.

17.10.

ANSWER 2.

17.5.
17.8-9.

ANSWER 3.

Coding Systems. Coding of items, for ease of identification, is well established in many areas independent of the use of Computers. A popular type of coding system is the 'Facet Code' where, the characters of the code are sub-divided into groups, each of which has a meaningful interpretation. Take, for example, the postal codes assigned to every address in the U.K. The first two characters indicate the district, eg. SO for Southampton, BH for Bournemouth, the next two digits identify the local area within the district, and so on down to a group of houses. This is also an example of a hierarchical code.

The Need for Coding Systems. The computer is unable without very sophisticated programming, to match successfully names or descriptions. This can be seen quite easily by considering the type of name which may be given to accounting codes. Even allowing for mis-spelling, names may vary when in common use, either by abbreviation or by paraphrase so it is better to assign a unique code which will not vary and is also, as a general rule, much shorter than the corresponding description.

Advantages from the use of Meaningful Codes.

a. As already discussed there is recognition without ambiguity.

b. The code may assist in computer file organisation. For direct access files a part of the code number may be used to generate the sector or bucket address. For serial access files, the code may be used to determine the sorted sequence of the file and hence assist in the organisation of the tabulations by ensuring that items are grouped together in respective categories.

c. A meaningful code assists the users in assigning the correct identifier to a transaction.

d. In addition, the user may undertake, possibly unknowingly, a feasibility check on the code if, say, goods are being supplied to a code which indicates something other than a customer.

e. The elements of the code may be further subjected to validation by the computer input program. This may extend the feasibility checks mentioned in the previous point and also include tests for format, range and check digit.

ANSWER 4.

Validation (17.8-9).
Data prep. (12.6-7; 12.10).

Chapter 18.
ANSWER 1.

INTRODUCTION.
1. Data has to be presented to the computer in a form which is acceptable as input (so called machine-sensible form). This *capturing* of data can be accomplished in many ways, using different input media. A summary of the main methods and media is given below:

NO	METHOD OF DATA CAPTURE	MEDIA USED
1	On-line (to computer)	Data transmission terminals, plastic badges etc.
2	Character recognition	Source documents using OCR; MICR or OMR.
3	Manual encoding	Magnetic tape (using encoders).
4	Manual encoding	Magnetic tape via disk (using Computer-controlled Data Entry Systems).
5	By-product	Cassettes/Diskettes, paper tape, tally rolls with cash registers, typewriters, etc.

STAGES INVOLVED IN DATA CAPTURE.
2. a. Clerically produced source documents.

b. Transcription into machine-sensible form.

c. Verification of transcription stage.

d. Getting source data or input to processing centre.

e. Finally input to computer (possibly not *strictly* regarded as data capture as such).

BASIC PROBLEMS.
3. a. **Accuracy and validity** of data when finally input to computer.

b. **Form of source data** which in many cases means a clerically produced document and indifferent document standards.

c. **Cost** of machinery, operators and buildings etc. which sometimes equals that of the computer system itself.

d. **Time.** Many of the methods outlined are cumbersome and very time consuming.

e. **Volumes of data.** Increasing volumes of data, indicating the need for more sophisticated methods of data capture.

f. **Movement of data** (in raw or transcribed form) to the central processing point present problems of packaging, delay, loss etc.

g. **Control.** With so many stages involved with some methods the problem of controlling and co-ordinating the whole is far from easy.

DISCUSSION OF PROBLEMS AND SOLUTIONS.

4. a. **Accuracy.** This problem is most acute with method 3 which requires *verification* to reduce errors made by punch operators. Even so errors will creep through and there is a necessity for a computer check of input. Limited *validity* checking can be carried out by the *computer.* Methods 4 and 5 (especially 5) claim increased accuracy and certain validity checks can be done *off-line.*

b. **Form of source data.** On-line systems can do away with source document, which is the ideal solution. Method 2 (character recognition) avoids the need for transcription especially with the use of the *"turn around"* document. Method 6 (By-product) also enables the source data to be produced in a machine-sensible form. (Example – Cash Registers equipped with Paper Tape rolls which capture data as sale is entered). Kimball tags also obviate the need for a manually scribed document.

c. **Cost.** Each method is going to cost a great deal but Computer-controlled Data Entry is probably more cost effective in large installations than its predecessor – Manul Key Punching (fewer operators, but higher machine costs).

d. **Time.** Method 1 gets over this problem by capturing data at source and putting it *directly* into computer. The methods which employ more machinery and fewer humans are likely to be more efficient in this respect.

e. **Volumes.** Similarly increased volumes point to the choice of on-line systems, Character Recognition, or Computer-controlled Data Entry as appropriate.

f. **Movement.** The solution is the use of on-line system or something approaching it.

g. **Control.** The methods which eliminate the most stages in data capture will be the answer. This points again to on-line systems and to a lesser degree Character Recognition, and Computer-controlled Data Entry (and possibly By-product).

CONCLUSION.

5. The capture of raw data for use within a computer system is a time-consuming and costly affair. The basic underlying problem is the interface of the slow human with the high speed computer.

The ultimate solution must be to capture data at its point of origin in a machine-sensible form, thus eliminating the many stages involved at present in getting it into such a form.

However it is as well to appreciate that very often *cost* and the *appropriateness* of a method of data capture to a particular application will be very important factors influencing choice.

ANSWER 2.

6. a. **Data Communication** is concerned with the physical transportation of both input and output data or information as well as the automatic transmission of digital data over telephone networks to remote location either on-line or off-line.

The context of the question is assumed to be the latter. Off-line transmission means data transmission by equipment not under the control of the central processor. For example, a branch office may use by-product paper tape as the means of data capture in an order processing system. At the end of the day, and using cheap rates for transmission, the tape may be loaded into a paper tape reader and transmitted to the central office for a daily sensitive sales analysis. On-line transmission implies that the equipment is under the control of the central processor, for example the many airline and hotel reservation systems.

b. The equipment is shown in the diagram and consists of a terminal device, a modem, transmission lines, and a multiplexor or front-end processor.

Terminals may vary from the conventional teletypewriter and visual display units through the complete range of input and output peripheral devices to the use of small computers themselves as terminals as, for example in the British Rail TOPS system where remote minicomputers are used in marshalling yards for local processing as well as being used as intelligent terminals for the receipt and transmission of information on-line to the central computer.

Transmission Lines fall into three main categories, a local line which is sometimes termed 'hard-wired' since it is a direct line from terminal to computer although it will almost certainly have a plug on each end for possible exchange with another system. This line is only suitable for distances of up to a hundred feet or so, the quoted distance varies between sources and is really a matter for local conditions to determine in practice. The second type of line is the BT telegraph line on the Telex system either using the public network or a private line which may be cheaper for heavy use and less prone to interference in signal. This service is called Datel 100 and is, in practice, limited to speeds of about 10 characters per second. The third type of line is the STD speech network, again either on a public or a private line and this will cope with much faster transmission speeds but requires a special interface unit called a modem.

Modems are required for transmission of data over the STD network. Their basic function is to convert the signal from the terminal or computer into different form suitable for transmission over long distance on the STD line, essentially into a sound. The models of modem vary in specification and price according to the required transmission speed.

Multiplexor, although having a special meaning, is a general term used to describe the special piece of hardware required on the computer to receive and decode the messages received from a number of different terminals and, when a complete message has been collected, to pass it on to the central processor for action. This function may be very complex and on some systems there is a separate computer processor devoted to this activity and this is called a "front-end processor'.

c. The use of this equipment is, by no means, confined to bureaux and is used extensively in banks, airlines, schools and colleges for processing student programs, and in many large companies with branches linked to a central computer service.

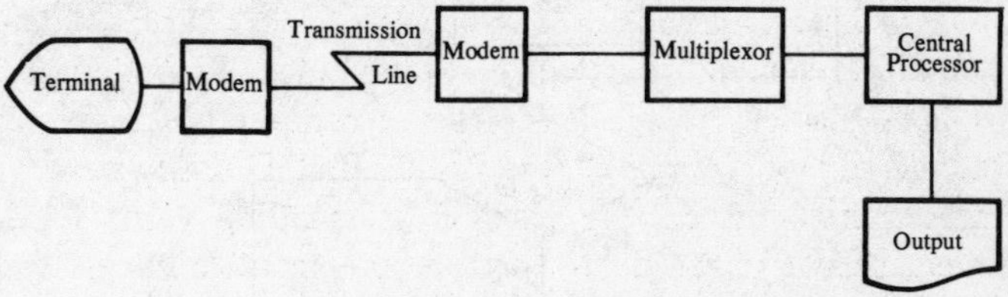

ANSWER 3.

(18.8 & 18.12).

ANSWER 4.

(18.10-18.11).

Chapter 19.

ANSWER 1.

(19.19) Pseudocode.

Chapter 20.

ANSWER 1.

a. i. Flowchart (showing the clerical procedure for working out discount entitlement).

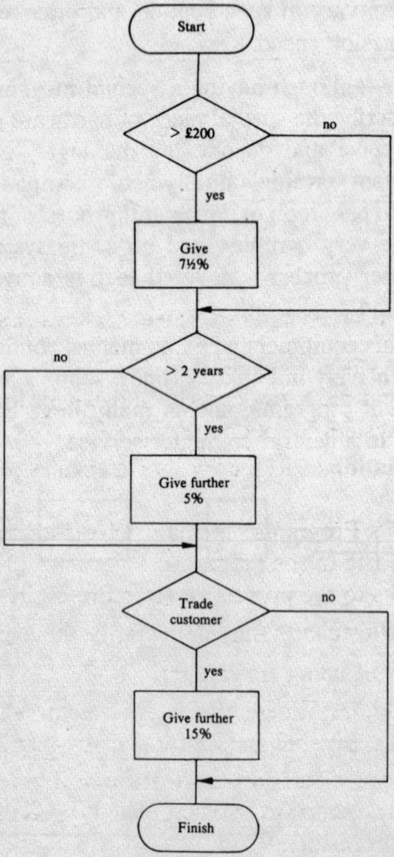

a. ii. Limited entry decision table.

CONDITIONS	RULES							
	1	2	3	4	5	6	7	8
> £200	Y	Y	Y	Y	N	N	N	N
Customer for over 2 yrs	Y	Y	N	N	Y	Y	N	N
Trade customer	Y	N	Y	N	Y	N	Y	N
ACTIONS								
Nil								x
5%						x		
7½%				x				
12½%		x						
15%							x	
20%					x			
22½%			x					
27½%	x							

Key:-	
	Y = Yes N = No x = Action to be taken.

1. b.

Advantages and disadvantages of flowcharts and decision tables.

1. Advantages of using flowcharts.

a. **Communication.** Flowcharts are a visual aid for communicating the logic of a system to all concerned.

b. **Documentation.** Flowcharts are a means of documentation because:-

i. Analysts/Programmers may leave the firm or they may forget the logic of the program.

ii. Changes to the procedure are more easily catered for.

c. **Analysis.** Flowcharts may help clarify the logic of a system.

2. Disadvantages of using flowcharts.

a. **Complex logic.** Where the logic is *complex,* the flowchart quickly becomes cluttered and lacks the clarity of the decision table.

b. **Link between conditions and actions.** It is not always clear, when looking at an action to be taken, exactly what the conditions are for that action to result.

c. **Alterations.** If alterations are required, the flowchart may require re-drawing completely.

d. **Reproduction.** As the flowchart symbols cannot be typed, reproduction of Flowcharts is often a problem.

e. Also see 18.19.

3. Advantages of using decision tables.

a. **Condition rules.** All possible combinations of conditions can be mathematically worked out. It is therefore possible to ensure that the *right number* of combinations have been considered. It is also possible to ensure that each combination is unique.

b. **Format.** The format is standardised, thus aiding training and communication.

c. **Reproduction.** As the tables can be typed, reproduction is not a problem.

d. **Link between conditions and actions.** It is simple to see the conditions applying to particular actions – consequently the *testing* of the logic is simplified.

4. Disadvantages of using decision tables.

a. **Total sequence.** The total sequence is not clearly shown, ie. no *overall* picture is given as with flowcharts.

b. **Logic.** where the logic of a system is *simple*, flowcharts nearly always serve the purpose better.

ANSWER 2

a.

CONDITIONS	RULES							
	1	2	3	4	5	6	7	8
Acceptable Academic Qualifications	Y	Y	Y	Y	N	N	N	N
Completed Training Course	Y	Y	N	N	Y	Y	N	N
Recommended by head	Y	N	Y	N	Y	N	Y	N
ACTIONS								
Grade 'A'	✓		✓		✓			
Grade 'A' Under Review		✓						
Grade 'B' Provisional							✓	
Grade 'B'				✓		✓		✓

b. (See answer to 1(a.)).

Chapter 21.

ANSWER 1.

```
BEGIN
  IF  Order > 200 THEN
        Give 7½% discount
  ENDIF
  IF  Period of ordering > 2 THEN
        Give further 5% discount
  ENDIF
  IF  Trade customer THEN
        Give further 15% discount
  ENDIF
END
```

ANSWER 2.

The types of validation checks that would be applied depend upon the actual details of the order. It is assumed that the following are entered customer number, quantities ordered, catalogue numbers, size codes, colour codes (with first and second choices where appropriate) cash paid, type of order (cash, credit), date of order.

1. **Invalid characters.** All fields would be examined for invalid characters, eg. the customer number field would be checked to make sure that all characters were numeric.

2. **Range check.** A check would be made to ensure that numbers came within specific ranges, eg. that the catalogue numbers were between say, 20000 and 60000.

3. **Reasonableness check.** A check would be made on order quantities, to ensure that abnormal amounts have not been punched in error, eg. 10 pairs of the same shoes.

4. **Completeness check.** A check would be made to ensure that all the fields that *must* have an entry *do* in fact have an entry, eg. that an entry *has* been made in the "cash paid" field but not necessarily in a "second choice" field.

5. **Control totals.** Control totals of quantities ordered and/or number of items in a batch would be compared with an accumulation during the validation run.

6. **Order quantity availability.** A check would be made on the availability of stock or second choice where applicable.

7. **Credit control.** A check would be made on credit requirements, eg. that a satisfactory deposit has been received relative to the size of order.

8. **Check digit verification.** Check digit calculations would be made on the account number and catalogue numbers.

ANSWER 3.

21.23-31.

ANSWER 4.

a. A series of repeated program instructions (Fig. 19.8).

b. A point in a program where alternative actions are selected according to the result of testing a condition (as in the start of an IF-THEN. . . Fig. 19.8).

c. 21.27.

d. A point in a program where the sequence of instructions is always changed to continue at another point.

e. A data value to be taken literally eg. "N".

Chapter 22.

ANSWER 1.

The advantages and disadvantages of high level languages are:-

Advantages.

a. Program writing is less complex because of the use of vocabulary which is relatively simple to learn.

b. As program writing takes less time, programmers are therefore more efficiently utilised.

c. Amendments during program writing are easily incorporated and subsequent revision of the whole program is readily accomplished.

d. Extensive use of macros and sub-routines (both those of the manufacturer and the user) is permitted.

e. High level languages are independent of the computer compared with low level languages.

f. Source programs can be understood by people other than the person who wrote them.

Disadvantages.

a. A large number of rules have to be adhered to.

b. Object programs tend to be less efficient in terms of main storage utilisation and running time. (This occurs because of the generalised nature of the compiler's operation).

ANSWER 2.

SOFTWARE.

1. In its general form software is the term used to describe *all* programs. More specifically it describes those programs supplied by manufacturers or software houses and thus excludes user application programs.

2. Software (using the specific meaning) can be divided into:

a. **Systems software** such as:-
   - i. Compilers.
   - ii. Operating systems.
   - iii. Service programs eg. sort, media conversion.

b. **Application packages** such as:-
   - i. Payroll.
   - ii. Network analysis.

3. a. Systems software is designed with a particular family of machines in mind.

i. **Compilers.** This is an item of software which translates the source programs into the language of the machine thus making for better utilisation of programmers.

ii. **Operating systems.** This is the controller of programs and makes possible more efficient use of the hardware.

iii. **Service programs.** These perform a range of utility operations which every user has a need for in his installation.

b. **Application packages.** These are "off the peg" application programs which save the user having to write them himself.

c. **Data Base Management Systems.** These programs create, maintain and retrieve data from a data base.

SUB-ROUTINES.

4. A sub-routine (or sub-program) is a standard set of instructions designed to perform a specified task. Very often a particular set of instructions will be performed at several different *points* in a program and by many different *programs.* Such instructions are formed into a sub-routine and stored on a direct access storage device. At the point in a program when the sub-routine is required it will be "called" into main storage. A branch is made from the main program to the sub-routine and the particular instructions are executed, whereupon a branch is made back to the main program.

5. Examples of a sub-routine. One designed to check for errors in transmission of data between an input unit and the central processing unit. Each time a 'read' instruction is executed a "read error" indicator is examined. If the indicator has been turned "on" the computer is instructed to enter the sub-routine which will attempt to correct the error.

LOOPS.

6. a. A loop is a series of program instructions which are executed repeatedly until a certain condition is reached, whereupon a branch is made to another part of the program. The number of times the loop is repeated can be determined by a counter.

b. A computer program itself can be thought of as a loop because it is cycled through once for each of a batch of transaction records that is processed. Within each program will be smaller loops. Consider the set of instructions required to locate a particular master record on a tape file. The program will go round the loop reading successive records into main storage until the appropriate record is found.

COMPILER.

7. a. Programs are now written in a "source" language which is convenient to the programmer (eg. COBOL). The source programs are then translated into the language of the machine in order that they may be used in the computer.

b. The translation process is actually done by a computer and is briefly described:-

i. The source language program is created in a source program file by using an Editor.

ii. The source program is used as input to a "compilation" run. source program translated into machine language.

c. The 'translation' program used in this process is called the COMPILER.

AUTHORS' COMMENTS.

1. The examiner only required notes on two out of three, but all three were included for the students' benefit.

ANSWER 3.

a. "Characteristics of" – 22.18.
"Advantages of" – See Answer 1.

b. Fig. 22.3.

ANSWER 4.

22.18.
22.25.

Chapter 24.

ANSWER 1.

Amend Fig. 24.7 and convert into flowchart form using Fig. 19.8. The amendments are quite small ie. you need only change the procedure "Process-the-transaction".

Chapter 25.
ANSWER 1.

a.

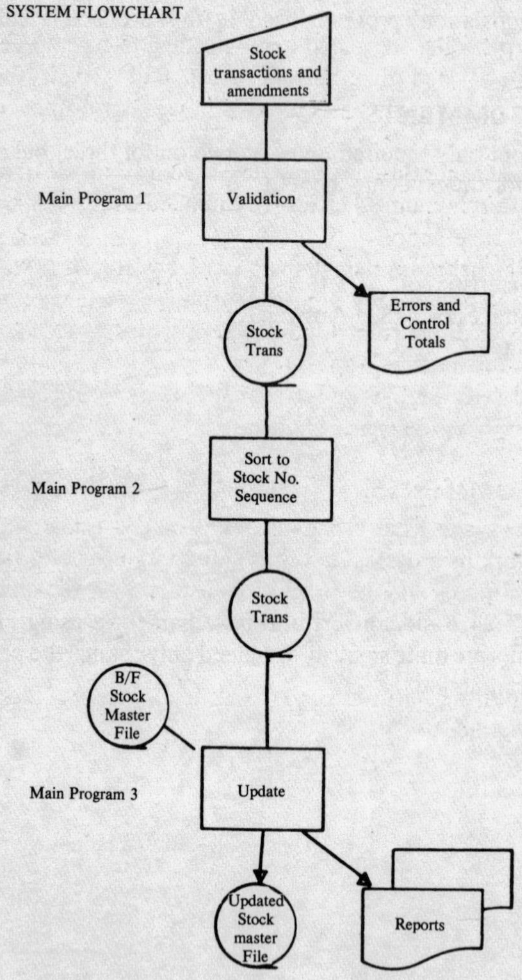

b. i. **Receipts.** Details of goods received, via goods received notes, for increasing the stock level, and reducing 'on order' level.

Allocations. Details of goods earmarked for a particular purpose (but not yet issued), to decrease 'free stock'.

Orders. Details of goods on order, via purchase orders, for increasing 'on order' level.

Master file amendments. Changes to the 'standing' data on a stock file eg. new stock item; change in maximum/minimum stock level.

ii. **Re-order list** suggested items needing to be re-ordered, in the light of lead time/current 'free stock' level. Probably provided on a weekly basis to cover a weeks worth of re-order work.

Stock exception report. Items going outside limits eg. maximum/minimum stock levels. Supplied each processing run for immediate action.

Order progress list. Items on order where 'progress' date reached. Supplied each processing run for immediate action.

Outstanding order value. Value of all orders outstanding to aid cash forecasting. Supplied monthly.

Audit trial. A list of all movements on each stock record, for audit purposes. Supplied monthly.

AUTHORS' COMMENTS.

Stock control systems can be very complex indeed, especially where raw material, work in progress and finished stocks are held. Issues of standard product parts may be 'exploded' before passing against the stock file and there may be links between a suggested re-order requirements file and the supplier file to provide suggested suppliers.

Magnetic tape has been used for the stock master files but disks could be used if appropriate.

ANSWER 2.

a. Fig. 8.1.

b. 13.26.

Chapter 26.

ANSWER 1.

a. 26.7-8.
b. 26.31.
c. 26.9-23.

ANSWER 2.

a. 26.7.
b. i. Data is pooled.
   ii. Consistency of stored data.
   iii. Controlled redundancy.
   iv. Access control.
   v. Program independence.
   See also (26.31).
c. i. The DBMS requires additional processor time – slowness.
   ii. The generalised nature of the stored data created an overhead in data storage and retrieval.
   iii. The implementation requires special analysis and design skills.
d. As in 11.3.

Chapter 27.

ANSWER 1.

27.6 a-d.
27.7-32.

Chapter 28.

ANSWER 1.

28.20b.
28.21-28.

Chapter 31.

ANSWER 1.

A critical examination is needed because there are reasons for carrying out each step in the present system. These reasons must be discovered and questioned to see if they *need* to be incorporated in the new system.

ANSWER 2.

a. Three from:
   - i. Interview.
   - ii. Questionnaires.
   - iii. Observation.
   - iv. Record inspection.

b. (31.4).

Chapter 32.

ANSWER 1.

Basically the choice of output depends on its subsequent use, or the type of application.

CHOICE ACCORDING TO SUBSEQUENT USE.

1. Output can be produced for use by humans or for use by machine:-

a. **Use by humans.** Output for use by humans must be in a form understood by humans so we have the following:-

   i. **Printed output.** Either on pre-printed stationery or plain paper and in various formats.

   ii. **Visual display.** Output in the form of script or graphs etc, displayed on a screen.

   iii. **Microform.** Output required for storage and subsequent reference.

b. **Further use by machines.** Output for use by machines will be prepared in a machine-sensible form. The following are examples:-

   i. **For subsequent re-input into computer.** Such output can be prepared on magnetic tape, disk etc. as appropriate. For example, output which goes directly to another run as input.

   ii. **Output converted off-line to another medium.** Magnetic tape may be used for output from an updating run which is subsequently printed as an off-line operation.

iii. **Transmission of output.** Output to be transmitted over communication lines will need to be in a form acceptable to the transmission device.

CHOICE ACCORDING TO TYPE OF APPLICATION.

2. Choice of output will vary with applications, one type of output being more appropriate to one application than another:-

a. **Batch processing.** Output will be on magnetic tape or disk if spooling techniques are used.

b. **Real-time processing.** The use of data communication devices is essential so that output can be transmitted immediately to the control point (a terminal).

c. **Interrogation or enquiry.** A visual display or terminal is the choice where immediate response to enquiries for information held on master files is required. These can be located locally or at a remote point.

d. **Turnaround document.** Used where output subsequently re-enters the computer system without there being any intermediate off-line coding process. To achieve this, output documents can be prepared in optical characters. Such documents can also be read by humans.

Note:
There is an obvious overlapping between 1 and 2.

ANSWER 2.

INTRODUCTION.

1. Even in these days of increasing automation, labour can still represent a *significant* proportion of overall production cost. Therefore no effort should be spared in using scientific methods to get maximum utilisation of this expensive commodity in pursuance of the production objective.

Undoubtedly the use of a computer will enable control information to be produced more *quickly* than before, thus enabling decisions to be made on more *up-to-date* information.

Also, analysis will be possible to a far *greater extent* with a computer because of its ability to sift *large* volumes of data at electronic *speeds.* Therefore plans, which are the basis of control, can be laid with far greater precision and confidence and are, as a result, more realistic.

Although we are concerned here, only with "labour control", to be successful any system of control must be integrated ie. labour, material, machinery and finance.

CONTROL INFORMATION SPECIFIED.

2. Routine.

a. Budgeted labour requirements in terms of man-hours and cost based on production budgets. This will be broken down by departments shop etc. and type and grade of labour.

b. Departmental and shop efficiency reports for period including comparisons with previous periods. These will show (in terms of actual and budgeted):

- i. Labour cost per unit of output.
- ii. Output per operator hour.
- iii. Labour rates.
- iv. Bonuses.

c. Analysis of labour cost into direct and indirect.

d. Analysis of *indirect* labour cost by category eg:

- i. Maintenance.
- ii. Supervison.
- iii. Materials handling.
- iv. Inspection.

Where possible, utilisation of *indirect* labour should be linked to *levels of activity* as a means of control.

e. Indices of operator performance highlighting persistent "below par" individuals. These are especially important when workers are paid a guaranteed rate.

f. Reports on *overtime* premiums paid.

g. Information on mis-use of grades of labour (eg. expensive high grade labour employed on low grade work).

h. Analysis of *idle-time* by cause eg:

- i. Machine breakdown.
- ii. No work etc.

i. Absenteeism and lateness reports.

j. Labour turnover analysed by age, sex, department, etc.

3. Ad Hoc.

a. Alternative *labour utilisation* as a result of major machine breakdowns or material storage.

b. Effect on *labour planning* of additional production requirements.

c. Effects of increased wages award on costs of production.

d. Breakdown of labour force, by age, sex, grade/trade, department.

CONCLUSION.

4. Not all information would be provided in the same amount of detail. The foreman would require detailed reports on a weekly, if not a daily, basis while higher levels of management would receive more summarized information probably at larger intervals of time.

The main thing to recognise is that the computer is able to sift large amounts of data, taking into account all variables and provides the information necessary for day to day running of the shop floor, and also for the longer term manpower planning.

DRAFT OUTPUT DOCUMENT.

5.

OPERATOR PERFORMANCE ASSEMBLY DEPT				WEEK NO 4			
CLOCK NO	NAME	STD HRS PRODUCED	HRS WORKED	% EFFICIENCY			
				WK 4	WK 3	WK 2	WK 1

AUTHORS' COMMENTS.

1. Almost any output document could be compiled along lines indicated in your answer. The one illustrated would serve to highlight below-par performers and enable the reasons to be investigated.

ANSWER 3.

The major principles of good form design – 32.9c.

Any form, that you have used, can illustrate:-

To: Managing Director — Form No. 1234

AREA SALES ANALYSIS — March 1976

	THIS MONTH			THIS YEAR		
	Budget	Actual	Variance	Budget	Actual	Variance
	£'000s'	£'000s'	£'000s'	£'000s'	£'000s'	£'000s'
London						
Birmingham						
Bristol						
Other						
TOTALS						

Illustrates:- Brief Explanatory Title; Vertical Spacing; Column Widths; Standard Size (A4/A5); Pre Printing of Standard Details.

Chapter 33.

ANSWER 1.

(33.7 – 33.10).

ANSWER 2.

SOURCE PROGRAM.

1. a. A source program is a computer program written in a *symbolic* language, which is subsequently translated into a machine language program.

OBJECT PROGRAM.

b. The machine language program referred to in a. above is known as the object program.

RELATIONSHIP BETWEEN SOURCE AND OBJECT PROGRAMS.

2. a. The "language" a computer understands consists of the particular machine codes built into its design.

b. Earlier computer programs were prepared in this *actual* machine language. This was time consuming and prone to error and today programs are first written in some form of symbolic language and *then* translated into the machine code.

c. This translation process is actually carried out by the computer using a translation program called a compiler, and is very simply illustrated in the following diagram.

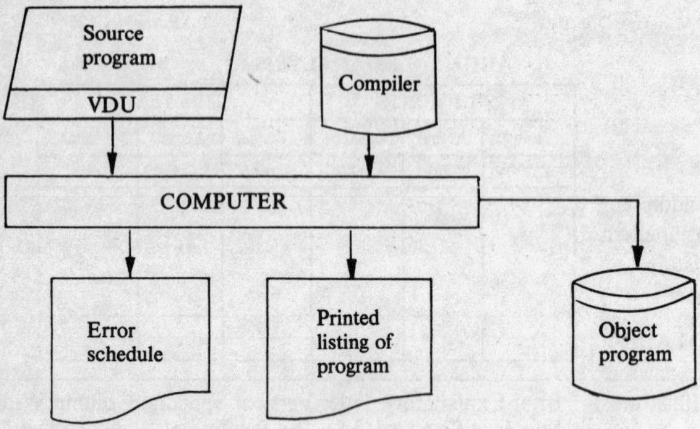

PREPARATION OF FULLY TESTED OBJECT PROGRAM.

3. Steps in preparing a fully tested object program are:

a. Prepare program coding sheets in symbolic language, from the program flowchart or pseudocode.

b. Check and enter symbolic statements using an editor.

c. The compiler program is loaded into the computer.

d. The source program is treated as input data to the compilation process and an object program is produced as output.

e. A printed listing of the object program is also produced as output; also a schedule of errors.

f. The object program, with the compilation errors rectified is then subjected to a test of its logic using test data.

g. Any logic errors are now put right and the compilation procedure repeated if necessary.

h. The tested and proved object program is then ready for operational running.

Note:

1. The errors found during compilation will have occurred during the writing of the program in accordance with the "rules" of the particular language. Such errors are called "errors of syntax".

2. The errors found during testing (3f) will be "errors of logic" ie. the program as written does not accurately reflect the procedure.

AUTHORS' COMMENTS.

1. Note the three main elements:-

a. Source program.

b. Object program.

c. Compiler/assembler.

2. Generally speaking an assembler is used for translating source programs written in low level languages and a compiler is used for translating high level language source programs.

3. Para 3 of answer was started from the program flowchart point because this was thought appropriate; you will appreciate however that the beginning of the story starts with deciding the logic of the problem and preparation of systems flowchart etc.

ANSWER 3.

1. a. **What is a package program?**

To take advantage of the similar information needs of large numbers of businesses, generalised packages have been developed by computer manufacturers and software houses.

An application package is a program or set of programs of a generalised nature designed to solve a particular problem. The package is so designed that it can be used by a large number of organisations.

The programs can be supplied in media such as punched card, magnetic tape, or disk and are accompanied by comprehensive documentation to assist the user.

b. **Advantages of using a package program.**

i. All the programming effort that is entailed in writing a custom-built program is saved. This gives savings in cost and man power.

ii. The user has a tried and tested set of programs, free of error and which can be used with confidence. It follows that a lot of computer time which is associated with the testing of programs is saved.

iii. Following on from ii. above, good reliable information can be available very quickly.

iv. A side-effect, which can be construed as an advantage, is the discipline enforced on those responsible for input procedures.

It should be remembered, however, that because some packages are designed for a wide range of users, it may well be necessary to modify the package to suit the user's needs, (in this case the "80 heading analysis").

A compromise would be to alter the company's information requirements to *fit the package.*

2. **Transfer of records to computer files.** Assuming records are at present held manually the steps involved are as follows:-

a. A thorough examination of all the manual documents to ensure a high standard of documentation which was possibly not a critical factor previously.

b. Data necessary to form the master file is taken from batches of documents and entered at a keyboard of key-to-diskette system say. (alternatively the data could be manually transcribed onto OMR documents)

Static data such as "name", "clock no" would be entered during early stages. The entry of data which by its nature is subject to change (eg. "total pay to date") would be left until the latest possible moment.

c. Batch details are listed on the printer and a visual check made of listings against documents (where this is possible).

d. Diskettes are used as input data to the computer and master files are created by the "File Creation Program".

e. A printed copy of the newly created file is examined and errors rectified (and re-input as necessary).

f. The file is now ready for use in testing procedures prior to operational use.

The major organisational problem is concerned with the length of time taken for the successful completion of the whole transfer process.

It is important to ensure that once a record has begun the transfer process, all subsequent changes to the date contained in that record are carried through to the computer file.

Overall control would be exercised by batching documents, possibly by department; and control/hash totals calculated for checking at the various stages. (eg. numbers of documents; hash totals of employee clock numbers etc).

A timetable for all these operations would be drawn up and progress monitored. The systems analyst would have the responsibility for this task.

Because of the high work-load involved it may be necessary to use a Bureau for the data preparation stage.

AUTHORS' COMMENTS.

1. Payroll packages, being application orientated, have a wide range of potential users. There are many such packages available, some of which will have been designed for use with a *particular range* of computers.

2. Difficulties arise because each company's requirements differ in terms of significant details; this is particularly so where there is an inter-relationship of applications as in this question ie. between payroll and labour cost analysis.

3. It may well be necessary to modify the user's information requirements to suit the package, especially if the package is one designed by a manufacturer.

4. However some Software Houses design packages on the modular principle and thus are able to accommodate the user's requirements, if not too outrageous.

ANSWER 4.

O & M can be described as the systematic investigation into selected procedures or operations, in order to suggest alternatives which are more suitable, both technically and economically.

STAGES OF THE EXERCISE.

1. Confirm terms of reference. The O & M team must be clear as to the aims of the exercise, so that time is not wasted investigating areas outside the scope of the objectives. The objectives must be set by management as it is only they who can say what information is required to aid them in their task of planning and controlling the business.

2. Fact finding and recording. By using such techniques as interviewing, direct observation, questionnaires, and studying procedure manuals and organisation charts, all the relevant facts can be obtained. Recording techniques such as flowcharts and string diagrams are used to aid analysis; the aim being to find out the 'who', 'where', 'which', 'what', and 'when' of the area under study.

3. **Examination.** A critical examination of the facts so collected will now take place. It is important that nothing goes unchallenged, including why the particular tasks are carried out *at all.* Then the tasks are looked at in relation to personalities, place, manner, time and equipment.

4. **Alternatives.** Alternatives must be designed and presented in a form suitable for management to choose between them. The number of alternatives presented will depend upon the ease with which the objectives could be achieved eg. there may be five or six feasible alternatives for processing invoices, but perhaps only one for providing exception reports in the time scale required for effective action to be taken upon them.

5. **Installation.** The method best suited to achieving the objectives will be selected and installation proceeded with. Equipment may need to be ordered, specialist staff recruited, or retraining of existing staff undertaken etc.

6. **Maintenance.** The final stage occurs when the new methods have been adopted and consists of checking that they are in fact being carried out according to plan eg. if duplicate records were being maintained after their planned elimination then the reasons for this must be discovered. The results of checking are also used to aid future exercise.

The stages listed above occur whatever the objectives of the exercise. The differences are only of degree within the stages eg. the objective "to improve customer service by despatching goods within 24 hours of receipt of the order" would probably indicate the use of an expensive real time computer system – in which case detailed fact finding and examination of existing steps might well be fruitless, when completely new procedures would need to be installed and major alternatives would not be possible; the objective "to reduce the number of accounts clerks" may require detailed fact finding and examination and produce alternatives ranging from better manual methods, through the use of accounting machines to a tape oriented computer system.

The stages are also not completely isolated on a time scale. For example, whilst obtaining the facts about a procedure from a particular manager, his true requirements may be discovered and used in the design of alternative methods.

The stages will also be carried out at different levels of detail according to the decisions required. For example, the first three stages of the exercise may have been done on an outline basis to provide sufficient information for the board room decision to have an in-house computer and repeated afterwards on an increasingly detailed basis for the decisions required to be taken by the lower levels of management in implementation.

AUTHORS' COMMENTS.

1. When the term 'O & M' is applied to an individual or a department eg. "O & M officer" or "O & M department" it normally indicates a specialisation in manual or mechanically assisted methods of data processing. The term "Systems Analyst" or "Systems Analysis" is applied to the specialisation in computer methods of data processing. There are many areas of work which could be carried out by conventional methods or electronic methods, and all feasible alternatives must be considered. This indicates that a close liaison is necessary between the two specialisations.

ANSWER 5.

a. Systems Analysis Part Introduction 3.

b. Investigation – 31.2-5 inclusive.
Analysis – 31.7-14.
Design – 32.

ANSWER 6.

32.29.

ANSWER 7.

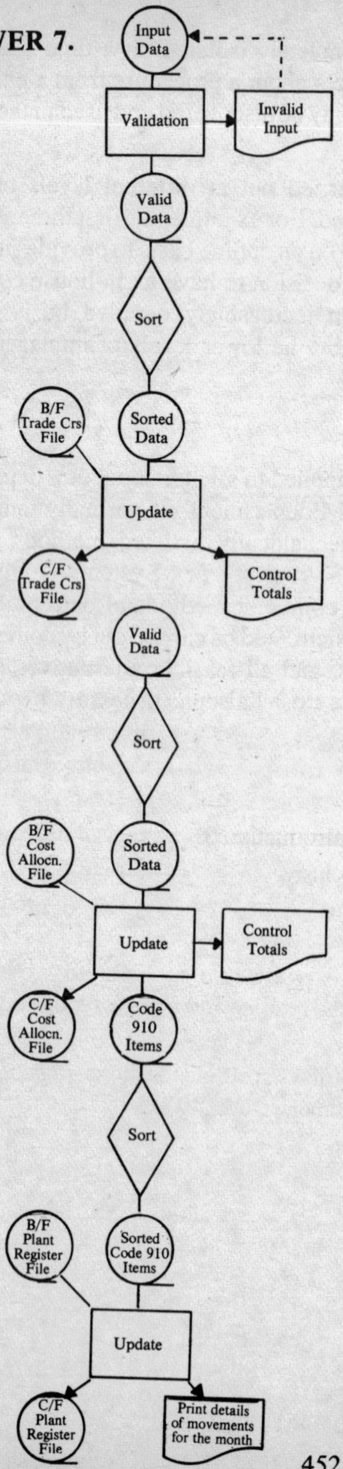

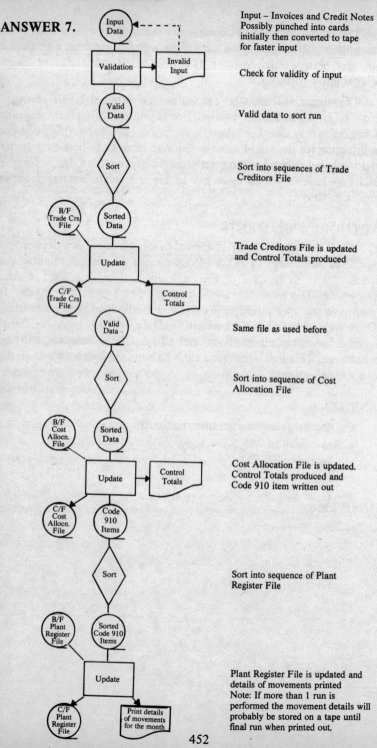

Input – Invoices and Credit Notes
Possibly punched into cards initially then converted to tape for faster input

Check for validity of input

Valid data to sort run

Sort into sequences of Trade Creditors File

Trade Creditors File is updated and Control Totals produced

Same file as used before

Sort into sequence of Cost Allocation File

Cost Allocation File is updated. Control Totals produced and Code 910 item written out

Sort into sequence of Plant Register File

Plant Register File is updated and details of movements printed
Note: If more than 1 run is performed the movement details will probably be stored on a tape until final run when printed out.

ANSWER 8.

31.3-5.

ANSWER 9.

Chapters 29-32 (summary needed).

Chapter 34.

ANSWER 1.

ADVANTAGES OF DISK STORAGE.

1. a. **Addressable medium** – each record can be located independently; this is not possible with magnetic tape which is essentially a serial storage medium.

b. **File organisation** – files can be arranged sequentially or in a random manner, whereas magnetic tape is confined to serial file organisation.

c. **Access** – access to records stored on disk may be sequential (using an index) or random. Time taken to locate a record is independent of the position of that record.

d. **Storage capacity** – disk packs of the removable type have a high capacity. 1 such pack holds up to 60 million characters.

e. **Data transfer speed** – this is high and much faster than all except the latest model tape devices. Current disk units have data transfer speed of about 312 thousand characters per second.

f. **On-line real time processing** – This is only possible using disk storage because of the features described in 1a.–c. above.

g. **Information availabilty** – requests for information can be answered quickly and at random.

h. **Low activity** – disk is a suitable medium for low activity processing. No time is wasted reading and writing redundant records as with magnetic tape.

i. **Software etc, storage** – disks are ideal for the storage of program libraries, rate tables and Supervisor software.

ADVANTAGES OF MAGNETIC TAPE STORAGE.

2. a. **Cost** – reels of tape cost £10 (approx) as opposed to disk packs which cost £250 (approx), and are therefore, much cheaper. Costs of associated drive units are not significantly different from those used with disks.

b. **Storage capacity** – potentially relatively high. Each reel has 40 million character capacity but typically it is not utilised to the same extent as with disk.

c. **File security** – physically different brought-forward and carried-forward tapes are used in processing and therefore a measure of file security can be said to be built-in.

d. **High activity** – tape is suitable for high activity batch processing applications because of the serial nature of the medium.

e. **Off-line storage** – tape reels represent a cheap form of off-line storage (see 2a. above).

f. **File maintenance** is facilitated because it is relatively easy to insert, delete or amend records on tape.

g. **Software** – no complicated software is required to handle files on tape as can be necessary with disk.

h. **Source data** can be keyed directly on to tape using a Magnetic Tape Encoding machine. This is not possible with disk which requires use of the computer.

EXAMPLES OF FILES FOR WHICH EACH METHOD IS BEST SUITED.

3. a. **Disk.**

i. **Master stock file** – where it is necessary to interrogate the file at random and where quick response is required.

ii. **Commodity prices file** – during an invoice run, the need to have direct access to commodity prices would arise.

iii. **Program or subroutine file** – storage of such a file on disk would enable the computer to choose any program or subroutine automatically at the appropriate time during processing.

b. **Magnetic Tape.**

i. **Transaction file** – file containing transactions would be used as input to a processing run.

ii. **Report files** – these files represent output from a processing run eg. error schedules or information which will subsequently be printed (as an off-line operation or using SPOOLING technique).

iii. **Copy or dump files** – such files would be used for security purposes or in conjunction with error checking routines.

Essentially the major feature of disk storage is direct access and if the management information system requires quick response to random requests then the use of disk is indicated.

The main feature of magnetic tape lies in its inherent characteristic of serial storage.

AUTHORS' COMMENTS.

1. One might be led to think the answer was required in report form. However it is considered that a report would contain advantages, disadvantages, conclusions, and recommendations, and therefore anything else would be unrealistic – a generalised approach was therefore used.

2. This was a straightforward question in which a tabulated approach was essential.

ANSWER 2.

a. 34.16-34.19.

b. 34.18.

c. eg. Cost Sheets, Balance Sheets, Statements of accounts.

Chapter 35.
ANSWER 1.

a.

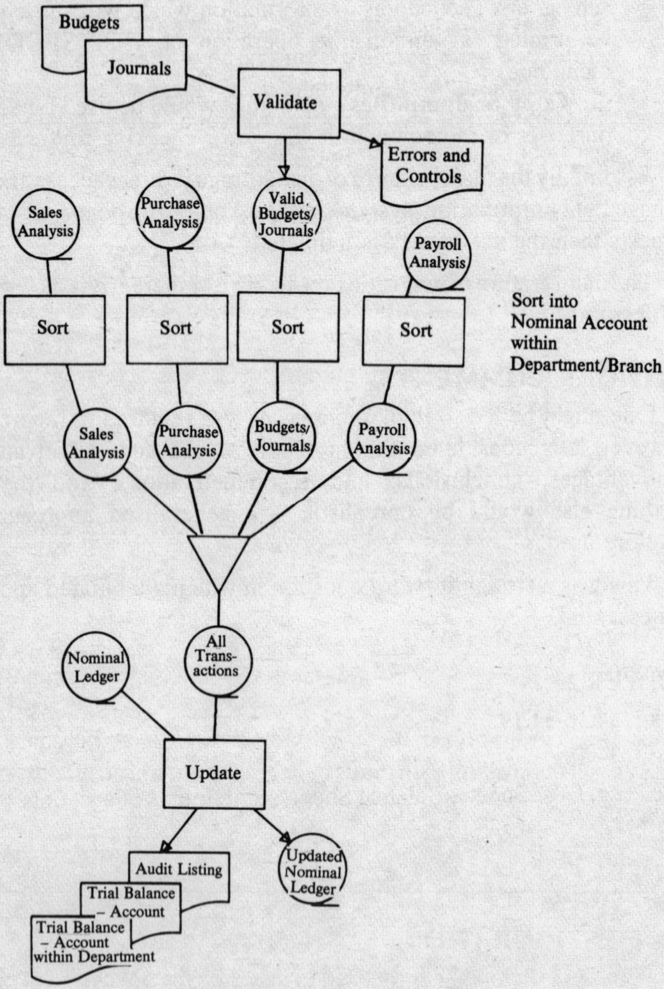

b. i. **Sales.** Debtors control totals and sales/cost of sales information. Probably provided automatically from the sales ledger system.

Purchases. Creditors control totals and purchase analysis information. Probably provided automatically from the purchase ledger system.

Payroll. Departmental and/or job payroll figures. Probably provided automatically from the payroll system.

Journals. All adjustments to accounts (errors in sales/purchases, pre-payments, accruals etc.) and payments/receipts not going through the purchase ledger (eg. capital items/petty cash). These would probably be input directly.

Budgets. Departmental/sales budgets input either monthly or once annually. Input most probably direct.

ii. **Validation checks.** Checks would be carried out on direct input (the validation checks on those passed over from other systems having been carried out within those sytems).

Range. Account numbers and department numbers coming within pre-determined range of figures.

Character. Each field would be checked to ensure characters were punched correctly eg. having a numeric character where required.

Completeness. Each record would be checked for the right number of characters.

AUTHOR'S COMMENTS.

Nominal ledger systems vary widely – the degree of automaticity depending upon the degree of computerisation of subsidiary systems. Thus other systems (cash book, petty cash book, sales/purchase ledger) may be self controlling with totals only being journalised into the nominal ledger.

Chapter 36.

ANSWER 1.

a. CONFIGURATION.

1. Configuration is the term used to describe the collection of physical units of machinery (otherwise known as hardware) to be found in a computer installation.

2. Example.

i. **Central Processing Unit.** The CPU consists of an

Arithmetic Logic Unit, Control Unit, and Main Storage (usually).

ii. **Console.** This provides external control over the processing system. Usually associated with it, is an electric typewriter.

iii. **Magnetic Disk Storage Unit.** This provides large capacity backing or auxiliary storage, and is also used for input and output to/from CPU.

iv. **Magnetic Tape Unit.** This provides input and output facilities and magnetic tape provides means for off-line storage.

v. **Line Printer.** This provides the means of producing the output reports generated by the system.

vi. **VDU terminals.** These provide on-line facilities for data entry, file enquiry etc.

b. RANDOM ACCESS.

1. The term random access is used to describe the ability to locate a record held in a storage device, independently of other records within the file. Storage devices which provide the facility are magnetic disks or drums. The methods of file organisation allowing random access are "indexed sequential" and "random".

2. An airline ticket reservation system is an example of an application using the technique of random access. A centralised computer maintains records of all flights on direct access storage devices. Reservation offices world-wide are linked to it by terminals. On receipt of information from a reservation point the flight record is *immediately* accessed and *updated* to show the current seating availability. This would not be possible without this random access facility.

c.

1. ON-LINE.

i. The term on-line is used to describe the situation when peripheral units (eg. tape units) are connected to, and under the control of, the central processing unit. Thus data can be read directly into or out of main storage from/to a device which is on-line.

2. OFF-LINE.

i. Conversely the term off-line is used to describe the situation when peripheral units are *not* under control of the central processing unit.

ii. The advantage of off-line output working is that the comparatively slow task of printing is done independently of the computer's central processing unit thus leaving it free to carry out more profitable processing of data.

iii. The term off-line is also used in connection with tape reels and exchangeable disk packs kept in the tape library. They are said to be stored off-line.

AUTHORS' COMMENTS.

1. To be strictly correct a configuration should specify the number of units required eg. 2 printers, 4 disk units and also the amount of main storage eg. 16K (16 x 1024 Bytes).

2. The concept of on-line can be extended, and the term used to describe those data processing systems where the means of input are linked to the computer by the use of data transmission facilities. The air-line ticket reservation example quoted could be described as being an "on-line system" as could the system operated by the big clearing banks.

3. With the advent of multiprogramming the printing of output can be done using Simultaneous Peripheral Operations On-line (SPOOL) and thus obviates the need for off-line printing facilities.

ANSWER 2.

a. 28.39 and 28.10.

b. 36.5-9.

ANSWER 3.

25.9-15 inclusive.

36.1-9 inclusive.

Chapter 37.

ANSWER 1.

One of the difficulties in selecting the computer best suited to a company's needs is how to evaluate what each manufacturer has to offer. What a company must attempt to do is to match its objectives against the capabilities of the computer systems offered by the manufacturers. The following criteria are suggested but it must be remembered that each user will place a different emphasise on the individual criterion.

a. Cost.

b. Delivery time.

c. Support –
   i. personnel supplied by manufacturers to aid user.
   ii. education of user's staff.

d. Software supplied with system – cost and ease of implementation.

e. Reliability – the manufacturer to supply performance data.

f. Modularity – the ability to add to system later.

g. Conversion – The ease with which conversion from existing system could be accomplished.

h. Experience – the manufacturer's experience with systems of the type that company is installing.

ANSWER 2.

The contents of a Systems Specification are *included* in a feasibility report, to the level of detail required by management to make a decision between alternative ways of satisfying the objectives (eg. use of bureau v own computer). The feasibility *report,* apart from containing an *introduction, current situation statement,* etc. would also, therefore, include details of *alternatives.*

ANSWER 3.

The review of a computer system must not be regarded as a once only task and ideally should be carried out periodically. The main question to be asked is "have the objectives been achieved"? This assumes that these were clearly defined in the first place. Thus, if the objective was "to reduce stock levels by 10%" or "to produce invoices one day earlier", the reviewer must judge the effectiveness of the new system against the achievement of these objectives. Some of the detailed areas which would occupy the attention of the reviewer are:-

a. Costs – are these in line with budgeted costs?

b. Staff – with regard to retraining, redeployment and morale. Are staff happy with the new system?

c. Are any parts of the "old" system which should have been dispensed with still in use?

d. Standards of input and output.

e. Feedback from the company's customers.

ANSWER 4·

a. 37.1-13.
37.39 a-b.

b. 37.14-38.

Chapter 38.

ANSWER 1.

Before entering into a discussion about the impact of computers in business it is necessary to define the functions of management.

Stated simply the functions of management are to *plan* the use of resources at its disposal, to *motivate* the company's work-people and to *co-ordinate* and *control* the activities necessary to carry out the plans. These functions of management have not changed with the advent of the computer, but the ways in which they are carried out have. To carry out these functions effectively managers need information. Information is the product of the processing of data, the amount and variety of which is increasing year by year.

Computers have the ability to process large amounts of data at high speed and with a high degree of accuracy. They relieve the human of a great deal of routine labour. Information is more reliable, is more up-to-date and as a result the quality of decision making is improved.

The use of computers in business allows a greater use of management by exception techniques. The computer only notifies those variations from plan which require management action. This saves the time of managers and helps to focus attention of matters which require attention.

It should be remembered however that the exercising of powers of judgement, leadership and initiative remains the prerogative of the human.

Information requirements at the highest level of management involve many external factors (government actions, competitors plans etc.) and the scope is wide. Nevertheless the use of computers have made possible better integration of plans and enabled quicker response to changed circumstances. Plans can be more frequently reviewed by the provision of more up-to-date information. The computer is invaluable in using models to test the validity and consequences of particular courses of action.

At the lower levels of management, information requirements are largely internal (dictated from above) and therefore quantifiable. The computer's great storage capacity, speed of processing, aid retrieval of data, and the ability to program for quantifiable factors enables it to have a great impact on the functions of co-ordination and control at this level. For example, the information needed to make a good decision on order acceptability includes up-to-date stock level and credit worthiness details. A computer, using terminals, direct access storage and integrated procedures, can provide this information quickly and accurately.

Managers must be fully aware of the criteria upon which the computer system producing the information, is based. For example, a buyer may be supplied, by the computer, with the details of the three most suitable suppliers for him to decide amongst. This is a very good aid to the controlling function as long as he appreciates that, for example, the stability of the suppliers was not considered by the computer. He is then able to exercise his judgement on the outstanding factors.

All levels of management carry out the functions but with the emphasis placed more on one than another eg, top management spend more of their time on planning than on motivating, whereas the converse is true of lower levels. The computer does not change the functions, but by providing the quantifiable factors required in exercising those functions, can leave the manager, at whatever level, more time to consider those areas for which the computer is not suited, ie. man management and innovation.

AUTHORS' COMMENTS.

1. This question emphasises the need to know a definition of management from which to work (!).

2. It is very easy, in a question like this, to wander off the main theme or say the same thing, in different ways, over and over again. You must jot down the points under which you are going to write.

ANSWER 2.

'Organisation chart' – Fig. 30.2 Part 2.

Main duties – 38.8-24.

'To whom . . . responsible' – 38.4-7. Note that the suggestion is that he should be responsible to the Managing Director to ensure that no departmental boundaries prevent desirable integration of systems to take place.

Chapter 39.

ANSWER 1.

ASSUMPTIONS.

a. A medium sized in-house computer has been assumed to be the subject of this answer.

INTRODUCTION.

Some costs are easy to identify precisely eg. hardware but others are less easy to measure. A suggested division is:-

a. Development costs.
b. Installation costs.
c. Conversion costs.
d. Running costs.

DEVELOPMENT COSTS.

a. Initial and feasibility studies – staff and associated overheads.
b. Detailed systems study and design – systems analysts etc.
c. Program writing and testing – programmers and analysts.
d. Selection, training and education of personnel.
e. Software.
f. Support.
g. Manuals etc.

INSTALLATION COSTS.

a. Buildings – new or structural alterations to existing buildings.
b. Computer hardware.
c. Ancillary equipment – data preparation etc.
d. Environmental costs eg. air conditioning.

CONVERSION COSTS.

a. File creation and conversion.
b. Conversion program writing.
c. Changeover.

RUNNING COSTS.

a. Staff.
b. Maintenance of buildings and equipment.
c. Storage of data.
d. Insurance.
e. Stationery.
f. Power – light etc.
g. Rental charges if appropriate.

Notes:

a. A distinction should be made between 'one-time' and 'running' costs.

b. Recovery of 'one-time' costs will be linked to a period of a number of years.

ANSWER 2.

1. A proposal to consider the use of computers in solving a company's business problems would have led a company to set up a preliminary study. This study would have determined the application areas and would have enabled computer objectives to be formulated. Before the company commits itself to the adoption of computer methods it will need a great deal of information on which to base its decision.

2. The **feasibility study** is undertaken to provide the information referred to above. It sets out to investigate the practicability of using computers and to assess the effects on the company both in economic and social terms. At the conclusion of the study, which could occupy months, a report will be prepared containing the study group's recommendations. This will then be considered by the board and a decision taken on whether or not to undertake computer methods.

3. The contents of the report were described in 37.11.

AUTHORS' COMMENTS.

1. The amount of time and effort required before the feasibility report can be produced depends upon the nature and complexity of the business activity under study.

2. Although the term 'feasibility study' is the term in general use, it is misleading in that most business activities can be carried out by computers (or by conventional methods). A more appropriate term might be justification study.

3. All possible alternative solutions whether involving the use of computers or not, should be included in the report.

ANSWER 3.

WHEN SHOULD A SYSTEMS STUDY TAKE PLACE?

1. A systems study will follow a recommendation to proceed further with investigation into the use of an alternative system to achieve company objectives. It has been assumed that the alternative system involves the use of a computer.

This recommendation could have come as a result of a preliminary study.

STEPS INVOLVED IN A SYSTEMS STUDY.

2. The systems study will be developed from all information gathered in the preliminary study previously carried out, but will require a considerable amount of further enquiry in order to reveal possible alternatives,etc. Steps and work involved in such a study are as follows:-

a. **Outline planning.** Make all administrative arrangements. The project leader should be in possession of authority to approach appropriate departments. Study must be publicised and supported by top management.

b. **Definition of task.** There must be precise identification areas to be studied. Objectives must be clearly stated and expected duration of project will be indicated. Although study must not be too protracted, any attempt to work to a tight schedule will almost certainly fail.

c. **Investigation.** This will include getting all the *facts* about the present system, using techniques such as interviewing, examination of records and procedures, and use of questionnaires as appropriate.

Data collected in this way will be recorded and documented using appropriate media, where possible facts should be *verified.*

d. **Analysis and classification.** This involves the sifting of the data gathered and analysing and classifying it into a meaningful form.

In doing this the analyst must be clear about the objectives of system and of any constraints. Controls to be built into the new system must be considered. Any weaknesses revealed should not be allowed to enter the new system.

e. **Outline design.** An outline design of new system will be drawn up, taking into consideration output requirements in terms of timeliness, accuracy, form etc.

Alternatives, both involving computer and, where appropriate, conventional methods, should be explored for economic justification. Up-to-date comparative costs should be included.

f. **Recommendations.** The results of the study together with recommendations will be presented to the Steering Committee.

If acceptable the report could form the basis of a specification to be forwarded to manufacturers for the purpose of inviting tenders.

COMPOSITION OF SYSTEMS STUDY TEAM.

3. A study covering all the commercial activities of a company would take a considerable amount of time. Such a study undertaken in a motor car manufacturing company for example would entail investigating sales, purchasing of raw materials, stock control etc.

When studying each such system a representative with the detailed technical knowledge of that system would be co-opted in order to ensure that its requirements were made known and understood by the other members of the team. This involvement of the user department is important when the implementation stage is reached.

One team member should have a good knowledge of the information needs of the business and the need for co-ordination. This member would be from the Management Services department.

Someone with a grasp of the technicalities of data processing and a knowledge of computer systems would be needed. This would be a systems anlayst. He must have those attributes essential to the maintenance of good relations with his superiors and those people who will be the subject of his investigation. His ability to overcome the natural resistance to change which will be encountered will be vital to the success of the project.

AUTHORS' COMMENTS.

1. When a computer configuration is decided upon there would follow a more detailed systems study resulting in:-

a. A detailed systems design. This would entail a fully detailed statement of the clerical and computer procedures required in the new system.

b. The writing and coding of the computer programs.
c. Implementation of the new system.

2. This is an area which lacks uniformity of terminology. The systems study referred to here is usually called a feasibility study. The study process as a whole consists of:

a. Preliminary study.
b. Feasibility study.
c. Detailed systems study.

It is a continuous process almost, with each study (or phase) developing from the previous one.

3. It should be understood that a company's approach to the introduction of any new system (especially one involving computers) will depend upon the size of the company, the complexity of its operations, and whether or not it already has well-established procedures.

ANSWER 4.

Time

0945 ASSEMBLY – COFFEE.

1000 Introduction by the Seminar Leader outlining the events. Objective of seminar to be stated, which is to make the board aware of what the proposed system will do and to invite suggestions on what additional information is required to suit their needs.

Questions will be dealt with during the discussion period but if it is considered appropriate board members may put a question during the talks.

1010 The head of the Computer Planning Committee will relate the background history leading up to the decision to install a computer.

1025 The computer manufacturer's representative will give general information about the computer and its capabilities particularly in relation to the company's applications.

1100 The head of Management Services will outline the objectives, the details of the various phases by means of which these objectives will be met, and the time-table to be followed. Emphasis will be placed on their relationship to strategic planning and management control. The need for top management to inject their ideas at this stage will be brought out in order that they may be incorporated into the management information system.

1200– 1400 LUNCH.

1400 A film demonstrating similar applications in other companies, if available, or a film illustrating the use of PERT techniques as applied to the installation of a computer system; the showing of this latter film is designed to make the board aware of the difficulties and problems involved.

1430 Discussion on the film and any matters arising out of the previous speakers topics. This discussion is to be conducted by the Seminar Leader. (Refreshments will be served during this time).

Remarks.

1. A programme will have been prepared in advance and will emphasise the main points to be put over.

2. The atmosphere should be informal.

3. The time-table should be adhered to.

4. It would be desirable at some stage in the discussion session after lunch to bring in the heads of the divisions who are going to be affected by the computer planning and also if not already present the member of the consultancy firm who assisted in any of the studies.

5. The time, place, and the name of the seminar leader, should be noted in the programme.

6. Avoid over-emphasis on technical details about the machine, but concentrate more upon what it can do in relation to the activities of the business.

7. The aim must be to get the directors thoughts turned towards future developments and how best they may be exploited for the benefit of the company.

8. It is recommended that a visit to the manufacturer's premises be arranged in order that the hardware may be viewed.

ASSUMPTIONS.

1. A decision has been taken to install a computer and an order has been placed for a particular system.

2. The Data Processing Manager designate will be present during the seminar, also the person responsible for carrying out the feasibility study.

AUTHORS' COMMENTS.

1. It cannot be emphasised too strongly that continued top-management involvement in computer planning is vital to its success.

2. Top-management must give its full support to those whose task it is to carry out the plans that they have sanctioned, and to some extent at least, become involved in the implementation of the new systems.

3. The seminar and all other talks, discussions etc. will be designed with these points in mind.

4. It is sometimes helpful in a seminar of this kind to pick a venue away from the company's premises in order to concentrate fully on the matters concerned.

ANSWER 5.

a. In a system of business control the management by exception technique is used to isolate those facts which relate to the area in which a decision has to be made.

Computer based systems are ideally suited to this task in the following circumstances:-

i. When large volumes of data, possibly originating at various geographical points, need to be collected and processed in order that relevant information may be extracted.

ii. When speed of processing is essential to provide management with more timely information in the planning-control feedback cycle.

iii. When a high degree of accuracy is required.

iv. When a greater amount of information is required.

v. When the capacity for discrimination is required to a high degree.

An application (reflecting the circumstance at (i) above) is found in stock control where there are many (possibly thousands) stock items and a high stock turnover. The stock records are kept on magnetic storage including, for each type of stock, the balance on hand, reserved stock, re-order quantity, re-order level etc. A demand for stock is compared with the balance on hand, taking into account reserved and ordered stock, and only if the stocks need replenishing will the computer issue a report to management, otherwise the record is updated accordingly.

Additionally the computer can be programmed to print out reports of stocks with a turnover below a certain percentage.

b. **Factors to be observed to ensure the system is a viable one.**
1. **Economy.** Checks should be made to ensure that the objectives are being achieved within the economic limits laid down in the systems study.
2. **Source data.** The system depends on a high standard of accuracy of source data.
3. **Program.** The logic of the computer program must be checked to ensure that no exceptions are missed.
4. **Review.** The system must be constantly reviewed to ensure that exceptions are still being selected using up-to-date criteria.
5. **Communication.** Managers must be fully aware of the criteria upon which the exception system is based and must have confidence and understanding of the methods.
6. **Flexibility.** The system must be capable of responding to changing circumstances indicating the need for new information.

AUTHORS' COMMENTS.

1. This was not an easy question. Management by exception is, however, fundamental to management studies in general and is a technique for which the computer is ideally suited.

ANSWER 6.

Chapter 39.

Chapter 40.

ANSWER 1.

INTRODUCTION.

1. The number of computer bureaux in this country is growing and more and more companies are turning to them as an alternative to installation of an "in-house" machine.

The services they offer are becoming more comprehensive, and now range from data preparation to consultancy.

ADVANTAGES.

2. a. **Capital outlay.** The company does not have the problem of finding a large capital sum for computer hardware, software, buildings etc. There are often many "hidden" costs associated with computer acquisition. Provided a reasonable contract is agreed with the bureau, costs will be known.

b. **Effect on organisation.** The installation of a computer is invariably accompanied by a major organisational upheaval. Although there may well be organisational changes when using a bureau the effect will not be so upsetting.

c. **Computer experience.** Using a service bureau is a good way of obtaining experience in computer work. This will give staff knowledge of input and output requirements, and an understanding of the capabilities and limitations of computers in general. It also provides the opportunity to make an assessment of particular systems, with a view to possible subsequent installation of an "in-house" machine.

d. **Hardware.** A company has access to a wide range of machinery; from the most powerful and up-to-date hardware down to visible record computers. It has no worries about the obsolescence of machinery; that is the concern of the bureau. It thus benefits from the most up-to-date technical innovations without having to pay out the large sums which would be involved with an "in-house" machine.

e. **Software.** A wide range of software is available from bureaux, Application Packages for example. Some bureaux specialise in the provision of such packages for particular industries. Thus, much of the programming development costs and effort are considerably reduced if not eliminated.

f. **Staff.** Experienced data processing staff are in short supply and expensive to recruit. By employing the services of a bureau a company will have at its disposal, high calibre personnel who are specialists in many fields, and expert help will be forthcoming to help solve the company's problems.

g. **Speedy implementation.** The computer system can be put into operation more quickly, especially if well tried standard packages are used.

h. **Machine utilisation.**

i. If large processing power is only required for relatively short periods of time, then it may be more economical to turn to a bureau and thus avoid the problem of having expensive facilities laying idle between times.

ii. The load put on to a bureau may be increased when the need arises. Seasonal variations also are no problem to the bureau.

i. **Complete service.** A recent arrival on the scene is the "turnkey" operation whereby the bureau contracts to provide a comprehensive data processing service from systems analysis right through to implementation.

DISADVANTAGES.

3. a. **Distance from user.** Source documents or input data may have to be transported over long distances to get to the bureau. This could raise problems of delay or loss.

b. **Confidentiality.** When using a bureau a great deal of company information has to be revealed to the bureau, and the computer files themselves will be processed outside the company's control. This raises problems of security of the company's affairs.

c. **Reliability.** The possibility of the bureau not meeting the deadlines laid down is also a consideration. This could have disastrous consequences for the company in the possible loss of customer goodwill or a discontented work force (in the case of a payroll application).

d. **Control.** The possibility of loss of control over some of the operations certainly exists. This can be overcome by working very closely with the bureau throughout all stages of the particular project.

e. **Company knowledge.** Not all bureaux will have the knowledge of your particular company. This can be a problem but bureaux have recognised it and many now recruit commercial and management specialists to back up their computer and systems staff.

f. **Staff resentment.** There may well be resentment on the part of staff towards the introduction of bureaux personnel into the company. This could be especially so when a bureau is used for consultancy purposes. This is an age-old human problem experienced in other fields and will be overcome by education and clear lines of communication.

g. **Schedules.** Work will be scheduled and these schedules adhered to. Bureaux can in some ways be regarded as inflexible in this respect. Their livelihood depends on tight scheduling of all cusotmer business and they would expect compliance on the users' part. They would find it uneconomic to work on any other basis.

h. **Costs.** Charges made by bureaux vary a lot and the problem is to decide whether the varying standards of service are reflected in the different prices.

AUTHORS' COMMENTS.

1. A fairly comprehensive list has been given for students benefit.

2. The Computer Services Association (CSA), provides a code of conduct for its members, who have to maintain high standards.

3. Contracts. These must spell out the particular arrangements between the parties. Responsibility for errors, late arrival of data, failure to keep to dead-line and method of payment for services must be pinpointed.

ANSWER 2.

a. 40.2.

b. i. Clock cards – for variable details eg. hours worked, jobs worked on.

Manual payments – eg. employee leaving suddenly with no time to go through bureau.

Joiner/Leaver info. – standing details eg. name, number, tax code number plus 'start' information, date, tax to date etc.

ii. Payroll/Slips – for control/communication to employees

Coin Analysis – for cash breakdown.

Labour Analysis – for departmental/job/efficiency information.

Chapter 41.

ANSWER 1.

1. Check digit – 17.9 g.

Limit check – 17.9 c. Note: 'Range check is also known as a 'limit' check ie. checking that prescribed limits have not been exceeded eg. number of hours worked in a week.

Parity check – 7.15.

Password – 41.21 b.

Tape mark – 5.27 d.

Conversational Mode – 28.20 f.

Batch Mode – 36.33 e.

Turn around document – 14.16.

ANSWER 2.

41.1–21 inclusive. Note that you should use the sub-headings within this chapter as the main headings in your answer.

ANSWER 3.

A benchmark test is a test program which is run on a number of computers to compare the processing time to assist in selection of the best system for purchase or use.

The best known benchmark test is the 'Gibson Mix' which has a fixed proportion of each of the common instruction types such as load/store, test, add and subtract etc. In addition the Analysts and Programmers of a Company may choose to develop their own benchmark programs to assist the assessment of the likely performance of the competing computers in their own company environment.

The benchmark test may be applied to develop selection criteria in a number of ways. First, as indicated above, to time the performance of two different processors. Secondly to time the corresponding peripherals and thirdly to time the performance of standard software packages such as sort routines and compilers. In addition there may be a requirement to test under multiprogramming conditions or to test performance with a number of terminals operating simultaneously. As well as timing, the benchmarks may be used to test qualitative aspects of software packages.

Advantages of benchmarks are that they enable a direct comparison to be made even when the two computers are of wildly contrasting concept and architecture.

Disadvantages include the fact that they only compare the performance on the benchmark which may not be realistic in the live running of the whole range of company systems. It is also difficult, even with a Gibson Mix type, to compare accurately the performance, say, of a byte machine with a word machine, especially if one has a three address assembly code and the other uses one address with, perhaps, indirect addressing instead of index registers and the prices of the two differ by, say, 25%. However used with caution it does, at least provide a basis for comparison.

AUTHORS' COMMENTS.

A straighforward question but on a rather specialised topic which may not have been studied by all candidates. Like many questions it invites the student to follow a set structure in the answer.

ANSWER 4.

a. i. and ii. 41.13–21.

b. i. and ii. 6.

ANSWER 5.

a. 41.21.

b. 41.13–20 inclusive.

ANSWER 6.

41.14–16 inclusive.

Appendix 2 Questions without Answers

This appendix is for use in the classroom situation.

Questions have been take from recent papers of the ICA, ACA, ICMA, IAS/AAT, SCCA and IDPM and grouped according to the respective Parts of the manual.

INTRODUCTION TO DATA PROCESSING.

1.

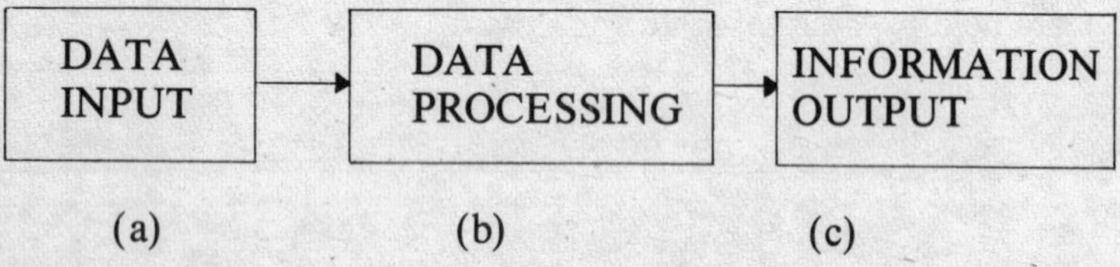

The above diagram illustrates in a simplified way, the three phases of Data Processing irrespective of whether the system is a manual or computerised system.

You are required to:

i. define for a. what is meant by data, giving examples, and to state the two sources from which an organisation could obtain data input;

ii. briefly list the processing carried out under b.;

iii. for c. to explain, why Management requires information;

iv. distinguish between data and information.

(IAS)

INTRODUCTION TO INFORMATION TECHNOLOGY FOR DATA PROCESSING.

1. a. Define data processing.

b. Indicate the major data processing stages.

c. Compare each of these stages in a manual system with similar stages in an electronic system.

(SCCA)

HARDWARE.

1. When reporting to Management, the lineprinter is possibly the most used output peripheral.

You are required to give two other methods for providing readable output and to briefly describe, or illustrate, how the output is produced. (IAS)

2. Describe, with the minimum of technical details, the main features of three devices for obtaining output from a computer and indicate the kinds of application for which the devices you describe are suitable. (ACA)

3. ABC Limited, a company which markets a range of consumer durables, operates a computer-based inventory control system. Goods are held in three separate warehouses.

Required:

a. List, and briefly comment on, FOUR items of source data and FOUR printed reports which, as input and output respectively, you would expect to find incorporated in the system.

b. Draft, with a line of sample entries, the form on which warehouse staff record details of goods received from suppliers.

(ACA)

COMPUTER FILES.

1. a. Define the term 'master file' and identify the various elements which may constitute such a file.

b. Describe how such a file would be updated on magnetic tape. (IDPM)

2. Although in the earlier days of computerisation the majority of files were held on magnetic tape nowadays magnetic disks are more common.

Describe the characteristics of the two storage media given above and discuss some of the problems of storing and accessing records on tapes and on disks. (ICMA)

3. a. Define, with a suitable example, the term master file. Your answer should show that you understand the distinction between static (or standing) data and variable (or current) data.

b. Explain, with the aid of a diagram, how a master file on a magnetic medium is created from existing non-computerised records.

(ACA)

4. a. Define the term "Master File" and list the various elements which may constitute such a file in a Stock Control application.

b. Describe how this file with a dynamic growth pattern would be updated on a disc.
(IDPM)

DATA COMMUNICATION AND CONTROL.

1. a. Briefly describe Optical Character Recognition (OCR) as a method of preparing data for computer input.

b. Name THREE advantages and THREE disadvantages of this method.

c. Identify and briefly explain THREE applications for which OCR is suitable.
(ACA)

2. The usefulness of a data processing system depends on the accuracy of data submitted to it for processing. Give an account of the methods which can be used to ensure that input data is correct and that corrupt data is identified for correction.
(IDPM)

3. a. Describe THREE different methods of data preparation that could be used for a large payroll application. What hardware will be required for each? (15 marks)

b. How will each method affect the organisation of the D.P. Department that runs the job on a central mainframe? (5 marks)
(IDPM)

SYSTEM DESCRIPTION AND PROGRAMMING.

1. In the process of producing a useable program, a number of distinct stages are involved. What are these stages?

Briefly describe what is involved at each stage. (IAS)

2. Programming has become less machine oriented and more problem oriented. Define these terms and explain how changes in programming languages have made this possible. (ICMA).

3. Compare and contrast high-level and low-level languages as methods of programming data processing applications. Illustrated your answer by reference to programming languages which you have used. (IDPM)

4. State the major types of computer software (programs) and describe the purpose and some of the characteristics of each. (SCCA)

Write FULL explanatory notes on the following terms:

a. Macro instruction.
b. Conditional branch.
c. Compiler.
d. Emulator.

(ACA)

5. Because of ever increasing development costs many companies are using packages for routine applications.

a. What are application packages?
b. What are their advantages and disadvantages?
c. What major factors should be examined when considering the use of a package?

(ICMA)

6. What methods are used in computer installations, including those using remote terminals, to:

a. guard against the effects of poor security, and
b. validate input data and the processing of that data?

(ICA)

7. 'A modern computer covering both batched operations on conventional peripherals and terminal based demand processing is as much dependent on software as it is on hardware. Ideally it has only minimal dependence on the human being.'

8. Discuss the roles of operational software and the human element in the context of this quotation. (ICMA)

9. The modern processor has a very small cycle time, but the speed of input and output peripherals is limited. What procedures can be employed to obtain a balance between these marked differences in speed of operation? (IDPM)

10. An installed computer application must be "maintained".

i. Explain what is meant by maintenance from the programmer's point of view.
ii. Describe the procedures involved in maintenance programming.

iii. Indicate how maintenance programming should be organised within a computer department.
(IDPM)

11. With the increasing use of microcomputers, one of the most widely used programming languages is BASIC (Beginners Allpurpose Symbolic Instruction Code) which is a relatively simple example of a particular type of programming language.

You are required to:

a. state what type of programming language is BASIC and the main features of this type of language; (6 marks)

b. explain why languages of this type were developed and are being increasingly used today; (6 marks)

c. state what other level of programming languages are available and the circumstances in which such languages are used. (8 marks)

(ICMA) **(Total: 20 marks)**

FILE PROCESSING AND DATABASE SYSTEMS.

1. a. Describe flowcharting.

b. List the various stages in compiling a systems flowchart.
(SCCA)

2. An accounts department utilises clerical labour and mechanised facilities (ie. Accounting Machines) to produce for management monthly departmentalised trading and profit and loss accounts, and a company balance sheet.

The month end accounting statements are produced on average between fifteen and seventeen working days following the month end to which they relate.

You are required:

a. to suggest five advantages that could possibly result from the computerisation of the accounting systems;

b. to draw a systems flowchart which broadly indicates
   i. the data inputs (eg. Purchase data);
   ii. the outputs (eg. Balance Sheet)

to be produced by the computer system.

(*Note:* Only an outline chart is required).
(IAS)

3. Part of a particular computer program consists of reading the daily sales totals for each of 80 departments of a retail store and printing out the store daily and weekly sales totals.

The first day's sales in department sequence are in the computer main store commencing at address 000 followed by the next day's sales commencing at address 080 and so on for the six day week. Minus sales can occur.

You are required to:

a. prepare a flowchart of a program to print-out daily and weekly store sales totals and

b. name and describe the techniques you have used to reduce the number of instructions contained in the program.
(ICA)

4. A Manufacturing Company employing approximately 2,500 uses a computer to deal with payroll accounting. The system is designed to meet the requirements of weekly and monthly paid employees.

Prior to the main weekly or monthly computer runs an employee master file (held on disk) is updated. There are about 200 transaction records giving details of changes to be made to the master file each week.

You are required to:

a. give five reasons for updating the master file;

b. name three outputs other than weekly and monthly payroll that could be produced from the computerised payroll systems;

c. draw a systems flowchart for the master file update.
(IAS)

5. In updating records held sequentially on magnetic tape, transaction record keys are compared with the keys of records on the brought forward master file and, depending on the result of the comparison, different processing paths are followed.

Required:

Draw an outline flowchart which shows the matching operations and the processing which normally takes place as a result of them. Your flowchart should provide for the situation when the last records (numbered 99999) of each of the files are read. You are not required to show the logical processes when amendments, deletions and insertions are made to a master file; your chart should deal only with transaction data. (ACA)

6. A warehouse operates the following stock control procedures.

A free stock balance (physical stock plus outstanding replenishment orders less unfulfilled orders) is compared with the re-order level and if it is at or below re-order level a replenishment order is placed. If a replenishment order has already been placed, a standard progressing letter is sent.

If the free stock balance is at or below the emergency level, any replenishment order will be subject to the emergency progressing procedures. If no replenishment order is outstanding a rush order will be sent. If the free stock balance is greater than re-order level but below maximum level and a replenishment order is outstanding, the delivery of the replenishment order is delayed for one week.

If the free stock level is at or above maximum level, any replenishment order outstanding is cancelled. If the free stock level goes above the maximum level more than once in any month, all levels and re-order quantities for that item are reviewed.

You are required:

a. to construct a limited entry decision table covering the above procedures;

b. to state the circumstances in which systems analysts would prefer to use decision tables rather than flowcharts.

(ICMA)

7. An alternative term sometimes used for commercial data processing is file processing.

a. Define file processing.

b. Describe master and transaction files.

c. Give the major considerations which govern the choice of the type of hardware storage for a given file. (20 marks)

(ICMA)

8. a. What is the function of a Database Administrator? (8 marks)

b. Describe briefly any THREE of the following:

i. Indexed Sequential Files (4 marks)
ii. Inverted Files (4 marks)
iii. Hierarchial Files (4 marks)
iv. Hashing. (4 marks)

SOFTWARE.

1. a. The terms compiler and interpreter are often used in the area of computer software.

Compare and contrast the operation of a computer program using these two methods. (10 marks)

b. Explain the difference between an assembly language and a high level language, illustrating your answer by referring to a high level language with which you are familiar. (10 marks)

(ACA)

2. What is an operating system? (3 marks)
Why is it necessary? (3 marks)
What functions does it perform? (14 marks)
(Total 20 marks)

SYSTEMS ANALYSIS.

1. Explain how a systems analyst might undertake the task of investigation and analysis of a non-computerised business system. You may assume that management have already approved the feasibility study and authorised ongoing development. (IDPM)

2. What are the essential factors a systems analyst should consider when designing financial information systems? (SCCA)

3. If is not uncommon for system designers involved in the introduction of computer based data processing to encounter resentment and oppostion from existing employees.

For what reasons may employees react in this manner? What steps can the system designer take to reduce this resistance? (ICMA)

4. 'Errors in a program are of two main types: errors due to incorrect use of the programming language and errors due to incorrect logic in the solution of the problem.'

Explain this statement and show fully how errors of both types are detected and amended. (ACA)

5. List, and comment on, the principal factors which the systems analyst should take into consideration when designing the output to be produced by a computer-based system. (ACA)

6. XYZ Ltd maintains its sales ledger system on a mini-computer. The sales ledger master file is held on magnetic disk. Accounts, which contain the usual standard data, are kept on a brought forward balance basis with the total balance analysed over current month, month 1, month 2, month 3 and month 4 and over. Visual display units are employed for the entry of transaction data and for the retrieval of data for answering enquiries. A variety of printed reports is produced on the line printer.

Required:

a. Identify and briefly explain FIVE items of transaction data which would be input to the system.

b. Draft, with TWO lines of sample entries, the Credit Limit Excess and Aged Balance report which is produced monthly for the Accounts Manager. Your answer should be in the format of a typical computer-produced line-printer report.

(ACA)

7. The auditors have asked that a section of each system specification used by your company should be devoted to the control aspects of the process of data capture through to transfer by the computer on to the magnetic storage media.

Using, for purposes of illustration, a sales order system, which commences with the completion of sales order forms by sales representatives in the field, prepare the section of the systems specification referred to above. (ICMA)

8. Taking a typical sales invoicing system as your subject matter:

a. illustrate the application of the system design formula:
Output data – Input data = File data + Calculated data;

b. state how you would then determine the contents of the file or files required by the system producing the invoices.

(ICMA)

9. a. What are the major tasks to be undertaken in systems analysis and design? (Your answer should be a concise explanation – excessive detail is *NOT* required).

b. As a method of systems changeover explain what is meant by parallel running and state its disadvantages.
(IAS)

10. A firm of chartered accountants has a time recording system on its in-house tape-based computer. The system reports include the following:

a. Staff report, showing for each employee for the current week and year to date, the chargeable hours, the charge out value of those hours, the non-chargeable hours and value and the percentage of non-chargeable hours to total hours. This is printed in employee sequence, within departments.

b. Fee report, showing for the current week, the amount of each bill in client number sequence, together with the total hours and value written off against each bill and the amount of over/under recovery compared with the scale charge.

c. Work in progress report, showing for each client, the total hours and value of those hours unbilled at the end of each week. This is prepared in client number sequence.

The system includes the following files:

i. Employee charge out rate file.

ii. Employee history file which includes, for each employee, name, chargeable hours and value to date and non-chargeable hours and value to date. Non-chargeable time is time not charged to a client, for example, holidays, study leave and courses.

The input consists of time sheets and draft bill forms which show the information to complete the fee report.

You are required to prepare computer run flowcharts for both types of input and for the printing of the staff report, the fee report and the work in progress report. (ICA)

11. Seymour Spectacles Limited is the sole United Kingdom distributor of a French manufacturer's spectacle frames and its objective is to provide an ex-stock delivery service to its optician customers. This service is seldom achieved and it now aims to carry sufficient stock of each variation of frame to cover the estimated sales of the ensuing eight weeks.

A weekly order is placed on the French manufacturer for delivery in four weeks' time.

The sales manager has been instructed to prepare the necessary estimates of future weekly customer orders for each stock line.

The company has an in-house disk based computer and it is proposed that a weekly computer report should be produced suitable for the purpose of stock ordering.

You are required to:

a. express the elements of information which are required to calculate the number of units of each stock line to be ordered each week, in the form of an order formula,

b. draft a form of "weekly stock order requirement report" containing these elements, and

c. prepare a flowchart illustrating only the computer run required to produce the report and specify, in supplementary notes, the input into each of the files accessed in the run.

(ICA)

12. A manufacturer wishes to maintain a computer based file of all customers' orders outstanding.

A typical order from a customer comprises the following information:

		Maximum number of characters
Customer's name		30
Date of order		9
Delivery date requested		9
Customer's order number		10
Product group	6 ×	9
Size code	6 ×	9
Description	6 ×	30
Quantity	6 ×	3

Each week the master file of outstanding orders will be updated by:

	Approximate number per week
i. Addition of new orders	200
ii. Deletion of despatches including partial despatches	220
iii. Order amendments including cancellations	50

The outstanding orders master file will contain approximately 1,000 outstanding orders.

You are required to specify a complete data processing system which will provide the following facilities:

1 weekly updating of master file;

2 weekly report all outstanding orders in order number within customer number within product group sequence;

3 weekly report showing total value of new orders for each product group;

4 weekly report of despatches for week showing total value per customer for each product group;

5 monthly report showing the total value of outstanding orders per size within delivery date.

At a minimum your specification should include:

a. an outline of the computer configuration required, listing the main items of equipment;

b. a systems flowchart containing or supported by brief narrative;

c. details of the file(s) you intend to maintain;

d. details of the minimum inputs necessary.

Any facts or figures not given above, which you feel are necessary in designing your system, may be included in your answer but must be clearly specified. (ICMA)

13. A company is to introduce a computer based production control system. As part of the overall system the weekly production activities are to be planned as follows:

a. The production controller determines quantities for each assembly to be manufactured for the following week. This is termed the 'assembly build progamme' (ABP).

b. For each assembly on the programme (approximately 300 per week) the assembly number and quantity are entered to magnetic tape on a key/tape system.

c. The data processing procedure is as follows:

   i. Input data are read and validated and an error report is produced.

   ii. Input data are checked for the feasibility of ABP, to determine components required for each assembly and to access/update component stock to produce the following two reports:

      1. made-in components in short supply report, showing components needed for ABP, in component number sequence;

      2. bought-out components report, in component number sequence.

d. Updated component stocks are processed to produce two reports:

   i. made-in component manufacturing programme, showing economic batch quantity for each component that has less stock than minimum stock level;

   ii. similarly, a bought-out components purchasing programme.

e. Check made-in component manufacturing programming data for feasibility, to determine the raw material requirements and availability of raw material for each component to update raw material stock file and to produce the following reports:

   i. made-in components with raw materials shortage report, in component number sequence;

   ii. raw materials in short supply report, in raw material code sequence.

f. Process updated raw material stocks and produce stock report for items having less stock than minimum stock level.

It may be assumed that the main files have already been determined as follows:

Assembly master file on disk pack A
Indexed sequential form in assembly number sequence containing the breakdown of components per assembly for 3,000 assemblies.

Component master file on disk pack B
Indexed sequential form in component number sequence sub-divided into bought-out and made-in component sub-files. There are 6,000 bought-out component records containing details of suppliers, prices and other information. also there are 12,000 made-in component records containing details of raw materials, production processes, tools required etc.

Component stock file on disk pack C
Indexed sequential form in component number sequence sub-divided into bought-out and made-in component sub-files. The file contains details of current stock balances, re-order levels, batch quantities, stores locations etc.

Raw material stock file on disk pack C
Indexed sequential form in raw material code sequences containing current stock balances, re-order levels, batch quantities, stores locations etc.

The computer configuration consists of a medium size central processor, two magnetic tape units, three exchangeable disk units and a line printer.

You are required to:

a. Design and flowchart a system for processing the information and producing the results specified above. Your answer should contain sufficient narrative to explain adequately the system you have designed.

b. Note that the system flowchart requested in a. above is but one part of the documentation required for a full specification of the system. Describe, briefly, three other items which would be required for the complete recording of the system, but do not fully specify them.

(ICMA)

14. An engineering group consists of eleven branch factories located within a 30 mile radius of its head office.

The group already possesses a medium sized computer with both serial and direct access backing storage. This is used for a variety of production control and accounting work. It is proposed to introduce a computer based plant register and maintenance accounting system for all items of works equipment, machine tools, office machinery and vehicles. Each item of plant is identified by a ten digit code of the following format.

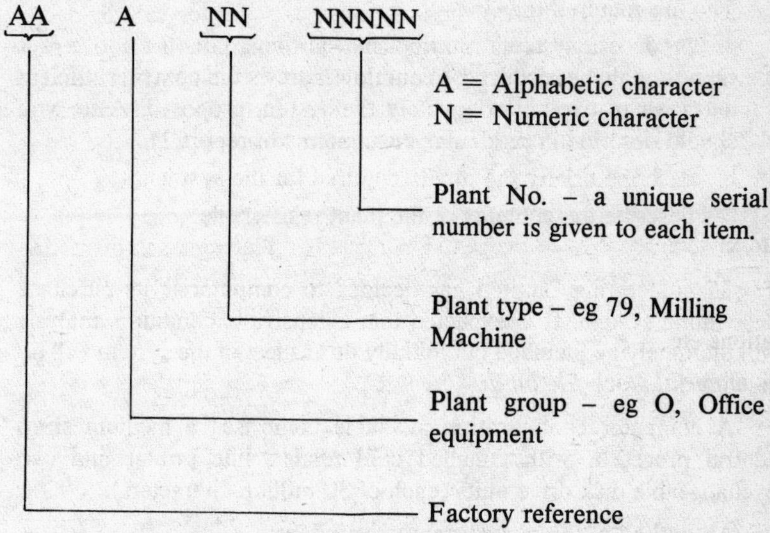

There are some 16,000 plant items in the group which are each serviced under the planned maintenance system approximately once each month. In addition to the planned servicing, approximately 25% of the machines require some intermediate form of attention.

Approximately 10% of the plant items are replaced each year. At a minimum the system must provide for the following reports:

Report 1 (weekly)	Plant maintenance statement showing labour and material costs per item serviced distinguishing between planned and unplanned servicing, in plant number sequence.
Report 2 (monthly)	Machine performance report providing information that will enable management to decide whether it is more economical to replace existing plant items. This

	report to be in plant number sequence within plant type for each plant group.
Report 3 (monthly)	Cost summary showing (totals only) current written down value and past month's maintenance and repair costs per plant type within plant group within factory sequence.
Report 4 (annually)	Plant depreciation report in plant number sequences.

You are required to:

a. produce a systems run flowchart showing how the above four reports could be produced; (Your flowchart should contain sufficient narrative to explain adequately the system proposed. Also, you should describe in particular the contents of report 2).

b. describe briefly the inputs required for the system;

c. describe the contents of the plant register file.

(ICMA)

15. Manufacturing Limited has decided to computerise its purchase accounting system. It is expected that extensive expenditure analysis will ultimately be included but initially this aspect of the system will be restricted.

A computer configuration available comprises a medium sized central processor with punched card reader, line printer and two exchangeable disk drive units (each of 30 million characters).

An outline of the new system is as follows:

Source Document

A source document will be created clerically from purchase invoices passed for payment. The contents of this document will be:

source document reference number
supplier identification code number
supplier's own reference number
invoice date

expense code amount value added tax rate	} occurs {	minimum × average × 1.2 maximum × 5

Output

This source data will be processed to produce these outputs:

i. Purchase daybook, being a daily listing of all prime data input, in source document reference number sequence.

ii. Remittance advices, containing supplier name and address and full details of invoices being paid in supplier identification code number sequence.
iii. Credit transfers, containing payer and payee bank details and amount, in supplier bank reference number sequence.
iv. Supplier analysis giving total expenditure for this month and this year to date per supplier, in supplier identification code number sequence within supplier category (note: suppliers are categorised according to the type of goods supplied, eg. raw metal, stationery, lubricating oils).
v. Expense code anlaysis giving total expenditure per each expense code.

It will be noted that i. above will be produced daily, while ii., iii., iv., and v. will be produced at the month end.

Predicted Volumes

Purchase invoices per day	200
Suppliers	2,000
Expense codes	70

Any facts or figures not given may be assumed provided each assumption is clearly stated.

You are required to submit the following:

a. computer system run flowchart(s) with brief narrative for the purchase accounting/expenditure analysis system;

b. a description of the main files required;

c. a suggested lay-out for print-out iv. above, the monthly supplier analysis.

(ICMA)

APPLICATIONS AND COMPUTER SYSTEMS.

1. Specify and describe hardware and software required for a real time computer application system. (IDPM)

2. As systems manager you have been asked to prepare a report on simulation for the board.

Your report should cover amongst other things:
i. a full definition of simulation;
ii. the process by which simulation exercises are developed;
iii. possible areas where simulation could usefully be employed;

iv. ways in which the efficiency of a simulation exercise can be judged;

v. the role of the computer in simulation.

(ICMA)

3. An increasing number of organisations are contemplating installing, or have installed, systems involving a data base. What factors have led to these developments and what are the characteristics of an efficient data base? (ICMA)

4. 'The different nature of Batch and Real Time processing requires a completely different approach to the subject of data validation.' Discuss. (IDPM)

5. What contribution can the modern microcomputer make to data processing applications? Explain the advantages and disadvantages of this type of equipment for data processing work. (IDPM)

6. a. Identify, and briefly explain, FIVE of the characteristics of the minicomputer which distinguish it from the larger main-frame machine.

b. Define 'distributed data processing' and explain the role played by the minicomputer in a distributed data processing system. (ACA)

7. 'Modern hardware developments are causing a movement away from centralised data processing systems to dispersed systems operating at or close to actual business activities.'

Describe the hardware developments referred to in this quotation.

What are the advantages and disadvantages of this movement? (ICMA)

8. You have been asked to prepare a report for the board of directors explaining the general features of Teletext systems (e.g. Ceefax and Oracle) and Viewdata systems (e.g. Prestel). Your report should also include an assessment of the likely commercial uses (if any) of the systems.

(20 marks)

(ICMA)

MANAGEMENT OF EDP.

1. XYZ Limited is about to consider for the first time the use of a computer for data processing work. A small steering committee of senior managers, under the chairmanship of the managing director, has been set up to exercise overall control of this development.

2. What advice would you give the committee to help ensure that computerised systems will be successfully introduced into the company? (ACA)

a. What are the characteristics of a business system which signify that the system is potentially suitable for transfer to computer operation?

b. 'A computer may be used for financial modelling,' Explain this statement.

(ACA)

3. A production planning and control system is being investigated with a view to computerisation. The systems investigators have been asked to include a financial justification for the new system in their report. What would such a justification include and how might the financial effects of the system be monitored after installation? (ICMA)

4. You are the accountant at XYZ Ltd. Budgetary control is in operation and quarterly accounts are prepared for presentation to management.

Required:

Draft a specimen Budget Performance Report for XYZ's Computer Department. Your form should show clearly the main heads of expenditure with the principal items of expense under each head. SAMPLE ENTRIES ARE NOT REQUIRED. (ACA)

5. a. Describe with the aid of a diagram the route which a typical batch processing job would take through the various sections of a computer operations department. (The diagram should start *and* end in the outside user department).

b. Explain the functions of the Data Control staff with respect to the above job.

(IDPM)

6. a. Produce an organisation chart for a typical medium sized computer department.

b. Describe four of the jobs that appear on your chart.

(ICMA)

7. ABC Ltd's computer department contains some 35 members of staff, including the computer manager. Analysts and programmers work together in project teams under team leaders.

Required:

a. Draft what in your opinion would be a typical organisation chart for this computer department. The distribution of staff should be clearly shown.

b. Identify the principal responsibilities of the operations manager in a computer department.

(ACA)

8. Your organisation is about to install a computer system but your auditors have written to you expressing their concern over the proposal as they fear that the audit trail may be lost.

9. Draft a reply to your auditors responding to their concern and, in addition, pointing out ways in which the computer can assist the audit process. (ICMA)

a. List and comment on the criteria used in deciding whether or not a particular application is suitable for computer processing, and

b. describe the features of an application for a wholesale stockist which you consider ideally suited to computer processing and state how it meets the listed criteria.

(ICA)

10. You have been asked to advise a local firm of Solicitors over the operation of their accounting procedures, which are at present done manually. Required:

a. Assuming that your advice is to computerize the operation of its accounting procedures, outline three different options open to the firm. (8 marks)

b. Explain the problem that will be met in file creation and conversion due to the computerization of the firm's records. (6 marks)

c. Explain three different types of changeover that can be related to the computerization of the accounting procedures. (6 marks)

(20 marks)

(ACA)

11. Your DP manager is concerned about security of your company's programs, data and equipment. What measures would you suggest to minimise problems in these areas?

(IDPM Part II)

12. File conversion (or file creation) is always a major practical problem when a new computer-based system is being implemented.

Assume that a new computer-based accounting system is to be implemented and source data are at present held in various types of clerical files in several locations.

You are required to describe:

a. the objectives of file conversion; (5 marks)

b. the typical problems that would be encountered in the situation outlined; (8 marks)

c. the way the file conversion process should be planned and controlled. (7 marks)

(ICMA) **(Total: 20 marks)**

GENERAL.

1. The advent of the mini-computer represents a threat to both the business of computer bureaux and to the sales of full scale computers.

Discuss this statement and compare the relative advantages and disadvantages for the smaller business of owning a mini-computer or of using a computer bureaux. (ICMA)

2. a. The introduction of an 'in-house' data processing system incurs costs at different stages.

You are required to:

i. suggest four stages under which costs could be grouped;

ii. for any stage given in i. to briefly describe the costs incurred (eg. clerical costs);

iii. suggest possible measures of systems performance (eg. cost reduction) which could be used where a 'Sales System' has been computerised.

b. What is meant by timesharing? Where timesharing facilities operate, what kind of backing store is required and why?

(IAS)

3. Write explanatory notes on the following data processing terms:

a. Magnetic ledger cards.

b. Turnaround documents.

c. Conditional branch.

d. Application packages.

(IAS)

4. In regard to a computerized system, define and describe the main features of each of the following:

a. utility programs;
b. serial access;
c. kimball tag;
d. trailer label;
e. optical scanning, and
f. parallel running.

(SCCA)

5. State

a. the various types of inputs to and
b. the various reports produced by

an efficient information system for the management accounting function in a manufacturing business. (SCCA)

6. The master record of a computerised stock control system consists of the following fields:

Field Name	*Number of Characters*	*Type*
Stock Code	4	9
Stock Description	30	A
Bin Number	3	9
Supplier Code	4	9
Balance Data:		
Orders on suppliers	5	9
Bin Stock	5	9
Price (Average)	4	9
Stock Value	8	9

Note: Type 9 = Numeric
A = Alphanumeric

The three transaction records processed relate to 'Orders Placed on Suppliers'. 'Goods Received from Suppliers' and 'Goods Sold to Customers'.

You are required to design the layout for an input card or cards which would be processed to update the master record.

Assuming the 'Balance Data' for stock item number 5,000 at the commencement of the update run to be:

Orders on Suppliers	10,000 units
Bin Stock	25,000 units
Price	£1.50
Stock Value	£37,500

Illustrate the effect on the master record where

a. an order for 2,500 units has been placed on a supplier;

b. a delivery of 7,500 units has been received from a supplier at £1.50 unit;

c. 5,000 units have been sold to a customer.

(IAS)

7. In regard to a computerized system, define and describe the main features of each of the following:

a. multi-programming;

b. magnetic disk;

c. executive program;

d. real time;

e. test pack, and

f. grandfather–father–son principle.

(SCCA)

8. In regard to a computerized system, define and describe the main features of each of the following, indicating its purpose:

a. buffer;

b. application package;

c. assembler program;

d. optical character reading;

e. real time processing, and

f. visual display unit.

(SCCA)

9. a. State briefly your understanding of the terms 'data processing' and 'systems design'.

b. Why do you consider that the Association of Certified Accountants includes these topics for study in its scheme of examinations?

(ACA)

10. a. Explain what is meant by the term 'Software', and give examples of the various types. (8 marks)

In the situation of an Organisation having its own programmers who write, test and develop programs written in a high level language, what would be the minimum software required by the Organisation? (4 marks)

(Your answer should indicate any assumptions made.)

b. The 'O and M' analyst and 'systems' analyst are both concerned with the efficiency of systems and the application of 'standards'.

What is a standard, what are the two main types and what purpose do they serve? (8 marks)

(Total 20 marks)

(AAT)

11. a. Control in a data processing department is maintained by setting 'Standards' and the provision of adequate systems documentation.

i. What are the two types of standards created and what do they seek to ensure? (4 marks)

ii. Why is documentation necessary? Give five reasons. (10 marks)

b. One of many services provided by a bureau is 'Timesharing'.

Explain what is meant by this term and how the user gains access to the computing facilities. (6 marks)

(Total 20 marks)

(AAT)

12. A critical stage in the implementation of any new computer-based system is initial file creation.

You are required to explain:

a. the objectives and general approach to initial file creation;

b. the control and security procedures necessary at this stage;

c. the particular problems involved when the data for file creation emanate from various sources and how these can be overcome.

(ICMA) **(20 marks)**

13. In the early days of computers a major problem was the high cost of the hardware involved. With the falling real cost of hardware, attention is increasingly being focused on the costs and time involved in developing appropriate software.

You are required to:

a. identify the developments which have led to the situation described; (7 marks)

b. describe possible ways in which a user organisation can minimise the problems and costs involved in software development. (13 marks)

(ICMA) **(Total: 20 marks)**

14. Using for illustrative purposes an inventory control system, **you are required to:**

a. outline the stages in the analysis, design and implementation of an appropriate data processing system; and

b. explain how management control of the project would be achieved. (20 marks)

(ICMA)

Appendix 3.

Details which have been omitted from the text in the interests of clarity.

Appendix 3.1. Check Digits

INTRODUCTION.

1. a. A check digit is a means of ensuring that a number (eg. a customer account number) maintains its validity.

b. It is calculated using a modulus. Various moduli are used in practice and each has varying degrees of success at preventing certain types of errors. MODULUS 11 (eleven) is used here.

2. Check digits are calculated by a computer in the first place and are generally used in conjunction with *fixed* data (ie. customer's number etc). As a result of a test done on Modulus 11 it was discovered that it detected all transcription and transposition errors and 91% of random errors.

CALCULATING THE CHECK DIGIT.

3. a. Original code number 4214

b. Multiply each *digit* by the *weights* 5432

c. Product = $(4 \times 5) = 20$
$(2 \times 4) = 8$
$(1 \times 3) = 3$
$(4 \times 2) = 8$

d. Sum of products = 39

e. Divide by modulus (11) = 3 and 6 Remainder.

f. Subtract *remainder* from modulus (ie. $11 - 6) = 5$.

g. *5 is the check digit.*

h. Code number now becomes 42145.

CHECKING OF NUMBERS.

4. When the code number is input to the computer precisely the same calculation can be carried out (using weight of 1 for right-most/or junior digit) and the resultant remainder should be 0. If not then the number is incorrect:-

$$42145 = (4 \times 5) + (2 \times 4) + (1 \times 3) + (4 \times 2) + (5 \times 1) = 44$$

Divide by 11; remainder = 0.

Note:

1. Where appropriate this check can be carried out off-line using a machine called a CHECK DIGIT VERIFIER. This machine is sometimes linked to an accounting machine to ensure validity of the account number etc., included in data captured as a by-product in paper tape for subsequent processing by a computer.

2. Students should have a ready worked example of a check digit in order to impress examiner in an appropriate answer.

3. An original code giving rise to the check "digit" 10 is normally discarded.

Appendix 3.2. System Flowcharts

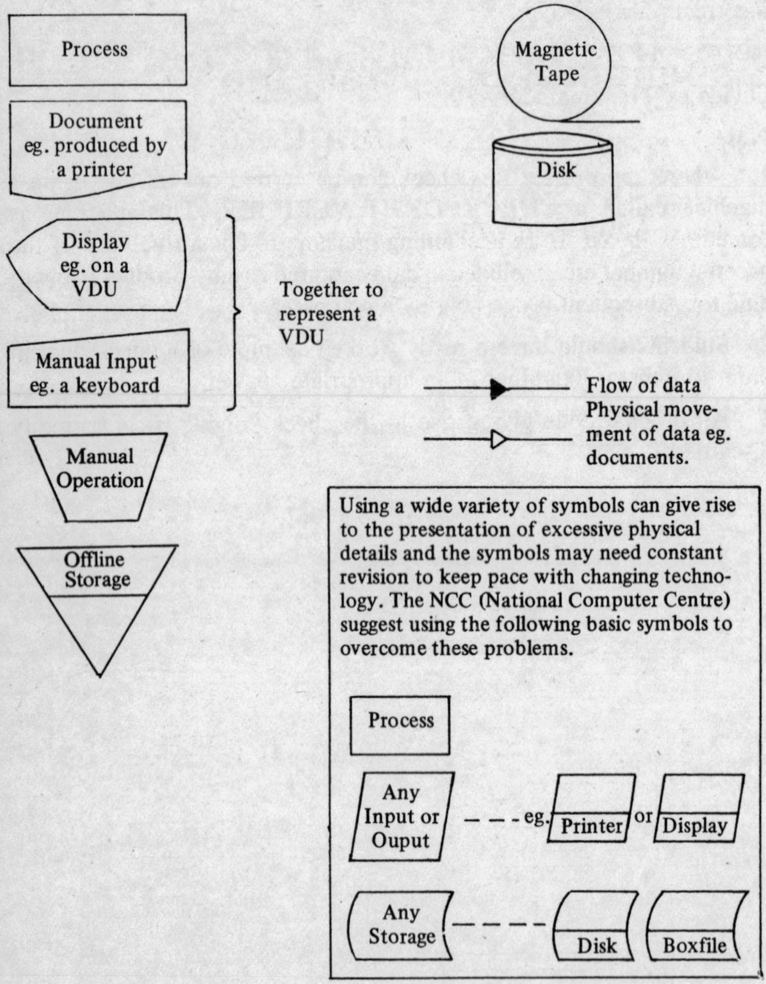

(Consult your examination regulations to see which symbols you should use in your examination).

SYSTEM FLOWCHART SYMBOLS.

A system flowchart may show what the data processing procedures are, and how the procedures are arranged into sequences, but it will *not* show how the procedures are carried out.

Appendix 3.3. Machine Language

1. The details given here supplement those given in chapter 22.

2. The example in Fig. 7.2 was based upon a fictitious 16-bit machine which is described in detail in "Computer Studies" by C. S. French, Pub. DP Publications.

3. The execution of instructions can be understood more fully by reference to this diagram:-

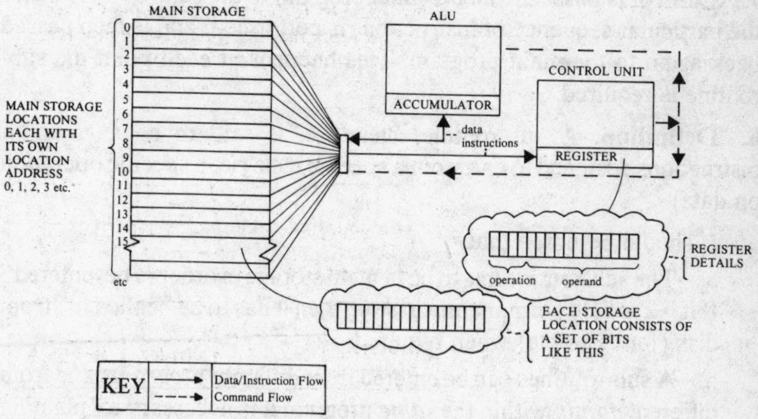

SOME DETAILS OF THE PROCESSOR AND MAIN STORAGE RELEVANT TO MACHINE LANGUAGE EXECUTION.

Note

a. Instructions are fetched from main storage into a register where they can be interpreted by the control unit which then sends the appropriate commands to the hardware.

b. Data can be "loaded" into "accumulators" in the ALU. Once it is in the accumulator, various arithmetic and logic operations may be performed on the data. Results are transfered back into main storage.

MACHINE LANGUAGE SUBROUTINES.

4. Subprograms (21.27) in machine language are normally called "subroutines". Further details of subroutines, directly related to machine language, are given here.

5. A particular processing operation will very often be performed at several *different* points in a program. The particular group of program instructions necessary to carry out the operation *could* be included at *each* of the different points. This is wasteful of storage space especially if the operation involves a *large* number of instructions.

6. A technique used in these circumstances is *not* to include the instructions in the *main program* but to have them in *another* part of main storage. Such a group of instructions is known as a sub-routine. Examples of sub-routines are PAYE, N.I., etc, calculations.

7. Control is passed from the main program to the sub-routine (where the particular sequence of instructions is performed) and is then passed back again to the main program. This happens at each point the sub-routine is required.

8. Definition. A sub-routine, therefore, is said to be a group of instructions designed to carry out a specific task. (ie. a specific operation on data).

It should be noted that:-

a. The sub-routine has to be in main storage in order to be 'entered'. If it is *not* held permanently in store then it has to be "called in" from disk (for example) when required.

b. A sub-routines can be entered from different *programs* and from different *points* within the *same* program it is necessary to 'plant' in the sub-routine the address in the main program to which return must be made.

9. The sub-routine described so far is a *closed* sub-routine. Sometimes the distinction is made between this type and an *open* sub-routine. An open sub-routine is actually included as part of the main program itself. Students should assume *closed* sub-routines in an examination question unless otherwise directed. See the following diagram (Appendix 3.4).

Appendix 3.4. Examples of Sub-routines (SR)

1. **OPEN.** 2. **CLOSED.**

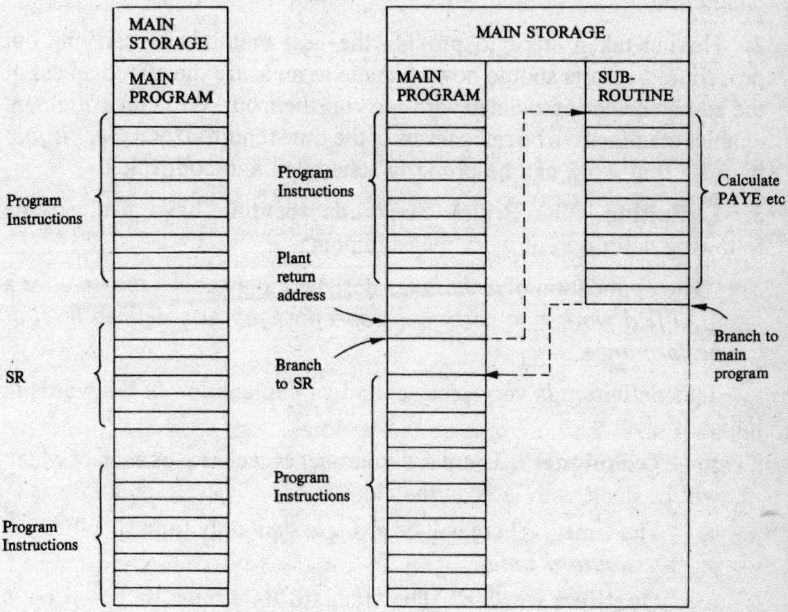

Note:

The open SR really becomes part of the program.

Note:

1. SR must be in main storage before branch is made.

2. The last instruction in SR will be a "BRANCH". *Before* entering SR the main program will modify the operand of this instruction by planting there the address in the main program to which control will pass on completion of the instructions contained in SR. Note this is an example of address modification.

3. The procedure above could be repeated several times during the execution of the main program and therefore return address will be *different* each time.

4. When the main program is *compiled* it must include an indication that the particular SR will be required during running of *object* program so that compiler can include necessary linkage instructions required during running of the program.

Appendix 3.5. Work Measurement

1. This material may be related to the discussion of O & M given in chapter 30.

2. Having taken steps to provide the best methods of carrying out procedures, efforts should now be made to measure the effectiveness of the human beings associated with carrying them out. Work measurement enables standards to be set in terms of the time required for a *specific job,* in order that work can be properly scheduled and controlled.

3. Definition. The British Standards Institute have evolved the following definition of work measurement:-

"The application of *techniques* designed to establish *the time* for a *qualified worker* to carry out a *specified job* at a defined *level of performance.*"

This definition is very precise, and an explanation of the words in italics is given:-

a. **"Techniques".** There are a number of techniques each of which will be dealt with later in the chapter.

b. **"The time."** There will be a *single time* only for a specified job ie. the *standard time.*

c. **"Qualified worker".** The standard time must be based upon workers skilled and experienced in their job.

d. **"Specified job."** The time must be related to a job which is clearly defined, ie. the *method* of carrying out the job must be laid down with the *starting* and *finishing* points of the job clearly stated.

e. **"Defined level of performance".** The *pace* at which the work is to be carried out must be a defined *standard pace.*

The pace at which a person is working can be judged, by an expert O & M practitioner, against what he considers to be a standard pace. For example, by observation, the O & M practitioner could judge that a particular worker is operating at 80% of standard.

In compiling the standard time, the *pace* at which the specified job has been judged will be equated to standard pace, eg. if a specified job is timed at 60 seconds, with an observed *pace* of working of 80%, then the time for the job at *standard pace* is 48 seconds (80% of 60 seconds).

4. Techniques of work measurement. (Conforming to British Standards Institute definition).

a. **Time study.** A trained observer times the job (or elements of the job if it can be suitably broken down into constituent parts) with a stop watch, over many cycles. An average time is then produced for the job. The *pace* of working is also judged.

The standard time is then compiled by:-

i. Adjusting the *observed time* taken to one at *standard pace.*

ii. Adding necessary allowances, eg. relaxation etc.

b. **Synthesis.** The time for a job is built up by accumulating time for *elements* of the job which have been previously time studied.

c. **Pre-determined time systems.** The time for a job is built up by accumulating times of basic human motions (such as 'reach', 'grasp' etc). Many systems have been developed whereby the basic human motions have been timed by time study or film analysis and tables of the time compiled. Through recognition of the motions involved in a particular job, the standard time can be built up by consulting the tables.

d. **Rated activity sampling.** A large number of random observations are made over a period of time. A note is made of the actual work being carried out at the time of the observations, and the pace of the individual. The technique is based on the premise that a random sample, if sufficiently large and representative, will reflect the behaviour of the whole. Statistical methods provide the means of establishing the minimum size of sample required to achieve a given degree of reliability.

e. **Analytical estimating.** The time for a job is built up by accumulating times for *elements* of the job which have been *estimated* through knowledge and practical experience of the elements concerned.

Notice that the techniques listed above all conform to the British Standards Institute definition. The standard times are produced as a result of trained observers adjusting the observed pace of workers to a standard pace, using qualified workers carrying out a defined job.

5. Other techniques of work measurement. The British Standards Institute (BSI) definition was evolved in terms of work measurement on the factory floor, where work is *routine* and *repetitive.* Many data processing jobs could well be measured using one of the techniques conforming to the BSI definition. However, as there are many jobs *not* suited to measurement by such techniques, others have been developed.

a. **Time surveys.** Time sheets are filled in by a clerk or an O & M practitioner observing the work being done, (eg. filing 25 documents in 7 minutes; sorting 1000 documents in 25 minutes) and standard times for the job are established.

b. **Activity sampling.** This is similar to Rated Activity Sampling except that no attempt is made to judge the pace of working.

c. **Historical data.** Use is made of past records to show the time required for particular volumes eg. "1000 invoices actioned in one week by one clerk."

It is emphasised that the techniques listed above do *not* attempt to judge the pace of working.

6. **Choice of technique.** The nature of the work largely determines the particular technique to be used. Where the work is routine and repetitive (eg. copy typing), techniques such as Time Study or a pre-determined system could be used and precise standards set. Where the work is not so routine or occurs only once or twice a month (eg. balancing the accounts) a technique such as Time Survey or the use of Historical data would be more appropriate and less stringent standards set.

Control. Once standards have been set, work can be scheduled and controlled. Control registers, graphs, gantt charts, and batching of work can all be used, as appropriate, to aid control.

7. **Place in O & M.** Ideally, a study of the method should first be carried out. After agreement for the new method has been arrived at, the work should be measured in order that appropriate standards may be set. Therefore in the overall stage of O & M, work measurement fits in *after* agreement of the method but *prior* to implementation. In some cases, the most apropriate *method* to be adopted may be dependent on the *time taken* by alternatives (eg. sorting by machine or clerk), in which case work measurement techniques are required at the fact finding stage. If there is not sufficient *time* to investigate alternative *methods,* work measurement *can* be applied to the *current method.*

Note:

a. Study of Method and Work Measurement do tend to overlap, but for examination purposes can be thought of separately – a concluding paragraph in an answer stating the places of overlap is often a good ploy.

b. In Work Measurement, there are the clearly distinguishable types of work; routine, repetitive work for which accurate standards can be set if *required,* and irregular work, or work occupying only an hour or so a week, for which less stringent standards are appropriate.

Appendix 4

1. This appendix contains notes on:

a. Using the questions and answers provided in the manual.

b. Effective study.

c. Examination technique.

Appendix 4.1 Questions and Answers

INTRODUCTION.

1. Two types of question are provided in this manual.

a. Questions set at the ends of chapters *with answers* provided in Appendix 1.

b. Questions *without answers* set in Appendix 2.

QUESTIONS WITH ANSWERS.

2. These questions are either

a. questions intended to test the understanding of the points arising out of the particular chapter

or

b. examination questions inserted at a stage where it is considered the student will be best able to give a reasonable answer.

3. Most answers are given in outline but some examination answers go a little further in order to provide greater guidance and provide students with the basis for study.

4. Where answers are *comprehensive* you couldn't be expected to write them in the time allowed. *Do not worry* if you feel you couldn't write such answers; you are not expected to. But you *must* grasp the *main* points or principles involved which will form the basis for good marks in an examination.

5. Do not worry if your answer differs, there is often more than *one* approach. You must satisfy yourself however, that it is *only* the approach that differs, and that you haven't missed the fundamental principles.

6. Authors' Comments. These have been included to give *additional* points or to elaborate on matters arising out of the subject covered by the question to which it is felt you should give some thought.

USING THE ANSWERS.

7. Have a shot at each question yourself *before* consulting the answer; you will achieve nothing if you don't do this. Write your answer out in full or jot down the main points. *Do not* hurry to the answer.

8. Look at the answer. (See para 5 in the case of examination answers). Study the particular area *thoroughly* now making sure of your understanding. *Repeat* the process outlined in para 7 and this para after a suitable interval. You *must* do this to get any benefit at all. Make sure the main points *stick.*

9. Just browsing through the answers will really get you *nowhere.* You *must* test yourself by *writing* down your version of the answer.

QUESTIONS WITHOUT ANSWERS.

10. The questions are provided in Appendix 2. They are intended for use in conjunction with classroom tuition. The questions, taken from papers of the ICA, ACA, ICMA, IAS, AAT, SCCA, IDPM, are grouped according to Parts of the Manual.

Appendix 4.2 Effective Study

INTRODUCTION.

1. These notes are intended for those who are new to studying for examination subjects, although those who are not may also benefit. They have been written in relation to study involving the reading of *text books,* and they apply to *all* subjects. It is often extremely difficult to pick out the important principles from such books. As the DATA PROCESSING MANUAL *is* an INSTRUCTIONAL manual your DP studies should be made much easier. Nevertheless careful reading of these notes will be of benefit even in studying the manual.

GENERAL.

2. Study means more than *just reading* a piece of literature. It means *close concentrated reading* with a *notebook* at your side. Unless you're one of a *few* people don't kid yourself you can absorb material by *just one* general read through it, you cannot!

3. Read a small area, *making notes* as you go along. Then ask yourself – what have I just learnt? *Write* down what you think it was all about. Then look again and you may be surprised to find you've missed a *key* point or points – they *must* be down in your notebook and eventually in your head.

COMPILATION OF NOTEBOOK.

4. A *well compiled* NOTEBOOK is a must. Use block capitals or different colour inks to *headline* the main areas and subdivisions of those areas. Notes made during lectures or private study should *not* go straight into your NOTEBOOK. Take them down on "rough" paper and write them in your NOTEBOOK *as soon as possible* after the lecture or study period, *thinking* about what you are writing. This does not apply to studying the DP manual which itself can be used as your notebook.

MEMORY AIDS.

5. **Mnemonics** are very useful – if the sequence of points in the text book *isn't* significant, *change it* if it makes for a better mnemonic.

6. **Association** of the points with familiar objects which will serve to recall them is also useful.

7. Some people memorise things by *saying* them over and over *out loud,* other have to *write* them down *time* after *time.*

8. Many students have *small blank cards* and using one side of each card for each study area, put down the main points. They carry the cards *everywhere* with them and use every opportunity to study them. As they are small they are easily carried. It is surprising how much of your day can be utilised in this way.

PROGRAMME.

9. Map out a programme for yourself; set targets and *achieve* them. One thing is certain, studying is not easy but it is *not* too difficult if you go about it in an orderly purposeful way. Many students fail their examinations through *bad preparation.* Tackle your studies as you would a project at work, *systematically.* Allocate a number of hours each week to each subject. Try fixing *specific times* for each subject, then *keep to them* by refusing to let *anything* keep you from your planned task.

REVISION.

10. Revise periodically. The nearer the examination gets, the more you should concentrate on the major headlines in your notebook and less with the supporting details.

Appendix 4.3 Examination Technique

FIRST IMPRESSIONS.

1. However well prepared you may be, you are still likely to look at the paper on the day and say to yourself, after a quick look at the questions, "There's not much *there* I can do".

2. The atmosphere of the exam room has something to do with this. Try to blot everything from your mind other than the job in hand. *Concentrate* hard. If you feel a bit panicky (most people do – despite the apparent looks of serenity around you) grip the table, take a deep breath, and *get on with it.* Remember things are *never* as bad as they seem!

TIME ALLOCATION.

3. *Allocate* each question *time* appropriate to the number of marks. At the end of the allotted time for a question *go on to the next* – remember, the *first* 5 or 10 marks on the *new* question are more readily picked up than the *last* 1 or 2 on the *previous* question.

4. The *temptation* will be to say "I'll write just *one* more sentence", but before you know where you are you'll have written *several* more and probably just managed to scrape another mark, whereas the same time spent on the next question could have earned 5 or 6 marks. TIME ALLOCATION IS IMPORTANT.

5. If you *are* running out of time write down the *main headings first,* leaving a few lines between each – at least the examiner will see that you had the overall picture. *Then* go back putting in as much supporting detail as you can.

GENERAL APPROACH.

6. Read the *instructions* at the top of the paper.

7. Read the question paper once through. Make your choice of questions *quickly.* Pick the easiest (if one appears so) and *get on with it.*

INDIVIDUAL QUESTION.

8. Read the question again carefully. The question will involve a *key principle or set of principles.* What are they? It is so easy to make the wrong decision at this stage, so read the question, underlining what appear to be the *key words.* This should help you. Irrelevancy has been *heavily* criticised by examiners.

9. Do not rush into action with your pen *yet.* Jot down on a piece of scrap paper the *main headings* you will use in your answer. All this will *take time* – about 5 minutes or more, but the *careful thought* and *outline answer* represent *marks* already earned.

10. If the question is *set out* in a particular sequence, ie:-

a. . . . .
b. . . . .
c. . . . . etc.

then answer it *in that sequence* or you'll have a *hostile examiner* to cope with.

11. Use the particular terminology *used in the question,* the examiner can then *link the points* in your answer to the relevant parts of the question.

12. Assumptions are sometimes required (for example because of the lack of standardisation of terminology in this subject). Having stated your assumptions, make sure that what you write is *consistent* with them. Do ensure, however, that your assumptions *are valid* and are *not* just a device for changing the *meaning* of the question to suit your knowledge!

LAYOUT OF ANSWER.

13. Tabulate where appropriate, using block capitals for your main headings and underline subheadings. Underline *words* or phrases which require emphasis. *Use a ruler.*

14. Leave a line *between* your paragraphs and subparagraphs. This makes for a *good* layout. However, do *not* write on every other line within paragraphs, or on one side of the paper only – examiners are waste conscious!

15. The use of different colour pens, where appropriate, is useful but *don't* overdo it. In fact one black and one red felt-tip pen would be sufficient (use the felt-tip pens which have a *fine point*).

CHARTS AND DIAGRAMS.

16. A descriptive heading or title must be given to each diagram (using the one in the question if indicated).

17. Do not squeeze a diagram into a corner – *spread it out.*

18. Do not clutter your diagram up with too much detail – this defeats the object, which should be clarity.

19. Give a *key* to the symbols and the different lines you've used, and again – use a ruler.

END OF EXAMINATION PROCEDURE.

20. Have a quick look at each answer, checking for grammatical errors and badly formed letters.

21. Ensure each answer sheet has your *number* on it and *don't* leave any lying on the table.

CONCLUSION.

22. Good technique pays a *large* part in examination success; this is a *fact. Refuse* to be panicked, keep your head, and with reasonable preparation you *should* make it.

23. Remember – you don't have to score *100%* to pass.

24. A final point; once you're in the examination room *stay there* and make use of every minute at your disposal.

25. Practise your technique when answering the questions set in the manual.

Index